Conservation of Building and Decorative Stone

Butterworth-Heinemann Series in Conservation and Museology

Published titles:

Artists' Pigments *c.* 1600–1835, 2nd Edition (Harley)
Conservation and Exhibitions (Stolow)
Conservation and Restoration of Works of Art and Antiquities (Kühn)
Conservation of Building and Decorative Stone (Ashurst, Dimes)
Conservation of Glass (Newton, Davison)
Conservation of Historic Buildings (Feilden)
Conservation of Library and Archive Materials and the Graphic Arts (Petherbridge)
Conservation of Manuscripts and Paintings of South-east Asia (Agrawal)
Conservation of Marine Archaeological Objects (Pearson)
Conservation of Wall Paintings (Mora, Mora, Philippot)
The Museum Environment, 2nd Edition (Thomson)
The Organic Chemistry of Museum Objects (Mills, White)
The Textile Conservator's Manual (Landi)

Related titles:

Manual of Curatorship
Materials for Conservation
Museum Documentation Systems

Conservation of Building and Decorative Stone

Editors

John Ashurst D.Arch, RIBA, EASA (Hon)
Formerly Principal Architect, Research and Technical Advisory Service, Historic Monuments Commission for England. Now private consultant in the field of historic building repair.

Francis G Dimes MSc BSc FGS
The late Francis Dimes was a Consultant Geologist in private practice, and formerly Curator of Building Stones at the Geological Museum in South Kensington, London.

Butterworth-Heinemann
Linacre House, Jordan Hill, Oxford OX2 8DP
225 Wildwood Avenue, Woburn, MA 01801-2041
A division of Reed Educational and Professional Publishing Ltd

 A member of the Reed Elsevier plc group

OXFORD BOSTON JOHANNESBURG
MELBOURNE NEW DELHI SINGAPORE

First published 1990 in two volumes
Paperback edition 1998

British Library Cataloguing in Publication Data
A catalogue record for this book is available from the British Library.

Library of Congress Cataloguing in Publication Data
A catalogue record for this book is available from the Library of Congress.

ISBN 0 7506 3898 2

Composition by Genesis Typesetting, Rochester, Kent
Printed and bound in Great Britain

Series Editors' Preface

The conservation of artefacts and buildings has a long history, but the positive emergence of conservation as a profession can be said to date from the foundation of the International Institute for the Conservation of Museum Objects (IIC) in 1950 (the last two words of the title being later changed to Historic and Artistic Works) and the appearance soon after in 1952 of its journal *Studies in Conservation*. The role of the conservator as distinct from those of the restorer and the scientist had been emerging during the 1930s with a focal point in the Fogg Art Museum, Harvard University, which published the precursor to *Studies in Conservation*, *Technical Studies in the Field of the Fine Arts* (1932–42).

UNESCO, through its Cultural Heritage Division and its publications, had always taken a positive role in conservation and the foundation, under its auspices, of the International Centre for the Study of the Preservation and the Restoration of Cultural Property (ICCROM), in Rome, was a further advance. The Centre was established in 1959 with the aims of advising internationally on conservation problems, co-ordinating conservation activities and establishing standards and training courses.

A significant confirmation of professional progress was the transformation at New York in 1966 of the two committees of the International Council of Museums (ICOM), one curatorial on the Care of Paintings (founded in 1949) and the other mainly scientific (founded in the mid-1950s) into the ICOM Committee for Conservation.

Following the Second International Congress of Architects in Venice in 1964 when the Venice Charter was promulgated, the International Council of Monuments and Sites (ICOMOS) was set up in 1965 to deal with archaeological, architectural and town planning questions, to schedule monuments and sites and to monitor relevant legislation.

From the early 1960s onwards, international congresses (and the literature emerging from them) held by IIC, ICOM, ICOMOS and ICCROM not only advanced the subject in its various technical specializations but also emphasized the cohesion of conservators and their subject as an interdisciplinary profession.

The use of the term *Conservation* in the title of this series refers to the whole subject of the care and treatment of valuable artefacts both movable and immovable, but within the discipline conservation has a meaning which is distinct from that of restoration. *Conservation* used in this specialized sense has two aspects: firstly, the control of the environment to minimize the decay of artefacts and materials; and, secondly, their treatment to arrest decay and to stabilize them where possible against further deterioration. Restoration is the continuation of the latter process, when conservation treatment is thought to be insufficient, to the extent of reinstating an object, without falsification, to a condition in which it can be exhibited.

In the field of conservation conflicts of values on aesthetic, historical, or technical grounds are often inevitable. Rival attitudes and methods inevitably arise in a subject which is still developing and at the core of these differences there is often a deficiency of technical knowledge. That is one of the principal *raisons d'être* of this series. In most of these matters ethical principles are the subject of much discussion, and generalizations cannot easily cover (say) buildings, furniture, easel paintings and waterlogged wooden objects.

A rigid, universally agreed principle is that all treatment should be adequately documented. There is also general agreement that structural and decorative falsification should be avoided. In addition there are three other principles which, unless there are overriding objections, it is generally agreed should be followed.

The first is the principle of the reversibility of processes, which states that a treatment should normally be such that the artefact can, if desired, be returned to its pre-treatment condition even after a long lapse of time. This principle is impossible to apply in some cases, for example where the survival of an artefact may depend upon an irreversible process. The second, intrinsic to the whole subject, is that as far as possible decayed parts of an artefact should be conserved and not replaced. The third is that the consequences of the ageing of the original materials (for example 'patina') should not normally be disguised or removed. This includes a secondary proviso that later accretions should not be retained under the false guise of natural patina.

The authors of the volumes in this series give their views on these matters, where relevant, with reference to the types of material within their scope. They take into account the differences in approach to artefacts of essentially artistic significance and to those in which the interest is primarily historical or archaeological.

The volumes are unified by a systematic and balanced presentation of theoretical and practical material with, where necessary, an objective comparison of different methods and approaches. A balance has also been maintained between the fine (and decorative) arts, archaeology and architecture in those cases where the respective branches of the subject have common ground, for example in the treatment of stone and glass and in the control of the museum environment. Since the publication of the first volume it has been decided to include within the series related monographs and technical studies. To reflect this enlargement of its scope the series has been renamed the Butterworth–Heinemann Series in Conservation and Museology.

Though necessarily different in details of organization and treatment (to fit the particular requirements of the subject) each volume has the same general standard which is that of such training courses as those of the University of London Institute of Archaeology, the Victoria and Albert Museum, the Conservation Center, New York University, the Institute of Advanced Architectural Studies, York, and ICCROM.

The authors have been chosen from among the acknowledged experts in each field, but as a result of the wide areas of knowledge and technique covered even by the specialized volumes in this series, in many instances multi-authorship has been necessary.

With the existence of IIC, ICOM, ICOMOS and ICCROM, the principles and practice of conservation have become as internationalized as the problems. The collaboration of Consultant Editors will help to ensure that the practices discussed in this series will be applicable throughout the world.

Preface

In presenting this book, John Ashurst and I have many people to thank, particularly Ian Bristow for his admirable introduction to the subject of conservation on which successive contributors have built; and David Honeyborne, whose name has long been associated with pioneering work in the field of stone weathering. Many others are owed much, and it is a debt which cannot adequately be repaid.

For my part I must thank John Ashurst, first and foremost for the constant aid and encouragement he has given. Without him the shoe leather would not have hit the pavement carrying the wearer to yet another building to add to the record. Chapters 2 to 6 owe much to Murray Mitchell, one of Britain's foremost geological editors, who spent many hours reading the script, correcting it, improving it and removing the double-negatives. The script was better for it. Especial thanks are due also to a friend and former colleague, Gilbert Green, for his great patience in straightening out my understanding of Bath Stone. The section on that stone owes much to him.

My erstwhile colleagues at the Geological Museum have helped, probably more than they realize, in answering the questions asked of them. Ron Roberts, Alan Timms, Peter Clough, Alan Jobbins and Robin Sanderson all had the kindness not to plead other engagements when they saw the question coming.

Inevitably Chapters 2 to 6 of Volume 1 are to some degree a compilation of existing, scattered knowledge. Many of the examples given are quoted from other books. They are listed in the References. There are examples, however, which may be said to be in the public domain. Should any of my friends have passed an example to me and I have not acknowledged it, I offer them my apologies.

It has not been possible to check every example given of the use of stone. I should be grateful, therefore, if any reader would let me know of any which are incorrect and, indeed, I should be pleased to learn of new outstanding uses. None of this might have happened but for one person to whom both John Ashurst and I must express the deepest debt of gratitude. Sadly he is no longer with us. Donovan Purcell, a former Surveyor to the Fabric of Ely Cathedral, a friend in all senses of the word, gently taught me what it was that an architect wanted to

Donovan Purcell

know from a geologist. To both John and me he demonstrated what limitless enthusiasm for a material could achieve. As founder chairman of the Standing Joint Committee on Natural Stones he opened a dialogue again between the masonry trade, the quarrying industry, the training establishments and architects and surveyors, contributing in no small way to a new unity of interest and purpose which has been foundational to the revival of the stone industry of the United Kingdom. To a great extent this book is part of his memorial.

John Ashurst and I have learned much from the band of dedicated people who have made their knowledge available and who have contributed largely to Volume 2. John particularly remembers with great pleasure the many discussions with these contributors on the philosophy of repair, consolidation and conservation. That this book is in two volumes is simply a matter of convenience. There is no division between an understanding of the nature of stone and the study of its repair and conservation in buildings.

Finally I must thank Janet, who came into the life of this book – too late! – and Margaret, who has lived with this book – too long!

Francis G. Dimes
Kingston Vale,
September 1990

Preface to paperback edition

Frank Dimes died on 8 October 1995. He and I both hoped to see *Conservation of Building and Decorative Stone* in a paperback edition and he would have been delighted to see that hope fulfilled. Had he been here I know he would have wanted to enlarge and enrich his sections of the book; he was always collecting new material with unabated enthusiasm and we discussed many 'improvements' over pints of Young's Special. These additions were not, as it happens, to be possible, but his work stands still as a testament to Frank's enormous experience and lucidity. Through his writing, some of which has been published posthumously (*The Building Stone Heritage of Leeds* with Murray Mitchell) and some of which may still be published, he is still able to educate and inspire and to entertain as he did throughout his professional life. He is still sadly missed by his wife Margaret and their daughters, by all his many friends and associates, and not least by me, remembering him as my greatest mentor. I am proud to have known and worked with him.

John Ashurst
Epsom
November 1997

Part 1

Contents

1 An introduction to the restoration, conservation and repair of stone 1
Ian Bristow

2 The nature of building and decorative stones 19
Francis G. Dimes

3 Igneous rocks 37
Francis G. Dimes

4 Sedimentary rocks 61
Francis G. Dimes

5 Metamorphic rocks 135
Francis G. Dimes

6 Determination of a sample 150
Francis G. Dimes

7 Weathering and decay of masonry 153
David B. Honeyborne

Illustrations of weathering and decay phenomena 179

Index 185

1

An introduction to the restoration, conservation and repair of stone

Ian Bristow

Introduction

> Whoever expects to find a stone that will stand from century to century, deriding alike the frigid rains and scorching solar rays, without need of reparation, will indeed search for 'the philosopher's stone'.[1]

As C.H. Smith, who delivered these lines at a lecture to the Royal Institute of British Architects in 1840 realized, stone, despite its image as the eternal material, has a limited life. Its decay may be caused by a number of factors, including polluted acidic atmospheres, which lead to surface erosion, flaking, and exfoliation. Eventually this may impair the aesthetic appearance of a building or affect its structural stability, and proper remedial measures will be needed.

The traditional method of repair has been to cut out and renew all weathered or otherwise defective stones, but in the case of historic buildings this process is, in effect, destructive both of the ancient fabric, with its archaeological interest and, no less importantly, of the character of age such a structure will inevitably possess. The loss of either will concern equally those who are interested in the history of a building and those to whom the qualities of its age are important. It is therefore necessary to adopt a special attitude to the repair of historic stonework, soundly based on a carefully considered philosophy. The approach adopted in any given case will vary, but should spring from consideration of a number of points, most importantly:

1. the age and character of the building;
2. the structural function of the individual stone in question, and the nature and cause of its defect;
3. a careful assessment of its rate of decay, taken in the context of the building as a whole.

The last of these, the much overlooked dimension of time, is in many ways the most difficult. It needs experience and an outlook which is foreign to many architects and building contractors, especially today; but it was much neglected too in the nineteenth century, and many churches received over-drastic restoration as a result.

The first essential in approaching an historic building in need of repair is to determine the cause of decay, and, where possible, remove it or minimize its effect. If surface disruption is caused by acidic air pollution, there is little the individual can do, although governmental action in a national or international context could be of the very greatest importance. Poor selection or incorrect bedding of stones is also without simple remedy, but it is sometimes possible to improve poor detailing without alteration to the appearance of a building, as, for example, by the provision of a drip on the underside of a projecting window sill. Where a material change in appearance would result, however, it is often necessary to accept the defect and any consequent tendency to decay in order to preserve the integrity of the historic fabric.

The effects of overloading can, on the other hand, often be remedied inconspicuously. For example, the detached marble shafts employed in thirteenth-century churches and nineteenth-century buildings of the same style often become overcompressed through settlement of the more frequently jointed adjoining masonry, and the stress may be simply relieved by sawing out their joints and repointing. To remedy the spalling resulting from concave beds, or the decay caused by juxtaposition of incompatible stones is, however, more problematical; but action can be taken to control plant growth in masonry, rusting and contingent expansion of iron cramps or window ferramenta, damage caused by mason bees, leaking gutters and rainwater goods, rising damp, and unsuitable uses and human activities.

In practice, one of the most important responsibilities of anyone faced with the care of an historic building is to anticipate trouble before it happens. Not only must maintenance, especially the cleaning out of gutters and downpipes, be carried out thoroughly and regularly, but potential trouble spots should be eliminated. If a bend can be removed from a rainwater pipe it will lessen the chances of a blockage; and where there is important internal masonry, such as a carved freestone or marble wall monument, any exterior downpipe should be resited as far away from it as possible. Care should also be taken to ensure that any repointing is carried out in a suitable mix, and that impervious paints and plasters, which will inhibit the free evaporation of moisture, are not used to the detriment of the masonry. Heating pipes should be sited well away from historic carving or wall bases in order to avoid rapid decay through increased evaporation of moisture within the fabric.

The birth of a conservative approach to repair

The need for careful maintenance was recognized by the fifteenth-century Florentine architect Leone Battista Alberti, who exclaimed that he was often filled with the highest indignation when he saw buildings going to ruin owing to the carelessness of their owners.[2] From the mid-sixteenth century, however, the growing English fashion for Italianate architecture led to a contempt for the Gothic style, and its consequent neglect. The seventeenth-century diarist John Evelyn, for example, spoke disparagingly of Henry VII's chapel at Westminster, as being composed of 'lame *Statues, Lace* and other *Cut-work* and *Crinkle Crankle*';[3] and at the same period many mediaeval churches, already despoiled by puritanical fanaticism, fell into poor repair. The Civil War too brought in its wake a toll of destruction to many castles, and a large number were slighted to prevent their continued use for military purposes.

The resulting ruins, together with those of classical Italy, soon became a poignant reminder of the past; and their fascination to the eighteenth-century mind is splendidly revealed in the following lines from David Mallet's poem *The Excursion* of 1726:

> Behind me rises huge an awful *Pile*,
> Sole on this blasted Heath, a Place of Tombs,
> Waste, desolate, where *Ruin* dreary dwells,
> Brooding o'er sightless Sculls, and crumbling
>   Bones.
> Ghastful *He* sits, and eyes with stedfast Glare
> The Column grey with Moss, the falling Bust,
> The Time-shook Arch, the monumental Stone,
> Impair'd, effac'd, and hastening into Dust.[4]

The particular qualities of ruins eventually became incorporated formally into aesthetic theory. In the 1750s, the philosopher Edmund Burke had postulated two characters, the Sublime and the Beautiful, the latter expressed by smooth outline and flowing lines, the former by jagged outline and grandeur of scale, a quality with which ruins would no doubt have been identified.[5] By the 1790s, however, this simple duality had come to seem unsatisfactory, and Sir Uvedale Price added a third character, the Picturesque, describing the way a beautiful building with its smooth surface and even colouring was converted by time into a picturesque ruin:

> First, by means of weather stains, partial incrustations, mosses, &c. it at the same time takes off from the uniformity of its surface, and of its colour; that is, gives it a degree of roughness, and variety of tint. Next, the various accidents of weather loosen the stones themselves; they tumble in irregular masses upon what was perhaps smooth turf or pavement, or nicely trimmed walks and shrubberies; now mixed and overgrown with wild plants and creepers, that crawl over, and shoot among the fallen ruins. Sedums, wall-flowers, and other vegetables that bear drought, find nourishment in the decayed cement from which the stones have been detached: Birds convey their food into the chinks, and yew, elder, and other berried plants project from the sides; while the ivy mantles over other parts, and crowns the top.[6]

The late eighteenth and early nineteenth century greatly enjoyed the qualities offered by decay of this nature, and the preoccupation with its pleasing character is well expressed in engravings of the period, such as that of St. Giles's Church, Little Malvern, Worcestershire (*Figure 1.1*). In it may be seen the evident pleasure of the artists in the ivy-clad ruins at the east end and on the southern side of the chancel of this fifteenth-century building, besides the truncated tower with its pyramidal roof which replaced the earlier parapet.

In parallel with this enthusiasm for the aesthetic qualities of ruins, an academic interest in the study of the remains of mediaeval architecture developed. The eighteenth-century classical architect Sir William Chambers, for example, made a plea in his *Treatise on the Decorative Part of Civil Architecture* (1791) for 'a correct elegant publication of our own cathedrals, and other buildings called Gothick, before they totally fall to ruin',[7] which was answered rapidly by a whole series of publications. Under the auspices of the Society of Antiquaries, John Carter

Figure 1.1 Pleasing decay. A view of St Giles's Church, Little Malvern, Worcestershire. (Engraving by J.le Keux from a drawing by J.P. Neal in their *Views of the most interesting Collegiate and Parochial Churches in Great Britain* (1824-1825), volume 2)

produced his superb folios of measured drawings of cathedrals, including those of Durham, Exeter, Gloucester, and York, and the abbeys of Bath and St. Alban's; whilst in 1811 John Milner published his *Treatise on the Ecclesiastical Architecture of England,* a work followed in 1817 by Thomas Rickman's *Attempt to discriminate the Styles of Architecture in England*, which formed the foundation of nineteenth-century scholarship. Perhaps the most prolific publisher of the period was John Britton, whose *Architectural Antiquities*, which contained splendid engravings of ancient buildings, appeared in five volumes between 1807 and 1826, and whose series of *Cathedral Antiquities*, which dealt with fourteen English cathedrals, was produced between 1814 and 1835. The latter volumes were distinguished by containing, besides a selection of general views and details, carefully executed measured drawings of the buildings. This was also a feature of the vitally important volumes of *Specimens* and *Examples of Gothic Architecture* produced by Augustus Pugin in 1819–1822 and 1828–1838 respectively. Together with others, these formed primary source books for the revival of mediaeval architectural styles, a subject outside the scope of the present chapter, but brilliantly charted by Charles Eastlake in his *History of the Gothic Revival* (1872). It had, though, an important parallel which is of great moment in the present context, the revival by the Tractarians of the ancient dignity of Christian worship.

In 1827, the author of *Notes on the Cambridgeshire Churches* wrote:

> The dilapidation of churches is a delicate subject to speak of ... but when the archdeacons abandoned their duty ... peculation, ruin, and desolation stalked abroad... and corruption and decay withered all around... The established places of worship have become unfit and unsafe for Christians to meet in; the churches are cold, comfortless, unhealthy; the haunts of colds, catarrhs, and rheumatism; the receptacle frequently of filth, and the abode of toads and reptiles. Congregations... are deterred from entering... by the dread of the fevers and consumption that they know lurk within... [and] are driven into dissenting places of worship.[8]

A few years later, Augustus Pugin's son, Augustus Welby Northmore Pugin, complained that the font at Selby Abbey, Yorkshire, was disused. The transept chapels were filled with rubbish, one even being used as a coal hole, and the eastern aisle windows were disfigured by having two large stove pipes carried through them.[9] The engraving of the interior

Figure 1.2 The neglected state of St Peter's, Cambridge, in the early nineteenth century (provenance unknown)

of St. Peter's Church, Cambridge, illustrated in *Figure 1.2*, shows the appearance of just such a neglected church; and it was not long before a concerted effort was made to remove the offending bric-a-brac from them, to repair their roofs and restore their damaged masonry in order to permit seemly and proper worship within. A large number of churches had, of course, been refitted in the eighteenth century, most generally by the installation of box pews, a reredos, pulpit, and galleries; and certain major structures, such as Milton Abbey, Winchester and Salisbury Cathedrals and Henry VII's Chapel, had been restored by architects such as James Wyatt, whose thoroughgoing approach had been the subject of controversy at the time.[10] To those who wished to revive the ancient dignities of worship, however, such crass alterations were anathema, and the resulting movement to put matters to rights led in 1839 to foundation of the Cambridge Camden Society. This event was of profound significance and was soon to have a devastating effect on ancient structures throughout the length and breadth of Britain.

The Society was formed by a group of undergraduates, notable amongst whom was J.M. Neale, who dedicated themselves not only to the study of mediaeval ecclesiastical structures, but, most importantly, to undertake their restoration. They started their programme for the latter in a small way with the font at Coton, a village church very close to Cambridge,[11] and in 1841 reported their repair of the font at St. Peter's. This had been broken into pieces, some of which had been lost;[12] the restored bowl with its sculpture pieced-in by the Society can still be seen in the church today. In June 1840, they paid to have the rough-cast removed from the tower of St. Bene't's, Cambridge, in order to expose 'the interest of its Anglo-Saxon construction',[13] and the following year embarked on their largest project, the 'thorough restoration' of the Church of the Holy Sepulchre,[14] which, on account of the impact it was to have elsewhere, is worth considering in a little detail. The opportunity for the Society's involvement was provided by the collapse of part of the vault of the circular aisle, caused by settlement of the perimeter wall which had been undermined by grave-digging. This had occasioned movement in the round tower, and the remedial measures instigated in 1841, under the direction of the architect Anthony

Figure 1.3 Church of the Holy Sepulchre, Cambridge, before restoration (from John Britton, *The Architectural Antiquities of Great Britain* (1807-1826) volume 3 (1812), plate facing page 90)

Salvin, involved not only rebuilding the wall and vault, but also the removal of the upper storey of the tower which had been added to the Romanesque structure in the fifteenth century (*Figure 1.3*). In addition, 'Plain single Norman lights' were 'substituted for the unsightly Perpendicular insertions which disfigured, as well as weakened, the walls of the circular Aisle'. The liaison in this statement between a return to a structurally perfect condition and restoration to an earlier physical state is significant; and in parallel with this, the box pews and other later furnishings were removed from the interior.

Such an approach typified a large number of later restorations at other churches inspired by the activities of the Cambridge Camden Society, the nineteenth-century debate surrounding which has been ably charted by Stephan Tschudi Madsen in his recent book *Restoration and Anti-Restoration* (Oslo, 1976), to which the reader is referred for greater detail of this important issue. From the point of view of the present chapter, however, the most important facet of the Holy Sepulchre restoration was the smoothing and redressing of the remaining ancient stonework both within and without, a matter the Society reported with enthusiasm.[15] The transformation effected by the works may be seen in the post restoration photograph (*Figure 1.4*), the final product, bereft of patina and 'scraped' clean, presenting a tidy and perfect face to the world, thus testifying to its new found health in the care of what was seen by its authors as a revitalized Christian witness.

Although the Cambridge Camden Society was disbanded in 1846, it was refounded the following year in London as the Ecclesiological Society and continued its activities, which included publication of the periodical, the *Ecclesiologist* (1841–1868). Through this, the principles of restoration advocated by the Society swept the country, and church after church was subjected to thoroughgoing works of the kind seen at the Holy Sepulchre. The enthusiasm of the clergy, which stands in marked contrast to their general apathy towards historic buildings today, ranged unchecked over ancient fabric; and gradually the picturesque face of the English parish church became transformed into a scraped and tidy blandness, scarred too with the harshness of new stone which was often cut with a soulless precision unknown in the Middle Ages. Restoration thus came inevitably into conflict with artistic sensibilities, and, furthermore, with archaeological interests as genuine mediaeval work disappeared in favour of somebody's more or less scholarly notion of what seemed correct.

The most notable reaction to this process was that of John Ruskin, who was horrified at the destruction of ancient fabric which was taking place. In 1849 he expressed his concern with considerable force in the 'Lamp of Memory', which formed Chapter VI of the *Seven Lamps of Architecture.* He characterized restoration as 'a Lie from beginning to end' and wrote:

> You may make a model of a building as you may of a corpse, and your model may have the shell

Figure 1.4 A nineteenth-century photograph showing the Church of the Holy Sepulchre, Cambridge, after restoration

> of the old walls within it as your cast might have the skeleton... but the old building is destroyed.

To lose the original surface, albeit weathered, was tragic; and its replacement totally unsatisfactory. How could one, he demanded, copy a surface that had been worn half an inch down, since the whole finish was in the half inch that had gone. The old, he insisted, still had some life, some mysterious suggestion of what it had been, and of what it had lost. All in all, he remarked:

> Neither by the public, nor by those who have the care of public monuments, is the true meaning of the word *restoration* understood. It means the most total destruction which a building can suffer.[16]

In both the *Seven Lamps* and the *Stones of Venice*, which succeeded it a few years later in 1851–1853, Ruskin showed himself to be not only an extremely sensitive observer and draughtsman of the patina of decay, but also an astute analyst of mediaeval fabric. The irregularities of setting out which he discovered at Pisa and elsewhere were just the sort of thing liable to be missed and made uniform by a restorer,[17] and the almost unique way in which he combined picturesque artist *and* archaeological scholar was quite remarkable.

The force of his arguments come to be accepted only gradually, to the great regret of many architectural historians today, but by 1861 the architect William Butterfield was writing in connection with his restoration of the tower of the Chapel at Winchester College:

> I should carefully save and reuse every old moulding and surface stone which is at all likely to last, even though it may be in some respects in an imperfect state;[18]

whilst about five years later George Edmund Street, faced at Monkland, Herefordshire, with tufa 'so rough, and... so rude, that most men would have proposed to build an entirely new church', rebuilt the nave 'with every wrought stone put back in its old place'.[19] One of the most revealing of these later restorations was the *anastylosis*, carried out by Sir Gilbert Scott in about 1875, of the fragments of the shrine of St. Alban which had been discovered in 1873. This was later praised even by such a critic as E.S. Prior, who remarked that we are

> fortunate in the taste and good sense with which the remains have been put together and treated, as such monuments should be, with the sole intention of the preservation of the beauties they have left.[20]

Scott himself wrote that the Shrine was, 'by the ingenuity of the foreman and the clerk of the works,

Figure 1.5 St Alban's Abbey, Hertfordshire, the shrine of St Alban after reconstruction in the 1870s. (From *Architecture*, volume 2 (1897), p. 77)

set up again, exactly in its old place, stone for stone, and fragment for fragment: the most marvellous restitution that ever was made'.[21] The illustration (*Figure 1.5*) shows the result, with no attempt to replace missing features, nor, most importantly, to renew damaged or defective stones. Of it, Gilbert Scott's son, George Gilbert Scott wrote:

> In that one structure, as it now stands, is summed up the history of english church architecture as a living fact, and of the death which finally overtook it. The one is seen in the exquisite finish and beauty of the monument thus recovered from its ruins; the other in the marks, which it bears upon it, of the crowbar-blows which shattered it into splinters, starring the finely-wrought marble, as ice is shivered by a mattock.[22]

In this passage a profound change from the attitude of the Ecclesiological Society may be noted. No longer is it necessary to present perfection of form as a living testimony to the Christian witness, its continued life is asserted *despite* the damage inflicted by the wreckers of the past.

Nevertheless, restorations of earlier type continued, notably under the direction of Lord Grimthorpe (formerly Sir Edmund Beckett Denison, QC). In 1877 matters came to a head over Tewkesbury Abbey, where the aged Scott, despite the sensitivity he could bring to mediaeval masonry, proposed to remove the seventeenth-century furnishings. To a younger generation, they too were part of the building's history, and over this issue William Morris founded the Society for the Protection of Ancient Buildings and published its *Manifesto*. This important document, which still forms the basis of the Society's policy, represents a milestone in thinking about the repair of historic buildings, and has dominated attitudes in England for over a century. It has also had considerable influence abroad. In it, Morris proscribed the restoration of a building to an earlier stage of its development, as had been done at the Holy Sepulchre and vast numbers of other mediaeval churches, and emphasized the need for careful and consistent maintenance, or 'daily care'. He stressed too the need to preserve the patina of age. However, unlike Ruskin, whose total opposition to tampering with historic fabric had led him to prefer demolition to repair,[23] Morris, in the *Manifesto*, implicitly acknowledged the need for renewal of decayed stone; but, he insisted, where this was done the new should be clearly distinguishable from the old.

The working out of this dictum in practice has been a matter of concern to many architects. In fact, the idea was not completely new, and in restoring the arch of Titus in the Forum Romanum in the early nineteenth century, the architect Giuseppe Valadier had distinguished his new architectural mouldings by omitting the enrichments, and by simplifying the new Ionic capitals whilst retaining the overall form of the antique survivors.[24] A similar approach was adopted about 1880 in the reconstruction of the shrine of St Frideswide in Christ Church Cathedral, Oxford (*Figure 1.6*), where the piers supporting the fragments of the canopy are uncompromisingly cut to show their status as new elements. Other examples of this may be seen on the exterior of many buildings, most notably where sculptured corbel-tables or label stops have been renewed but left uncarved as simple projecting blocks of stone. For plain areas of masonry, on the other hand, a convention arose of replacement, not in stone, but with tile, in order to differentiate the repair from

Figure 1.6 Christ Church Cathedral, Oxford, the shrine of St Frideswide as reconstructed about 1880 (F.H. Crossley/Courtauld Institute)

Figure 1.7 Buttress repaired by the tile method, St Mary's Church, Higham, Kent

surviving mediaeval work. An example may be seen in the detail illustrated of a buttress at St Mary's Church, Higham, Kent (*Figure 1.7*), and the technique became widely used in the early years of the present century. Brick had often been employed for the same purpose but for different reasons in the eighteenth century, and it was no doubt felt that the use of tile would result in a similarly pleasing patchwork. Soon, however, it became clear that the character of large areas of mediaeval masonry was being transformed in a way just as assertive as insensitively inserted new stone; and an alternative was therefore developed in which the tile was recessed half an inch from the wall face, and its surface rendered to provide a closer colour match to the adjoining old masonry. The revised method was strongly advocated by A.R. Powys, who, in his book *Repair of Ancient Buildings* (1929), from which *Figures 1.8 to 1.11* are taken, linked it especially with the work of William Wier.[25] The first two illustrations show repairs carried out in this way to a buttress, and the second pair the same technique employed in the repair of a mediaeval window at Limpsfield Church, Surrey, in 1927.

Closely related to this method is the use of 'plastic stone', a specially constituted mortar reinforced and keyed back to sound stone with copper wire or dowels used to make up defective areas. This too, was widely used between the wars, but has problems of its own, and shares with the rendered tile method a tendency to discoloration over a comparatively short period of years, so that even if there is a good match with the old stone when first completed and dried out, it will often weather to produce a disfiguring piebald appearance. The material also requires great care in mixing to avoid being too strong and impervious, and whilst in skilled hands it can be a useful solution in some circumstances, it has acquired a poor reputation amongst many architects since where the mix is too strong it will eventually crack away from the backing stone owing to the effects of salt action. When this happens (*Figure 1.12*) it will often pull away a further inch or more of old stone with it. For success, the mixture must thus be quite weak; and the material cannot, therefore, be used for the repair of structural or weathering elements. Indeed, it has always been best used for the simple filling of cavities, rather on the principle adopted by the dental profession. In this connection it is interesting to see that Powys seems to have acknowledged that the rendered tile method too was unsuitable for weathering elements, since in his drawing showing the repair of a buttress (*Figure 1.8*) he shows a new stone for one of the water-tablings. Undoubtedly, however, the greatest danger in the use of plastic stone is the tendency for every blemish, however tiny, in a wall to be 'repaired'; and examples may be found where masonry has been so over-treated with the material that it has lost the patina of age, and thus presents an unpleasant smoothness to the observer.

Attitudes towards the repair of stonework today

From the chronological résumé above it will be seen that the repair of masonry has a history of its own, and is not simply a mechanical operation which can be tackled in a purely utilitarian way. Rather, the architect must educate himself to understand the art-historical and archaeological importance and character of the particular structure with which he is concerned, and develop a sensitivity towards the preoccupations of the different groups and disciplines interested in its continued preservation. Inevitably too, he will come to see his own operation not only in the historical perspective of the individual building, but also in the context of the philosophical developments of the last two or three hundred years.

Perhaps the greatest lesson to be learned from the observation of work carried out during the eighteenth and nineteenth centuries is that the least

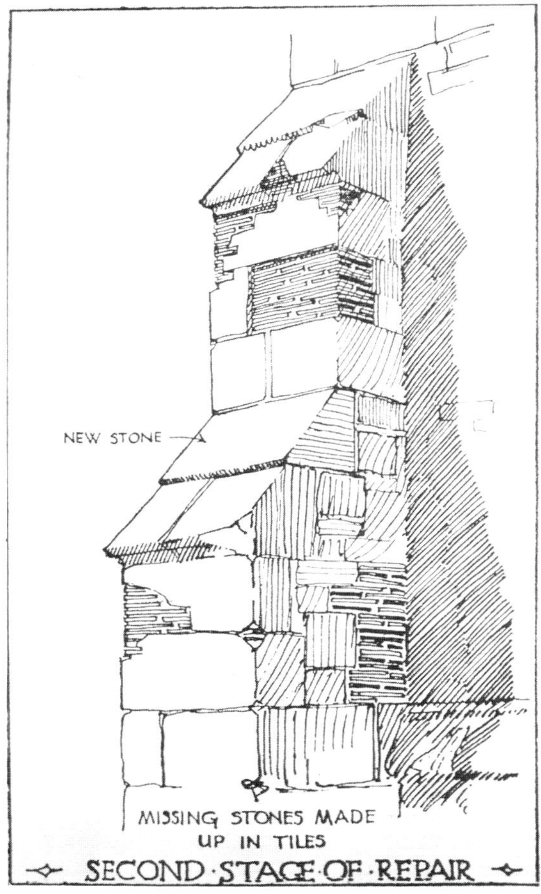

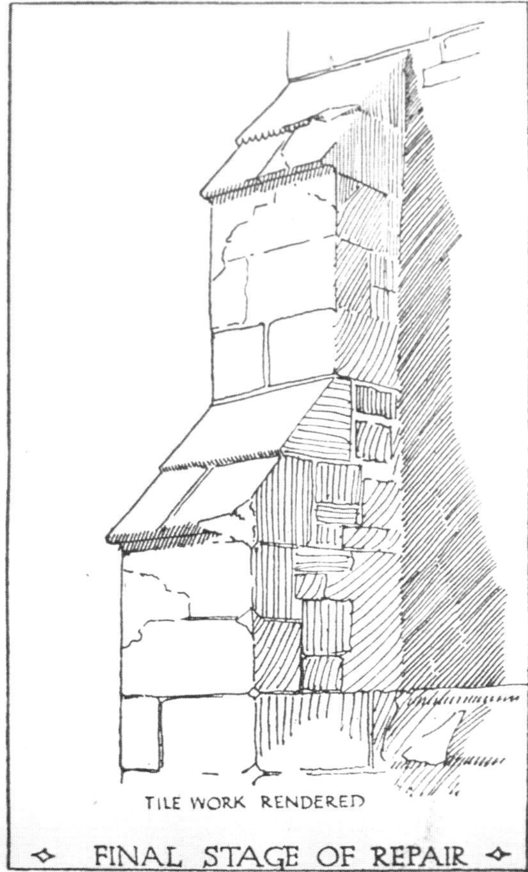

Figures 1.8 and 1.9 Rendering of tiles; diagrams showing stages in the repair of a buttress. (From A.R. Powys, *Repair of Ancient Buildings*, figures 11 and 12. Reproduced by kind permission of Mrs Eleanor Walton)

possible amount of stone renewal, whatever material is selected to replace it, makes for the fewest problems and greatest preservation of historical material. The crucial decision to be made is what to repair and what to leave alone, a critical matter which must be approached in a careful and organized way and not simply left to be made at the last moment by someone on site. Just as an elegant mathematical proof will do only what is *necessary and sufficient*, so too the historic-buildings architect should adopt the same criteria with respect to aged masonry. The first stage, as emphasized in the first section of this chapter, is a painstaking survey leading to historical appreciation of the structure and careful and thorough diagnosis of any defects which are found. These, as stressed, have to be set into the context of the building as a whole, in dimensions of both space and time. Obviously too, any major structural movements which are progressive must be attended to at an early stage; but even here careful thought is necessary, and where cracks are the result of movement which took place early in a building's history and have since remained static there may be no need for action, obviating any need to disturb the archaeological integrity of the wall or its foundations. Where work is necessary, on the other hand, it is important it should be carried out using a method which will involve the least damage to historic fabric, not necessarily by the cheapest available. Thus, the use of bored rather than driven piles may avoid damage through vibration; or in instances where facework has become detached from the main mass of a wall and is bulging, a method of tying it back *in situ* (with, for example, resin anchor bolts concealed

Figures 1.10 and 1.11 Limpsfield Church, Surrey. A window in the north wall during and after repair in 1927. (From A.R. Powys, *Repair of Ancient Buildings*, figures 14 and 15. Reproduced by kind permission of Mrs Eleanor Walton)

Figure 1.12 Plaxtol Church, Kent. A failed cement repair to the belfry window

in the joints) will often be preferable to taking the face down and rebuilding it. Again, it is often possible to avoid rebuilding dangerously leaning walls by jacking them back into a vertical position or by stabilizing them with concealed reinforced concrete members. For examples where this has been successfully done, the reader is referred to *Old Churches and Modern Craftsmanship* by A.D.R. Caroe (1949), *The Care of Old Buildings* by Donald W. Insall (1958), and the same author's *The Care of Old Buildings Today* (1972).

Once the problems presented by such major structural faults have been resolved, the wall may be looked at in terms of its individual components. The architect should consider each defective stone in turn, asking if it is doing its job in the wall as a load-bearing or weathering member. Just because the face of a stone is weathered it does not mean it has become incapable of supporting the masonry above: after all, it may have lost half an inch of its face in the course of one or more centuries, but there may well be considerable substance remaining which could be allowed to weather further for a material period before renewal becomes necessary. Even where a stone is fractured, this does not mean of itself that it is no longer fulfilling its function and must be cut out and replaced. A cracked lintel in the Temple of Zeus at Athens has been cited as an instance of this: the fractured block of marble now acts as an arch rather than a beam and thus remains structurally completely stable.[26] Other fractures are often caused by the rusting of buried iron dowels or cramps which can be carefully removed and the disrupted stone repaired by gluing the broken pieces together using a suitable masonry adhesive.

The special techniques now available for the consolidation of decaying architectural sculpture are discussed in Volume 2, but these are not always applicable to ordinary building elements. Nevertheless, a conservative approach may still be adopted for structural members even when they have failed. Thus, it may be possible to flash the pitted upper surface of an eighteenth-century cornice with lead in order to restore its weathering capabilities, or use the same method to provide a drip at its leading edge when that on the soffit of the corona has decayed. Other defective stones may be carefully pieced in to avoid the need to renew the whole, although the situations in which this can be done successfully must be chosen with care in order not to introduce a distracting pattern of fresh joint-lines into the masonry. A good example of the technique in practice is the work recently completed on the western towers of St. Paul's Cathedral, London. Here (*Figure 1.13*) the corona had weathered, but the mouldings of the cornice which it had sheltered were in good condition. Rather than renew the whole cornice, it was therefore decided to renew only its upper half, making a new joint in the angle beneath the corona where it was concealed in shadow. A similar instance may be found in the 'half-and-half' technique for the repair of window mullions and tracery which have weathered where exposed to the elements. In such instances, it is often possible simply to cut back the decayed stone to the glazing line, and dowel or glue back a new outer face to the old inner half. This technique was used in St. Anselm's Chapel at Canterbury Cathedral at some date prior to 1845,[27] and has been used recently with great success in the Lady Chapel and western tower at Ely (*Figure 1.14*). Here too, the new joint is concealed, this time by the glazing groove.

This careful approach, seeking always to retain every old element that can possibly continue to do its job, is the hallmark of the competent historic-buildings architect, and contrasts strongly with the attitude commonly displayed by the inexperienced.

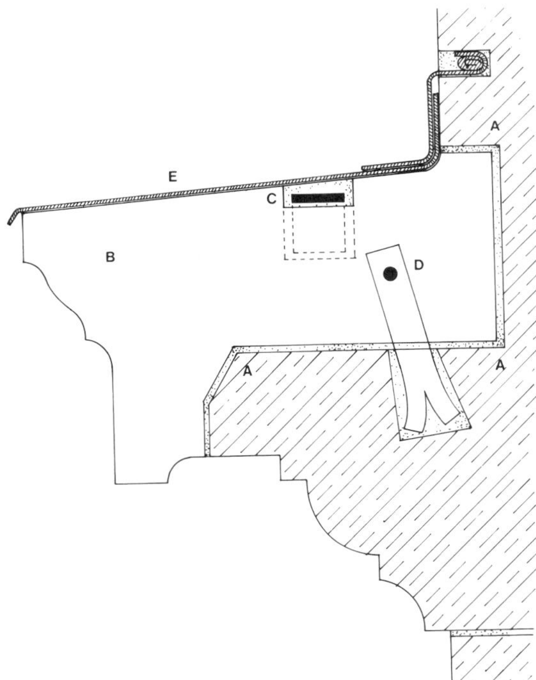

Figure 1.13 Section through a cornice, St Paul's Cathedral, London, showing the method of renewing the decayed corona. (Illustrated by kind permission of Robert Potter) (*a*) Original stonework cut back; (*b*) new stone; (*c*) stainless steel dog cramp across each joint; (*d*) stainless steel fishtail cramp and dowell; (*e*) lead weathering

Figure 1.14 The half-and-half technique used for repair of a mullion, west tower, Ely Cathedral. (Architects: Donovan Purcell and Peter Miller)

Figure 1.15 Decayed but sound masonry, south porch of St Michael's Church, East Peckham, Kent

Figure 1.16 Repaired drip mould, west window of south aisle, St John's Church, Wateringbury, Kent. (Architects: Purcell Miller Tritton and Partners).

For example, some years ago, a restoration of the fine fifteenth-century doorway of the south porch of St Michael's Church, East Peckham, Kent (*Figure 1.15*) was proposed. Looking critically at the masonry, however, and asking whether each stone was still capable of doing its job showed not only that the arch, although weathered, was structurally sound, but also that the drip provided by its label mould was in a fully functioning state. In this instance there was therefore no need for any stone repair, with a consequent saving not only to parish finances but, most importantly, to the historical integrity of the masonry and its wonderful state of picturesque decay. At St John's Church, Wateringbury, Kent, on the other hand, the drip mould of the west window of the south aisle had decayed to a point where renewal was necessary for the preservation of the window masonry beneath; but at the same time it was clear replacement could be restricted to parts of this element only (*Figure 1.16*). Furthermore, no attempt was made to repair the weathered tracery beneath, beyond careful pointing of its open joints and a few unimportant fractures.

The decision to renew any stone must in every case be taken on an individual basis, and only after a close inspection has been made. One should never think in terms of *areas* for renewal. Final decisions about stones at high levels can, accordingly, only be taken once the necessary scaffolding has been erected, and the repair specification must be written with this in mind. There is no place in historic-buildings work for the architect or other professional who remains on the ground, since defects will very often appear in a totally different light once close access is possible, and decisions over renewal should never be delegated. It has also been stressed above that the need for renewal must be assessed in the context of the building as a whole, seen both in its own timescale and that of the progress of its weathering, that is, its overall rate of decay. It must constantly be kept in mind that the purpose of repair is to hand down to the next generation the maximum possible quantity of historic fabric, not to put all defects or potential defects in the masonry to rights and obtain a textbook example of sound construction. Frequency of access, however, plays an important part in decisions over what is 'necessary and sufficient' at any given time, and when the expense of scaffolding is involved it is common to plan for an anticipated period of, say, fifty years before further repairs are needed; whilst for masonry at lower levels it is easy to go back and do a little more in ten or twenty years should this become necessary. The condition of stones on a tall spire or high parapet may, therefore, be rather more critically assessed than those on parts of the building to which more frequent access is possible.

Looking at a building and its decay in both space and time also means that there will be a different assessment of need for renewal of individual stones in a ruin, such as the east wall of Tynemouth Priory, Northumberland (*Figure 1.17*), where erosion is part of the character of the building, and in an eighteenth-century ashlar façade in good condition. As suggested above, the ruin may be considered to reflect Burke's character of the Sublime; whilst in the case of the ashlar façade, its smoothness, corresponding with his notion of beauty, is paramount. Both are

Figure 1.17 Eroded masonry as part of a ruined character. Tynemouth Priory, Northumberland

characteristics whose retention should be sought, and whilst there would be little point in renewing any of the drip mouldings at Tynemouth in an attempt to slow down the overall rate of decay, there would be a very good case for renewing a defective stone in an ashlar façade if this would help to prevent the imminent decay of the stone below. Similarly, a nineteenth-century church or extension to an eighteenth-century house will have a character of its own which will call for sensitivity in its preservation. The architect must train himself to respond to this by constant visiting and observation (perhaps aided by drawing or photography) of a wide range of historic buildings.

Altogether, the most important judgement an architect must bring to bear is his assessment of the rate of decay of an individual element. This requires experience, often gained by the quinquennial survey and resurvey of churches under the Inspection of Churches Measure 1955, and there is no quickly available substitute, although the comparison of old photographs with the state of the structure today can often be helpful. Often, slow decay may be left to take its course for a few more years before repair becomes necessary, and it is the ability to differentiate this from rapid decay which is important. The expertise required for historic-buildings work is thus very different from that needed in ordinary architectural practice. Much damage has been done to historic fabric by inexpert misjudgement and unnecessarily panicky action. The inexperienced individual, faced with the repair of a masonry structure for the first time, should have no qualms about obtaining a second opinion from an experienced architect.

When a decision has been made to replace a particular stone, it will either be cut out completely or to a certain depth. Once the destruction of historic fabric which this involves has taken place, it seems, perhaps, a little academic to consider what is selected to go in its place. Nevertheless, a great deal of discussion over this matter has taken place in the past; and a case can be made out for each of the methods reviewed. Today the choice rests generally between natural and 'plastic' stone, since the use of tiles is generally out of fashion although renewed interest has been shown by one or two individuals over the last few years. Some of the practical considerations affecting the choice between the genuine and the artificial product have been outlined above, the most important undoubtedly being that 'plastic' stone cannot be used for structural or weathering purposes, and can only be used to fill cavities. In many instances, therefore, it may be appropriate to employ both new and 'plastic' stone on the same job, using the former where necessary for structural reasons, and the latter to enable the minimum of old stone to be cut away where a little 'dentistry' will suffice.

Much of the nineteenth- and twentieth-century opposition to the use of new stone has come not merely from over-renewal, but also from its often hard appearance in a weathered wall. Mid-nineteenth-century masonry in particular often exhibits this insensitive character, and it is important that the architect should learn, by observation of old work, to specify replacements correctly. Mediaeval stonework was often comparatively crudely set out, especially in curved work, and the contrast between work of this nature and that of the nineteenth century may be seen clearly in the arcade running round above the wall benches in the Romanesque chapter house and vestibule at Bristol Cathedral (*Figure 1.18*). Early stonework was, moreover, dressed by hand from the rough block, and it is virtually impossible to obtain the same effect by taking a modern piece sawn die square and tooling or 'distressing' its surface and arrises (*Figure 1.19*). Of particular importance is the bed joint, which in mediaeval times was often only very roughly dressed, so that as the face of the stone weathers gently back an irregular, undulating joint line is constantly

Figure 1.18 Irregular setting out of Romanesque work (right) compared with the nineteenth-century renewal (left). Chapter House, Bristol Cathedral

Figure 1.19 The unsatisfactory appearance of distressed masonry, Jumièges Abbey, Normandy

exposed rather than the hard, mathematically precise network which would result from flat, truly-sawn beds and perpends. The point may be appreciated instantly in connection with paving if the old slabs in a London street, with their hand-dressed edges, are compared with new sawn replacements (*Figure 1.20*). It is vital that the architect learn to recognize that such irregularities have nothing to do with weathering, and are a product of the original craftsmanship; when looking at a wall with a view to its repair, the two must constantly be distinguished. The stones illustrated in *Figure 1.21* for example, were laid in 1410, and still bear their original tooling, although it is slightly eroded by time. In no way would a modern piece of the same stone weather to the same appearance in five or six centuries if finished with a sawn or rubbed face, and it is not good enough, therefore, to slap in a new stone and hope that it will weather to match the old. Careful attention must be paid to the specification of finishes on both face *and* joints so that the character of the old masonry is matched and the new blends happily and unobtrusively with the old even before weathering has commenced.

Even after great care has been taken with specification, it is essential that the detailed attention which must be given to individual stones is borne upon the contractor and carried through into execution. The way the masonry trade is organized today, however, makes this extremely difficult to achieve since stone is seldom dressed on site. Instead, one man will visit the building to take measurements and profiles which are transferred to cards showing the banker mason the shape and dimensions of the new stone required. The latter will then dress the stone in a shop which may be miles from the building under repair, without ever having visited the site himself, and is thus completely unable to gain any feeling for the character of the masonry and its individual needs. The stone will be fixed by a third man, who all too often is not a mason, and may simply regard the stone as an inconveniently large form of brick. This is a most unsatisfactory state of affairs, but one not easily resolved in many instances. In the case of a large and important historic building, however, a directly employed team of craftsmen may be available, whilst for smaller jobs it may be possible to employ a small local firm who can bring the necessary individual attention to bear.

Great care is also necessary in the specification and execution of pointing, not just from the point of view of mortar mixes, but also on account of the impact the style of pointing will have on the final appearance of the work. Where one or two individual stones are to be replaced it should not necessarily be assumed that the entire wall needs to be repointed, and just as conservative an approach should be brought to bear here as in the renewal of stone. After all, the mortar is as much a part of the archaeology of the building as the building block. In such cases, the aim should be to match the original pointing as closely as possible, and experiments and sample panels for approval should be allowed for in the specification. The same is true where a whole

(a)

(b)

Figure 1.20 (*a*) Hand-dressed edges of old York stone paving, City of London; (*b*) sawn edges of new York stone paving

wall has to be repointed, but here, if the existing pointing is at variance with the character of the building, there is an opportunity to change to another style. This is most commonly done where a building was furnished with 'ribbon' or 'snail-creep' pointing in the nineteenth century, and a change to a more seemly variety is desired. For many mediaeval walls this replacement may be of the 'Ancient Monuments' type, where the mortar is kept back slightly from the faces of the stones to allow their arrises to read fully; but this is not always appropriate, and the architect should familiarize himself with the whole range of alternatives, both modern and historical. Above all, he should be aware of the damage that can be done to masonry in the removal of old pointing, especially where Portland cement has been used in it, and avoid the use of terms such as 'hack out' in his specification. Where possible, the

Figure 1.21 Weathered tooling of 1410, St Bartholomew's Church, Tong, Shropshire

term 'rake out' should be employed; but where forced by the hardness of the pointing to use the expression 'cut out' the architect should stipulate that this is to be done with a hammer and chisel used along the direction of the joint and not across it, in order to avoid damage to the arrises.

Finally, a word must be said about the desirability of preparing record drawings of any wall of archaeological importance both before and after repair. Record drawings may, in any case, be a vital prelude in approaching repair, especially where renewals and alterations have been carried out in the past, and will enable a proper understanding by the architect of the historic masonry under consideration. It may, indeed, lead him to stay his hand in certain particularly sensitive areas; or, conversely, indicate where repair can be carried out with impunity. It is only recently, for example, that a proper study has been made of the city walls at Canterbury, Kent. Comparison of the photograph (*Figure 1.22*) with the record drawing (*Figure 1.23*) will show how features overlooked for centuries have been revealed. Besides the plotting of the individual stones making up the wall, their types were also determined, and examination was extended to the mortars used in the different phases of the wall's construction. The most notable discovery has been the row of early battlements which are believed to be of Roman date, repaired in the early Norman period, and later built into the nave wall of the twelfth-century church of St Mary Northgate. Many more items of interest have been revealed by careful studies of this nature.[28]

The post-repair drawing, on the other hand, will be of the very greatest value to those who follow fifty years or a century later, enabling historians to distinguish replacements from old stone with great ease and providing valuable information to whomsoever has the job of supervising the next round of repairs. It may also, incidentally, be useful when

Figure 1.22 The north wall of the twelfth-century nave of St Mary's Church, Northgate, Canterbury, Kent, built on the earlier city wall (*Kentish Gazette*)

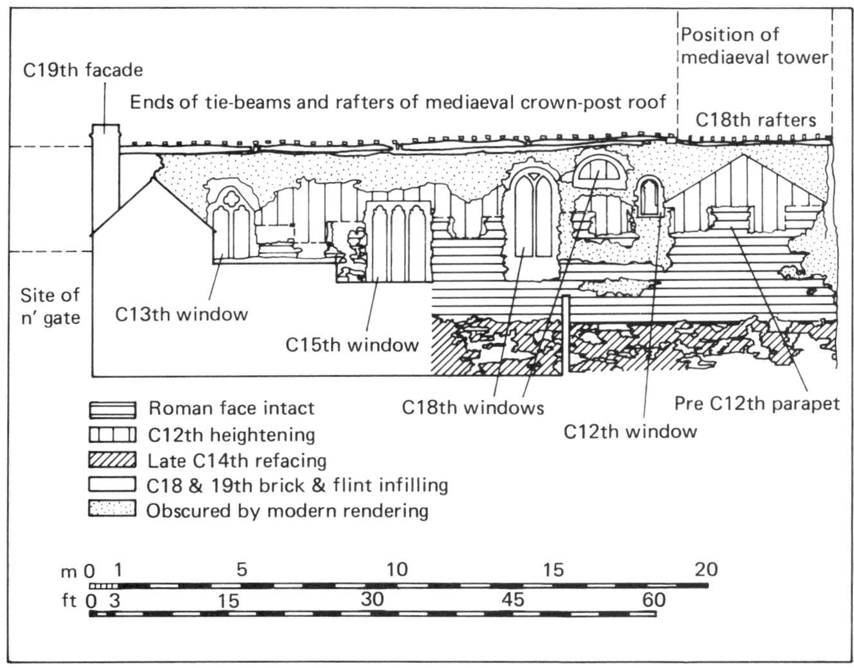

Figure 1.23 Interpretation of the wall shown in *Figure 1.22* (Canterbury Archaeological Trust)

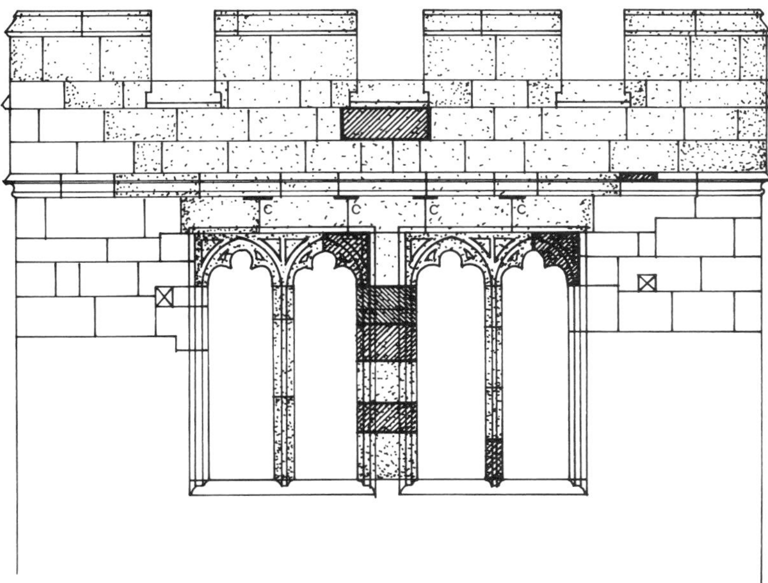

Figure 1.24 Head of the tower, north face, St Margaret's Church, Horsmonden, Kent. Areas dismantled and rebuilt are shown dotted; new stones are hatched; 'C' marks positions of concealed stainless steel cramps (By kind permission of Purcell Miller Tritton and Partners)

explaining to a client where his money has been spent, since in a good repair the renewals should blend into the wall and be difficult to see. Although in many ways the greatest compliment that can be paid to an architect is that the building after repair looks no different than before work commenced, he may still be concerned that there is little to show for what may have been considerable expenditure. Record drawings of this nature need not be particularly elaborate or costly to produce. Those made when the parapets and facings of the upper part of the tower of St Margaret's Church, Horsmonden, Kent, was dismantled and rebuilt in 1971 (*Figure 1.24*), for example, were prepared as a matter of routine during the course of the contract. They show not only the areas of masonry taken down, but also the locations of the new stainless steel ties and cramps inserted and the very small number of new stones which had to be used.

Altogether, it must be stressed, historic buildings are important artifacts, which provide a wealth of data about past habits, manners, techniques, and aspirations. In some cases they may be the only documents left by a defunct civilization. It is essential, therefore, that the architect entrusted with their repair neither seeks to leave his mark upon them nor forces them to conform with modern standards and practices, but labours instead to preserve, without distortion, the full range of evidence and enjoyment they can provide. An ill-considered refacing of the stretch of the Canterbury City wall illustrated in *Figure 1.22*, for example, would have completely destroyed the archaeological evidence it contained, leaving it bereft of its historical interest and the life given it by antiquity. In the same way, poorly-matched renewals can be equally destructive of the homogeneity of an eighteenth-century wall (*Figure 1.25*). The repair of masonry should accordingly never be undertaken in a wanton manner, but must be a carefully considered process aimed at the preservation of both archaeological data and the aesthetic qualities of the building, including those owing to its age.

Figure 1.25 Poor piecing in an eighteenth-century ashlar wall

References

1. Smith, C.H., 'Lithology; or, Observations on Stone used for Building', *Transactions of the Royal Institute of British Architects*, **1**, Pt. 2, 1842, 129
2. *The Architecture of Leon Battista Alberti* (tr. James Leoni), **2**, f.99*v*, 1726
3. John Evelyn, *A Parallel of the Antient Architecture with the Modern*, 2nd edn., 1707, 'An Account of Architects and Architecture', p. 10
4. *Op.cit.,* 1728, p.23
5. Edmund Burke, *A Philosophical Enquiry into the Origin of our Ideas of the Sublime and the Beautiful*, 1757
6. Price, Uvedale, *An Essay on the Picturesque*, new edn, 1796, pp. 62-63
7. *Op.cit.,* p. 24
8. *Op. cit.,* pp.11–13
9. Pugin, A.W.N.,*Contrasts,* 2nd edn, 1841, p. 74
10. *Vide* Eastlake, C.L., *A History of the Gothic Revival*, 1872, p. 120 sqq.
11. *Report of the Cambridge Camden Society for MDCCCXL*, Cambridge, 1840, pp. 9, 15
12. *Report of the Cambridge Camden Society for MDCCCXLI*, Cambridge, 1841, p. 40
13. *Ibid.,* p. 39
14. *Report of the Cambridge Camden Society for MDCCCXLII*, Cambridge, 1842, p. 23
15. *The Ecclesiologist*, **1**, 1841–2, pp. 5, 29, 143
16. *Op.cit.,* pp. 179, 180
17. *Ibid.*, p. 144 sqq.
18. Letter in Winchester College archives from Butterfield to Sir William Heathcote dated 1st or 17th June 1861 (quoted from Paul Thompson, *William Butterfield*, 1971, p. 416)
19. *The Ecclesiologist,* No. CLXXV, August 1866. p. 212
20. Prior, E.S., *A History of Gothic Art in England*, 1900, p. 289
21. Scott, Sir Gilbert, *Personal and Professional Recollections* (ed. G. Gilbert Scott), 1879, p. 325
22. Scott, George Gilbert, *An Essay on the History of English Church Architecture*, 1881, p. 147b
23. Ruskin, John, *The Seven Lamps of Architecture*, 1849, p. 180
24. *Vide* Linstrum, Derek, 'Giuseppe Valadier et l'Arc de Titus'. *Monumentum* **25**, No. 1, 43–71, March 1982
25. *Op. cit.*, p. 77
26. Heyman, Jaques, 'The Gothic Structure', *Interdisciplinary Science Reviews,* **2**, No. 1, 151–164, March 1977, fig. 23 (p. 163)
27. Willis, Robert, *The Architectural History of Canterbury Cathedral*, 1845, p. 116
28. Tatton-Brown, Tim, 'Canterbury', *Current Archaeology*, **6**, No. 3, 78–83, June 1978

2

The nature of building and decorative stones

Francis G. Dimes

Introduction

Stone, the primary building material taken from the crust of the Earth, has been used since the earliest times for convenience, endurance and visual impact. Its use began when man gave up the nomadic lifestyle of a hunter-gatherer and began to build permanent setttlements.

Much of the history of the world's civilizations is recorded in stone. In many instances it is almost the only remaining tangible evidence of a past occupation. The monuments include for instance, the great four-mile long, grey granite menhir avenues of Carnac, the gneiss monoliths of Callanish, the sandstone trilithons of Stonehenge and the volcanic tuff and scoria colossi of Easter Island.

The Egyptians were the earliest people to use stone in large quantities for building.[1] The pyramids are estimated to contain more than two million blocks of limestone each weighing approximately 2.5 tonnes. Stone was considered to be so important that at one time all the quarries were in royal ownership. Granite, limestone, dolerite, quartzite, schist and breccia are some of the stones used to construct the tombs, temples and palaces along the valley of the Nile.

From the early masonry achievements in Egypt, commencing before 3000 BC and extending over three millennia, an impressive catalogue can easily be assembled which demonstrates clearly the importance of stone to man in his building endeavours. There are the alabaster and limestone reliefs and sculptures of Assyria; the alabaster blocks of the Minoan palaces; the marble and limestone architecture of Greece and Rome. Many stones were

Figure 2.1 The coarsely foliated nature of gneiss is well displayed in the monoliths of Callanish, Isle of Lewis, Scotland. (Photo: John Ashurst)

Figure 2.2 The Parthenon, on the Acropolis, Athens, Greece. Parian marble, from the Isle of Paros was used for the roof (courtesy of R.H. Roberts)

Figure 2.3 The sculptured wall by the Terrace of the Leper King, Ankor Wat, Cambodia (now Kampuchea) is built of sandstone and of laterite (courtesy of E.A. Jobbins)

exploited during the expansion of the Roman Empire and the building of the great frontier wall of China. There is a profusion of stone buildings and trachyte sculpture left by the Mayan culture as well as the incomparable close-fitting masonry of Cuzco, the Inca capital of Peru. The Angkor Wat (*Figure 2.3*) and other vast laterite and sandstone buildings of the Khmers of Cambodia are covered with narrative reliefs. Nearly 15 000 tons of drystone walling carved with chevron patterns form the palace site on the granite hill known as Zimbabwe. The cathedrals and fortifications of medieval Europe, Russia and Scandinavia and of Saracenic Syria, North Africa, Turkey and India involve almost every building and decorative stone known. Stone was the material for the great houses and palaces of the Renaissance and the Classical and Gothic revivals which followed them. These styles were often used for public buildings, industrial buildings and churches in North America, Australia and South Africa as well as in Europe. Even modern buildings are frequently clad in thin stone facings in a way which the Assyrians, Romans or Moguls would have understood.

The repair, maintenance and preservation of this vast heritage of stone is an enormous and sometimes costly business. There are also major problems associated with decay and weathering with which this book is largely concerned. However, the principal characteristics of stone emerging from a study of masonry buildings are those of durability, versatility and of beauty. When man built, and indeed builds, for permanence and for impact, stone is the material chosen.

Definitions

Dimension stone is the term used for a rock that can be quarried, cut and worked to a specified size or shape for use in a building as a structural unit or for use purely as decoration. In this sense the term rock is defined in the dictionary as the solid part of the Earth's crust and the term stone is defined as any piece of rock which has been detached from the Earth's crust. All rocks are aggregates of minerals. Thus such materials as clay, coal and sand are recognized geologically as rocks.

Minerals, in strict scientific definition, are natural inorganic substances with symmetrical crystal forms which reflect internal atomic structures and which have defined chemical compositions. Over 2500 minerals have been identified and named. Many of them are rare. Only about twenty-five, either singly or in association, make up the physical bulk of most rocks used for building.[2]

Criteria for use

Three criteria may be considered to determine whether stone should be used in any particular situation. Firstly, it should be sufficiently durable for the intended purpose. In the past the durability of a stone was discovered from experience of its use, a method of assessment which should not be forgotten today. Now physical and chemical tests can provide valuable additional indications of likely durability (see Chapter 10). Secondly, it should be economically available and easily quarried and worked to the desired profiles. This criterion is still important but is less critical now than in the past because of improvements in transport systems and increasing sophistication of cutting equipment. Thirdly, it should be pleasing to the eye. Because stone is a natural material all types may claim to satisfy this criterion, although it may be noted that some man-made juxtapositions of stone are not aesthetically pleasing.

It may usually be assumed that in the past availability was of paramount importance. Other historical factors relating to political boundaries, ownerships, trade agreements and conditions of instability and war have obviously influenced the use and choice of particular stones.

Geological factors

Geological factors now decide whether a stone may be used within the determined criteria. Geology is the fundamental science which determines not only the scenery of any region but also its architecture. It is the science of the prime natural materials used for building and is the determining factor of regional forms of building. It is immediately apparent that the shape and size of flint, whether used as 'field flint', 'cobble' or 'squared flint', largely dictates the method of construction and is a major influence on the style of building. The main factor limiting the construction method and determining the appearance is the size of the flint blocks that can be obtained and used. The size of these blocks is a direct reflection of the mode of formation, or the genesis, of flint. Similarly, other building stones can only be obtained in sizes which are a reflection of their geological history. It follows, therefore, that any stone chosen for building must be obtainable in blocks large enough for the desired purpose. It should be free from fractures. It should be sufficiently tough and free of minerals which may break down chemically or by weathering. Hardness is not necessarily a requisite, although when a stone is to be used for paving or steps resistance to abrasion is a desirable quality. The distinction between toughness and hardness should be noted. A tough stone is not necessarily hard.

In some instances, for example where stone is to be used for internal decorative facing, it should be capable of taking a polish. The colour of the stone and its 'figuring' then become important characteristics. Depending upon the architectural detailing of a building, low water absorption, and a macroporous structure may be desirable qualities. It should be noted particularly that no two blocks of stone, even if quarried side by side, are absolutely identical any more than, for example, two planks of oak are. The differences may not be discernible and may be of no practical importance; but they may be substantial. The differences may also contribute greatly to the attractiveness and beauty of the stone and can be exploited to show the material to its best advantage.

Distribution

A purely superficial glance at the geological map of Great Britain[3] shows that the country has a great variety of rocks. This is a reflection of the geological history of the country. All rocks have been used in one manner or another for building purposes. The vast variety of rock types and the sometimes restricted area in which some occur and were used precludes mention of them all; a meaningless catalogue would result. Discussion has been confined, therefore, to those stones which have been used on any scale for building and to those which have

Figure 2.4 In an area without a supply of rock suitable for building, any stones available may be used. The 'conglomerate wall' enclosing the Nursery, Battersea Park, London, in addition to bricks and tiles has been built of many pieces of different types of stone, mostly gathered from around London's docks

particular qualities worthy of note. Many of the stones discussed here are from British sources. But, because Britain is made up of rocks which belong to the majority of all the known types, the geological considerations discussed may be applied world-wide.

On the Geological Map of the United Kingdom, published by the Ordnance Survey for the British Geological Survey, a sedimentary formation is shown as one colour throughout the length of its outcrop. This must not be interpreted as indicating that the type of rock is consistent throughout that outcrop. This is because the map shows the *age* of the formation, not necessarily its lithology. The type of stone in any area cannot be identified by reference to the map alone.

Classification

Despite the apparently bewildering variety of rocks, any one can be placed into one of three groups; all rocks within any one group have common characteristics which are unique to that group. The groups are igneous, sedimentary and metamorphic rocks.

Igneous rocks

The rocks within the lithosphere (the solid outer shell of the Earth, which includes the crust) are normally solid. They melt only when there is a decrease of pressure or there is an addition of other material. The molten rock material then formed is termed *magma* and it may originate at different levels within the Earth. It is essentially a fluid silicate melt with water-vapour and other volatiles. In geologically favourable conditions, magma may rise through the crust, becoming lighter through expansion and increasingly mobile. On cooling, at whatever level in the Earth, it forms an *igneous* rock. Some of the magma may have poured out on the surface as *lava* during a volcanic eruption and the resultant rock is known as *volcanic* or *extrusive* igneous rock. Magma which cools and consolidates within the Earth is termed an *intrusive* or *plutonic* igneous rock and is seen only when the encompassing *country rock* has been weathered away. No matter where they are found, igneous rocks have characteristics directly arising from the cooling and consolidation of magma. The form, or shape, will depend on where the magma came to rest. The rate of cooling also depends, to a great extent, upon the position of the magma within the Earth. If poured out onto the surface the magma will cool rapidly and glassy or very finely crystalline volcanic igneous rocks will result. Many cubic kilometres of magma within the lithosphere may be contained in chambers. It cools slowly and coarsely crystalline plutonic rocks result, the crystals of which normally can be individually distinguished by eye. In some instances, the magma cooled at variable rates and large crystals,

Table 2.1 Classification of igneous rocks

Position of emplacement	*Chemical composition*			
	Acid	*Intermediate*	*Basic*	*Ultra-basic*
Volcanic (extrusive) (glassy or very fine-grained)	Normally these rocks are glassy or too fine-grained for individual crystals to be seen			
	◄—— Tuff ——►			
	Pumice Obsidian* Rhyolite	Andesite	Basalt*	
Minor intrusions (fine-grained or medium-grained)	Quartz obviously present	Some quartz may be present	No quartz seen	No quartz seen
	Quartz-porphyry	Porphyry*	Dolerite†	
Plutonic (medium grained or coarse-grained)	Granodiorite* Granite*	Diorite* Syenite*	Gabbro*	Serpentinite* Peridotite

*The geological names of rocks which have been used on any scale for building, either structurally or decoratively
†Quartz dolerites do exist

termed ***phenocrysts*** were formed first. The remaining magma cooled more slowly and the phenocrysts may be surrounded by smaller crystals.

Igneous rocks, therefore, can be classified using the position of emplacement as the criterion. However, this does not take account of the chemical composition of the original magma, which can be deduced from the chemical composition of the minerals which crystallize from it.

Igneous rocks are essentially assemblages of silicates. When they are chemically analysed the proportion of silicon dioxide (SiO_2) present may be used as a basis of classification. Those rocks yielding a high percentage of SiO_2 are termed *acid*. These rocks contain the mineral quartz, the crystal form of silica. The term acid refers to the chemical composition of the rock and does not imply that the rocks have a corrosive quality.

Rocks which yield a low percentage of SiO_2 are known as ***basic*** and as ***ultra-basic***. The terms basic and ultra-basic refer only to the chemical composition of the rocks and not to their origin.

Purely arbitrary limits may be set for the percentage of silica present. A common classification is shown below:

Rock type	*Per cent SiO_2*
Acid	>65
Intermediate	55–65
Basic	45–55
Ultra-basic	<45

It should be noted, however, that there may be a continuous mineral variation in igneous rocks. Rocks which are genetically related may fall, therefore, into different divisions of a classification.

Nevertheless, using the criteria of emplacement and of chemical composition, a classification can be constructed to accommodate most igneous rocks (*Table 2.1*).

Sedimentary rocks

The geological processes of weathering and of erosion produce sediments, the raw material of sedimentary rocks. All rock types when exposed to the atmosphere are susceptible to weathering, the mechanical or chemical breakdown of the rock, and to erosion, the process of removal and of transport of the products of weathering.

The material of the sediments, often reworked many times through the long period of geological time, originated from igneous rocks which formed the first primitive crust of the Earth. The processes can be illustrated by considering the weathering of a granite, an acid plutonic igneous rock. By definition, for a rock to be termed granite, three essential minerals must be present: feldspar, mica and quartz. The mineral quartz is hard. It is not easily cleaved and is highly resistant to chemical attack. It becomes broken into smaller and smaller fragments; the size depends on the length of time during which the fragments are exposed to the mechanical processes of weathering.

Mica is the name given to a family group of silicate minerals, which differ from each other in detailed chemical composition. They are individually named. Examples include biotite mica and muscovite mica. Mica is not very hard and is brittle. It has perfect cleavage which enables it to split into very thin plates, and is resistant to chemical attack and to weathering. It breaks down into smaller and smaller flakes until eventually they are of sub-microscopic size.

Feldspar is the name for a group of minerals with the general formula of $X(Al,Si)_4O_8$ where X = Na, K, Ca or Ba. They are named depending on their chemical composition, e.g. Orthoclase, Plagioclase. The feldspars are the most abundant of all the minerals. Feldspar, especially when acted upon by slightly acid water, breaks down to give soluble salts of potassium (K), sodium (Na), and calcium (Ca) with a clay mineral, kaolinite, hydrous aluminium silicate ($Al_4Si_4O_{10}(OH)_8$). It is the breakdown of feldspar which releases the grains of quartz and mica.

Basic igneous rocks weather in much the same manner, but more soluble material is produced and, under certain conditions, more clay. However, no quartz grains will be produced (see *Table 2.2*).

The weathering products may not be transported any distance and may remain to blanket the bedrock from which they were derived. More normally, however, they are transported and during transport are reduced in size by abrasion. They are more or less changed during their journey and finally deposited as a layer or bed (if very thin, *laminae*) of sediment (*Figure 2.5*). Running water is the most common transporting medium. Most, but not all, sediments come to rest in the oceans. Water movement sorts the sediments and tends to concentrate similar materials together.

The small, insoluble flakes are deposited as beds of *mud*; the quartz grains as beds of *sand*. The salts are added to the water where some may reach sufficiently high concentrations for them to be chemically precipitated, to form for example, a *lime mud*.

Sedimentation is not continuous; thus a series of beds of sediment is built up. The sediments are converted into sedimentary rocks, by the process of lithification, either shortly after deposition or at a later stage. Lithification includes dewatering, compaction, welding of the constituent particles and the natural cementation of the grains by other mineral matter. The form of a sedimentary rock and its unique characteristic is a roughly horizontal layer or *bed*. The major cementing minerals are calcium

Table 2.2 Classification of sedimentary rocks

Rock type	*Name*	*Main constituents*	*Remarks*
Rudaceous (rubbly rocks mainly composed of large fragments of older rocks)	Breccia	Large fragments of any rock type	Broken, *angular*, mostly unworn fragments set in finer material and held together by natural cement; often a cemented scree.
	Conglomerate	Large fragments of any rock type	*Rounded* fragments in finer material and held together by natural cement; a cemented gravel.
Arenaceous (sandy rocks)	Sandstone*	Quartz grains	Bedded, composed of rounded quartz grains, fine to medium grained, usually with grains cemented.
	Grit (stone)*	Quartz grains	Bedded, composed of angular quartz grains, usually medium to coarse grained. May contain small pebbles. Generally coarsely bedded.
	Flagstone*	Quartz grains and mica flakes	Finely bedded, fine-grained rounded quartz, with layers of mica flakes lying along bedding planes.
	Arkose*	Quartz grains and feldspar, commonly partly decomposed	Sandstone or grit, medium to coarse grained containing over 25% feldspar. Mostly terrestrial deposits.
	Quartzite*	Quartz grains	Composed almost entirely of quartz grains, closely fitting and naturally cemented with silica.
Argillaceous (clayey rocks)	Clay	Clay mud	Very fine-grained, flaky minerals, structureless.
	Mudstone	Clay mud	Clay with much water squeezed out; very fine grained, massive and structureless.
	Shale	Clay mud	Laminated, commonly finely compacted mudstone. Splits along laminae which are in the direction of the original bedding.
Calcareous (carbonate rocks mainly of calcium and magnesium carbonate) Some calcareous rocks are chemically precipitated.	Limestone*	Calcium carbonate, (calcite)	Bedded, composed essentially of calcium carbonate
	Oolitic limestone*	Ooliths of calcium carbonate	Limestone composed mostly of small spheroidal calcareous grains.
	Magnesian limestone*	Magnesium carbonate and calcium carbonate	Limestone, with a high proportion of dolomite; massive, granular, saccharoidal.
	Tufa*	Calcium carbonate	Deposited from saturated limey waters; friable, porous (spongy) structure.
	Travertine*	Calcium carbonate	Similar to tufa, but more compact, more dense, not friable.
Organic	Coal Lignite Peat	Organic remains	Bedded rocks formed from vegetable matter.
Evaporites	Gypstum (includes Alabaster*) Anhydrite Rock salt	Hydrated calcium sulphate Calcium sulphate Sodium chloride	Chemically precipitated from evaporating waters
Chemical precipitates	Chert *† Flint* Jasper (some limestones are chemical precipitates)	Silicon dioxide with greater or lesser amounts of impurities	

*The geological names of those rocks which have been used on any scale for building, structurally or decoratively

†There is geological controversy about the origin of chert and allied rocks which are listed here as chemical precipitates

Figure 2.5 Well marked horizontal bedding in alternating shales and limestones of the Lower Lias, Jurassic. Southerndown bay, Glamorgan

carbonate, especially in the form of calcite, the crystalline form of calcium carbonate ($CaCO_3$); silica, commonly in the form of quartz (SiO_2); iron, commonly as limonite ($2Fe_2O_3{\cdot}3H_2O$); and the calcium magnesium carbonate, dolomite ($CaMg(CO_3)_2$). Groundwater circulating through the sediments before or after lithification, may take mineral matter existing in the sediment into solution and re-deposit it, normally around some kind of nucleus to form a *concretion*.

It is possible, by using grain size and the nature of the constituent grains of a sediment as criteria, to construct a classification (*Table 2.2*). It should be remembered, however, that few sediments are composed exclusively of one type of constituent grain.

Metamorphic rocks

Any rock within the Earth's crust may be affected and modified by natural heat or by intense pressures, or both, generally resulting from stresses generated when large plates of the lithosphere move against each other. The mineral matter of the rocks may be re-formed to produce larger crystals of the original mineral or it may be recrystallized to form new minerals that are stable in the new environment. It is important to note that the rocks remain essentially solid during these processes and may retain some of their original characteristics. There are two categories of metamorphism which are of interest. The first type is that caused by heat alone from, for instance, an igneous intrusion. This is termed *contact metamorphism*. The second type is caused by high temperatures or by great stresses or both, generated within great fold belts found within the Earth's crust. This is termed *regional metamorphism*. In general the type of metamorphism is of little practical importance when considering types of building stones. Products of the two types of metamorphism which ,are most commonly used for building or decoration are marble (contact metamorphism) and schist (regional metamorphism).

Contact or thermal metamorphism is a matter of simple baking. When subjected to heat and contained by other rocks, particles of limestone ($CaCO_3$) and fossils are gradually recrystallized into roughly similar-sized interlocking crystals of the mineral calcite. The rock is then known as *marble*. If the limestone was not confined by other rocks the calcium carbonate of the limestone would disassociate following the reaction $CaCO_3$ + heat → CaO (lime) + CO_2 (carbon dioxide).

A limestone with little or no mineral matter other than calcium carbonate converts into a pure white granular marble. However, if other mineral matter is

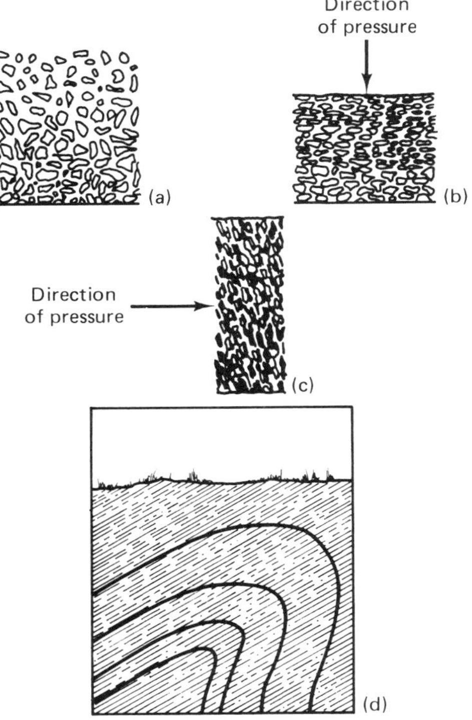

Figure 2.6 When first deposited, the submicroscopic flaky clay minerals are arranged in random order (a). With increasing pressure they tend to turn to be at right angles to that pressure (b). When regional pressure is applied the flakes tend to reorientate at right angles to the new applied pressure. Some mineral matter rearranges itself to form new minerals which grow at right angles to the pressure and slaty cleavage is imposed. If the beds of clay were folded before metamorphism, the slaty cleavage may have a direction different from that of the original bedding. The difference between bedding and cleavage should be noted. (© Nat. Mus. Wales, reproduced by permission)

present in the original limestone, it too is altered to develop new minerals which give the colour and figuring to many marbles. Marbles produced solely by thermal metamorphism are not of major importance. However, calcareous rocks subjected to regional metamorphism taking place over extensive areas recrystallize to produce fine-grained marbles. The coarseness of grain is dependent on the degree of metamorphism.

Regional metamorphism is widespread and takes place in areas of mountain building. Two factors control the processes; heat and pressure. Each of these may be acting alone or in any combination.

If a clay is subjected to sustained regional pressure at low temperature, the flaky materials present tend to reorientate at right angles to the direction of strong stress. Some recrystallization also occurs and small flakes of new minerals, mostly mica, and chlorite, a hydrated silicate of aluminium, iron and magnesium, $((Mg,Fe,Al)_6(Si,Al)_4O_{10}(OH)_8)$, grow at right angles to the direction of principal stress. A new rock, termed a *slate*, is formed and it has a parallel orientation of planar minerals impressed upon it. It has *slaty cleavage* along which the rock may be easily split. This is not the same as bedding of sedimentary rocks (see *Figure 2.7*).

The form of metamorphic rocks depends on the form of the original rocks from which they were derived. Any pre-existing rock may be metamorphosed. Characteristically all metamorphic rocks have a foliated structure. This may not always be observed on a macroscopic scale, but may possibly be seen on a microscopic scale. The rough alignment of the interlocking crystals of calcite in a marble (*Figure 2.8*) is one example.

Figure 2.7 The parallel arrangement of sheet-shaped minerals enable the rock to be split easily along the direction of slaty cleavage. Penrhyn Quarry, Caernarvonshire. (Courtesy of R.H. Boyle)

Table 2.3 Classification of metamorphic rocks

Sedimentary origin	*Regional metamorphism*			*Contact metamorphism*
	Low grade	*Medium grade*	*High grade*	
Pelitic rocks (from argillaceous or muddy sediments	Slate*	Schist[1]	Gneiss[2]	Hornfels
Psammitic rocks (from arenaceous, or sandy sediments)	Quartz-schist	Quartzite[3]*	Quartzite*	Quartzite*
Calcareous rocks (from calcareous, or limey, sediments)	Marble*	Marble*	Marble*	Marble*
Igneous origin				
Basic rocks (dolerites, basalts)	Schists[1] and Gneisses[2]			
Acid rocks (granites)	Schists[1] and Gneisses[2]			

[1]Finely crystalline, commonly with much mica and will split relatively easily in one direction
[2]Coarsely crystalline, with crystals roughly streaked out in one direction
[3]The term quartzite is descriptive and does not indicate mode of origin
*The geological names of rocks which have been used on any scale for building, either structurally or decoratively

Figure 2.8 A coarse foliation in marble seen in a roadside section on Mount Jagro, Carrara, Italy, is picked out and emphasized by vegetation

The degree of metamorphism to which a rock was subjected is expressed by its *grade*. Complicated classifications can be constructed to take account of the many variables. Here (*Table 2.3*) a classification adapted from H.H. Read and J. Watson.[4] based on the original nature of the rock is used.

Joints

The size of a block which can be wrought from the quarry is controlled by *joints*, the chief structural feature of any rock. A joint is a parting plane within the rock which separates or tends to separate the contiguous mass into two parts. Groups of parallel joints form a *joint set* and intersecting sets of joints form a *joint system*. Joints may be only a short distance apart (*close jointed*) or may be a considerable distance apart (*wide jointed*). Persistent joints which are maintained over considerable distances are *master joints*. One or two sets of joints provide the master joints. The others are interrupted and normally are not continuous although they retain their essential parallelism. A joint is distinguished from a fault, which is a fracture within the rock mass along which the rock on one side has been displaced relative to the rock on the other side. Displacements up to thousands of metres are known.

All consolidated rocks are jointed. The joint system controls not only the shape of the quarry but also the shape and size of the blocks which can be extracted. Joints and joint systems are themselves a direct reflection of the mode of formation of the rocks in which they are found and are best considered and discussed under the major classifications of igneous, sedimentary and metamorphic rocks.

Joints in igneous rocks

Discussion on joints in igneous rocks may conveniently be divided into those found in volcanic rocks and those found in plutonic rocks.

Volcanic rocks are those poured out originally as lava sheets on the Earth's surface. The molten lava sheet cannot contract overall, and thus shrinkage commonly takes place around equidistantly spaced centres which, because they are in a more-or-less geometrical system, lead to a regular pattern. These joints usually occur at right angles to the cooling surfaces and thus the sheet is divided into hexagonal columns. The pattern is produced by contraction towards roughly equally spaced centres. Horizontal cross joints are developed to lesser extent and these divide the columns into shorter lengths. One of the most spectacular manifestations of hexagonal jointing is seen in the columnar jointing of the fine-grained basalt of the Giants' Causeway in Northern Ireland.

Figure 2.9 Weathering has accentuated the widely spaced joints in the granite of Hay Tor, Dartmoor, Devon

Minor intrusions, commonly in the form of sills and of dykes (*Figure 2.10*) show a similar, but usually not so well developed, style of jointing. Columns, if produced, are at right angles to the cooling surfaces; the joint system is regularly arranged with respect to the walls containing the magma.

Major plutonic intrusions show a complex joint system caused by the interaction of contraction on cooling, stresses caused by emplacement and by pressure release when the overlying rocks are removed by weathering. When the cooling mass of magma reaches a sufficient state of rigidity, joints are formed in patterns related to the form of the intrusive mass.

Three sets of joints are developed. Two are vertical and roughly at right angles, while the third,

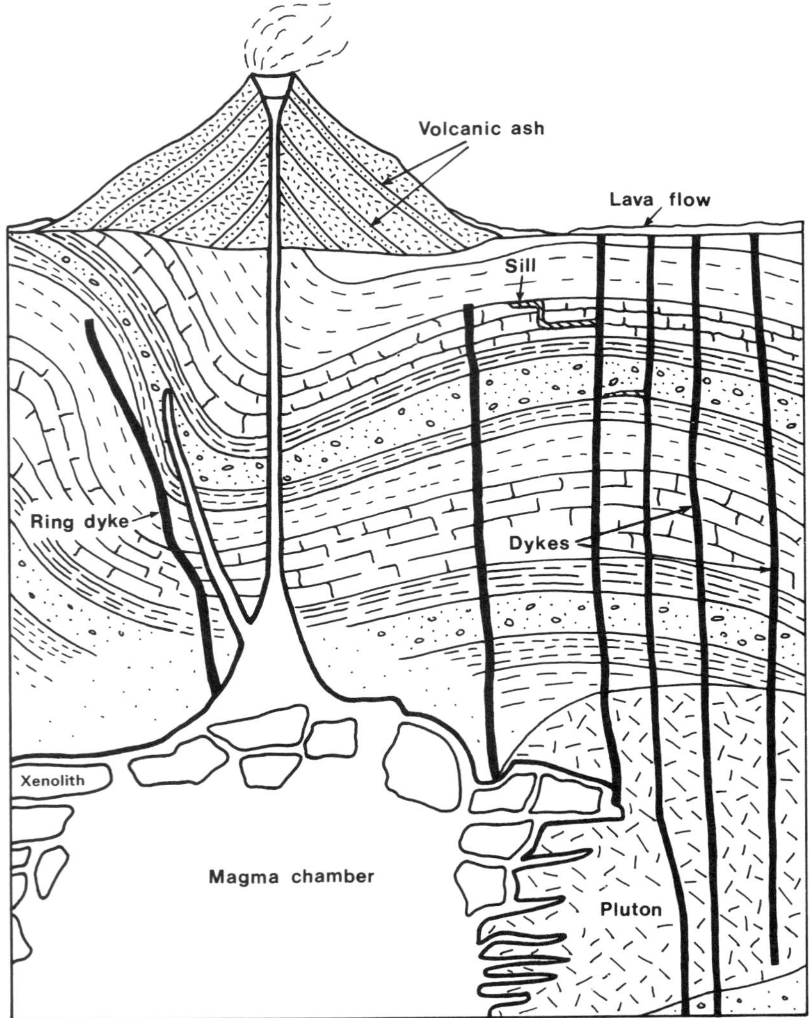

Figure 2.10 Igneous intrusion masses

termed *sheet jointing*, is horizontal, and follows the average contour of the ground surface.

Most granites, when worked in a quarry, will exhibit a direction along which the rock shows a tendency to split more easily than along other directions. This plane is known as the *rift*. Its origin is obscure; it may be due to a rough alignment of the constituent minerals of the rock or it may be a reflection of a rough orientation of the cleavage planes of the constituent minerals. A plane approximately at right angles to that of the rift and along which the rock will break with an ease second only to that of the rift, is known as the *grain*. The rift and grain follow the two intersecting vertical joint sets. When exposed to the natural agencies these joints normally are opened by weathering. Incipient joints, however, which are still mineralogically continuous may manifest themselves as thin, dark, discontinuous lines most easily distinguished on polished slabs.

Joints in plutonic igneous rocks can be widely spaced. The Duke of Argyll offered a monolithic shaft of the Ross of Mull granite 150 feet (45.7 m) long as a memorial obelisk to the Prince Regent.[5] Cleopatra's Needle in London, 68 feet 5½ inches (20.9 m) long, is one of the longest unjointed stones known.[6] An incompletely quarried obelisk at Aswan, Egypt, is 137 feet (41.7 m) long (*Figure 3.13*).

Joints in sedimentary rocks

The unique feature of sedimentary rocks is the bed. Each bed is the product of a single episode of sedimentation. A bed is bounded by two surfaces, one at the top and one at the bottom, called *the bedding planes*.

A bedding plane indicates a pause or change in the main sedimentation. During that pause the surface of the bed may have been marked by ripples, be rain pitted, dry and show sun-cracks or lie quietly under or above water level where very fine material will settle on it to form a thin layer.

Because the bed below and the bed above differ, if only very slightly, in composition, compaction, or grain size, they will not be exactly similar. The upper surface of each bed forms a plane of separation, the bedding plane. With the deposition of successive beds a series is built up which is called the *bedding* or *stratification*. Most sedimentary rocks consist of sediments laid down on the sea floor, and thus, the bedding is essentially horizontal. However, some sedimentary rocks result from the deposition of sediments in deltaic environments, sand banks, along the edges of lakes or seas, or from wind blown material. In these instances the bedding is at often acute angles to the general overall horizontal structure of the formation. This bedding, which may be conspicuous, is termed variously *false bedding*, *current bedding*, *cross bedding* or *dune bedding* (*Figures 2.13 and 2.14*). It is an important original

Figure 2.11 Joint system in Portland stone is well displayed on the bedding-plane surface. Portland Bill, Isle of Portland, Dorset

Figure 2.12 Vertical joints, roughly at right-angles, determine the width and depth of block that can be extracted at Weldon Quarry near Corby, Northamptonshire. The height on bed can vary considerably

Figure 2.13 Markedly cross-bedded (false-bedded, current-bedded) sandstones of the Coal Measures Carboniferous, exposed in cliffs near Seaton Delaval, Northumberland

Figure 2.14 Massively bedded Millstone Grit, Carboniferous, is exposed in Johnsons' Wellfield Quarry near Huddersfield, Yorkshire. The Millstone Grit was deposited in deltaic conditions and as a result wedge-bedding can be seen

which arises from the nature of the sedimentation. It is due to the currents which deposited the sediment.

As a sediment dries out, *shrinkage joints* develop because it is physically impossible for a bed of sediment to shrink overall laterally. The shrinkage joints are limited by the bedding planes. Commonly, two joint sets are produced, approximately at right angles to each other and at right angles to the bedding planes. Irregular, subordinate joints may be developed at an angle to the main joint sets to give irregularly shaped blocks. Some joint sets are produced by tectonic movements and result from stresses imposed upon the rocks. Commonly these joints are strongly developed and persistent and cross several beds. They are termed *master joints*. The shrinkage joints are subservient to the master joints. Generally master joints run in two sets and may be the main factor which determines the manner in which sedimentary rocks are quarried.

Joints are found in all sedimentary rocks except for some of the most recent. They control not only the height on bed of the block of stone that may be quarried but also its width and depth. The nature and spacing of the joints, therefore, is of economic significance. Well jointed rocks are more easily extracted.

Joints in metamorphic rocks

Metamorphic rocks arise from the change of existing rocks caused by heat or stress or the action of chemically active fluids, normally during the complex processes of mountain building. The rocks remain essentially solid during these processes. To a greater or lesser extent they retain their pre-existing joint patterns, but in addition have joints which result from the extreme stresses of tectonic movements imposed upon them. Complex joint systems may result. The important and, indeed, fundamental structure however, is *foliation*, the more or less parallel arrangement of the minerals.

Metamorphic rocks in which the mineral grains are roughly orientated are said to show a *schistose* texture. The foliation of a schist, the most common metamorphic rock, is seen as discontinuous layers. Some schists are the product of the metamorphism of clays. A succession may be traced from a clay, to a slate, to a schist.

If the minerals are coarse grained and segregated into rough bands the rock is termed a *gneiss*. A gneiss shows a lesser tendency to split along the bands than does a schist.

Marble results from the metamorphism of limestone. The presence of carbon dioxide apparently aids the formation of a granular structure and a rough, microscopic schistosity may be imposed. Because the calcite grains develop an interlocking structure, large blocks, the desired feature for building purposes, may be extracted from between the pre-existing joint system in areas which are not otherwise tectonically disturbed. The alignment of the calcite grains normally is not seen in pure marbles, but other coloured mineral matter may give an indication of a foliation.

Metamorphic rocks, therefore, are chosen for two contrasting characteristics. For example, slate is used because it will cleave into thin sheets and, marble is chosen because it may be obtained in large, homogeneous blocks.

Jointing and quarrying

As has been seen, the joints in any of the three major types of rock determine not only the size of the block extracted but also its shape. Because joints and bedding planes are the planes along which rocks will most easily part, their spacing and frequency are a determining factor in the quarrying of rock for dimension stone.

Stone has been extracted in many ways, including pulling out blocks, 'jumping' and digging out. However, two main methods are employed; plugs and feathers are used to quarry all types of stone, and flame-cutting is used for some igneous rocks.

For the first method a series of holes is drilled in a line parallel with one of the joint sets, and, with igneous rocks, parallel with the sheet jointing direction. The diameter of the holes, their depth and their distance apart differ from quarry to quarry and will depend on the nature of the rock being quarried and, mostly, on experience. A pair of 'feathers', shaped, semi-circular steel pieces, is inserted into the holes. A wedge-shaped 'plug' is driven between the 'feathers'. Normally the 'feathers' are shaped so that as the plug is driven down by a sledge-hammer the 'feather' stays parallel with the side of the hole, thus exerting even pressure along its length. The 'plugs' are driven in in sequence until eventually the stone splits along the line of the holes (*Figure 2.15*).

Flame-cutting (*Figure 2.17*), used only for igneous rocks, depends on the spallability of the rock. Heat will cause certain rocks to spall and the degree to which they will do so has been determined to depend on:

1. Large linear thermal expansion at temperatures below 700 °C;
2. High thermal diffusivity at temperatures below 400 °C;
3. The presence of an equigranular interlocking structure with little or no fine-grained clay or mica alteration products;

(a)

(b)

(c)

Figure 2.15 (a) Plugs and feathers are inserted into holes in the rock parallel with a joint set. (b) Plugs are driven down in sequence between the feathers to exert an even pressure along the line of the holes drilled into the rock. Eventually the rock splits along the line of the holes. (c) Plugs and feathers may also be used to lift a block of stone along the line on the bedding-plane

Figure 2.16 Plugs and feathers have been used in holes drilled parallel to the widely spaced joints in granite at Merrivale Quarry, Dartmoor to produce blocks which can be handled by quarry machinery

4. The lack of significant amounts of soft, low-melting, or elastic minerals or materials which yield after thermal decomposition.[7]

The method uses a long blowpipe through separate conduits in which oxygen, fuel (usually hydrocarbons such as paraffin, kerosene or fuel oil but acteylene and propane have been used for concrete surface treatment); and water are passed to a burner. An exhaust flame with a temperature between 3500 and 5000 °F (1900–2800 °C) is produced with a velocity of about 5300 ft./s (1600 m/s). The high velocity of the flame wash clears the spalled pieces of rock. The water cools the nozzle of the burner and the rock surface around the flame and helps remove spallings.

Flame cutting has distinct advantages in producing a 'free end' in a widely jointed granite mass. The channel, however, is best aligned with one of the

Figure 2.17 Flame-cutting is used to produce a 'free-end' in widely jointed granite at De Lank Quarry, St Breward, near Bodmin, Cornwall (courtesy of G.H. Setchell)

joint sets. The noise level of the process is up to 120 dB and this has been regarded as a disadvantage.[8]

The colour of rocks

The colour of a rock may be its most striking visual characteristic. Colour depends on the reflection of some of the vibrations of white light seen by the human eye. It is one of the most difficult characteristics to describe. Nevertheless, it may well be the deciding factor in the choice of a stone, particularly for decorative purposes. The description of a stone as 'light salmon-coloured, coarsely crystalline, having a slightly mottled appearance' conveys little.

Increasingly used by geologists is the *Rock-Color Chart*.[9] Any given hue (colour) is expressed in terms of value (property of lightness) and chroma (degree of saturation). Both are numbered and thus a colour may be given a numerical designation. For example, pale greenish yellow is 10Y8/2; that is, hue 10Y, value 8, saturation 2. The *Rock-Color Chart* was prepared by the Geological Society of America. It uses the terms pale and light to quantify colours. Except where direct quotation is made from this chart, pale will be used here to refer to colour. The term light will be used to refer to weight.

If the accurate expression of a rock colour is desired it is recommended that the *Rock-Color Chart* is used. It must be remembered, however, that because rocks are a product of natural processes, they will rarely be uniform in colour overall. Stone from the same bed in a quarry may provide a variety of hues. Colour changes or variations, which may be marked as with 'blue-hearted' stones, should be considered early in the planning stages of a building and provision made to accommodate them. Stones capable of being polished may show a highly accentuated hue or, indeed, appear entirely different from the unpolished stones.

Names of rocks

The object of giving a name to any substance whether animal, vegetable or mineral is that when that name is used it is immediately and universally recognized as relating to a defined material with identifiable characteristics which distinguish it from all other materials. The name should be unique to the substance. Unfortunately, in the stone trade many stones are given names which do not accord with that principle and which also do not accord with geological scientific nomenclature.

For example, 'Ingleton Granite' of the stone trade is actually a grit (a sedimentary rock) from Yorkshire. 'Onyx' is a name which has been used for at least three widely different materials.[10] 'Pearl', 'Pearl Granite' or 'Blue Pearl Granite' is a syenite from Norway. Verde Issorie and Tinos which are advertised as marbles, are serpentinites.

The scientific name of a stone is of importance as was recognized by J.G.C. Anderson[5] some years ago when he wrote

> ... for purely commercial purposes a nomenclature more in accordance with strictly scientific practice would be an advantage. It is being realized that the properties of a rock are, to a considerable extent, functions of its mode of formation, composition and texture—factors that are taken into account in petrological nomenclature. If, therefore, the latter is made use of in industry, the purchaser giving a particular specification stands a better chance of getting the type of rock best

suited for his purpose, while the quarry owner is enabled to supply the product most likely to prove satisfactory.

In Chapters 2 to 6, in order to maintain geological integrity the names used are those which are scientifically appropriate with the popular name given in parenthesis if it differs widely from scientific usage.

Seasoning of rocks

The importance of allowing a stone to season, that is letting the blocks stand for some time before use, has been commented upon since early days. '...let the stone be got out two years before, not in winter, but in summer, and let it lie and stay in exposed places', wrote Vitruvius in 1 BC.[11] It is well recorded that Wren insisted that the blocks of Portland Stone used to rebuild St. Paul's Cathedral, after the Great Fire of London in 1666, should be seasoned for at least three years.[12] Most stones when first taken from the quarry contain, to a greater or lesser extent, groundwater or *quarry sap*. In this condition the stone is known as *green*. This water contains small amounts of mineral matter in solution. It was thought that when the stone was exposed to the atmosphere the water evaporated and the mineral matter was deposited between the grains within the surface layers and so acted in small degree as an additional natural cement.

Such experimental work as has been undertaken shows that the variability in specimens makes it difficult to come to definite conclusions. Recent investigations now show that the degree of cementation is not significant. For Portland Stone the reduction in pore space is less than 0.09 per cent. However, there is no doubt that the uniaxial compressive strength of a block of stone increases as the block dries out. It becomes more difficult to work after seasoning, when it is often said by masons and others to have 'hardened'. Even granite is reputed to work more easily when first extracted from the quarry. As the 'hardening' is not due to the chemical processes of cementation, it is evidently due to a physical change. The 'hardened' (sometimes called 'case-hardened') nature of 'old blocks' is commonly used as a reason for not re-using blocks already used in a building. There is, however, no evidence to indicate that second-hand stones or 'old blocks' are in any way inferior to newly quarried stone; it may be that they are just more difficult to work.

Hardness of rocks

Hardness is an important physical property of materials and each specific material has a hardness which is defined as its resistance to abrasion. It may be measured quantitatively by the diamond indentation method. Hardness (H) is the product of the packing structure of the atoms, and it is expressed by a number on Mohs' scale of hardness. In 1812 Friedrich Mohs arranged ten minerals in such an order that each one would scratch those lower in the scale. The scale, with explanatory notes, is given in *Table 2.4*. It must be noted that the scale does not advance in any regular steps; it is quite arbitrary.

It is difficult to express the hardness of some rocks because rocks are aggregates of minerals, and each mineral has a specific hardness. In granite, the mineral quartz has a hardness of 7, feldspar about 6, and mica about 2.5. The actual hardness depends on the type of feldspar and of mica. It is thus only possible to define the hardness of a rock in relative terms. Granite appears hard because quartz (H=7) is the mineral which binds the others together. It should be noted that hardness should not be equated with the difficulty of breaking. Many hard materials are brittle.

Table 2.4 Mohs' scale of hardness

*Hardness**		*Notes*
10	Diamond	Diamond is the hardest mineral but artificial substances harder than diamond are now known 9½ Boron carbide 9¼ Carborundum
9	Corundum	
8	Topaz	
7	Quartz	Quartz will scratch window glass. Flint may be used for quartz
6	Feldspar	A good pocket knife blade will scratch feldspar but not quartz
5	Apatite	
4	Fluorite	A copper coin will just scratch fluorite
3	Calcite	A knife blade easily scratches calcite
2	Gypsum	2½ A fingernail will scratch gypsum, but fingernails differ in hardness
1	Talc	Softest mineral

*When performing a hardness test several precautions should be observed:

1. The point of a sharp blade should be used; a definite scratch must be produced. Wet the scratch to remove the powder then use the edge of a finger-nail to feel the scratch;
2. A pocket knife may leave a line on the harder mineral if the blade has been scratched in the test;
3. In granular rocks such as sandstone the individual grains may have only been disturbed, but not scratched;
4. Some minerals may have broken because of their brittleness and not because of their hardness.

Eras	*Periods*		*Age in million years**	*Notes*	*Orogenies and major intrusions of igneous rocks*
Quaternary	Holocene			Recent = Today	
	Pleistocene		1.6	The Ice Age	
Tertiary	Pliocene				
	Miocene				Alpine: Widespread basalt lava flows. Large deep seated igneous intrusions, e.g. in Skye, Mull, Mourne Mountains and Lundy
	Oligocene				
	Eocene				
	Palaeocene		60		
Mesozoic	Cretaceous		135		
	Jurassic		205		
	Triassic		250	New Red Sandstone	
Palaeozoic	Permian		290		
	Carboniferous	Coal Measures		In USA: Pennsylvanian	Hercynian: Devon and Cornwall granites†
		Millstone Grit		Mississippian	
		Carboniferous Limestone	365		
	Devonian		409	Includes Old Red Sandstone	Caledonian: Newer Granites, Cairngorms, Aberdeenshire, Galway, Donegal and Lake District
	Silurian		439		
	Ordovician		505		Volcanic rocks of Lake District and Wales
	Cambrian		570		
Precambrian			c. 3800		Older Granites Volcanic rocks of Charnwood, Grampians and elsewhere

*Based on *The Phonerozoic Time Scale,* Geological Society, London.
†It is possible to date any given specimen of granite rock. But as the mass was injected in a fluid state over a period of time, specimens taken from the mass give ages ranging from about 254 my to 303 my.

List of building Stones adapted from reference 14.

Figure 2.18 Geological time scale

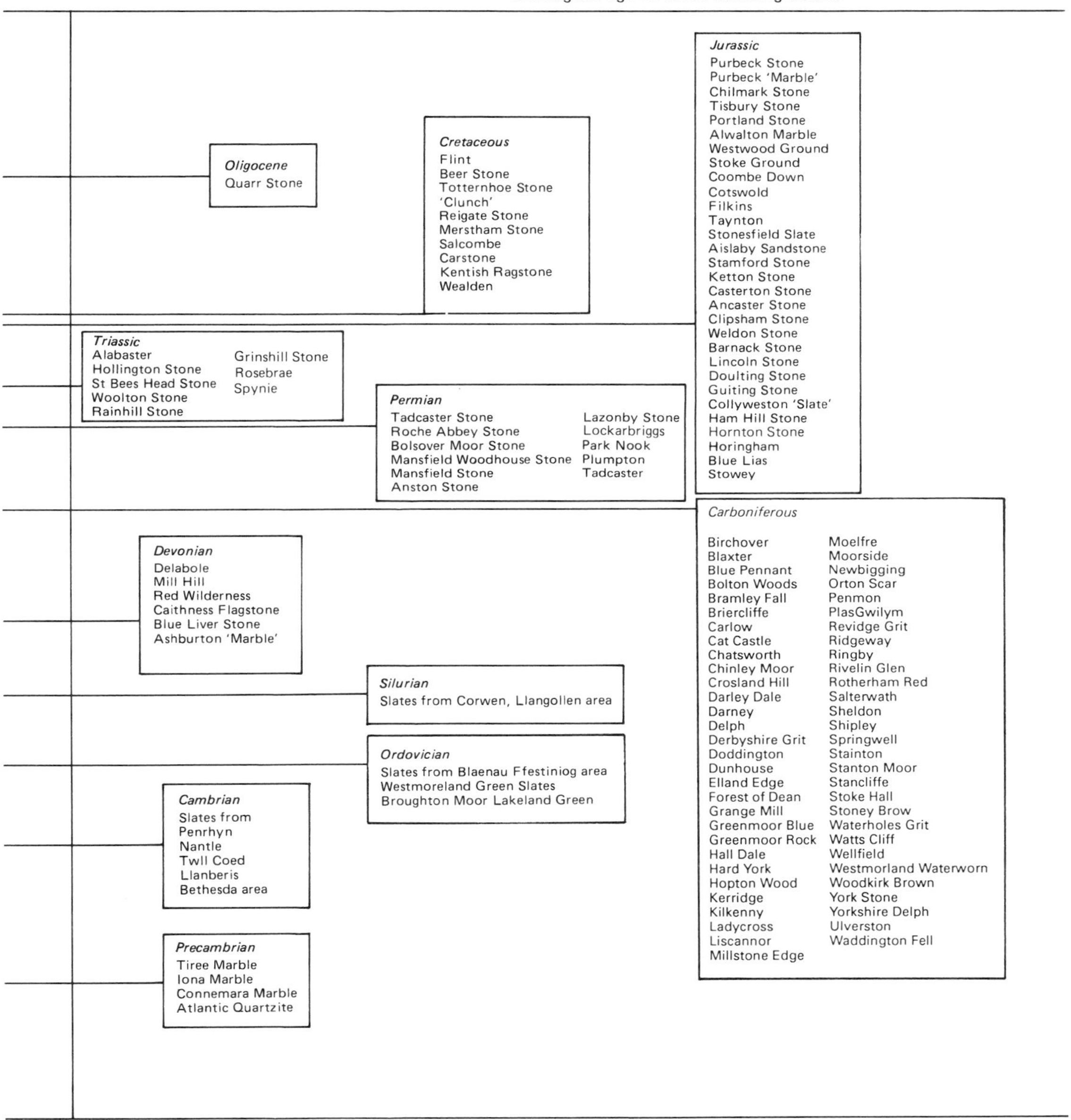
Geological age of some building stones
Jurassic
Purbeck Stone
Purbeck 'Marble'
Chilmark Stone
Tisbury Stone
Portland Stone
Alwalton Marble
Westwood Ground
Stoke Ground
Coombe Down
Cotswold
Filkins
Taynton
Stonesfield Slate
Aislaby Sandstone
Stamford Stone
Ketton Stone
Casterton Stone
Ancaster Stone
Clipsham Stone
Weldon Stone
Barnack Stone
Lincoln Stone
Doulting Stone
Guiting Stone
Collyweston 'Slate'
Ham Hill Stone
Hornton Stone
Horingham
Blue Lias
Stowey
Oligocene
Quarr Stone
Cretaceous
Flint
Beer Stone
Totternhoe Stone
'Clunch'
Reigate Stone
Merstham Stone
Salcombe
Carstone
Kentish Ragstone
Wealden
Triassic
Alabaster
Hollington Stone
St Bees Head Stone
Woolton Stone
Rainhill Stone
Grinshill Stone
Rosebrae
Spynie
Permian
Tadcaster Stone
Roche Abbey Stone
Bolsover Moor Stone
Mansfield Woodhouse Stone
Mansfield Stone
Anston Stone
Lazonby Stone
Lockarbriggs
Park Nook
Plumpton
Tadcaster
Carboniferous
Birchover
Blaxter
Blue Pennant
Bolton Woods
Bramley Fall
Briercliffe
Carlow
Cat Castle
Chatsworth
Chinley Moor
Crosland Hill
Darley Dale
Darney
Delph
Derbyshire Grit
Doddington
Dunhouse
Elland Edge
Forest of Dean
Grange Mill
Greenmoor Blue
Greenmoor Rock
Hall Dale
Hard York
Hopton Wood
Kerridge
Kilkenny
Ladycross
Liscannor
Millstone Edge
Moelfre
Moorside
Newbigging
Orton Scar
Penmon
PlasGwilym
Revidge Grit
Ridgeway
Ringby
Rivelin Glen
Rotherham Red
Salterwath
Sheldon
Shipley
Springwell
Stainton
Stanton Moor
Stancliffe
Stoke Hall
Stoney Brow
Waterholes Grit
Watts Cliff
Wellfield
Westmorland Waterworn
Woodkirk Brown
York Stone
Yorkshire Delph
Ulverston
Waddington Fell
Devonian
Delabole
Mill Hill
Red Wilderness
Caithness Flagstone
Blue Liver Stone
Ashburton 'Marble'
Silurian
Slates from Corwen, Llangollen area
Ordovician
Slates from Blaenau Ffestiniog area
Westmoreland Green Slates
Broughton Moor Lakeland Green
Cambrian
Slates from
Penrhyn
Nantle
Twll Coed
Llanberis
Bethesda area
Precambrian
Tiree Marble
Iona Marble
Connemara Marble
Atlantic Quartzite

The distinction between hardness and toughness also should be observed. Some limestones are described as hard. But all limestones are made up essentially of calcium carbonate in the form of calcite. The hardness of all limestones, therefore, is about $H=3$, which is relatively soft on Mohs' scale of hardness. But some limestones are friable, some are compact and it is this quality which determines the ease with which they can be worked—their apparent hardness. A sandstone made up of grains of quartz ($H=7$), and thus hard may appear soft because the grains are not well cemented and the rock can be powdered in the hand. Toughness, or the ability to resist abrasion generally, is a more desirable quality than hardness. An old, simple but nevertheless effective and quick test may easily be performed to give an indication of the hardness of a rock. Rub a piece of the rock on an old file. A soft rock will leave much powder on the file and will make little noise; a hard rock will leave little (if any) powder and will screech.

It does not follow that a hard rock will be better suited for building purposes than a soft rock. The crushing strength of a rock is a preferred guide to its suitability for building purposes, but the geological factors of the rock *in situ* must always be borne in mind.

The age of rocks

Geological time is the expression used to denote the period since the formation of the Earth, some 4800 million years ago. The oldest rock so far found is a pebble of volcanic ash in a conglomerate in Greenland. The pebble is about 3824 million years old.[13] During that time, sediments have been laid down, life has emerged and evolved, mountains have been built and destroyed. Obviously, all this did not occur at the same time. From the apparently simple observation that one bed of sediment overlies another and therefore must be younger, a sequence of events was established and a *relative* time-scale was developed. The sediments deposited during geological time differ one from the other but it is possible to group together sequences of deposits which have some common characteristics of lithology or of fossils. A universally applicable system of time and rock divisions has been agreed. This geological time scale, or geological column, is given (*Figure 2.18*).

Since the discovery of the radioactivity of the element uranium in 1896, it has been realized that the decay of unstable elements could be used to give rocks an *absolute age* in terms of years. These ages have been added to the geological column in *Figure 2.18*.

The geological column is the fundamental reference document of the geologist. If a building is described as Georgian, it may be concluded that it was built after Elizabethan buildings and before those of Classical Revival. The building has been given a relative age and it may be implied that it will also have a certain style of architecture with specific characteristics. In the same manner, if a rock is described as Permian it can immediately be concluded that it was laid down after a series called Carboniferous and before a series of rocks called Triassic. It has been given a relative age. It can be implied also that it will have certain forms of fossils and other characteristics which, if the rocks are used as building stones, will determine to greater or lesser degree its value as a building stone and also the architectural style in those regions where the rock is found.

References

1. Bromehead, C.E.N., 'Geology in Embryo (up to 1600 AD)', *Proc. Geol. Assoc.*, **56**, Pt. 2., 1945
2. Anon. *Glossary of Terms for Stone used in Building*. British Standard 2847, British Standards Institution, London, 1957
3. British Geological Survey *Geological Map of the United Kingdom*: 1 : 625,000, Ordnance Survey, Southampton, 1979
4. Read, H.H. and Watson, J., *Introduction to Geology*, Volume 1, Macmillan & Co. Ltd. London, 1962
5. Anderson, J.G.C., 'The Granites of Scotland', *Memoirs of the Geological Survey, Special Reports on the Mineral Resources of Great Britain*, **33**, HMSO, Edinburgh, 1939
6. Burgess, S.G. and Schaffer, R.J., 'Cleopatra's Needle', *Chemistry and Industry*, **30**, pp. 1026–29, 1952
7. Rolseth, H.C. and Kohler, R.H., 'Rocket-jet burners cut time and costs in granite quarries', *Mining Engineering*, **21**, no. 7, 1969
8. Anon., 'Jet channelling at Hantergantick', *Mine and Quarry Engineering*, **28**, No. 8, 1962
9. Rock-Color Chart Committee, *Rock-Color Chart*, Geological Society of America, Boulder, Colorado, 1979
10. Dimes, F.G., 'What is Onyx?' *Stone Industries*, **12**, No. 5, pp. 14–16, 1977
11. Vitruvius, *De Achitectura* quoted in Bromehead, C.E.N., 'Geology in Embryo (up to 1600 AD)', *Proc. Geol. Assoc.*, **56**, Pt. 2, 1945
12. Watson, John, *British and Foreign Building Stones*, University Press, Cambridge, 1911
13. Thackray, J., *The age of the Earth*. HMSO, London, 1980
14. Anon., *Natural Stone Directory, 7th edition, 1987*, Stone Industries, Ealing Publications Ltd, Maidenhead, 1987

3

Igneous rocks

Francis G. Dimes

Introduction

> The style of a national architecture may evidently depend, in a great measure, upon the nature of the rocks of the country.
> John Ruskin, *The Stones of Venice*

> Good quality stone is still one of the most permanent of all building materials, as it is beyond doubt the most beautiful and, where local material is used, the most congenial to the surrounding landscape.
> Alec Clifton-Taylor, *The Pattern of English Building*

The accuracy of Ruskin's observation may be demonstrated with little difficulty. The soft nature of the limestone known as the Chalk allowed the exuberance of carving seen in the Lady Chapel of Ely Cathedral, Cambridgeshire (*Figure 3.1*). Tough and intractable Kentish Ragstone led to random walls, or walls roughly brought to courses (*Figure 3.2*). The tough and hard nature of the granites of south-west England is apparent in the square, undecorated churches of the area (*Figure 3.3*). The easily worked red sandstone of Cheshire was used in large blocks, even for cottages.

Figure 3.2 Because of its tough, intractable nature little decorative work was undertaken in Kentish Ragstone. As a result flat walls with the stone brought roughly to courses are seen as at Knole House, Sevenoaks, Kent. The obtrusive repairs are of Portland Stone

Figure 3.1 Ease of working allowed elaborate carving of Chalk used in The Lady Chapel, Ely Cathedral. Purbeck 'marble' was used for the columns of the arcade

When there was a local supply of suitable stone, it was natural for it to be used for all building. Aberdeen is for ever associated with granite; Burford, Oxfordshire and the villages around, with Costwold Stone; Buxton, Derbyshire, with limestone and with grit. The buildings themselves are a reflection of the geological diversity of the country. Geology provided the very material of the buildings and the material determined the nature of the architectural style of the cities and of the villages. The manner in which stone was and is used is a manifestation of its genesis. It follows that the nature of the stone is of prime importance. In discussion of examples and uses,

Figure 3.3 Little decorative carving is found on granite which because of its intractable nature led to square, blocky buildings. The castellation of St Sennon Church near Land's End, mimics the castellated weathering of the Land's End granite mass. The wall around the church is of granite boulders–moorstones–picked up off the surrounding moors

therefore, consideration is given under each of the three main groups of rocks, following the classification given in Chapter 2. This chapter will concentrate on igneous rocks as building stones. Building stones from sedimentory and metamorphic rocks will be discussed in Chapters 4 and 5.

Basalt is probably the most abundant extrusive igneous rock occurring on the *surface* of the Earth. It forms the large plateaux of Northern Ireland and the Deccan of India and it covers most of Iceland, much of Washington State, USA and elsewhere. Yet in relation to its abundance, it has been little used for building, primarily because of its close-jointed nature.

In contrast, granite and closely allied rocks, which comprise about 95 per cent of the intrusive igneous rocks *within* the Earth's crust, have a limited outcrop. Nevertheless they are undoubtedly the most widely used of the igneous rocks.

Acid plutonic igneous rocks

Granite is the one rock name known to all. The grenadiers of the Consular Guard were so called because at the battle of Marengo in 1800, when the French had given way, they stood like granite. It is the connotation for all that is hard, resistant and durable. The name granite probably is more misused in the stone trade than any other rock name. Petit Granit, or, as it is known in Germany, Belgian Granite, is a limestone which is cut and polished and sold as marble! Granit de Rocq is a limestone from France; Granito Nero a Swiss marble; Andes Black Granite is a gabbro; Black Diamond Granite, from South Africa, is a syeno-gabbro; Swedish Black Granite is a gabbro; and Blue Pearl Granite and all the other varieties of Imperial Pearl, Dark Pearl and Light Pearl, is a syenite from Norway. Blue Granite from Guernsey, much used in the past in London for kerbs, paving and steps, is a quartz-diorite. The list is seemingly endless and the names are not synonyms. The desirability of calling these stones by their proper, scientific names, is immediately apparent.

Granite is a strictly defined rock. It is an acid plutonic igneous rock, which has a fairly limited range of composition. The granite family includes members which contain varying proportions of quartz, acid plagioclase feldspar, potash feldspar and a dark-coloured ferromagnesian mineral, which is generally either biotite mica or hornblende. A granite containing a fair amount of hornblende is known as a hornblende-granite. Other accessory minerals may be present, but never in great amounts, unless as purely local concentrations.

Granites contain a high proportion of pale-coloured minerals. Quartz usually is found to be colourless. However, in the main mass of the rock, it appears to be grey, although it may sometimes have a pale purple hue. The dark brown mica, biotite, is evenly scattered throughout the mass and, if the pale-coloured mica, muscovite, is present, it is distinguished by a silvery appearance.

The mineral present in the greatest quantity is feldspar. Two varieties of feldspar are common, orthoclase and plagioclase. They may occur together in the same rock, but plagioclase is less common when quartz is present. Orthoclase is usually white to flesh pink but may be red; plagioclase is white to grey or, more rarely, yellowish, brown, or pink. Because feldspar makes up the bulk of the rock, this mineral determines the overall colour of the stone. It is possible, by detailed mineralogical study of hand specimens, to suggest the provenance of some granites. Muscovite is commonly found in association with biotite in the granite of Devon and Cornwall, England. It is unusual to find muscovite in granites of western Scotland. The mineral sphene occurs particularly in granite from Dalbeattie. Large, rounded, brownish potassic feldspar, mantled with white-coloured oligoclase feldspar, is characteristic of Baltic Brown granite from Finland. It has what is known geologically as a Rapakivi texture.

Although some granites are considered to have been formed by ultrametamorphism, most are found in the form of huge, intrusive masses, called batholiths, in the cores of old, eroded mountain chains. The outcrop of granite, consequently, is limited and is defined geographically. It is considered here on that basis.

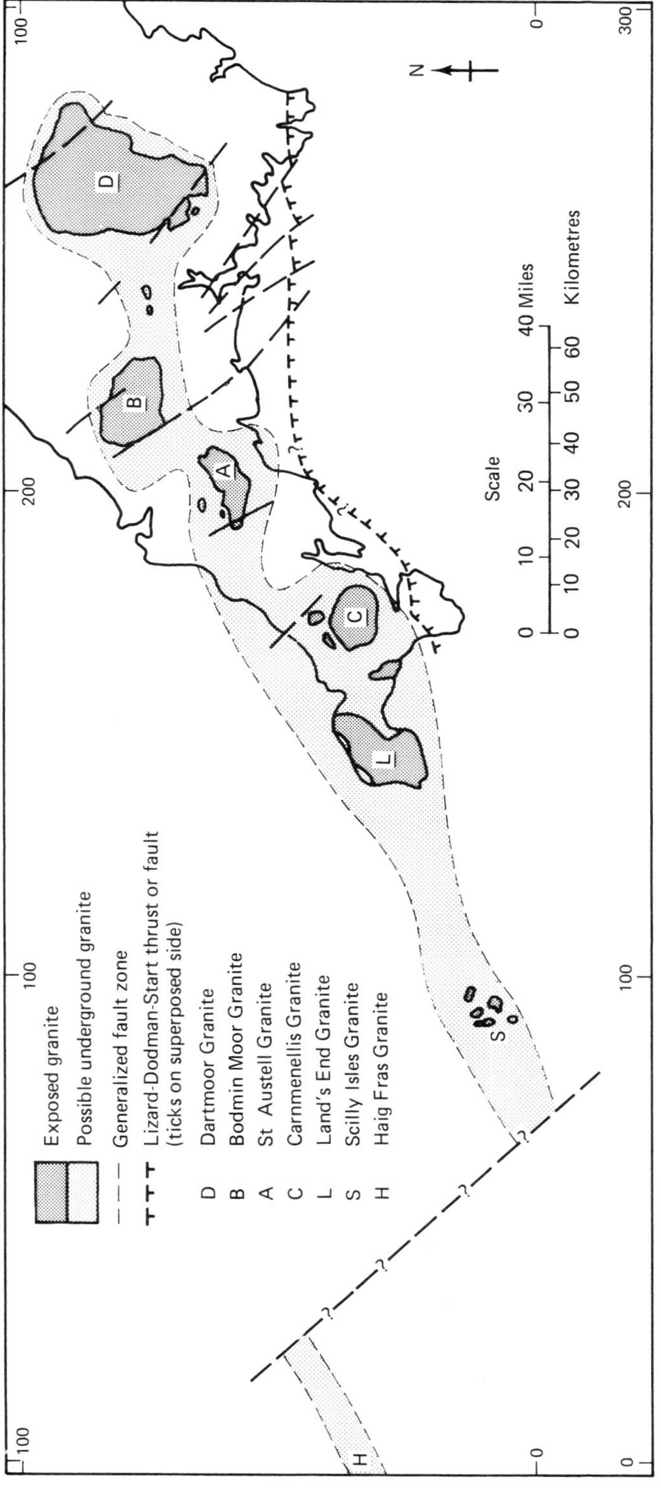

Figure 3.4 South-west England batholith. (From E.A. Edmonds *et al.*, *British Regional Geology: South-west England*, 4th edn, HMSO, 1975. Crown copyright, reproduced by permission of the Controller, HMSO)

South-west England granites

The series of granite outcrops in south-west England, which stretch from Dartmoor westwards to the Isles of Scilly, are the visible tops of bosses rising from a single, elongated batholith (*Figure 3.4*). All the granites quarried in the region are genetically related. Generally they are chemically and mineralogically in accord, although, in some areas, the rock may be slightly more acid (SiO_2–rich) than in others. All the varieties contain quartz, feldspar and mica, which is predominantly brown biotite, with some white muscovite. Tourmaline is a common accessory mineral. The texture of the granite may range from fine-grained to coarse-grained, or 'giant'-granite. Coarse-grained granites, which contain conspicuous, large feldspar crystals, up to 7 inches (175 mm) long, are termed megacrystic varieties[1,2]. The large crystals probably grew within the solid rock[3]. All granites quarried now and in the past differ principally in the abundance of feldspar megacrysts. All stone currently quarried is an overall silver-grey in colour. At one time, a pink stone was extracted at Cheesewring quarry, near Liskeard, Cornwall, and a red-coloured granite occurs in the St Austell mass.

Iron Age structures of granite are known, but, because the rock is hard and was difficult to work, most buildings constructed in the early days were of blocks picked up off the moor. These were more or less rectangular in shape, as a consequence of the joint system. The name Moorstone was given to these stones. Unfortunately, the name is also used in non-granite areas for other types of stone. The name Surface Granite is also used, particularly in Cornwall.

In general terms, granite may be described for building purposes as a compact, crystalline rock, with a generally uniform structure. It has a range in colour, is hardwearing, resistant to polluted air, impervious to water and is capable of taking a high polish. This is a specification that few, if any, other materials can meet.

Figure 3.5 Flanged granite blocks were used to guide horse-drawn wagons carrying blocks of granite from quarries near Hay Tor, Devon, on the first stage of their journey to London

In the country around Dartmoor granite is used almost without exception for the churches, but, because of its hardness, elaborate working and carving was difficult in the early days. The carving on the church at Plympton St Mary, Devon and on Launceston church, Cornwall, is remarkable, because such carving would have demanded considerable money and time. Not until the development of power tools in the middle of the eighteenth century was it possible to work granite on any scale. Since then, granite from south-west England has been widely used, much of it for civil engineering purposes. An interesting use was in the 'forgotten granite railway'. Between 1820 and about 1860, stone was sent from Hay Tor Quarry on Dartmoor, near Bovey Tracey, Devon, to London. The stone was taken from the quarry, loaded onto barges at Teigngrace, then taken to Teignmouth, where it was transhipped for London. The 'railway' line from the quarry is made of granite blocks up to 8 feet (2.5 m) long, with an inside flange, which is normally on the wheel, on the blocks (*Figure 3.5*). In London, the stone was used in the National Gallery, in the British Museum and for London Bridge[3]. Stone from Princetown Quarry, Dartmoor, was also used for the 1831 London Bridge and for its widening in 1902. Another famous landmark in London, Nelson's column, is built of Dartmoor granite taken from the Foggintor quarries. A markedly megacrystic variety quarried by convicts from the Prison quarry, Dartmoor, was used for Norman Shaw's New Scotland Yard (1888-1899), on The Embankment, London (*Figure 3.6*). Stone from the nearby Merrivale Quarry which, although no distance from the Prison Quarry, yields a poorly

(a)

(b)

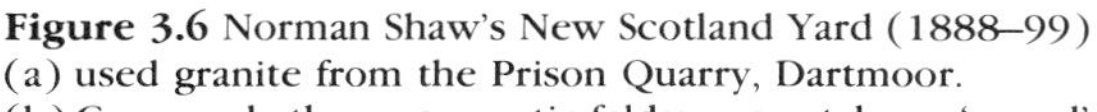

Figure 3.6 Norman Shaw's New Scotland Yard (1888–99) (a) used granite from the Prison Quarry, Dartmoor. (b) Commonly the megacrystic feldspar crystals are 'zoned' and contain small amounts of other minerals which outline the crystal shape

megacrystic stone was used to clad the present (1967) New Scotland Yard in Victoria Street. This has now been replaced by stainless steel. Stone from this quarry was used also for part of Unity House, Euston Road (1914) and more recently, for British Petroleum House and Ashdown House, both in Victoria Street, London and for the polished parapets of the new (1973) London Bridge. In the quarry, distances of up to 16 feet (5 m) between joints have been measured, with 8 feet (2.5 m), or more, between the sheet jointing.

The Cornish granite masses of St Austell and Land's End are characteristically megacrystic, while those of Bodmin Moor and Carnmenellis are poorly so. Cornwall, however, is best known for its giant crystal granite, exemplified by stone from Cheesewring Quarry, near Liskeard, which is now no longer in production. It was used for major civil engineering works, such as the piers of Westminster Bridge; for Tower Bridge (with repairs in 1981 in Merrivale granite); and for the Duke of Wellington's tomb in St Paul's Cathedral. The bases of the statues at the Guards Monument of the Crimean War, Waterloo Place, London, are also in stone from this quarry.

Carnsew Quarry, near Penryn, supplied a medium grained stone for the plinth of the railings at the British Museum, Bloomsbury. In the dressing yards at Penryn in 1956 rough stone for monumental work and for ashlar was first shaped up by hand. The operation was known locally as 'taking the wind out of the stone'. The Cornish granites are so similar that most geologists, when asked to identify the granite in *situ* on a building, will say only that it is south-west England granite. Also, it is not easy to determine the provenance of hand specimens, without detailed microscopic study. Granite quarry workers, however, claim to be able to distinguish between granites from different quarries. Because of the similarity of the stone from one quarry to another, several quarries would operate together in supplying stone for large contracts and stone from a number of quarries might well be worked in a common yard. Many quarries in Cornwall are now supplying stone for the new town of Milton Keynes[4].

Stone from the De Lank Quarry, near St Breward, Bodmin, is renowned for its use for the Eddystone Lighthouse (1756) and the Beachy Head Lighthouse (1828). It has also been used elsewhere, for example, for the plinth of the Nurse Cavell Monument, Charing Cross Road, London (1922) and for the plinth of the Churchill Memorial, Parliament Square, London. It may be seen as polished slabs cladding the Marks and Spencer store in Sheffield. Both the De Lank Quarry and its immediate neighbour, the Hantergantick Quarry, produce coarse-grained granite, with small megacrysts, which show a foliation

Figure 3.7 The architect Edwin Lutyens used granite structurally for Castle Drogo, Devon. In places the walls are 2 metres thick

defined by a generally planar disposition of feldspar and mica[2]. Stone from Hantergantick Quarry may be seen on the ABN Bank, Threadneedle Street, London.

Pelastine granite, quarried at Mabe, was taken to Penryn for dressing. It has also been used for civil engineering works; between 1949 and 1958, much was used for the South Bank wall of the River Thames. It was also used for cladding, as on the Bank of England, King Street, Leeds.

Edwin Lutyens' Castle Drogo, Drewsteignton, Devon, 'the last granite castle' (*Figure 3.7*) was built entirely in granite, including some of the bathroom furniture! It has walls 2 m (6.5 ft.) thick to the Chapel. Stone from a quarry opened in nearby Whiddon Park was used, with some stone from Pew Tor, south-west of Merrivale[5].

To some extent, all the South-west England granite masses were altered when extremely hot solutions and gases were squeezed out during the last stages of cooling and consolidation. These chemically very active, mobile emissions penetrated fissures in the consolidating granite and the surrounding rocks. Complex chemical changes took place and most of the granite mass was either kaolinized, a change that led in extreme cases to china clay, or was gneissened, a process that led to a quartz-mica rock, with some topaz and feldspar, or tourmalinized. By and large, the changes are of little interest when dealing with building and decorative stones. However, around Luxulyan, Cornwall*, tourmalinization has produced a highly decorative rock, named Luxullianite. Originally, the granite contained large crystals of feldspar; the rock now has pink-coloured feldspar megacrysts in a purplish-black background consisting mostly of dark-coloured tourmaline. Apparently the only use of the stone is for the sarcophagus of the Duke of Wellington in St Paul's Cathedral, London[3,7,8]. This fact is often recorded.

Closely associated with the granites is a series of quartz-porphyry dykes with a few sills, the well known elvans. One granite in the region stands out geologically as an oddity, the mass that makes up most of Lundy Island. It has been age-dated at 50 to 55 million years, which is middle Eocene (see *Figure 2.18*). It is considerably younger than the granites so far considered. The stone is light grey in colour and varies from fine- to coarse-grained, with some large feldspar crystals. The sheet-jointing is conspicuous. Between 1864 and 1870, it was much used in the Embankment, London. The island quarry was re-opened to rebuild the Marisco Tavern (the old hotel building) and to build the Agent's bungalow in the traditional Lundy manner in 1983.

*The Ordnance Survey Atlas of Great Britain, published by Ordnance Survey/Country Life Books 1982, has been taken throughout as the authority for the spelling of place names. Spellings found elsewhere do not always agree with this source.

Welsh granites

Wales, which is a geologically complex region in some parts, has a tradition of building with stone. Granite masses, however, are not a major component and the stone has had little impact. Note may be made of Trevor granite, from the Eifl quarry, Clwyd, which is used for curling stones.

Igneous rocks from Leicestershire

An igneous mass at no great distance from London, in an area of mostly poorly consolidated sedimentary rocks is bound to assume an importance which might be regarded as out of proportion to the size of its outcrop. So it is with the igneous rock masses which occur in Charnwood, north of Leicester. At Markfield, Groby and Bradgate, a geologically interesting type of syenite, named Markfieldite, was quarried, but of more interest for building is the granite from Mount Sorrel. In geological terms, this stone is actually a granodiorite. The distinction is a mineralogical one; in granite *sensu strictu*, the amount of orthoclase feldspar (a potassium, aluminium silicate) is more than that of plagioclase feldspar (a sodium, calcium, aluminium silicate). In granodiorite, plagioclase exceeds orthoclase. The rock, however, belongs to the granite family. This stone was used locally for building[9], but developed a much greater reputation for use as setts, which Elsden and Howe[7] record were not used until the later part of the eighteenth century in London's roads. The so-called 'Euston Pavement' was of setts 3 inches square by 4 inches deep of Mount Sorrel granite. A drawback, however, of some of the more compact, tougher stones used for this purpose is that they develop a slippery surface when subjected to heavy wear. Mount Sorrel stone varies in colour from grey to dark red-brown and contains large, pale crystals of feldspar.

Cumbrian granites

Shap granite, from another small outcrop of only three square miles (8.7 square km), is one of the most widely known of the British granites because it is easily recognizable. Although there are many other granite intrusions in the Lake District area, the one known above all others is that from the Shap Quarries, Cumbria. This granite contains many accessory minerals, but it is immediately recognized visually by the distinctive megacrysts of pink feldspar, set in a much finer groundmass. Two varieties may be distinguished, Dark Shap and Light Shap, which are seen to grade one into the other. The dark variety occurs in bands 2.5–16 feet (0.75–5 m) wide on each side of the master joints. The megacrystic pink feldspar crystals are prominent and, apparently, were unaltered when hot vapours penetrated the master joints after consolidation of the granite and altered the minerals of the groundmass. Characteristic of Shap granite is the number of dark dots, varying in size and shape and which may have very ill-defined margins. They are known by the quarrymen as 'heathens', or, less frequently, as 'foreigners' and are geologically termed xenoliths (*Figure 3.8*). They are incompletely assimilated fragments of pre-existing rocks, which were caught up by the magma before it solidified. All stages from 'fresh' to almost completely digested fragments may be seen. These blotches are an original feature of the granite. They are not flaws, nor do they in any way affect the quality of the stone. Most granites will be found to contain xenoliths and these add character and interest to the stone.

Figure 3.8 Monolithic bollards, some of which contain xenoliths, are used to surround St Paul's Churchyard, London. Feldspar and quartz crystals may be seen in the xenolith indicating that magmatic fluids had permeated the fragment of country rock

It is apparent that the San Grita granite from Poland which clads the National Westminster Bank, Brompton Road, London, was chosen because of the effect created by the xenoliths. Shap granite has been used in villages around Shap for quoins and lintels. However, because there is little local demand, it has been used far more widely outside its own area. Fine blocks of Dark Shap for the Tyme (formerly Jean Renet) shop on the corner of Bond Street and Piccadilly, London; dark and light varieties for the columns to the hotel entrance portico, St Pancras Station, London; monolithic bollards, some with excellent xenoliths, around the west entrance of St Paul's Cathedral, London; columns for the Irish Life Assurance Company building, King Street, Manchester; and in the west portal of St Mary's Cathedral, Edinburgh, are a few examples. An unusual use is for large paving slabs in the entrance to the Central Library, St Peter's Square, Manchester.

Figure 3.9 Flesh-coloured Peterhead granite was used for this fine example of a drinking fountain near the Royal Exchange, London

Scottish granites

Scotland is rich in granite. It has been used widely in Scotland and it has been exported to neighbouring England and to many countries overseas. Large masses crop out in the Grampian Highlands, the Southern Uplands, the Western Isles and in the Northern Highlands. The granites range in age from Precambrian to Tertiary. Most of them, however, are associated with the Devonian-Carboniferous Caledonian orogeny, which was marked by the production of large granite masses, known as the Newer Granites. Within the Grampian Highlands, an important series of these masses crop out in a semi-circle, stretching southwards from about Inverness to the Cairngorm Mountains, eastwards, via Hill of Fayne, to Aberdeen and north-west to Peterhead and to Strichen. The chief rock type is a biotite-granite, with little, or no, muscovite, although muscovite does appear in the Kemnay granite in the northern part of the Hill of Fayne mass. Aberdeen was, at one time, the granite centre of the world, but it is, perhaps, the Peterhead granite which is more widely known and the most famous.

Most of the stone taken from the Peterhead mass is coarse-grained and dark or pale flesh-coloured. It consists mainly of quartz and orthoclase feldspar, with only a little biotite mica. Hornblende may be present and, in some places, it completely replaces the mica. The stone is noted for its characteristic dark-coloured xenoliths. It was used widely in its own area, and is responsible for the 'gleaming red' town of Peterhead. With the development of the railways in the 1880s, it was exported in vast quantities to the rest of Britain. Fine columns of this stone may be seen in the East Carriageway, St Pancras Station, London, and the Duke of York's column, (except for the base), provides an outstanding

Figure 3.10 Peterhead granite matched with Rubislaw granite, a favourite combination of the Victorians, used here for the Baynard Castle public house, Queen Victoria Street, London

example. Pillars of the stone can be seen in the entrance hall of the Fitzwilliam Museum, Cambridge and stone from the Stirlinghill Quarry, which is known for its fine xenoliths, was used for the base of the main building (1906) of Strathclyde University, Glasgow. The lower floors of the Midland Hotel, St Peter's Square, Manchester, provides another example. There the stone is matched with bands of Dark Shap. In some areas of the Peterhead mass, the stone is dark grey in colour and is fine-grained, with scattered irregular, larger crystals of pale-coloured feldspar. Strictly, it is a granodiorite. Cairngall Quarry was the best known of those quarries supplying this grey stone, which is commonly called Blue Peterhead. It may be seen in the plinth of the statue of Wellington, Queen Street, Glasgow; in the base of the fountains, Trafalgar Square, London; and is renowned for supplying a 30-tonne block for the sarcophagus of the Prince Consort at Frogmore, Windsor, Berkshire. Eight 20 foot (6 m) high polished columns in St George's Hall, Liverpool, are each made of one block of the stone. Another dark grey-coloured, medium-grained stone quarried at Rora, about one mile north of Aberdeen, was used for ornamental work. Pillars of it are recorded at Cambridge[6].

Aberdeen, the city of the 'glitter of mica at windy corners', typifies a city built of granite. The enormous 155 m (380 ft.) deep hole, Rubislaw Quarry, which is said to date back to 1721 and which supplied the stone to build much of Aberdeen, is now surrounded by the city. The stone from Rubislaw is blue-grey in colour, medium-grained, and contains orthoclase, plagioclase, quartz, much biotite and a little muscovite, with xenoliths. The biotite mica flakes in it have a marked orientation. If the stone is cut to be polished, the cut should be at right angles to the orientation. If the mica flakes lie parallel with the exposed, polished surface, the natural mineral cleavage of the mica leads to a pitted appearance. This can be seen on most other types of polished granite surfaces, but, because the mica flakes are not always orientated, the effect is usually less noticeable. The feldspars often show a swirling texture. This stone has been widely used from an early date. St Machar's Cathedral, Aberdeen, is generally credited with being the earliest, large scale use of granite for building. As with most other granites, it was used also on a large scale for civil engineering works including, Waterloo Bridge (in part 1817), Portsmouth Docks, and Bell Rock Lighthouse (or Inchape Rock), which is 131 feet (40 m) high and was designed by Robert Stevenson and Rennie in 1807. Many other quarries, such as Dancing Cairns, Sclattie and Persley, in the Aberdeen mass also supplied stone for building work generally, but, unless a record exists of the stone used, it is not possible by casual inspection to do more than determine that the granite is Aberdeen, or Rubislaw.

Granite from around Aberdeen used to be exported to many other countries. It is on record that dark grey, even-grained stone from Dyce Quarries, five miles north-west of Aberdeen, was used in the Bank of Australia, Melbourne (pre-1911). As a relief from the uniformly grey colour in Aberdeen, the pink and red of Corrennie and Peterhead granite may sometimes be seen. The outcrop of granite which makes up the Hill of Fare mass, 15 miles (24 km) inland from Aberdeen, is included in the Aberdeen granite. Two widely known stones were taken from it, Kemnay and Corrennie. Kemnay, pale silver-grey, with a yellowish tinge from the colour of the feldspar, is quartz-rich and contains both biotite, which is orientated, and muscovite mica. It was used for the granite houses of Kemnay and for Kemnay House itself (seventeenth century). More importantly, stone was quarried in large quantities and was used for several bridges spanning the River Thames. This stone forms the base of the Queen Victoria Monument outside Buckingham Palace, London. It is renowned for its use in the building claimed to be the second largest granite building in the world, Marischal College, Aberdeen, 'a poem in stone'. El Escorial, outside Madrid, Spain, is claimed to be the largest. The Kemnay Quarry, apart from being the first to use steam and electrical firing, is noted as the first to use Blondins, an aerial cableway used to bring blocks of stone to the surface from the bottom of deep quarries.

The Corrennie Quarries supplied, in contrast, a warm red-coloured stone, coarser-grained and quartz-rich, with bright, pink-red feldspars. In addition to its use for decorative shop fronts, for example, in Bond Street, London, it is best known for its use in the base and for the balustrade of the City Chambers, Glasgow (1887). In places, Corrennie stone has a streaked texture. Associated bodies of a more basic (lower SiO_2 content) nature occur in this rock and a quartz-diorite forms grey patches and bands throughout part of it. Blocks may even be half pink and half grey. An entirely grey stone was quarried from nearby Tillyfourie. Further to the west, Balmoral Castle is built of light grey 'local granite' and roofed with slates from nearby Foudland.

It was not unusual for granite to be used for the decorative effect given by the variety of colours displayed. This was a consideration with, for example, the Albert Memorial, Kensington Gardens, London. The wide range of colour shown by Aberdeen granites can be seen in the nineteen columns of the pulpit of Crathie church (1895), near Balmoral, which, it is recorded, was built at the desire of Queen Victoria.

Many of the smaller granite masses in the Grampian Highlands have been used mostly locally. Occasionally some have been more widely used, such as that at Ballachulish, a locality more commonly associated with slate. Ballachulish granite, notable for a frequent abundance of xenoliths, was used in part for the monument outside the Geology Building, Glasgow University. The stone was obtained from a demolished railway bridge.

Brief mention should be made also of Ailsa Craig, Firth of Clyde, Ayrshire, the remnant of a volcanic core. Most of the island is of a fine-grained micrograrite, which contains the dark blue mineral riebeckite, instead of hornblende. Used on the island for building, it is much better known for its use as curling stones. It also supplied good quality setts.

In the Southern Uplands, an important, large intrusive granite mass and a very narrow vein were the sources for two well known, widely used stones. The first is the Criffel mass, Dumfries and Galloway. On its western edge are the quarries of Dalbeattie. The stone is pinkish-grey coloured, medium-grained, and contains oligoclase, plagioclase, biotite mica and hornblende, with many accessory minerals, particularly a clove-coloured sphene (a calcium titanium silicate ($CaTiSiO_5$) mineral), which is brown and greenish-yellow, grey, or black. It is widely found as an accessory mineral. The composition of the granite differs throughout the mass.

Because the quarries are near the sea, the stone was shipped far and wide, including to Ceylon. Examples in Great Britain, apart from the light grey town of Dalbeattie itself, include pillars at St Pancras Station, London; the lower Mosley Street side of the Midland Hotel, Manchester; part of the Albert Memorial, London; and the George V Bridge, Clyde, Glasgow. It is used as a facing stone for the Bank of Scotland, 30 Bishopsgate, London. Sweetheart Abbey, New Abbey, Dumfries and Galloway, uses 'Crifell Granite', which is not otherwise localized, as a contrast to the mass of the red sandstone building. Perhaps the best known use is for the lower part of the Pearl Life Assurance building, Holborn, London.

The silvery-grey coloured Creetown granite was quarried from an outcrop about 650 feet (200 m) wide and only about a mile (1.6 km) long. Because the quarries were also near the sea, the stone was shipped out widely. Records of its use, however, are scarce. Mersey Docks, part of the Thames Embankment, Aldermary House, Watling Street, London, and the Marks and Spencer store (1966), Argyle Street, Glasgow which also used Rubislaw granite, are some examples.

A number of famous quarries on the southern peninsula, or ross, of the Island of Mull, Inner Hebrides, supplied a red stone that became known generally as Ross of Mull granite. In fact, the mass, some twenty square miles (50 square km) in outcrop, ranges from a hornblende-biotite-diorite, to a muscovite-biotite granite and from a grey to a red colour. It is the red stone which has been widely used. It is pale to deep red-coloured, coarse-grained

Figure 3.11 The piers of Blackfriars bridge are models of the font of the former Blackfriars monastery. They were so designed at the wish of Queen Victoria who opened the bridge in 1869. The three drums of the columns are of solid Ross of Mull granite

Figure 3.12 The statue 'Asia' of the Albert Memorial, London, is of Sicilian Marble (see p 147) and has an inset slab of Ross of Mull granite. Much importance was given to the colours of the many granites used in the memorial. Ross of Mull granite was one of the earliest quarried in Scotland

stone, composed of pink to red orthoclase feldspar, brown biotite mica, and, in some places, white muscovite mica, which may be replaced by hornblende. The stone is noted for its flow-structure and for a blotchy appearance, caused by a rough clustering (clotting) of the feldspar. It is renowned for its widely spaced joints. Its earliest use was for Iona Abbey (seventh century), which is just across the Sound of Iona from the granite mass. Loose blocks, deposited by glacial action on the island, were incorporated into the structure. The joint system allowed large blocks to be won. The stone may be seen as pedestals on Holborn Viaduct, London; in the piers of Blackfriars Bridge, London (*Figure 3.11*); as columns in the Albert Memorial, London (*Figure 3.12*); and as pillars flanking the main south entrance of the University, Glasgow. In this city, Ross of Mull granite on the lower part of buildings was commonly combined with red sandstone above[10]. In the Northern Highlands, granite has only been used locally.

Irish granites

Important granite masses are found in Ireland, all of which have been worked at one time or another. The most important is probably the Wicklow-Leinster mass. The outcrop trends roughly south-west to north-east, and is 60 miles long by about 10 miles wide (100 by 16 km). In general, the stone is a grey-coloured, coarse-grained granite, with muscovite. A pink variety is known. Many quarries were opened in the rock and much grey Wicklow granite was used for buildings in Dublin. Blocks were also supplied to help build the Thames Embankment, London. Stone from Ballyknockon Quarries, County Wicklow, was used for the Wellington Monument, Phoenix Park, Dublin, for Trinity College (1832), Dublin; and for part of Dublin Station.

The Newry granite, stretching through County Armagh and into County Down, is best known for the Newry, Bessbrook and Castlewellan stones. The towns of Newry and Bessbrook were both built of local granite from an early date. The Newry granite is a complex of intrusions and the rock varies considerably. In general, the stone is a pale grey-coloured, fine-grained granodiorite, with biotite mica. However, there is a concentration of biotite in some areas and of hornblende in other places. As a consequence, the stone assumes a dark appearance as at Castlewellan, County Down. Stone from quarries in Northern Ireland was used in the base and pedestal and for some of the columns of the Albert Memorial, London. Newry granite road setts were once characteristic of Belfast streets and the stone has been used also for buildings, such as the Ulster Bank, Waring Street, Belfast. Stone from the Castlewellan Quarry, specifically, may be seen as columns on the Water Commissioners' Building, Donegall Square, Belfast. Bessbrook granite has been used for the base of the pilasters of Abbey-Life House, 1–3 St Paul's Churchyard, London[11].

The nearby Mourne Mountains granite is a complex of five separate intrusions, which show only slight differences. In places, the edge of the mass is of a finer grain. This enabled good setts to be produced, which are said to have 'paved Lancashire[12]. Mourne granite was used for the base of Telephone House, Belfast.

Masses in County Galway yielded a pink-coloured, fine-grained stone for the top, and a dark grey, medium-grained stone for the bottom, of the Parnall Monument, Dublin. Shantallow Quarry supplied many setts in Dublin. All the polished granite for the new Post Office for South Kensington, in Exhibition Road is reported to be of Galway granite and so is the base of the Fontenoy Memorial, Belgium. In the main, however, this mass was so intensively glacially rotted that it erodes easily. Stone taken from it should be selected with care.

Channel Islands granites

The Channel Isles, Jersey and Guernsey, have exported granite to the British mainland for a long time, mostly for kerbs, paving and setts. Jersey granite varies a good deal in character, from pale red to pink in colour and from fine- to coarse-grained. Stone from La Moie Quarries, near St Helier, was used for Chatham Docks. Guernsey supplied a stone known locally as Bird's Eye, which was exported to London as Blue Granite. It is a diorite type rock. Columns in Goodwood House, West Sussex, are recorded as being of Guernsey granite.

Imported granites

Granite may be found in many other countries, but it seems that it was not until the middle of the nineteenth century that foreign granite began to be imported into Britain on any scale. In 1864, granite from Sweden was imported in quantity, to help build the Thames Embankment, London, in which many other granites were also used. A variety with noticeably blue coloured quartz, quarried at Vanevik, Sweden, may be seen in the Coliseum Theatre, St Martin's Lane, London. There are few, if any verified references to the use of imported granite in ancient monuments and historic buildings. Since the 1860s, however, much has been imported and some varieties seem to have become fashionable for a period. Most of these varieties are not discussed in detail here. There are some, however, that deserve more than a brief mention.

Italy, not immediately brought to mind as a granite

supplier, has a number of granite quarries. Those at Baveno have acquired more than a local reputation. Pale rosy-pink in colour and fine-grained, this stone was used widely at least as far back as the sixteenth century. The Italian island of Sardinia supplies a lot of granite which is widely exported. Sardinian Grey and Sardinian Beige, Coral and Pink are the chief varieties. Sardinian Grey was used for the Ismaili Centre, South Kensington, London, with spectacular effect.

Egypt has supplied stone from Suwan, known as Syene by the Greeks and now as Aswan, since at least from 4000 BC. It is a hornblende granite, pink coloured, and composed of plagioclase and orthoclase feldspar, quartz, a small amount of aggregated muscovite mica and hornblende, with magnetite as an accessory mineral. It is known world-wide as the stone of the twenty-two Cleopatra's Needles. One is in London, one in Central Park, New York, USA and another in the Place de la Concorde, Paris, France.

Figure 3.13 'An uncompleted Cleopatra's Needle'. A monolithic obelisk, abandoned by the early Egyptian quarriers, as yet not released from the granite bedrock at Aswan (Syene), Egypt. Blocks of this granite were used for the many 'Cleopatra's Needles' now scattered around the world. (Courtesy of Dr C. Welch)

Norway has also exported much stone to Great Britain, particularly since the early 1900s. The Stock Exchange, Manchester, is an early example.

At one time, Aberdeen was a centre for granite processing of both British and imported stone. Many of the imported stones were given British-sounding names; for example Balmoral Red, Royal Grey, Braemar Grey and Abergeldie Grey are from Finland. Grey Royal granite is from Norway and Imperial Red is from Sweden. The trade name of the stone cannot be taken as giving an indication of its provenance.

Two recently imported granites, currently being widely used for cladding demonstrate how a stone becomes available and then fashionable. The first, from Millbank, South Dakota, USA, called Imperial Mahogany in Great Britain, is a dull red-brown colour. It is coarse-grained, and shows a marked foliation and streaking out of the feldspars, which may be picked out by wisps of mica. It is one of the Older Granites, which have suffered later deformation and mineral alteration. It may be seen as polished slabs cladding, for example, Blackfriars Station, London and Lloyds Bank, Victoria Street, London. The second example is from quarries in Finland, about 0.5 miles (0.8 km) from the border with Russia, on the Kotka to Leningrad road. Sold in Britain as Baltic Brown, it has large, flesh-coloured potassic feldspars, which form rounded crystals up to a few centimetres in diameter which are mantled with white sodic plagioclase, and, in some instances, rhythmically zoned with orthoclase. These feldspars are embedded in a matrix of normal texture, which consist chiefly of quartz and some coloured minerals. The stone exhibits Rapakivi texture (*Figure 3.14*). Polished slabs clad the main Lloyds Bank building, Leeds.

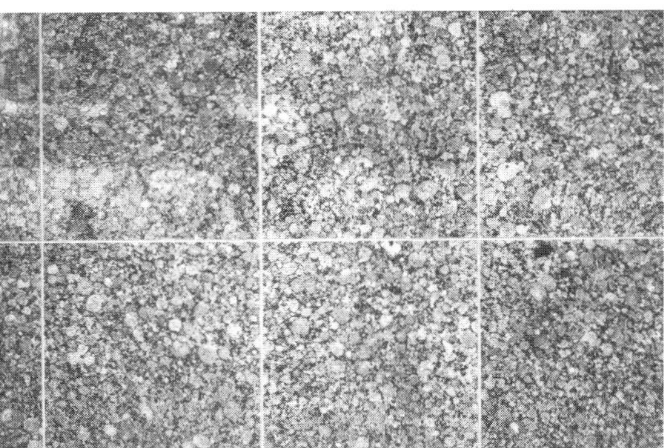

Figure 3.14 Rapakivi structure is well seen in 'Baltic Brown' granite from Finland. The boundary between Finland and the USSR runs across this granite mass and similar stone may be seen used in Leningrad and other towns near the border

Intermediate plutonic igneous rocks

Syenite is not a common rock in Great Britain. The original type is comprised mostly of hornblende and orthoclase feldspar and comes from near Dresden, Germany. It is one of the quirks of geology that the rock at Syene in Egypt, from which the name was derived is actually a hornblende granite. Syenite, an intermediate plutonic igneous rock which is pale-coloured grey to reddish, occurs in relatively small masses. It may be thought of as a granite without quartz. Despite its relative rareness compared with granite *sensu strictu*, it is probably more noticeable in all the major cities of the world than any other rock, because of the popularity of one particular type, larvikite (from Larvik, Norway), which has been sold on the world market for many years as Pearl Granite, Imperial Pearl, Light Pearl, Dark Pearl, Royal Blue and several other varietal names. This rock contains large rhomb-shaped feldspars of different types intergrown with one another. Indeed, the rock may be made up almost entirely of feldspar. Because of the peculiar structure of the intergrown feldspars, light is reflected from different layers within the crystal which results in interference patterns and an iridescence, termed *schiller*. The bright play of colours is enhanced by polishing and the difference between an unpolished and polished surface is marked. The polished appearance, however, cannot be expected to appeal in every instance of its use. The stone has been widely used for shop fronts, and public house fascias. It may be seen used sculpturally for the monolithic 'Elephant and Calf', at the Philadelphia Zoo, Pennsylvania, USA (*Figure 3.15*).

Figure 3.15 'Elephant and Calf' carved from a monolithic block of larvikite. Philadelphia Zoo. Pennsylvania, USA

Other instances of its use are: the Henry and Edsel Ford Memorial Auditorium, Detroit, USA, the new Mitsui Building, Tokyo, Japan, the entrance to the Mayfair Hotel, London, the Innocenti Building, Milan, Italy, the DGB Building, Dusseldorf, Germany, in the remarkable suspended staircase, of General Motors Research Staff Building, Detroit, USA, and for the interesting modelling of a ship's prow on the new National Employers Federation Building, Bury Street, London. It has also been used with startling effect in the perfumery department of Harrods, London, where the ceiling is set with 250 lights directed to stimulate the schiller. The stone commonly is recorded as granite.

A visually attractive syenite containing the azure-blue mineral sodalite (a sodium aluminium silicate with chlorine) comes from Bahia Quarry, São Salvador, Brazil. Called Blue Bahia it is also known, inevitably it may be thought, as 'blue granite'. Sodalite-syenite adequately describes the stone, which, of course, can be given any name. It is currently being used with marked effect for the Ismaili Centre, South Kensington, London. An interesting stone in this family is a nephaline-syenite known geologically as foyaite because the original type described was from Mt. Foya, Portugal. It is worked in the Sierra de Monchique, Algarve in Portugal and shows radiating clusters of fine feldspar laths. It is sold as a syenite and is recorded as used in the Bank of Abu Dhabi, at the entrance to Stewart Wrightson's, Camomile Street, London[13].

Swedish Green 'Granite', a dark grey-coloured syenite has a greenish cast caused by the green coloured mineral epidote (a calcium aluminium iron silicate). It has been used decoratively.

Diorite is a fairly abundant intermediate plutonic rock but is of limited occurrence in Great Britain. Characteristically it is speckled black and white because the dark minerals are in clots. It is coarse-grained and composed mostly of plagioclose feldspar and hornblende. It may contain one of the pyroxenes (a group of complex silicate minerals). The stone may have a deep green cast from iron-silicate minerals which were altered very early on in the formation of the rock, and thus may be confused with Swedish Green 'Granite'. The mineral quartz may be present in diorite. In that instance the stone is termed a quartz-diorite and thus grades into grano-diorite. Diorite has been imported into Great Britain for decorative use. The best known is Ebony Black Granite from Sweden, which is even black in colour with shiny opaque metallic flecks. The lower façade of the Empire State Building, New York is clad with this stone, as is the Institut Français du Pétrole, Rueil Malmaison (Seine), France (1959). It has also been used by Milles for the sculpture of his eagle at Worcester, Massachusetts, USA; and it forms the base of the renowned US Marine Corps War Memorial in Washington, DC, USA. A similar stone, Black Swede H, is spectacularly used in the Imperial Theatre, Tokyo where it is teamed-up with Imperial Red Granite, also from Sweden.

Bon Accord Black 'Granite' from Sweden which is classified between diorite and gabbro is medium-grained and was, at one time, extensively worked in

Aberdeen. It has been used principally for shop fronts and for head stones. Black Diamond 'Granite' from South Africa is also used mainly for cladding. It is a syeno-gabbro and is uniformly black-coloured with shiny feldspar laths up to 1 cm long. It may be seen on the VIth Inn, Crown Square, Manchester. 'Andes Black' from South Africa, is a similar stone.

A geologically interesting rock named Kentallenite from the Scottish town of Kentallen, may be considered here amongst the Syeno-gabbro types. Coarse to medium-grained, it exhibits large shining plates of biotite mica. This 'handsome dark... ornamental stone' is recorded[14] as having been quarried as 'black granite' and sent to Aberdeen for processing, but no record of its use has been discovered.

Basic plutonic igneous rocks

Gabbro typically is a mottled dark-grey to black coloured, coarsely crystalline rock composed essentially of the minerals labradorite (a complex type of feldspar) and augite (a complex silicate of calcium, magnesium, iron and aluminium of variable composition). Iron-bearing minerals are common accessory minerals and because the rock is often rich in them it tends to weather more easily than some of the acid igneous rocks. The mineral olivine (a magnesium iron silicate, $(Mg, Fe)_2 SiO_4$) may be present to give the rock (an olivine-gabbro) a green cast. Olivine also weathers readily.

Gabbro is a rare rock in Great Britain. The Cuillins of Skye is the largest mass and it is not common elsewhere. The 'Black Granite' from Herrestad, Sweden is the best known example. The use of this stone in a highly polished state in the interior of the Ritz Hotel, London, is so often recorded that this appears to be its only use. It is usually mistaken for a marble. Recently, Indian Ebony Black, a related type of rock, has been imported into Great Britain and has been used for decorative cladding[10] and monumental work.

Ultrabasic igneous rocks

Serpentinite (or serpentine rock), a rock made up mostly of the mineral serpentine (hydrated silicate of magnesium and iron, $Mg_3Si_2O_5(OH)_4$), has resulted from the alteration of rocks such as peridotites and picrites which are rich in the mineral olivine. It is a secondary rock, formed by the *serpentinization* of other ultrabasic rocks. Therefore it is conveniently considered here.

Serpentinites are found in those areas of the crust which have been tectonically affected. The change probably occurred when the original rock within the Earth's lithosphere was forced upward, and became hydrated in the process. They are soft but variable ($H = 2\frac{1}{2}$ to 4), heavy, mottled, streaked and banded from virtually black, through red, green and grey to dirty white. The stone will take a good polish, but weathers readily to a poor-looking dingy grey when exposed. The name serpentine is from the supposed resemblance of the rock to the skin of a serpent. The best known mass in Great Britain is found in The Lizard, Cornwall where the rock was once extensively wrought. It was used on a massive scale for interior decoration, particularly in churches. St John's College Chapel, Cambridge has columns of serpentinite. It may also be seen in the floor at Peterborough Cathedral, in the pulpit and twelfth-century doorway of Landewednack Church on The Lizard[3], as blocks for steps and as columns in Truro Cathedral, and as innumerable, mostly Victorian, fonts in many churches. Because the stone weathers readily it is unsuitable for outside work. Nevertheless, interestingly, it has been used for columns on the shop front of (now) Mappin & Webb and of Loewe, Bond Street, London. The stone appears in many church monuments.

A narrow sill of serpentinite which outcrops on the shore and in the cliffs at Portsoy, Banffshire is the source of the so-called Portsoy 'Marble'. Predominantly darkish-green with lighter yellowish-green blobs and streaks, the stone now is worked, as is that at The Lizard, for small ornamental pieces and tourist knick-knacks. In the past it supplied the stone for a magnificent fireplace in nearby Cullen House[15]; and for fireplaces in the Palace of Versailles, France[16]. Other masses are found in Fetlar and in Unst, Shetlands. Stone from Unst was used locally and was also the source of soapstone and talc, minerals closely related to serpentinite.

Serpentinite is found also in Anglesey. The principle outcrop is near Rhoscolyn and it is a serpentinized gabbro, dark green, brecciated with some patches of the white-coloured mineral calcite ($CaCO_3$).

The stone was produced apparently in limited quantity, and was known as Anglesey Serpentine, Mona Marble, and Verde Antico. However, in this instance Verde Antico was used to indicate its appearance, not its provenance. It was used, as was most serpentinite from elsewhere, for 'marble-topped' tables, wash-hand stands, chests and so on. Many other stones were similarly used and the determination of the stone may occasionally help with the determination of the provenance and date of a piece of furniture. The best known use of 'Mona Marble' is in the chancels of Truro Cathedral. The shafts supporting the pulpit in the nave of Worcester Cathedral also are of this stone, and pieces of furniture in the Victoria and Albert Museum, London are topped with it. Llys Delas House, Anglesey has a fireplace made of 'Mona Marble'.

The areas of Piedmont, Italy and Thessaly, Greece are important sources of decorative serpentinite, not only in the past but also at the present. The stone is brecciated. This was caused, it seems, by big pods of the original rock being squeezed up into the cores of mountain belts. The stone is composed of small or large angular fragments, red, purple, green, grey and rarely black in colour, which are much veined, with the veins swelling and narrowing, some with contrasting white calcite. There is a profusion of names which depend on the quarry from which the stone is taken. Verde Antico (*Lapis Atracius* of the Romans) from near Larissa, Greece, is the classic and classical variety, noted for patches of calcite. *Rosso di Levanto*, from near Levanto, Italy, the other main type, is predominantly red to reddish purple in colour, with occasional white veins of soapstone (called sapone by the Italians).

The Greek and Italian serpentinites have been extensively used for ecclesiastical work, decoration, inlay and furniture. They may be found worldwide and are used decoratively for shop fronts and like purposes (*Figure 3.16*).

The island of Tinos, Greece is the source of a marble known as Tinos (Tenos, or Vert Tinos). It is a serpentinite with irregular whitish veins and it has been variously classified as a serpentinous marble or as ophicalcite. It was quarried in classical times by the ancient Greeks who used it extensively. It has been used for monolithic columns and for plinths, pavements and panels. It was used for sixteen columns in the semi-circular hall of the New Sessions House, London, built in 1907[6]. It is also used in the National Gallery, Trafalgar Square, London.

Figure 3.16 A green serpentinite, *Verde* (or *Verte*) *Fraya*, used decoratively for a shop front in Regent Street, London

A serpentinized picrite, quarried at Polyphant (Polyfant, Pollaphant, in older spellings), Cornwall is a minor building stone in regional terms. Because it is found in an area where other available stones such as granite or slate were either hard to work or not suitable, it became widely used and widely known, out of all proportion with the size of the outcrop. A very dark ultrabasic hypabyssal igneous rock, it probably resulted from the upward migration of peridotite. The stone is fine-grained and grey to dusky-green-blue with white specks and reddish to yellowish brown spots. As it may be easily worked it has been used for dressings, almost as a freestone. It is recorded that Saxon and Norman arches in Cornwall are made of the Polyphant stone[6]. It may also be seen as shafts of the columns in Truro Cathedral, where it is used to provide the colour contrast in the same way that Blue Lias and Purbeck Marble are used in other parts of the country. Additionally it was used for columns in the church at Pampisford and for the Celtic Cross (1914) at Bartlow, Cambridgeshire; as well as for some piers in Exeter Cathedral. A recent, spectacular use is for the new (1983) font, designed by John Skelton, in Chichester Cathedral. It is the stone used for the war memorial, a copy of an old Cornish cross, at Haverfordwest, Dyfed. Another fine example of its use is provided by Archbishop Temple's tomb in Canterbury Cathedral.

A similar stone, also a serpentinized picrite, was formerly quarried at Duporth (2 miles (3.2 km) east of St Austell, Cornwall), where two small intrusions which cannot be traced very far inland occur on the beach. Although it is now largely forgotten, this stone also was used in Truro Cathedral[17] for some of the vaulting shafts in the choir and transepts, in the baptistry, and in the shafting in the triforium. Duporth Stone, was used in the Cathedral '... with great effect ... and it might hold up its head and claim to be quite as handsome and suitable to the purpose as the Purbeck Marble that was found in churches in other parts of the country.' It is possible that some determination of Polyphant Stone should properly be of Duporth Stone.

Serpentinite may grade into a serpentinous marble depending on the quantities of the minerals present. Such a marble is known as an ophicalcite. Ophicalcites commonly result from the metamorphism of a limestone containing other mineral matter.

Asbestos

The substance commonly known as asbestos has been found in mortars used in countries around the Aegean Sea. It is known that the asbestos came from Cyprus. The name asbestos, however, is given today to a number of minerals which have different chemical compositions but which have one characteristic in common, they crystallize into long, thin fibres which can be fairly easily separated. Since these fibres are flexible, they may be woven into a fabric. Additionally the minerals are resistant to heat to different degrees.

The asbestos found in Cyprus is a fibrous form of serpentine which has been named crysotile (magnesium iron silicate, $(Mg,Fe)_3Si_2O_5(OH)_4$). This form provides about 90 per cent of the world's asbestos. In Cyprus it is found as veins intimately associated with ultrabasic rocks.

The perpetual lamp wicks of the Vestal Virgins were of amianthus, the name for asbestos used by the Greeks and by the Romans. It is derived from the Greek word for undefiled, a reference to the way in which it could be cleansed by fire. Interestingly, the quarries where the asbestos is extracted and the village nearby on Mount Troodos, Cyprus, are named Amiandus.

Rocks from minor intrusion

Among the smaller, finer-grained igneous intrusions the rocks named porphyry are of importance in relation to building and particularly to decorative stones.

The name porphyry is derived from the Greek word for purple. Pliny in his Natural History describes *Porphyrites leptopsephos* (white-spotted) from Egypt and it was this stone, Imperial Porphyry that was taken in quantiy to Imperial Rome as *Lapis porphyrites*.

A similar stone, but in this instance green, quarried in Greece during classical times was known at the time of Pliny as *Marmor Lacedaemonium Viride*.

Porphyry is an igneous rock of any composition that contains conspicuous, relatively large, crystals, known as phenocrysts, set in a fine-grained groundmass. The phenocrysts are normally of quartz (quartz porphyry) or feldspar (feldspar porphyry) or both (quartz-feldspar-porphyry).

The elvans

The granites of south-west England are intimately associated with a series of quartz-porphyry dykes called elvans. Elvan and grey elvan are names given by Cornish quarrymen and miners to dyke and sill rocks around the granite masses which are up to 150 feet (46 m) thick. These dykes are mostly of quartz-porphyry and it is to this rock that the name elvan should be restricted. Geologists continued the use of the stone workers' perfectly adequate classification and nomenclature. Later writers have tended to misuse the term. The term blue elvan was given to other rock types, principally to greenstone, which is now determined as dolerite (diabase), and to rocks such as serpentinized picrite. In the past many elvans were quarried for local building, for example at Mayon and Douglas near St Austell; Helland, St Neot, Lanivet and Witheal near Bodmin; Trevailes and Roseorow near Penryn. In some instances elvans from several different localities were introduced into a building. One example is Truro Cathedral which used Pentewan, Wild Duck, Newnham and others.

Figure 3.17 A porphyritic granite, a microgranite and an elvan, all quarried locally, were used for the School of Mines, Camborne, Cornwall

(a)

(b)

Figure 3.18 (a) Blue-grey coloured elvan from Landrake was used by the Normans for the spectacular arch of St Germanus, Cornwall; (b) it was used also for the nearby much more recent entrance lodge to Port Eliot

Elvan from the Tarton Down Quarries, Landrake, Cornwall was used by the Normans for the magnificent west door entrance of the Church of St Germanus in St Germans, four miles away. All Norman stonework in this area is of this eye-catching blue-grey-green stone. It may be seen also in the nearby entrance lodge to Port Eliot, which is much more recent (*Figure 3.18*).

The most widely known elvan appears to be Pentewan Stone (Pentuan in earlier spelling), which certainly was used from an early date. A Roman inscribed stone built into the wall of Tregomy Church is a rough block of it. This stone is pale buff grey in colour. All elvans are more or less kaolinized and under the microscope the feldspar of Pentewan Stone is seen to be of minute scales of kaolinite with some quartz. These rather softer powdery masses commonly weather out from the stone to give it a characteristic pock-marked appearance. However, this is not detrimental. In fact it probably owes its good qualities as a weather resisting stone to the ground mass of quartz and white mica.

Pentewan Stone has a long history of use as a building stone. Clifton-Taylor[9] lists several houses built of it, for example a house at Travithen, Antony House, Torpoint, and Trevice House, near Newquay. The church at Fowey also is of Pentewan stone. In 1985 blocks of Pentewan stone were recovered from the beach near the original quarry and were used for repair and restoration work at St Austell Church, Cornwall. A warm yellow quartz-porphyry quarried near St Columb Minor was used for the local church and several houses around.

Greek and Egyptian porphyries

Of considerable importance, particularly in the archaeological context is the Green Porphyry of Greece and the Red Porphyry of Egypt. Both have been widely used as ornamental stones since at least the early days of the Roman Empire. The stone from the Marathonisi Quarries, Laconia, Greece, the *Marmor Lacedaemonium Viride* of Pliny was later known as *Porfido Serpentino*. This is unfortunate because the stone is not a serpentinite. Pausanias (second century AD) calls the stone Verde Antique and describes it as '... hard to work, but once worked (it)... might grace sanctuaries of the gods'. It was very popular in Rome and was also exported elsewhere. It was commonly known as *Porfido Verde Antico*. It was quarried at Demos Krokeae, in western Laconia and is renowned for the lighter green porphyritic labradorite feldspar crystals conspicuously set in a darker green fine-grained groundmass. It is sometimes found to have been used in Roman villas in Great Britain and in Ireland. As may be expected, it has been extensively used in Rome; for example in the church of St Giovanni in Fonte; St Maria Maggiore and St Pietro in Vincoli; St Vitali at Ravenna and for two columns in the Ava Coeli. Watson[18] also records an 'elaborately carved tombstone of white marble, erected in 1903, in the churchyard of Dullington, a village in Cambridgeshire, is inlaid with this rock'. Probably the most often visited example is the plinth of Napoleon Bonaparte's tomb in Les Invalides, Paris.

The Green Porphyry of Greece often is used with the famous Red Porphyry, the Imperial Porphyry or Porfido Rosso Antico, of Egypt. The Imperial Porphyry is as spectacular as the Green Porphyry. It differs in colour because it has a dark purplish-red groundmass caused by the presence of the mineral haematite in which are set pale-red, or pink to white laths of feldspar. The stone was first quarried from Lykabettus, north of the hill Gebel Abu Dakhan in the eastern desert of Egypt apparently by the Romans and not by the Egyptians. This is the only known locality where this rock occurs. Columns nearly 40 feet (12 m) high were sent from Rome for use in St Sophia, Constantinople. Other columns may be seen in Venice (*Figure 3.19*). A slab is used in the tomb of Henry III in Westminster Abbey and it was used for the cross behind the altar in the Chapel of St Andrew, Westminster Cathedral. One of the steps up to the Chancel in the spectacular Church of St Mary, Studley Royal, Yorkshire is made of sizeable blocks of this 'Stone of Rome'.

Figure 3.19 'The Tetrarchs', in Venice, Italy are carved in Imperial Porphyry from Egypt. Note the unfortunate repair of the right-hand side lower leg and foot in an obviously geologically inappropriate stone. (Photo: John Ashurst)

Dolerites

Dolerite is a common intrusive rock type in north-east England and in the Midland Valley of Scotland. Smaller sill and dyke masses are found elsewhere. The rock may also be called diabase, particularly outside Great Britain. It is a dark coloured rock consisting mostly of plagioclase feldspar and augite (calcium magnesium aluminosilicate, $(Ca,Mg,Fe,Al)(Al,Si)_2O_6$), a dark green to black pyroxene mineral. In many instances the markedly green mineral chlorite (one of a group of silicates which are related to the micas) may be present. Because of the presence of this mineral, field occurrences of dolerite were given the generic name of greenstone. This name, however, includes other rock types. Dolerite is medium-grained, dark, and heavy. The minerals can be distinguished normally with the unaided eye. Although dolerite has not been widely used in building it does provide striking examples of the local use of local material. Undoubtedly the biggest mass in Great Britain is the Great Whin Sill of northern England which may be traced from the Farne Islands, off the Northumberland coast at Bamburgh, across Northumberland through Teesdale to the western facing scarp of the Pennines. The Great Whin Sill is comprised mostly of quartz-dolerite. Much material has been taken from this sill and used as crushed rock and as setts. The names Whin and Trap have been used for the stone, but it should be noted that those names have been applied to other types of rock. The Romans built part of the renowned Hadrian's Wall along the sharp scarp crest of the Great Whin Sill and used stone from the sill itself as the building material. Blocks from the sill, used as part of the rubble filling the centre of the wall, are locally called Bluey. Not all of the Wall, however, is of quartz-dolerite from the Sill. Across the country the stone of which the Wall is built changes with the geology. The Romans used any suitable stone quarried close to the Wall.

A thick well-joined dyke of olivine-dolerite crops out at Carrickfergus, Co. Antrim, Ireland. It supplied the stone for the Castle which stands on it.

Thick sills of dolerite, up to 150 feet (46 m) thick cap Titterstone Clee Hill and Brown Clee Hill, north-east of Ludlow, Shropshire. They have been much quarried for roadstone, for setts which are used extensively in London and elsewhere, and may be found in local buildings. Large blocks are incorporated in the Iron Age camp on Titterstone Clee. The extraordinarily close jointing of a dolerite-type rock found at Corndon Hill, Shropshire, which allows it to be thinly laminated, enables it to be used as a tilestone; that is a stone, other than slate, which is used for roofing. It was used as far away as Llandrinio, Powys[19], at least as early as the mid-fifteenth century.

Around Exeter, Devon, a number of basic igneous rocks are known generally as the Exeter Traps or Exeter Volcanic Series. Some are of dolerite and closely related rock types. These have been extensively used in the city of Exeter for the City Wall, the mediaeval bridge, and the almshouses in Magdalen Street and in Gordon Road (*Figure 3.20*). The main quarries are at Pocombe and Thorveton. The Thorveton Quarry was worked by the Romans. A sill of somewhat serpentinized dolerite (greenstone)

Figure 3.20 A dolerite-type rock from the Exeter Volcanic series which crops out locally was used for the Almshouses, Magdalen Street, Exeter

Figure 3.21 Font of Clataclews stone. Church of St Petroc, Padstow

which runs through Rock, Padstow and which clips Cataclews (Catacleuse) Point, comes from a quarry at the Point. It is a fairly easily worked, dark greenish-blue-grey stone which was used locally for building. For example, it was used in the Norman parts of the church of St Petroc, Padstow (*Figure 3.21*) and for much of the mullions, tracery and font of the present-day church. Prior Vyvyan's Tomb in Bodmin Church provides a fine effigy. Clifton-Taylor[9] records that the effigies of Lord Marney and his son at Layer Massey, Essex are of this stone.

Confusingly, brown slatey-siltstones of Devonian age have also been quarried near Cataclews Point and they are sometimes referred to as Cataclews Stone in Church and other local guides.

Tuffs

Although it might be expected from a consideration of their genesis that volcanic igneous rocks would not provide stones suitable for building or for decoration, nevertheless, some have been used, particularly in those areas where other stones are not readily available. The glaringly white andesite tuff and lava known universally by the Peruvian name of Sillar, was used to build Arequipa, the 'White City' of Peru. Easy to work, the stone lends itself to elaborate carving as on the church of La Campagna in that city (*Figure 3.22*).

Tuff is the term used for consolidated fine-grained volcanic ash of whatever composition. The classification is on grain size, but it is possible to relate it to the original lava type, for example, andesitic tuff, or

Figure 3.22 Arequipa, the 'White City', Peru, is built substantially of a white andesite tuff, *sillar*. It may be easily carved as seen on the church of La Compagna. (Courtesy of Dr C. Welch)

(a)

(b)

Figure 3.23 (a) The eye-catching green-coloured altered volcanic ash from Hurdwick used for the Town Hall, Tavistock has, unusually, granite dressings (b)

Figure 3.24 Tuff is the material of the Etruscan necropolis of Cerveteri, near Rome. (Photo: John Ashurst)

basaltic tuff. Commonly tuffs are layered and thus superficially may resemble sediments.

Tuffs have been rarely used in Great Britain. However, a tuff from Dennis Hill caps the buttress of the west Tower of St Petroc, Padstow. The best known example is the somewhat altered ash, green-coloured, and very free-working tuff from Hurdwick used to build much of Tavistock, Devon (*Figure 3.23*).

Tuffs occur on continental Europe, particularly in the Brohl valley and the Nette valley of the Eifel, Germany, and near Rome, Italy (*Figure 3.24*). That found in the Eifel is a grey to cream coloured, somewhat fragmented rock with much pumice-like dust of trachytic composition; that is, rich in silica and poor in dark minerals, with much feldspar. It is known locally as Trass and is of importance in that it is used as a building stone. It is also used, after being finely ground and added to lime, to give a hydraulic cement, which is a type of cement which sets quickly even under water and hence can be used for hydraulic works. It produces a compact and chemically resistant cement with a low setting temperature. Trass, because of its porous nature and light weight may be confused with pumice which was formed from a highly gaseous, rapidly cooled lava. Surprisingly sand suitable for building purposes is not readily available near Rome, Italy. Consequently a trachytic volcanic ash, was used. It is this material, named Pozzolana or Pozzuolana, which was crushed and mixed with lime to produce a hydraulic cement. When the cement is mixed with crushed tuff and travertine is added as aggregate, a cheap, strong and long lasting concrete was formed. The name Pozzolana is derived from the seaport Pozzuoli where a similar volcanic ash is also found (*Figure 3.25*). Compact varieties of the tuff were used as a

Figure 3.25 Layers of Pozzolana in cliffs near Tivoli, Rome may on casual inspection appear to be of sedimentary rocks because of an apparently bedded appearance. (Photo: John Ashurst)

Figure 3.26 A cut block of 'Peperino' at Marino, near Rome clearly shows dark coloured scoriae 'peppercorns', pieces of other pyroclastic material and markedly angular pieces of light coloured marble. (Photo: John Ashurst)

building stone in Rome. Another variety, Peperino, or Peparino Tufaceo is so named because it contains small dark pieces of pumice-like material (scoriae) fancifully thought to resemble peppercorns (*Figure 3.26*).

Many materials are pozzolanic. The term is used for any substance which although not itself cementitious, will combine with lime mortar to give hydraulic properties and strength. Little pozzolanic rock is found in Great Britain. Pozzalana recorded from France and from the Azores, Santorin Earth from Greece, and Tosca from Teneriffe, Canary Islands are a few other examples.

Volcanic glass

In certain conditions acid lavas which were poured out onto the Earth's surface cooled so rapidly that the lava did not crystallize. Instead it solidified to form a natural glass, obsidian. If it had cooled slowly at depth, a granite would have resulted. Very rarely is obsidian completely non-crystalline, very small incipient crystals are present. Volcanic glasses from past geological periods show devitrification, the very slow process of crystallization. The rock, when fresh, is shiny black, hard (H = 5-5½), brittle, with a marked conchoidal fracture giving extremely sharp edges. Although dark coloured, thin fragments are light and transparent. It was worked for use as an ornamental ('gem') stone by the ancient Greeks and the Romans. The stone is found in the Lipari Islands, Iceland, Central Anatolia, the USA and in great quantities in the Valley of Mexico. It appears not to have been used for building as flint was elsewhere but was prized as a material for arrowheads, sickle blades, knives and so on. The Middle East imported the stone at least as early as 7000 BC from Central Anatolia. American Indians of every tribe worked spearheads and arrowheads from it. Small pieces shaped and worn for personal adornment are known as Apache Tears. Because of its glossy lustre it was fashioned into mirrors. Some examples up to 15 inches by 12 inches by 1 inch thick (38 cm × 31 cm × 2.5 cm) from the Valley of Mexico are in the Smithsonian (Natural History) Museum in Washington, DC, USA. Obsidian artifacts have been found in Great Britain and it would not be unexpected to discover the stone in an archaeological context.

Pumice is a highly vesicular, froth-like, volcanic glass, similar in composition to obsidian. In the Lipari Islands the bottom part of a lava flow may be of solid black obsidian passing up into white pumice in the upper part. Mostly the stone is ground to a fine powder for use as an abrasive, but it has also been used as a lightweight insulating material in building. Blocks have been found at archaeological sites in Great Britain.

Basalt

A prominent, and probably the commonest, rock in the world is basalt, a basic igneous volcanic rock, dark grey to black in colour. When fresh it weathers to a reddish colour. It is heavy, fine-grained, and composed mainly of plagioclase feldspar and usually augite. It often has grains of magnetite (metallic iron ore, Fe_3O_4). It may contain other minerals such as olivine and thus olivine-basalt. Normally fine-grained, the crystals cannot be distinguished by the unaided eye. It may be vesicular, and thus exhibit small vesicles where gas was trapped. It may also be scoriaceous or slaggy, and resemble clinker. Some exposures show vitreous basalt. Basalt occurs in flows of vast extent. The Deccan of India is a basalt plateau of over 500 000 square miles (1 300 000 square km). The Columbia Plateau, covering parts of Oregon, Washington State and Idaho, USA, covers some 200 000 square miles. The Antrim Plateau of Northern Ireland originally covered an area that stretched to Iceland and to Scotland (*Figure 3.27*).

Columnar jointing is a common feature in basalts. Because the columns could be easily taken apart, quarries between Bonn and Coblenz, Germany, were able to supply ready dressed columns that were merely put together again and extensively used for sea defence work notably in Holland. Watson[6] records that Blackpool, Clacton-on-Sea, Southend-on-Sea, Hartlepool and Hastings, all in Great Britain, used Renish basalt columns for a similar purpose. An undated advertisement issued by the London Basalt Stone Co. Ltd. states that Rhinish (*sic*) stone had been used in England since 1895.

Figure 3.27 Columnar jointing in basalt of the Giant's Causeway, Northern Ireland. The polygonal joint pattern is very marked when viewed from above. (Photo: John Ashurst)

Figure 3.28 The sandstone (seen here) of Cologne Cathedral has weathered more than the basalt, the other main stone used in its construction. (Photo: John Ashurst)

Basalt from the Eifel area was also used to great effect, largely to build Cologne Cathedral (*Figure 3.28*). The Cathedral is built of many other types of stone including sandstones and limestones. The rock first used was a trachyte from Dranchenfels. It is the sandstone which is weathering badly and it is

Figure 3.29 The columnar structure of the basalt of the Giant's Causeway is neatly mimicked in its use for the public lavatories nearby. In 1986, these lavatories were under threat of demolition as being obtrusive in an environmentally sensitive area (courtesy of R.H. Roberts)

planned to replace most of it with basalt which is still available and which is far more durable in today's polluted atmosphere[20].

The Mayen in the Eifel region is also the source of the widely known Niedermendig lava. It is markedly vesicular in texture and as a consequence it was much used, at least since about 1200 BC[21] for millstones, querns, and saddle-stones. The stone is frequently found not only in Great Britain but also across continental Europe on archaeological sites.

A dark, fine-grained basaltic rock from Mount Tmolus, Lydia is the original Touchstone. The earliest method of assaying gold was devised by the Lydians and known as trial by the Lydian Stone. Later other stones were used and they became known as Touch Stone or the Touch. The purity of the gold was judged by the colour of the streak left on the stone.

Recent research, however, indicates that the black pebbles known as 'Lydian Stone' from the River Tmolus are not a kind of black basalt. The River Tmolus was not known to ancient geographers. The river Pactolus which rises on Mt. Tmolus is believed to be in the Boz Dagh area of the Menderes massif, Turkey. There is no basalt in this massif. A full discussion is given in reference 22.

Although not widely used for building as its commonness would suggest, when used basalt has been used to great effect. The Giant's Causeway, Northern Ireland is renowned for the hexagonal pillars produced by the jointing system. This outstanding characteristic is neatly captured by the architecture of the public lavatories nearby which are built of basalt from the lava flow (*Figure 3.29*). Although this basalt flow covers a substantial area of Northern Ireland the rock has been little used. It is used locally for rubble-masonry and is seen occasionally roughly squared and dressed in Belfast. In the

Figure 3.30 Parliament Building, Reykjavik

Figure 3.31 The Cathedral, Funchal, Madeira, is of slightly differently coloured basalt blocks

Figure 3.32 Rough blocks of particularly scoriaceous basalt lava flow from nearby were used dramatically for the Holiday Inn, Grants, New Mexico. (Photos: John Ashurst)

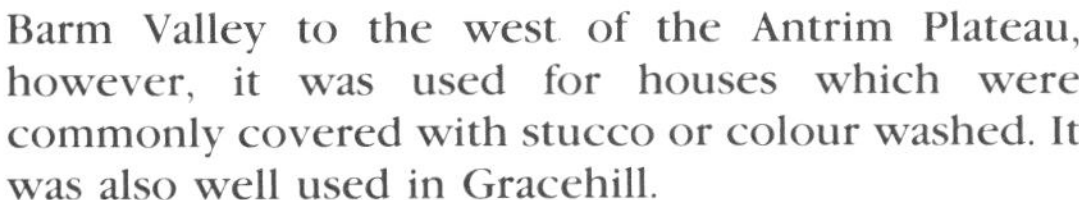

Barm Valley to the west of the Antrim Plateau, however, it was used for houses which were commonly covered with stucco or colour washed. It was also well used in Gracehill.

Although Iceland, a country that developed architecturally from the turf-hut directly to reinforced concrete, is practically entirely of basalt and closely-related rocks, only one building is stone-built. This building illustrates the thesis that when man builds for status and to impress, he builds of stone, for it is the Parliament Building in Reykjavik (*Figure 3.30*).

The island of Madeira also illustrates this thesis. Most of the island is of basalt, which here and there yields blocks large enough for building. It may be seen used for the Cathedral, Funchal, for banks and public buildings, and occasionally for church statues. See *Figure 3.31*.

Basalt outcrops are found in the Galilee area of Israel and the stone has been used extensively in that area. The Church of the Primacy on the shore of the Sea of Galilee is mostly of basalt with light-coloured limestone dressings. The drab-grey dolomitic limestone of the Central Post Office, in Jerusalem, is heightened visually by the contrasting use of basalt.

Basalt covers extensive areas of the USA, and may be found used directly as a building stone as in the Church at Flagstaff, Arizona; or in a modern manner as in the Holiday Inn Motel, Grants, New Mexico where a particularly scoriaceous vesicular stone from a basalt lava flow which forms much of the surrounding country has been used (*Figure 3.32*). The Devil's Post Pile, California shows a fine example of columnar jointing, comparable to the Giant's Causeway.

Igneous rocks were not always used in their natural state. An interestingly curious process used Rowley Rag, a doleritic rock capping Rowley Hill, Shropshire, England, which is similar to that of the Clee Hills. The stone was melted and then cast in moulds to produce steps, windowheads, slabs for tables and sideboards and mantlepieces. This reworked stone is believed to have been used in Handsworth and in Edgbaston. However, the process was not a financial success.

Classification

There are at least 400 named types of rock. Obviously it is not practical to place them all on the classification in *Table 2.1*. In any event a classification is an artificial construction in many respects. Rocks are placed into the classification on the basis

Figure 3.33 Basalt blocks with rusticated finish (with sandstone above) used for Parliament House, Melbourne, Australia. (Photo: John Ashurst)

Figure 3.34 Chamfered and rock faced rustication of basalt blocks is seen in the Treasury Building, Melbourne, Australia

of some characteristics which cannot be seen in a stone used in a building. It may not be possible, for instance, to determine some of the constituent minerals. For an accurate identification to be made it may be necessary for a specimen of the stone to be made into a thin section for microscopic examination. The descriptions in this and later sections should not be used as a basis for the determination of a stone in a building.

References

1. Hawkes, J.R. and Dangerfield, J. 'The Variscan Granites of south-west England: a progress report', *Proc. Ussher Soc.*, **4**, Pt. 2, 1978
2. Dangerfield, J. and Hawkes, J.R. 'The Variscan Granites of south-west England: additional information', *Proc. Ussher Soc.*, **5**, 116–120, 1981
3. Edmonds, E.A., McKeaven, M.C. and Williams, M. *British Regional Geology, South-West England.* 4th Edn., HMSO, London, 1975
4. Burton, M. (Ed.), 'Cornish Granite: traditional material for new contracts', *Stone Industries*, **14**, No. 10, 1979
5. Trinick, M., *Castle Drogo, Devon,* The National Trust, 1981
6. Watson, J., *British and Foreign Building Stones,* University Press, Cambridge, 1911
7. Elsden, J. and Howe, J.A., *The Stones of London,* Colliery Guardian Company Ltd., London, 1923
8. Ashurst, J. and Dimes, F.G., *Stone in Building,* The Architectural Press, London, 1977
9. Clifton-Taylor, A., *The Pattern of English Building.* Faber and Faber, London, 1972
10. Lawson, J., *Building Stones of Glasgow,* Geological Society of Glasgow, Glasgow, 1981
11. Robinson, E. and Bishop, C. 'Geological Walks around St Paul's', *Proc. Geol. Assoc.*, **91**, Pt 4, 1980
12. Whitlow, J.B., *Geology and Scenery in Ireland,* Penguin Books, Harmondsworth, 1974
13. Robinson, E. 'Geological walks around the City of London—Royal Exchange to Aldgate, *Proc. Geol. Assoc.*, **93**, Pt. 3, 1982
14. Anderson, J.G.C., 'The Granites of Scotland', *Special Reports on the Mineral Resources of Great Britain,* **32,** HMSO, Edinburgh, 1939
15. McLaren, M., *The Shell Guide to Scotland,* Ebury Press, London, 1967
16. Muir Wood, R. *On the Rocks: A Geology of Britain,* BBC, London 1978
17. Worth, R.N., *The Rocks and Minerals of Cornwall and Devon*, 54th Ann. Rep. R. Corn. Polytech. Soc., 1886
18. Watson, J., *British and Foreign Marbles and other Ornamental Stones,* University Press, Cambridge, 1906
19. North, F.J., *The Slates of Wales,* National Museum of Wales, Cardiff 1946
20. Seneviratne, G., 'Novel cement for Cologne Cathedral', *New Scientist*, 8 April 1976
21. Röder, (ed.), 'The Quern-quarries of Mayen in the Eifel', *Antiquity,* **29**, No. 114, 1955
22. Moore, D.T. and Oddy, W.A., 'Touchstones: Some aspects of their Nomenclature, Petrography and Provenance', *J. of Archaeological Science,* **12**, 59–80, 1985

4

Sedimentary rocks

Francis G. Dimes

Introduction

Igneous rocks, it has been estimated, form about 25 per cent of the exposed surface of the Earth's crust but occupy about 90 per cent of the volume. Sedimentary rocks, in contrast, form about 75 per cent of the surface, but only 5 to 10 per cent of its volume. Sedimentary rocks thus cover extensive tracts of the surface of the continents. Argillaceous rocks are by far the most abundant sedimentary rocks, occupying about 45 per cent of the area, with sandstones forming about 30 per cent and limestones about 28 per cent of the surface. It is not surprising, then, to find that sedimentary rocks have been widely used for building and decoration and that sandstones and limestones are the predominant rock types used.

Figure 4.1 The large stone standing on the Hanger, Selborne, Hampshire is a quartzite. Such blocks, scattered across southern England are known as sarsens.

Sandstone

A sandstone, by definition, is a rock in which the dominant mineral grain is quartz between 2 to 0.07 mm in diameter. It is formed by the lithification of a sand made up predominantly of rounded quartz grains. The word sand is commonly used to indicate a number of materials. The grains forming the beach at the sea, river or lake side are popularly referred to as sand regardless of their nature. However, a sand made up of the broken fragments of shells would be classified as a limestone if lithified. Sands made up of grains of the mineral zircon, volcanic ash or corundum are known. Coral sands are common in some parts of the world. Olivine sands are found in the Bay of Naples.

Commonly the grains have been naturally cemented, and the cementing material is deposited on the surface of the grains where it partially or completely fills the interstices between the grains. If the cementing material is quartz and the original sand is thoroughly indurated with it, a hard, tough, resistant rock termed a *quartzite* is formed. The well-known sarsens of southern England provide an outstanding example of quartzite (*Figure 4.1*). There are quartzites which are igneous and metamorphic in origin (see *Tables 2.1, 2.2, 2.3*). The term quartzite describes the type of rock. It should not be used to imply a mode of origin.

Calcite is a common cementing material and may give a crystalline texture and appearance. If sufficient calcareous cement is present the rock is known as a *calcareous sandstone*. Many sandstones are cemented by one or more of the iron compounds, normally the red iron oxides or the brown iron hydrates, or both. They are known as *ferruginous sandstones*. Usually these are light red to deep

Figure 4.2 Strongly iron-cemented sandstone–carstone–resists weathering to form the Devil's Jumps, Surrey

Figure 4.3 A sandstone in which the grains are angular is known as a grit or gritstone. They may be massively bedded as in Bramley Fall Quarry near Leeds in the Millstone Grit

brown in colour. The colour is caused by the nature and amount of iron cement present. When iron minerals are present in substantial amount, the sandstone may be called *carstone* (*Figure 4.2*). The mineral gypsum is a less frequent cementing medium. The mineral dolomite is more commonly found as discrete grains and not as a cement. When it is present either as cement or as grains, the stone is termed a *dolomitic sandstone*. Mansfield Stone, of Permian age, from Mansfield, Nottinghamshire, provides a matchless example of a dolomitic sandstone.

Rarely are sandstones pure, that is made up solely of quartz grains with silica cement. Other mineral grains, as distinct from the mineral cementing medium, are present in greater or lesser amounts. Feldspar, commonly in a partially chemically decomposed state and derived from a disintegrated granite, may be present in considerable amounts. If it makes up a third or more of the rock the name *arkose* is used. Most arkoses are terrestrial deposits. Flakes of mica lead to a *micaceous sandstone*. Grains of the mineral glauconite (a complex potassium, iron silicate, $K(Fe, Mg, Al)_2(Si_4O_{10})(OH)_2$), present as small, rounded, green-coloured aggregates give the rock, particularly when wet, a green cast. The rock is termed a *greensand* when glauconite is present in any quantity. Other minerals such as gypsum and barytes may rarely be the cementing medium but may locally be present in noticeable amounts. Clayey material occurs in some sandstones and, if present in quantity, is not a desirable constituent because *argillaceous sandstones* are susceptible to frost action. All these cementing materials were carried into the original loose, incoherent sand by circulating waters. A sandstone is produced by deposition of material from solution to bind the sand grains together.

In some sandstones most of the individual grains are well sorted, that is they are all about the same size and are rounded. This is a reflection of the mechanical erosion which they have suffered. Larger pebbles may occur. If the grains are angular the rock is then termed a *grit* or *gritstone*, and it is normally, but not necessarily, coarse-grained (*Figure 4.3*).

The term *gritstone* has no unique definition. It is often used for a rock of any composition with grain size between 0.5 to 1.0 mm. The mica flakes in a micaceous sandstone are commonly concentrated along bedding planes with their long axes aligned parallel to the bedding. The rock is *fissile* and will readily split along these planes. If the bedding planes are closely spaced, splitting produces a *flagstone*. The name is believed to be derived from flaggstone, a name given by the Vikings to the flat stone which they found in Scotland. Some flagstones owe their fissility to thin layers of clay material. Commonly flagstones show ripple marks and suncracks. Sandstones may contain fossils.

Local concentrations of mineral matter, commonly but not always the same as the cementing material, may form around a centre or nucleus after the sediment was deposited. Such growths are known as concretions and result from the solution of material at one point and its redeposition elsewhere. In form concretions may be quite irregular but they are commonly found to be flattened ovals in section. They often lie along the direction of the bedding because water travels more easily along the bedding planes. If concretions are hollow, they may be internally lined with crystals. These types of concretions are called *geodes*. Concretions may also be called *doggers*. Frequently they contain fossils, which originally acted as the nucleus which triggered the deposition of mineral matter. They are a similar colour to the host rock but usually of a deeper shade. Local quarrymen's names have been given to these concretions. For example, ferruginous concretions in the Huddersfield White Rock, a sandstone of the

Millstone Grit Series, are known as Mare Balls. The name Galliard Balls is given to similar concretions found in the Woodkirk Quarry, from which a sandstone of Upper Carboniferous (Coal Measures) age is taken.

Examples and uses

Most sandstone nowadays is crushed for aggregate[1]. In the past it was widely used for building stone and pavements and is still used extensively today where it contributes greatly to the character of many buildings, particularly in the northern parts of Great Britain. Sandstones occur commonly throughout the geological column and most are used locally.

Precambrian to Silurian sandstones

The Precambrian age Torridonian Sandstone is an arkose in places and adds dramatically to the scenery of north-west Scotland. It has been used, for example, in the walls of Iona Abbey, Argyll. Until the middle of the nineteenth century, nearly all building in Scotland was of sandstone. Ordovician age sandstones were worked for flagstones near Pomeroy, Northern Ireland. Sandstones of Precambrian, Cambrian, Ordovician and Silurian age, however, have not been used generally outside the areas in which they occur. Even so, their use occasionally is eye-catching and thus more widely remarked. One example is the purple-coloured feldspathic Caerbwdi Sandstone of Cambrian age which gives the Cathedral of St Davids, Dyfed its most unusual purple appearance. The Ordovician age Hoar Edge Grit, named from Hoar Edge near Cardington, Shropshire, is somewhat coarse in grain, shelly and slightly calcareous. It was used not only as slabs (tilestones) on the Prior's Lodge, Much Wenlock (*see Figure 4.4*), but also as blocks for the Church at Church Stretton. It is one example of a sandstone that is suitable stone for both flagging and block stone.

Figure 4.4 The fissile nature of the Hoar Edge Grit, Ordovician, enables it to be split into slabs for use as tile stones as on the remarkable roof of the Priors Lodge, Much Wenlock, Shropshire

Devonian sandstones

The Devonian is the oldest period to have yielded sandstones that were used on a large scale outside the areas where they crop out. The Old Red Sandstone is the name given to a series of rocks deposited mostly on the land surface; it is the continental facies of the Devonian. They consist of red, brown, chocolate and white sandstones, all with beds of coarse quartzitic conglomerates, thick beds of usually red-coloured marl and some impure limestones. They represent deposits laid down in a semi-arid climate in inter-montane environments and this led to distinctively different rocks in the areas where they crop out.

Over a large part of Hereford and Worcester, Gwent, Powys and Shropshire sandstones of Old Red Sandstone age are found. They have been extensively used. Because so much was used in and around the city of Hereford the general name Hereford Stone was given to them. Unfortunately that name gives no indication of closer provenance within this area. The massive tower (1300) and some of the remainder of Hereford Cathedral is of local Old Red Sandstone. However, the Cathedral was largely restored in Alton Mottled Stone, a sandstone from the New Red Sandstone, from Staffordshire in 1901–1905. The famous and magnificent Kilpeck Church, Hereford, with its spectacular south doorway is of Old Red Sandstone quarried from nearby (*Figure 4.5*).

Some beds of the series are a remarkable quartz conglomerate containing grey, yellow and red pebbles with pieces of decomposed igneous rock and jasper. They were the foundation of a massive millstone industry along the southern Welsh borders, and millstones of this type are of common occurrence at archaeological sites. In some areas beds of grey, green, yellow and reddish-brown micaceous flaggy sandstones, known geologically as The Tilestones, were once used for roofing in Gwent and in Hereford. They were normally laid, because of their weight, at a low pitch, sometimes down to 30°[2]. Red-brown and grey, compact, fine-grained stone, some of it flaggy and some thickly bedded, was at one time quarried near Hay-on-Wye, Powys. It was used for tilestones and buildings and was known as Racephas Stone. Red Wilderness Stone, which is a red-brown coloured, fine-grained and slightly micaceous sandstone from near Mitcheldean, in the Forest of Dean,

Figure 4.5 The Old Red Sandstone from nearby was used for Kilpeck Church, Hereford, with its spectacular south doorway renowned for the tympanum

Figure 4.6 Stone taken from many quarries in the Old Red Sandstone such as the Red Wilderness Quarry near Mitcheldean, Gloucestershire (seen here), was widely used in the Welsh Borderlands, and is commonly known as Hereford stone

Gloucestershire, was extensively quarried and used for many churches and houses in that area (*Figure 4.6*). Because of its reputation as a durable stone for sills, steps and flags it was used in the Cathedral in Liverpool (1908) and is recorded as used in Harrow School, Middlesex. Red sandstones of Old Red Sandstone age also have been quarried in Dyfed, Wales and near Edinburgh, Nairn and Elgin, Scotland. Near Edinburgh, the Old Red Sandstone was quarried for much useful building stone. The Craigmillar Quarries are the best known. The stone is purplish-white and cream in colour and is tough and markedly pebbly. It was used for Heriot Hospital (seventeenth century), Leith Docks (1876) and for kerbs. In many buildings in Edinburgh it has probably been confused with the much more widely used Carboniferous sandstones. Dull red, reddish-brown to bright red stone, with sporadic patches of feldspar grains and mica flakes occurs around Carmyllie, Angus. Flaggy sandstones and flagstones were once worked on a large scale. The flagstones are the source of the renowned Arbroath pavement. At one time, however, the most important stones were those taken from the Caithness Flagstone Series. Flagstone groups within this series provided pale greenish-white and pale ochre to blue, flaggy sandstones which were used in huge quantities for paving. The best flags were taken from finely fissile calcareous sandstone seams or beds, locally known as 'fouls', around Thurso. Caithness Flags were used extensively in London where some may still be seen. They were also used

> ...all over the world. Baron Liebig's great establishment on the River Plate, in South America, for the manufacture of his well-known meat extract, is floored throughout with Caithness flags.[3]

They are, in general, a compact, tough blue-grey stone. Large flags may still be seen vertically set into the ground as fences between fields in Caithness. The flags may contain fossil fish scales and fragments of fish.

Probably the most often seen, although certainly not the most widely recognized, piece of Old Red Sandstone is The Coronation Stone, the Stone of Destiny or Stone of Scone, in Westminster Abbey, London. This rectangular mass of coarse-grained, reddish-grey sandstone contains small pebbles of porphyrite or andesite about the size of a pea. There is little doubt geologically that the stone was quarried near the ancient seat of the Pictish monarchy at Scone, Perthshire. It was once thought that because the stone was once kept at Dunstaffnage Castle, Argyll, it was quarried near there. The rocks in that area, however, are quite dissimilar from that of the Stone. It is thought that the stone originally may have been a portable altar. The other Coronation Stone at Kingston-upon-Thames, Surrey is of sarsen (a quartzite).

The Eday Sandstone of the Orkney Islands, a thick sequence of yellow and of red sandstone was quarried at Fersness, Eday and used as building stone in Kirkwall and elsewhere on the Islands. It was used to build St Magnus Cathedral, which has a marked contrasting red-yellow look. The fine, yellow ('white') freestone was much prized.

Old Red Sandstone is also found in Ireland. The main outcrop is in the south-west of the island. Red-brown and yellow sandstones were used for much building and are probably seen to best effect in Tralee, Kerry.

Carboniferous sandstones

The Carboniferous System is one of the most important sources of sandstones in Great Britain. The system has been split geologically into three major divisions:

Coal Measures }
Millstone Grit } (Upper Carboniferous)
Carboniferous Limestone (Lower Carboniferous)

These major divisions are split into many subdivisions. The index of a recent geological map and recent literature shows a more complicated division. The divisions do not always refer to rocks laid down at the same time, but they are retained here for ease of explanation. It is possible to have many different types of rock laid down at the same *time* depending on geographical and environmental conditions. However, an apparently continuous bed of the same type of rock which extends across many square kilometres may have been deposited over a considerable period of time.

All the main divisions yield sandstones of major importance. The Carboniferous Limestone division, in southern England and the Midlands is predominantly a limestone. However, when traced northwards, into northern England and Scotland it is found to contain an increasing number of sandstone beds especially in its upper part. This has led to the apparent anomaly that an enquirer may be told that a piece of sandstone is from the Carboniferous Limestone.

Lower Carboniferous sandstones

Sandstone beds up to 50 feet (15 m) thick occur in Yorkshire (the Yoredale Series). They vary greatly from one place to another but have provided important building stones from many small quarries close to most villages in the northern Pennines. Locally, flagstones with surprisingly smooth surfaces were produced to provide tilestones.

> Most building stones have been used near where they were quarried, as can easily be seen from the comparison of a geological map with a survey of the fabric of farms, field walls, and the older parts of villages and towns.[4]

In Northumberland sandstones of the Yoredale Series have a far wider significance and helped to make that county, perhaps more than any other, a county of sandstone buildings. The change in the proportion of limestone to mudstone and sandstone which begins in Yorkshire becomes more marked in Northumberland. In Northumberland there is considerably more sandstone present and the name Carboniferous Limestone is really a misnomer. A particularly important sandstone is the Fell Sandstone. It consists of pink-coloured, false-bedded and coarse-grained sandstones which are up to 1000 feet (300 m) thick. Another horizon in the upper part of the Carboniferous Limestone of Northumberland yielded flagstones, known as the Slate Sills, which were widely used as tilestones throughout the county.

Prudham Quarry at Fourstones, near Hexham, Northumberland, supplied a cream to brown, coarse-grained, slightly micaceous stone which is perhaps the best known of the Northumberland sandstones. The stone is famous because of its use for the Roman wall. In its heyday the quarry 'employed possibly 200 men[5]. The stone was used extensively in Tyneside as well as in Newcastle-upon-Tyne, where it was used in the central railway station (1850) and the General Post Office (1870). The stone was even exported to London and to Edinburgh, a city with its own ample supply of fine sandstone. In Edinburgh it may be seen in houses in Craighall Gardens (1885–1890) and in Heriot Watt College (1886). It was used much more recently in the new office block above the bus station, St Andrews Square (*Figure 4.7*). The extensions to University College (1882–1883), London were also carried out in this stone.

Figure 4.7 Prudham stone, a sandstone from the Carboniferous Limestone series, was used for the Norwich Union Building, St Andrew Square, Edinburgh (courtesy of R.W. Gransbury)

Stone from Doddington Quarry, near Wooler, Northumberland, is no less well known. Fine-grained, and pink- to purple-grey, it is distinguished by being composed of up to 97 per cent quartz grains with the mineral haematite (iron oxide, Fe_2O_3) giving the gentle pink colour. When in green condition it is soft on extraction and easy to work (see also the account in reference 5).

Restoration of St Andrew's Church (1894), is in this stone. It was widely used elsewhere in Newcastle-upon-Tyne (*Figure 4.8*) and was also sent

Figure 4.8 Doddington Stone forms the wall in the school of Architecture, Newcastle University, Tyne and Weir. Note rising salt soiling. This wall was very poorly spun clean

to Edinburgh where it was used in St Giles Industrial Museum (1897) Observatory and the Wesleyan Hall, for example. It was also used for the Cathedral at Dunblane, Perthshire. It has been used recently (1984) for a building development in Lovett Lane, London. Buff-coloured Blaxter Stone from north-west of Newcastle-upon-Tyne is also used in this development. These stones make an interesting addition to the list of stones used in London, which otherwise has used little sandstone.

Dozens of quarries operated in the past and many are still working today[5]. Another local stone of interest is the Black Pasture Stone from quarries near Chollerford, Northumberland. Buff coloured with brown specks, this tough, fine-grained sandstone was used in the Roman Wall, for buildings in Newcastle-upon-Tyne and for some restorations at Durham Cathedral. It was also used for the Mitchell Library (1907) in Glasgow although Glasgow has an ample supply of local stone.

In the Midland Valley of Scotland the Carboniferous Limestone is divided into a Calciferous Sandstone Series overlain by a Carboniferous Limestone Series. Major sandstone horizons are found in each member and they are mostly light coloured and generally fine textured. Some have been extensively quarried and used.

If Aberdeen is the granite city then Edinburgh is the sandstone city, the 'Grey Metropolis of the North'. Undoubtedly the best known is Craigleith Stone from a quarry which, when originally opened, was outside Edinburgh but now is surrounded by the city. It was the stone used for nearly all building in Edinburgh. It is taken from the Calciferous Sandstone Series and is tough, tight and fine-grained. It is drab coloured, slightly calcareous and virtually unaffected by the weather. Because so much of Edinburgh was built of local sandstones the city has an entity not seen in most other cities. Craigleith Quarry is renowned for supplying large blocks.

> In 1823, there was excavated a stone of such dimensions and weight as to be without parallel in ancient or modern times. In length it was upwards of 136 feet, averaging 20 feet in breadth and its computed weight was 1500 tons. It was longitudinal cut from a stratum of very fine rock. The greater part of it was conveyed to the Calton Hill, where it now forms the architrave of the National Monument, and the rest was sent by sea to Buckingham Palace.[6]

The Register House (1776–1826) in Edinburgh, together with St Andrews Church (1785) and the Old University (1789–1834) provide local examples of its use. The stone was also used for the floors and stairs of The British Museum, London (1828) and the old Bank of England, London (1770). Undoubtedly the most spectacularly visible use of Craigleith Stone is for the statue of Nelson on top of his column made of granite from Foggintor, Dartmoor which stands in the middle of Trafalgar Square, London (*Figure 4.9*). Some distance from Craigleith, a quarry at Barnton Park also supplied 'Craigleith Stone' which was used for the now demolished Imperial Institute, London (1880). However Barton Park Quarry was better known for a stone named Blue Liver Rock which is tough, dark blue-grey and medium-grained. Hailes Stone is also widely used in Edinburgh. Hailes Quarry supplied a white, a blue (blue grey, grey) and a red (pink) stone which were noted for their regular laminations caused by the amount of mica flakes the rock contains. Because of its strength the stone was highly regarded for foundations. It was used as a building stone for Dalry School (grey, 1876), Plewlands Villa (blue, 1878), Red House, Cluny Gardens (red, 1880), Free Church Assembly Hall (blue, 1846), and the Royal Infirmary (pink, 1875), all in Edinburgh. It was recorded that 'Large quantities are now being exported to London'[7] but verified examples of its use there have not been found.

Glasgow is built on, and mostly surrounded by, the Upper Limestone Group of Upper Carboniferous age, which contains beds of sandstone. These provided much of the stone first used to build the city, although the sites from which the stone was taken

Figure 4.9 Craigleith stone, used here for the statue of Nelson, Trafalgar Square, is one of the few sandstones used in the capital. The stone has weathered very little. (Courtesy of Mrs C. Bennett)

are now a matter of geological conjecture. Important quarries still remain in use. The best known is probably that supplying Newbigging Stone from Burnt Island. The stone is renowned for its use for Gothenberg Cathedral, Sweden. Hopetown in West Lothian is a currently active quarry in the Calciferous Sandstone Series. Important in historical context is Giffnock Stone (Giffneuk) from near Glasgow. This is a pale grey, fine-grained stone with a reputation of not weathering well in a smoky atmosphere. It was used widely in Glasgow. The stone was exported to Ireland and may be seen in the Customs House, the Assembly Buildings and elsewhere in Belfast.

Upper Carboniferous (Millstone Grit) sandstones

The Millstone Grit must be reckoned as possibly the most prolific source of sandstones in Great Britain, and architecturally, probably the most important. Sandstones from the division have an unparalleled reputation for durability and for use in large civil engineering works. It has been used from the earliest times; many castles, cathedrals, churches and houses were built of stone from this formation.

Geologically the Millstone Grit of northern England comprises a series of gritstones and sandstones interbedded with shales and mudstones. A number of grit groups are distinguished; the Silsden Moor Grit, the Kinderscout Grit, and the Rough Rock are important members. In the main the quartz grains comprising the grit groups are markedly angular in form. Because of this the stones were eminently suitable for use as millstones; hence the name for the formation. Millstone Edge is a well-known locality in south-west Yorkshire. In many places the Millstone Grit is remarkably fissile and was used, mostly locally, for flagstones and tilestones. Characteristically, the Millstone Grit is current-bedded. This is the result of the deposits being laid down under deltaic conditions. In some areas the stone contains a lot of feldspar and is lithologically an arkose.

Figure 4.10 A millstone made of stone from the Millstone Grit, used because of the angular grains of quartz, marks the boundary to the Peak National Park, Derbyshire

All the grit groups have been used locally in buildings. Usually the fissile beds were used as tilestones, but some stones taken from the formation obtained a much wider repute. Darley Dale, sometimes known as Stancliffe Stone, which was taken from a number of quarries near Matlock, Derbyshire is generally regarded as the classic stone. Pale brown in colour, compact and close-grained, normally with darker brown ferruginous specks, feldspathic, with occasional flakes of mica, it was widely used because of its strength and toughness. The capitals of the columns of the canopy of the Albert Memorial are of the stone which was noted as 'perhaps the finest building stone in the kingdom'. King's College Hospital (in part), London is another example of its use. St George's Hall, Liverpool, was built from Stancliffe Stone which was taken from Stancliffe Quarries in the Dale. Darley Dale Stone was used by Henry Moore for his dramatic *Three Standing Figures* (1947) which stood in Battersea Park, London. Hall Dale Stone from the same area is a pink-coloured, fine-grained stone which was used for the Manchester Town Hall extension in 1938.

Whatstandwell Stone, used by George Stevenson for much of his railway construction, is another stone from the Dales. Coarser-grained than most and pinkish in colour, it was used for the original Euston Railway Station, London. It is intimately known by a certain proportion of the population because it was used for the prison at Leicester (1828) as well as the prison at Birmingham (1849).

Birchover Gritstone, quarried at Stanton Moor, Derbyshire, is also from the Dales. It is medium-grained and pink to yellowish-buff in colour. Its height-on-bed in the quarry may reach 9 feet (2.7 m). It has been extensively used, notably for public works in Lancashire, bridges over the Birmingham to Preston motorway, the Royal Insurance Building, Kircaldy, the Newport Civic Centre, and for many churches.

Bramley Fall Stone, the name of another of the classic stones, was used at one time as a general name for a number of stones wrought from an area north-west of Leeds, Yorkshire. The stone was taken from the Rough Rock Grit group, which is made up of the Rough Rock Flags, also known as Greetland Stone at Greetland, near Halifax, Yorkshire, overlain by the Rough Rock Grit. In general terms the Rough Rock Flags are a variable succession of generally fine-grained flagstone and sandstone beds with thin shale partings. The Rough Rock itself is mainly a massive, current-bedded gritstone which is often pebbly. The pebbles are chiefly quartz and are often of large size, up to 2 inches (0.8 cm) or more. Because of its great strength, its massive bedding and the large-sized blocks which could be obtained, it was used extensively for engineering works. Millwall Docks, London is one example. The Town Hall (1853–1858) and the Roman Catholic Cathedral (1904) Leeds, abutments of Southwark Bridge, London (Rennie, 1819), and the plinth course of the town bridge, Stamford, Lincolnshire, which has local limestone overlying, are other examples. Its best known use, however, must be for the Euston Arch, London, unpardonably now demolished.

Spinkwell Stone, from an horizon named the Gaisby Rock, is quarried near Bradford, Yorkshire and is nowadays known as Bolton Wood Stone. The Gaisby Rock provides excellent flagstones and building stone. Overall it is grey in colour. It is compact and fine-grained, with occasional flakes of white muscovite mica. It was used for the Town Hall, Manchester (1868–1876).

Huddersfield, Yorkshire, and the villages around are mostly of Crosland Hill Stone, a general name for stones taken from a number of quarries on Crosland Moor, above the town. The stone, taken from the Rough Rock member of the Millstone Grit, is brown-grey in colour, and fine-grained with occasional quartz pebbles, which may be of some size.

The stone was used for the majority of public buildings in the area around Huddersfield. It is stated to have weathered well except in Huddersfield Parish Church 'due to the frequent error of laying the stone oblique to the bedding planes'[8]. Known nowadays as Wellfield Stone or Johnsons Wellfield (*Figure 4.11*), recent use includes the University of

(a)

(b)

Figure 4.11 Massively bedded Rough Rock of the Millstone Grit taken from Johnsons Wellfield Quarry, Crosland Moor, near Huddersfield (a) is guillotined into regular sized blocks which may be easily laid for walls (b)

Edinburgh, Oldham Civic Centre, the restoration of entrance portico, Assize Court, York, the Free Trade Hall, Manchester, and the New Civic Buildings, Newcastle. This stone is now often used in Edinburgh for new works and as a replacement for Craigleith and Hailes Stones, which are no longer available. Waterholes Grit Stone, quarried a short distance from Wellfield Stone, is similar in character.

The Millstone Grit becomes less important for building stone when traced northwards. In central Scotland it contains very few beds of gritstone, but does produce important fireclays. In North Wales the Cefn-y-fedw sandstone of Millstone Grit age has been used locally for building. It was not more widely used because it was remote from transport. Stone quarried at Minera, west of Wrexham was used for the Bank of New Zealand, Queen Victoria Street, London (*Figure 4.12*). This is an interesting use in a city that has used little sandstone. Millstone Grit has been used locally in Ireland for flagstones.

Upper Carboniferous (Coal Measures) sandstones

Despite the name, only about five per cent of the thickness of the Coal Measures is coal, and it has yielded some important sandstones. Many of the sandstones from the Coal Measures have layers of mica flakes and are so highly laminated that they may be split into slabs an inch (2.5 cm) or less thick. They occur particularly in the southern part of Yorkshire (the former West Riding) and the general name York Stone has been given to them. Unfortunately this name is also widely used for almost any sandstone coming from Yorkshire.

Figure 4.12 The Cefn-y-fedu sandstone of Millstone Grit age was uniquely used in London for the Bank of New Zealand, Queen Victoria Street. The pattern of dirt soiling is typical of coarse-grained sandstone

The Elland Flags undoubtedly were, and still are, the most important of the York Stones. The Flags form a well-marked, bold escarpment running from Mountain, through Pule Hill, Stump Cross, Bank Top near Halifax, Elland Edge itself, to Cowcliffe, Sheepridge and the Colne Valley. They have been extensively quarried and, where massive, were occasionally mined for building stone. Where the stone is flaggy it is used for paving and tilestones. The flagstone may be split into slabs from one to fifteen inches (2.5–38 cm) thick and many feet in length. The Elland Flags were wrought in the area around Northowram, Southowram, Hipperholme, and Brighouse. They are still worked extensively around Halifax, Huddersfield and Leeds. The Elland Flags are known by other names in other parts of the country; for example they are also called Brincliffe Edge Rock and Greenmore Rock. They are known as the Rockdale or Upholland Flags in Lancashire.

The flags have been extensively used for paving; at one time much of London's pavements were made of them. The City of London Corporation still makes extensive use of York Stone. It 'is considered to be the near ideal paving material as it is strong, colourful and remains non-slip throughout its long life'[9].

The paving of the floor of Westminster Hall and that outside the York City Art Gallery (*Figure 4.13*) are considered typical examples. York Stone was recently used for a paved floor at the mews conversion at the Royal Crescent Hotel, Bath (1983). The stone is also used for kerbs, as at Colchester, Essex. Although, as Clifton-Taylor[10] pointed out, the Elland Flags are not suitable for roofing because they hold so much moisture, they were used on the roof of the Gatehouse at Kirklees near Brighouse. The Elland Flags have also been used on a smaller scale for domestic building. For example, several houses in Ryder Gardens, Leeds, Yorkshire are partly built of the Elland Flags. The Grenoside Sandstone from the Sheffield area is probably the equivalent of the Elland Flags.

The importance of the York Stone flags should not overshadow the many dimension stones taken from the Coal Measures. Bolton Wood Stone was used for the Town Halls of Bradford and Leeds. Woodkirk Stone, from Morley near Leeds, Yorkshire supplies a fawn- to brown-coloured, massive, fine-grained sandstone which has been used for the Halifax Building Society's new headquarters building in Halifax,

(a)

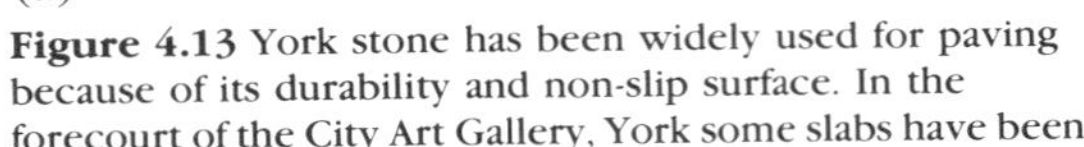

(b)

Figure 4.13 York stone has been widely used for paving because of its durability and non-slip surface. In the forecourt of the City Art Gallery, York some slabs have been shot frame sawn, a process which it is claimed improves the non-slip quality

Yorkshire and for the Sheraton Inn, Stockton-on-Tees. The Royal Bank of Scotland, Falkirk and Beaver House, Manchester are two other examples of its recent use.

In the county of Durham, sandstones from the Coal Measures are of prime importance. They crop out over much of the county. Dunhouse Stone, quarried near Darlington is fine- to medium-grained and brown in colour. For many years it has been used for restorations to the magnificent Durham Cathedral (*Figure 4.14*). In the original cathedral building many other Coal Measure sandstones were used[11].

Figure 4.14 Most of the structure of Durham Cathedral is of Coal Measures sandstone from the Kepier Quarry but a couple of miles away to the north-east. Black Pasture sandstone (see p.66) and for the last fifty years Dunhouse Stone have been used for repairs and restoration.

Dunhouse Stone is renowned for supplying large blocks of stone and it was also used for Bowes Museum, Barnard Castle, and for the Town Hall, Middlesborough, Yorkshire. The Technical College, Sunderland, Durham is a more recent example of its use. It was also the stone chosen for restoration work at Castle Howard, Yorkshire, and for Birmingham Cathedral. Stainton Stone, from near Barnard Castle, is fine- to medium-grained and creamy-brown in colour. It is eye-catching because of the localized large swirling streaks due to concentrations of iron-oxide minerals which are otherwise seen as specks generally spread across the surfaces. It was used for the extension to the Bank of England, Glasgow.

Auchinlea Stone, from Cleland, Lanarkshire is an example of a sandstone from the Coal Measures of Scotland. White-cream in colour, often with small, brown specks and medium- to coarse-grained, it was easily wrought but toughened considerably on exposure to the air. Its use is recorded in South Buchanan Street, Roseburn Terrace and Trinity in Edinburgh, as well as in Glasgow and in Carlisle.

The Pennant Sandstone is of Coal Measures age but has considerably different characteristics. It forms much of the South Wales coalfield and is also found in the Forest of Dean, Gloucestershire, and in Monmouth. It is dark-grey, blue-grey or pinkish-grey in colour and generally massively bedded, micaceous and feldspathic. The sandstone or grit grades in places to an arkose. Much of the series is false-bedded and in some areas it is conglomeratic.

Stone from the Pennant Sandstone or Grit is hard and durable. It has been extensively used for building. However, because the stone tends to weather to a rusty-brown colour it contributes, especially when used with dark-coloured slate roofs, to the drab and depressing look of the towns and villages in the South Wales valleys. The stone has been used on a large scale in Bristol, where it is commonly used as a plinth, with limestone above; Bristol Gaol may be cited as an example. Records indicate it was used in London[3,12], for example in the New Sessions House, Old Bailey. It was also used in Cardiff and South Wales generally. Because of its strength and durability Pennant Stone was widely

Figure 4.15 Bwlch-y-Maen farm, Craig-yr-Allt, Glamorgan, built of locally quarried Pennant Grit, is in part tallow white-washed

Figure 4.16 The gigantic sham of Castell Coch, Glamorgan, is built in Pennant Grit

used for civil engineering works such as the New Dock, Avonmouth (Forest of Dean), Cardiff New Pier (Forest of Dean), Bideford Bridge (Pennant), and the bridge at Littleton, Middlesex (Forest of Dean). The use of Pennant Stone for Caerphilly, the biggest castle of its type, and for the rebuilt Castell Coch, Glamorgan—that 'gigantic sham, a costly folly'—illustrate its use for monuments ancient and modern (*Figure 4.16*).

In North Wales, the Cefn Rock of Coal Measures age was the most important building stone in the area. It was extensively quarried, from its outcrop at Cefn-mawr and at Broughton, Clwyd since at least mediaeval times. The stone is also known as the Bryn-teg Freestone from the quarries of that name. Light-drab to buff-coloured, fine- to medium-grained with some interstitial decomposed feldspar, stone from the Cefn Rock is recorded as being used for the Parish Church, Wrexham, Ruabon Church (thirteenth century), the Free Library and Museum (1859), the Walker Gallery (1877), Liverpool, and for the 'new' University College, Bangor (1908).

Suitable sandstones of Coal Measure age were commonly used on a very restricted local scale. Stone taken from a bed known as the Big Flint Rock was used for railway bridges on the Wellington to Colebrookedale line, Shropshire. The stone is brown to greyish-white in colour and massive and false-bedded. This stone was used for the stone piers of Ironbridge.

Permian and Triassic sandstones

It may be argued that the Carboniferous System, and particularly the Millstone Grit and the Coal Measures, are the major sources of sandstone in Great Britain. This however, ignores the many famous sandstones from the next two younger Systems, the Permian and the Triassic. In their own areas and, indeed, outside, they have had just as marked and as dramatic an effect because they are mostly red in colour. Stones taken from the Permian and Triassic red sandstones have many points of similarity, as do the beds from which they are taken. Permian and Triassic sandstones may be found grouped together as the New Red Sandstone because the allocation of some of the beds to one System or to the other is the subject of geological discussion.

Collyhurst Stone, from Collyhurst a north-east Manchester suburb, is Permian in age and was the chief building stone of early Manchester[13]. In some places this sandstone is well known for its abrupt changes in thickness and reaches 800 feet (244 m) thick. It may be brecciated. It has well-rounded, not very well cemented quartz grains which have a distinctive purplish-red colour due to a coating of iron oxide. The stone shows marked dune-bedding. St Ann's Church, St Ann's Square, Manchester (1709) displays the character of the stone well. A great deal of other sandstone has been used for later restoration of this church and 'the mixture is unique and fascinating'[13].

Mansfield Stone, from Mansfield, Nottinghamshire, has been the source of confusion in nomenclature. It is a fine-grained dolomitic sandstone of Permian age consisting of angular and sub-angular quartz grains cemented by dolomite and, to a lesser extent,

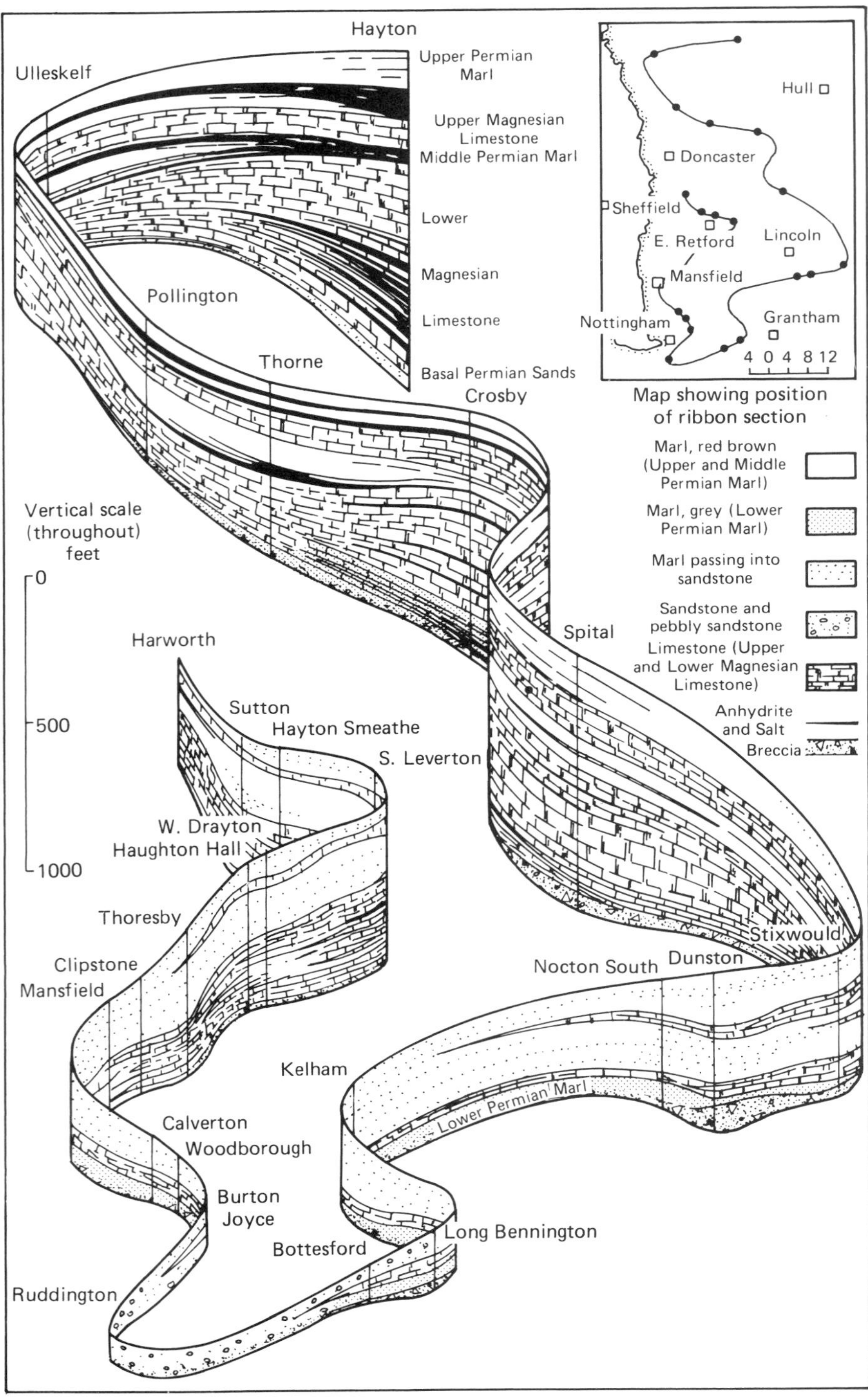
Hayton
Ulleskelf
Upper Permian Marl
Upper Magnesian Limestone
Middle Permian Marl
Lower
Magnesian
Limestone
Basal Permian Sands
Pollington
Thorne
Crosby
Hull
Doncaster
Sheffield
E. Retford
Lincoln
Mansfield
Nottingham
Grantham
4 0 4 8 12
Map showing position of ribbon section
Marl, red brown (Upper and Middle Permian Marl)
Marl, grey (Lower Permian Marl)
Marl passing into sandstone
Sandstone and pebbly sandstone
Limestone (Upper and Lower Magnesian Limestone)
Anhydrite and Salt
Breccia
Vertical scale (throughout) feet
0
500
1000
Harworth
Sutton
Hayton Smeathe
S. Leverton
Spital
W. Drayton
Haughton Hall
Thoresby
Clipstone
Mansfield
Stixwould
Dunston
Nocton South
Kelham
Lower Permian Marl
Calverton
Woodborough
Burton Joyce
Bottesford
Long Bennington
Ruddington

Figure 4.18 Dolomitic sandstone from Gregory's Quarry, Mansfield, Nottinghamshire is quarried from a formation, named the Magnesian Limestone, of Permian age. It was used in part for St Pancras Station, London and in restorations at Chichester Cathedral (1861)[3]

by calcium carbonate and silica. It is a true sandstone and should not be confused with Mansfield Woodhouse Stone which is a dolomitic limestone. The sandstone was supplied as 'White' (or 'Yellow') and 'Red' Mansfield. The yellow variety is commonly yellowish-white when quarried but tends to weather white on exposure. The stone is fine- and even-grained, current bedded freestone (see p. 129). The two colours are used well outside its local area. Red Mansfield forms the capitals and piers alongside the Shap Granite columns at St Pancras Station, London (1873)[3]. It also forms part of the pavement of the Albert Memorial, London. Slabs of Red and White Mansfield Stone were originally used for paving in Trafalgar Square, London, but some of the white was replaced with Portland Stone. Both Red and White Mansfield Stone have also been used as block stone for construction. The Keep, or Little Castle (1612-1621) of that impressively-sited large house, Bolsover Castle, Derbyshire, provides an unrivalled example. The outstanding example of the use of White Mansfield Stone is for Southwell Minster, Nottinghamshire, 10 miles (17 km) south-east of Mansfield. Watson[3], records its use for the Municipal Buildings (1852) in Windsor, Berkshire.

Penrith Stone is taken from sandstones of Permian age known as the Penrith Sandstone. The stone is bright red to pink and buff in colour and moderately coarse-grained. Many of the quartz grains are of the millet-seed type which indicates a desert sand origin. The stone is noteworthy because many of the grains have secondary outgrowths of quartz which are in optical continuity with the grains. Penrith Red is widely known and has been extensively used. Not unexpectedly, much of Penrith, Cumbria is built of it. Often the stone displays a sparkling surface. Lazonby Red (Plumton Red) from Lazonby, Cumbria is also from the Penrith Sandstone. It is red to pink in colour, with some buff (white Lazonby) beds, and medium- to fairly coarse-grained. Because of its gritty character it was sometimes known as the Lazonby Grit. St Adrian's Church, Carlisle (1900) is made of it.

Figure 4.17 The ribbon diagram shows that considerable variation may be found both vertically and laterally in the lithology of a geologically named rock series. In the Permian rocks of Yorkshire and the East Midlands a local development in the Magnesian Limestone yields sandstones–Mansfield white (or yellow) and Mansfield Red (see p. 73). At Mansfield Woodhouse (about 3 km north of Mansfield) a fairly coarse, granular, somewhat crystalline limestone is found. This stone was used for part of the Palace of Westminster. (Diagram reproduced by courtesy of The Director, British Geological Survey. Crown Copyright reserved)

(a)

(b)

Figure 4.19 Old barn (a) and recent house (b), both of Penrith sandstone from Strangeway's Quarry (seen in background in (a)), Halfway Wells, Great Salkeld, Cumbria

Permian sandstones form the country around Dumfries in Scotland and the stone taken from the quarries at Locharbriggs is renowned. It was used to build much of Dumfries, the 'Queen of the South'. Light-red in colour, medium-grained, it 'once provided about half the freestone used for building in Scotland'[14]. Much of the red city of Glasgow results from the use of the stone. The Kelvingrove Art Galleries in Glasgow is one example. Care must be taken, however, not to confuse the Locharbriggs Stone with Old Red Sandstone which is also used in Glasgow. It was exported to Canada and the USA. In Montreal, Canadian architects preferred 'the brighter New Red Sandstone from Great Britain'[3] to a local sandstone.

Lochabriggs Stone was used for the Museum for the Burrell collection, Glasgow (*Figure 4.20*), which won the Stone Federations' New Building Design Award for Natural Stone in 1983. There it was teamed up with Lazonby Stone which was used for paving. The stone was also used in Edinburgh.

Figure 4.20 Lochabriggs Sandstone with Lazonby stone paving was used for the Burrell Collection building, Glasgow. The wall incorporates a masonry doorway, part of the Burrell Collection

The Mauchline Sandstone which tops the Ayrshire coalfield also provides an excellent building stone. The Ballochmyle Quarries produced a bright red-coloured, fine-grained stone with wind-rounded grains, similar to the sandstones of Dumfries and Galloway. Mauchline Sandstone was also used in St Vincent Place[15], Glasgow, and in Edinburgh[7]. Unless documentary evidence is available, it is extremely difficult to determine whether Lochabriggs Stone, Mauchline Stone from Ballochmyle or Penrith Stone has been used in a building. Appropriately The Burns Monument (1879), in Kilmarnock, is known to be of Mauchline Sandstone. The stone was also exported to North America.

The red sandstones in Dumfries and Galloway have been extensively used elsewhere in the west of Scotland. Remarkably soft when green, they are an example of a stone which is too weak for use as aggregate, but nevertheless provides an excellent and enduring building stone.

Around Hopeman, Grampian, an outcrop of pale-fawn coloured sandstone is considered to be Permo-Triassic but its geological horizon is uncertain. The stone is quarried under the names Greenbrae, Clashach and Hopeman Stone. Greenbrae Stone was used by the North of Scotland Hydro-Electric Board for many of its works and Board Houses. Clashach Stone may be seen in the Old Course Hotel, St Andrews. Permo-Triassic sandstones crop out in a broad sweep from around Annan, Dumfries and Galloway eastwards into the Vale of Eden, and around the northern edge of the Lake District. The Corsehill Quarry near Annan supplied a warm-red coloured, fine- and close-grained, slightly micaceous and finely laminated stone, taken from the Annanlea Sandstone which is certainly Triassic in age and is the equivalent of the St Bees Sandstone further south. Records reveal a surprisingly wide geographical range for its use including Liverpool Street Railway Station, London (1875), Cadogan Square Mansions, Chelsea, London, Jews' Synagogue, Great Portland Street, London[12], and 'there are several buildings in New York'[3]. Locally, large blocks have been used in building for houses and cottages. Its suitability for carving is illustrated by its use by Henry Moore for his *Figure* (1933-1934) and his *Reclining Figure* (1935).

The New Red Sandstone crops out in south-west England. Many quarries existed in the past including Broadclyst, Dainton, Exminster and Ugbrooke, in Devon. Many red sandstone churches may be seen, for example, in the lower Exe Valley. An important building stone is the Heavitree Conglomerate, found to the north around Exeter. It was used in Exeter with notable effect in the Cathedral Close (*Figure 4.21*). It was also used for Rougemont Castle in

combination with local stone and in conjunction with other stones in the great red city wall which was begun about 200 AD by the Romans.

A remarkably coarse and bright red local conglomeratic sandstone, well exposed in the colourful cliffs, might, at first sight, be considered unsuitable for building, but was used for the charming late mediaeval Kirkham House, Paignton, Devon.

Red sandstones of Triassic age occur in Scotland, but are of more importance in England. The Spynie Sandstone is quarried near Hopeman under the names Spynie Stone and Rose Brae Stone. St Bees Stone, or Red St Bees, has been quarried near St Bees, Cumbria from early times. Carved Roman pieces of it have been found, and the Ancient Monument of Furness Abbey (1127 and later), Cumbria is an example of the use of the stone in extremely adverse climatic conditions. It is stated to have been used in Windsor Castle, Berkshire, but so is almost any other stone!

St Bees Stone is chocolatey-brown-red, fine-grained with slight laminations and is occasionally micaceous. Quarries on the northern edge of the Lake District at Aspatria, Cumbria supplied stone much like St Bees. It was used for the De Vere Hotel, Kensington, London and as dressings for St Polycarp's Church, Belfast. Another very similar stone taken from the St Bees Sandstone is known as 'Barbary Plane'. It was quarried near Langwathby, Penrith, Cumbria and used for the Library, Manchester.

The West Lancashire Plain and the Cheshire Plain are, to a great extent, underlain by rocks of Triassic age which include useful, important and widely used sandstones. Freestones in nature, most of them could be obtained in large blocks which can be seen in many local buildings. Stone from near Storeton, Wirral Peninsula, Cheshire was widely used, particularly in Liverpool, for many public buildings including the Customs House (1828), the Wellington Monument (1863), and the Lime Street Railway Station (1871)[3]. Better known, however, are Woolten Stone and Rainhill Stone, which were quarried near Liverpool, Merseyside. Both are dull-red in colour and fine- to medium-grained. Woolton Stone was used for all the work of the external walls of the Liverpool Anglican Cathedral and Rainhill Stone was used for the internal walls. In a building where red sandstone is an integral part of the architecture, Red Wilderness Stone (Devonian) was used for pavements and steps and Penrith Stone (Permian) was used for some string courses[3].

Figure 4.21 At first sight an unlikely stone for use in building, the Heavitree Conglomerate (Permian in age) is used with dramatic effect in the church of St. Pancras, Exeter

Dull light-red coloured, medium-grained stone from Runcorn, Merseyside was of importance not only locally and in Liverpool, but also in Manchester where it was used in St Ann's Square for restoration of St Ann's Church and in the newer building of Chetham's Hospital School.

In the Yorton, Clive and Grinshill areas of Cheshire and particularly on Grinshill Hill many old quarries can be found. One of them, now Grinshill Stone

Figure 4.22 Highly false-bedded, brick-red mottled greenish, Red Grinshall stone of Triassic age used for the Castle, Shrewsbury. Weathering has accentuated the bedding planes

Quarries Ltd., is said to have been in unbroken production since Roman times. In the past, Triassic sandstone, named the Ruyton and Grinshill Sandstone, was extensively quarried and a 'Red Grinshill' and a 'White Grinshill' stone was produced. 'Red Grinshill' was used for many of the older buildings of nearby Shrewsbury, Shropshire, including the castle (*Figure 4.22*), the abbey and town walls. More recently the red stone has been replaced by 'White Grinshill' a whitish-grey coloured, brown-specked, fine-grained sandstone. It was used for St Mary's Church, with its magnificent spire, which is one of the three tallest in England. Perhaps the best known Triassic stone is Hollington Stone, quarried at Hollington, near Uttoxeter, Staffordshire. The stone is dull red, white, or mottled. The white stone is in fact yellow and the mottled stone was formerly said to be 'salmon' in colour. It is fine- to medium-grained and is remarkably easy to work when 'green' but toughens considerably on exposure. It was used for the incredible Alton Towers (1812 onwards) which is now a massive fun-fair. Hereford Cathedral was restored (1901–1905) with the stone which was supplied as Red Mottled or as Brown Alton Stone. Bracken House, Queen Victoria Street, London, until recently the headquarters of the *Financial Times* newspaper, which is printed on pink paper, is partly clad with Red Hollington Stone and some blocks show excellent cross-bedding. Without doubt the most spectacular example is the use of the stone for the new Coventry Cathedral (1954–1962), the same stone as was used for the old Cathedral, so fearfully destroyed in 1940 (*Figure 4.23*).

Banked up against the Carboniferous Limestone of the Mendips is a local deposit called the Dolomitic Conglomerate. It is extraordinarily variable in composition and ranges from a grey and red, coarse-grained sandstone to a massive rock made up of

Figure 4.23 Hollington stone is the common bond between the old Coventry Cathedral to the left and the new cathedral (right). The choice of the same stone by Sir Basil Spence, architect of the new cathedral, is a testament to a stone which at first sight might not be considered to be of use for building

boulders. Many of the boulders, which are of limestone and dolomite may weigh several tons. Many of them are markedly angular in form and set in a sandy matrix. The conglomerate could, with complete justification, be classified as a limestone.

The formation represents a thick scree which accumulated on and masked old mountain slopes. Although it is usually unsuitable as a building stone, the deposit has been worked at Draycott, near Wells, Somerset where it has a reddish tinge. Because it is possible to polish the stone it was sold as Draycott Marble or under the trade name of Bryscom. It was known locally as millstone or millgrit rock and was used for gateposts of farms and houses. It was notably used in Wells Cathedral for four tall pillars at the western end of the nave, and for the newer parts (1860) of Temple Meads station, Bristol. A table top made of the stone, 9 feet 2 inches by 4 feet 1 inch (2.8 × 1.2 m) is on view at Longleat House, Wiltshire. The inn at Rodney Stoke, Somerset deserves study if only for the fine use of the stone.

Triassic sandstone of variable colour and quality was worked in Northern Ireland, particularly at Scrabo Hill and at Dundonald. Reddish-brown in colour, well-jointed and cross-bedded stone from quarries on Scrabo Hill, known as Scrabo White, Scrabo Pink, Ballycullen and Glebe was widely used in Belfast. The Albert Memorial is of Scrabo Sandstone, as is St Enoch's Church. Cook's Centenary Church is built of sandstone from Glebe Quarry.

Jurassic sandstones

The Jurassic System has yielded a few sandstones, which in general, did not travel far. However, two must be especially noted. In the county of Northamptonshire, a division of the Jurassic known as the Inferior Oolite Series contains a member called the Northampton Ironstone or the Northampton Sand Ironstone (*see Figure 4.24*). It is mostly an oolitic ironstone deposit but in places is a ferruginous sand. It has a buff or brown colour derived from the contained iron minerals. North of Duston, on the outskirts of Northampton good building sandstone was obtained. Many quarries were opened around the town as well as in the neighbourhood of nearby Harlestone and of Moulton. It is stones from these or from other long-forgotten quarries in the same rocks, which are responsible for the warm russet-brown hues of Northampton itself and of many villages around. The Church of St Peter and St Paul, Moulton, serves as an example. Harlestone Stone was used for setts and for kerbs, and at Duston some beds are flaggy.

A pale-yellow, slightly calcareous, fine- to medium-grained sandstone from the district around Aislaby, near Whitby, North Yorkshire was used for Whitby Abbey (thirteenth century), the old Covent Garden, London, parts of University Library, Cambridge, and for 'the foundations of the old Waterloo Bridge and

Figure 4.24 The variability of the Northampton Sand Ironstone adds interest to buildings made of it, as at Ecton, Northamptonshire

Figure 4.25 In many buildings stone of local importance is used, illustrating the intimate relationship between geology and building. The charming Scarborough museum was built in 1829 to the design of William Smith (the 'father of English geology'). The side wings were added in 1861. The stone used was Hackness Stone (Jurassic), typically a calcareous sandstone, which came from the 'Great Quarry', west-north-west of Scarborough

London Bridge'[16]. Other similar sandstones of Jurassic age were worked and locally used in and around the Howardian Hills.

Cretaceous Sandstones

The Cretaceous System is commonly regarded as having no important building stone. To an extent that is true; but some Cretaceous stones are still available. Others must be noted because they are architecturally and historically important and were widely known, particularly across southern England, an area which, by-and-large, lacks good building stone.

The Wealden Series, the lowest part of the Cretaceous System, yielded slightly calcareous sandstones which were of importance in the Weald area which is otherwise mostly clay or chalk. Stone has been taken from the Ashdown Sand, the Tunbridge Wells Sand and the Lower Greensand. In the main, stone from the Ashdown Sand and the Tunbridge Wells Sand is usually buff- to brown-coloured, fine-grained, somewhat friable, and massively bedded with cross-bedding common. Scattered small pebbles may be locally present.

Where suitable stone was found many quarries were opened. Most are now long lost and impossible to trace. Many buildings throughout the Weald made use of the sandstone and it is not possible to suggest a provenance for the stone without supporting archival or documentary evidence. A fine-grained Wealden sandstone is commonly the best that can be suggested.

Sussex Sandstone and Wealden Sussex from near West Hoathley, Sussex are still available. They are fine-grained, and brown-yellow in colour. Stone from the Ashdown Sands quarried nearby was used for the small, but grand, Bodiam Castle, Sussex. A similar stone from near Hastings was used for restorations at Battle Abbey (pre-1911), Sussex.

In some areas, the Weald Clay, a formation within the Cretaceous contains calcareous sandstone beds which split readily. The best known and most important is a bed up to 30 feet (9 m) thick found near Horsham, Sussex. This stone was once extensively worked and was used for paving slabs and roofing under the name Horsham Stone. The sandstone was originally deposited in shallow waters and

(a)

(b)

Figure 4.26 Ripple-marked slabs of fissile Horsham Stone (a) were used not only for non-slip paving but also for tilestones on the church at Mickleham, Surrey (b)

many slabs have ripple markings. Such slabs were sometimes used for paving stables and stable yards, thus providing a non-slip surface for the horses. The nineteenth century Army Depot in Horsham was paved with these slabs. The Horsham Stone has been widely used as a tilestone and may be seen on many houses around the area (*Figure 4.26*). The roofs of the old Grammar School Building, Guildford, of the Church of St John, Wotton, and of St Katherine,

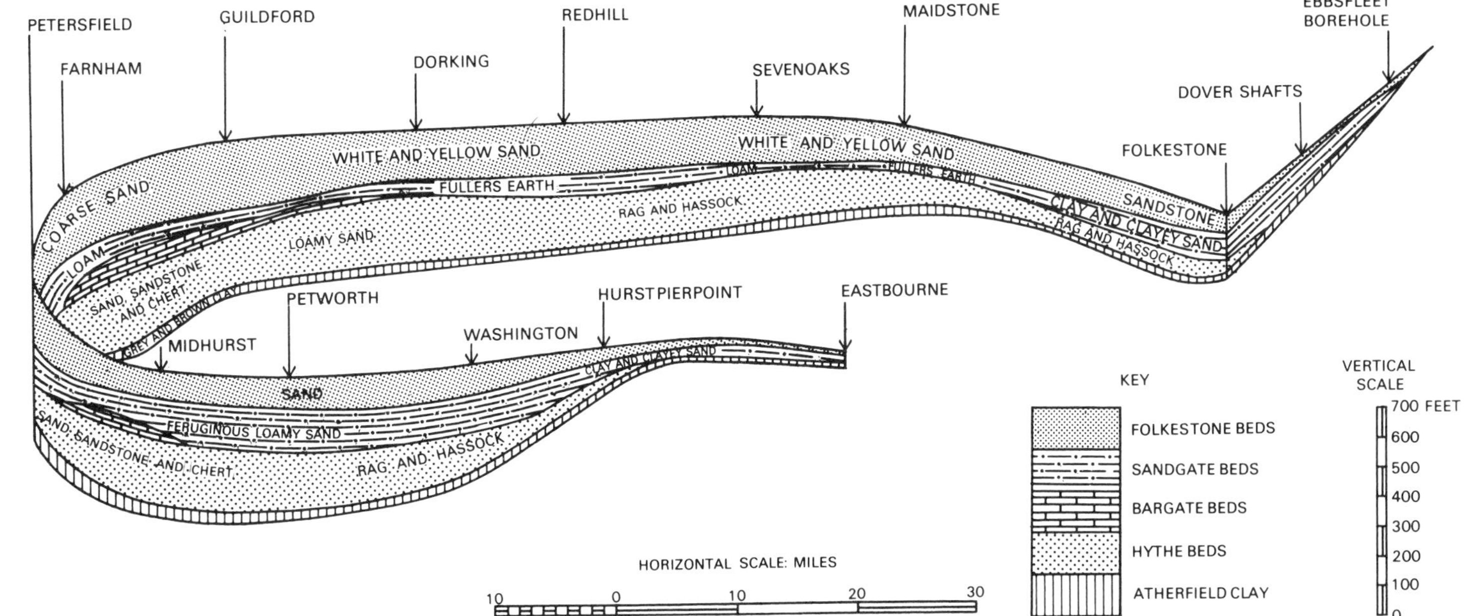

Figure 4.27 The major divisions of the Lower Greensand vary in thickness and lithology. In some areas they may yield stone useful for building which is not found elsewhere along the outcrops (see p.80). (Reproduced by courtesy of The Director, British Geological Survey. Crown copyright reserved)

(a)

(b)

Figure 4.28 (a) House near the Silent Pool, Albury, Surrey is of Bargate Stone (light coloured) and of irregular blocks of carstone from nearby Folkestone Sands (see page 81). (b) The house 'Tankards' in Eashing, Surrey, uses carstone as gallets ('nails') between blocks of Bargate Stone

Merstham, are three examples in Surrey. Locally known as healing stones, they were used at least as early as 1425 to roof the Draper's Guild Hall[17].

Stones from the Lower Greensand (Lower Cretaceous age) differ considerably one from the other, not only in thickness but also in geographical distribution (*Figure 4.27*). The Lower Greensand is divided into a number of formations, but is considered here as a unit and discussed on a geographical basis.

An outcrop which shows considerable lithological variation occurs west of Dorking, Surrey, over a large tract of country south-west of Guildford particularly around Godalming, and extends eastwards in a belt beyond Churt and into Sussex. It consists of a variable group of calcareous and glauconitic sands with discontinuous layers and lenses of cemented pebbly calcareous doggers which may be locally rich in comminuted shell debris. It also contains some cherty lenses. At one time many small quarries were opened to secure the pebbly doggers known as the Bargate Stone, and it was an important building stone in Surrey. The great tower of Guildford Castle (twelfth century) is mostly of Bargate Stone with flint and chalk courses. Bargate Stone is recorded as used for the Royal Grammar School, Guildford (Edward VI), and was used by P.C. Hardwick for Charterhouse School. It is renowned for its use by Sir Edwin Lutyens for Munstead Wood and Tigbourne Court, *'Lutyens'* gayest and most elegant building'[18]. Easebourne Quarry, near Midhurst, Sussex was worked to supply stone to the surrounding Cowdray estate and for bridges in the area[19]. Querns found at Danebury Ring, Hampshire, have been petrologically traced back to the Lower Greensand at Midhurst where, in a long abandoned quarry, there is evidence of a type of production line for their manufacture.

Some beds of the Lower Greensand are locally rich in the green-coloured mineral glauconite. At Ightham, Kent, the Ightham Stone, a vividly green hard chert, with a glassy appearance, was occasionally used. In the early nineteenth century, it was used as road metal in London. Stone from another very restricted occurrence of a glauconite-rich sandstone was used with spectacular effect for the Church of St Mary at Husborne Crawley, Bedfordshire. Irregular seams of ferruginous sandstone in the form of sheets, tubular masses or box stones occur sometimes in some of the sands which are found in the Lower Greensand. The seams are commonly brown to red, friable or well-cemented, medium-grained sandstone. The sand grains are coated and cemented either lightly or heavily with ferruginous minerals. They are commonly known as carstone, or box stone, if box-shaped. Such rocks are not uncommon through the geological column, but they are found particularly in Mesozoic and Tertiary rocks. They are of common occurrence in the Folkestone Beds in Surrey and Kent, where they may exist as veins only an inch (2.5 cm) thick which run randomly across the bedding, or as veins a foot (0.3 m) or so thick with an interlaced 'wasp nest' structure. Blocks of over two feet (0.6 m) thick are known.

Unlikely though it looks, carstone has been extensively used for building; many cottages and houses at Wrotham, Kent (*Figure 4.29a*) and at Eashing and at

(a)

(b)

Figure 4.29 (a) Cottages of carstone, Wrotham Hill, Kent. (b) Brick dressings with carstone ('gingerbread stone') were used for HM The Queen's Stud, Sandringham, Norfolk

Albury, Surrey (*Figure 4.28*) are built of it. In Limpsfield and in Westerham, Kent, it has been used for paving with the stone set on end with the bedding planes vertical[20]. Along the Lower Greensand ridge from about Farnham, Surrey to around Wrotham, Kent, small pieces of carstone were, and still are, pushed into the mortar between the stones of the buildings. This technique is known variously as garnetting, galleting or nailing (*see Figure 4.30*). 'The nailed wall' was noted by Gilbert White[21] who wrote in Letter IV,

> From a notion of rendering their work the more elegant, and giving it a finish, masons chip this stone into small fragments about the size of the head of a large nail, and then stick the pieces into the wet mortar along the joints of their freestone walls; this embellishment carries an odd appearance, and has occasioned strangers sometimes to ask us pleasantly, whether we fastened our walls together with ten penny nails.

Other stones are similarly used; for example, Kentish Ragstone to the east of Sevenoaks, Kent, and flint, which was used in the magnificent Goodwood House, Sussex. Small outcrops of the Lower Greensand occur around Ely, Cambridgeshire, and the Cathedral is built on one of them (*Figure 4.31*). Carstone also occurs and it has been used in the arcading of the cloister near the south transept door and in the outside wall of the south transept.

A distinctive ginger-brown coloured carstone is seen in the cliffs at Hunstanton, Norfolk. It has been found to be at least 58 feet (18 m) thick[22] in inland borings. It is conglomeratic, with quartz and chert pebbles and may be current-bedded. Finer grained and well-jointed carstone has been quarried over a long period of time near Snettisham, Norfolk. This is the 'gingerbread stone' which was used for the stables of Houghton Hall[10] and for many other buildings. An outstanding example is its use for HM The Queen's Stud, Sandringham, Norfolk. Cottages and walls in that area have been built using small slabs and large blocks.

Ferruginous sandstones other than those from the Lower Greensand may also be called carstone. Wimborne Minster, Dorset is often stated to be built of carstone and other stones. However, the stone is from an entirely different set of beds, the Agglestone Grit, in the upper part of the Bracklesham Group which are Eocene in age. Canford Magna Church, near Wimborne Minster, is made of blocks of grit collected from the heaths and from the Agglestone and the Puckstone. Local buildings, walls, barns and houses also used the stone.

The Upper Greensand (Lower Cretaceous) around Reigate, Merstham, Gatton and Godstone in Surrey contains beds of compact sandstones. Some of these rocks are known as firestone, malmstone, malm rock or Burrystone, others are called hearthstone. The Upper Greensand outcrop extends westwards through Surrey and into Hampshire. Throughout this area the rock is commonly referred to as malmstone. Hearthstone is a friable greenish-grey sandstone which was sold in blocks for household scouring purposes. Firestone, named from its property of resisting heat without decrepitating, occurs as massive, compact beds about two feet (0.6 m) thick. It is a calcareous, greenish-grey sandstone with muscovite mica and large amounts of glauconite. In places it becomes a siliceous limestone. Sponge spicules are abundant in the stone as fragments or as casts, which may be filled with glauconite or with silica in amorphous form. These stones were widely used and known under the general name of Reigate Stone or Merstham Stone. Merstham, Gatton and Godstone Stones are similar in nature. It is not possible to determine the provenance of a block used for building by visual inspection because the stone from these localities has no unique characteristics. Stone has been obtained from the north-east Surrey area possibly since Saxon times[23]. The stone was so

(a)

(b)

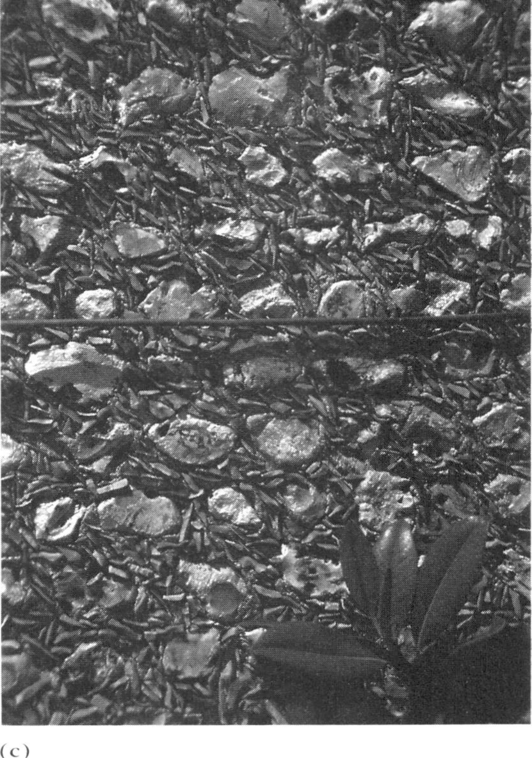

(c)

Figure 4.30 (a) Carstone 'nails' were used between blocks of Upper Greensand at Selbourne, Hampshire; (b) chips of flint have been pressed into the mortar between blocks of sarsen at Windsor Castle and flint has similarly been used on a massive scale between irregular blocks of flint for Goodwood House, Sussex (c)

Figure 4.31 Rough blocks of carstone from the Lower Greensand on which Ely Cathedral stands were incorporated into the exterior wall of the south transept

important to Royal building programmes that during the reign of Edward III (1312–1327) the quarries of Reigate Stone were considered as valuable Crown property[12]. Despite its poor weathering properties it was extensively used in London because it was quarried nearby and could be easily carved (*Figure 4.32*). From the 'eleventh century to the sixteenth, large quantities were dragged by ox cart across the Home Counties'[10] Interestingly, the world's pioneer public horse-drawn and freight-only railways connected Wandsworth with Croydon, with a branch from Mitcham to Hackbridge. Its extension, the Croydon, Merstham and Godstone Railway (CMGR), which operated from 1805 to 1843, continued the line '...to a terminus at...underground firestone quarries at Merstham...'[24]. In 'Almost all old buildings [in London] we find occasionally introduced

(a)

(b)

(c)

(d)

Figure 4.32 Reigate Stone was used extensively in the Tower of London, seen here in the arch of the entrance to the Bloody Tower with Kentish Ragstone forming much of the wall (a). It was also used for a delightful doorway arch in Deans' Yard, Westminster Abbey, (b). In each of these instances note obtrusive replacements with stones which are not geologically appropriate. (c) Beech house of Gatton Stone with brick dressings, Godstone, Surrey. (d) Side wall of White Hart Hotel, Godstone, also of Gatton Stone. This shows carstone galleting into poor and inappropriate re-mortaring which is leading to decay of the stone (see Volume 2).

large portions of stone from the vicinity of Rygate and Godstone'[25]. The Black Prince's Palace at Kennington (*c.* 1388), the vaulting of the crypt of Guildhall, the Tower of London and Henry VII's Chapel, Westminster, all bear witness to that statement. It was also used in Windsor Castle and Eton College (1443), Berkshire. Gatton House, supposedly built on the lines of the Corsini Chapel in Rome, and Gatton Church are local examples. In the 'Town Hall' nearby, there is an urn in memory of the deceased (and obviously a very rotten) borough.

The Malmstone outcrop to the west of Reigate has been quarried along its length for building stone. Examples may be seen in Farnham Church and the walls of Farnham Castle, Surrey. Much of Wiston

Figure 4.33 Eastbourne parish church, Sussex, built of Eastbourne Green Stone dug from reefs on the shore of the town

House, Susssex, is of malmstone, locally known also as malmrock. The Firestone was used extensively for fire places in, for example, the original house of Manresa, Roehampton, London and in Duntish Court, near Sherborne, Dorset.

Eastbourne Stone (Eastbourne Green) was taken from outcrops between tidemarks at Eastbourne, Sussex. A fairly tough, markedly green coloured sandstone, it was used for part of Pevensey Castle, Sussex. Perhaps it is to maintain the balance, that catapult balls found at Eastbourne are of the same stone.

The Upper Greensand of the Isle of Wight at one time yielded what was regarded as by far the best building stone on the Isle. It was quarried in many places, but principally in the neighbourhood of Ventnor and of Shanklin. The most important bed is a freestone three to five feet (0.9-1.5 m) thick, confined to the Southern Downs and seen in the cliff between Bonchurch and Black Gang. It is speckled pale-green to blue-grey in colour, and fine-grained with a varying amount of glauconite and of mica. The freestone was sawn into blocks as well as into lengths for mullions. It has a reputation for durability and it was used for ornamental and for structural work. On the Isle of Wight many houses in Ventnor, Bonchurch and Niton are built of it and it may be seen in Carisbrook Castle. An outstanding example of its use is for the detached bell tower of Chichester Cathedral in Hampshire. Winchester Cathedral was restored in part with the stone in 1825.

Tertiary sandstones

The Tertiary System has yielded few sandstones suitable for structural work. In general Tertiary sandstones are not consolidated enough for use in building. There are at least two exceptions, however, although they may be regarded as oddities. Sarsens, also known as grey-wethers, Druid stones or bridestones, are found as individual boulders which are often of considerable size, in an area south of a rough line from the Severn estuary stretching to Lowestoft, Suffolk. Two types may be distinguished; highly siliceous cemented sandstones (quartzites) and conglomerates of well cemented flint pebbles in a matrix of sarsen-like sandstone known as puddingstones. The sarsens of southern England, south of the River Thames are predominantly quartzites although some are markedly pebbly, with angular rather than round flint pebbles. They are far more widely distributed than is generally realized. The greatest concentration is in Wiltshire and Berkshire, where they often occur as 'valley trains'. They are also found in Dorset, Hampshire and Sussex. Generally they are white, fine-grained and well-cemented, sometimes with rootlet holes. They may have noticeably irregular surfaces.

They were much more naturally abundant in the past. They have been used for building from prehistoric times until recently for structures of all types. Stonehenge and Avebury Circle, for which over 600 sarsen stones were used, are the outstanding examples. The Megalithic monuments of White Horse Stone and Kit's Coty, Kent are also made of this stone. It was used too in Windsor Castle, Berkshire, where some walls are galleted with chips of flint. Some churches in Surrey made use of sarsen, and it has been used more mundanely for the wall alongside the car park of the public house at Avebury Village.

Properly, the name puddingstone should be applied to a conglomerate in which the contained pebbles and the cementing matrix are of equal hardness so that when broken, a smooth surface results. Most conglomerates break around the surface of the pebbles. Unfortunately the name puddingstone is commonly applied indiscriminately to all types of conglomerate. The Hertfordshire Puddingstone, of Tertiary age, is a classic example of a true puddingstone. It is composed of round flint pebbles up to two inches (5 cm) or so, set in a siliceous ground mass of sand grains and small flint fragments, all cemented by silica. Because of the shortage of stone suitable for building in Essex, puddingstone was widely incorporated in buildings and walls. It was also commonly used for millstones and for querns, one of which has been dated to 1500 BC[26]. Bradenham Puddingstone, locally known as pebble stone, is similar although less abundant. It has poorly-rounded irregular flints. It, too, was incorporated into local buildings, and was used 'in connection with rockeries, etc.' at Whipsnade Zoo[27].

Many local names, some restricted to a valley or two in Hertfordshire, have been used for Hertford-

(a)

(b)

(c)

Figure 4.34 (a) A 'valley train' of sarsens is spread along the valley bottom at Piggledean, near Avebury, Wiltshire. From sites such as these, stones were taken for the great monuments such as Avebury Circle, Wiltshire (b). (c) An inscribed sarsen, presented in 1967 to the City of Salisbury by the National Association of Master Masons. It stands near to the spot, indicated by an upturned cannon, from which the trigonometrical survey of Britain was begun

shire Puddingstone. Woe Stones, Hag Stones, Breedingstone, Growing Stone and Mother Stone are some examples[26].

Imported sandstones

Britain is plentifully endowed with sandstone and little is imported. The imported stone is mostly in the form of quartzite, which is of limited occurrence in Britain. However, one exception is a sandstone known as Grès de Vosges from the Department of Vosges, France. This fine- to medium-grained, yellowish to light olive grey (between 5Y 8/1 and 5Y 6/1), impure, slightly micaceous sandstone of Triassic age has been used, but as a colour match only, as a substitute for Kentish Ragstone.

Figure 4.35 In Hertfordshire, blocks of the locally occurring puddingstone may be found incorporated into walls and buildings. The stone has also been used ornamentally

Flint, chert and jasper

Although not always neatly placed into a classification, flint, chert and jasper may be conveniently considered here because they are composed mainly of silicon dioxide (SiO_2) the main substance of sandstones and closely allied stones.

Flint is found as nodules, layers of nodules and more rarely as bands in the top part of the middle and throughout the upper division of the Chalk formation. It is compact cryptocrystalline silica. All flint, whatever its immediate source, originated from the Chalk. This primary flint is black or dark blue-grey in colour and it breaks with a conchoidal fracture, a characteristic valued by early man because it provided a very sharp edge of use for cutting and scraping. It is possible also to split or 'knap' flints so that a moderately flat surface is obtained. Flint has long been used for building and many local names describe the immediate origin and form of use of it; for example field flint, squared flint, cobble, chequerwork and flushwork. Flint pebbles (cobbles, boulders, shingle, nodules, beach stones) and knapped flints have been, and are, still widely used for building. It is a difficult and intractable material which was used because no other suitable material was available in the areas where it is found rather than because of its intrinsic qualities. It is used for structural purposes and as a veneer.

Many examples of flint building may be seen in Kent, Surrey, Sussex, Suffolk and Norfolk. The Roman Wall of London incorporates much flint along with many other stones in an area where no building stone is found. Goodwood House (*c* 1790-1800 by James Wyatt) is an impressive example in West Sussex. It is 'one of his very few dull designs' according to Ian Nairn and Nikolaus Pevsner[28], but is nevertheless a magnificent use of what might be regarded as an unpromising material. Burpham Lodge, Arundel, West Sussex, which is much modernized is of large knapped flints. It is East Anglia that must take pride of place for the use of flint. Many churches in that area are entirely of flint. The Guildhall, Norwich, is an excellent example of the celebrated chequer work using flint and Caen Stone (*Figure 4.36*).

The name chert or hornstone is also applied to nodular silica which may be difficult to distinguish from flint. Generally the name is used for silica beds, layers and nodules which occur in limestones other than the Chalk. Any form of silica that can be used in the pottery industry is called flint in the Americas. The name flint is used outside the United Kingdom for silica deposits which would be called chert inside the UK.

Normally chert is thought of as being an impure flint, but the distinctive differences between flint and some chert are not immediately apparent. Generally chert has a hackly fracture compared with the markedly conchoidal fracture of flint. The name chert is often used for thick beds of massive chalcedony (SiO_2) which is a compact variety of silica made up of microscopic, or cryptocrystalline, quartz crystals with submicroscopic pores. Chert is prominent at some levels in the Carboniferous Limestone, the Jurassic Portland Beds and in the Lower Cretaceous Upper Greensand.

Chert has only been used locally and on a limited scale for building. The Old Grammar School, Chard, which is built of chert from the Upper Greensand, and the use of chert from the Carboniferous Limestone in walls and houses in Richmond, North Yorkshire are two examples[29]. Chert was mined until the end of 1968 by the Bakewell Chert Company, Derbyshire for use mainly in grinding mills in the Potteries.

Jasper, an opaque form of impure chalcedony even when very thin, is the name usually given to a red-coloured variety. Yellow, brown and green varieties are known. Lenticles of a dark-pink ('blood red') with large streaks and patches of darker red jasper occur in rocks of Precambrian age in Gwynedd, North Wales. At one time they were quarried two miles (3.2 km) north of Aberdaron. It was used for a Celtic cross nearby. Despite its hardness, toughness and the extreme difficulty of working it, an amazing use was made of jasper for the Norwich Union Insurance Group building on the corner of St James's Street and Piccadilly, London (*Figure 4.37*).

Limestone

Limestones consist chiefly of calcium carbonate ($CaCO_3$) in the form of the finely-divided mineral calcite which was originally a calcareous mud. Limestones were formed either directly or indirectly from mineral matter dissolved generally, but not always, in sea water and may be made up of as much as 99 per cent calcium carbonate. However, other mineral matter may be present in significant amounts. Limestones are very widespread and usually have a marked bedding. They are commonly richly fossiliferous.

Complicated classifications may be constructed, but for the purposes of discussion the classification used here is based on their mode of origin:

Chemical
Organic
Clastic or detrital

Chemical limestones are formed directly by precipitation of calcium carbonate from water. Calcium carbonate is only slightly soluble in water. However, most circulating ground waters contain carbon dioxide. Rain water, which is the source of most groundwater, also contains carbon dioxide. These

(a)

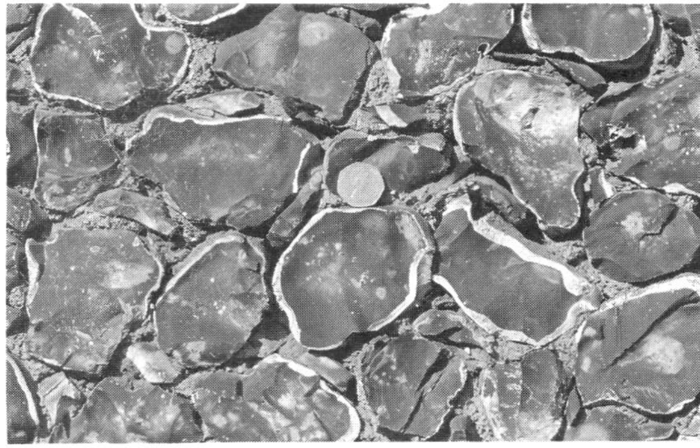
(b)

(c)

(d)

(e)

(f)

(g)

Figure 4.36 Some of the faces of flint. (a) Blocks of chalk containing nodules of flint were used, with blocks of basalt, for the harbour wall, Waterfoot, County Antrim; (b) split nodules of flint from the wall of St Peter's Church, Croydon; (c) nodules of flint, with dressings of Ham Hill stone, were used for Training College, Salisbury; (d) two adjoining cottages at Rustington, Sussex show contrasting styles of use of flint. That on the right uses split flint nodules, that on the left has round, evenly graded pebbles brought neatly into courses; (e and f) flints knapped to remove most of the cortex (the 'white skin') from some and to leave it on others, then grouped, lead to an interesting chequerboard pattern. This is seen on the church of St Thomas, Andover sub Foxcotte, Hampshire; (g) knapped flint with Caen stone produces the spectacular diaper flushwork on the Guildhall, Norwich

Figure 4.37 Jasper, which occurs as lenticles in rocks of Precambrian age around Aberdaron, North Wales, was used in 1905 for the Norwich Union building, Piccadilly. This building was one of the first in London to use Pentelikon marble from Greece

Figure 4.38 Ooliths result from the concentric deposition of calcium carbonate around a nucleus in highly carbonate-charged waters. The recent ooliths on the right were collected from the Great Salt Lake, Utah. The picture on the left shows an identical structure on the surface of Ketton Stone, from Ketton, Northamptonshire, an oolitic limestone about 175 million years old (Courtesy British Museum (Natural History))

waters convert calcium carbonate into calcium bicarbonate ($CaCO_3 + CO_2 + H_2O \rightarrow Ca(HCO_3)_2$) which has a much higher solubility and exists only in solution. When the charged ground waters reach the atmosphere at the surface the loss of carbon dioxide leads to the reprecipitation of calcium carbonate in the form of *tufa* or of *travertine*. The dividing line between these two is a matter of fine judgement. The name tufa is commonly used for a spongy, cellular, porous calcium carbonate deposit formed around seeps, springs and in streams flowing off limestone country. More compact, tougher forms, with a greater or lesser proportion of voids, generally regarded as having been deposited from hot springs[30] are named travertine. The name travertine is derived from Italian and is a corruption from the term *Tiburtinus*, the stone being found in great quantity at Tibur, near Rome, Italy and named by the Romans *Lapis Tiburtinus*.

Similar deposits may be formed by the dripping of water charged with calcium bicarbonate from the roofs of caverns in calcareous rocks. Layers of the mineral calcite are deposited one over another to build stalactites. The counterparts, rising from the floor, are stalagmites. In some instances layers of calcite encrust the walls or floors of caves. The encrustation is called *flow-stone*, *dripstone*, *cave onyx* or, more rarely, *waterstone* or *water marble*. As with stalactites, it is characteristically banded. *Onyx marble* is also a chemical precipitate. It is generally thought to be deposited from standing sheets of water and, in a sense, may be thought of as a horizontal stalagmite.

Chemically precipitated limestones were also formed in sea waters. In some areas, such as around the Bahamas, around the Florida Keys, in the Persian Gulf and in the Great Salt Lake, Utah, USA, richly charged, warm, tide-swept and wave-agitated shallow sea water in tidal channels and in lagoons precipitates calcium carbonate in concentric layers, commonly round a fragment of shell or a grain of sand which acts as a nucleus. These small, mainly spherical carbonate grains are known as *ooliths* (*see Figure 4.38*). Some limestones are found to be composed nearly entirely of ooliths; they are called *oolitic limestones* or, *oolites*. Commonly the ooliths are about 1 mm, more rarely up to 2 mm (0.08 in) in diameter. In some rocks they are about the size of a pea; the name *pisolite* is then used.

Organic limestones consist largely or entirely of the fossilized shells of one or more organisms. The organisms removed calcium carbonate from the water in which they lived and used it for their shells or skeletons. Reef limestones, for example, are composed of a number of organic components; algal limestones originated from algae which secrete lime. Shelly limestones are made up dominantly of the fossil remains of shellfish. Coral limestones may contain complete coral colonies; crinoidal limestones are made up of fragments of crinoids (sea lilies), which are animals related to sea urchins and starfishes. The spaces between the fossilized organisms may be filled with broken shell matter or with calcareous mud. The fossils in a limestone may range from complete, unbroken shells to those that are completely broken up (comminuted). Many commercial 'marbles' are shelly limestones.

Clastic or detrital limestones result from the erosion of pre-existing limestones. The fragments range from fine-grained calcareous mud to pebbles of the original limestone, later consolidated and normally cemented with calcareous material into a new coherent rock.

The Lower Lias (Jurassic) Sutton Stone, from Glamorgan, South Wales was derived mainly from the Carboniferous Limestone, which it overlies in places. Draycott marble is a clastic limestone in some places. Many commercial 'marbles' which are called 'breche' are clastic limestones. Limestones may be *close* or *massively* bedded.

When pure, or nearly so, limestones are white in colour, as, for example, the upper part of the Cretaceous Chalk. Few limestones, however, are composed entirely of calcium carbonate. Most contain other mineral matter which will determine its overall colour. Clay is one of the commonest non-calcareous constituents of limestone. The lower the amount of contained clay the better the polish which can be given to a limestone. Limestone, probably more so than other rocks, shows gradations to all other sediments; a clayey limestone easily grades into a calcareous shale or calcareous clay, that is, a marl. Many other minerals may be present in limestones.

Dolomite, a calcium magnesium carbonate, ($CaMg(CO_3)_2$), may be present in considerable amounts. It may have originated as a chemical deposit, but more probably formed by the chemical alteration, termed dolomitization, of the original limestone by the replacement of calcium by magnesium. Pure dolomite rock is rare. The Carboniferous Limestone is dolomitized irregularly, sometimes on a considerable scale. Nearly all the limestones of Permian age in England contain dolomite. The Magnesian Limestone is a particularly well-known formation. The font at Coventry Cathedral is a boulder of dolomitized Chalk brought from Israel.

In general, dolomitic limestones are more resistant to weathering than pure limestones, but they are particularly vulnerable in heavily polluted atmospheres.

Quartz in the form of sand grains may also be present, either by itself or in association with other minerals. If there are large amounts of sand the limestone is called a sandy limestone. In some instances, complete removal of the calcium carbonate in a siliceous limestone leaves behind a 'skeleton' of silica. This is known as rottenstone and it has been used for polishing and as an abrasive. The dolomitized patches in the Carboniferous Limestone were also called rottenstone by men quarrying for limestone.

Rarely, a limestone may be rich in one of the iron minerals. Some oolitic limestones of Jurassic age in Lincolnshire and in Northamptonshire are rich in iron minerals, commonly *siderite* (chalybite, iron carbonate, $FeCO_3$) and *chamosite* (iron silicate, Mg, $Fe''_3Fe'''_3(AlSi_3)O_{10}(OH)_8$). If these minerals are present in sufficient concentration the rock is termed an oolitic ironstone and may be worked as an iron ore.

The complex iron-silicate, *glauconite* is an occasional constituent of limestones but it is not as widespread in limestone as in sandstones.

Pyrite (iron disulphide, FeS_2) may be present and in disseminated form contributes to the dark colour of some limestones and to the hydrogen sulphide smell which some of them emit when struck. Watson[3] records that stone from the Carboniferous Limestone of the Mendip Hills, Somerset is popularly known as Stink Stone because, when newly quarried, it emits a strong fetid odour. Manganese minerals, normally in the form of *manganite* (hydrated manganese oxide, MnO(OH)), may have a dramatic effect even when present in small quantities. It appears as attractive dendritic patterns on the joints or bedding-planes particularly of fine-grained limestones.

Although limestone is not quarried for dimension stone on the same huge scale that it is for crushed rock and for industrial use, it has, nevertheless, contributed greatly and sometimes dramatically to the appearance of many British buildings and towns.

Limestones are widely distributed geographically and, like sandstones, are of common occurrence throughout the geological column. They are less common in the older systems, but increase in prominence in younger rocks.

In the stone trade in Great Britain and in most other countries overseas it is usual to call any calcareous rock which can be cut and polished a 'marble'. This does not accord with the strict geological definition which is adhered to here.

Silurian and older Limestones

Geologically interesting limestones are found in the Precambrian, Cambrian, Ordovician and Silurian Systems. Although they were used locally for building they were not of commercial importance. The Wenlock Limestone, of Silurian age, became more widely known, not only for its fossils, including the 'Dudley locust', but also for polished slabs sold under the names of Fossil 'Marble', Ledbury 'Marble'[17] and Shropshire 'Marble'. The limestone was rarely used for building but it may be found in Dudley Castle, Worcestershire and in some churches around the area.

Devonian limestones

The Devonian System has yielded limestones which have had wide use. The principal beds occur in the Middle Devonian in a belt extending from Plymouth across to Torquay, Devon. Babbacombe, Petit Tor,

(a)

(b)

Figure 4.39 Unpolished blocks of Devonian Limestone used naturally for the Town Hall, Plymouth, with a south-west England granite plinth and serpentinite infill panels on entrance (a). Slabs of the limestone form an attractive pavement outside the town hall (b)

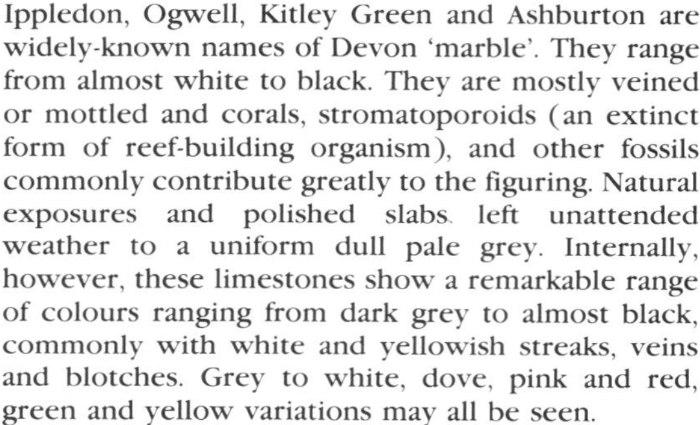

Ippledon, Ogwell, Kitley Green and Ashburton are widely-known names of Devon 'marble'. They range from almost white to black. They are mostly veined or mottled and corals, stromatoporoids (an extinct form of reef-building organism), and other fossils commonly contribute greatly to the figuring. Natural exposures and polished slabs left unattended weather to a uniform dull pale grey. Internally, however, these limestones show a remarkable range of colours ranging from dark grey to almost black, commonly with white and yellowish streaks, veins and blotches. Grey to white, dove, pink and red, green and yellow variations may all be seen.

The limestone has been used for building in Torquay. In Plymouth, where it was used for the post-war rebuilding, it may be seen beautifully applied for the Town Hall and for the matching surrounding paving (*Figure 4.39*).

It was more for its decorative effect, however, that vast amounts were quarried in the past. The last producing quarry at Ashburton, Devon recently ceased production of dimension stone. It yielded a dark-grey to black stone with white, yellow and red patches and veins. Ashburton 'Marble' was widely used as an internal and external decorative stone. It was exported to northern America where it is known as Renfrew 'Marble'. It was recently used for the Royal Bank of Canada, Port of Spain, Trinidad. It has also been widely used for internal ecclesiastical work, often as supporting pillars. For example, it is used purely for decorative effect for some pillars in Chichester Cathedral, Sussex. It may be seen on many shop fronts and was used for some steps and floors of the (now) British Telecom Tower, London. It is spectacularly used in the entrance of the Geological Museum, London, where the foyer, stairs and entrance arch exemplify the attractive use of British decorative 'marbles.' The wide range and variation of colour shown by the Devonian limestones makes it difficult to attribute any given example of its decorative use to a specific quarry because at one time several varieties may have been produced from any quarry. Commonly the best determination that can be given is Devonian limestone as in, for example, Salisbury Cathedral, Hampshire, where some original shafts presumed to have been of Purbeck 'Marble' were replaced by Devonian limestone shafts.

The limestones of Devonian age were noted not only for their beauty but also for their durability. As North[17] remarks '... greater used could be made of the ornamental varieties, because much of the domestic "marble" can withstand the British atmosphere better than many of the foreign crystalline marbles that are imported, into this country.' At one time Devon 'marbles' were widely exported to Europe as well as to Australia, America and South Africa.

Carboniferous limestones

The Carboniferous System is the first in the geological column in which limestones, named the Carboniferous Limestone, form a major constituent. The Carboniferous Limestone is responsible for many of the areas of outstanding natural beauty in Great Britain including the Mendips, the Peak District, and much of the Pennines. In these areas the limestones are extensively and attractively used both for building and for walling. It provides more limestone for industrial use in the chemical, pharmaceutical, cement, iron and steel and agricultural industries than any other geological formation. It also provides many building stones, which are usually cut and polished, then sold as marbles. However, the variety sold now is by no means as great as in the past.

Figure 4.40 Haddon Hall, Derbyshire is constructed of Carboniferous Limestone with dressings of Millstone Grit. Both stones were quarried from nearby the house

The overall appearance of the Carboniferous Limestone differs greatly from one locality to another. The differences are the result of the contained fossils and small amounts of other minerals disseminated through the stone. Much of the limestone is compact, tough, mainly massive, well-bedded grey-coloured rock with greater or lesser amounts of fossils, of relatively low porosity and very low permeability.

Porosity and permeability are important characteristics of building stones. Limestones are generally thought of as being porous, but they are not necessarily permeable. Permeability is the capacity of a rock to allow the passage of fluids such as water or oil through it. Permeability is measured by the rate of flow, that is, the amount of fluid passing through the rock in a given time. Porosity is the percentage of free space in a given volume of rock. A porous rock is not necessarily permeable. Permeability depends on the size and arrangement of the pores. To be permeable a rock must have pores which form continuous through channels for the passage of fluid. For example, pumice is very porous, but not permeable. This can be demonstrated by the fact that it floats on water. If the pores were connected, the rock would fill with water and would sink.

Limestone can be virtually impermeable. A mock-up of a spandrel below a window sill to be used as part of a wall in Arundel Great Court, London, was constructed of six-inch (15 cm) thick Portland Stone. It was subjected to simulated driving rain for 24 hours. At the end of the test only small drops of moisture were found on the internal face (Personal communication by J.B. Forrest, lately of Frederick Gibberd Coombes and Partners.). Compact Carboniferous Limestone is sometimes used for water butts (*Figure 4.41*).

Compact, massive, grey-coloured Carboniferous Limestone has been widely used usually as block stone for structural building work in all the areas it is found. The many dry stone walls of the Pennines and elsewhere, testify to its robust durability. The delightful Haddon Hall, Derbyshire was built of blocks quarried from nearby, with dressings of Millstone Grit also quarried on the estate (*Figure 4.40*). The walls of Cardiff Castle, South Glamorgan, made of stone from nearby Wenvoe, provide another example. Carboniferous Limestone may be seen similarly used for many buildings in Ireland, notably in Galway City.[31] It is, however, the varieties of other colours and which contain fossil matter which have received more attention and which have been used for decorative effect. One of the classic Carboniferous Limestone stones is Frosterly 'Marble', which was

Figure 4.41 Contrary to widely held belief, many limestones, particularly the compact types, are virtually impermeable. The water butt at Lindale Trough, Cumbria (left) was carved from a solid block of Carboniferous Limestone. The butt at Whitehaven, north of Raw, Cumbria (right) is of slabs of Carboniferous Limestone with lead seals. (Courtesy of M. Mitchell)

formerly quarried at Frosterley on the banks of the River Wear, Durham. Dark grey to black in colour with eye-catching pale- to white-coloured sections of fossil corals, the stone was one of the first to be used in northern England for decorative effect. The fantastic columns in Durham Cathedral are an outstanding example of its use. A massive block was used for the tomb of Sir Thomas Gresham in the Church of St Helens the Great, London. Other blocks form the steps and the base of the alabaster font in St George's Chapel, Windsor Castle, Berkshire. Elsden and Howe[12] recorded that large slabs are used as radiator covers in the National Portrait Gallery, but apparently these covers have now been removed. The stone was also used for the step up to the High Altar in Peterborough Cathedral; and in Bristol Cathedral. It is recorded as having been exported for use in the base of the pulpit in the Cathedral at Bombay, India.[32] The stone was known also as Stanhope Black 'Marble'.[32] A tombstone slab by the south door of St Albans Cathedral, Hertfordshire has spectacular sections of corals (*Figure 4.42*).

Figure 4.42 An old tombstone slab, St Albans Cathedral, of Frosterly 'marble'. Fossil corals, white in colour, contrast vividly with the black of the limestone

Another classic and rarely seen stone is Duke's Red from Rowsley, Derbyshire. The stone is found on the estate of the Duke of Devonshire and the 7th Duke, fearful that the stone would be quickly exhausted, ordered that it should all be quarried and stored.[32] It is a deep red-coloured, fine-grained stone. It was given by the Duke of Devonshire and was used for the columns round the apse of St John's College Chapel, Cambridge. Not unexpectedly, it is used decoratively inside Chatsworth House, Derbyshire, the seat of the Dukes of Devonshire.

Derby Fossil, from Coalhill, and similar stones known as Derbydene or Derbydene Fossil or Monyash 'Marble' from around Wirksworth, Monyash and Cromford in Derbyshire are probably the most

(a)

(b)

(c)

Figure 4.43 Fossil crinoids in Carboniferous Limestone (seen here in Steeplehouse Quarry, Wirksworth, Derbyshire), are enhanced by cutting and polishing to contrast with the limestone in which they are embedded (a). The stone is used decoratively for (b) a plateau (standing on a table of onyx marble edged with serpentinite) in Chatsworth House, Derbyshire and (c) for flooring in the British Museum (Natural History) Geological Museum, London

widely used of the decorative Carboniferous Limestone stones. The stones are grey- to dark-fawn in colour and, when cut, sections of lighter coloured crinoids are prominent. Probably the most seen but least observed example is in the Royal Festival Hall, London where the entrance, stairways and foyers are clad with it. It has been widely used elsewhere, for example for the base of the columns in Chichley Hall, Buckinghamshire, inside 30 Gresham Street, London, in many London churches, in Westminster Cathedral and in the now sadly demolished Imperial Institute, South Kensington, London. It was used for the balastrade at the visitors entrance of Chatsworth House, Derbyshire (*Figure 4.43*). Many window sills are also made of it. A red-coloured variety is used for an eye-catching plateau in the Chapel corridor of Chatsworth House. Derbydene, specifically from Dene Quarry, Matlock, is recorded as used in Thorn House, St Martin's Lane, London. Matlock Fossil is a visually similar stone, quarried from near Matlock, Derbyshire. These crinoidal limestones occasionally are called screwstone.

Deepdale Fossil, from Deepdale, Yorkshire is light-brown to dark-grey in colour with many fossil markings. Swale Dale Fossil, from Barton, Yorkshire is pale brown in colour with many fossils. Orton Scar, from Orton Scar, Cumbria, is pale fawn with darker veins. Salterwath, from Crosby Ravensworth Fell, Cumbria, is dark brown with fainter markings. These stones demonstrate part of the range obtainable from the Carboniferous Limestone.

Hopton Wood Stone, a cream-coloured fine-grained crinoidal limestone, has been extensively used as a decorative and a building stone. It was beloved and extensively used by monumental masons and by artists. Barbara Hepworth's *Image* (1951-1952) is hewn from it as is Henry Moore's *Reclining Nude* (1937). A fine slab cross over five feet high (1.5 m) high and based on an early Celtic cross made of Hopton Wood Stone was erected at Heilbron, Orange River, South Africa. The stone has been used extensively in many public buildings including the Town Hall, Manchester, the Municipal Buildings, Leeds, St George's Hall, Liverpool and Chatsworth House, Derbyshire. It was also used for the paving of the river terrace of the Palace of Westminster, London and of the Bank of England in London. The fragments of crinoids appear as scattered darker spots within the compact fine-grained stone. This characteristic led to its use for headstones and this stone was one chosen by the War Graves Commission for military cemeteries of the First World War. In the past it was also used for kerbs and setts. Hadene Stone, quarried close to Hopton Wood is from the same geological formation and is visually indistinguishable.

Penmon Limestone from Penmon, Beaumaris, Anglesey is pale brown with darker veins and patches, blue-grey or grey-white in colour and is a close-grained, compact limestone. It is widely known as Penmon 'Marble'. It was used for Beaumaris Castle, and by the Mersey Dock and Harbour Board. It was also used for Edward I's spectacular Caernarfon Castle, Gwynedd, where it is banded with local Carboniferous brown sandstone to resemble the fifth-century walls of Constantinople.

In the past, many other stones were taken from the Carboniferous Limestone. Derby Black or Ashford Black warrants special mention. Near Ashford-in-the-Water, Derbyshire, beds of limestone never more than 2 feet thick (0.6 m) interspersed with shale partings outcrop over an area of about four square miles (10 square km). These limestone beds are very dark grey to black in colour, very fine-grained, somewhat muddy and, importantly, commonly unfossiliferous, although some beds are crowded with fossils. The stone will take a high polish. The stone was wrought mainly from underground and an industry which is now 'dead and almost forgotten'[33] was based on it. It provided stone used for 'chimney-pieces to table tops, from vases to jewellery, and from statuary to church flooring. At least one highly-polished slab was used as a mirror'.[33] The Derby Inlay Work (*see Figure 4.44*), or *pietra dura* was also based on it. The earliest recorded use is prehistoric; a skeleton was found with its skull adhering to a 2 foot long, 9 inches wide, 6 inches thick (0.6 × 0.2 × 0.15 m) dressed slab.[33] Hardwick Hall, Derbyshire has fireplaces of Derby Black; Chatsworth House, Derbyshire used much of the stone for decoration and structural work. In addition, quantities were

Figure 4.44 A magnificent example of the renowned Derby inlay work shows various coloured stones inlaid into a block of black Carboniferous Limestone (Derby Black 'marble'). (Courtesy of E.A. Jobbins)

'sold rough to other workers for finishing'.[33] Because of its uniform black colour, its fine-grain and its ability to take a high polish '... it is popular, preferred by many sculptors and marble workers to the Black Marbles of Ireland and Belgium'.[33] It is possible that this black 'marble' is more widespread than is commonly recognized. There were three black 'marble' producing areas: Ireland, Belgium and Derbyshire.

In Ireland the Carboniferous Limestone has an outcrop area about three times that of the United Kingdom and important black 'marbles' are taken from it, principally in Galway, Kildare, Kilkenny and Limerick. The local black Galway 'Marble' may be seen in the Cathedral of Galway and was 'used by Sir Christopher Wren in 1700 for the staircases of Kensington Palace'.[32] Kildare Black seems to have been used for little else than local walls and small buildings. Kilkenny's famous black and white 'marble' was used to face many buildings in Kilkenny. The white colour is due to veins of calcite and the sections of fossils. Kilkenny Black is well known from its use in 1872 to replace earlier Blue Lias columns on the west front of Wells Cathedral, Somerset. It has also been used for a fireplace in the White Swan Tavern, Chestertown, Maryland, USA, which was recently restored (1981) with the same stone. The walls of Limerick are 'of marble blocks...'.[34] In general all these varieties show white patches caused by fossil fragments or, occasionally, by larger, nearly complete fossils. Irish Black Marble appears to have been widely used during Victorian times.

Belgium has been and still is one of the world's leading producing countries of 'marble'. The industry dates back to the twelfth and thirteenth centuries. It should be remembered, however, that much stone was imported into Belgium, processed and then exported. Therefore, a reference to a stone being from Belgium may be misleading. Black coloured stone has been taken from the Carboniferous Limestone around Tournai since very early times. It has been imported into England since at least the twelfth century. Normally referred to as Tournai 'Marble', the stone is known to have been used for archaeologically and artistically significant fonts and for memorial slabs. Seven important Norman fonts of Tournai 'Marble' are known in Great Britain. They are at the Church of St Peter in St Mary Bourne, Hampshire, the Church of All Saints, East Meon, Hampshire, the Church of St Michael, Southampton, Hampshire, Winchester Cathedral, Hampshire, the Church of St Lawrence, Thornton Curtis, Humberside, Lincoln Cathedral and the Church of St Peter's, Ipswich, Suffolk. There seems little doubt that these fonts were fashioned in Belgium and imported into England in their finished state. To reach some of the churches the fonts must have been laboriously hauled overland for many miles. Undoubted memorial slabs made of Tournai 'Marble' also are known; Bishop Nigel's tomb slab in Ely Cathedral, Cambridgeshire is one example (*Figure 4.45*).

Figure 4.45 Tournai Marble, a black stone from the Carboniferous Limestone of Belgium, acquired ecclesiastical significance in Britain. It was used for memorial slabs, such as that of Bishop Nigel, Ely Cathedral (a), and for fonts, such as that in the church of St Michael, Southampton (b)

There is, however, no unique test which will distinguish between the black limestones of Carboniferous Limestone age from Derby, Ireland and Belgium although the Irish Black commonly is speckled with fine white spots. It is possible that the study of the microfossils in a thin section may determine the provenance of a specimen, but any given section may not contain the microfossils on which a determination can be based. The study of a thin section implies that a sample must be removed from the object under investigation which may not be practicable. Purely visual inspection of black 'marble' does not enable the varieties to be distinguished. Carboniferous black 'marble' is sometimes confused with a black limestone of Devonian age. 'Plymouth Black marble forms the dark columns in the pulpit of St Paul's Cathedral, ...'[12], 'Derby Black ... probably occurs in many houses and churches'[12]; '... Thin black slab ... probably came from Tournai ...'[35] are extracts which point up the difficulty. The definite attribution of a black 'marble' is better based on archival or other written evidence. Black 'marble' was not commonly used by the Romans. Two Greek quarries were well known, one in Laconia and one on Lesbos. Other black stones were reported from Varro in Africa, Gaul (France) and Algeria. The Carboniferous Limestone of Ireland also yields other 'marbles.' The best known are Armagh Red and Cork Red (Victoria Red). They are partially recrystallized and red-stained, probably with hematite. Occasional crinoid ossicles may be present. Large quantities of both Armagh and Cork Red were used for mantelpieces and other decorative work. Armagh Red was used for the Armagh Catholic Cathedral (1873) and for some columns in St John's College Chapel, Cambridge (1869).[32] Cork Red may be found in the Exchange, Liverpool and the Exchange, Manchester. The red columns of the pulpit in St Paul's Cathedral, London (1861) were made of Cork Red.

Permian limestones

The Permian System includes marls, sandstones, conglomerates and limestones. One of the Permian limestones, the Magnesian Limestone, has been the source of many excellent and famous building stones and the cause of great controversy and of the appointment of a Committee of Parliament.

The story of the choice of Magnesian Limestone from the Bolsover Moor Quarry for the Palace of Westminster (the Houses of Parliament) in 1839, the substitution of indiscriminately selected Anston Stone and its subsequent deterioration is well known. (See for example, references 10 and 12.) The account given here is based mostly on Elsden and Howe[12]. Following the destruction of the Palace of Westminster by fire in 1834, a Commission of Parliament was set up to select a suitable building stone. The stone chosen was Magnesian Limestone from Bolsover Moor Quarry, Derbyshire. It was later discovered that the quarry could not supply blocks of stone of the size required. Another quarry, Mansfield Woodhouse Quarry, Nottinghamshire, also in Magnesian Limestone was also unable to supply the stone in the sizes required. However Mansfield Woodhouse Quarry did supply 20 000 cubic foot which was used and 'has since been found to have worn well'. Anston Stone from Kiveton Quarries near Sheffield, Yorkshire, only eight miles from the Bolsover Moor Quarry, was substituted. 'The Anston quarries ... were worked indiscriminately from the surface to the bottom of the formation to a depth of 35 ft., the stone lying in 17 beds varying in thickness from 1 ft. to a few inches ... The whole of the beds were used, no particular beds were followed horizontally, no supervision at the quarries was provided for, and no seasoning of the stones took place ... The whole building, except the upper part of the towers and the front towards Abingdon street, was done with Anston stone. It cannot be denied that a great part of the Anston stone was of the first quality ... It is thus perfectly clear that the Commissioners' choice was not so much at fault as the supervision of the quarrying and the selection of the stone. The services of an expert were actually offered, for the modest salary of £150 per annum, to exercise supervision over the quarrying and delivery of the stone, but this offer came to nothing, because it could not be agreed who was to be responsible for the payment of this trifling amount ... the blocks used ... were selected by masons indiscriminately ... and no particular care was taken to mark the bedding, so that a great many stones were surbedded, an example of unpardonable slackness'.

In marked contrast, when the Museum of Practical Geology was built (1837–1848) in Jermyn Street, London, Sir Henry De la Beche, then Director of the Geological Survey and of the Museum, personally selected blocks of Anston Stone to be used in the building. When the Museum was demolished nearly one hundred years later in 1935, the stone was reckoned to be as good as new (*see Figure 4.46*). The Geological Museum has now been administratively transferred to the British Museum (Natural History) in Cromwell Road, South Kensington, London.

The Magnesian Limestone consists of upper and lower limestones separated by beds of marl. It crops out in a strip, rarely six miles (9.65 km) wide, from Nottingham, through Mansfield and Tadcaster to Darlington where it widens to the coast at Hartlepool, Sunderland and South Shields. The best building stones come from the lower limestones. They differ greatly from place to place.

Bolsover Moor Stone, from quarries on the moor, Derbyshire, a warm yellowish-brown, fine-grained dolomitic limestone was used for Southwell Cathedral, Lincoln Cathedral and Bolsover Castle, Derbyshire but not for the Palace of Westminster in London. Anston Stone, from Kiveton Quarries near Sheffield, Yorkshire, is pale brown to cream in colour, compact and fine-grained and was used to

(a)

(c)

(b)

(d)

Figure 4.46 Much Magnesian Limestone was used in York where it was known generally as Tadcaster Stone. It was used appropriately, for the City Gate, Tadcaster Road (a). (b) The Anston Stone entrance door of the Museum of Practical Geology (now the Geological Museum in South Kensington), opened in 1851 in Jermyn Street, was 'as good as new' when the building was demolished in 1935; (c) Bolsover Castle is of Bolsover Moor Stone, the stone originally chosen for the Palace of Westminster; (d) Roche Abbey is of stone taken from the Magnesian Limestone which crops out nearby. (Photo (b) courtesy British Museum (Natural History))

restore some flying buttresses of Westminster Abbey, London in 1847. The new (1851) Record Office, Fetter Lane also was built of this stone with limestone from Babbacombe, Devon and Kentish Ragstone. Anston Stone was used as recently as 1967 for repair work on the Palace of Westminster.

Mansfield Woodhouse Stone, Nottinghamshire is yellowish-brown in colour, somewhat crystalline and generally fairly coarse and granular in nature, although some of the stone is very fine-grained. It was used for paving in Westminster Hall, London and for the Martyrs' Memorial, Oxford.

Stone from Parliament Quarry on the west side of Common Lane, Mansfield Woodhouse is reputed to be that used for the Palace of Westminster. Huddleston Stone, from Yorkshire, is minutely cellular (micro-oolitic) or finely granular and pale grey to cream coloured. It was used widely and may be seen in York Minster, Selby Cathedral and Huddleston Hall. It was teamed with Red Mansfield Stone, a dolomitic sandstone, for the original Eleanor Cross, Charing Cross, London.

The famous Eleanor or Norman crosses were erected after 1290 by Edward I on his way to

Westminster with the body of his wife Eleanor of Castile. He erected a memorial cross at each place where his wife's body rested for a night. There were originally ten or more built. Those at Geddington (1291–1294) and Hardingstone, south of Northampton (*c.* 1295) are restored originals. They are made of Weldon Stone. Only a stump remains at Waltham, which was the last cross before London. The cross at Charing was destroyed in the seventeenth century. The present cross in the courtyard of Charing Cross railway station is a Victorian copy.

Roche Abbey Stone, from Roche Abbey, Yorkshire, which is white coloured, granular and sugary-looking, shows another variety of the Magnesian Limestone. Apart from Roche Abbey itself, the stone was used for Tickhill Castle, Yorkshire, which was licensed by Richard Lionheart and ruined by Cromwell, for Tickhill Church with its outstanding 124 foot (38 m) tower, and for many other churches in the area.

Tadcaster Stone was quarried to the west of Tadcaster, Yorkshire. It was used there for local building and transported to York to build the Minster. The well-known quarries of Jackdaw Crag and Lords and Smaws supplied stone for many important buildings including York Minster, Ripon Minster, Beverley Minster (Humberside) and many other churches.

It is a testimony to the Magnesian Limestone, which commonly has been noted to wear and weather well (although some did weather badly), that for the recent restoration of York Minster, Huddleston Quarry near Sherburn-in-Elmet, Yorkshire, which dates back to Roman times, was reopened.

The close correlation between building stone and geology may be especially observed from the use of the Magnesian Limestone. Many towns and most villages along and near the outcrop of the limestone are built of stone taken from it. The Romans and the Normans used it extensively.

Jurassic limestones

The Jurassic System has probably furnished more important, more enduring and more widely used limestones than any other system. Taken as a whole the Jurassic rocks are clays, shales, sands, sandstones with some ironstones and subordinate limestones (see *Figure 4.47*). Many of the limestones are markedly oolitic in character. As seen on p. 88, an oolite (properly an oolitic limestone) is a particular type of limestone. But the word is also used as part of the name of some specific formations, for example the Great Oolite, and the Inferior Oolite which have oolites as a major component. Many writers use the terms Lower, Middle and Upper Oolites as divisions of the Jurassic. This can cause confusion. Here the Jurassic section is divided simply into the Lias (lower Jurassic) and Oolites (middle and upper Jurassic).

Liassic limestones

The Lias formation consists mainly of clays with predominantly thin-bedded limestones in the lower part which provide hydraulic limestones in the south Midlands. There is a general tendency for the Lias to be more calcareous in the south of Britain and sandier in the north, where sandstones and oolitic ironstones may be found. The White Lias is a white to cream calcite-mudstone or rather impure limestone. It provides a dramatic example of a stone which although it has a very restricted outcrop, influences architecture both for style and appearance.

The allotment of the White Lias to the topmost beds of the Triassic System or to the bottommost of the Lias formation of the Jurassic is a matter of geological discussion. They are here assigned to the Lias, following the British Geological Survey usage.

Around Radstock, Somerset, the White Lias, a series of white, cream to pale-grey fine-grained limestones and calcite-mudstones, reaches 20 feet (6 m) in thickness. In that area it has been quarried for building stone on a large scale and its architectural effect is immediately obvious when entering Radstock (*Figure 4.48*). It has limited use elsewhere, for example as pinnacles between shafts of Blue Lias on tombs in the church at Curry Rivel, Somerset[35]; for small carvings in the voussoirs of the main West Door, Wells Cathedral[35] (*Figure 4.49*) and for rough building near Castle Cary, Somerset. The lowest part of the Lias, particularly in southern England, consists mainly of clays and marls with prominent thin-bedded limestones which are widely known as the Blue Lias. The limestones have been extensively used where they crop out for building and for ecclesiastical work, notably for instance, in some detached shafts, bases and capitals in Bristol Cathedral and for some shafts in the entrance porch of its near neighbour, the church of St Mary Radcliffe. Blue Lias was also used for shafts flanking the doorway at Wells Cathedral, and for shafts of the blank wall arcading in Exeter Cathedral[36], which is some way from its source. It has also been extensively used for paving slabs, kerbs and for tombs. The tomb in Wells Cathedral of Bishop Button II (died 1274), thought to be the earliest incised tomb in England, is a slab of Blue Lias. Blue Lias was also used for paving in both Wells Cathedral and in the Palace of Westminster. Kerbstones of the limestone may be seen at Chickerell and Lyme Regis, Dorset, and in many other towns and cities. As Donovan and Reid remarked[35] 'the stone commonly is misdescribed as Purbeck'.

Banked-up against the Carboniferous Limestone

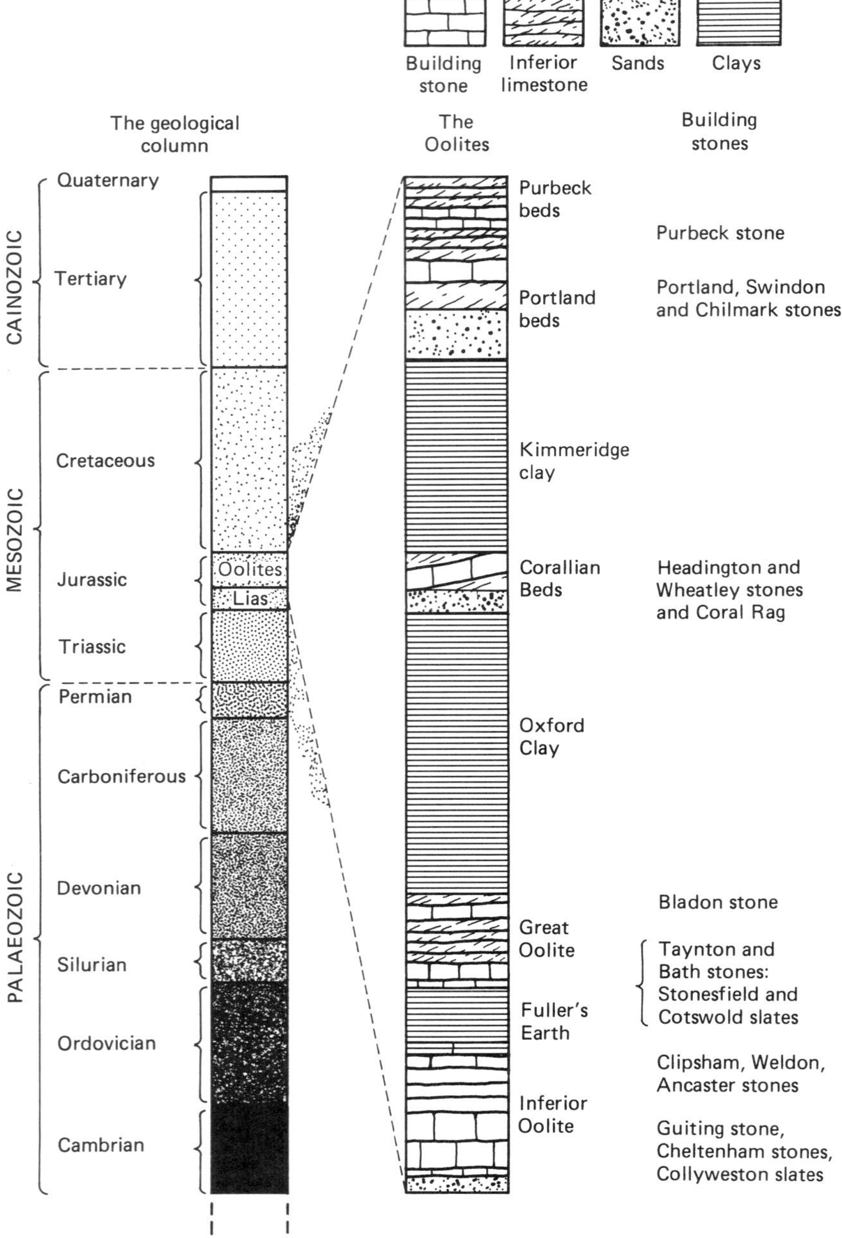

Figure 4.47 The generalized succession of the Jurassic rocks, together with the names of some of the building stones quarried from the major horizons. (After W.J. Arkell, *Oxford Stone*, Faber and Faber, London, 1947)

Figure 4.48 The direct relationship between geology and architectural appearance of buildings is demonstrated at Radstock, Somerset where the light coloured White Lias directly influences the street scene

Figure 4.49 White Lias was used for the small figures, mostly now decapitated, on the West Door of Wells Cathedral, Somerset

Figure 4.50 Much Blue Lias was used for the chapter house of Llandaff Cathedral, near Cardiff. Sutton Stone, Dundry Stone, Coombe Down, Clipsham, Doulting, Beer, and Hornton Stone may also be found, with a roof of 'Westmorland Green' slate. Other stones have been used also and Caen Stone was used for some memorials and detailing. Few, if any, cathedrals are exclusively of one stone, the different stones commonly indicating building periods

which makes up the Mendips, the Lower Lias appears as a pale cream-grey, coarse-grained limestone composed mainly of comminuted shell matter. At one time the Lias was quarried near Shepton Mallet, Somerset as Downside Stone. It was used for buildings in Shepton Mallet, in Wells Cathedral and for Nunney Castle, Somerset. A similar stone, also from the Lower Lias, was formerly quarried on the north side of the Mendips near Downside, south of Bristol. It was known as Brockley Down Stone or Bastard Downside.

Sutton Stone, quarried near Bridgend, West Glamorgan is a massive whitish somewhat conglomeratic limestone which contains occasional large boulders of the underlying Carboniferous Limestone. Like Downside Stone it is a littoral (near shore) deposit of the Lower Lias. It was used in Llandaff Cathedral.

An important limestone from the middle part of the Lias is Hornton Stone which was quarried at Edge Hill near Banbury, Oxfordshire. The colour may be blue-grey or brown with a greenish tint which is sometimes described as sage green. It crops out over the plateau area south of Edge Hill, capping the Burton Dassett or Little Bourton ridge. Lenticles of highly calcareous stone reach 1 to 2 feet (0.3-0.6 m) in thickness and may extend several yards. They commonly contain pockets or colonies of brachiopods. In the vicinity of Edge Hill the stone has been used for building and ornamental purposes (*Figure 4.51*). Further south, because of its ferruginous content, it has been exploited as a low grade

Figure 4.51 House of Hornton Stone (by Forsyth Lawson) with Painswick Stone dressings and Stonesfield slate roof. (Courtesy of J. Forsyth Lawson)

Figure 4.53 Unusually used in London, Ham Hill Stone from Somerset is found in Hampshire House, Bayswater Road

Figure 4.52 Memorial figure 1945–46 by Henry Moore, carved in Hornton Stone, Dartington Hall, Devon

calcareous iron ore. The best building stone is the least oxidized because it breaks into large blocks up to several tons in weight. The stone was often used by the sculptor Henry Moore, for example for the *Memorial Figure* at Dartington Hall, Devon. It was also used for his *Mother and Child* (1924), *Reclining Figure* (1947), *Square Form* (1936) and other pieces (*Figure 4.52*). Hornton Stone was used for the reredos of Ampleforth Abbey Church, Yorkshire, in the church at Harold Wood, Essex, the War Memorial, Staff College, Camberley, Surrey, the Moat House Hotel, Stratford-on-Avon, Warwickshire (where fine nests of Terebratulids can be seen in the stone), and elsewhere. This popular stone was used far more widely than is generally realized. The thirteenth century church at Hornton, Oxfordshire is a prime example of the use of the greenish brown variety.

Ham Hill Stone, from the upper part of the Lias, quarried at Hamdon Hill, near Norton-sub-Hamdon, Somerset, is a lenticular mass of detrital shelly limestone about 90 feet (27 m) thick although only about 50 feet (15 m) is worked for building stone. It has been worked at least since Roman times and some Roman coffins are made of it. A richly-toned brown in colour, it consists mostly of broken fossil shells with a ferruginous cement. Although the formation may be more or less sandy in places, the stone is correctly classified as a limestone, rather than a sandstone. Two beds were worked in particular. One was pale brown or buff in colour and known as the Yellow Bed. The second was darker in colour and known as the Grey Bed. It is a durable building stone which is most widely known for its use for the classic masterpiece, Montacute House, Somerset built in 1603. It was used also for Sherborne Abbey, Dorset. The window arches, quoins and coping stones of the west front, and the turrets of the tower, which are contrasted with a grey-coloured Devonian limestone, of Buckfast Abbey, Devon, are of Ham Hill Stone. Hampshire House, Bayswater Road, London (*Figure 4.53*) and the Ladbroke building, Piccadilly, London, are also of this stone. Its use was also extended to vernacular architecture, as seen unexpectedly in Hamstone House, Weybridge, Surrey. The outcrop of the stone extends southwards from Hamdon Hill to North Perrott, Dorset where it was wrought under the local name of North Perrott Stone.

Middle and Upper Jurassic limestones

Without doubt the limestones obtained from the series of Beds above the Lias (see *Figure 4.47*) have had a greater effect on the general appearance of towns, especially in southern England, than any other stones. Clay is the major constituent of the beds above the Lias and is of great importance for the production of bricks. However, the limestone members, primarily because of their ease of working and general consistency, have been extensively used especially in southern England. One of these, the Portland Stone, has been used country-wide.

The limestones crop out over a large sweeping curve from the Dorset coast, through the Cotswolds where they form a prominent escarpment. The outcrop continues in a wide band through Oxfordshire and Northamptonshire, and forms a very narrow band north of the River Humber to sweep round to the coast near Redcar.

These Middle and Upper Jurassic limestones are generally oolitic in nature, but there are important exceptions. However, because the name 'oolite' is so familiar many of the important non-oolitic limestones are incorrectly referred to as oolites.

One of the important non-oolitic beds occurs at the bottom of the Lincolnshire Limestone, a unit within the Inferior Oolite. Inferior Oolite is the geological name for a formation which is found stratigraphically below the Great Oolite (*Figure 4.47*). It *does not* indicate that the stone is inferior in quality.

Around the village of Collyweston, Northamptonshire a sandy fissile limestone occurs at the base of the Lincolnshire Limestone. The fissile character is localized; in some directions the bed is found to become non-fissile. The bed varies in thickness. It is commonly 6 inches (15 cm) thick, but swells rarely to 3 or to 4 feet (0.8-1.2 m). The stone is wrought by removing sand (the Northamptonshire Sand) from beneath it and supporting the stone with wooden props. When the bed has been undercut, the props are knocked away and the limestone falls as large blocks known as 'logs'. From time to time the fall must be assisted by inserting wedges. The 'logs' are laid in the open with the bedding planes horizontal, and are kept liberally soaked with water, especially on the edges until frost is imminent. At that time the laid-out slabs are almost swamped with water. On freezing all of the 'logs' become a mass of ice. Under ideal conditions there should be a hard frost at night followed by a slow thaw during the day to 'move' the stone. Under those conditions water enters the bedding planes. When the next frost occurs further splitting takes place. After 'frosting' the stone may be 'clived' or split along the bedding planes. Once clived, the thin slabs are dressed for use and sold as Collyweston Slates, for use as tilestones (*Figure 4.54*).

(a)

(c)

(b)

Figure 4.54 When frost is forecast, horizontally laid 'logs' of Collyweston Slate are soaked with water (a). (b) After freezing the slabs may be split. This is known in Collyweston as 'cliving'. The split slabs are used as tilestones and may be seen extensively in Collyweston, where local oolitic limestone has been used for the houses (c). Note the obtrusive and unpleasant use of 'artificial stone' quoins seen behind an equally obtrusive electricity pole!

It is still widely believed that if the stone is not kept watered before frosting and is allowed to dry out it loses its fissile character. During mild winters the stone was sometimes taken back underground, covered with the dug-out sand, and the drift-mine sealed to prevent the 'logs' drying out. However, Honeyborne[37] demonstrated as long ago as 1975 that it was possible to get moisture back into a dried-out stone. If the moisture is re-introduced the 'logs' once again are susceptible to frost.

The stone commonly is bluish in colour but weathers to a familiar buff-colour. In the past the 'slates' were hung on wooden pegs; more recently nails were used. The size of the hole may be used as an indication of the age of use of the 'slate'.

Collyweston slates have been used since Roman times and are widely used for roofing in their own area. These tilestones may also be seen on Guildhall, London. They cover the roofs of a number of colleges at Cambridge including the First Court of Christ's College (1505–*c.*1511), and Caius Court of Gonville and Caius College (1565–1569). They were also used elsewhere[38], for example on Oakham Castle (1383) and on Phipps Mansion (1906), Westberry, Long Island, New York, USA. Over an acre of Collyweston slates cover the roof of the Haycock Hotel, Wansford-in-England, Peterborough.

Other historically important stones taken from the Inferior Oolites are also not markedly oolitic. Dundry Stone was worked from mines and quarries at Dundry Hill, south of Bristol, where traces of ancient workings may be seen. The old quarries were at the highest point of the hill just west of the village. The freestone is approximately 15 feet (4.6 m) thick, but the bed worked for building stone is only about six feet (1.8 m) thick. It overlies about 40 feet (12 m) of rag beds, which are stones which break with a ragged fracture and are not easily worked. The stone consists mostly of fragments of fossils. Fresh surfaces appear markedly granular and are commonly described as sugary. The stone was used for the great Gothic church of St Mary Redcliffe in Bristol, for St John's Church, Cardiff, in Llandaff Cathedral, and in several churches in the Republic of Ireland where its use may be traced along the waterways. An exceptional example of its use is in the Biconyll tomb (1448), Wells Cathedral. This is the only instance of its use in that Cathedral.

Doulting Stone, from Doulting near Shepton Mallet, Somerset is an exceptional pale-brown in colour and coarse-textured. It is described as a massive, granular, wedge-bedded bioclastic limestone in which fossils are uncommon.[39] Found on the south side of the Mendips, the building stone beds are about 45 feet thick (14 m) and only locally slightly oolitic. In places the character of the stone approaches that of the Lower Lias Downside Stone. Doulting Stone may have been formed, in part at least, by the erosion of the Downside Stone and other Lower Lias deposits.

In the past it was worked as two varieties; the Fine, Brown Bed or Brambleditch, and the Cheylinch (Chelynch), Grey or Weather Bed. The main example of the use of Doulting Stone is for Wells Cathedral (*Figure 4.55*). Elsewhere it has been used for restorations to Llandaff, Bristol and Exeter Cathedrals, for the interior nave and aisle of Guildford Cathedral, for the New (1898) Naval Barracks, Portsmouth, Hampshire, and as facings to some bridges on the M2 motorway.

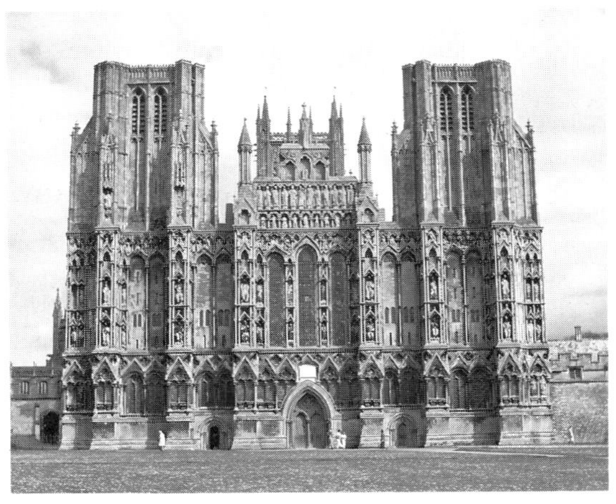

Figure 4.55 The bulk of the fabric of Wells Cathedral, Somerset is of Doulting Stone, a granular limestone of Inferior Oolite age. Many of the Blue Lias limestone columns were replaced with Kilkenny Black 'marble' taken from the Carboniferous Limestone, near Kilkenny, Ireland

The Inferior Oolite at one time supplied such vast quantities of stone from quarries along the scarp of the Cotswold Hills at such places as Birdlip Hill and Cleeve Hill, near Cheltenham that the general name Cheltenham Stone was used.

Near Cheltenham and Gloucester a part of the Inferior Oolite is named the Lower Freestone. It is a pale-coloured oolitic limestone, commonly tough and compact and, on the whole, sufficiently free from fossils for it to be used readily for both building and carving. The Building Freestone reaches 130 feet (39 m) in thickness at Leckhampton Hill. Stone from Leckhampton Hill was used for Regency Cheltenham and for The Cross, Gloucester. Similar Cheltenham Stone was used for Tewkesbury Abbey, Gloucester.

Guiting Stone, from Guiting, Gloucestershire, warm-brown to yellow (Yellow Guiting) or white-cream (White Guiting) in colour is a coarse fossiliferous oolite which has been used in the north

Cotswolds since Norman times. It is taken from roughly the same geological horizon as Cheltenham Stone. Stanway House (*c.*1630), Gloucestershire provides an outstanding example of its use. It may be seen also in Prinknash Abbey, Gloucestershire, the Royal Oxford Hotel, Oxford, and Abbey Bridge, Worcester.

Other Inferior Oolite stones, mostly named from where they are quarried, were also used outside their immediate area and thus achieved a wider renown. Painswick Stone, used for Gloucester Cathedral, is an example. Nailsworth Stone was widely used locally.

During Inferior Oolite times a basin of deposition ran northwards through Rutland, Lincolnshire and Northamptonshire, in which thick deposits were laid. Rocks deposited in this basin are known as the Lincolnshire Limestone. They crop out at Kettering and thicken rapidly northwards to reach a maximum of about 130 feet (39 m) at Sleaford. From here the deposit thins towards Market Weighton, and is recognizable north of the River Humber as the Cave Oolite which is 38 feet (12 m) thick.

The Lincolnshire Limestone is divided into two parts, with the upper beds resting on an eroded and channelled surface of the lower beds. These features strongly resemble modern carbonate deposits in shallow seas and the channels were probably formed under water by currents on the shoals of ooliths.

The Lincolnshire Limestone is not a homogeneous deposit, either vertically or laterally. The building stone is wrought mainly from the Upper Lincolnshire Limestone. Because the section exposed in any one quarry may vary considerably both laterally and vertically stone from one quarry may often resemble stone from another. The practised eye, however, may be able to distinguish the stone taken from the different quarries.

Without doubt, Barnack Stone, no longer obtainable, from Barnack, near Stamford, Lincolnshire, is the classic stone taken from the Lincolnshire Limestone. Coarse-textured and shelly, this stone was so highly regarded that the Abbots of Peterborough maintained quarrying rights on it. It was one of the earliest of the stones worked from this formation, which was known to have been quarried from at least the Roman period until the fifteenth century, when it seems to have been worked out.

Barnack Stone was used for Peterborough Cathedral and is particularly known for its use for Ely Cathedral (*Figure 4.56*). It was identified as the stone of the Losinga statue in Norwich Cathedral and the Romans re-used large blocks of it for the recently discovered (1976) river wall along the Thames. Burghley House, Cambridgeshire (formerly Huntingdonshire) is built of it.

Ancaster Stone from near Grantham, Lincolnshire varies within the quarry, as do most stones. Two main varieties may be distinguished; a cream-buff

Figure 4.56 The magnificent Prior's Door, Ely Cathedral is a magnificent testament to the enduring qualities of Barnack Stone

coloured oolite, usually fine grained, but with some slightly coarser beds with broken fossil matter; and a coarse shelly variety with a large amount of crystalline calcite, known as the Ancaster Rag. Ancaster Stone may be locally rich in small, rolled gastropods and may be pisolitic.

Ancaster Stone was used for part of Lincoln Cathedral, for numerous mansions and churches in Lincolnshire, and in the Town Hall, Holborn, London. It was also used for some Cambridge colleges including the Chapel, St John's; Tree Court, Gonville and Caius; and Trinity Hall.

Casterton Stone, also called Stamford Stone, from near Stamford, Lincolnshire, is beige-coloured and somewhat coarser grained than others in this group. It was used for many buildings in Stamford, notably for its Town Hall. It was reputedly used for Pembroke and for Trinity College, Cambridge. Elsewhere it was used in Truro Cathedral, Cornwall, Oundle School, Northamptonshire, and the Post Office, Cambridge. At one time the stone was sold as

Stamford Grit. A compact, usually blue-hearted, sparsely oolitic variety, was smoothed, rather than polished, and sold as Stamford Marble.

Ketton Stone from Ketton, near Stamford, Lincolnshire is generally very pale cream to yellow-buff in colour, with some blocks a distinct pink. In some beds it is beautifully regular medium-grained oolite. Other beds, called Ketton Rag, are more heavily cemented with crystalline calcite and the ooliths are more variable. The Ketton oolite and Casterton Stone may be difficult to distinguish. A characteristic feature of Ketton Stone is the absence of crystalline calcite as a matrix. This is in marked contrast with other oolites from the Lincolnshire Limestone.

The fine Ketton oolite has been used in Downing College, Cambridge, where pink-coloured blocks are prominent (*Figures 4.57 and 4.58*), for repairs to the Palace of Westminster, in the City Hall, Norwich, for Cotterbrook Hall, Northamptonshire, and for Martins Bank, Coventry.

Clipsham Stone, from Clipsham, near Oakham, Leicestershire is a buff- to cream-coloured, medium-grained oolite with shell fragments. It is possibly the most widely known of the Lincolnshire Limestones because it was used in the past by the Romans. More recently it was used for restoration work on the Palace of Westminster and for the Berkeley Hotel, London. The London Stone, which, until 1960 was incorporated in the south wall of St Swithin's Church, Cannon Street, London is of Clipsham Stone. The London Stone is now set in a niche in the wall of the Bank of China on Cannon Street. The Stone has been in existence since at least 1198 when it was known as the Lonnenstane.

Many blocks of limestone, notably some blocks of Clipsham stone and other Jurassic limestones, are found to be blue-hearted. This means that the centre of the block is blue-grey in contrast to the buff-brown colour of the surrounding stone. Normally any iron minerals in sediments are oxidized and a brownish colour is seen in the subsequent rock. However, iron minerals in the reduced condition, which have been deposited in an oxygen-free environment, have a blue-grey colour. These blocks are commonly rejected as flawed, although they are thought by many masons to be more durable than the cream-coloured stone[40].

Figure 4.58 Ketton Stone, including some pink coloured blocks, used for the north (or 'Wrens') door during the rebuilding of the north-east corner of the north transept of Ely Cathedral in 1699, provides a strong and unpleasant contrast with the Barnack Stone used for much of the fabric. Although both stones are taken from the Lincolnshire Limestone, due regard must be paid to the colour and structure of the stone when restorations are carried out

Figure 4.57 The remarkably fine oolitic limestone from Ketton, Northamptonshire was used for Downing College, Cambridge. Blocks of pink stone are noticeable

Blocks of blue-hearted limestone are often not used because they are not homogeneous. However, Donovan Purcell deliberately used blue-hearted Clipsham Stone for replacement columns in the Galilee Porch of Ely Cathedral to provide a contrast and to avoid a dull uniform appearance.

Blue-hearted blocks of limestones, like all limestones, eventually weather to a grey-coloured surface.

Weldon Stone, from near Corby, Northamptonshire, is thought to have been used for the old, pre-Fire St Paul's Cathedral, London, although some authorities think that the imported Caen Stone was used. It is a pale-brown to buff-coloured, fine even-grained oolite with variable amounts of shell matter and an open texture. There are at least three varieties: Fine Bed, Coarse Bed, which is generally shelly and has voids, and Hard Rag, which occurs intermittently through the beds. The stone is said to be particularly resistant to frost. Blocks re-used in Roman times were found in the river wall, London. Kirby Hall, Northamptonshire provides an outstanding example of its use and many Cambridge colleges including Kings College Chapel, Cauis, Jesus, Clare Hall, and Sidney Sussex used the stone. Boughton House, Northamptonshire, and Rushton Hall, Northamptonshire testify to its popularity, as does the new building in the Market Place, Northampton.

The Cave Oolite is a well-cemented, compact oolitic limestone within the Lincolnshire Limestone. It has a considerable number of patches of a crystalline calcite, much of it in optical continuity, which cements ooliths of varying size. It crops out

(a)

(b)

(c)

(d)

Figure 4.59 (a) Weldon Stone from a quarry immediately behind was used for this delightful Quarry Master's House, near Corby, Lincolnshire; (b and c) Edge bedded Weldon Stone (pp.104, 120) has weathered badly at Kirby Hall, Northamptonshire; (d) The Eleanor Cross (p. 97), mostly of Weldon Stone, at Geddington, Northamptonshire, although much restored through the years is one of the two crosses which now remain substantially complete

from the River Humber through South Cave and Newbald. There it occurs as a considerable spread and was quarried on a large scale west of the village. It was used in Beverley Minster, Humberside where it was called Newbald Stone and Cave Marble. It was also used for interior work around Brough, for Holderness Monastery and for Hull Docks, all in Humberside.

Higher up in the Jurassic, the Great Oolite Series contains many well-known and widely used oolitic limestones. At the base of the Great Oolite Series is a thin-bedded fissile sandy limestone, remarkably similar in appearance to the Collyweston Slates at the base of the Inferior Oolite. These are the famous tilestones known as the Stonesfield Slates.

The Stonesfield Slates are light brown in colour and were formerly mined near Stonesfield, Oxfordshire. They were frosted in a similar manner to those from Collyweston. They appear to have been used since Roman times, but some authorities, for example Arkell in his book *Oxford Stone*[41] doubts whether the Romans discovered the 'frosting' process. Stonesfield Slates were once widely used in the Cotswolds. They are now unobtainable and old buildings are bought just to obtain the 'Slates' for re-use on new buildings. They are renowned for their use for the roofs of many of the colleges in Oxford. It is doubtful if many people could distinguish between a Stonesfield and a Collyweston Roof from ground level.

The name Stonesfield Slate should properly be restricted to the stone taken from the Stonesfield Slate horizon. These beds are thin and are restricted to a small area around the village of Stonesfield. Further afield similar stone of about the same horizon may be found along a line which extends roughly from Andoversford through Naunton to Stow-in-the-Wold. These 'Slates' are better known as Cotswold Slates and probably many identifications of Stonesfield Slate should be Cotswold Slate.

From place to place, naturally laminated beds occur in thicknesses which make them suitable for use as tilestones. They are commonly known as Presents.

(a)

(b)

Figure 4.60 The Stonesfield slate, geologically similar to Collyweston slate, was used widely around the village of Stonesfield, seen in (a) on Home Close, High Street; (b) a cottage outhouse roof of Stonesfield slate in Filkins, Oxfordshire is reputed to be 300 years old

Bath Stone

Bath Stone, the most famous of the stones wrought from the Great Oolite Series, was at one time quarried and mined on a large scale around Bath, Avon. The stone was named from the localities where it was quarried; for example, Stoke Ground, Winsley Ground, Westwood Ground, Box Ground (or St. Adhelm Stone) and Bradford Stone.

There is no unique characteristic which distinguishes one variety from another. It is possible, however, to group them into three distinct horizons (see *Figure 4.61* and *Table 4.1*). Coombe Down Stone has fine veins of crystalline calcite running through it, as does the equivalent stone to the east, Box Ground. The veins are a very good indicator, but not an absolutely unique characteristic of these varieties. Allen Howe[42] states that ' ... Coombe Down Stone ... is liable to contain thin veins of calcite and small iron-stains ...', while Arkell[41] maintains 'the test for Bath Stone in a building is the presence of fine vertical calcite veins. These are infallibly present in Box Ground Stone and are called "watermarks" by the Oxford masons ... They never run parallel to the bedding, and when they appear to do so in a building it is a sign that some of the blocks have been joint-bedded'.

Bath Stone has been used since Roman times; some Roman buildings, now nearly 2000 years old, are still in use. A fine example of the use of Bath Stone, and certainly the most easily seen, is Apsley House (The Wellington Museum) at Hyde Park Corner, London (*Figure 4.62*). It was originally built of brick and was

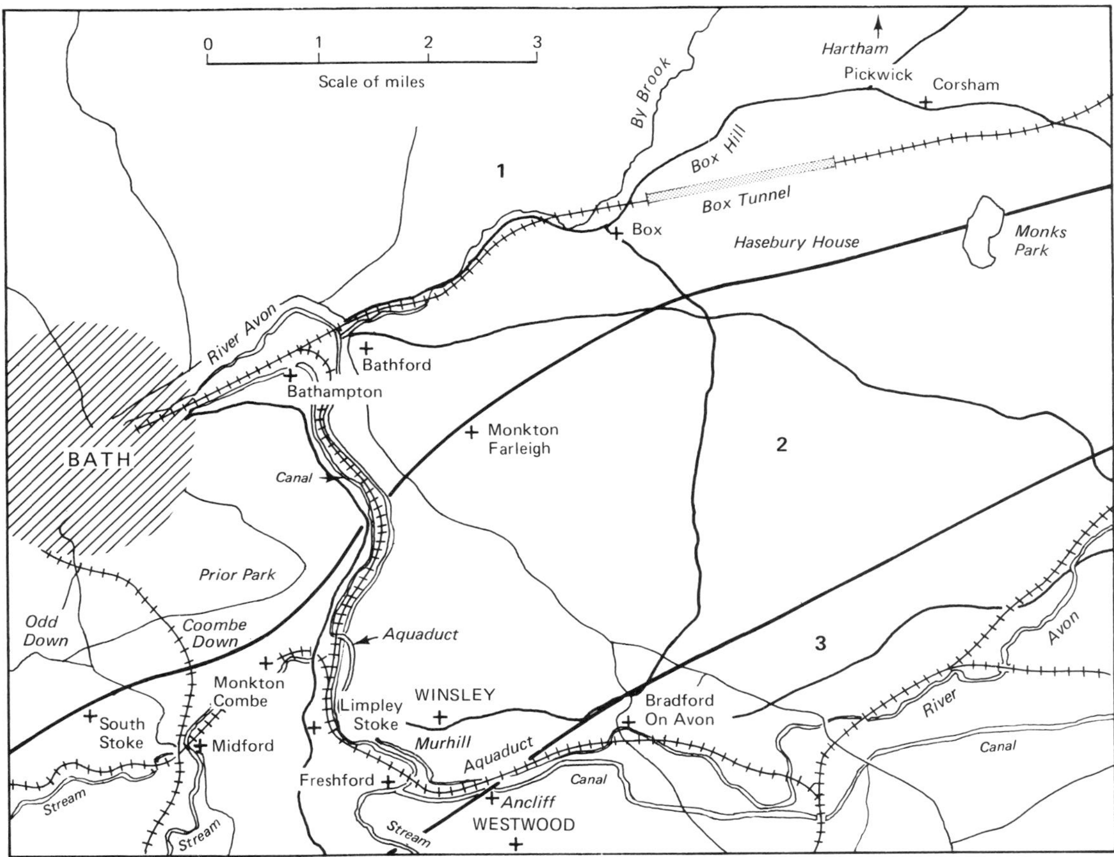

Figure 4.61 The lines on the map showing the principal Bath Stone Quarry locations separate the groupings shown in Table 4.1. (After W.J. Arkell, *Oxford Stone*, Faber and Faber, London, 1947)

Table 4.1 Characteristics of Bath Stone

Stratigraphic position	*Name of variety**	*Characteristics*
3: Higher than 2 stratigraphically	Bradford Stone	Characteristically of poor quality, very shelly with shells in well marked layers. markedly current bedded.
2: Upper	Farleigh Down Bathampton Down Winsley Ground Freshford Ground Stoke Ground Westwood Ground	Characteristically soft, not shelly (but there are rare large shells) and usually rather finely and evenly graded. Farleigh Down is typically brown, the others are paler.
Straddles levels 1 and 2	Monk's Park	Cement characteristically crystalline, paler and finer in grain than others.
1: Lower	Coombe Down Odd Down Box Ground (in Corsham-Box area)	Characteristically shelly/fragmental and medium grained.

*Many other local names have been used for different varieties of Bath Stone. It appears that the varieties Monk's Park, Ridge Down and Corsham Down were not widely used until the Box Railway Tunnel, near Bath, was built[43].

(a)

(c)

(b)

Figure 4.62 (a) Perhaps the most seen example, Apsley House ('No 1, Piccadilly') is clad, over brick, with Box Ground Stone variety of Bath Stone; (b) the minarets of the Royal Pavilion, Brighton. Originally of Bath Stone these were replaced with glass reinforced fibre, and are now being replaced again with Bath Stone; (c) Bradford Stone, a coarse, shelly variety of Bath Stone quarried at Bradford-on-Avon, Wiltshire, was used for the walls of this cottage in Bradford-on-Avon; finer grained Bath Stones form the quoins with Ham Hill Stone dressings

covered in 1828 with Box Ground Stone, shortly after it was presented by the grateful nation to the Duke of Wellington. An interesting contrast is seen between the Box Ground Stone of the house and the Portland Stone pillars supporting the railings. Monk's Park Stone was used for Salisbury House, London, the Polytechnic, Battersea, London, the Town Hall, Capetown, South Africa, and more recently for the Sun Alliance House, Bristol. Coombe Down Stone was used in the northern and western faces of Buckingham Palace, London and for restoration of Henry VII's Chapel, Westminster Abbey in about 1923.

Many other buildings in other cities are recorded as being built of one or another variety of Bath Stone, but it is difficult to distinguish the varieties when they are in a building. As Arkell wrote in *Oxford Stone*,[41] 'There are many varieties of Bath Stone and not even the experts can tell them apart'. Bath Stone (as a generic term) was used widely for dressings for churches. Many housing estates of the Victorians and later, employed the stone for window-sills and for copings to walls. For example, '... it has been used with excellent effect as dressings in red-brick residences on the Westbury Estate, Putney (London)'[12].

Cotswold Stone
Other oolitic limestones of Great Oolite age were formerly available on a wide scale from so many quarries in the Cotswolds that the general name Cotswold Stone was given to them. Care must be taken to distinguish them from the geologically older Cheltenham Stone of Inferior Oolite age.

Taynton Stone, quarried at Taynton, Oxfordshire, is one of the best known and earliest used of the Great Oolite stones. Brown in colour with paler brown streaks, it is coarse in texture and shelly. It is renowned for its use for the Wren church of St Stephen Walbrook in the City of London, and for the interior of St Paul's Cathedral, London. Stone for both of these buildings was supplied by Thomas Strong who had '... a reputation ... for being a progressive craftsman, expert to a degree rare among country-bred masons ... up-to-date in his methods capable of executing designs ... with intelligence and fidelity'[44]. The stone was also used for some early Oxford Colleges, including Magdalen, Merton and St John's, and for Eton College (1448–1450). It was also spectacularly used for most of Blenheim Palace in Oxfordshire. A similar type of stone was quarried at Minchinhampton, Gloucestershire.

Although unrecognized for many years, Alwalton 'marble' has now been identified as the stone of the columns in the entrance porch of Peterborough Cathedral. It was also used for some of the columns in the Galilee Porch of Ely Cathedral and in the lowest storey of St Hugh's Choir, Lincoln Cathedral.[38]

The stone is an extremely oyster-rich limestone from the Great Oolite. It crops out as a tough blue-grey bed along the Alwalton Lynch on the banks of the River Nene at Alwalton near Peterborough, Northamptonshire. The 'marble' polishes to an interesting, attractive and distinctive surface which is commonly recorded as Purbeck 'marble', although it is, in fact, quite different. The 'marble' was certainly known to and used by the Romans at nearby Castor. The Abbey of Peterborough held the workings.

The recumbent effigy of Abbot Benedict (1177–1193) in Peterborough Cathedral is made of Alwalton 'marble'. The twelfth century font is also a fine specimen. The font is supported on pillars and a base made of Purbeck 'marble', and the difference

Figure 4.63 New Purbeck 'marble' columns (front) with drums placed 'in bed', with original Alwalton 'marble' columns (rear) in Galilee Porch, Ely Cathedral

Figure 4.64 Alwalton 'marble' was wrought from a thin bed exposed in the banks of the River Nene, at Alwalton Lynch, Northamptonshire, where fallen blocks may still be found

(a)

(c)

(e)

(b)

(d)

(f)

(g)

Figure 4.65 (a) The thick bedding and widely spaced joints of Portland Stone are seen in the cliffs at Portland Bill, Dorset; (b) Portland Roach clads the Economist Building, St James's Street, London. It may contain masses of the fossilized alga *Solenopora* (c); (d) Portland Stone slabs are used to remarkable effect on the domes of the Victoria and Albert Museum, South Kensington, London; (e) the characteristic black and white weathering found on Portland Stone, particularly in polluted atmosphere, may lead to distressing patterns. Architectural detailing should ensure that rain water does not flow across surfaces; (f) the copy of The Magna Carta, presented by Great Britain to the United States of America on its Bicentennial, rests on a slab of gneiss from Ardivachar Point, North Uist (the oldest rock in Great Britain), which in turn rests on a slab of Portland Stone; (g) the colour difference, accentuated by weathering, is displayed in Lloyds Bank, Stamford, Lincolnshire which used Portland Stone, bottom storey, Bath Stone above and Portland Stone, uppermost storey

between the two stones may be easily seen. Similar stones have been worked as Raunds Marble north-east of Northampton and as Stanwick Ragstone near Higham Ferrers near Raunds.

Portland stone

Towards the top of the Jurassic another important oolitic limestone, the Portland Stone, is found. The Portland Beds, from which stone is taken for building, form the tilted tableland of the Isle of Portland, the two arms of Lulworth Cove, Dorset and the cliffs of the Isle of Purbeck. The Portland Stone beds are remarkably well jointed.

The stone is a fine- and even-grained oolite and may be so fine-grained that it is sometimes difficult to see that the stone is oolitic in structure. A very pure limestone, it is about 95 per cent calcium carbonate. When first quarried the stone is warm cream in colour. However, particularly when used in smoke-polluted atmospheres, it weathers to a characteristic black and white colour. The sheltered side is blackened and a skin of calcium sulphate develops underneath.

The various beds of the Portland Stone series differ in character and in thickness. The building and quarry trade names of Base Bed or Best Bed, Whitbed and Roach are generally applicable to types of stone rather than to precise geological horizons.

A typical generalized section through the Portland Stone series is:

Strati-graphic level	*Bed name*	*Thickness*
Top	Roach	3 feet (0.9 m) or more
	Whit Bed	7 to 15 Feet (2–4.6 m)
	Flinty Bed	2 feet (0.6 m)
	Curf	0 to 4 feet (0–1.2 m)
	Little Roach or Base Bed Roach	0 to 3 feet (0–0.9 m), notably impersistent
	Base Bed or Best Bed	5 to 10 feet (1.5–3 m)
Base	Chert Beds	60 to 70 feet (18–21 m)

Not all of the beds are necessarily present in any one quarry and the beds may vary greatly within limited areas.[45] If the Flinty Bed and Curf are present, the Whit Bed and Base Bed may easily be differentiated. If they are absent it may not be possible to distinguish between the two. Base Bed Roach may be replaced by fine oolite. Veins of calcite, called Snailcreep, may be found running through the stone. Snailcreep is similar to the watermarks seen in Bath Stone.

Roach is normally found at the top of the Portland Stone series. It is a cream-coloured oolitic limestone, honeycombed by mostly empty moulds of fossils. In some of these moulds the internal casts of shells may remain. In particular, internal casts of lamellibranchs (*Trigonia*) are known locally as 'orses 'eads. Internal casts of gastropods (*Aptyxiella*) are known as Portland Screws. The term roach has been applied to a number of different rocks in various parts of the country. It has been used for a conglomerate and the Old Red Sandstone in the Lake District, for rock in the Coal Measures of Staffordshire and for other rocks elsewhere. To be unambiguous the particular roach should be specified, for example Portland Roach.

The Portland Roach, not widely used before 1939, has, since the end of the 1939 to 1945 war, been increasingly used for its decorative appearance. It has been used to great effect in The Economist Building, St James's Street, London, for the Commercial Union House, Birmingham; and recently (1982) for Finwell House, Finsbury Square, London. The French Lieutenant met his woman on blocks of Portland Roach making up The Cobb at Lyme Regis, Dorset.

The Canadian Pacific building, in Finsbury Square and St Paul's Cathedral Choir School are other examples. The Assize Courts, Cumberland House, Crown Square, Manchester is a fine example, faced with an unusual type of Portland Roach containing masses of algal origin (*Solenopora*).[46]

'The earliest known users of Portland Stone were the Romans in about 55 BC',[47] and columns of Portland Stone were found at Dorchester, Dorset. The oldest known building of Portland Stone (undifferentiated) is Rufus Castle, on the Isle of Portland itself, which is generally dated at 1080 AD. The stone was sent to Exeter and to London in the fourteenth century[48] where it was used in the Tower of London (1349) and in London Bridge (1350). Following its use, first by Inigo Jones for Banqueting Hall, Whitehall, London (1610) and secondly by Christopher Wren for the re-building of St Paul's Cathedral London after the Great Fire of 1666, Portland Stone became generally popular.

Its use is more widespread throughout the British Isles than any other Jurassic oolitic limestone. It has also been used on a large scale elsewhere around the world. It '... is the only limestone found in the city of Newcastle'.[49] It was used for the Metropolitan Cathedral of Christ the King, Liverpool, for the engraved plaque commemorating Eric Gill at Hopkin's Crank, Ditchling Common, Sussex and, unusually, as tilestones covering the domes of the Victoria and Albert Museum, London. It was also used for building in Colonial Williamsburg, Virginia, USA.

Although the Portland Beds are named from the Isle of Portland, they are thicker, better exposed and geologically more interesting in the Isle of Purbeck where the Portland Stone reaches 115 feet (35 m) in thickness. The stone was quarried on the Isle of Purbeck from early times and is known as Purbeck-Portland. Two freestones, called the Pond and the Under Freestone were worked. Stone from quarries at Seacombe, near Swanage, Dorset was used for paving, kerbs and steps. The staircase of the Sedgwick Museum, Cambridge is made of it[3]. Portland-Purbeck is recorded for use for the lighthouse at Margate, for part of Dover Pier[3] as well as for local churches.

Stones of the same age as Portland Stone but of totally different character are quarried in the Vale of Wardour, Wiltshire, under the names Chilmark Stone, Tisbury Stone and Vale of Wardour Stone. The fact that these stones are of Portlandian age has led to a number of misconceptions that the stone is similar to that found on the Isle of Portland itself. Although some sandy oolitic beds of Portlandian age are recorded in the Vale of Wardour, the Chilmark, Tisbury or Wardour stones are sandy, glauconitic limestones. They were quarried and mined near Tisbury, Chilmark, Chicksgrove, Wockley and at Lower Lawn, Wiltshire. The most extensive galleries were those at Chilmark. Many individual beds were named including the Trough, Hard or White Bed, the Green Bed and the Fretting Bed. However, after exposure, when stone from these beds is dry, it does not seem possible to recognize any differences between them.

The Vale of Wardour stones have been recorded as used in many important buildings (*Figure 4.66*). Salisbury Cathedral (thirteenth century) is built of

Figure 4.66 Grains of the mineral glauconite in Chilmark stone, a sandy limestone, are responsible for the green cast seen in Salisbury Cathedral

Chilmark Stone. This stone specifically was also used for Hampshire County Council Offices (1910) and extensions (1932), the West Gate, City of Winchester, restorations by His Majesty's Office of Works (1932), and by Sir Gilbert Scott for restorations to St Albans Abbey, Hertfordshire. Chilmark Stone was used for the remarkable 125 feet (38 m) high church spire at Teffont, Wiltshire. The south front of Wilton House, Wiltshire is of stone from the Chilmark Quarries. It may be directly compared with stone from the nearer Upper Greensand used for the east front. The Chilmark Trough Bed was recorded as having been used for the renovation (1867) of the Chapter House, Westminster Abbey, London.

The stone of Blandford Forum church, Dorset, is said to be from the Tisbury Quarry but has been called incorrectly Wiltshire Greensand. Tisbury Stone, specifically, was used for Winchester College, Hampshire.

Purbeck 'Marble'
The Purbeck Beds of the Isle of Purbeck, the Isle of Portland, the Vale of Wardour and elsewhere, which overlie the Portland Stone beds, consist of a varied series of limestones, shales, shellbeds and mudstones. The famous Purbeck 'Marble' is part of this series. More than twenty beds of limestone were recognized and named individually by quarrymen including Laning, Red Rag, Shingle, Spangle and Upper Tombstone Bed. Each bed is said to have its own particular uses, for example, tombstones, kerbstones, many of which can still be identified in use, flooring, setts and steps. Some of the limestones can be easily split into thin slabs which were used as tilestones.

There are many fossils in the Purbeck Beds. Certain fresh-water snails (*Viviparus*) occasionally built laterally extensive, but not very thick beds, of limestone which now constitute the Purbeck 'Marble'. The 'marble' occurs as two thin beds near the top of the Upper Purbeck. Each bed never exceeds four feet (1.2 m) and seldom is more than one foot (0.3 m). The 'marble' was used by the Romans, but after that period, there appears to have been little demand for it until the twelfth century. The quarry at Worth Matravers, Dorset, is mentioned in about 1190 and after that the fashion for the stone seems to have caught on.

The notable examples of its use include parts of Salisbury Cathedral, Wiltshire (*Figure 4.67*), and the beautiful choir columns of Ely Cathedral, Cambridgeshire, where the stone is seen properly in bed (*Figure 4.68*).

Purbeck 'Marble' has been used for many of the columns of the choir of Exeter Cathedral. They have recently been cleaned and, oddly, left unpolished to reveal a dull-grey surface. This does not show to best advantage the surface pattern for which the marble

Figure 4.67 Small figures at the base of the central column of the Chapter House, Salisbury Cathedral, show the typical surface pattern of Purbeck 'marble' caused by countless small fossilized gastropods ('snails')

Figure 4.68 The variation in Purbeck 'marble' is seen in the columns in the south choir aisle, Ely Cathedral, which are constructed of drums laid, properly, in bed

is best known or display a contrast with the main stone of the fabric. It seems to negate the purpose for which the stone was originally chosen.

Exeter Cathedral is possibly one of the best recorded examples for the use of stone. The use of Beer, Ketton, Doulting, Bath, Salcombe, Caen, Ham Hill and Portland are all well documented (see, for example, reference 40).

The 'Marble' was used as far north as Durham for some shafts in the Galilee Chapel of the Cathedral and is recorded in Normandy, France. Apart from its use as a structural element, the 'Marble' has been used extensively for effigies, coffins, incised slabs and other ecclesiastical adornments. They are extensively monographed by Rosemary Leach[51].

Cretaceous limestones

The Cretaceous system has yielded some limestones which, while not widely used, have attained a degree of importance particularly in southern England.

Lower Cretaceous limestones

The Weald Clay near the base of the Cretaceous contains subordinate beds of shelly limestone and beds of slightly calcareous sandstone. Two main varieties of limestone are found known as Small-*'Paludina'* and Large-*'Paludina'* limestone. They are composed of either small or large species of the freshwater mollusc *Viviparus*. Small-*'Paludina'* limestone contains the small species, *Viviparus elongatus* and the Large-*'Paludina'* limestone contains *V. sussexiensis*. These beds of Wealden Marble are rarely one foot (0.3 m) thick. In many areas they are a maximum of about six inches (15 cm), but commonly are only two or three inches (5–8 cm) thick. They have been quarried for a long time and have been used both as a structural and an ornamental stone. They are usually known by the name from where they were wrought. The Large-*'Paludina'* limestones include Bethersden 'Marble' (Kent), Petworth 'Marble' (Sussex), Sussex 'Marble' and Laughton Stone (Sussex). The Small-*'Paludina'* Marble was quarried at Charlwood, Surrey.

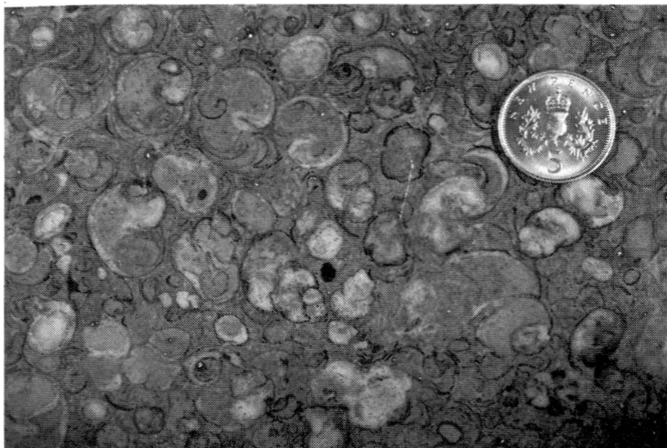

Figure 4.69 Cross sections of the large species of the gastropod *Viviparus*, of which the Large-*'Paludina'* 'marble' is mostly composed, distinguish Wealden from Purbeck 'marble'

Large-*'Paludina'* occurs only in the Weald Clay and does not occur in the Purbeck. Therefore, the presence of Large-*'Paludina'* is diagnostic of a Wealden Marble even if it is not possible to suggest a provenance. Small-*'Paludina'* limestone from the Weald Clay and Purbeck Marble may easily be confused, especially when seen isolated as slabs or columns in buildings. Other limestone beds within the Weald Clay may contain the fossils *Margaritifera (Pseudunio)*, (the *'Unio* Marble') or *Filosina (Cyrena)*. Slabs of these beds are often seen in paving and sometimes as columns and steps. They were no doubt passed off originally as one of the Wealden 'Marbles'.

The Wealden 'Marbles' do not appear to have been used extensively for building. It is generally recorded that some thin shafts and the old steps to the altar in Canterbury Cathedral are of Bethersden 'Marble'. However, at least some of the blocks which make up the steps are of *'Unio* Marble'. Bethersden 'Marble' may also be seen in Bethersden Church, Kent and in the fifteenth century tower arch of Biddenham Church, Kent. Wealden Marble (Large-*'Paludina'* limestone known locally as winkle stone)[52] was used for Petworth House. Presumably this is Petworth Marble dug from nearby.

All Saints' Church, Staplehurst illustrates well the use of locally quarried Small-*'Paludina'* limestone which is only one to two inches (5 cm) thick by the Normans as well as its use through Early English times. Large-*'Paludina'* 'Marble' was used in the church during the Perpendicular period[53]. In this church these Wealden limestones may be directly compared with Purbeck 'Marble' used for some Early English moulded bases and little bell capitals.

Otherwise unspecified Wealden 'Marble' of the Large-*'Paludina'* type was used as slabs in the floor of the Painted Hall, Naval College, Greenwich, London where it is referred to as Purbeck (*Figure 4.70*). Chest tombs of Wealden 'Marble' may be seen in the churchyard of St Mary, Reigate, Surrey.

Kentish Ragstone, taken from the Hythe Beds of the Lower Cretaceous Lower Greensand Formation is an important building stone especially in south-east England. The main quarries were around Maidstone, Kent and are still in use today (*Figure 4.71*). The stone occurs in beds up to two feet (0.6 m) thick, which alternate with sands known as hassock. Kentish Ragstone is a sandy glauconitic limestone which is dark-blue to green-grey in colour. The

Figure 4.70 Although stated to be of Purbeck 'marble', the floor of the Painted Hall at the Royal Naval College, Greenwich, also contains many slabs of Wealdon 'marble'. This is distinguished by the appearance of Large-*'Paludina'* (see p. 114)

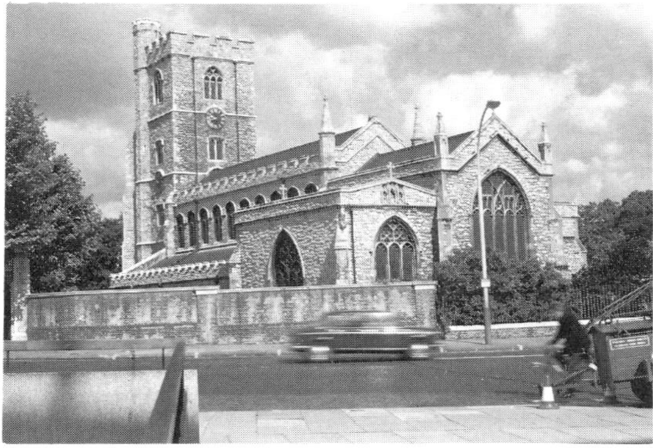

Figure 4.72 Kentish Ragstone was used in large quantities by the Victorians, particularly for ecclesiastical building in London. Commonly, Bath Stone was used for the dressings because of the intractable nature of the ragstone, as seen in the church of St Mary, Fulham. No entirely satisfactory substitute stone has been found for restorations to buildings of Kentish Ragstone

Figure 4.71 Resistant beds of Kentish Ragstone stand out from the friable, more easily eroded 'Hassock' in Furfield Quarry, Kent

lithology is essentially limestone containing up to 90 per cent or more of calcium carbonate with 5 per cent or more silica and glauconite grains. The proportions of these minerals may differ considerably and the lithology varies considerably along its outcrop. In some instances the proportion of silica is substantial and the stone may be called a chert.

Kentish Ragstone was widely used in London in Roman and in mediaeval times. Most of it probably came from the Maidstone area and was carried by boat down the River Medway and then up the River Thames. The Roman ship discovered at Blackfriars, London[54] was carrying a cargo of Kentish Ragstone which was almost certainly from the Maidstone area. Tough and intractable, it is not freely worked, but nevertheless has been used effectively for countless churches in London, (*Figure 4.72*) and earlier for the walls of Londinium. It was also used for the Tower of London, and for the New City Prison, Holloway (1849-1852), but it had the uncomfortable reputation of sweating when used on interior walls. No better example of its use exists than the great house of Knole in Kent[10].

Kentish Ragstone and Hassock grade into each other. In general terms Hassock is more friable, and is normally classified as a sandstone because it is loosely-cemented, calcareous, argillaceous, glauconitic and sandy. Occasionally it is sufficiently cohesive to allow it to be used as a freestone, and not uncommonly ragstone walls were lined with Hassock. It is said that fireplaces were made of the stone.

Upper Cretaceous limestones

The Cretaceous System takes its name from the major formation within it, the Chalk (*Creta*), a limestone that may be up to 98 per cent pure calcium carbonate. It is white to pale-grey in colour and very fine-grained. The Chalk is uncemented and soft in southern England, cemented and tough in northern England and exceptionally tough and impervious with recrystallized calcite within the pore spaces in Northern Ireland. Although the Chalk in Northern Ireland, known as the White Limestone, proved unsuitable for building, Chalk has been used elsewhere on a considerable scale for building.

Boynton Stone, from near Bridlington, Yorkshire was used in that area[17]; Amberley Quarry, Sussex,

(a)

(b)

(c)

(d)

(e)

Figure 4.73 Although Chalk is not noted for weathering resistance, it has been widely used, particularly where no other suitable stone was available. It needed however, to have its 'feet dry and head covered'. Not unusually walls were thatched as at Hendon, Wiltshire (a); (b) the Chalk walls of a cottage at Lenham, Kent stand on an impervious flint plinth. Undoubtedly the cottage was thatched originally; (c) built of Totternhoe Stone, Woburn Abbey was quite inappropriately patched with Bath Stone, leading to a disastrous appearance; (d) beautifully proportioned Ashdown House, Berkshire, has walls of locally dug Chalk; (e) offering little resistance to the mason's chisel, Chalk is easily worked, leading to a riot of carving as seen in the arcading in the Lady Chapel, Ely Cathedral

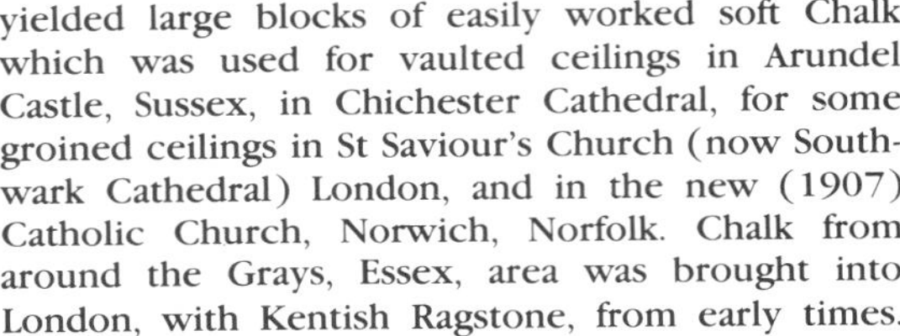

yielded large blocks of easily worked soft Chalk which was used for vaulted ceilings in Arundel Castle, Sussex, in Chichester Cathedral, for some groined ceilings in St Saviour's Church (now Southwark Cathedral) London, and in the new (1907) Catholic Church, Norwich, Norfolk. Chalk from around the Grays, Essex, area was brought into London, with Kentish Ragstone, from early times. Chalk with no certain provenance but probably from Beer, Devon is noted for its use in St Stephens' Chapel, Westminster, London and in the crypt of Lambeth Palace, London.

Many cottages, barns, houses and walls built of Chalk may be found along its outcrop. These buildings and walls were commonly thatched and had deep eaves so that water was thrown clear of the wall to prevent excessive weathering. The delightful Ashdown House, Berkshire is an example of the use of Chalk on a larger, grander scale.

In detailed lithology the Chalk differs considerably in its characteristics both laterally along its outcrop and vertically. Certain types were recognized from an early date as of particular use for building. These types became used through a wider area than was locally dug Chalk.

Beer Stone, taken from near the base of the Middle Chalk is probably the best known of the Chalk building stones. It is a creamy grey-coloured, highly calcareous variety made up of minute, irregular, apparently corroded fragments of shells cemented by a calcareous matrix which appears largely crystalline in form. Occasional larger pieces of fossil matter are seen, and grains of glauconite with a lesser amount of quartz grains are scattered throughout the rock. The stone has been worked at Beer, Devon, apparently since Roman times; a 'Roman quarry' existed in 1932. It was also quarried in Hooken Cliffe, west of Beer Head. It was worked from open quarries until the overburden of other Chalk beds became too great. Tunnels were then made to extract the stone. The Beer freestone bed is up to thirteen feet (4 m) thick. It hardens considerably on exposure 'and is altogether much stronger than Bath Stone and very much superior to Caen Stone which was once so much used in England'[55].

Beer Stone has been widely used. It may be seen in St Ann's Cathedral, Belfast, Northern Ireland and in the altar and reredos of Christ Church Cathedral, St Louis, Missouri, USA.

In Britain its use dates back to Norman times when it was used for the doorway of Axminster Church, Devon. It was used more recently for Peak House, Sidmouth, Devon, which is entirely of Beer Stone. The Grandison tombs at Ottery St Mary, Devon, dated at 1360 testify to its durability. Perhaps its best known use is for Exeter Cathedral, Devon which dates back to Norman times.

Totternhoe Stone, from near Dunstable, Bedfordshire is also widely known. Greenish-grey in colour, it contains an abnormal amount of small fragments of the fossil bivalve *Inoceramus.* This results in it having a gritty feel, which has led to the stone being described incorrectly as sandy. The stone is taken from a well marked bed within the Lower Chalk. It appears to set in as a thin bed in Berkshire, continues through Oxfordshire and Buckinghamshire, reaches 15 to about 25 feet (4.6–7.6 m) thickness through Bedfordshire, Hertfordshire and Cambridge, and thins through Suffolk and Norfolk to only 2 feet (0.6 m). Its texture is compact and fine-grained and it is worked as a freestone.

Totternhoe Stone is renowned for its use in the twelfth century Woburn Abbey, Bedfordshire, for the organ screen in Peterborough Cathedral, for St Albans Abbey, and for the parish church, Luton and the Priory Church, Dunstable.

Burwell Stone (or Rock) of Cambridgeshire, is the same geological horizon as Totternhoe Stone. At Burwell the stone was dug from pits and it had long been worked for building material. The uppermost bed was called the bond or bondstone and said to be the best stone. Burwell Stone was quarried near the village of Burwell, Cherryhinton (formerly Hinton), Eversden and elsewhere around Cambridge. Many early buildings of Cambridge University used the stone, including the unparalleled King Edward's Gateway (1426).[38] The Lady Chapel of Ely Cathedral is a *tour de force* of carving in a stone which provided no obstacle for the mason's chisel.

Chalk is commonly called clunch by the mason and others. This term should be restricted to the types of Chalk found in East Anglia. The origin of the term is obscure and the word is often applied to other types of rock.

Tertiary limestones

Limestones are poorly represented in rocks of Tertiary age and in Britain only one is of any importance architecturally.

Quarr Stone, from the eastern end of Quarr Wood, near Quarr Abbey, Isle of Wight was quarried from the Bembridge Formation which comprises the Bembridge Limestone, overlain by the Bembridge Marls. The limestone is freshwater in origin and up to 26 feet (8 m) thick. It is pale grey but with a green cast and massively bedded. It is made up of molluscs, which normally are represented by casts or moulds. The shells are replaced by calcite in some instances. A most unlikely looking stone for building purposes,

Figure 4.74 Most of the stone quarried at Quarr, Isle of Wight, was used on the mainland for many churches, notably for the interior of Winchester Cathedral, and for Beaulieu Abbey. On the Isle it was used for the small but delightful Quarr Abbey

it was extensively worked and used during the Middle Ages. It was highly esteemed and was used in many churches in Sussex, in Winchester Cathedral, for the Priory at Lewes and in Chichester Cathedral. It has also been identified as one of the many stones used in Westminster Hall, Palace of Westminster, London. More compact and less carious limestone from the Bembridge Limestone, which characteristically contains the nucules, variously ornamented small globular bodies about the size of a large pinhead, of the lime-secreting freshwater alga *Chara*, also has been quarried in the past on a fairly large scale, principally at Binstead, near Ryde, Isle of Wight. Quarr Stone passes laterally into Binstead Stone. Binstead Stone has been used locally on the Isle of Wight. On the mainland it may be found in Winchester Cathedral and in many Sussex churches. It was also used for the external walls of the imposing Beaulieu Abbey, Hampshire, which at the Dissolution, was used as a quarry to supply stone to build some nearby houses.

Septarian nodules

Septarian nodules (concretions or septaria) are brownish- to greyish-coloured, calcareous nodules ranging in size from a few centimetres to a metre or more in diameter. They occur particularly in clays and are notably common at some horizons within the London Clay. They are usually more-or-less bun-shaped and are frequently found to have a flat bottom with a convex upper surface. Their characteristic feature is an internal arrangement of cracks which are arranged concentrically and radially to form the boundaries of roughly polygonal masses which were supposed to be seven sided. It is said that this is the origin of the name septaria.

The cracks are filled with distinctive yellowish-brown calcite but some may be found to be open. In some instances the nodules are found to have no cracks. The cracks arise from shrinkage of the nodules which are then infilled by the deposition of calcite by percolating water to fill or partially fill the cracks. Commonly on weathering the calcareous clayey matter of the nodule is worn away more quickly than the calcite veins, which then stand out as ribs in a distinctive honeycomb pattern. The septaria may be richly fossiliferous. Septaria have also been called beetle stones, turtle stones and cement stones.

At one time septarian nodules from the London Clay were collected together to make cement (Roman Cement or Parker's Cement) because the proportions of calcareous and argillaceous matter were about right for the process. Polished slices were used as tops of ornamental tables[17]. They were used for building in parts of East Anglia where no other suitable building stone exists. The church at Wrabness, Essex, on the banks of the River Stour, the

Figure 4.75 In an area devoid of other building stone, septarian nodules from the London Clay were used for Orford Castle, Suffolk

church at Chelmondiston, Suffolk, just off the banks of the River Orwell, the church at Frinton-on-Sea, Essex, and the Norman church at Clacton-on-Sea, Essex are built substantially of septaria. One of the best examples of septaria masonry work is stated to be Orford Castle, Suffolk (*Figure 4.75*). Colchester Castle Museum is another excellent example. The septaria were taken from pits dug in the London Clay or from nearby river or sea beaches where they had been washed out from the clay. The river beach at Wrabness is a well-known locality for the concretions.

Tufa

Tufa, which is principally calcite, and contains iron oxides responsible for yellow and red colours, is a spongy, porous rock which forms from carbonate charged waters, around springs and seeps and in streams. Commonly it will contain leaves, stems, gastropods and other organisms, or their remains.

Local deposits of tufa are well known in Great Britain and it is still being deposited. The carbonate is commonly deposited on plants, and on other objects, hence the petrifying springs such as those at Matlock, Derbyshire. Tufa is the term restricted mainly to the recent deposits of spongy nature.

Streams from springs issuing from the Hythe Beds, the Chalk in Kent, the Lincolnshire Limestone, and elsewhere are still depositing tufa. There are many occurrences in Kent. For example, at Wateringbury at least eight feet of tufa fills a channel in a small valley. At East Barming a tufa deposit 14 feet 9 inches (4.5 m) thick has been measured.

Tufa was known to the Romans when they came to Britain, since there are extensive deposits in Italy. It is frequently found in the remains of Roman buildings where it has been used as a light-weight, insulating material. Some buildings seem to have been constructed largely of tufa. However, because of its lightness, it was used mainly to fill the webs of high ribbed vaults, for example.

The vaulting above the high choir in Gloucester Cathedral is of tufa from deposits at nearby Dursley. The vaulting of the nave and choir roofs of Sherborne Abbey, Dorset used tufa, known locally as French Pummy[56]. It was also commonly used in Norman buildings. Leeds Church Tower, Kent (twelfth century) is of tufa as are mediaeval buildings in East Malling. Tufa was also used in Cliveden House, Buckinghamshire.

Travertine

Travertine is the name normally given to the more compact form of tufa. Like tufa it is characterized by the presence of many irregular cavities. It is usually opaque in thin slabs and may be banded. It is being deposited at the present day from hot springs in places such as in Yellowstone Park, USA. Deposits of travertine are quite common and occur in a number of countries. Travertine as known in the stone trade ranges from very pale cream, through yellow to dark brown and is banded and compact with some cavities.

The Cannstatt Travertine from near Stuttgart, Germany has a limited outcrop but has been widely used worldwide. It was used for façades of buildings in Berlin, in Buenos Aires, in the Hague, as well as for internal work including the Hotel Winthrop, New York, USA. It has also been used for monumental works such as the William III monument at Breda, Holland and the mausoleum of August Thyssen, Mülheim, Ruhr, Germany.

Large deposits of travertine are found in the Sienna and Tivoli districts of Italy and important deposits exist near Rome, Naples and Florence. It was the

(a)

(b)

Figure 4.76 (a) Travertine, of different colours, set with bedding planes vertical, used as cladding for flats in Turin; (b) statue by Henry Moore, outside the UNESCO building, Paris, of traventine with horizontal bedding

Figure 4.77 Travertine used structurally, was the stone chosen by the Romans for the Colosseum. (Photo: John Ashurst)

(a)

(b)

Figure 4.78 (a) Onyx-marble used for decorative external cladding on a bank front, Charing Cross Road; (b) Vase of onyx-marble, Chatsworth House, Derbyshire

material used by the Romans for the Colosseum in Rome (*Figure 4.77*) and for many other buildings.

Travertine has been imported into Great Britain and many other countries in vast quantities for flooring, walling and cladding. Most comes from the renowned quarries at Tivoli and Sabino near Rome. It is particularly recommended for paving and treads because it is claimed that it is non-slip and has a non-fatiguing effect upon pedestrians. These qualities are attributed to the voids in the stone. The voids are frequently filled or 'stopped', in the modern use of the stone, which is often for cladding without regard to the bedding.

Travertine is said to resist abrasion remarkably well. This is borne out by its use at St James's Park Underground Station, London. The stone was used for the Cloaca Maxima, Rome. Tivoli travertine was recently used in a private hospital in St John's Wood, London. Roman travertine was used by Henry Moore for *Reclining Figure* (1957–1958) seen outside the UNESCO Building in Paris.

Onyx and onyx-marble

Despite many papers and articles,[30] considerable confusion exists in the use of the names onyx and onyx-marble. The two substances are different in appearance and different in chemical composition.

Onyx is a cryptocrystalline variety of quartz (SiO_2) and is the name given only to a banded black and white form, which has probably been produced by artificial colouring.[30] Onyx cannot be scratched with a penknife blade because its hardness is about H=6.5.

Onyx-marble is an exceptionally fine-grained, generally translucent variety of calcite ($CaCO_3$). It is normally banded and it ranges in colour from nearly white, through ivory, yellow, green, reddish, red-brown to brown. It can be scratched with a penknife because its hardness is approximately $H=3$. It has been highly prized since early times, not only for its translucent property, but also as a luxury material for 'marble' bathrooms.

Onyx-marble now is produced in many countries including Italy, Argentina, Algeria (possibly the largest producer), Turkey, Iran and Pakistan. Mexican onyx-marble, used by the Aztecs, is highly prized and was used in the entrance hall of the Trocadero Restaurant, London, now sadly demolished. Onyx-marble from Argentina is usually sold as Brazilian Onyx. This illustrates the point made by P.A. Males[57] that 'One should always be suspicious of the accuracy of names that include a locality. Although not always the case, a large number of such names do prove to be mineralogically incorrect'.

Watson[32] records the use of Algerian Onyx-Marble in the Grand Opera House in Paris and in the Credit Lyonnais building, Rue du 4 Septembre. Onyx-marble is often used for small ornaments such as table lamp stands, clock cases, ash-trays, statuettes and particularly eggs, apparently from a very free-laying bird. Decorative table tops, both ancient and modern, are commonly partly or wholly of onyx-marble. A fantastic use of onyx-marble from Turkey may be seen in Barclays Bank, Piccadilly Circus, London. Gibraltar Stone or Gibraltar Onyx, which, in the past, was mostly used for small tourist knick-knacks, is from stalagmitic deposits in the limestone caves of Gibraltar.

Imported limestones

There is a wealth of limestone to be found in Great Britain and its suitability as a building and as a decorative stone was recognized at an early date. It seems surprising, therefore, that much limestone is imported. Most is cut and polished and sold by the stone trade as decorative 'marble'. Colour is normally the principal factor controlling its choice.

French limestones

The earliest known imported limestone, Caen Stone, was used structurally. It is probably the best known of the French limestones in Great Britain.

Traditionally the stone has been imported since Norman times and it is recorded as being used by Paul of Caen, Abbot of St Albans, in 1077. The stone was quarried at Caen, Calvados, Normandy from underground galleries where it is 90 to 100 feet (27–30 m) thick. The quarries are of great antiquity; Merovingian coffins made of the stone have been found around Caen. It is also amusing to read that protests at its import 'not withstanding almightie God hath so blessed our realms in a most plentiful manner [with limestone]' were made as early as 1577 by William Harrison in *Description of England*[17].

Caen stone is often described as an oolitic limestone which resembles Bath Stone, Painswick Stone or other stones. In fact, it has no direct equivalent in Britain. M. Dunham and K.C. (now Sir Kingsley) Dunham[58] wrote that the stone consists 'of pellet limestone, having rounded and ovoid pellets of cloudy calcite mud up to 0.15 mm diameter set in a matrix of clear calcite crystals of rhombic habit, averaging about 0.1 mm but in places ranging up to 0.6 mm in breadth. The remains of a small, multi-chambered foraminifera constitute a microfauna in the rock'.

In hand specimen Caen Stone is a fine-grained limestone, yellowish to yellow-white or quite white in colour. It was used extensively in ecclesiastical and royal works. Canterbury Cathedral, Kent is a good example of its use. It is recorded that it has also been used in Salisbury Cathedral, Winchester Cathedral, Chichester Cathedral, Worcester Cathedral, Norwich Cathedral, Rochester Cathedral, Durham Cathedral (The Neville Screen), the altar of St Mary's Roman Catholic Church, Belfast, the font of St Peter's Church, Antrim Road, Belfast and the Church of St Margaret, Walmgate York. It is teamed with knapped flint in the Guildhall, Norwich (see *Figure 4.36g*). It has been used, in part at least, for Windsor Castle, Hampton Court, Buckingham Palace (particularly the east façade), and the interior of Beaulieu Abbey, Hampshire. At one time it was used in London for building monumental structures to the exclusion of all other material. Its uses included such buildings as the Junior Athenaeum Club at 116 Piccadilly (1849), the Carlton Club, Pall Mall, and the columns supporting the main floor of the Museum of Practical Geology (now demolished), Jermyn Street, London. Caen Stone was used by the Normans for the central White Tower of the Tower of London, finished in 1097.

When seen in a building where the light may be poor and the surface dirty and rubbed it may not be possible to differentiate between the Upper Cretaceous Beer Stone, fine-grained Upper Jurassic Portland Stone and Caen Stone. Care must be taken in determination and a freshly broken surface is preferred for study.

Caen Stone is no longer available and as there is a requirement for repair and other building work on existing structures of Caen Stone, a number of French limestones are imported. They are sometimes offered as a matching stone but none of them is. There is also a tendency to call them all oolitic but only a few are. They are imported under many names, for example St Maximin (Oise), Moulin à

Vent (Meuse), Richemont (Charentes-Maritimes) and Lepine (Vienne). In general they are Jurassic in age and are mostly pale-buff in colour and fine-grained. Longchant Stone which is pale-buff and fine-grained is markedly oolitic. Euville Stone (Meuse), a pink-beige coloured, medium-grained, bioclastic limestone was once used extensively in Paris, although St Vaast Stone, from near the city itself, is commonly said to be the 'stone that built Paris'. Tuffeau Stone from south-west Paris was used for the Palace of Versailles (Seine-et-Oise). The Catacombs of Paris are exhausted limestone quarries.

France produces both true marbles (marbres) and limestones (pierres marbrières). The limestones are mainly pale-coloured. Many of those produced in the Ardennes, near the Belgian frontier, are virtually identical with the Belgian stones.

Over 200 French 'marbles' are known. A comprehensive survey of French masonry limestones together with an assessment of their possible behaviour was undertaken by Honeyborne in 1978[59]. In the past, French limestones were imported into Great Britain. Their use is not always recognized. For example, Birmingham Council House used a variety known as Gris d'Alesia, from near Dijon, which is of similar appearance to Carboniferous Hopton Wood Stone. Similarly Forêt des Brousses, Burgundy, was polished like marble and used for the interior decoration of the New York Central Railway Station in 1917. The more compact limestones are worked primarily for decorative purposes. In the Boulonnais, Napoleon Stone and the closely allied Lunel, Notre-Dame A and B and Rubane Stones, which are virtually indistinguishable, have been exported widely. They were used mostly for decorative cladding of shop fronts.

The Campan group of 'marbles' are principally quarried from the Espiadet quarries, Campan Valley, Hautes Pyrenées, France. In the past this Department was an important centre for French 'marble' and it was largely developed during the reign of Louis XIV. The stone from the quarries has nodules of limestone which have been drawn out and later cemented with a mainly greenish chloritic matrix. Pink, brownish and red coloration is also found.

The colour determines the name given to the stone. Campan Vert is one of the best known. The dominating colours are light and dark green with irregularly shaped white markings. Campan Rouge is similar but red in colour. Campan Mélange is a mixture of the two colours.

The Trianon in Versaille, France is thought to have been called the Marble Trianon because of its external decor of Languedoc marble pilasters. However, some of them are of Campan Rouge and Campan Vert, which are known to have been extensively used by Louis XIV at Versailles. Campan Marble may also be seen in Westminster Cathedral, London and it 'is popular for making the tops of the tables that may be seen in the numerous restaurants and cafés in Paris'.[32] It has also been used as a decorative stone in Roman baths in London. It is also used in the entablature of the Chapel of the Sacred Heart, Brompton Oratory, London and was used in pavements in Peterborough and Bristol Cathedral.

Belgian limestones

Belgian 'marbles' are limestones of Carboniferous age. Belgium is one of the world's leading 'marble'-producing countries. A large amount of limestone is quarried, but large amounts of stone are also imported. The imported stone is processed and may then be exported as 'Belgian marble'.

Some of the well known Belgian stones include Rouge Royal, Rouge Griotte, St Anne, Bleu Belge and Petit Granit. In spite of its name, Petit Granit is a limestone which is sold as a 'marble'. In the past a marble effect was achieved on porcelain by dabbling the glaze with sponges which may have been wrapped in linen. This porcelain was known as Rouge Royal and it was commonly used in Victorian lavatories. The Rouge Royal 'marble' had a similar use and the distinction between the two is sometimes not obvious.

Italian stones

Italy is renowned for marble, especially Carrara Marble. It also produces much limestone. The five major regions which produce marbles and limestones are:

1. The area around Carrara, Tuscany, which produces true white marbles and 'blue' marbles such as Bardiglio, Italian Dove and Bleu Turquin;
2. The area around Sienna, Tuscany, which produces yellow limestones (known as Sienna 'marbles') and travertine;
3. The area around Veneto and Lombardy which produces limestones of Jurassic age including Red and Yellow Verona;
4. Piedmont which produces many of the modern 'green-marbles' which are serpentinite;
5. The area around Istria (now partly in Yugoslavia) which produces limestones of Cretaceous and Tertiary age.

There is production elsewhere, but normally not on a large scale. Some areas have a substantial output of a particular stone, for example, travertine from near Rome.

Although Italy is thought of as a marble-producing country, much of the output is not marble. This is now recognized in recent Italian literature[60] which classifies output as:

1.1 True marbles (recrystallized calcareous rocks);
1.2 Polishable calcareous rocks;
1.3 Polishable calcareous breccias;
1.4 Serpentines and ophicalcites;
2.1 True granites and other igneous rocks;
2.2 Gneissic metamorphic rocks;
3 Travertines;
4 Stones.

Many references in literature, building records and archives to marble from Italy should be treated with considerable reserve. Many of the stones are not marbles in strict geological definition. In addition, Italy has a long tradition of importing stone, processing it and then exporting it around the world. Many Italian limestones are colourful and have been used for decorative panels as well as wine coolers, vases, table tops and other items of furniture. Italian marble was used decoratively for the famous sixty-six columns of 'Yellow Marble of Sienna' for the Throne Room of HM the King of Siam in Bangkok, Thailand.

Many of the Cretaceous limestones from the Istria peninsula are known in Britain as Roman Stone. In general the limestone is a cream-grey colour with greater or lesser amounts of broken fossils which gives it a spotted appearance. Where there is a considerable amount of fossil matter the stone has a marked brownish spotted appearance. The limestone is also known by its Italian name Bianco del Mare. Aurisina is a well known type of Istrian limestone and Nabresina is a variety of it. The name Veseljie Stone has also been used. An attempt was made to launch the stone under the name Jubilee Stone at the time of HM Queen Elizabeth II's Jubilee in 1977.

Superficially the stone resembles the Carboniferous Hopton Wood Stone and Hadene Stone and was accepted as a substitute for them. Istrian stone has been quarried since at least the time of Imperial Rome. It has been widely used and is recorded[33] as being freely used in England for ornamental work. It is seen in Vienna and extensively in Venice.

The Cretaceous rocks of the Trieste area also provide a series of decorative limestones under the name Repen. For example Repen Zola and Repen Classico. Some of these stones may be confused with some of the Aurisina series and, in fact, they are all from the same series of beds. Repen Zola was used for internal decorative work in St George's Hall, Liverpool, Merseyside (1848), for the ballustrades of the main staircase in the Law Courts, Hull, Humberside (1908) and was freely exported to the USA.[32]

Swedish limestones

An interesting Swedish limestone was used on the half pace of the west end steps of St Paul's Cathedral, London. There are two varieties; one is a fine-grained reddish muddy limestone and the other is a fine-grained greenish-grey muddy calcareous siltstone. Both contain the distinctive fossil cephalopod *Orthoceras*, which is seen in section in the paving. Detailed study of the fossils in the stone indicate that it is of Ordovician age, with a strong possibility that it came from Sweden.

Swedish literature records that dressed building stone was exported from Gotland and Øland to Germany, Denmark and England during the fifteenth, sixteenth and seventeenth centuries.[61] Documents dealing with building work by Christopher Wren record that he used 'Swedish' or 'Swedes' stone and 'Denmark' stone or 'Red Denmark'.[62] There is now little doubt that these references are to red and grey *Orthoceras* Limestone of Ordovician age from the Island of Øland, Sweden.

The stone was widely used in Scandinavia, Germany and Holland. There does not seem to be much recorded information about its use in England, but the cloisters at Hampton Court Palace and the paving at Somerset House, London are made of it.[62] 'Swedish Marble' is recorded as being used for the floor of St George's Hall in Windsor Castle.

Similar rocks of the same geological age crop out in several other places in Sweden. Quarries at Brunflo, Järntland produced large amounts of stone since the end of the nineteenth century. This stone is still available today, but the limestone from Øland is now quarried on a more modest scale.

The slabs on the half pace of the steps of St Paul's Cathedral are made of stone from the Brunflo quarries (*Figure 4.79*). The same stone was also used to replace some paving at Hampton Court Palace, at Somerset House and at the Royal Hospital, Chelsea. An eye-catching modern use of the Øland limestone is on the shop Henning Glahn in Sloane Street, London.

Figure 4.79 Transverse and longitudinal cross sections of *Orthoceras* provide distinctive white markings in the Swedish Limestone used on the half landing of the west end steps, St Paul's Cathedral

Records of Swedish Stone, Denmark Stone or Orthoceras limestone suggest that the stone was quarried in Sweden. However, to determine the exact provenance of a stone detailed petrological and palaeontological study is necessary.

Spanish limestones

Spain has a massive output of 'marbles', many of which are limestones which have been used since Roman times. One, Brocatella, is a classic decorative stone. It is red and yellow mottled with small white patches which are made up of the broken up remains of fossils. It has been used for ecclesiastical work and may be seen among the many decorative stones used in Westminster Cathedral, London.

A very unusual Cretaceous limestone from Arteaga, Spain contains rudists (a highly aberrant type of lamellibranch which mimics a form of coral). One variety, which appears to have yellow nodules on a reddish ground, is used for infill panels beneath the ground floor windows of the Norwich Union building, St James's Street, London. It was also used as flooring in the entrance to Fluor House, Euston Station, London. The same stone forms the floor of the Louvre in Paris. Red and Grey varieties were used for the map of the world on the Embankment of the River Tagus, Lisbon, Portugal, near the monument of Henry the Navigator.

Portuguese stones

Portugal has lately been developing its decorative stone production. The stones have been classified, scientifically by the Direcção-Geral de Geologia e Minas.[63] Limestones of Jurassic age are worked. A good example is Emperor's Red (Encarnado), which has been used in Britain for ecclesiastical decorative work.[32]

Israeli limestones

Perhaps the most widely known and certainly the best recorded 'marbles' are those used by Herod Antipas, Herod the Great and Pontius Pilate. The use of 'marble' in Palestine is recorded in the Bible and 'marble' has been used through the centuries. Israel has lately increased its quarrying capacity and has been actively exporting stone, particularly to Belgium and Great Britain. The limestones are nearly all of Cretaceous age, roughly equivalent to Lower and Middle Chalk of Great Britain. The font of Coventry Cathedral is a three tonne boulder of dolomitized Chalk brought from the Valley of Barakat, near Bethlehem[64]. Unfortunately this font, 'more ancient than the Christian Faith itself', is recorded as sandstone in the early edition of a glossy guide to the Cathedral[64]. 'Marble' of Eocene age is also known.

Stylolites are a common feature in some limestones from Israel. They appear as darker, wavy sutured lines, roughly parallel with the bedding and consist of a minute column-like development roughly at right angles to the bedding. Stylolites are believed to have formed due to solution and pressure acting together along original bedding-plane surfaces within the rock. As a result the insoluble material in the limestone was concentrated along bedding planes. An interlocking suture may be seen on polished slabs and although if hammered the stone probably would break along that line, it will not fall apart as is sometimes feared by those unfamiliar with the feature. In fact, Perlato de Sicilia (Sicilian Pearl) from near Trapani, Isle of Sicily, which is currently fashionable in Great Britain is noted for its stylolites, and this is one of the characters for which it is chosen.

Many Biblical buildings of Israel remain as enduring evidence of the durability of the stones used, especially in that climate. Little is recorded of the origin of the stone of the First or Second Temple, but Herod used blue-green veined stones of the Cretaceous Hatrurian Formation for the House. The Western, or 'Wailing' Wall, is of huge blocks of Cenomanian dolomitic limestone. Ninety per cent of the present-day output of all building stone is used in Jerusalem[65].

Stone from Israel is decoratively used on the fronts of some shops of the Marks and Spencer chain of stores. It was used also on the Banco di Roma, Brussels.

'Marbles' from other countries

Apart from the countries and examples described here, most countries in the world produce 'marbles' and many of them are now major producers. Many of them appear on the British market from time to time. However, in dealing with ancient monuments and historic buildings due regard must be paid to history because at any time only certain stones were available. Nevertheless, unusual decorative stones, normally in small quantities, were occasionally brought in by the dilettante completing his 'grand tour'.

Evaporitic rocks

A number of rocks, widely dissimilar in chemical composition, are grouped together and treated as sedimentary rocks because they have one thing in common: they were precipitated from ancient seas and lakes due to evaporation in arid climates. These rocks are known collectively as evaporites. Rock salt (or halite), potash, anhydrite and gypsum are included in this group. The precipitation of these minerals implies concentrations of elements far greater than normally found in sea water. Modern theories suggest that their formation is due to a recycling action whereby the evaporating waters are continually replaced rather than simple evaporation. Some uncommon elements may also rarely be found as evaporites.

Some evaporites are of importance in building and in decorative work. In this context they may be regarded as monomineralic rocks.

Alabaster

Gypsum, hydrated calcium sulphate ($CaSO_4 \cdot 2H_2O$) has a hardness of $H=2$, that is, it may be scratched easily with a finger nail. It, and the closely allied mineral anhydrite ($CaSO_4$) named from the Greek 'without water', are commonly found interbedded with shales, marls and limestones and may occur as persistent beds over considerable distances.

Gypsum occurs in a number of varieties. One form, found filling some veins, consists of fine, parallel, fibrous crystals with a silky lustre. It is known as satin spar and has been used for necklace beads and other ornaments. The variety selenite, named, because of its pellucid appearance, after Selene, goddess of the Moon, occurs as colourless transparent or whitish translucent flat, tubular crystals. An unusual type of gypsum which is widely known because it is sold as a tourist souvenir, is the Desert Rose. It is found only in arid areas and is apparently formed by the evaporation of ground waters drawn by capillary action to the surface. It consists of clusters of platey crystals. The crystals typically contain sand grains and commonly assume complicated shapes to resemble whatever the observer wishes to imagine. At one time Desert Roses were thought to be petrified flowers.

Alabaster is the name used for gypsum in its massive, fine-grained granular compact form, which is suitable for carving. This is the variety which has been used widely for building, monumental, gemmological and artistic purposes.

Thick beds of gypsum are found in many areas including North and South America, continental Europe, particularly Spain, and Great Britain. Italy is now the major supplier of the variety alabaster. The alabaster is mined in the Volterra district as ovoid masses up to a metre and a half in diameter from limestones interbedded with marls. It is cut, then commonly artificially stained and polished at Pisa, Florence and Volterra. It is made into table lamps, ash trays, statues and other knick-knacks. Because thin slabs of alabaster are translucent they have been used as windows in the Mediterranean area from an early date. One of the most famous examples of alabaster windows are those in Galla Placidia's Mausoleum in Ravenna. They are yellow orange in colour and are the only source of indoor light.

At one time British alabaster was much sought after and was extensively wrought. Gypsum and anhydrite occur in many areas in Great Britain.[66] It is possible to collect pieces of the variety alabaster, which may be suitable for carving, from any of the places where gypsum crops out. For example, the pink Welsh Alabaster found in thin bands along the coastal cliffs of Glamorgan in Wales can be carved. Two places renowned for the supply of good quality block alabaster are Fauld, Staffordshire and Chellaston, Derbyshire. At Chellaston the Tutbury Gypsum beds were once worked on a large scale. The Fauld mine now supplies only a limited quantity.[67] At Fauld the mineral is found in a series of beds, not all of which are worked. The bed which is worked consists of discontinuous lenticular masses, several metres in diameter and about 2.5 metres thick, which are separated by marl. The thick nodular beds are known as 'floors'. The smaller masses are called 'cakes'.

The purest form of alabaster is white and translucent, but traces of ferric oxide produce light brown, orange- and red-coloured veins, bands and patches. Alabaster has been used in Great Britain since the earliest days. The second rim of the arch of the Norman west doorway of Tutbury Church, Staffordshire, dated 1160 is made of it, as is an effigy of a cross-legged knight in the parish church of Hanbury, Staffordshire dated about 1280 to 1300. Alabaster altar pieces, panels and other pieces were produced in quantity and generally were painted.[68]

Since about 1400 vast amounts of alabaster have been supplied from Tutbury, Chellaston and elsewhere to 'the factory at Nottingham'. There alabasterers were employed to carve effigies and panels. Nottingham was particularly known for its plaques of the head of St John the Baptist. The first reference to this industry dates from 1367 and mentions an alabaster altar-piece.[68]

Nottingham was an important centre for international trade. Mediaeval altar-pieces were exported from there to Iceland, Italy, Spain and elsewhere. The fame of British alabaster spread rapidly. In May 1382 King Richard II allowed Cosmato Gentilis, Pope Urban II's collector, to export four alabaster images. British alabaster was so sought after that blocks were exported. The industry suffered a blow during the Reformation when images of 'stone, timber, alabaster, or earth, graven, carved or painted' had to be defaced or destroyed. The production of effigies for tombs was excepted. The use of alabaster for building is magnificently seen in the so-called Marble

(a)

(b)

(c)

Figure 4.80 (a) Alabaster, richly gilded and painted, forms the bulk of a monument (part of the inscription on which reads 'The Marble Selfe Doth Weepe') in the church at Amersham, Buckinghamshire; (b) intricately carved alabaster forms the canopy above the High Altar, Peterborough Cathedral; (c) balustrade of staircase in alabaster supporting a marble handrail. National Liberal Club, London

Hall of Holkham Hall, Norfolk, and for the twenty 25-feet high columns of Kedleston Hall, Derbyshire. The alabaster for these columns was quarried at Red Hill near the confluence of the River Soar and the River Trent. Each column is made up of three blocks which are so well matched that the joints are not easily distinguished. Jacob Epstein's sculpture *Consummatum Est* (1937) is a direct carving in alabaster. The uses of alabaster are well recorded, see for example Cheetham[68] and Dimes.[69]

Gypsum easily loses and gains water. When heated the water is driven off and the resulting powdered product is Plaster of Paris. When water is added, gypsum is reformed and sets as a rigid mass.

Plaster of Paris is named from its early use in France. Extensive beds of gypsum up to 100 feet (30 m) thick were worked, notably at Montmarte, then to the north of Paris. When Henry II of England visited Paris in 1254 he was much impressed with the fineness and whiteness of this plaster and he introduced it into England. Soon after English sources of gypsum were exploited. A plaster made from calcined gypsum was used in the pyramids of Egypt, over 4000 years ago.[70]

Gypsum is used extensively in plaster and mortar and is also added to Portland cement to delay the setting time.

Marmo di Castellina is alabaster which has been placed in water, gently heated nearly to boiling point and cooled. The translucency of the alabaster is deadened to resemble, it is claimed, fine Carrara marble. As such it was sold to tourists. At one time many carvings sold to tourists in Mexico as jade were made from alabaster which was dyed green.

The use of large blocks of alabaster for structural purposes is familiar to many because it is mentioned by the tourist guides at the Palace of Knossos, Crete. Gypsum is also used in the process of burtonization of beer. Therefore, it may be appropriate that the balustrades of Messrs Bass's offices in Burton-upon-Trent are recorded as being of alabaster.

Bitumens

Bitumens are a series of substances, essentially mixtures of hydrocarbons, with a wide variety of names including asphalt, tar, pitch and bitumen. They have the general formula of C_nH_{2n}, but most hydrocarbons are mixtures of different series usually with impurities. Surface seeps, tar pools, and asphalt lakes occur relatively commonly. Their source is mostly a matter of speculation. They appear to have been left behind by the evaporation of the more volatile hydrocarbon content and thus are sometimes described as residuals. Hydrocarbons are invariably generated and accumulate in sedimentary rocks.

The peculiar deposit of elaterite, at Windy Knoll, near Castleton, Derbyshire, is known to generations of geologists. The natural bitumen seep in the Coalport tar tunnel, near Ironbridge, Shropshire is now a tourist display. The Athabaska Tar Sands, North-West Territories, Canada, are well known. The 114 acre (46 hectare) Pitch Lake near La Broa, Trinidad has been used since at least the time of Sir Walter Raleigh (*Figure 4.81*).

Figure 4.81 'Pitch' from The Pitch Lake, Trinidad, used by Sir Walter Raleigh, today is packed in cardboard barrels and mostly exported. (Courtesy of Mrs J. Hay)

In Mesopotamia and Palestine bitumens were used in the production of mortar. Bitumen mortars, bitumen cements and cements made with pitch are known. The bitumen acts as a bonding agent. Apart from its use for caulking ships, bitumen, or asphalt, has been used for paving and for roofing. Bitumen has been found used as a mortar in the river walls of the old Palace of Westminster, London. Modern asphaltic concrete is produced by mixing stone fragments with a precisely measured amount of bitumen.

Coal, Cannel Coal and jet

Coal is a sedimentary rock of organic origin; it is the result of the accumulation of plant material which was altered to greater or lesser degree. Coal is largely made up of carbon, oxygen and hydrogen. Beds of coal have closely spaced vertical jointing known as the *cleat*, with a less well developed jointing at right angles known as the *end*. This joint pattern leads to the development of the familiar cube-shaped pieces of coal when the coal is extracted.

Unlikely as it may seem, coal has been used as a decorative material. Occasionally large blocks of coal are secured and they have been carved into intricate objects displayed during miners' fêtes, village open days and the like. They have little, if any, practical use. A cube of coal with faces three feet (0.9 m) square sits atop a column in Newcastle, New South Wales, Australia, a monument to the development of the South Maitland coalfield. The Coal Seat, in Osborne House, Isle of Wight, is the ultimate fanciful conceit. In addition to its brittleness the danger of damage by fire is immediately apparent.

Cannel Coal is dense, lustreless, blackish and typically shows concoidal fracture surfaces. Under the microscope it is seen to be composed largely of spore and pollen remains, small resin bodies and fragments of leaf cuticles. It is considered to be a drift coal. It ignites easily and burns with a very smokey yellow candle-like flame (cannel is Scots dialect for candle). Recent examination revealed that a small section of the original floor in the Lady Chapel of Lichfield Cathedral amazingly was laid lozengy of Cannel Coal and alabaster. Such a floor is thought to be unique. (Personal communication by M. Stancliffe.)

Jet is a lustrous black substance which is easily worked and which will take a high polish. In Great Britain it is found particularly in the Upper Liassic age Jet Rock Series in the cliffs at Whitby, Yorkshire.

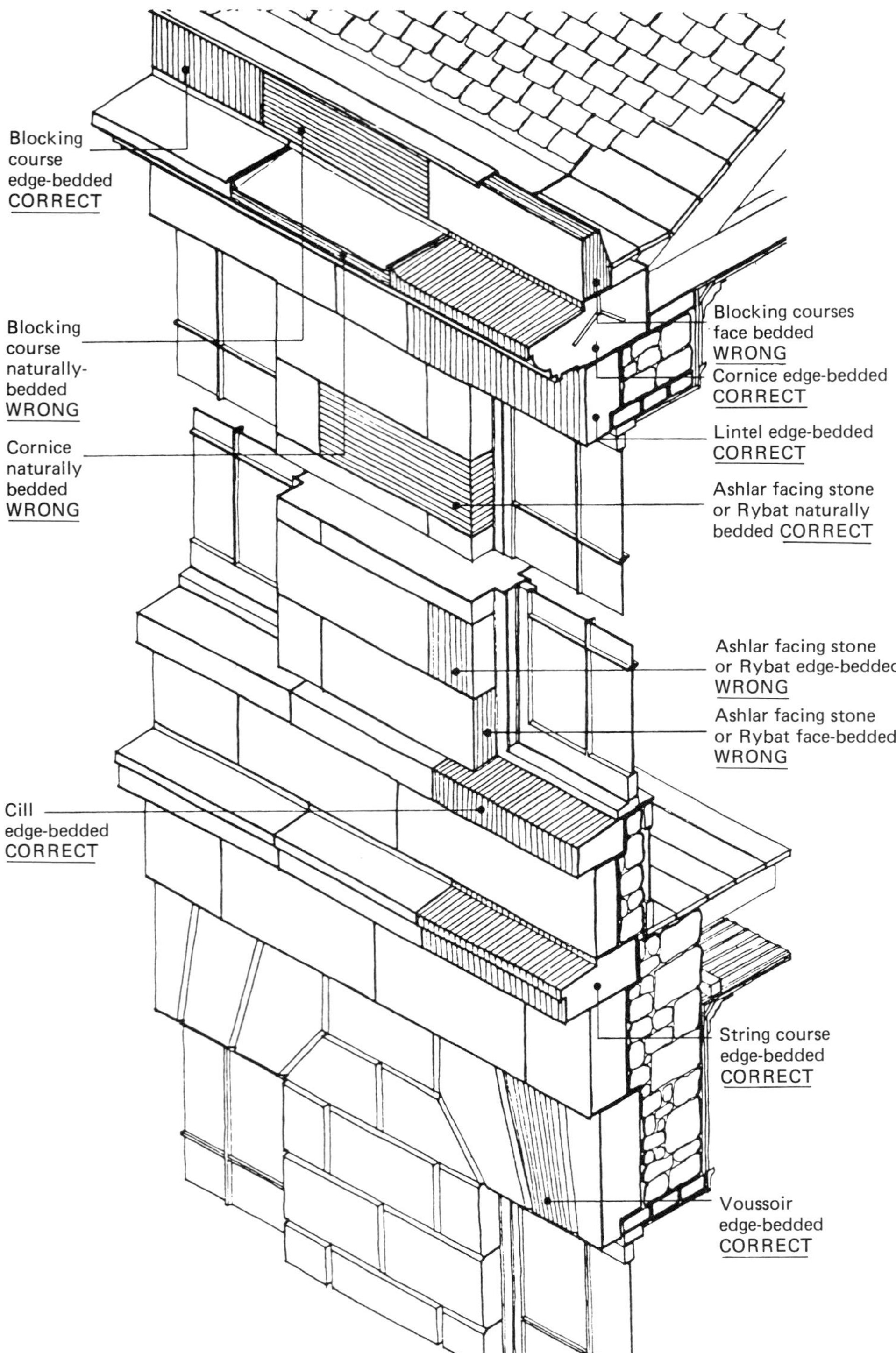

Figure 4.82 The placing of a sedimentary stone into a building. The bedding planes should be at right angles to the thrust imposed on them. (From reference 75)

It occurs as sporadic lenticular masses and is derived from pieces of drifted wood buried in isolation which did not pass through a peat phase and thus were not coalified, but underwent decomposition and retained their cellular structure.

Jet was known in the Bronze Age. The Romans thought very highly of it and they established a jet workshop in York. It has since been widely used for personal adornment and jewellery. It was very popular in Victorian times for mourning jewellery.

Much folklore is attached to jet and it is said to protect against the evil eye, against serpents and dogs. It cures toothache, hysteria and epilepsy. It is also a love token and if a woman was given water into which jet had been dipped and she remained continent she was pure. It shatters during acts of infidelity. Proof of these properties has yet to appear in scientific literature.

Special considerations

Placing stone 'in bed'

The bed and the bedding plane are unique characteristics of sedimentary rocks. A block of stone from a quarry can be placed in a building in one of three attitudes in relation to the bedding (see *Figure 4.82*).

There is now no doubt that stone will resist weathering far better if it is 'in bed' than if it is oriented in any other direction. In effect the thrust on the stone should be at a right angle to the bedding, (see *Figure 4.82*) and this also seems to apply to having the stone the right way up. In many sedimentary stones the bedding is immediately apparent, but in stones taken from rocks which are massively bedded and wide-jointed the bedding direction may be difficult to determine by eye. Therefore, the way-up of the stone should be marked on each block removed from the quarry face and the mark should be maintained on the stone until it is finally fixed. The disastrous consequences of ignoring the bedding are all too easily seen (*Figure 4.83*). Even when stones are markedly cross-bedded way-up criteria should still be applied. The phrase 'built on cant' is used particularly in Scotland for stone which has been placed with the natural bed in a vertical position. It was noted that this stone wastes very quickly.[71]

The importance of placing blocks of building stone 'in bed' was recognized by the Romans when they built Rome. Blocks of travertine, an excellent building stone when laid on its bed, were sometimes set the wrong way and had speedily to be replaced '... the rostra in the Forum are an example'.[72] The lesson seems to have been forgotten. Many times a stone is thought to be unsuitable or of poor quality or to decay easily because due consideration was not paid to the bedding planes of the stone.

Freestone

Any stone, specifically those taken from sedimentary rocks, that can be freely worked in any direction is commonly referred to as a freestone. The term does not give any indication whatever of the nature of the stone. When used in the southern part of Great Britain, a freestone will almost certainly be a limestone, while in the Midlands and northern England it will be a sandstone.

Incompatible stones

Although different types of stones for building may be mixed with impunity, associations of some stones used without due regard to architectural detailing may lead to associative decay. This applies especially to limestone and sandstone association. If a limestone in a building is placed above a sandstone, it will normally be found that the sandstone will decay.

Limestone is essentially calcium carbonate, which is only slightly soluble in pure water. However, water which contains carbon dioxide, which most rain water does, will dissolve calcium carbonate to form calcium bicarbonate, which only exists in solution. Thus when rain falls on the limestone surfaces of building stone some calcium carbonate is dissolved into the water in the form of the bicarbonate, which is unstable. When it reaches the sandstone below, the rain water is absorbed, and, as the water evaporates, calcium carbonate is redeposited within the interstices. The grains of the sandstone are forced apart and the stone disintegrates. This process does not operate when sandstone is used above a limestone because the silica grains of the sandstone are virtually chemically inert. Associative decay has been noted widely in Bristol, which is sited in an area where the Pennant Grit and Carboniferous Limestone were both readily to hand.

If there is no alternative but to use the two types of stone, careful architectural detailing should endeavour to ensure that rain water is thrown clear of the sandstone.

Soiling by wax

Sandstones, many limestones and marbles are absorbent. Surfaces of these stones which are subjected to constant touching, rubbing or smoothing will absorb grease from human hands, sometimes to a significant degree. The wax will oxidize and darken on exposure to air, as will all polishes.

Most igneous and metamorphic rocks, because of their close, tight-grained nature do not suffer. Normally it is only the surface which is dirty. Integral

(a)

(b)

(c)

(d)

(e)

Figure 4.83 (a) The blocks of Portland Limestone from the Isle of Purbeck used for a seawall at Hotwells, Portsmouth are laid with due regard for the bedding; (b) further along the wall, one of parapet stones has been laid with its bedding planes horizontal, and as a consequence has failed; (c) blocks of Bath stone forming the parapet of a wall on the roof of St Pancras railway station were laid with bedding planes horizontal; (d) markedly false-bedded stones should be laid to observe way-up criteria, Old Red Sandstone, Goodrich Castle, Herefordshire; (e) current bedding in Coal Measure Sandstone used for the York City Art Gallery is emphasized by layers of small mica flakes along the bedding planes. The stone is correctly positioned to fulfil its function in the structure of the building. (Photos (a) and (b) courtesy R.H. Roberts)

Figure 4.84 The castle walls of York were built of Millstone Grit and of Magnesian Limestone. The topmost five courses are of sandstone, with eight courses of limestone below. No associative decay is seen. However, the next nine courses of sandstone below are badly decayed because rainwater, charged with calcium bicarbonate from the Magnesian Limestone above, is able to soak into the sandstone. Note that the lowest courses of limestone are unaffected

Figure 4.85 Traditionally, visitors to the inner area of the Temple at Angkor Wat, Cambodia (now Kampuchea), gently stroke the Apsaras (statues of the guardian women). The ingrained deposit of wax from human hands shows the favoured areas. (Courtesy of E.A. Jobbins)

handrails to stairs may appear appreciably darker than the adjoining stone and this may not necessarily be regarded as a desirable feature. Architectural detailing should take account of this factor.

Statues in museums, which are not regularly cleaned, show those areas favoured by the visiting public; it provides an illuminating study. In the past, some stone structures were painted or polished. The oil of the paint or the wax may well have penetrated to some depth. Although it may be possible to clean the pigment from the surface of the stone it is not possible to remove the wax or oil from any depth. Paint was used on the White House in Washington, DC, USA. It has penetrated several centimetres and now cannot be removed without removing the surface of the stone.

Effects of fire

Little detailed study has been made on the effects of fire and heat on a range of building stones. Normally the other materials burn to leave stonework still standing although it may be weakened by the destruction of other structural elements. The immediately apparent effect is a reddening of the stone, but not all reddening of stones is due to fire. Red coloration at the base of the Parthenon in Athens, Greece, once was thought to be due to fire. The effect of fire is dramatically demonstrated in Hafod Chapel, near Devils Bridge, Dyfed, Wales, and in the central tower of Tewkesbury Abbey, Gloucestershire. The reddened bases of the columns of the aisle in Gloucester Cathedral still witness the ferocity of the 'mighty fire' of 1122 AD.

Stone does not burn, with the obvious exceptions of coal and allied material, but it is damaged by the burning of other substances. The rate of heating is an

Figure 4.86 Fire-reddening and surface spalling on an external wall of Westminster Hall, London resulted from the fire of 1974. (Photo: John Ashurst)

important condition; temperatures of about 1000 °C may be reached within an hour in a not particularly vicious fire. By comparison a Bunsen burner flame reaches about 500 °C. The spallability of the stone determines whether small flakes, a few millimetres at the most, will spall off. Overall, the thermal expansion of rocks is very small.

The coefficients of linear expansion (α) given by Kaye and Laby[73] are: granite, 6–9 $\times 10^{-6}$, marble, 3–15 $\times 10^{-6}$, slate, 6–12 $\times 10^{-6}$, sandstone, 5–12 $\times 10^{-6}$ and Portland Stone, approximately, 3 $\times 10^{-6}$. The coefficients are all of a similar order and about the same as those for porcelain and glass.

The coefficient of linear expansion may also be expressed more directly in millimetres per metre per degree C. Typical figures[60] are:

Name of stone	*Type*	*Locality*	*mm/m °C*
Bianco p.	Marble	Carrara, Italy	0.0029
Bianco venato gioia	Marble	Carrara, Italy	0.0063
Cipollino apuano	Marble	Lucca, Italy	0.0077
Potoro macchia fine	Calcareous breccia	La Spezia, Italy	0.0050
Travertino ascolano striato	Travertine	Ascoli Piceno, Italy	0.0050
Rosso antico d'italia	Serpentinite	Genova, Italy	0.0061
Verde issorie	Serpentinite	Val d'Aosta, Italy	0.0058
Granito rosa baveno	Granite	Novara, Italy	0.0075
Sienite balma	Syenite	Vercelli, Italy	0.0042

In Great Britain the range of temperature from solar gain that might be expected in stone cladding, depending on its type and colour, is from −20°C to 65°C. Taking Cipollino Apuano as an example and using the worst possible case temperature difference: 85 × 0.0077 = 0.6545 mm expansion per metre of stone.

The thermal conductivity of rocks is minute. Reports of stone being 'red-hot' can be dismissed as sheer invention. Stone may be regarded as the ideal fire-proof natural material. Laboratory tests on limestone containing iron oxides show that intense heating causes the limestone to pass through a cycle of colours including pink, purple, grey and cream. It is not possible, however, to use the colours as an indicator of temperature because too many variables are involved. The colour will depend on the type of stone and its mineral composition, which may vary substantially from one part to another.

With a fairly pure limestone with little other mineral matter and with practically no iron oxide minerals the calcium carbonate will dissociate according to the reaction:

$$\underset{\text{calcium carbonate}}{CaCO_3} + \text{heat} \rightarrow \underset{\text{lime}}{CaO} + \underset{\text{carbon dioxide}}{CO_2}$$

Depending on specific conditions dissociation will occur at about 900°C (1652°F).

Further reactions may occur. If firemen's hoses are played onto the dissociated limestone:

$$\underset{\text{lime}}{CaO} + \underset{\text{water}}{H_2O} \rightarrow \underset{\text{slaked lime}}{Ca(OH)_2}$$

Other reactions are now possible, for example:

$$\underset{\text{slaked lime}}{Ca(OH)_2} + \underset{\text{sulphuric acid (acid rain)}}{H_2SO_4} \rightarrow \underset{\text{gypsum}}{CaSO_4 2H_2O}$$

or:

$$\underset{\text{slaked lime}}{Ca(OH)_2} + \underset{\text{carbon dioxide}}{CO_2} \rightarrow \underset{\text{calcium carbonate}}{CaCO_3} + \underset{\text{water}}{H_2O}$$

The likelihood of all of these reactions occurring is remote. In any event, because of the low thermal conductivity of stone any of these effects would be purely on the surfaces of the stone, much of which will not have been exposed directly to heat. However, the surfaces which are affected may be important. For example, the fire inside Westminster Hall in 1974, which was quenched with large amounts of water, left the eleventh century wall surface with a thin superficial layer split from the face. In some areas this layer was fragmented.[74]

In laboratory tests, limestone heated to 900 °C throughout passed through an unstable stage. The cooled specimen eventually fell into a white powder after several days in the atmosphere. Other specimens heated to 1085 °C and to 1250 °C remained stable for several weeks before they disintegrated.

Other chemical effects

Instances are known of limestone ribs, bosses, string courses and the like in a church decaying and becoming unsafe. No immediate cause was found but in the past the church was lit by acetylene lamps.

When acetylene (C_2H_2) is burnt, carbon monoxide (CO), carbon dioxide (CO_2), and water (H_2O) are produced. Within a closed building acidic vapours, particularly carbonic acid, which is very much like an industrial smog, will be concentrated. This undoubtedly would have a deleterious effect on the limestone over the years. Acid gases may have a number of effects:

$$\underset{\text{calcium carbonate}}{CaCO_3} + \underset{\text{sulphuric acid}}{H_2SO_4\ (=H_2O + SO_2)} \rightarrow \underset{\text{calcium sulphite}}{CaSO_3}$$

or:

$$\underset{\text{calcium carbonate}}{CaCO_3} + \underset{\text{oxygen}}{O} \rightarrow \underset{\text{calcium sulphate}}{CaSO_4}$$

Cautions

Repair, restoration and replacement of stonework may destroy other important evidence. The reddening of stone used in ancient buildings may be of historical and of archaeological significance, and may help to date the development of the building. Care must be taken, however, to determine whether the fire-reddened stone has been re-used from earlier building.

The displacement of drums of stone making up columns of buildings may be evidence of an earthquake. It provides not only data for the architectural behaviour of a type of construction but also evidence of an event which is of both geological and archaeological importance.

It may be of great interest to maintain damaged stonework. The pock marks in the Portland Stone of the front of the Geological Museum, Exhibition Road, London are an emphatic reminder of the effect of German high-explosive bombs on masonry. The pitted giant monolithic granite columns of St Isaacs Church Cathedral bear grim witness to the 900-day siege of Leningrad, USSR. The grooves worn by wheels in the slabs forming the roadway, which is part of the Roman Wall, at Housesteads, Northumberland tell more about life at the time than does unworn stone. In these instances history has been impressed upon the stone rather than lying within it.

Figure 4.87 The drums of the columns of Pentelic marble have been displaced by earthquake activity at the Temple of Hephestos, Athens

References

1. Harris, P.M., *Mineral Dossier No. 17. Sandstone*, HMSO, London, 1977
2. Penoyre, J. and Penoyre, J., *Houses in the Landscape*, Readers Union, Newton Abbot, 1978
3. Watson, J., *British and Foreign Building Stones*, University Press, Cambridge, 1911
4. Smith, E.G. In Rayner, D.H. and Hemmingway, J.E., eds., *The Geology and Mineral Resources of Yorkshire*, Yorkshire Geological Society, 1974
5. Crane, T., *Newcastle Stone*, Ealing Publications Ltd., Maidenhead, 1979
6. Anon., *Edinburgh Weekly Journal*, November 1923 *quoted in* Craig, G., On Building Stones used in Edinburgh; their Geological Sources, Relative Durability, and Other Characteristics, *Trans. Edin. Geol. Soc.*, **6**, 1893
7. Craig, G. On Building Stones used in Edinburgh; their Geological Sources, Relative Durability, and Other Characteristics, *Trans. Edin. Geol. Soc.*, **6**, 1893
8. Wray, D.A., Stephens, J.C., Edwards, W.N., and Bromehead, C.N., 'The Geology of the Country around Huddersfield and Halifax', *Mem. Geol. Surv. G.B.*, HMSO, London, 1930
9. Mills, P., 'York Stone Paving', Letter in *The Times*, 13 January 1975
10. Clifton-Taylor, A., *The Pattern of English Building*, Faber and Faber, London, 1972
11. Pevsner, N., *The Buildings of England: County Durham*, 2nd edn, Penguin, Harmondsworth, 1983
12. Elsden, J. and Howe, J.A., *The Stones of London*, Colliery Guardian Co. Ltd., London, 1923
13. Simpson, I.M. and Broadhurst, F.M., *A Building Stones Guide to Central Manchester*, University of Manchester, Manchester, 1975
14. Whittow, J.B., *Geology and Scenery in Scotland*, Penguin, Harmondsworth, 1977
15. Lawson, J., *Building Stones of Glasgow*, Geological Society of Glasgow, Glasgow, 1981
16. Kent, Sir Peter, *British Regional Geology: Eastern England from the Tees to the Wash*, HMSO, London, 1980
17. North, F.J., *Limestones: Their origins, distribution, and uses*, Thomas Murby & Co., London, 1930
18. Nairn, I. and Pevsner, N., *The Buildings of England: Surrey*, 2nd edn, Penguin, Harmondsworth, 1971
19. Thurrell, R.G., Worssam, B.C., and Edmonds, E.A., 'Geology of the Country around Haslemere'. *Mem. Geol. Surv. G.B.*, HMSO, London, 1968
20. Dines, H.G., Buchan, S., Holmes, S.C.A., and Bristow, C.R., 'Geology of the Country around Sevenoaks and Tonbridge', *Mem. Geol. Surv. G.B.*, HMSO, London, 1969
21. White, G., *The Natural History of Selborne*, J. Fisher ed., Cressert Press, London 1947
22. Larwood, G.P. and Funnell, B.M., eds., *The Geology of Norfolk*, Paramoudra Club, Norwich, 1970
23. Anon., *Merstham Firestone Quarries: an interim account*, Croydon Caving Club, Carshalton, 1976
24. Osborne, B.E., 'Early Plateways and Firestone Mining in Surrey; an interim report' *Croydon Natural History and Scientific Society*, **17**, Pt. 3, Feb. 1982
25. Sowan, P.W., 'Stone Mining in East Surrey' *Surrey History*, **1**, No. 3, Phillimore, Chichester, 1975

26. Appleby, J.W., *Hertfordshire Puddingstone*, St. Albans Museum, 1978
27. Davies, A.M. and Baines, A.H.I., 'A Preliminary Survey of the Sarsen and Puddingstone Blocks of the Chilterns', *Proc. Geol. Assoc.* **64**, Pt. 1, 1953
28. Nairn, I. and Pevsner, N., *The Buildings of England: Sussex*, Penguin, Harmondsworth, 1965
29. Clifton-Taylor, A. and Ireson, A.S., *English Stone Building*, Gollancz, London, 1983
30. Dimes, F.G., 'What is Onyx?' *Stone Industries*, **12**, No. 5. Sept/Oct 1977
31. Whittow, J.B., *Geology and Scenery in Ireland*, Penguin, Harmondsworth, 1974
32. Watson, J., *British and Foreign Marbles and Other Ornamental Stones*, University Press, Cambridge, 1916
33. Ford, T.D., 'The Black Marble of Ashford-in-the-Water, Derbyshire', *Liverpool and Manchester Geol. J.*, **2**, Pt. 1, 1958
34. Whittow, J.B., *Geology and Scenery in Ireland*, Penguin, Harmondsworth, 1974
35. Donovan, D.T. and Reid, R.D., 'The Stone Insets of Somerset Churches' *Proc. Somerset Archaeological and Natural History Soc.*, **107**, 1963
36. L.S.C. and F.S.W. *The Stones of Wells Cathedral*, Wells Natural History and Archaeological Society, Wells, n.d.
37. Bainbridge, C., 'Cold comfort for the village of slate', *The Times*, 9th August 1975
38. Purcell, D., *Cambridge Stone*, Faber and Faber, London, 1967
39. Green, G.W., and Welch, F.B.A., 'Geology of the Country around Wells and Cheddar', *Mem. Geol. Surv. G.B.*, HMSO, London, 1952
40. Purcell, D., *The Stones of Ely Cathedral*, 2nd edn., The Friends of Ely Cathedral, Ely, n.d.
41. Arkell, W.J., *Oxford Stone*, Faber and Faber, London, 1947
42. Howe, J.A., *The Geology of Building Stones*, Edward Arnold, London, 1910
43. Perkins, J.W., Brooks, A.T., and Pearce, A.E. McR, *Bath Stone: a quarry history*, University College Cardiff and Kingsmead Press, Bath, 1979
44. Lang, J., *Rebuilding St Paul's after the Great Fire of London*, Oxford University Press, London, 1956
45. Arkell, W.J., *The Geology of the Country around Weymouth, Swanage, Corfe and Lulworth, Mem. Geol. Surv. G.B.*, HMSO, London, 1947
46. Simpson, I.M. and Broadhurst, F.M., *A Building Stones Guide to Central Manchester*, University of Manchester, Manchester, 1975
47. Brown, P.R., Rudkins, G.F., Wheldon, P.E., 'Portland Stone', *Chartered Civil Engineer*, January 1954
48. Edmunds, F.H., and Schaffer, R.J., 'Portland Stone: Its Geology and Properties as a Building Stone', *Proc. Geol. Soc.*, **43**, Pt. 3, 1932
49. Crane, T., *Newcastle Stone*, Ealing Publications Ltd., Maidenhead, 1979
50. Allan, J., *Restoration and Archaeology in Exeter Cathedral*, Devon Archaeology No. 1, 1983
51. Leach, R., *An Investigation into the use of Purbeck Marble in Medieval England*, Privately Printed, R.A. Leach, Devon, 1978
52. Thurrell, R.G., Worrsam, B.C., and Edmonds, E.A., *Geology of the Country around Haslemere, Mem. Geol. Surv. G.B.*, HMSO, London, 1968
53. Worssam, B.C., *Eight Centuries of Stone*, Eagle Printing Works, Cranbrook, n.d.
54. Marsden, P.R.V., *A Ship of the Roman Period, From Blackfriars, in the City of London*, Guildhall Museum Publication, n.d.
55. Jukes, Brown, A.J., *'The Cretaceous Rocks of Britain', Vol. III, The Upper Chalk of England, Mem. Geol. Surv. G.B.*, HMSO, London, 1904
56. Fowler, J., *The Stones of Sherborne Abbey*, Friends of Sherborne Abbey, n.d.
57. Males, P.A., 'Mexican Onyx and other Marbles'. *Australian Lapidary Magazine*, February 1974
58. Dunham, M. and Dunham, K.C., 'The Stone of the Neville Screen in Durham Cathedral, *Durham University Journal*, March 1957
59. Honeyborne, D.B., 'The building limestones of France', Building Research Establishment Note, Department of the Environment, 1978
60. Catell, M. *et al.*, *Italian Marble—Technical Guide.* F. Lli Vallardi Editori, Milan, 1982
61. Lundbohm, H., *Några öpplysningar om Sveriges stenindustri*, Stockholm, 1888
62. Wilson, E., 'Swedish limestone paving in 17th and 18th century English buildings', *Post-Medieval Archaeology*, **17**, 1983
63. Anon., *Rochas Ornamentais Portuguesas.* Ministério da Indústria e Energia, Direcção-Geral de Geologia e Minas, Lisbon, 1982
64. Anon., *Coventry Cathedral*, Reprinted from Shell—BP News, The Staff Magazine of Shell-Mex and BP Ltd.
65. Shadmon, A., *Stone in Israel*, Ministry of Development, Natural Resources Research Organization, Jerusalem, 1972
66. Notholt, A.I.G., and Highley, D.E., *Mineral Dossier No. 13, Gypsum and Anhydrite*, HMSO, London, 1975
67. Anon., *Natural Stone Directory* 7th edn, Stone Industries, Ealing Publications, Maidenhead, 1987
68. Cheetham, F.W., *Medieval English Alabaster Carvings in the Castle Museum, Nottingham*, The City of Nottingham Art Galleries and Museums Committee, Nottingham, 1973
69. Dimes, F.G., 'Alabaster—soft option for sculptors', *Stone Industries*, **14**, No. 6, July/August 1979
70. Watson, J., *Cements and Artificial Stone*, Heffer and Sons, Cambridge, 1922
71. Anon., 'The Architectural Use of Building Materials, *Post-War Building Studies No. 18*, HMSO, London, 1946
72. Bromehead, C.E.N., 'Geology in Embryo (Up to 1600 AD)', *Proc. Geol. Assoc.,* **56**, Pt. 2, 1945
73. Kaye, G.W.C., and Laby, T.H., *Physical Constants*, Longmans, London, 1959
74. Anon., 'Resins for Repair', *Stone Industries*, **19**, No. 2, March 1984
75. Davey, A. *et al., The Care and Conservation of Georgian Houses*, 3rd edn. Butterworths, London, 1986

5

Metamorphic rocks

Francis G. Dimes

Introduction

Metamorphic rocks are formed by the crystallization or recrystallization of pre-existing rocks at elevated temperatures or at elevated pressures or both beneath the Earth's surface. The original constituent materials of the rocks, which may have been formed under widely different conditions, are rearranged mechanically or chemically, usually with the development of new minerals. During metamorphism the original rocks lose many, if not all, of their original characteristics. Any pre-existing rock may be metamorphosed. Thus there are many types of metamorphic rocks. The common types are given in *Table 2.3*. Most of the metamorphic rocks used in commerce are the product of regional metamorphism. By far the most widely used are slate and marble. However, one stone which is the result of thermal metamorphism is of interest both from a geological and from a visual point of view.

Thermal metamorphic rocks

Ematita Granite, known also as Verde Ematita, Madreperla, or Labradorita, is from the Andean Cordillera, north of San Juan, Argentina[1]. It is a high grade metamorphic rock, described as a cordierite-silimonite-phlogopite-plagioclase-quartz rock. Blue-grey to greenish in colour it has been used particularly for Marks and Spencer shops in Northampton, Sheffield, Cardiff and in the eastern end of Oxford Street, London. A striking example of its use is for St Peters' Hill House, Carter Lane, London.

Regional metamorphic rocks

Schist

Schist is one of the most abundant of the metamorphic rocks. Much of Scotland, for example, is underlain by it. The aligned arrangement of platy and other elongated minerals commonly gives a structure known as schistosity. The alignment of the platy minerals appears to the unaided eye as a marked layering.

Many varieties of schist exist. They are named after distinctive minerals which may be present, for example, garnet, chlorite, graphite and talc. By far the most common type is mica schist. Mica schists commonly have a second mineral. Garnet-mica schist and hornblende-mica schist are also common. Biotite mica is an important constituent mineral of most schists. Because of the ease with which schist will part along the lamination it has only been used locally for building. However, some quartzites of the stone trade are schists in strict geological definition. They differ from other quartzites in that a laminated structure is produced by aligned planes which are commonly of mica flakes.

Otta Slate, from Norway, known also as Rembrant Stone (or Quartzite) and as Pillaguri Slate after the mountain peak near which it is quarried half-way between Oslo and Trondheim. It is a garnet-hornblende-biotite-muscovite-quartz schist. It is blue-black in colour. The mineral hornblende appears as needle-like streaks up to 2 inches (5 cm) long. The garnets appear as small red spots. Some of the stone may be found without hornblende. The stone can be polished and a peculiarly fascinating three-dimensional appearance is obtained. The top

(a)

(b)

Figure 5.1 (a) Slabs of Otta Slate clad columns at Tenter House, Moorgate (Cippolina marble in background); (b) needle-like hornblende crystals and red spots of garnet are responsible for the characteristic appearance of the schist. Rutherford House, George Street, Manchester

layers of the quarry, where the schist has been exposed to the weather, yield rust-coloured slabs. The stone has been recently used in Britain; the Nationwide Building Society, High Holborn, London is an example. It was also used for Bergen Hospital, Norway, for floors, risers, and treads in Unilever House, Rotterdam, Holland and for Klöcknen-Humbolt-Deutz AG, Cologne, Germany.

Barge Quartzite also known as Sanfront Stone or as Italian Quartzite, is a mica-quartz schist from Mount Bracco, Italy, in which the quartz content may be as high as 95 per cent or more. Grey, gold, amber and olive colours are available. Many modern examples of its use are found, usually for flooring or for cladding. Examples include the Bear and Staff public house, Charing Cross Road, London, Radiant House, Gas Company, Liverpool and facings of Tower Block and Bridge, Shell House, London SE1.

Gneiss

A gneiss is a foliated rock normally composed of feldspar, quartz, biotite or muscovite mica or both and sometimes hornblende. The minerals are arranged alternately in fairly large-scale, roughly parallel layers known as gneissose banding. This tough, massive and, in some instances, decorative rock has been used locally for building purposes. Because its mineral composition and appearance is similar to some granites, gneiss usually is sold as granite. Alps Grey Granite, from Switzerland, is a biotite gneiss, which is white and dark-grey to black in colour. Pink Parys Granite is a gneissose granite from Parys, Transvaal, South Africa. It was used for the spectacular cladding on Irongate House, Dukes Place, London (*Figure 5.2*).

Quartzite

A quartzite is produced when a sandstone is metamorphosed. The constituent grains of quartz are recrystallized to an interlocking mosaic of quartz as distinct from quartzites of sedimentary origin. Mica flakes are commonly present, occasionally with other minerals.

Alta Quartzite or Altazite, with some varieties known as Crystalite, is a silver grey-green somewhat micaceous quartzite. It has been quarried since 1919 from the mountains around Alta Fjord, Norway, well inside the Arctic Circle. It has been widely used since then for paving and steps. The floor of the Chapel of the Daughters of the Cross, Stoodley Knowle, Torquay, Devon and of The Weald Inn, Burgess Hill, Sussex provide contrasting examples. The Driver and Vehicle Licensing Centre, Swansea, South Wales is another example of its use.

Diamant Quartzite (Diamantzite, or Allied Quartzite) shows a variation of colour from white, through grey-blue to beige-ochre. It is also used for paving and steps. It is quarried in Namaqualand, South Africa and, like most quartzites, is tough and hard-wearing. Mica is found along marked planes resulting in a very smooth cleavage. The stone could be classified with some justification as a schist. A fine example of its use is seen in St Joseph's Oratory, Montreal, Canada. It paves the British Telecom Monarch telephone exchange, London, and may be seen in the Nationwide Building Society, Edinburgh. Safari Quartzite, from the Transvaal, South Africa is a similar stone.

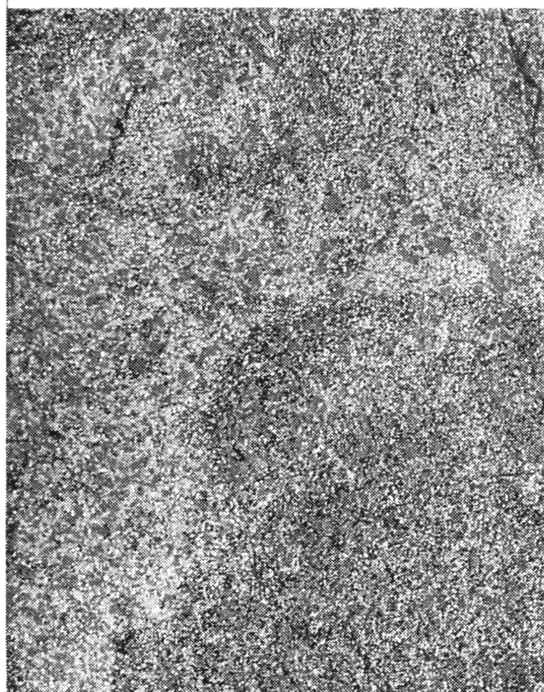

Figure 5.2 Granite from Parys, Transvaal, South Africa, used for Irongate House, Dukes Place, London, is strongly deformed and now shows gneissic structure

Slate

Slaty cleavage, the characteristic feature, imposed upon a clay during the processes of regional metamorphism may be of variable thickness (see *Figure 2.6*). Some slates are produced from fine-grained sediments which are not clay in strict sense. The thinner that a slate can be cleaved, the finer it is reckoned to be. The original bedding may sometimes be seen as coloured bands running at a different angle to the cleavage surface. Slaty-cleavage may be parallel to the original bedding, but normally it is not. The pattern of quarrying is determined by the cleavage. In North Wales the cleavage way is the direction along which the slate will most easily split. The pillaring way is more or less at right angles to the cleavage. In the Lake District the terms backs and ends are used. 'A back runs with the natural cleavage of the slate .... and an end close to right angles'.[2] The name slate has also been used for manufactured roofing tiles which are not true slates. Because slate can be cleaved readily and smoothly into thin or thick sheets, and is impervious and virtually chemically inert, it is widely used for roofing, stair treads, flooring, cladding, table tops and acid tanks among other things.

Slate is derived from completely or virtually sand-free sediment, which may have contained a considerable quantity of fine-grained volcanic ash. Individual crystals cannot be seen by the naked eye. The stone is compact and non-porous. It may be almost any colour from nearly white, through grey, blue, green, red and black.

Because slate, which is microcrystalline in nature with highly developed slaty-cleavage, is generally composed of particles less than 1 micron (0.001 mm) in diameter, it is difficult to study in petrographic thin section. Normally X-ray, electron microscope, thermal and chemical techniques must be employed. Consequently an analysis of the slate, unless the requirement is strictly defined, may prove to be costly. In general terms slate is a complicated network of sub-microscopic scales of clay minerals, which are mostly varieties of mica with other platy minerals.

Platy crystals of the green mineral chlorite (a hydrated silicate of aluminium, magnesium, iron; $(Mg,Al,Fe,Mn)_6(AlSi)_4O_{10}(OH_8)$ are commonly responsible for the green colour of many slates. Hematite (iron oxide, Fe_2O_3) gives many slates their red colour and graphite (carbon, C) disseminated through the stone is responsible for the intense black of many slates.

The platy crystals have a marked parallelism, which leads to the development of planar cleavage. The more nearly parallel the orientation of the crystals, the better developed is the slaty cleavage. The planes may be only microns apart. Apart from pyrite and calcite, which are sometimes present, slate minerals are insoluble and resistant to acids. Thus slates do not weather very much through the years.

In Great Britain, which once was a large slate producer, slate is found chiefly in Scotland, the Lake District, North Wales and Cornwall. Vast reserves exist to meet any foreseeable future demand.

Scottish slates

Ballachulish Slates from the Scottish Highlands were worked as early as 1761 but are not now in production. They are blue-grey to black in colour. At one time, a mottled green and purple coloured slate was sold with the trade name Tartan. Some horizons were noted for containing perfectly formed cubic crystals of the brassy-coloured mineral pyrite (iron disulphide, FeS_2), which were known locally as diamonds. Unfortunately pyrite, particularly when exposed to the natural elements, decomposes to form the mineral melanterite ($FeSO_4 \cdot 7H_2O$) which is normally found as a white, powdery efflorescence. Because melanterite like all secondary minerals occupies a greater volume than the pyrite, slate containing pyrite frequently is disrupted. In many instances crystals fall out of the slate to leave characteristically cubic-shaped voids. However, this does not have any effect on the structural strength of the slate in use.

Only about 2 to 5 per cent of the slate quarried is recovered for economic use as is evidenced by the massive tips seen around the workings. The tips at Ballachulish were known to the many motorists patiently waiting to cross Loch Leven on the ferry. The land renewal scheme at Ballachulish is a model of site reclamation. The former 63-acre site was once an eyesore. Other slates in Scotland were quarried in the past, some on a large scale such as the Macduff Slates, Grampian. However, they were rather thick[3].

The Island of Easedale, Strathclyde was famed for its slate quarries. The slates from this island were exported to the Inner and Outer Hebrides. They were also used for the re-roofing of Iona Abbey. Characteristically the slates are blue-grey in colour and, like Ballachulish Slates, may have brassy-coloured pyrite crystals.

Slates from the Lake District

The Lake District is a major producing area for slates. There are two main sources. Perhaps the better known are those which were generally known in the past as Westmorland Green or Lakeland Green. Some of these slates were, in fact, quarried in the former counties of Lancashire and Cumberland.

The history of their origin is but one of the fascinating stories of geology. During Ordovician times (439–505 million years ago) a massive outburst of volcanic activity blew vast quantities of ash, lava and pieces of the existing country rocks into the air. The rock sequence produced in this way is known as the Borrowdale Volcanic Group. The fine-grained ashes settled in the waters of the surrounding seas as a mud which consolidated into the volcanic ash rock known as tuff. During the Caledonian mountain building episode (around 400 million years ago), tuffs were subjected to regional pressures and were metamorphosed into slates.

The Westmoreland Green or Lakeland Green slates, which are generally green in colour, are produced from two main areas. One area is around Honiston. The second is around Coniston, along the Broughton Moor, Coniston, Tilberthwaite and Langdale belt.

Broughton Moor, Buttermere, Cumbria Green, Elterwater, Kirkstone Green, and Spoutcrag are names which the different green (olive, light sea, pale barred, silver-grey, hailstone and rainspot) slates are sold by the different producers.

Green slates from the Lake District have been widely used in Great Britain and they are also known world-wide. They were used on Mullard House, Tottenham Court Road, London, the Observer building, Queen Victoria Street, London, Hotel Leofric, Coventry, and ICI Research Laboratories, Alderly Edge, Cheshire. In Longridge House, Manchester, they make a 'splendid display .... Many of the panels reveal stratification ... and small scale faults'[4]. The Bank of New Zealand, Christchurch, New Zealand; and the 3.5 acres (1.4 hectares) of cladding on the Canadian Imperial Bank of Commerce, Imperial Square, Montreal, Canada provide eye-catching examples abroad.

These slates were used for roofs across the country; for example on the roof of the Geological Museum, London (1935) and the adjoining British Museum (Natural History), which was partly re-roofed after the 1939–1945 war. The architectural use of Lakeland Green and other slates for copings, cappings and walls should not be overlooked.

Burlington Slate and Brathay Slate also are from the Lake District. The muds (geologically known as the Brathay flags) from which they were formed were laid down during the Silurian and were metamorphosed during the Caledonian mountain building episode. The slates are black to blue-grey in colour, and Brathay Slate has small amounts of the brassy-coloured pyrite.

Burlington Slate has been worked for over 300

(a)

(b)

Figure 5.3 (a) Lakeland Green slate clads the chapter house of Coventry Cathedral; (b) sedimentary structures may be seen in Lakeland Green slate slabs cladding The Observer building, Queen Victoria Street, London

years from quarries at Kirkby-in-Furness, Cumbria and may be seen cladding John Dalton house, Manchester (*Figure 5.4*). Slate steps and thresholds, beautifully polished by wear through the years, can be seen on old houses in Kirkby. Burlington Slate was also used for the Police Headquarters, Preston, Lancashire, the Strand underpass, London and the offices of Kalamazoo, Ltd., Birmingham. It has also been much used overseas, for example for the Congress Hall, Berchtesgaden, Germany, the State Library, Berlin, the Dupont Office Building, Delaware, USA and the Kaiser Office Building, Oakland, California, USA. Twenty-eight thousand 18 inch × 10 inch (46 × 25 cm) slates roof the church in the industrial town of Skellefteå, Sweden, on the Gulf of Bothnia, 125 miles (200 km) south of the Arctic Circle.

Brathay Slate is from near Ambleside, Cumbria. The quarry was worked originally during the reign of Queen Elizabeth I. It too has been widely used in Britain and abroad. In Britain it may be seen in The Standard Bank, St James's House, Manchester, an office block, Pilgrim Street, Newcastle-upon-Tyne, a shop in High Street, Newcastle-under-Lyme and the Lufthansa office, St Ann's Square, Manchester. Abroad it was used for the Unilever Ltd. Office, Vlaardingen, Rotterdam, the New Town Hall, Esslingen, West Germany and St Nicholaus Church, Eindhoven, Holland.

Welsh slates

At one time, Wales produced more slate than all the other slate producing areas in Great Britain put together, nearly four-fifths of British output. Welsh slate has been quarried since the Roman occupation.[5] 'Welsh slate is possibly the best in the world . . . it tends to be more durable in urban areas owing to the very low calcite content'.[6] The major producing areas in North Wales are around Corwen, Blaenau Ffestiniog, around Corris and along a belt extending from Nantlle to Bethesda. The slates are quarried or mined from rocks of Cambrian age (Nantlle, Penrhyn), Ordovician (Ffestiniog, Aberllefenni, Corris) and Silurian (Llangollen, Corwen) age. A much smaller amount was produced in the neighbourhood of Myndd Prescely, Dyfed, South Wales. There slates of Ordovician age were used at least as early as the thirteenth century. By the end of the sixteenth century they were being widely used and sent to many places including 'dyvers partes of Ireland'.[5] In colour they range from olive-green to silvery-grey, including a deep and characteristic purple colour.

The massive tips in North Wales stand as mute witness of the scale of former slate workings. The narrow belt of slate from Bethesda to Nantlle is of

Figure 5.4 Burlington Slate, a markedly black coloured slate from Kirby-in-Furness, was used with a riven surface (along the line of slaty cleavage) for John Dalton House, Deansgate, Manchester. The line of cleavage is more or less at right angles to the original bedding which can be picked out on some slabs. (Courtesy Dr F.M. Broadhurst)

Cambrian age. Perhaps the two best known workings are the famous Penrhyn and Dinorwic quarries. Several beds, locally known as veins, with poor slate and sandy beds between them are worked. The slates are mostly reddish-purple in colour with some blue and green. The house in Nantlle where Edward I stayed when he visited copper mines at Drws-y-Coed was roofed with slates from nearby Cilgwyn quarry. Slates of Cambrian age also have been quarried to the north-west of Arenig from the Dolgelly Beds. These are noticeably black in colour, but because of disseminated iron pyrites weather to a rusty brown colour. This meant they were not commercially acceptable.

By far the best slates come from around Blaenau Ffestiniog where Ordovician age slates may be obtained in very thin sheets because of the fineness of the cleavage. They were sometimes called Portmadoc Slates because they were mostly shipped from that port in the past.

Portmadoc Slates are very fine-grained, dark blue, blue-grey and sometimes intense black in colour. The Llangollen belt around Corwen yields slates of Silurian age which are dark grey-blue and paler blue-grey in colour. Much of the material from this belt, however, cannot be finely cleaved and large slabs, or flags, rather than slate in strict definition are obtained. Many of the beds split more easily along the bedding than along the direction of cleavage.

The identification of slates used for building and particularly for roofing presents complex problems, partly because few slates have been microscopically studied and compared. The determination of provenance is of more importance in the historical and in the archaeological context. The traditional use for slate is for roofing. It was the predominant material used in London. However, it is also used for other architectural purposes and increasingly cladding (*see Figure 5.6*).

The use of Welsh slate for roofing can be traced back to Roman times. It was used for mediaeval castle and ecclesiastical building through Tudor times to the present day. In extremely exposed areas it was not unusual to coat the roof with tallow whitewash, which eventually became so thick that it may be difficult now to see that the roof is of slate.

Slate from Penrhyn Quarry was used on St Asaph Cathedral, Clwyd, in the early seventeenth century. When 'after some 250 years, the roof was stripped owing to the failure of the timber, the slates were in such good condition that they could be used again'.[5] The Assembly Hall of the Blaenau Ffestiniog School (1936) shows the use of block slate for building. Welsh Slate has been extensively used. Some examples include the floor of St Bartholomew's Church, St Albans, Hertfordshire, and cladding tunnels on the Newport-Monmouth road. At Montparnasse Station, Paris, several thousand square metres of Welsh Red Slate was used to clad the pillars and the façades. The Environmental Museum, Llanberis, Gwynedd provides a magnificent example of the use of slate for building (*Figure 5.5*). At one time whimsical names were used for different sizes of slates not only in Wales but also elsewhere, including Collyweston, where they were applied to tilestones. Short Hag Hattee, Chits, Batchlers, Long twelves (which were 16 inches (40 cm) long) are some. More amusingly, many were named after the degrees of the aristocracy, including Lady, Countess, Duchess and Princess. During the period 1790–1830, Ladies cost 8 shillings, Countesses 13 shillings and Duchesses 23 shillings per hundred. Mr. Leycester, a Welsh Circuit

(a)

(b)

(c)

Figure 5.5 (a) The large scale of the slate quarry at Penrhyn, Bethesda, Gwynedd may be judged from the size of the quarrymen and the mechanical digger. Slate from this quarry was used for the Environmental Museum, Llanberis, Gwynedd (b) and for internal flooring and walling of the CEGB pumped storage scheme in the old Bethesda Quarry, Gwynedd (c). (Courtesy R.H. Boyle)

Figure 5.6 Modern shop front of slate slabs (otherwise unidentified) in Jermyn Street, London

Judge in 1839 incorporated the names into a poem part of which read:

> This countess or lady, though crowds may be present,
> Submits to be dressed by the hands of a peasant;
> And you'll see when her Grace is but once in his clutches
> With how little respect he will handle a duchess[7].

Leicestershire slates

In the Charnwood Forest area of Leicestershire, irregular outcrops of Precambrian rocks occur. The Swithland Slates, which form part of the succession, are mainly of siltstone grade and consist of white mica, quartz, chlorite and accessory opaque minerals. The slates are purple (blue-grey) and green-grey in colour and provide a remarkable contrast when graded slates are laid over the otherwise uninteresting red brick buildings of west and south Leicestershire[8]. They were quarried from an early date for roofing material. They do not, however, cleave as well as Welsh slates and when Welsh slates became readily available in the last century, the quarries in the Swithland Slate declined. Nevertheless, Swithland Slates are an attractive roofing material, so much so, that until recently, the roofs of old buildings were pillaged for their slates[9].

Figure 5.7 After some 150 years, the inscription on the headstone of Smithland Slate in The Churchyard at Rothwell, Northamptonshire, still remains crisply legible

Because of their fine grain and because they withstand the ravages of weathering, slates have been widely used for tombstones. Swithland Slate may be found widely distributed throughout Leicestershire and adjoining counties and many headstones over two hundred years old still retain crisp, readily readable inscriptions (*Figure 5.7*).

Cornish slates

Slates from south-west England were used from early times and were also exported to continental Europe. They have been found on many medieval sites in southern England and they were shipped to Brittany and to the Netherlands[10]. In 1187 800 000 slates were shipped from Devon to the King's Buildings, Winchester, Hampshire. In 1436 a Southampton man was granted a licence to ship Devon slates to Mont St Michel 'in satisfaction of a ransom'.

The belt of rocks which crop out between Launceston and Tintagel, Cornwall, has been quarried for slates on a large scale. The slates are of Upper Devonian age and are the geologically youngest slate produced in Great Britain. They are fine-grained, smooth, with a noticeable sheen, grey, green and rustic in colour. They are commonly very finely black-spotted. The spots are probably caused by small amounts of the mineral manganese. Slates of Devonian age also were quarried along the south coast of Cornwall[10]. The use of slates from south-western England has been plotted along the south coast of England and its hinterland to Dover and Canterbury where they have been found in mediaeval contexts by Jope and Dunning[10]. Of all the slate quarries undoubtedly the most renowned is Delabole, in north Cornwall. This huge hole, 'prob-

(a)

(b)

Figure 5.8 (a) Slate from Delabole Quarry, Delabole, Cornwall–'The biggest slate quarry in the world'–was used widely, particularly in Southern England, and also was exported; (b) the public house in the village is hung with slate from the quarry and is named after tools used by the quarrymen

Figure 5.9 Local slates of Devonian age were used to clad this cottage in Ashburton, Devon

ably the biggest slate quarry in the world', has been worked for at least 400 years and is now about 500 ft (150 m) deep. Slate from this and other quarries in these Devonian beds was used as slabs for walling, often with decorative effect. It was also used for cladding, for example on the picturesque slate-hung houses of south-west England (*Figure 5.9*). The quarries also provided roofing slates which were commonly crudely and disagreeably covered with a cement slurry. Local examples of these uses abound. Delabole Slate was used on the Victoria and Albert Museum, South Kensington, London and on Truro Cathedral, Cornwall. Padstow Church, Cornwall was re-roofed with them[5]. There is a demand for Delabole and other slates for restoration work. Interestingly, part of the cargo of the ship *James Matthews*, sunk in 1841 off the east coast of Australia, is of slates believed to be from Delabole.

Imported slates

Although excellent quality British slate is readily available and can satisfy the domestic requirement, slate from abroad which is 'cheaper, but also inferior'[5] has been imported. The early part of the Highbury housing estate, Cosham, Portsmouth, Hampshire, built in the 1930s, was roofed with French slates. By the 1950s trouble was reported with these roofs. The later parts of the estate used slates from North Wales (Personal communication, R.H. Roberts).

Slate is imported principally from France, Belgium, Spain, Portugal and Italy. Recently the greatest amount has come from Spain followed by Portugal and then Italy. In Great Britain there is a big market in second-hand slates, which some authorities have reckoned are probably more used than the total current output of the slate quarries.

France has a long tradition of slate working, particularly in the Ardennes, where records indicate that slates were being produced before 466 AD. These slates are Cambrian in age and are remarkably similar to the Cambrian slates quarried in North Wales. As in the Welsh slates various colours may be found including green, blue, purplish and red. Slate from the Ardennes was certainly exported to England 50 to 60 years ago, but the records of its use appear to have been lost. Some specimens may well have been determined as North Wales slate. A green slate, probably from Fumay, was found at the deserted mediaeval village at Hangleton, Derbyshire[10]. Ironically, in recent years the French have complained

(a)

(b)

Figure 5.10 (a) Slate roofs of cottages in Wadebridge, Cornwall may be found covered with cement slurry; (b) slate roof of house in Tonyrfail, Glamorgan coated with bitumen and slag chippings

(a)

(b)

(c)

Figure 5.11 Whilst slate from the mine at Chiavari, Italy, is still cleaved by hand for the production of billiard table beds (a), it is planed by machine to ensure a flat surface (b). The production of cills, skirtings and kerbs is almost entirely automatic (c)

about the amount of British slate being imported to re-roof historic buildings which were formerly roofed with Ardennes slate.

Slate also was produced in the Province of Anjou and the renowned grey slates were used for the Palace of Versailles. They are now replaced with slates from Spain or, sadly, with asbestos and cement tiles.

Spain has a vigorous industry and Spanish slates are currently being imported into Great Britain. Many historically important buildings in France are roofed with them, for example the cathedrals at Amiens and Liège.

Although Italy is inevitably associated with marble, slate also is worked. Italy claims to be one of the largest producers of clear, black slate. Production is concentrated almost entirely in the Province of Leguria. The underground quarry at Chiavari in slate of Ordovician age is one example. In addition to a large output of cills, tiles, hearths and skirtings the works produce 2000 to 3000 billiard table beds a month. Most of these are exported to the USA where the cost of a real billiard table is obviously not regarded as mis-spent.

Marble

Few countries do not produce marble, although many of the commercial marbles are limestones. The terms marble and limestone are wrongly and commonly confused. Limestone is a sedimentary rock. Marble is a *metamorphic* rock made up mostly of calcite ($CaCO_3$). In a marble the calcite is recrystallized to produce an interlocking granular mosaic of roughly equal-sized calcite crystals (*Figure 5.12*). Calcite is the name given to calcium carbonate when it is in crystal form. The recrystallization removes any of the original sedimentary structures and fossils. No true marble will have fossils. Non-calcareous mineral matter present in the original limestone will also be metamorphosed and new kinds of mineral assemblages will be created. Some marble is produced by thermal metamorphism but by far the greater amount is the result of regional metamorphism. Considerable temperatures and pressures are involved. As a result, the mosaic of calcite crystals shows a rough alignment which may not always be visible to the naked eye. It can commonly be seen on the gross scale and marble sometimes shows a rough schistosity (*Figure 5.13*). The length of time that the rock is subjected to metamorphic processes determines the coarseness of the grain size; the longer the time the coarser the grain size that may be expected. The process is aided by active pore fluids. In marble it is aided by carbon dioxide.

The granular structure of marble is often called sugary and viewed from some aspects a cut surface may look like sugar in the mass. As marble weathers, the bonds between the grains of calcite are loosened and the surface assumes a sugary appearance known as saccharoidal weathering. This feature may be used, with care, as one of the criteria used to decide whether a stone is a marble or a limestone. A limestone and a marble will weather in different manner. Because of the interlocking mosaic of calcite grains marbles have a very low porosity.

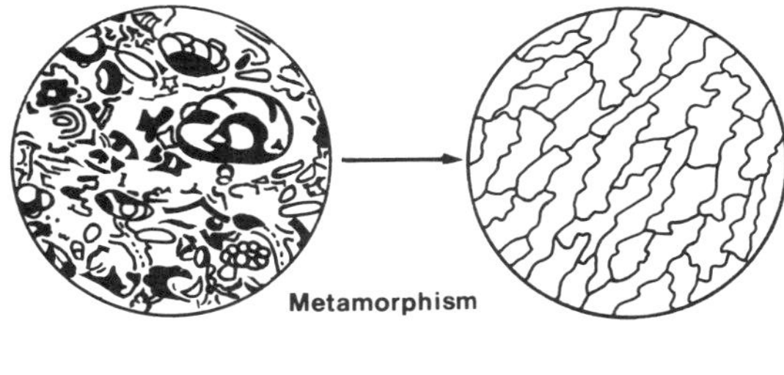

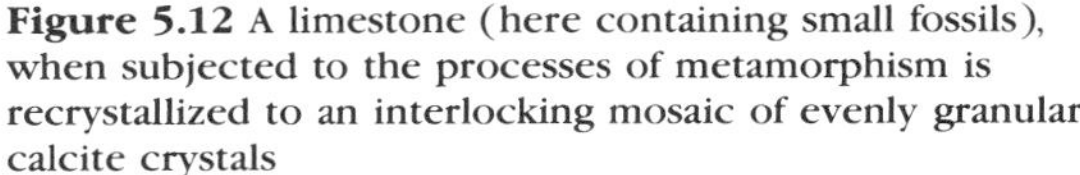
Figure 5.12 A limestone (here containing small fossils), when subjected to the processes of metamorphism is recrystallized to an interlocking mosaic of evenly granular calcite crystals

Figure 5.13 Schistosity, a characteristic feature of metamorphic rocks, is not normally seen in marble. However, it is shown on the large scale at Carrara, Italy, where it is picked out by vegetation

A pure marble, which is entirely or nearly of calcium carbonate, is a monomineralic rock. It is white in colour. Because the calcite crystals which make up the rock are normally transparent, slabs of marble up to about 1.2 inches (30 mm) thick may appear translucent.

The limestones which were metamorphosed to marbles usually contain other mineral matter and it is this which produces the colour seen in marble. It may be either evenly distributed or may give a blotchy, mottled look to the stone. It may also appear as veins. Some marble is highly coloured; black, grey, green, pink, red, and yellow marbles are common.

Serpentine (or serpentinous) marble, also known as ophicalcite, is a general name for marble containing a greater or lesser amount of the mineral serpentine. A serpentinous marble is characteristically streaked with the vivid green of serpentine.

The chemical equation for its production is[11]:-

$$2CaMg(CO_3)_2 + SiO_2 = Mg_2SiO_4 + 2CaCO_3 + 2CO_2$$

Dolomite + Quartz = Olivine + Calcite + Carbon dioxide

Water, if present, reacts with the olivine to form:

$$5Mg_2SiO_4 + 4H_2O = 2H_4Mg_3Si_2O_9 + 4MgO + SiO_2$$

Olivine + Water = Serpentine (removed in solution)

The water, which will be in the condition of a supercritical gas at the temperatures and pressures involved, is a hydrothermal fluid and is a very effective solvent and transporter.

Marble has acquired a reputation as a prestigious building and decorative material and was once even regarded as fit spoils of war. The statue of King George II standing in the middle of the Hospital Square, Greenwich, London was 'sculptured from a single block of marble seized from the French by Admiral Rooke'[12].

The choice of marble as a decorative stone as distinct from its use as a stone for cills, thresholds, cladding and other general building purposes, is based on colour. Panels of highly coloured and decoratively attractive marble may be seen hung on walls, rather as paintings would be. Marble was much used for fireplaces. Even if the limestones, cut, polished, and sold as marbles are discounted, the number of true marbles to choose from is large.

British marbles

In the British Isles, marbles are relatively rare rocks and most of them are only of geological interest. A few have acquired a greater than local importance.

Iona Marble, from the Isle of Iona, Strathclyde, Scotland is a serpentinous marble, white with green to yellowish-green streaks, bands and mottlings. At one time the outcrop of a vertical band 20 to 40 feet

(6–12 m) thick and about 100 yards (91 m) long was extensively quarried. Considerable quantities were sent to Leith and London[13]. Records of its use are regrettably sparse. Traditionally it is said to have been used for the old altar of Iona Cathedral (Abbey) and probably it was used similarly elsewhere in ecclesiastical buildings. A slab was sent to Johannesburg, South Africa, for the headstone of Lord Walter Campbell, a son of the Duke of Argyll. The marble may be seen in the pavement in St Andrews Chapel, Westminster Cathedral, London. A panel of Iona Marble which has religious significance is inset into the fantastic travertine cladding of the chancel of the Church of St Mary, Studley Royal, Yorkshire. Other examples of Iona Marble may have been confused with Connemara Marble, which it closely resembles.

Skye Marble, from the quarries near Torrin, on the Isle of Skye in Scotland is one of the few examples of a thermally metamorphosed marble. Limestone of Cambrian age was altered by an igneous intrusion of Tertiary age. The marble was worked briefly between the two world wars for statuary marble but because of many small igneous intrusions and extensive shattering of the rock, it mostly was worked for crushed rock and agricultural lime. There appear to be no records of its use for building or for decoration, but there are many white marble chip drives leading to cottages and houses both on the island and on the nearby mainland.

The Island of Tiree, Strathclyde, Scotland is composed mostly of metamorphosed sediments from which the highly decorative Tiree Marble once was quarried. This marble is unusually pink and is full of spots and clots of a dark green mineral, coccolite (a granular variety of diopside, $CaO.MgO.2SiO_2$). Although it is recorded as a 'well known . . . ornamental stone'[14] there appear to be no records of its use.

In Glen Tilt, near Blair Atholl, Tayside, Scotland a limestone, which is locally thermally metamorphosed was worked as the Glen Tilt Marble. It was esteemed for decorative work and was used for wash-hand stands and other items of furniture. It is a white marble with green blotches and streaks, which closely resembles Mona Marble from Anglesey. Because it is not well known it is likely that examples of its use are confused with Mona Marble.

Connemara Marble, from a number of quarries including Lissoughter, Derryclare and Streamstown in Co. Galway, Eire, is a metamorphosed dolomitic limestone of Precambrian age. It has a greyish groundmass in which varying amounts of light to dark green serpentine occurs as twisted and interlocking bands. In block the stone can range from almost white to nearly completely dark green. The stone had many names including Galway Serpentine, Irish Green, Irish White (a very light coloured variety), Recess Marble (from near Recess, Co. Galway) and Lissoughter Marble.

The marble has been used for decorative purposes from early times particularly for ecclesiastical work. Two fine columns of it stand at the entrance to the Chapel of St Wilfred, Brompton Oratory, South Kensington, London. It was used for wall panels in St Anselm's Church, Mayfair, London. It appears in the chancel pavement of Bristol Cathedral and occurs in Truro Cathedral and in Peterborough Cathedral. It was also used widely elsewhere.

Imported marbles

Because of the comparative rarity of marble in the British Isles as well as its limited range of colour, the geological difficulties of working and the remoteness of the quarries, marble has been imported since at least Roman times. There is little doubt but that much of it was chosen purely for its colour; *opus tesselatum*, *opus sectile* and *opus alexandrinum* depend on colour contrast for their effect.

It is also worth recalling that Roman Rome was a glistening city of marble. In addition to local sources, which were developed comparatively late, some 500 foreign marbles have been identified in the ancient city. However, many of these are in fact limestone.

Italian marble

Italy claims first place in the production of marble. The main producing areas are listed on p. 122. Without doubt the most widely known locality is Carrara in the Province of Tuscany. It is particularly known for the pure white, and to some, characterless and boring, marble. The marbles (metamorphosed Jurassic limestones) of the Apuan Alps which surround the production area around Carrara where most of the quarries are found, may be grouped as follows:

1. Statuario (Statuary Marble)
   a. First Statuary (white statuary), virtually pure white, fine-grained marble;
   b. Second Statuary, marble with some grey markings;
   c. Vein Statuary, marble with noticeable grey veining and grey areas.
2. Bianco Chiara (or Blanc Clair); white marble with only a few grey markings.
3. Bianco Chiara Venato (Bianco Venato, or Blanc Veine), white marble with stronger greyish markings which may have a distinct vein pattern.
4. Bardiglio (or Bleu Tarquin, Turquin, or Italian Dove), a blue-grey marble.

Commonly it is very difficult to distinguish between Second Statuary and Vein Statuary marble. Statuary marbles which are more heavily veined may be called Bastard Statuary. It may be difficult to distinguish Bianco Chiara from Vein Statuary marble.

Figure 5.14 Ornamental fountain in grey veined marbles (Second Statuary with Arabescato in rear), Carrara, Italy

Figure 5.15 Banking hall floor of Sicilian marble (white, grey veins and patches), Kilkenny 'marble' (black) and Bardiglio marble (grey), Dublin. (Courtesy J. Redmill)

Many names have been given to stone from individual quarries which differ in the pattern and strength of the figuring but are very similar to stone from adjoining quarries: '. . . certain marbles which owe their naming to pure fantasy . . .'[15]. Arabescato is white with grey markings. Parona is white with veinings of grey colour. Tulanto is described as white with a few grey lines which are not prominent. Sicilian has a white ground-mass through which run light grey veinings.

Only on the British market is the name Sicilian applied to general types of Carrara marble which are white with irregular greyish veinings and cloudy masses. In Italy these marbles would be known as Bianco Chiara. At least 1000 tons of Sicilian Marble was used for the Queen Victoria memorial facing Buckingham Palace, London. Marble Arch, London, also built of it.

The Carrara area has also produced some markedly coloured stone. Fior has a violet-coloured groundmass, and Red Carrara is reddish. Bardiglio Marble (Bardilla, Blue Turquin, Blue Fleuri) is one of the most important coloured types from Tuscany. It is best known in Britain as Italian Dove. It is dove-coloured (grey) with darker grey veins and bands. To some it appears drab. It is close-grained and hard wearing and has been used for flooring and paving as well as for decorative purposes. Many fireplace surrounds are made of it.

Carrara Marble is very widely used. The twelfth century Cathedral of Pisa and the Campanile (the 'Leaning Tower') are made of Luni Marble, which was known to the Romans as *Marmor Lunense*. When the Romans developed local marble quarries they founded a camp, named Luni, near the present town of Carrara in 177 BC. The use of marmor lunense was first cited by the historian Velleius Patercolus in the first century BC, on the occasion of the construction of the sumptuous home of the prefect Mamurra on Mt. Celio.'[15] It was Augustus who inherited a city of brick and left it a city of marble.

Greek marble

Not even the briefest review of marbles can ignore Greece. It produces the classic white marbles, Parian and Pentelic, as well as the highly coloured Skyros Marble. Parian Marble, from the Island of Paros, is considered by some to be the finest white marble in the world. Parian porcelain was named because it was considered to resemble the marble from the Island of Paros. Most of the island is of marble which was quarried from galleries driven into the sides of Mount Marpesian. The marble has a translucent appearance and, particularly in fresh faces, some of crystals reflect light with a sparkling play of colours, known by the Greeks as Lychnites. It was worked in the sixth century BC and was widely used by the Greeks for roofing, for example on the Parthenon on the Acropolis in Athens. Later the Romans quarried large quantities and the stone was widely used for building and sculpture. Pieces of the marble have been recovered from archaeological sites in Great Britain. Parian Marble was also used in the modern context. Watson[16] records its use in Draper's Hall, London (1898–1899).

Pentelic Marble, argued by some to rival Parian, is quarried from Mount Pentelikon in Attica. Classically the stone is known as *Marmor Pentelicum*. It is available as white or blue stone and was known commercially as Stavatovouni. White Pentelic (or Pentelicon) may be white or may have cloudy markings. The cloudy markings may contain finely disseminated iron pyrites in crystal form. Commonly the stone has a delicate, soft light golden cast, which is better demonstrated than described. This characteristic feature can, however, be used as a diagnostic feature for determination.

Pentelic Marble is the stone that was used for the Propylas which was built by Pericles 437 BC, and for the many other buildings in Greece. It is renowned for its use by Phidias for the Parthenon (447–438 BC). It was also used in Euston Tower, London, and for the interior floors and walls of the National Westminster Bank, King Street, Manchester. The Ceremonial Staircase to the Council Chamber, County Hall, London includes the marble. The Norwich Union Building built in 1905 on the corner of St James's Street and Piccadilly, London, is one of the first London buildings on which the marble was used. This listed building was not comprehensively cleaned and restored until 1980. This was done only because 'severe corrosion [of the structural steel members] had pushed the stones from position .... The Pentelikon marble was sound, apart from one course at fourth floor level which showed signs of movement caused by more rusty steelwork'[17].

Skyros Marble, from the Isle of Skyros in the Aegean Sea, is a markedly colourful stone. In general it has a white ground with strong orange, reddish, golden-yellow to brown and to violet veins and markings. Because of the variation in the veining and markings, specimens of this marble, in isolation, may look widely dissimilar. It is highly decorative and was used extensively for the late-lamented Lyons Corner Houses. It may now be seen in the offices of Canadian Pacific, Cockspur Street, London.

French marble

France has been a source of marble since Roman times. Most of the marbles are coloured. Some white statuary marble is found in the Pyrenees. The classic stone is Campan. Campan is not completely metamorphosed and the white calcite is crystalline, but the matrix is not (see p. 122).

Turkish marble

Asia Minor, principally Turkey, has supplied marble since the earliest days. The Romans used much marble from this area. White marble was taken from the Isle of Marmara. This stone was called *Marmor Proconnensus* after the classical name for the island. A fine, even-grained pure white statuary marble was obtained in addition to coarse-grained varieties. It was used in the Church of St Sophia in Istanbul, Turkey. Pieces of marble found on Roman sites in Great Britain have been identified as Marmara. A white marble with purple veins, widely known as Pavonazzetto, from Docimio, north of Synnada, Phrygia, was one of the first marbles imported into Rome. Other marbles from Turkey are known. The identification of a sample as Turkish White Marble probably from the Balikesir-Erdek district, was part of the evidence used to determine that the Worksop Giant was one of the missing pieces of the main frieze of the Great Altar of Pergamon[18].

Scandinavian marble

Norway exploits only a small amount of the marble available. Breche Rose (Norwegian Rose, Norwegian Pink) has a pleasant white and pink colour and is brecciated. It is deservedly popular for decorative purposes and was used for part of the altar of the Chapel of St Augustine in Westminster Cathedral.

Sweden, like Norway, has much marble but only a little of it is worked. The most important is called Swedish Green in Britain. It is known to have been quarried since 1650. It is a Precambrian ophicalcite and is quarried in the Norrköping area, in Southern Sweden. It is greyish-white with twisted bands, streaks or patches of green to brown. It was used for the floor of the Regimental Chapel, Manchester Cathedral, where it is matched with Roman travertine, and in the Coliseum Theatre, London. It may also be seen in the main entrance hall floor of the Victoria and Albert Museum, London. It is sometimes confused with Connemara Marble, a similar type of stone, which it may resemble.

American marble

Vast quantities of marble exist in the United States of America and Canada. Some American marbles are widely known. Examples include Georgia marble which is white, silvery grey, grey to black and white

Figure 5.16 The Washington Monument, Washington DC, was faced with three types of marble: Texas Marble (Maryland) below, then a band of four courses of Lee Marble (from Lee, Massachusetts), followed by Cockeysville Marble (Maryland). The band of Lee Marble separating the two others may be easily distinguished

Figure 5.17 The Lincoln Memorial, Washington DC, built to a plan resembling the Parthenon on the Acropolis, used a white marble with faint grey markings from West Elk Mountains, Colorado

and Tennessee marble which is grey and pink to brown. Texas Marble, from Maryland, Lee Marble, from Massachusetts, and Cockeysville Marble from Maryland, are white to pale grey. They were all used for the Washington Monument in Washington DC (*Figure 5.16*). Use of marble is so extensive that the USA also imports large amounts of marble from other countries. Much marble from Carrara, Italy as well as travertine from Italy is used in Washington DC. The marbles and other principal building stones used for many of the public buildings in Washington DC, have been excellently and comprehensively described in *Building Stones of our Nation's Capital*[19].

Marble from Australia and New Zealand

Australia has an inexhaustible supply of marbles. Those from New South Wales, Queensland and South Australia are particularly well known. At one time about forty different types came from New South Wales, where quarrying began some 185 years ago. However, some of these are limestone in strict geological classification. White, black and other coloured stone is found. They may be seen used for public buildings and monuments in Sydney, Adelaide, Melbourne and elsewhere. The stones were offered on the English market in the early part of the twentieth century but they do not seem to have been used, except for Australia House, London.

Kairuru Marble, a white, coarse-grained marble quarried in New Zealand, was used in Wellington. A light-grey variety may be seen in the interior of Parliament Buildings, Wellington. Other marbles also have been used locally.

Water marble

The homogeneous varieties of marble have long been a favourite of the sculptors and many famous works have been chiselled from it.

In the nineteenth century many mass produced pieces of statuary were made to stand in the gardens and the centre of ponds or fountain lakes of the *nouveau riche*. This is the origin of the name water marble. However, the name is not an indication of the type of stone used. Catalogues of these pieces were issued and they could be ordered from stock.

Although marble is commonly and popularly regarded as a luxury material, in those parts of the world where it is the stone of the country, it is used wherever stone is needed. For example, in part of South Africa, a pure white marble was used for pig sties.

References

1. Caminos, R., 'Some Granites, Gneisses and Metamorphites of Argentina', *Spec. Publ. Geol. Soc. S. Afr.*, **3**, 1973
2. Anon., 'Modern Slate Output in the Lake District', *Stone Industries*, **7**, September 1983
3. Read, H.H., *British Regional Geology, The Grampian Highlands*, rev. by A.G. Macgregor, HMSO, Edinburgh, 1948
4. Simpson, I.M. and Broadhurst, F.M., *A Building Stones Guide to Central Manchester*, University of Manchester, Manchester, 1975
5. North, F.J., *The Slates of Wales*, National Museum of Wales, Cardiff, 1946
6. Crockett R.N., 'Slate', *Mineral Dossier No. 12*, HMSO, London, 1975
7. Anon., 'Curious Facts About Slate', *Stone*, **28**, No. 3, August 1907
8. Penoyre, J. and Penoyre, J., *Houses in the Landscape*, Readers Union, Newton Abbot, 1978
9. Eastwood, T., 'Roofing materials through the ages', *Proc. Geol. Assoc.*, **62**, Pt. 1, 1951
10. Jope, E.M. and Dunning, G.C., 'The use of blue slate for roofing in medieval England', *The Antiquaries Journal*, **34**, Nos. 3, 4, 1954
11. Holmes, A., *Principles of Physical Geology*, Nelson, London, 1965
12. Oman, C., *Britain against Napoleon*, Readers Union, London 1943
13. Viner, D.J., *The Iona Marble Quarry*, Iona Community, Glasgow, 1979
14. Phemister, J., *British Regional Geology. Scotland: The Northern Highlands*, HMSO, Edinburgh, 1948
15. Anon., *Italian Marble Technical Guide*. Vallardi Editori, Milan, 1982
16. Watson, J., *British and Foreign Marbles and other ornamental stones*, University Press, Cambridge, 1916
17. Anon., 'Recut red Jasper is fit for a new life', *Stone Industries*, **15**, No. 4, May 1980
18. Haynes, D., 'The Worksop Relief', *Sonderdruck aus Jahrbuch der Berliner Museen*, **5**, 1963
19. Anon., *Building Stones of our Nation's Capital*. United States Department of the Interior, Geological Survey, Washington DC, n.d.

6

Determination of a sample

Francis G. Dimes

Introduction

The two commonest questions asked of a geologist by an architect are 'What stone is it?' and 'Where can I get some more?' They are not always easy to answer. Generalized descriptions of a rock as given in this book must not be used as a basis for the determination of a stone in a building. Unless a stone is seen to be taken from a quarry and placed in a building there is no absolutely certain way of determining its provenance.

Rocks are aggregates of minerals and the properties of a rock will depend on many unpredictable factors. The texture may differ from place to place because of a difference in grain size. A schist may appear to be an entirely different rock depending on which schistose layer is observed. The relative proportions of constituent minerals in a rock may differ from place to place. In short, because rocks are not homogeneous, laboratory determinations of their physical constants may not produce data of relevance.

General analysis

It is possible for the lithology of a stone from a building to be determined, for example whether it is a sandstone or a limestone. The determination of its provenance is by no means as easy. The reason is quite simple; similar environmental conditions of deposition lead to similar types of sediments being deposited. This results in similar types of rock. Commonly the best a geologist can do is to suggest a stone of similar lithology (e.g. sandstone or limestone), mineral content, colour and other characteristics. Because the sample is matched geologically the match will be a good one, although the stone may not look the same because the colour is different. This is because there is a marked difference in appearance between new and old, weathered stone which disappears with time.

The geologist must have a specimen of the building stone in order to identify it. It follows that a piece of the stone must be removed from the building. Care should be taken to ensure that the sample is of sufficient size to be representative of the building stone as a whole. A small specimen may not show features which are characteristic of the rock. As large a sample as possible should be supplied. Although determinations have been given on pieces no larger than the little finger nail, the smaller a specimen, the less secure the determination. Whatever the size of the sample it should be truly representative of the stone under study.

The comments made about the sample relate only to the block of stone from which the sample was taken; it must not be blindly assumed that the comments may be taken to apply to all stone used in the building. It is helpful if the sample is clean. The geologist will also like to know if the specimen may be broken further so that a fresh surface may be examined. Archival evidence is the way to determine the provenance and name of the stone, but archives may not record the type of the stone in petrographical terms.

A few simple observations and tests may be sufficient to establish the nature of the stone *in situ*. Observation with a hand lens, magnification ×10 is standard, should provide some answers. With a hand lens it should be possible to determine whether the stone is granular, compact, crystalline, coarse- or fine-grained. It should also be possible to decide whether the stone is igneous, sedimentary or metamorphic. However, some igneous rocks may be very fine-grained, and the grain size may be too fine to be properly resolved with a hand lens. The surface of the stone may have been rubbed to a flour, or covered with dirt, wax, polish, varnish or just the grime of ages. This will mask diagnostic features. A pocket knife with a blade of hardness $H = c.\,5\frac{1}{2}$, used with caution will give an indication. Limestones will scratch but sandstones and most igneous rocks will not.

A carbonate will effervesce when tested with dilute hydrochloric acid. The effervescence indicates only that a carbonate is present but does not identify the carbonate mineral. There are several carbonate minerals, but since copper carbonate (e.g. malachite) is green and magnesium carbonate (e.g. rhodochrosite) is pink the test usually indicates that calcium carbonate (as limestone or as marble) is being tested.

Commonly, these simple tests will be sufficient to determine the nature of the stone. They will not give any indication of provenance, but experience may be a valuable guide. The architect should use this information to look for a geologically compatible stone. If the integrity of the geology of a stone building is maintained, all else will be well. However, for historical or archaeological reasons, the determination of provenance may be required. In many instances, however, it must be recognized that the geologist is 'best-guessing'.

More detailed analysis

An analysis of a stone is rarely required. What is an analysis and will it give a useful answer? The architect, restorer, or conservator should discuss the purpose of the enquiry with the geologist. The geologist should be given as much information as is possible because a seemingly minor item may be crucial from his point of view. When a specimen has been submitted a simple systematic series of tests are possible. The tests used will depend on the sample and what information is required.

1. Macroscopic examination using a hand lens
   i. What is the texture?
      a. crystalline
      b. granular
      c. other
   ii. What is the grain size?
      a. is it uneven?
      a. any contained pebbles?
   iii. Are there any notable minerals or grains?
   iv. Are there any fossils present? (If the surface of a stone is moistened, the moisture will enhance the fossil.
   v. Is the stone compact or friable?
   vi. What colour is it? (The *Rock Color Chart* is of use)
   vii. Has it a lustre?
   viii. Is it transparent or translucent?
   ix. Has it any particular type of fracture?

2. Physical tests
   i. What is the hardness and toughness?
   ii. Is it
      a. compact
      b. friable
      c. fresh
      d. weathered
   iii. What is its density, does it feel heavy? In fact, this is of little help.)

3. Chemical tests
   i. Does it effervesce?
      a. A lot
      b. Little (There will be little if any effervescence with dolomitic limestone.)

4. Chemical analysis
   i. Partial
   ii. Total
   Chemical analyses are generally of little use in this context. They may indicate the presence of particular minerals, for example, dolomite, or gypsum, but there are easier ways of determination.

5. Microscopic examination
   i. Study of a thin section of the stone
   Undoubtedly this is the most useful method, particularly for igneous and metamorphic rocks. It will certainly identify the type of rock, for example, granite, dolerite, or micaceous glauconitic sandstone. It will not determine the provenance, although the information gained will be of great help in suggesting it.
   Thin sections are slices of rock about 0.8–1.2 in (2 cm by 3 cm) mounted on a glass microscope slide and ground down to a standard thickness of 30μ (micron = 0.003 mm). At this thickness all the common rock-forming minerals are transparent in transmitted light except the iron-oxide minerals which remain opaque. The optical properties may be determined and the quantity and relationships of the minerals may be studied. Thus, the mineral composition can be determined. This is an important factor especially in fine-grained rocks.

6. Special tests
   i. X-ray diffraction
   This may be used to determine the presence of dolomite, calcite, gypsum and other minerals but normally easier methods are available. This technique is of value when only the merest scraping of the object is allowed.

7. Geochemical fingerprinting and isotopic study
   A programme of geochemical fingerprinting would undoubtedly enable identification and determination of provenance in nearly every

instance. The programme involves the collection of specimens, both laterally and vertically across every outcrop to create a reference collection of specimens. Then any submitted specimen is 'fingerprinted' and compared with the reference specimens.

Some work already has been undertaken in the field of isotopic study which has shown that, when used with other analytical methods, it offers great possibilities of matching samples to quarry location.[1,2] The Craigs report[1], '. . . the Athenians scatter fragments of Pentelic marble around the Parthenon each winter, in order to provide material for the insatiable pillage by tourists. This marble is from modern quarries and is isotopically distinct from that of the classical quarries'.

Geochemical fingerprinting and isotopic study require sophisticated equipment and highly trained scientists. These are costly.

References

1. Craig, H. and Craig, V., 'Greek Marbles: Determination of Provenance by Isotopic Analysis *Science*, **176**, 28 April 1972
2. Coleman, M. and Walker, S., 'Stable Isotope Identification of Greek and Turkish Marbles' *Archaeometry*, **21**, Pt. 1, 1979

7

Weathering and decay of masonry

David B. Honeyborne

Introduction

If stone masonry is exposed to the weather, some changes must inevitably occur, however well the property is being looked after. The changes might be aesthetically pleasing or distressing, of no physical consequence or structurally hazardous and the rate of change might be very low or quite rapid. The word *weathering* is used to refer to all such changes. In specific cases where significant loss of substance or form occurs, the change is referred to as *decay*.

This chapter deals first with the basic causes of the weathering of stone masonry, including changes brought about by living organisms. Attention is then drawn to the influence that some design and construction errors have on the weathering of the masonry. Finally, the advantageous and adverse effects of possible actions by those using or looking after stone buildings is discussed. Some technical details that might be of interest are placed in an Annex.

Basic causes of weathering of stone masonry

Those responsible for the conservation of buildings or monuments in which stone masonry is decaying or otherwise deteriorating will wish to understand what is happening, if only to satisfy their curiosity. But there is more to be gained than that, for such understanding might well help them to reduce the rate of deterioration by improving the ambient conditions in some way. Moreover, an analysis of what is happening might permit some definition of the micro-climate immediately surrounding the masonry. This would greatly assist in the selection of suitable replacement materials, should such drastic action prove to be necessary.

There are several causes for the deterioration of masonry and each has a recognizably different effect. Some lead to a loss of substance of the stone or mortar; others lead to a disfigurement or a disruption of the masonry, not necessarily accompanied by any loss of substance. While it is generally recognized that disruptions can arise from excessive load concentrations, settlements, uneven thermal expansions and similar physical phenomena, it is not so widely realized that forces arising from chemical reactions can also cause them. Disruptions that have a chemical origin are dealt with here. A very detailed review of the chemistry and physics involved in all these phenomena will be found in reference 1.

Deterioration caused by decay

There are three main causes of deterioration involving loss of substance. These are:

1. salt crystallization,
2. attack by acidic gases in the air,
3. frost action.

Salt crystallization

Salt crystallization is the most important because it is potentially the most damaging. It attacks porous materials irrespective of their chemical composition and often enhances the effects of the other primary causes of decay. Also, it will occur in areas virtually free from frost or acidic air pollution. This cause of deterioration will therefore be dealt with first.

Limestones and sandstones

Table 7.1 gives a list of salts that are most frequently involved in crystallization damage to masonry, and lists some common sources for each of them. The main sequence of events giving rise to such damage

Table 7.1 Salts that have been known to damage stone masonry and their sources

Type of salt	*Common sources*
Sodium sulphate	Clothes washing powders; soil, some types of fired-clay bricks; some processed solid fuels; by action of polluted* air on sodium carbonate.
Sodium carbonate (washing soda)	Clothes washing powders; many domestic cleaning aids; some proprietary cleaners for limestone-faced buildings; fresh concrete and cement-based mortars.
Magnesium sulphate (Epsom salt)	Some fired-clay bricks; rain washings from dolomitic limestone affected by polluted* air.
Potassium carbonate	Fresh concrete and cement-based mortars; fuel ashes and ash-mortars.
Potassium sulphate	Some types of fired-clay bricks; by action of polluted * air on potassium carbonate.
Sodium chloride (common salt)	Seawater; road and pavement de-icing salt; salt used for preserving meat etc; soil.
Potassium chloride	Soil.
Calcium sulphate	Many types of fired-clay bricks; limestone and dolomitic limestone affected by polluted* air; gypsum-based wall plasters.
Sodium nitrate (Chile-saltpetre)	Soil; preserved meat; fertilizers.
Potassium nitrate (saltpetre)	Soil; fertilizers; gunpowder.

*Pollution in this context means pollution by oxides of sulphur or sulphuric acid.

is as follows. A solution of a salt, or mixture of salts, in water is transferred by some means to the pores or fissures of the stone. Under drying conditions, the water evaporates and the salt is deposited on the surface of the masonry, within its pores, or in both positions. A salty *growth* or *florescence* appearing on a surface is known as *efflorescence*. Crystallization that occurs invisibly within the pores of the masonry is called *cryptoflorescence*. It is not unusual for both forms of florescence to occur together.

Efflorescence is usually regarded as unsightly, but is, in itself, harmless. In contrast, cryptoflorescence causes some pressure to be exerted on the walls of the pores or fissures within the masonry. The magnitude of the pressure will depend partly on the kind of salt involved and partly on the size and arrangement of the pores. The process is not completely understood (see Annex for further information). However, if the pressure exceeds the internal strength of the stonework, some degree of damage will occur. The damage might be on a microscopic scale at first and cause no more than a slight loss of strength, but, after a sufficient number of cycles of wetting and drying, each leading to a redissolving and recrystallizing of the salts, a powdering of the surface will become visible. Occasionally, a large scale fragmentation takes place along some plane of weakness, but this is always accompanied by some powdering. Formation of powder is, therefore, the diagnostic characteristic of crystallization damage to masonry.

The dissolving phase of this damaging process need not always involve a direct wetting of the stone by liquid water. Many salts will absorb water from the air in sufficient amounts to dissolve if the relative humidity of the air becomes high enough. Conversely, they will lose water and recrystallize if the relative humidity falls low enough. Such salts are said to be *hygroscopic*. The relative humidity at which a salt or mixture of salts will just begin to pick up water from the air is known as the *equilibrium humidity* (EQRH) of the salt or mixture. *Table 7.2* gives the EQRH of a number of salts at a temperature of about 25 °C. The values may be different at other temperatures. There does not seem to be any accurate way of estimating the EQRH of a mixture of salts from the EQRHs of its components. Direct measurement in the laboratory appears to be the only satisfactory way of obtaining this.

A third way in which salt crystallization damage can occur is through changes of temperature. Some salt crystals, in contact with a saturated solution of that salt, will redissolve if the temperature rises sufficiently and will recrystallize if it falls again. Thus, once potentially harmful salts get into the pores of a stone, there are at least three ways in which crystallization damage might occur. This damage will continue to occur indefinitely.

The rate of decay induced by salt crystallization will depend not only on the types of salt involved

Table 7.2 The equilibrium relative humidity of a number of simple common salts

Salt	*Chemical formula*	*EQRH** (%)
Magnesium chloride hydrate	$MgCl_2 \cdot 6H_2O$	33
Potassium carbonate hydrate	$K_2CO_3 \cdot 2H_2O$	44
Sodium nitrate	$NaNO_3$	75
Sodium chloride	$NaCl$	76
Potassium chloride	KCl	85
Sodium sulphate hydrate	$Na_2SO_4 \cdot 10H_2O$	89
Sodium carbonate hydrate	$Na_2CO_3 \cdot 10H_2O$	90
Potassium sulphate	K_2SO_4	98

*The EQRH of a salt tends to rise with a fall in temperature. The effect is more striking with some salts than others. Exceptionally, the EQRH reaches a maximum at some mid-range temperature. The values given have been rounded off and apply approximately in the temperature range 20–25 °C.

and the frequency of the crystallization cycles, but also on the resistance offered by the stone. Clearly, the smaller the proportion of pore space in a piece of masonry, the better will be its chance of surviving salt crystallization attack. However, it is an apparent anomaly that some limestones of quite high porosity (say 28%) resist crystallization attack better than many with porosities as low as 16%. The pore space of those limestones that resist attack are comprised mainly of relatively large diameter pores. Susceptibility to attack is related closely to the fineness of the pores and this can be of greater importance than total pore volume over quite a large range of porosities (see Annex).

Sandstones also vary in their resistance to salt crystallization and the size of the pores also plays an important part in determining their resistance. However, the relationship is not quite so clear-cut as it is with limestones.

For types of stone with equal resistance to salt crystallization, the damage caused by a fixed number of cycles of crystallization will vary with the type of salt involved in a manner that is not well understood. The salts listed in *Table 7.1* are broadly in order of decreasing aggressiveness. However, mixtures of salts often behave more aggressively than the constituents alone. A common example is the mixture of table salt (sodium chloride) and calcium sulphate which has particular relevance to the behaviour of limestones in heavily built-up coastal regions.

Marbles and granites

The porosity (i.e. the ratio of the volume of pore space to the bulk volume) of a freshly quarried block of marble or granite is normally much less than one per cent. With such materials, contact with an aggressive salt might be expected to have little or no effect, or at least to take centuries to cause significant damage. However, heating and cooling can cause partial separation of some of the boundaries between the crystals of the rock. The consequent increase in porosity and reduction in cohesive strength may then be sufficient to permit the occurrence of salt crystallization damage within the lifetime of an historic building or monument.

Porosities greater than normal are also found in granites in which some of the feldspar has been converted to a clay mineral of the kaolin type. During the late stages of the consolidation of a magma highly reactive and mobile fluids and gases are squeezed out of the mass. During the emplacement of the mass in south western England acid solutions moved along the joints. They altered the crystals of plagioclase feldspar into aggregates of kaolinite. This process is called kaolinization. Purified kaolinite is generally known as china clay. Under conditions less favourable to this process, the kaolinization is far from complete and the resulting mixture is of little use to those industries. It is equally unsuitable for most building purposes.

Sources of salts

Unfortunately, there are many sources of harmful salts and many ways in which they can be transferred into masonry. Some indication of this has been given in *Table 7.1*.

Buildings near the sea will naturally tend to pick up sea salt. This consists of a very large range of salts, most of which are present only in minute quantities[2]. The main constituent of sea salt is sodium chloride and this is by far the most significant in the context of stone decay. Coastal regions tend to have a higher than average relative humidity. Hence the EQRH of sodium chloride (~76%) will be exceeded often enough to ensure that stonework contaminated with seawater will suffer some crystallization attack even when it has not been rained on. The resulting decay will become apparent most quickly on the *inside* faces of mullions, transoms and tracery of windows, where the thickness of the stonework is less than in the walls. However, after long exposure, much of the *external* masonry may also show decay. In all cases, this will take the form of powdering. It will primarily affect those surfaces from which most drying occurs.

The winter salting of roads and paths to reduce risks to traffic and pedestrians from hazards of ice and snow can provide a source of sodium chloride close to buildings and other structures. Even if a building has a damp-proof course, splashing can cause contamination that might result in the decay of the stonework.

Meat preserving has also led to crystallization damage in the past. At least one mediaeval stone wall is still decaying as a result of the storage of salted meat against it more than 100 years ago. The stonework of one mediaeval kitchen in a college has been replaced because blocks of cooking salt (sodium chloride) were once stored against it.

Fired-clay bricks, stored in close contact with a masonry wall and left uncovered or built as a backing in direct contact with stone masonry that becomes very wet, can introduce sulphates of calcium, magnesium, potassium or sodium, according to the type of brick involved. Fresh concrete or cement-based mortars in contact with stone can introduce sodium or potassium carbonates, which will be converted to sodium or potassium sulphates by the sulphur-based acids in our polluted air.

Preparations containing caustic soda or caustic potash are marketed for cleaning the external faces of limestone buildings. These materials will also be converted to sodium or potassium sulphates by the sulphur-based acids in the air. An exceptionally skilled operator might be able to clean limestone safely using such aids, but, in practice, their use has led to much staining and crystallization damage.

Damage can also be caused to other types of stone by rain-washings from limestone or magnesian limestone that contain sulphates, and which has been attacked by sulphur-based acids in the air and thus contains sulphates. This will be discussed in more detail in the next section.

Decay caused by acidic gases in the air

Over most of the highly industrialized parts of the world, the air is polluted with small particles of carbon or tar products and with acidic, sulphur-based gases. These are produced by the combustion of solid fuels and oils by industry, transport and domestic heating systems. Various industrial processes put other particles into the air. These, along with transport vehicles, produce nitrogen compounds that almost certainly add to the thunderstorm production of nitrogen-based acids[3]. Air pollution is an important cause of decay in building stones in the industrialized world, but where pollution is low, the effects described below will be minimal.

Limestones and marbles

The particulate pollution makes buildings dirty and the tarry matter occasionally causes staining. The acidic pollutants greatly enhance the rate of acid-based decay of limestones. However, even if there were no man-made pollutants, the carbon dioxide naturally in the air and the sulphur-based acids that are released during the decay of sea-weeds would be sufficient to cause some decay of this type of building material, though the rate of deterioration would be very slow.

The main aggressor in acid attack is sulphur dioxide gas (SO_2). This gas is very soluble in water, and reacts with it to form sulphurous acid (H_2SO_3). Two reaction paths may then be followed in the attack on limestone[4]:

1. Sulphurous acid + oxygen from the air could produce sulphuric acid (H_2SO_4), which would then attack the limestone ($CaCO_3$) to give calcium sulphate ($CaSO_4$) and water (H_2O). The calcium sulphate then takes up water as it crystallizes as the mineral gypsum ($CaSO_4 \cdot 2H_2O$).
2. Sulphurous acid can directly attack the limestone to give calcium sulphite ($CaSO_3$), which then combines with oxygen from the air to produce calcium sulphate. This also crystallizes as gypsum.

The first of these paths is probably the one more likely to be followed, particularly under damp, foggy conditions. However, there is evidence that some reactions along the second path must take place because the presence of some calcium sulphite in the gypsum coating of exposed limestone surfaces has been reported[5,6]. In any event, the gypsum coating slows up the attack. What happens next depends on how often the affected stone is washed by the rain or sprayed with water during cleaning.

The slightly soluble gypsum is steadily removed from those parts of a limestone-faced building that are frequently washed by the rain along with any dirt that has been fixed to the limestone surface by the gypsum when it first crystallized. The limestone is thus maintained in a clean state, because it is being slowly eroded. Those external parts of a limestone-faced building that are sheltered from the rain behave very differently. When there is no rain-water to keep these parts clean, droplets of acid in the polluted air will continue to condense on them under foggy conditions. The acid will react with any unchanged limestone surface and bind any available particulate pollutants to that surface. Thus, these areas become darker and the skin on them becomes less and less permeable. In urban districts, where the particulate pollution is high, the surfaces often become black. In rural districts, where particulate pollution is normally low, they are sometimes only a rich brown, even after more than a century.

What happens to this virtually impermeable skin depends on the resistance of the limestone to weathering. The most durable limestones appear to be able to retain a dirty, inert skin more or less indefinitely. Less durable limestones behave differently. On these, occasional blisters will gradually form. Sometimes, the blisters are very flat and their limits are not easily discernible. More often, they have a clear form and develop until they burst. They often look so much like miniature volcanoes that the word erupt is used to describe their formation. The stone immediately behind the skin of the blister has decayed to a powder or a pack of lightly connected flakes. Much of this decayed stone will fall away in time, thus presenting a fresh limestone surface for further attack. As with crystallization damage, coarse-pored limestones prove the most resistant.

In magnesian limestones, the mode of attack is slightly different. The mineral dolomite is a chemical association of 45.7 % by weight magnesite ($MgCO_3$) and 54.3 % by weight calcite ($CaCO_3$). The compositions of the magnesian limestones vary over a wide range, but usually the proportion of magnesite is lower than it is in dolomite. Magnesian limestones are sometimes called dolomitic limestones, but this term can be misleading unless their composition closely approaches that of dolomite.

In rain-washed parts of a building faced with magnesian limestone, acids derived from the sulphur-based gases in the air will normally attack the stone surface and produce calcium sulphate and magnesium sulphate. The rate of attack varies from one type of magnesian limestone to another and is believed to be at a minimum when the ratio of magnesium carbonate to calcium carbonate approaches that of a true dolomite[7].

As with the simple limestones, the stone remains clean in the rain-washed areas and the solution resulting from the acid attack is carried harmlessly to the ground or is absorbed by the more sheltered parts of the stonework or by other porous materials. Where the solution is absorbed by sheltered areas, the calcium sulphate often forms a skin of gypsum, which incorporates dirt, as do the gypsum skins on simple limestones. However, the magnesium sulphate penetrates further and crystallizes behind this skin. In most cases, the gypsum skin forms blisters which eventually break open to disclose a powdered area beneath the skin. Removal of the powder reveals a deep cavern caused by the crystallization and recrystallization of the magnesium sulphate. This is known as *cavernous decay*. Dirt accumulation, blistering and cavernous decay in sheltered areas of stonework also occur in the absence of rain-water running down from overlying exposed masonry, if moisture often condenses on the surface when there is fog. The rate of attack and accumulation of dirt is much lower in rural districts. The resistance of magnesian limestone to blistering and cavernous decay varies from one type to another. The pore structure is only one of the controlling factors. For a discussion of the other factors see Annex (page 174).

Because marbles consist essentially of calcium carbonate, they initially undergo the same chemical reactions as limestones when they are in moist air containing sulphur-based acids. A skin of gypsum is formed that can incorporate some dirt particles. As with limestones, what happens next depends on whether or not the marble is in a position that is well washed by rain. In well washed areas the gypsum is dissolved, no dirt accumulates and the marble surface is gradually weathered away. But, since the surface is usually nearly free from pores, there is normally no secondary damage resulting from recrystallization of gypsum. Hence, the rate of erosion is normally considerably less than that of limestone in the same environment, though polished marble will quickly lose its smooth surface.

In some circumstances, marbles decay more quickly and, although more research is needed, it appears that this is associated with considerable temperature variation. Excessive heating and cooling can result in movements at the boundaries of the calcite crystals which can lead not only to the bending of marble headstones that is sometimes to be seen in cemeteries, but also to an increase in the porosity of the marble. This enables recrystallization of the gypsum skin to occur below the surface. Weathering, often in the form of *sugaring*, then proceeds more quickly.

In sheltered areas of buildings in urban districts, marble, like limestone, will acquire a dirty coating. However, so long as the surface of the marble remains relatively free from pores, the dirty layer will not become nearly so black as a porous limestone, nor will its surface develop unsightly blisters.

Sandstones, slates and granites

The majority of sandstones consist of grains of quartz (a crystalline form of silica, SiO_2), cemented together by silica in a less well crystallized form. Iron oxides or hydroxides are sometimes present in the cement and the quartz grains are sometimes accompanied by grains of feldspars and micas. Quartz-based sandstones are very resistant to the sulphur-based acids in the air, but they can become very dirty. They tend to be dirtier in the rain-washed areas than in the sheltered parts of buildings. In this sense their behaviour is quite different from that of limestones or marbles. Very occasionally, sulphur-based acids in the air will attack one of the iron compounds in a sandstone and temporarily convert it to a soluble form. This can then migrate to the surface of the stone, where lime, derived perhaps from mortar, reconverts it to a rusty-looking insoluble form. Such deposits can remain unnoticed beneath the soot layer until the sandstone is cleaned by a mechanical or chemical process.

A small minority of sandstones used for building in the United Kingdom are cemented by calcite (*calcareous sandstones*). *Calciferous sandstones* are defined here as sandstones which contain calcite that does not take part in the cementing process. Sulphur-based acids in the air readily attack calcareous sandstones. These sandstones weather more severely than limestones in regions of high air pollution because the dissolving of a small amount of calcite will release many sand grains. Where the stone is heavily rain-washed, the surface will steadily powder away. When the stone is not heavily rain-washed, the acids attack some of the calcite converting it to the more soluble gypsum. Some of the gypsum is drawn towards the surface in solution and redeposited as the moisture dries out again. This produces a weakened layer roughly 4 mm below the surface of the stone which blocks the pores of the surface layer. As the temperature varies, the unrestrained gypsum expands or contracts about 1.7 times as much as sandstone. Changes of temperature will therefore create stresses that tend to break the gypsum-rich layer from the underlying sandstone. In time, these layers will peel off. The effect may be seen on the south wall of the old (bombed) Cathedral Church of St Michael, Coventry. A striking example of attack by acidic gases on calcareous sandstone on the mainland of Europe is at Strasbourg Cathedral[8].

Some sandstones are cemented with dolomite. In general, these withstand an acid-polluted atmosphere better than calcareous sandstones, particularly when there is a lot of cementing material present. This is probably because dolomite is much less readily attacked by acids than calcite. When a dolomitic sandstone seems to respond like a calcareous sandstone, the cement probably contains calcite as well as dolomite. It is usually the calcite that has been attacked by the acid.

Calciferous sandstones, where calcite plays no part in the cement, behave very like calcite-free sandstones, providing there are no complicating factors like the presence of clay. Sandstones containing substantial amounts of clay are known as *argillaceous sandstones* and have very poor resistance to weathering agencies. They tend to lose strength when wetted and dried, whether or not the air is polluted by sulphur-based acidic gases.

All sandstones, even those in which the grains are cemented by silica, are to some extent susceptible to salt crystallization attack. One common source of trouble is the calcium sulphate washed from limestone in urban districts by rain. Where sandstones are exposed to the washings they usually decay sooner or later. This is an indirect attack on sandstone by sulphur-based acidic gases in the air.

Closely allied to the attack by acidic gases on calcareous sandstones is the attack by such gases on some types of roofing slates that contain up to 13% calcite. Sulphur-based acidic gases in the air dissolve in rain-water and are held by capillarity 'between the lap', that is, in the overlap between adjacent slates in a roof. They form acids which attack the calcite in the slate, thus weakening it. The gypsum formed by this reaction causes further weakening by crystallization attack, so that in time the surface of the slates between the lap can be easily scratched by the finger nail. Eventually, the fixing holes become so enlarged that the slate slips from its position.

Another kind of slate contains pyrite (iron sulphide) in an unstable form, with some calcite. Rainwater alone is able to cause decay of this type of slate by reacting with the unstable pyrite. This forms a sulphur-based acid, which then attacks the calcite causing the slate to crumble. This type of slate will deteriorate on exposure, even if the air is virtually free from sulphur-based pollutants. Its use was abandoned many years ago because it failed even as a barrier to water when used as a damp proof course.

In complete contrast, acidic pollutants in the air are unlikely to cause any significant decay of granites used for building.

Two special cases

Two special cases of acidic air attack on stone deserve mention; stone exposed near the sea, and contour scaling.

It has been observed that limestones that are not much affected by acidic gases in inland cities, or by sea salt in crystallization tests in laboratories, can suffer serious decay when exposed to mild air pollution by sulphur-based acids in coastal regions. The effect is believed to occur because gypsum, the normal result of acid attack on limestones, is more soluble in water which contains common salt (sodium chloride), which is the main constituent of sea salt. In consequence, the crystallization damage caused by gypsum in the presence of sea salt is much greater than when gypsum alone is involved.

Important examples of this phenomenon have occurred in the Portland Stone used for the War Memorial at Southsea, Hampshire and the National Library of Wales, near Aberystwyth, Dyfed. Most of the blocks affected were of a quality that would have been expected to give good service in London and other large cities. In both cases, analysis revealed that the only soluble salts present were calcium sulphate and sodium chloride. Laboratory tests subsequently confirmed that stone is more affected by a crystallization test employing a combination of the two salts than by either of them on its own.

Contour scaling is a phenomenon first recognized in the United Kingdom about 1955, but not publicly reported until 1965[9]. In this form of decay, a crust of sandstone breaks away at an approximately constant depth of between 5 and 20 mm (0.2–0.8 in.). The crust follows the man-made contours of the block, rather than any of the natural bedding planes. The effect is most striking when it occurs in mouldings.

It was first thought that it could be explained in terms of *moisture rhythm*. This occurs when the stone is wet by rain, and water penetrates to a depth, which is a characteristic of the stone. Subsequent drying brings small amounts of the cementing material towards the surface. If continued over many years this cycle would result in a weakening of the structure at approximately the maximum depth of penetration. Even silica, the cement in the most durable sandstones, is sufficiently soluble in water for this mechanism to operate over a long period of time. In apparent support of this view, the examples found were always in buildings at least 35 years old and usually much older.

However, it was later discovered that in the few cases that were carefully examined, the detached surface of the sandstone had become completely blocked with gypsum. It was then supposed that the separation of the affected layer occurred as a result of fatigue failure of the stone just behind the choked layer. This was thought to arise because changes in temperature would affect the choked layer differently because of the high coefficient of thermal expansion of gypsum. The fact that the failures occurred as often in stonework fully exposed to the sun as in stonework that was in the shade raised doubts. It was also thought that the tendency of the unchoked stone to expand when wet and contract when dry would be sufficient to develop the necessary shear forces to lead to fatigue failure[10]. The problem was then to explain how the stone became wet and dry in view of the impermeability of the outer skin.

The presence of gypsum in the samples was not easy to explain because the sandstones were virtually free from calcite or other sources of lime that could be attacked by acidic gases in the air. However rainwater occasionally contains a very dilute solution of calcium sulphate. It was assumed that this arises as a result of a reaction between sulphur-based gases and particles of lime or limestone that escape from the stacks of lime and cement works and can be carried very far from the sources. The fall-out of calcium sulphate formed in this way could explain the presence of calcium sulphate in the pores of the sandstones in question. The fall-out would not be detected on bricks or limestones because these are contaminated with calcium sulphate in any event.

Therefore, on the assumption that the choking of the surface pores of some sandstones leads the development of contour scaling, the phenomenon appears to be related to air pollution.

Decay caused by freezing

Frost attack differs from attack by salt crystallization and air pollution in two striking ways: frost damages only those parts of a building that can become frozen when very wet; and the damage appears dramatically, in the form of cracking. Cracking can result in the production of a few large fragments of stone or many small pieces, but frost attack never reduces the stone to a fine powder or produces blisters. Its effects are thus distinctive from those of salt crystallization or to attack by sulphur-based acids.

Because frost damage will not occur unless a stone is very wet, it is seldom if ever seen in plain walling between damp-proof course and eaves. Instead it tends to be confined to features with surfaces that will catch the rain, or water from some other source. Copings, cornices, sills, string courses and window hoods are the features usually affected. Tops of plinths and steps are occasionally affected but many builders and architects now take care to ensure that such features are constructed from frost-resistant stone.

Broadly speaking, frost damage to stonework takes one of two forms, illustrated in *Figures 7.1a* and *b*. The commonest form involves the separation of a wafer or lens-like piece of stone from the most exposed surface of the block. This will normally be the top surface, but it can be the outermost surface when the block is part of a string course or sill. The break usually occurs at right angles to the line of maximum thermal gradient and the separating piece moves in the direction of greatest heat loss (*Figure 7.1a*). Sometimes, the separation is sufficient for ice to be seen between the separating pieces. The ice often appears to consist of a number of minute columns aligned along the direction of movement. Sometimes the appearance of separate columns is an illusion caused by lines of very small air bubbles trapped in the ice. Frost damage of this kind usually leaves the affected blocks disfigured, but otherwise functional. Many similar attacks can occur before they cease to serve any useful purpose in the building.

In the second and less common form of attack, the block of stone is often rendered useless, apparently in one single action. As shown in *Figure 7.1b*, cracks can radiate in many directions and a block can be reduced to several smaller blocks. As might be expected from the form taken by the damage, this kind of decay is associated with multi-directional cooling of the stone. It is much more likely to affect coping blocks, cornice blocks and balusters, which are very exposed to any cold winds and to clear night skies, than it is to affect sills, string courses and the like, which are much more shielded by the rest of the building.

The effects of frost damage are different if the stone has very marked weaknesses along its natural bedding planes. This can distort the pattern of radiating cracks that develop in the second form of frost damage and it might be mistaken for frost damage of the first kind.

The pore structure of a stone plays an important part in determining its resistance to frost. The fine-pored types of stone being more susceptible than the coarse-pored types. Pore structure has a similar effect on the resistance of stone to salt crystallization and acidic gas attack.

Causes of frost damage

Damage to metal water pipes caused by the freezing of the water in them is well known and the mechanism involved is well established, even if some of the details are not entirely understood. Under very cold conditions, ice starts to form within a pipe at the position where the temperature first falls to the freezing point of water (0 °C; 32 °F). This ice eventually forms a plug, trapping water between this point and a tap or valve. Sometimes water is trapped between another plug of ice formed at a second point.

At normal pressures, ice occupies about 9% more volume than the water from which it was formed. If the water cannot be pushed away to make room for this increase in volume, the pressure inside the pipe must rise. *Figure 7.2* shows the relationship between the pressure on the water and the temperature at which it will be converted to ice. As the pressure rises, the freezing point falls. The maximum pressure

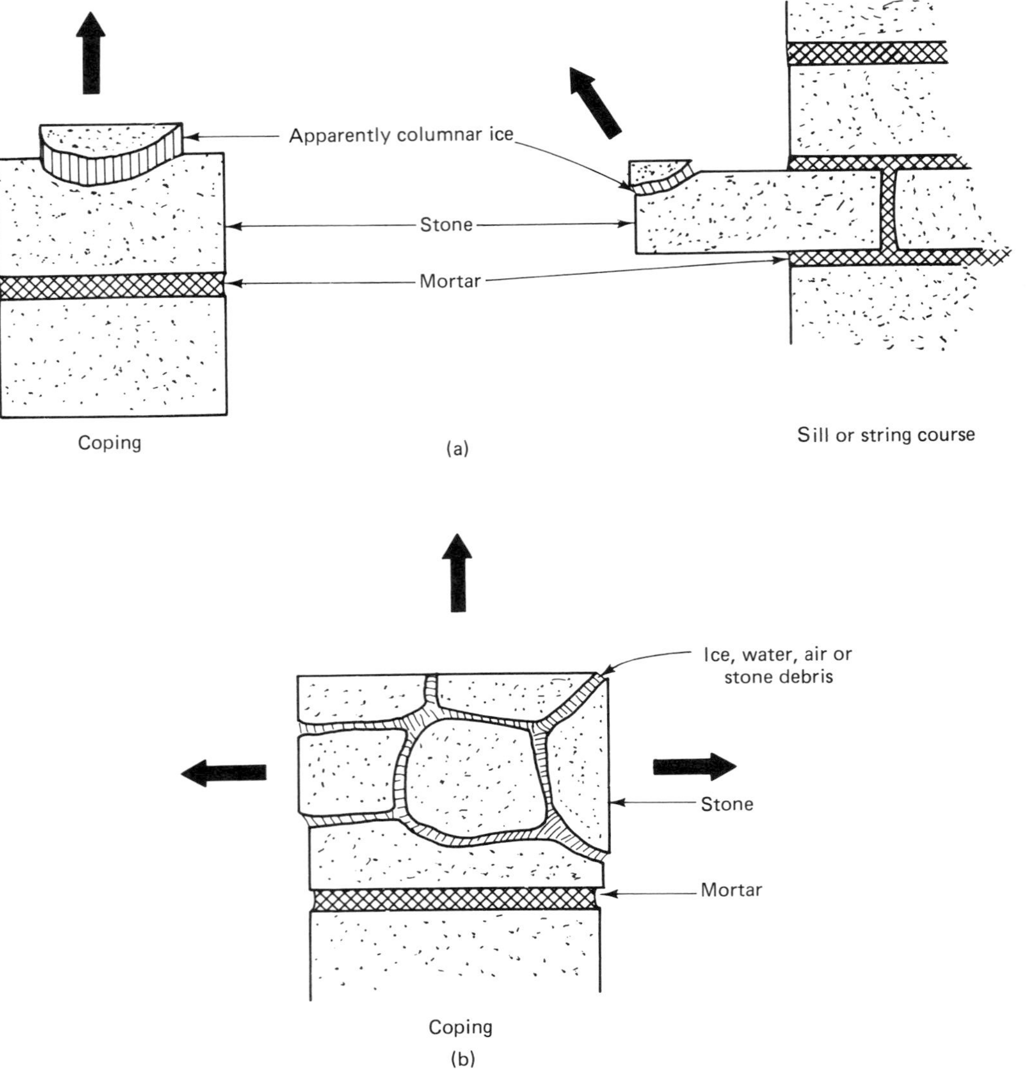

Figure 7.1 Forms of frost attack on stone (a) cross-section through blocks of stone showing examples of the common form of damage. Broad arrows show the direction of heat loss. (b) Cross-section showing an example of the less common form of frost damage

that can be developed by ice forming from water in a confined space of this kind is 207.4 MN/m^2 (2047 atmospheres) and the temperature needed to achieve this is −22 °C (−7.6 °F). At lower temperatures a different kind of ice forms, which occupies less volume than water, so the pressure would fall again. However, pressures far below this maximum are sufficient to burst all normal water supply pipes made of metal.

It is tempting to assume that all frost damage to stone occurs in the same way. For this to happen a block of stone would need to be frozen on all sides to produce an ice casing. The ice casing would have to trap water, and this water would then need to be frozen. It is just conceivable that this might happen to copings over balustrades but not to copings over solid walls, parapets, sills and other water-collecting features, where special circumstances are required before water can become trapped. However, the water held in the pores of a coping block on a wall

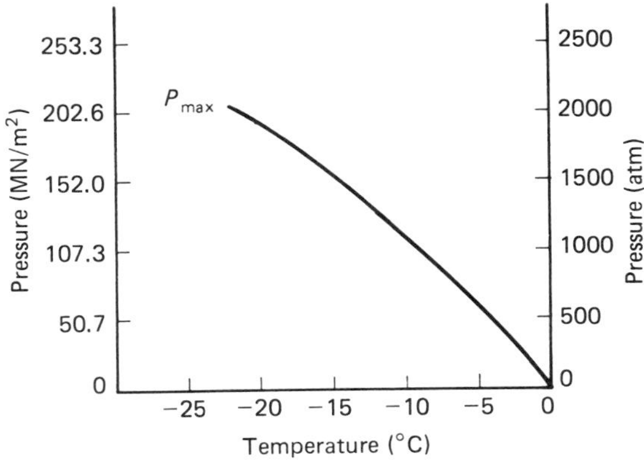

Figure 7.2 Pressures which may be developed by freezing completely enclosed water. P_{max} (= 2047 atm = 207.4 MN/m^2) is the highest pressure that can arise in this way. At lower temperatures a form of ice crystallizes out which occupies less volume than the water from which it is formed. It contracts on further cooling. The crushing strength of porous stone is usually in the range 7.5–56 MN/m^2. The tensile (bursting) strength is usually much lower. Reliable values of bursting strength are not available. Basic numerical data are taken from reference 2.

and in the top of the wall itself might freeze completely during several days of frost and then be covered by a coating of snow. Sunshine might melt the snow, which will help keep the stone very wet, and the ice in the block might partially melt but the bottom of the block will remain frozen. A very severe night frost might then case the top and upper parts of the sides of the block with ice, trapping the water that was thawed the previous day. Freezing of the trapped water could then cause a shattering of the block.

An alternative method by which shattering pressures might arise entails the formation of an ice casing on all faces but the bottom of a block of stone. If very rapid freezing of the remainder of the water occurs, the advancing ice front would force water through the pores of the bottom part of the stonework. If these pores were very fine, they would resist this flow very strongly and sufficient hydraulic pressure to shatter the stone may develop. This theory is attractive, because it explains why fine-pored stone is more susceptible to frost than coarse-pored stone.

The commoner form of frost damage (*Figure 7.1a*) has a different cause. It is related to the frost heaving of soils described by Stephen Taber[11] and the thermodynamical considerations discussed by D.H. Everett[12] and J.M. Haynes[13]. A more detailed discussion is given in the Annex (pages 174–177).

Everett[12] considered a wet, porous body subjected to severe cooling from one face only. If, as a result of this cooling, ice forms in a relatively large pore connected, on its warmer side, to a source of water through smaller pores, ice crystals will continue to grow in the larger pore so long as there is an unrestricted supply of water and no great pressure is exerted on the ice. However, if the ice is confined by the roof of the larger pore, pressure will begin to rise and, if nothing gives way, ice will begin to grow down the finer pore *after a certain critical pressure is reached*. While growth down the finer pore occurs there will be no further increase in pressure. For the sake of simplicity, let the larger pore be cylindrical, with a radius R and the smaller pore be cylindrical, with a radius of r. The maximum pressure that can develop in this case would be $\sigma(1/r - 1/R)$, where σ is a constant[12]. This maxi-mini pore system acts as if it were a miniscule jack of precisely limited lifting power. If many of these jacks act in unison along a plane within the stone, it is likely that fracture will occur, particularly if the stone has been weakened by previous attacks. This is a possible explanation for the lifting of wafers or lens-like spalls of stone from copings and the like, in the commonest form of frost damage. This theory also helps to explain why fine-pored stone is more susceptible to this kind of frost attack than coarse-pored types.

Taber[11] found that ice lenses grow initially in sandy or silty soil fed by water from fine-pored clay soil below. The direction of lens growth is determined by the direction of heat flow. No lens forms if all the soil below is sandy and hence coarse-pored (this is of particular importance in the designing and siting of cold stores). Everett's theory[12] fits these facts well, for it requires there to be a considerable difference between the magnitudes of $1/r$ and $1/R$ for large heaving pressures to be developed.

Only if stone is very wet will it suffer frost damage. If water is trapped by a coating of ice, pressure will be transmitted the moment more freezing occurs and the ice–water system begins to expand. If the casing has trapped a mixture of air and water, the easily compressible air will be able to accommodate some of the increase in volume of the ice–water system and, hence, further freezing. If there is much air present, all of the water present might be able to freeze without giving rise to sufficient pressure to cause damage. Where water is not encased by ice, but is being rapidly forced through a narrow escape area, the presence of air between the ice front and the escape area might also be sufficient to prevent the development of damaging pressures. When the frost heave mechanism is operating, the pores supplying the growing ice lens must be full of water. If air is present the growth of ice will cease and pressure will not be maintained.

It often happens that a frost attack will leave a

stone apparently unharmed, but internally weakened. In fact, it is usual for most types of stone that are eventually damaged by frost to suffer several weakening attacks before showing visible signs of damage. Stone that is visibly damaged after being caught in a very wet condition by a single frost is quite exceptional.

Unlike crystallization damage, which can affect all classes of porous stone, frost damage occurs much more often in limestones and magnesian limestones than in sandstones. In long term tests blocks of stone measuring 100 × 50 × 50 mm were exposed standing on end in trays that became filled to a depth of 50 mm each winter. The results after up to 22 years exposure at Garston, Watford, Hertfordshire, England were: limestones failed, 63.5%; sandstones failed 8% (ref. 14). Later unpublished results showed sandstones to be even more resistant.

Marbles, slates and granites

The types of marble, slate and granite normally used for building have porosities that are too low for them to be susceptible to frost attack. The porosity of marble, particularly statuary marble, can be significantly increased by prolonged heating and cooling. It is conceivable that increases of this kind might be sufficient to make the marble susceptible to frost attack, but this has not been observed. It is also conceivable that slates containing calcite that have been softened by acidic gas attack might become susceptible to frost attack, though such slates would be doomed in any event. Partially kaolinized granite might well be attacked by frost if used in susceptible features of a building, in the same way that it might be attacked if it became contaminated by soluble salts. Such types of granite are sometimes used because they are easily accessible, but they are really unsuitable for use externally in buildings.

Deterioration caused by staining

While the word decay implies a loss of substance, the word staining implies an undesirable addition of some material to the masonry. Most staining of masonry involves metal corrosion, but other factors are also important.

Effects of tarry pollutants

The blackening of stonework is caused by particulate air pollutants which consist of carbon and associated tarry matter. In particularly sheltered parts of limestone walls, these pollutants become cemented on to the wall by gypsum, formed as a result of chemical attack on the limestone by sulphur-based acids. Because gypsum is slightly soluble in water, any dirt that adheres to rain-washed areas of limestone is regularly removed, but, in the semi-sheltered areas, a heavy black deposit accumulates. If this remains untouched for many years, the tarry matter builds up in the pores of the stone to such an extent that any eventual removal of the sooty matter by artificial washing leaves the stone with a tarry, light brown stain. The stain becomes intensified as the limestone dries out. On stone that was originally pale in colour, this can be rather disfiguring.

Sandstones behave rather differently. The particulate pollutants are very firmly held by the sandstones even where the stone is washed by the rain. Artificial washing with water will not remove them. Tarry matter penetrates the pores of sandstones quite deeply. Artificial washing using special cleaning agents is possible, but tarry stains tend to remain. Fortunately, the average sandstone is darker than the average limestone and the staining is less obvious and more readily accepted.

Rain washings from limestones

Although rain washings from the exposed parts of a limestone building are normally deposited in more sheltered parts on the same kind of stone, they may be deposited on darker porous material, such as another limestone or a sandstone or brickwork. Deposits on the same kind of stone normally do not result in unacceptable staining. However, pale-coloured stains on a darker limestone can be disturbing and stains on sandstones or brickwork can be very disfiguring. They can also cause crystallization damage, unless the stones or bricks are highly resistant.

Effects from rising damp

Soil and subsoil often contain small amounts of coloured matter, derived from the decomposition of organic materials, that are sufficiently soluble in water to be capable of staining stone quite unpleasantly. When a building has no damp proof course, or has a defective damp proof course, the base courses often become stained. The effect is more striking, the paler the colour of the stone. When soluble salts are present, as they usually are in soil water, efflorescence will occur and pitting or powdering might add to the unattractive effect.

A similar problem is often found in porous stone retaining walls that have not been provided with any means of keeping the soil water away from the stone.

Effects from mortars containing hydraulic lime or Portland cement

Many types of limestone contain small amounts of organic matter that do not cause any staining, unless they are brought into contact with a highly alkaline solution. A possible contemporary source of this contamination is the effluent from washing powders which form highly alkaline solutions.

There are numerous records of the staining of stonework by alkaline solutions leached from fresh mortars based on Portland cement or hydraulic lime. The phenomenon was first recognized early in the present century by investigators searching for an explanation of the appearance of brown stains on Indiana limestone (see ref. 15). The stain is always brown and most noticeable on the paler coloured limestones.

Rich Portland cement mortars are unlikely to be used in the conservation of stone buildings, but hydraulic limes are often thought to be suitable. If hydraulic lime mortars are to be used with fresh stone, it would be advisable to carry out a staining test.

Effects from copper and its alloys

Copper is used externally on buildings for lightning conductors, flashings and the external skin of domes. After many years exposure to town air, copper acquires a stable patina, consisting of copper sulphate ($CuSO_4.3Cu(OH)_2$). Copper exposed near the sea acquires a patina of similar appearance, but which consists of copper chloride. In the interim stages of patina formation some copper is washed away, presumably as a dilute solution of copper sulphate or copper chloride. On contact with limestone or mortar, this alters to a less soluble, blue-green basic copper salt, which remains on the mortar or stone as a stain.

Analogous staining occurs on the stone pedestals of figures made of bronze or gun metal. Gun metal is an alloy of copper and tin; other forms of brass may contain additional ingredients. Elimination of the bluish-green stains is tedious, but not impossible. The methods are described in Chapter 11 in volume 2.

Effects from iron and steel

Rust, formed by the action of water and the atmosphere on iron and steel, produces the worst kind of staining on stonework. Rust is virtually insoluble in water, and it is not completely understood how it can be deposited on masonry some distance from the exposed iron or steel. What is well known is that the stain produced can be more intense than any other common stain on masonry and is more difficult and sometimes impossible to remove. Hence every reasonable effort should be made to avoid its occurrence.

Railings that have been left unpainted for some time after insertion, or have been maintained by an insufficiently frequent painting cycle, are a common source of rust staining. Neglected cast iron gutters, rain-water pipes, or their fixings are another. Old scaffolding poles, left where rain can run off them on to masonry, are a third source. Neglected iron or steel window bars are a fourth source. Buried cramps or dowels of steel or cast iron, that have been left unprotected in stone for a long period and have caused the stone to split are a fifth group. Cramps and dowels will not rust if they are set in a thick pad of mortar so long as the mortar retains its original high alkalinity and is free from sodium chloride. Both lime- and cement-based mortars lose this alkalinity in time as the carbon dioxide gas naturally present in air penetrates the pores of the masonry and neutralizes it. Any sulphur-based acids in the air will go further and gradually render the mortar acid. This will drastically increase the rate of corrosion of the metal and hence the production of rust.

An interesting example of the development of rust stains on stone occurred on the porphorytic granite facing of an important building in London some years ago. A granite which had been cut into slabs by a steel frame saw was coated with sulphuric acid to remove the specks of iron from the saw that had become embedded in the stone. As a result of production difficulties, a few slabs were inadequately rinsed with water to remove the acid. After installation, rust stains appeared on these slabs. Laboratory examination showed that a solution of iron sulphate ($FeSO_4$) was being held in minute fissures in the surface of the granite and was gradually working its way to the surface. On contact with limestone, lime or cement dust on the surface, rust was immediately formed[16].

Other causes of deterioration

There are a number of examples of deterioration caused by inanimate matter that do not fit into the above classification. These are discussed below.

Wind erosion

The idea that wind, carrying sand particles, can erode and shape large rocks in desert regions so catches the imagination that people often point to stone in buildings in Britain that has become furrowed in a spectacular manner as examples of wind erosion. However, it seems doubtful that wind erosion occurs to any extent in any building in Western Europe.

The buildings cited are nearly always ruins, cloisters or projections of buildings in arches or alleys. Wind passes at increased velocity over such features. In nearly all cases, the stone is a limestone which will accumulate calcium sulphate because of air pollution, or a sandstone in a coastal region. Hard driven rain will wet the stones thoroughly; and dry wind flowing past will dry them rapidly. These conditions favour salt crystallization attack. This, almost certainly, is the explanation for what has happened. The shaping is caused by the variation in drying rates with wind speed, which is higher where there is any narrowing of the gap. The additional furrowing seen in some sandstones is caused by the different resistance to crystallization attack shown by adjacent thin beds in the stone. There is no reason to postulate wind-blown sand as an important agent of decay. In fact, geomorphologists are now emphasizing the importance of salt crystallization in desert rock weathering[17,18].

Heating and cooling and wetting and drying

Stone slabs can be heated on one side so rapidly that parts of their surface will break away from the cooler, underlying mass. Flame-texturing of granite and dense limestones depends on this principle. The surface temperature involved is far higher than any likely to be reached by stone exposed to the sun. Nevertheless, it is theoretically possible for temperature gradients set up in stone by the heating effect of the sun to lead to surface decay, if repeated often enough. No decay purely from this cause has been recorded in buildings in Britain.

However, a closely related effect is known to cause trouble in marbles. Although marble is essentially composed only of one mineral, calcite, each calcite crystal expands along one crystallographic axis when heated and contracts along the other two, and thus behaves rather like a conglomerate of different minerals when heated. If heated to 300 °C and cooled a number of times, white Carrara marble will lose virtually all its strength. Kessler[19] found that a sample of marble, heated to 150 °C and cooled a number of times acquired a small permanent set after each cycle and started to bow. The effect is thought to be due to slippage of calcite crystals relative to one another. The bending of marble headstones and marble mantelpieces seems to be due to the same phenomenon.

General considerations suggest that a related effect must occur in granites because its three main constituents, quartz, feldspar and mica, have distinctly different coefficients of thermal expansion. On long heating and cooling, there appears to be sufficient micro-cracking at mineral boundaries to make the otherwise resistant granite susceptible to crystallization damage. Hockman and Kessler[20] carried out many heating and cooling and wetting and drying experiments on North American granites and concluded that the damaging effects may contribute to the deterioration of granites in monumental structures, but that they were probably not the cause of any deterioration of granites in normal buildings.

Heating and cooling probably also play an important part in the development of blisters on limestones once a sulphate skin has formed as a result of attack by sulphur-based gases in the air. The thermal expansion of gypsum is very much greater than that of limestone; the ratio is five to one[21]. Thus, it seems reasonable to assume that such differences should lead to a separation of the sulphated layer during a heating phase.

Wetting and drying is an inevitable part of the process leading to salt crystallization damage to stonework, even if the wetting phase sometimes involves water vapour rather than liquid water. Wetting and drying also accounts for the destruction of slate containing calcite and unstable pyrite. However, the part it plays is a subsidiary one. There is a widespread belief among building material technologists and geomorphologists that wetting and drying plays a considerable part in causing the decay of porous stone or the disintegration of porous rock. Porous stones expand when wetted and contract on drying. The theory is that fatigue failure must eventually occur, because of the shear forces that will frequently arise along any plane separating the wet from the dry material. This mechanism may account for contour scaling but, apart from this, the decay or disintegration of unconfined stone or rock can not be attributed to wetting and drying alone.

One of the more spectacular effects of heating and cooling or wetting and drying is when a wall of porous material is built under cool, dry conditions between two substantial abutments and its temperature or its moisture content later rises considerably. The attempt of the wall to expand may generate stresses severe enough to cause the masonry to bulge or even to crack diagonally, so that one part can oversail the other. Under extreme weather conditions, the wall will normally be either cold and wet or hot and dry. In consequence, thermal movement and wetting and drying movement tend to counteract one another, and little harm is done. Only

Table 7.3 Approximate thermal and moisture movement of masonry materials

Material	*Thermal movement* 0/000 for 10°C	*Dry to wet movement* 0/000
Porous limestones	0.028	0.083
Marble and dense limestones	0.038	0
Granite and other igneous stones	0.10	0
Slate	0.11	0
Sandstone	0.11	0.67
Concrete (dense)	0.11	0.33

exceptional hot and wet conditions cause trouble. If the wall is built of virtually pore-free material such as slate, only the temperature change will be significant and there can be no off-setting effect. *Table 7.3* gives the thermal and moisture expansions of some relevant building materials.

Fire

Broadly speaking, a building fire can have four relevant effects on stonework: blackening, shattering, decomposition and oxidation. Blackening is a result of the deposition of carbonaceous or tarry matter derived from the thermal decomposition of wood, or woollen, cotton or synthetic organic materials within the building on relatively cool parts of the structure. Blackening has no directly damaging effects on stone, but the processes used to remove it may well cause some damage, particularly if tarry matter has deeply penetrated porous limestone or sandstone.

Shattering of surface layers of stone is likely to occur when the flames heat up a previously cold surface very rapidly. The surface of marble is likely to 'sugar' under these conditions and the surface of granite may show some disintegration because of the many grain boundaries that separate different types of minerals with different coefficients of thermal expansion. Sandstones tend to suffer more than limestones when their surfaces are rapidly heated, probably because their main component, quartz, undergoes a sharp crystalline change at 573 °C. Porous limestones behave well by comparison. The temperature of decomposition of calcium carbonate is reached at about 550 °C. Even then, decomposition is very slow until temperatures of over 900 °C are reached, when quick-lime is rapidly formed. Quick-lime does not necessarily fall away to expose fresh limestone to the flames. Experience in World War II showed that many burnt-out buildings constructed of limestone remained structurally sound and could be re-used after the walls were scraped and the floors and roofs reconstructed.

Oxidation as a result of a fire changes the colour of limestone. Small quantities of some iron compounds that either attract no attention or contribute to the acceptable appearance of the limestone before a fire, are converted by fire to a highly oxidized and stable form that imparts a very enduring pink colour to the stone. On pale stones, this is very noticeable. It sometimes provides an interesting reminder of a fire that occurred in mediaeval times, as, for example, at Tewkesbury Abbey.

Chemically induced expansions

Some expansions of building materials are caused by chemical changes in the masonry itself. This cannot happen unless there has been some error in design or construction, but even conservators can make mistakes.

The splitting of stone by the rusting of iron or steel is a chemically induced expansion. Access of air and water to the metal is necessary for this rusting to take place and its associated pressure to develop. Attempts in the past to prevent access of air and water to the metal by coating it with tin, zinc or some form of bitumen have all had their disadvantages. Tin, once scratched, actually accelerates the rusting. Zinc, in the form of hot-dip galvanizing of the whole piece of iron, is quite good. Its life-time is dependent upon the thickness of the coating and the degree of acidic pollution of the ambient air. At best, it will serve for a small fraction of the expected life of a monumental building. Covering with a thick coating of bitumen reduces the effectiveness of the metal-to-stone bond. The traditional method of setting iron in the stone with molten sulphur, which has often been used for railings, has been known to lead to cracking of the stone[22]. Undoubtedly, the best method of reinforcing stone or of fixing railings to stone is to use a non-ferrous copper-based alloy, or an austenitic corrosion-resistant steel for the areas of contact between metal and stone.

The practice of burying iron in stonework has continued up to the present century, despite the recognition of its associated hazards early in the fifteenth century and the additional warnings that were given in the sixteenth century[23].

To understand why serious difficulties sometimes arise with mortars made from magnesian lime, it is necessary to have an outline understanding of the manufacture of a building lime by burning and slaking and the hardening process that takes place when lime is used in a mortar. Normal lime mortars are made by heating ('burning') limestone (calcium carbonate) until it decomposes and loses carbon dioxide gas to form quick-lime (calcium oxide). When the quick-lime is added to water (slaked), it is converted to slaked-lime (calcium hydroxide). When the slaked-lime is used to make mortar and the mortar begins to dry out, it absorbs carbon dioxide from the air and is reconverted to limestone. If some magnesium carbonate is present, as in a magnesian limestone, the magnesium carbonate goes through an analogous process and forms magnesium oxide, which is changed to magnesium hydroxide on slaking. When this magnesium hydroxide is used in a mortar, it combines with carbon dioxide from the air and reforms magnesium carbonate. The resulting mortar contains both calcium carbonate and magnesium carbonate. The result is excellent.

However, the 'burning' of magnesium carbonate has to be done much more carefully than the burning of calcium carbonate. If 'burning' is incorrectly done, the magnesium carbonate is converted to magnesium oxide, but will not readily hydrate to form slaked-lime. The lime is then said to be 'dead burnt'. If the slaked-lime obtained from normal limestone and dead burnt magnesium oxide are used in a mortar, the mortar apparently hardens in the normal way. The normal slaked-lime is converted back to limestone, but the magnesium oxide remains virtually unchanged. If it remains so for the life of the building, there is no problem. However, if the mortar is kept rather wet, the magnesium oxide will very gradually change to magnesium hydroxide and then to magnesium carbonate over the course of many years. There is a considerable increase in volume when magnesium oxide slakes and hardens and, though such an increase is easily accommodated when the mortar is still in the plastic state, it cannot normally be accommodated once the calcium hydroxide has hardened. The result of this late hydration and carbonation is normally a bending or disruption of the masonry and, eventually, a complete loss of strength of the mortar. Under optimum conditions, magnesium oxide will increase in volume by 240% on changing to magnesium carbonate.

It is unlikely that any 'dead burnt' magnesium limestones are produced today. Trouble still occasionally arises with nineteenth century buildings in which magnesian lime mortars were used. The problem is summarized in *Figure 7.3*.

Chemical expansion can also be caused by a reaction between a solution of calcium sulphate and a Portland cement-based mortar that has already set. Some hydraulic limes may produce the same effect. The setting of Portland cement gives rise to a number of products including calcium aluminate. Under wet conditions, calcium sulphate will react with this material to form a mineral called ettringite (calcium sulpho-aluminate), which occupies much more volume than the components from which it is made. The result is a considerable and powerful expansion, which can cause serious cracking in masonry[24]. If the damp conditions persist, this chemical reaction can continue until the mortar has lost its cohesion, whereupon the already-disrupted masonry might disintegrate.

Ettringite expansion has been observed mainly in brickwork in which the bricks were heavily charged with calcium sulphate. The effects have also been observed in a screen wall of flint work, surmounted by a capping of under-fired, and hence rather salty, bricks, sited in a very exposed position. Because of the degree of exposure, the architect had specified the use of a Portland cement-based mortar. After

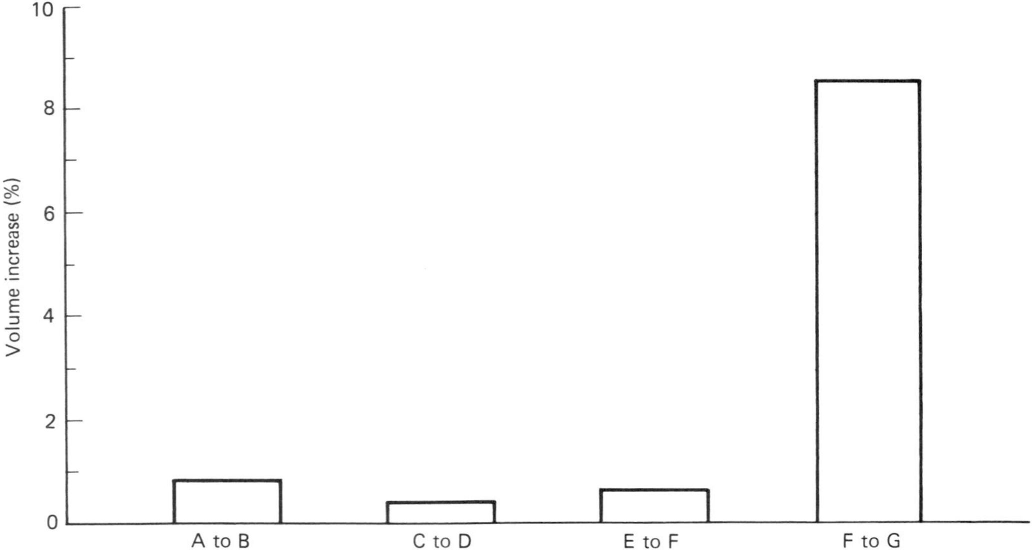

Figure 7.3 Theoretical volume increases in hardening of lime mortars. All mortars are composed of one part by volume slaked lime and three parts by volume sand. A ratio of one part by weight magnesium oxide to 2.48 parts by weight calcium carbonate is assumed. Less magnesium will give a smaller volume increase. Changes A to B, C to D and E to F occur mainly when mortar is in a plastic state. Change F to G takes place after the mortar is hardened, and may take decades. The risk of damage to the masonry is then much greater

about six months, the wall was leaning away from the wetter side, flints began to fall out and displacement of return walls became apparent. Almost complete rebuilding was essential. The use of bricks with a low soluble-salt content would have avoided the trouble. The simple use of a damp proof course between flintwork and the brick capping may have been sufficient and would have kept the flintwork drier.

Small amounts of calcium sulphate (gypsum) are deliberately added to Portland cement during manufacture to control the rate of setting because calcium sulphate acts as a set accelerator. Such additions do not cause disruptive expansions because any small expansion of the mortar in the plastic state is easily accommodated. However, if large amounts of calcium sulphate are added accidentally in making up a mortar for masonry the mortar will first set rapidly. The calcium sulphate then slowly acts on the set mortar to produce an extreme example of disruptive expansion. This mistake often arises because a particular kind of plaster based on calcium sulphate, Keene's Cement, has been inadvertently used with Portland cement for making up large batches of mortar. An error of this kind led to the disruption of a whole Gothic-style window in a matter of about three weeks and complete rebuilding was necessary.

Another form of chemical expansion involves certain concrete aggregates which contain a reactive form of silica that can swell in the presence of strong alkalis based, for example, on sodium or potassium. Alkali-reactive aggregates are rare in the British Isles and British Portland cements in the past have had alkali contents too low to cause trouble[25]. However, environmental protection pressures are forcing aggregate suppliers to look for fresh sources of aggregates, and alkali-reactive aggregates might come on the British market in the future. Moreover, the need for manufacturers to reduce particle emissions from their factories is causing a rise in the alkali content of British cements. In consequence, the risk of disruption caused by alkali-aggregate interaction in the British Isles is slowly increasing.

Disruption from this cause is more troublesome when the reactive aggregate is coarse than when it is finely ground. The minerals, not the whole piece of concrete or mortar swells and a swelling piece of aggregate in a non-swelling matrix will tend to crack the matrix. If all swelled equally, the total expansion might cause trouble, but there would be no disintegration. Thus the alkali-aggregate reaction can cause the collapse of structural concrete. If it occurs in a mortar, it will make repointing necessary and possibly cause some staining of stone round the joints but is not likely to lead to serious structural weaknesses in masonry. Therefore, it is not as serious a problem as sulpho-aluminate expansion.

Deterioration caused by living organisms

Certain plants, fungi, algae, lichens and bacteria have the potential to harm some kinds of stone or stonework. In some cases, the ability to cause serious damage has been well established; in others, it remains conjectural. The process by which deterioration might be caused varies considerably according to the type of organism involved.

Trees, climbers and creepers

It is a well-established fact that trees of some fast-growing species can progressively lower the average moisture content of clay soils and cause sufficient shrinkage to damage foundations of nearby buildings. Massive monuments are unlikely to be affected in this way, but smaller houses and the low parts of ruins are potentially at risk. Similar problems do not occur on fast-draining, sandy soils.

Sometimes, the seeds of a tree (e.g. Elder, *Sambucus nigra*) will germinate in soil or mortar dust that has collected in a cavity or ledge in the walls of an old building. As the tree's roots seek sources of moisture, ancient mortar will be further loosened and blocks of stone might eventually fall away if no action is taken to remove the tree. Ivy (*Hedera helix*) can be even more damaging, because its adventitious roots will eventually attack a multitude of weak points in the mortar system and an old tree will add very considerable weight to the weak parts of the wall. Schaffer[26] quotes parts of a poignant letter to *The Times*[27], in which Sir Martin Conway describes the partial destruction of Allington Castle, and the complete destruction of nearby Leybourne Castle by ivy. Evidence from old drawings and prints shows that this devastation was completed in about 100 years.

Growths of trees and climbers and creepers should be removed as quickly as possible, if damage to the structure is to be avoided. However, plants like Virginia Creepers and other *Vitis* species, which hold on to walls without the use of deeply penetrating adventitious roots, are probably not harmful. It is often argued that the leaf cover provided by such plants causes the wall to be moister than it would otherwise be. This is not necessarily harmful because the cover will shield the wall from heat loss by radiation so that frost attack is less likely to occur. Salt attack will also be reduced if the wall is kept moist for long periods because it is wetting and drying that causes crystallization damage. Admittedly, in an area of high air pollution, sulphur-based acid gas attack on damp limestone will be greater than on dry limestone.

Smaller flowering plants, ferns and mosses

Some smaller, flowering plants, such as Wallflowers (*Cheiranthus cheiri*) or the Ivy-leafed Toadflax (*Cymbalaria muralis*) and some species of grass, sometimes establish themselves on old walls. Their presence is an indication that soil-like dust is available for the plants to grow in. This may indicate that joints in the stonework should be repointed. These plants also indicate that some moisture is present. If the wall is unduly wet moss may be present. Ferns occupy an intermediate position as indicators, because some need damp conditions and others can thrive in moderately dry ones.

Algae

Algae form a group of plants that includes the seaweeds. Freshwater forms, particularly green algae, readily colonize stonework that remains damp for sufficiently long periods of time. Because they contain chlorophyll, they are able to manufacture most of the food they require by photosynthesis and, under the right conditions, they can multiply rapidly. The green appearance imparted to the stone is often considered to be disfiguring. Bravery[28] makes the point that, while the algae alone might not be considered to be too unsightly, their appearance is made much worse in an urban environment when dirt readily becomes entrapped in the algal mass.

Bachmann[29] suggested in 1915 that acidic by-products of the algae will attack calcareous stones, but no quantitative evidence has yet been cited to show that algae cause any significant increase in the rate of decay of limestones.

Fungi

Fungi have no ability to manufacture their own food by using the energy of sunlight and hence they cannot live on stone, even if it is permanently wet, unless some organic food is present. The waste products of algae and bacteria, or the dead cells of these organisms, can provide such food. Decaying leaves and bird droppings are other sources.

Several workers have isolated fungi from decaying stone where nutrients are present. Lepidi and Schippa[30] have found fungal hyphae (the food-seeking threads of a fungus) extensively penetrating the decayed parts of a limestone and apparently burrowing into otherwise sound stone. Fungi can produce organic acids such as oxalic and citric acids[31,32]. Both of these acids can dissolve calcium carbonate, the main constituent of limestones. Hence fungi are potential contributors to limestone decay. But it has yet to be shown what proportion of the total decay of limestones is attributable to their activities.

Lichens

Lichens are an intimate association of fungi and algae, in which the fungal hyphae seek the water and salts necessary for both organisms and the algal cells manufacture organic food for both of them by photosynthesis. Thus, it seems likely that lichen are more important contributors to limestone decay than either type of organism on its own. It has yet to be demonstrated that their contribution is significant in comparison with the amount of decay caused directly by salt crystallization, acidic gas attack and frost action. This may be because most lichens are killed by even moderate levels of air pollution by sulphur oxides[33], though Lloyd[34] has reported the rapid colonization of pre-washed asbestos cement sheets in central London.

Lichens have also been known to attack sandstones and even basalts and granites[35]. The attack appears to be mainly on micas in the granites and Bachmann[36] believed it to be chemical in nature. However, there are also reasons to believe that the damage is often the result of surface stresses induced when the lichens shrink on drying after remaining wet for long periods[37]. Drying gelatine can attack glass in the same way[38].

Despite the generally attractive appearance of lichens growing on old stonework and the lack of conclusive evidence that they contribute significantly to stone decay, there is a general feeling among conservation experts that lichens should be removed and the stonework treated to discourage re-infection. Bravery[39] gives a detailed account of toxic treatments.

Bacteria

Bacteria are a group of living organisms that are so small that their presence is normally recognized only by the chemical and biological changes that they bring about. Thus, unlike lichens, algae, fungi and higher plants, bacteria do not significantly change the appearance of stone by their presence. If they play a part in the decay of stonework, it is because they initiate or augment the production of chemicals that can attack stone or mortar directly.

As early as 1911, Anderson[40] suggested that bacteria might play this kind of role. Since then, many biologists have isolated bacteria from decaying stonework and shown that they are species that could almost certainly have contributed to the observed decay. The groups of bacteria most likely to be involved are those that can oxidize sulphur or one of its compounds to form sulphuric acid[41–43], which attacks limestone directly, those that oxidize ammonia in the air to form nitric acid, which also attacks limestone directly[44,45] and those that produce organic acids with the power to dissolve silicates[46–48]. However, in nearly all cases, little or no evidence has been produced to show that the decay caused by bacterial products is significant in comparison with the decay caused by salt crystallization, frost and the effects of air pollution.

From the practical point of view, those concerned with the conservation of stonework need take no more than an academic interest in the matter until it can be shown that the use of some bactericide can significantly decrease the rate of decay of stonework.

Birds and bees

Small birds can damage soft stone with their bills. In Britain, the species most commonly involved appear to be the Blue Tit (*Parus caeruleus*) and the House Sparrow (*Passer domesticus*) who appear to be seeking grit. They may also be seeking salt. The damage caused by their bills might not be very conspicuous on broad stretches of ashlar, but on carved features in soft stone it can become a matter for concern.

However, more damage is unquestionably done by the roosting and nesting of birds on masonry. Starlings (*Sturnus vulgaris*) and wild, feral and domestic pigeons are the main offenders. Decay is caused mainly by the accumulation of their droppings and nesting materials. These can form a compost, which breaks down as a result of bacterial action and releases acids which will attack limestone and calcareous sandstone. The compost also contains salts which might cause crystallization damage to any susceptible type of stone. This aspect has not been adequately investigated. Such troubles are likely to be most serious when the birds roost among statuary.

Mason bees, also, can harm stonework. The type involved in Britain bores holes in soft stone to provide a safe refuge for its eggs and grubs. The stones affected are mainly loosely bonded, possibly argillaceous sandstones. At one time, these creatures appeared to be active only in East Anglia, but more recently they have been reported from other parts of the country. A massive attack could result in highly disfigured stonework that is possibly so weakened that the stability of that part of the building is threatened. Such attack is, however, unlikely to make the stone more susceptible to frost, or to any other of the main causes of decay.

Effects of errors in design, specification or construction

Although it is a prime principle of conservation that the original should be changed as little as possible, there are occasions when errors in design, specification or construction of some part of a building lead to a degree of deterioration that begins to threaten the viability of the whole. If some alternative construction is essential for this part of the structure, it is equally essential to understand the reasons for what has happened, so that the original faults can be avoided in the remedial work.

This chapter is concerned with over-stressing that has a chemical origin. *Table 7.4* gives a list of design, specification and construction errors that can cause trouble.

Errors at the design stage

Water is involved in nearly all the processes that lead to deterioration or decay of building materials and a well-designed building will have arrangements for conducting the rain-water that falls on it harmlessly away from the building. If the building has no impermeable plinth or damp proof course, but depends instead on the good drainage of the soil on which it stands, it is better not to rely on simple shedding of rain-water. During heavy rainfall this may raise the water content of the soil around the building so that good drainage will become an insufficient safeguard and water and salts will enter the lower courses and cause damage by crystallization and general staining.

If the face of the building contains more than one kind of building material, damage might be caused before the rain-water reaches the soil. Water running over limestone on to brickwork or sandstone is likely to cause staining with subsequent crystallization decay unless the brick or sandstone is exceptionally resistant to the forces involved in the crystallization of the calcium sulphate that the rain-water extracts from the limestone. Conversely, rain-water flowing over brickwork on to limestone or sandstone is likely to cause crystallization damage to the limestone or sandstone as a result of the transfer of salts extracted from the brickwork by the rain-water. The effect will be significant unless the area of brickwork is very small compared with the area of the stone, or the bricks are exceptionally free from soluble salts.

The injudicious placing of corrodible metals such as iron or copper where rain-water can flow over them on to light-coloured stonework is likely to give rise to rusty-brown or greenish-blue stains that are impossible or extremely difficult to remove. The only iron-based metal that should be used in such circumstances is some suitable variety of corrosion-resistant steel. If this is unacceptable, the iron will need to be painted at regular intervals and the cost of maintenance might be high especially if the use of extensive scaffolding is required. The problem of preventing statuary in bronze or other copper-based alloys from causing bluish-green stains on the plinth of the statue or on other underlying stonework can

Table 7.4 Effect of errors in design, specification or construction

Error	*Possible harmful effects*
Design	
Design of building allows rain-water to flow over brickwork on to porous stone.	Crystallization damage to stone.
Design of building allows rain-water to flow over limestone on to brickwork or sandstone.	White staining and probable crystallization damage to brickwork and to sandstone.
Design of building fails to prevent soil water from entering stonework.	Stains and/or crystallization damage to stonework.
Design of building involves use of corrodible metals where rain-water can wet them and then run over stonework.	Staining of stonework; slight possibility of decay by crystallization attack.
Design of building involves use of iron or steel partially or completely but shallowly, embedded in stonework or mortar.	Cracking of stonework sometimes accompanied by rust staining.
Specification	
Specification of an unduly rich Portland cement-based mortar.	Alkali-induced staining of pale-coloured limestones; any crystallization damage occurs to stone rather than to mortar.
Specification of too dense a mortar (but not necessarily too cement-rich).	Any crystallization damage occurs to stone rather than to mortar.
Specification of stone of generally inadequate weather resistance.	General decay of stonework.
Specification of stone of adequate general weather resistance, but inadequate resistance to frost.	Failure of projecting features in stone unless they are protected by flashings of metal.
Specification of type of stone characterized by vents.	Usually no problem in plain walling; might lead to falls of stone from overhanging features or from fine, elaborately carved details.
Specification of stone characterized by soft seams.	Furrows in surface of stonework might appear early in the life of the building. Could be considered as 'character' but could lead to falls from overhanging features.
Specification of stone with shakes.	Question of aesthetics only; can adversely affect appearance; can provide 'character'.
Specification of stone with too high a permeability for cappings.	Undue rain penetration leading to staining or frost damage to underlying stonework.
Specification of unsuitable metal for cramps or dowels.	Staining or even disruption of masonry caused by volume of corrosion products.
Workmanship	
Unsuitable positioning of stone with shakes.	Aesthetic question only.
Use of blocks with soft seams in particularly exposed positions. (It is not always possible to distinguish these seams in unweathered stone.)	Unduly rapid erosion of the soft seams.
Failure to place a block of stone on its natural bed.	In general the consequences are not serious but if the bedding is strongly marked and the block is face bedded the rate of decay might be enhanced.
Bruising of stone during squaring up or carving.	Unduly rapid decay of affected surfaces where exposed to the weather.
Wrongly compounded mortar.	A whole range of consequences from rapid erosion of mortar to disruption of the masonry by expansion of the mortar.
Inaccurate positioning of cramps or dowels.	Cracking of stonework sometimes accompanied by rust staining.

sometimes be overcome by providing an inconspicuous metal tray beneath the statue that will collect rain washings and enable them to be led harmlessly away. The problem of avoiding staining of masonry by the copper of lightning conductors is one that has not been satisfactorily solved.

A more serious error is for the designer to include ironwork that is to be partially or shallowly embedded in stonework. The expansion accompanying the inevitable rusting almost invariably leads to the cracking of the stonework and to some degree of rust staining. It is better for the designer to plan for the use of corrosion-resistant steel in all such situations.

Errors in specification

A good design is often spoiled by inadequate specification of materials or components. It is an error to specify a type of stone that has inadequate resistance to the environmental conditions in the locality of the building. This could lead to unduly rapid deterioration of the external fabric. It is also an error to fail to allow for the fact that stone that is suitable for use in plain walling is not necessarily adequate for the harsher microclimate affecting projecting features such as copings, cornices and string courses in areas subject to frosts. Moreover, stone that is to be used in buildings near the coast must be of higher weathering resistance than stone that is just adequate for otherwise similar positions inland.

A type of stone that is characterized by the occasional occurrence of soft seams (seams of lower weather resistance) might be acceptable in plain walling if the furrowed appearance that develops is considered to give desirable character to the building. However, in buildings with much external carved work, development of furrows is usually an undesirable disfigurement. Such stone should therefore be specified only after cautious deliberation.

Similarly, stone containing vents, though often acceptable for plain walling, or walling with shallowly-cut decoration, will often prove to be quite unsuitable for stonework that is to be intricately carved because weaknesses along the vent planes will sometimes allow parts of fine decorative features to fall away.

If a permeable type of stone is specified for a building, the specification of a different stone, with slight or negligible permeability, should be made for features such as cappings. Otherwise, serious amounts of water might enter the underlying stonework and lead to staining, efflorescence or even penetration of water to the interior of the building.

It is as important to specify a suitable mortar or metal for use as a cramp or dowel as it is to specify a suitable type of stone. The specification of a mortar that is unduly rich in Portland-type cement is likely to result in alkali-induced staining of pale-coloured limestone. Moreover, the low permeability of such a mortar induces any salts present to crystallize in the stone rather than in the more expendable mortar. This can lead to crystallization damage to the stone. Similar damage can occur if the specification is for mortar that is rather dense, though not necessarily too rich in Portland-type cement.

Errors in workmanship

Even if the design and specification are beyond criticism, errors in workmanship can still cause serious trouble. They lead not only to defects in the building, but also to defects in the raw materials supplied to the building site. If, for example, mortar made with over-burnt magnesium lime is supplied due to an error on the part of the supplier the consequences can be severe and extensive damage can be caused to the masonry.

However, most errors of workmanship affecting a building occur on the building site. Some of them are aesthetic rather than material errors and have no effect on the life of the stonework. They reflect on the quality of the supervision rather than on the workman concerned. One example is the placing of a block of limestone with a shake in a position that is inappropriate in respect of the aesthetic appearance of the building. Because shakes are veins of calcite they do not detract from the strength of the block concerned or the masonry as a whole.

A materially more serious effect results from the use of a block of stone with a soft seam (even of poor weather resistance) in a very exposed position. Sometimes an expert mason can detect such seams in unweathered stone, but this is not always so. Where it is not possible, the mason cannot be blamed for inappropriate placing. Where the results of wrong placing could be serious, the use of stone types known to be subject to soft seams should be avoided until materials technologists have developed a reliable and non-destructive on-site test for them.

In most types of stone, the natural bedding is distinguishable and masons will normally place a block on its natural bed, except perhaps at cornices and other overhanging features, where joint-bedding may be used to reduce risk of frost damage. Problems arise at the corners, where a block that presents a joint-bed on one façade of the building must present a face-bed on the façade at right angles to it. Face bedding generally enhances the rate of weathering in the long term. It is a serious mistake for a mason to face-bed a block of stone unless it is well known that the type of stone can be safely face-bedded.

It is a more serious error of workmanship to bruise a stone during squaring up or carving by using too much force or dull tools. By creating microscopic fissures in the stone, bruising could lead to unduly rapid decay of the affected surface, particularly if the stone is to be used externally.

Inaccurate positioning of cramps and dowels is a fault of workmanship that could lead to fractures as a result of an increase in stress concentrations beyond the design level. If corrodible metal is involved, it could also lead to unduly rapid development of fractures resulting from the volume increase as the metal decays and to stains caused by the corrosion products.

Fixer masons need to be even more careful in preparing mortars than bricklayers because stone is generally more sensitive than bricks to mortars that are outside the intended range of compositions. Errors are most likely to occur with composition mortars which contain a hydraulic cement as well as lime and sand. Serious damage has arisen as a result of the use of a calcium sulphate-based plaster called Keene's cement.

Effects of behaviour of users and occupiers on the welfare of stone buildings

The owner of a stone building normally has responsibility for its welfare, but the owner is not necessarily the occupier and there can be other users besides the occupier. A cathedral building, for example, is owned by the appropriate church organization and used by those who conduct religious services and worship there, as well as those who visit the building to admire or study its architecture or to enjoy its historic atmosphere. All users will have some adverse effect on the building, but only the occupiers or regular users can reasonably be expected to exert a net positive benefit.

The effects of direct contact by visitors

For a building or monument that is visited by a very large number of people every year, the wearing down of paving and flooring materials by the passage of many feet is a well recognized hazard. In general, the damage is done by hard grit embedded in the soles or heels of shoes or boots. Damage will be greatest where people turn sharply[49].

In some circumstances, the damage can be minimized by arranging for people to have to take smooth curves rather than sharp turns. It may also be possible to lead the visitors along routes paved with hardwearing contemporary materials of no historical value. Eventually, it may be necessary to make it obligatory for visitors to wear slippers in some historic buildings. However, this is a matter of policy rather than of technology.

The rubbing of clothes against the fabric of a building can produce a polishing and staining of the surface. This is particularly noticeable in spiral staircases. Even granite can be affected in this way, but limestone and lime- and gypsum-based plasters are more quickly polished. In contrast, sandstones are relatively immune. Paler coloured materials naturally show staining more rapidly than dark ones. The staining is generally attributed to oil from woollen clothing. However, some of the staining might well be due to polishing in of dirt particles already on the surface.

Oil in the skin has a similar effect to oil from clothing and this can often be seen on stone handrails and on other carved features that people tend to finger out of curiosity. Some of the stains seen on marble, particularly white statuary marble, probably originate in this way. Oil stains of this kind will not lead to any deterioration of the building material and there is some evidence that the oil has a tendency to preserve stone. However, the stains are usually considered to be unsightly. The special techniques required for their removal are expensive and absorb funds that are usually needed for other conservation activities.

The indirect effects of visitors

Staining can be caused on marble counter and table tops by cigarettes that have been left smouldering in contact with them. A more widespread staining can occur as a result of a large number of people regularly smoking within a building. This has been established as being the most likely cause of otherwise unexplained staining of marble in at least one large building in London. There is no reason why tobacco smoke should not also cause stains on *porous* stone or brick surfaces, though such stains are likely to be noticed only if the surfaces are pale in colour. The removal of these stains from porous stone or brick would present grave difficulties. There is usually a ban on smoking in historic buildings because of fire risks and staining is another good reason why the ban should be maintained.

The presence of many people in a building alters the relative humidity of the air. The air exhaled in breathing will be much moister than the air inhaled. If a large number of people are involved, the relative humidity of the air in the building may rise sufficiently for condensation of moisture to occur on some of the colder surfaces. What happens to this condensed moisture depends very much on the nature of the cold surface on which it is formed. Moisture condensing on an impervious surface will initially be very pure and very reactive in a chemical sense. Although modern glass is unlikely to be significantly affected, mediaeval window glass, particularly that with a high content of potash, is likely to be slightly attacked. This process, often repeated, could eventually cause visible damage. Condensed water running down window panes can also cause damage to putty and to timber framing in the long run. If condensation runs over gypsum-based plaster, it can cause softening or the appearance of blisters on the plaster. If it runs into brickwork it can dissolve soluble salts in the bricks and may transfer them to other porous building materials which can be damaged if the salts crystallize when the water evaporates. Staining of the surface from which the evaporation takes place can also occur.

Condensation of moisture from the air can also occur directly on to porous materials. In the very finest pores condensation will occur at a slightly higher temperature, and hence more often, than it will on an impervious surface. In the absence of soluble salts, this is not likely to cause trouble. However, if soluble salts, particularly hygroscopic salts, which absorb water at relative humidities below those causing normal condensation, are present, they are likely to dissolve at the higher relative humidities brought about by visitors and to crystallize out again when the relative humidity returns to normal after the visitors have gone. If this cycle is repeated often enough, crystallization damage to the porous material can occur.

Effects of occupiers or regular users

The occupier or an informed regular user of a stone building of merit might reasonably be expected not only to avoid actions that might harm the fabric of the building but also to take positive action to help to conserve it. One of the simplest beneficial actions they might take is to ensure that all gutters, downpipes and other parts of the rain disposal system are free from blockage and are functioning correctly. This might be boringly obvious, but in practice it is often neglected. Rain-water, flowing where it was not intended to flow, will make some parts of the building wetter than normal. This can have many deleterious effects.

Areas that are normally dark because they are not much washed by rain will become paler as a result of the overflow. Correction of the fault will not cause the building to return immediately to its former appearance; the change might take years. If the overflow has given rise to more serious stains such as those caused by rust, it will be very difficult to put right. Extra water flowing over stonework might also lead to frost attack on those features that are normally not affected because their water contents never reach the critical value. Also the additional water might penetrate deeply enough into the stone to dissolve dormant salts within the structure. Under drying conditions, these salts could be brought to the surface where they may cause crystallization damage. Finally, the additional water may penetrate to the interior of the building and damage to wooden panelling, wall paintings, interior stonework and furnishings may occur.

If lead water channels become perforated penetration of stonework by water from defective guttering can occur without being accompanied by a gross overflow of water on to the exterior stonework. The perforation of lead channels by workmen wearing unsuitable boots or dropping hard metal objects such as scaffold poles can easily be prevented. However, water dripping on to lead from one point can eventually cause perforation, particularly if the rain-water has run over organic growths on the roof which might generate organic acids. Exposed lead normally survives because it quickly becomes covered by a protective film. Organic acids or constant dripping of water at one point can remove this protective film and permit penetration. Although this seems unlikely in view of lead's resistance to many other acids, it can be significant.

An occupier or frequent user of a building can also help to conserve it by preventing any tree, bush, creeper or other significant flowering plant from establishing itself on the stonework. Ivy is particularly harmful. Some lichens can slowly attack stone and their presence should be noted. Green algae might not do harm by themselves, but they are an indicator of persistent dampness, which should be investigated.

It is wrong to attempt to suppress an efflorescence of soluble salts that has appeared on the *inside* of stone window frames, mullions, or transoms by using a water-repellent treatment of any kind. These efflorescences usually affect windows facing seawards and the salt is usually sodium chloride. A palliative procedure is to treat the *outside* stonework of the window with a water repellent and to brush the efflorescence gently from the inside stonework until new efflorescence no longer appears.

It is also wrong to allow soil, solid fuel, stacks of bricks or bags of fertilizer to be placed in contact with a porous stone wall, particularly if they are in contact with stonework above a damp proof course or impermeable plinth. All are sources of salts of various kinds that will eventually cause crystallization damage to the stonework. For the same reason, it is wrong to use common salt as a means of removing any ice or snow lying in contact with the stonework. Any de-icing treatment of paths near the building should be carried out carefully, to avoid splashing salt solution on to the stonework.

Many household cleaning powders and cleaning grits contain salts that are harmful to porous stone and great care should be taken in cleaning stone floors, to prevent damage to the floors or to the walls which might become contaminated in the process. It would be ideal if special materials based on grits of appropriate size and detergents that are free from sodium, potassium and other alkali metals in any form were available. However, this is not the case. Laundry detergents are even more harmful and should not be used on stonework in any circumstances. For this reason, leaking drains that might allow discharge from domestic sinks or washing machines to contaminate stonework should be dealt with immediately. Treating stone with a solution of common salt on the grounds that it preserves meat, is a serious mistake.

Implements or stock materials, such as pipes that are made of copper, bronze or brass should not be left in contact with stonework for any considerable time, particularly in urban areas. This can lead to staining of the stonework. It should also be noted that an unwise choice of cleaning materials or of repointing mortar can lead to an increase in the rate of deterioration of the stonework.

Annex

Frost attack on stone

The work of Everett[12] and Haynes[13] attempted to explain the relationship between pore structure and resistance to decay in building stones. Their ideas are summarized below.

Fineness of pores

In the commoner form of frost attack, freezing is somewhat one-sided and the stone is not surrounded by a casing of ice. The effect of this type of attack may be stated *approximately* in the form of the equation

$$P_{max} = \sigma_{iw} \left(\frac{1}{r} = \frac{1}{R} \right) \qquad (7.1)$$

where P_{max} is the maximum excess pressure that can be developed during the slow freezing of water in a pore of radius R attached to a finer pore of radius r that has access to an *unlimited* supply of water that is free from any significant restraints on its movement. P_{max} is also the excess pressure at which ice will begin to grow in the fine pore (see *Figure 7.4a*). The constant σ_{iw} is the interfacial tension between ice and water, not the better known interfacial tension between water-saturated air and water.

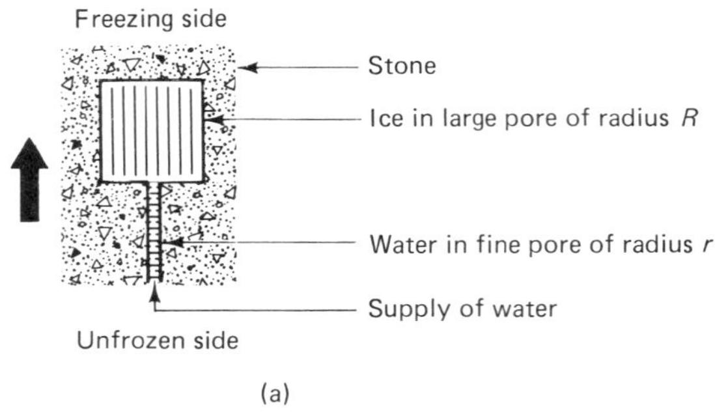

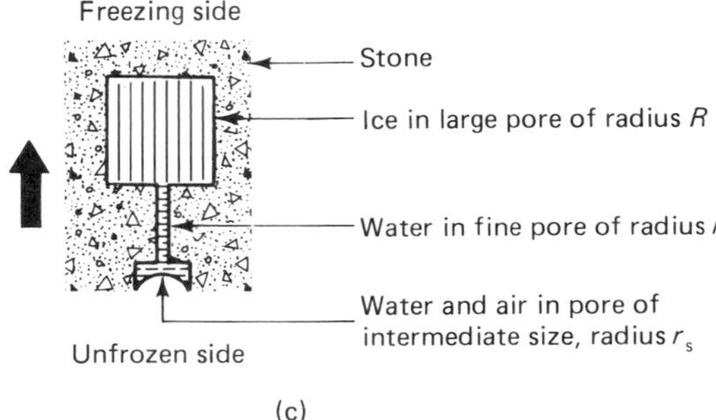

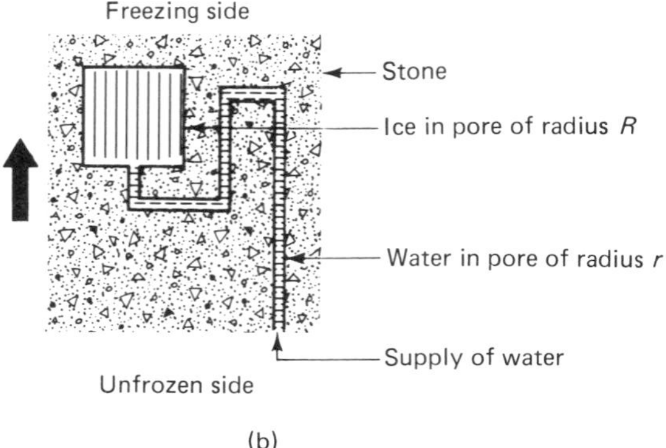

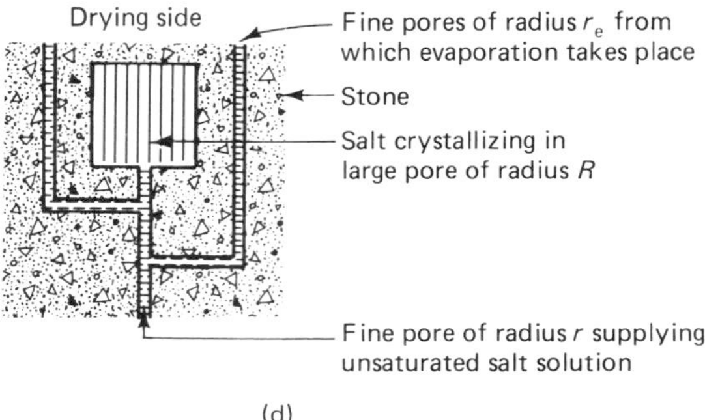

Figure 7.4 Everett's theory applied to frost and crystallization attack on stone (a) the simplest case of pressure development during one-sided freezing. Broad arrows show the direction of heat flow. The maximum pressure in the large pore is σ_{iw} ($1/r - 1/R$). (b) water freezes at a lower temperature in small pores so the supply is not necessarily cut off if the small pore passes through the freezing region. The maximum pressure in the large pore is σ_{iw} ($1/r - 1/R$). (c) effect of limited supply of water. Broad arrows show the direction of heat flow. The maximum pressure in the large pore is σ_{iw} ($1/r - 1/R$) − σ_{aw}/r_s. (d) pressure development by crystallization of salts caused by evaporation of water. As evaporation occurs, more solution feeds in from the pore of radius r and diffusion causes the solution in the large pore to become more concentrated and to attempt to form more crystals in the large pore. This further increases the pressure in the pore until the maximum possible pressure for that pore geometry is reached. This is σ_{ss} ($1/r - 1/R$)

The value of σ_{iw} is not known with certainty, but some experimental results[50] have indicated that it is about 0.032 N/m. The finer pore in the model need not be entirely on the warmer side of the freezing-point isotherm in the stone, because water in fine pores freezes at a lower temperature than water in wider pores. Hence a pore system of the kind shown in *Figure 7.4b* would still develop a pressure equal to $\sigma_{iw}(1/r - 1/R)$ before ice could begin to penetrate the finer pore. The open water in contact with the fine pore must be on the warm side of the freezing point isotherm. If it were situated on the cold side of the isotherm, it would freeze and cut off the supply of water before pressure could build up in the coarse pore.

It is clear from Equation 7.1 that potential excess pressure attributable to ice growth becomes greater as the fine pore becomes finer and the coarse pore larger. It would be unusual for any band lying along a freezing-point isotherm in a piece of stone to consist entirely of large pores fed by numerous small pores. A study of pore structure suggests that it is much more likely that the ratios of the radii of the coarse and fine pores will lie within the range 2 to 30. *Table 7.5* gives values of P_{max} computed for values of R/r ranging from 2 to 32 and for values of r ranging from 0.01 to 1.28 μm. The effect of the ratio of the radii becomes relatively unimportant when R/r is greater than 8. *Figure 7.5* shows the effect of changes in the value of r on P_{max}, when the radii ratio is 10. P_{max} rises rapidly as r falls below 0.1 μm. Therefore the fineness of the pore structure plays a large part in determining its frost resistance under conditions of one-sided freezing where there is an adequate supply of water on the warmer side.

Table 7.5 The maximum pressure in bars (pascals × 10^5) that can be developed in a pore of radius R connected to a smaller pore of radius r when water in the larger pore freezes. The pores are shown in μm. It is assumed that σ_{iw} = 0.032 N/m. σ_{iw} is the interfacial tension between ice and water. The small pores are assumed to have access to a free water supply

r= \ R=	r	2r	4r	8r	16r	32r
0.01	0	32	48	56	60	62
0.02	0	16	24	28	30	31
0.04	0	8	12	14	15	15.5
0.08	0	4	6	7	7.5	7.8
0.16	0	2	3	3.5	3.8	3.9
0.32	0	1	1.5	1.8	1.9	1.9
0.64	0	0.5	0.8	0.8	0.9	1.0
1.28	0	0.3	0.4	0.4	0.5	0.5

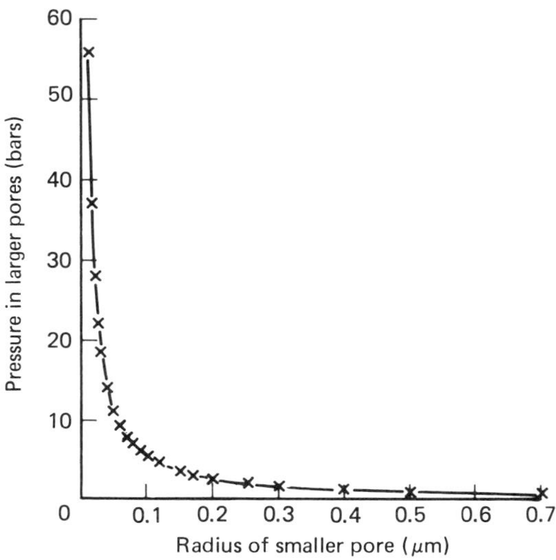

Figure 7.5 Theoretical pressure resulting from the freezing of water in a large pore connected to a smaller pore. The ratio of large and small pores was kept at eight

Water supply

If the supply of water is limited, Equation 7.1 must be extended:

$$P_{max} = \sigma_{iw}\left(\frac{1}{r} - \frac{1}{R}\right) - P_s \qquad (7.2)$$

where P_s is the negative pressure on the supply side. This is Everett's equation[12].

The pressure P_s could arise if all-round freezing cuts off the supply of water. If shortage of water causes the air/water interface on the warmer side to enter smaller and smaller pores:

$$P_s = \sigma_{aw}/r_s \qquad (7.3)$$

where r_s is the radius of the pores at the air envelope on that side, and σ_{aw} is the normal surface tension of water. This is also shown in *Figure 7.4c*.

This is why all-round freezing causes damage by a process that is distinctly different from that involved in one-sided freezing and why initial moisture content is so important in determining whether frost damage by one-sided freezing may occur.

Porosity

Under conditions of one-sided freezing, associations of coarse and fine pores can give rise to considerable local pressures. This acts like a miniscule jack. To cause damage there must be a sufficient concentration of jacks within the zone under attack to allow the development of a gross pressure that can overcome the cohesive strength of the stone. The probability of the occurrence of such a concentration is greater the higher the porosity of the stone. Moreover, the higher the porosity, the lower the amount of solid material within the zone and hence the lower the bursting stregnth of the stone.

In fact porosity is not the most important factor in determining frost resistance. Obviously, stone without pores cannot suffer frost damage, but even stone with a porosity of 40 per cent is not necessarily susceptible to frost attack. This is because the natural process that gives rise to porosity produces a fine pore system in the early stages and then proceeds by breaking down the pore walls, thus increasing the mean pore radius and hence reducing the number of jacks and the maximum pressure developable from each of them.

Salt crystallization attack

Because freezing is a crystallization process, Equation 7.2 may also be applied to salt crystallization attack on stone with only modest modification. Crystallization can take place as a result of cooling or evaporation of solvent (see *Figure 7.4d*). In both cases, the appropriate governing equation is:

$$P_{max} = \sigma_{ss}\left(\frac{1}{r} - \frac{1}{R}\right) - P_s \qquad (7.4)$$

where P_{max} is the maximum pressure that can develop in the larger pore, σ_{ss} is the interfacial tension between the salt and its solution, r and R are the radii of the small and large pores. P_s is the negative pressure in the finer pore caused by the entry of an air/water meniscus at the distant end due to shortage of water or salt solution or by the blockage of the distant end of the pore system by crystallization. At the beginning of crystallization attack, P_s will normally be zero.

In the freezing process, σ_{iw} will always be the same; in the crystallization process, σ_{ss} will vary with the salt involved. This explains why some salts are more aggressive than others. It is also clear from this theory why the coarser pored types of stone are generally more resistant to salt attack than the finer pored types. Unfortunately, in the absence of any experimental value of σ_{ss}, it is not possible to treat the problem quantitatively.

Acid gas attack on limestones

Everett's[12] theory does not directly apply to the attack on limestone, magnesian limestones, calcareous sandstones and calcareous slates by acidic gases in the air. Nevertheless, since the primary attack by these gases is normally followed by a crystallization attack, it has some relevance.

The good influence of coarse pores can be discerned more easily with ordinary limestones than with calcareous sandstones or magnesian limestones. This is because the loosening cause in calcareous sandstones by direct chemical attack on the calcium carbonate cement is so great that the effects of subsequent crystallization attack, which is influenced by pore size, is relatively minor. With magnesian limestones, the susceptibility to acid attack depends very much on their composition. It is lowest when the calcium carbonate/magnesium carbonate ratio is 1.19, as in the mineral dolomite. Variations in chemical resistance caused by variability in chemical composition tend to obscure the effects of pore coarseness on subsequent crystallization damage.

Blister formation on limestones

Attack by sulphur-based acids in the air can lead to the development of blisters on the surface limestones. Because this seems to occur mainly on limestones with finer-than-average pore structure, it is tempting to think that Everett's theory[12] is directly applicable and the blisters are forced up by crystals of gypsum growing in larger pores from supersaturated solutions fed through finer pores in which the gypsum cannot crystallize. However, the majority of limestone blisters are hollow beneath the skin, with no sign of crystals that could have forced the blister upwards. Instead, blisters appear to arise because the skin develops a larger surface area than the underlying stone. Hence, Scott Russell's explanation[21], that this occurs because the thermal expansion of gypsum is about five times as great as that of the unattacked limestone, seems sensible. Thus, when the temperature rises, the gypsum-rich surface skin will expand relative to the limestone below and cause a degree of shear failure. However, for a blister to continue to grow, it must not return to its original area on cooling. It has sometimes been thought that stone debris, formed as the crack extended, will prevent the skin from returning to its original position. However, the hollowness of most blisters on limestone belies this. Instead, the thermal expansion may enlarge some pores in the skin and allow the crystallization of more gypsum from the supersaturated solution held by the finer pores. The skin would thus increase in area and the blister bulge further away from the plane of the original surface with each significant cycle of heating and cooling. Everett's theory[12] may thus be invoked and the relationship between susceptibility to blister formation and the fineness of pore structure of the limestone may thus be explained. This process of blister formation has not been adequately studied experimentally in the past, but a new approach to this and to closely related problems is currently being made[51].

References

1. Amoroso, G.G. and Fassina, V., 'Stone Decay and Conservation' *Materials Science Monograph II*, Elsevier, Amsterdam, 1983
2. Dorsey, N.E., *Properties of Ordinary Water Substance*, p. 655, Reinhold, New York, 1940
3. Apling, A.J., Potter, C.J. and Williams, M.L., 'Air Pollution from Oxides of Nitrogen, Carbon monoxide and Hydrocarbons, *Warren Spring Laboratory Report LR 306*; Galloway J.N. and Likens G.E. 'Acid Precipitation: the Importance of Nitric Acid' *Atmospheric Environment*, **15**, 1081–1085, 1981
4. Serra, M. and Starace, G., *An Isotopic Method for Studying Absorption and Oxidation of Sulphur dioxide on Calcium Carbonate'*, CNR Centro di Studio Cause di Deperimento et Metodi di Conservazione delle Opere d'Arte, Rome, 1973
5. Kaiser, E., 'Skin Formation on Limestone', *Der Steinbuch*, **5**, 254, 1910; 'A Fundamental Factor in the Weathering of Rocks and a Comparison of the Chemical Weathering of Stone in Buildings and in Nature', *Chemie der Erde*, **4**, 342, 1929
6. Schaffer, R.J., 'The Weathering of Natural Building Stones', *Department of Scientific and Industrial Research Spec. Rep. 18*, pp. 28–29, HMSO, London, 1932 (available from the Building Research Establishment, Watford WD2 7JR, England)
7. Hull, E., *Building and Ornamental Stone*, p. 203, MacMillan, London, n.d.
8. Millot, G., Cogne, J., Jeannette, D., Besnus, Y., Monnet, B., Guri, F. and Schimpf, A., 'La Maladie des Grès de la Cathédral de Strasbourg', *Bull. Serv. Geol. Alsace Lorraine*, **20**, 131–157, Strasbourg, 1967
9. Anon. 'The Weathering, Preservation and Maintenance of Natural Building Stone, Part 1', *Building Research Station Digest*, **20**, Pt. 3, HMSO, London, 1965
10. Anon., 'The Decay and Conservation of Stone Masonry', *Building Research Digest*, **177**, Pt. 2, HMSO, London, 1975
11. Taber, S., 'The Mechanics of Frost Heaving', *J. Geol.*, **38**, 302–317, 1930
12. Everett, D.H., 'The Dynamics of Frost Damage to Porous Solids', *Trans. Farad. Soc.*, **57**, 1541–1551, 1961
13. Haynes, J.M., 'Frost Action as a Capillary Effect', *Trans. Brit. Ceram. Soc.*, **63**, 267, 1964
14. Honeyborne, D.B. and Harris, P.B., 'The Structure of Porous Building Stone and its Relation to Weathering Behaviour', *Proc. 10th Symp. Colston Research Soc. Bristol, March 1958*, p. 345, Butterworths, London, 1958
15. Huber, H. 'Staining and Efflorescence on Indiana Limestone caused by Moisture Seepage through Backing Masonry', *ASTM Proc.*, **28**, Pt. 2, 695–713, 1928
16. Department of Scientific and Industrial Research, *Building Research 1956*, p. 10, HMSO, London, 195
17. Evans, I.S. 'Salt Crystallisation and Rock Weathering: A Review', *Revue de Géomorphologie Dynamique*, **19**, 153–177, 1970
18. Cooke, R.W. 'Salt Weathering in Deserts', *Proc. Geol. Assn.*, **92**. 1–16, 1981
19. Kessler, D.W. 'Physical and Chemical Tests on the Commercial Marbles of the United States', *Technical Paper 123*, U.S. Bureau of Washington, 1919
20. Hochman, A. and Kessler, D.W. 'Thermal and Moisture Expansion Studies of some Domestic Granites', *US Bureau of Standards, Journal of Research*, **44**, 395–410, 1950
21. Scott Russell, A., quoted by Schaffer, R.J. Reference 6, p.32
22. Gaetani, L. de 'Cracking of Stonework by Cementing Iron Rods with Sulphur', *Giornale del Genie Civile*, 425, 1902
23. Rogers, F. *Specifications for Practical Architecture*, 2nd Edn. Crosby, Lockwood and Co., London, 1886. Quotes warning by Alberti (15th C) and de Orme (16th C)
24. See, for example, DSIR *Building Research 1952*, p.8, HMSO, London
25. Jones, F.E. and Tarleton, R.D. *DSIR National Building Studies; Research Papers 14, 15 and 17*, HMSO, London, 1951 and 1952
26. Schaffer, R.J., reference 6, p.76
27. Conway, Sir M. Letter to *The Times*, 11 May, 1929
28. Bravery, A.F. 'Preservation in the Construction Industry', in *Principles and Practice of Disinfection, Sterilisation and Preservation* (eds Hugo, Aycliffe and Russell), Blackwell Scientific Publications, Oxford, 1980
29. Bachmann, E. 'Kalklösende Algen', *Berichte der Deutschen Botanischen Gesellschaft*, **33**, 45–57, 1915
30. Lepidi and Schippa 'Some Aspects of the Growth of Chemotropic and Heterotropic Micro-organisms on Calcareous Surfaces', *Proc. 1st Int. Symp. Biodeter. Building Stones*, 143–148, 1973
31. Bachmann, E. 'The Phthalus of Calcicolous Lichens', *Berichte der Deutschen Botanischen Gesellschaft*, **10**, 30–37, 1892
32. Neculce, J. 'Some Aspects of Fungi in Stone Biodeterioration', *Proc. 6th Symp, Biodeter. and Clim.*, pp.117–122, 1976
33. Smith, A.L. and Hearing, G.G. 'Lichens', *Encycl. Britannica*, London, 1950
34. Lloyd, A.O., private communication to Bravery, reference 28, 1980
35. Lloyd, A.O. 'Progress in Studies of Deteriogenic Lichens', *Proc. 3rd Int. Biodegrad. Symp.*, (eds Sharpley, J.M. and Kaplan, A.M.) Applied Science, 395–402, 1976
36. Bachmann, E. 'The Relation Between Silica Lichens and their Substratum', *Berichte der Deutschen Botanischen Gesellschaft*, **22**, 101–104, 1904
37. Fry, E.J. 'A Suggested Explanation of the Action of Lithophytic Lichens on Rock (Shale)', *Annals of Botany*, **38**, 175–196, 1924
38. See, for example, *National Glass Budget*, **60**, 7, 1944
39. Bravery *loc. cit.*, reference 28
40. Anderson, T. 'The Decay of Stone Antiquities', *Museums Journal*, **10**, 100–106, 1911
41. Pochon, J. and Jaton, C., *Chem. and Ind.*, 25 Sept., 1587–1589, 1967
42. Jaton, C. 'Microbiological Aspects of the Alteration of Stonework of Monuments', *Proc. 2nd Int. Symp. on Deterioration of Building Stone*, 149–154, 1973

43. Paleni, A. and Curri, S. 'Biological Aggression on Works of Art in Venice', *Proc. 2nd Int. Biodeter. Symp.,* 392–400, 1972
44. Kauffmann, J. and Toussaint, J. 'Corrosion des Pierres: Nouvelles Experiences Montrant le Role des Bacteria Nitrifiantes dans l'Alteration des Pierres Calcaires des Monuments', *Corrosion and Anticorrosion,* **2**, 240–244, 1954
45. Jaton *loc. cit.,* reference 42
46. Duff, R.B., Webley, D.M. and Scott, R.O. 'Solubilisation of Minerals and Related Materials by 2-Ketogluconic acid-producing Bacteria', *Soil Sci.,* **95**, 105–114, 1963
47. Wood, P.A. and Macrae, I.C. 'Microbial Activity in Sandstone Deterioration', *Int. Biodeter. Bull.,* **8**, 25–27, 1972
48. Dumitru, L., Popea, F. and Lazar, I. 'Investigations Concerning the Presence and Role of Bacteria in Stone Deterioration of some Historical Monuments from Bucharest, Jassy and Vluj-Napoca', *Proc. 6th Symp. Biodeter. and Clim.,* p.67, 1976
49. See, for example, *Wear,* **10**, 89–102, 1967
50. Rennie, G.K. and Clifford, J. *J.C.S. Faraday 1,* **73**, 680, 1977
51. Price, C.A. and Ross, K. (Building Research Establishment, Watford), private communication, August 1982.

Illustrations of weathering and decay phenomena

1 Frost spalling of limestone

Detachment of lens-like pieces of stone in a saturated limestone viaduct record seasonal losses over many years. In the centre of the illustration is a frost spall which occurred the night before the photograph was taken and relates to water seepage through joints.

2 Fire damage to limestone

Of the several effects which fire may have on stone, shattering is the most obviously destructive. Rapid heating of previously cool surfaces will bring about the shattering illustrated here, after a fire following a bomb explosion. Rapid cooling of very hot surfaces, commonly brought about by quenching with water, will similarly encourage fracturing. The deeper tones in the photograph indicate areas which have undergone a colour change due to oxidation of iron compounds during the fire.

3 Marine salt damage to sandstone

Marine environments often provide ideal conditions for salt crystallization damage to take place. A ready source of salts (principally sodium chloride) and frequent wetting and drying cycles cause spectacular damage to the sandstones forming the sea wall defences of Berwick upon Tweed. Damage is most pronounced in the upper courses of the wall from which most drying occurs.

4 Calcium sulphate skin formation: washed and unwashed zones

Limestone which is regularly washed by rain, as indicated by the light coloured parapets, exposed ashlar and plinths in the illustration, often remains sound in spite of small-scale surface erosion. Sheltered zones, however, on which water sits in droplet form, are subject to the formation of skins of calcium sulphate, which become progressively darker and less permeable. In some cases, on the more durable limestones, these skins cause little problem. In other cases, the skin may split and blister.

5 Detail of splitting sulphate skin on Magnesian Limestone

Acid solutions derived from sulphur-based gases in the air attack the surface of Magnesian Limestone and produce calcium sulphate and magnesium sulphate. In sheltered zones, gypsum skins are formed but the magnesium sulphate penetrates more deeply and crystallizes behind the skin. The illustration shows a sheltered, blackened frieze of carved lettering on the Palace of Westminster, London, splitting and spalling.

6 Splitting and spalling of calcium sulphate skin on limestone

This recently cleaned limestone shows characteristic splitting and spalling of a calcium sulphate skin in a semi-sheltered position. The limestone is of moderate durability and had been exposed for about one hundred and fifty years.

7 'Cavernous' decay of Magnesian Limestone

Deep pockets in Magnesian Limestone created by crystallization and re-crystallization of magnesium sulphate. In this illustration the gypsum skin has largely disappeared.

8 Acid attack on argillaceous sandstone

Sulphur-based acids in the air readily attack calcareous sandstones, argillaceous sandstones and, to a lesser degree, dolomitic sandstones. Heavily rain-washed areas powder away dramatically because the dissolving of a relatively small amount of cementing material (calcite, clay or dolomite) will release many grains of quartz. The illustration shows the deterioration of an exposed detail of argillaceous sandstone.

9 Contour scaling of sandstone

Blocking of the surface pores of sandstones appears to be related to air pollution and to wetting and drying and heating and cooling cycles. In some cases which have been examined in detail, such as Tintern Abbey (Wales), shown in the illustration, the detached crusts had become completely blocked with calcium sulphate hydrate. The crusts break away at a constant depth independent of any bedding pattern.

10 Splitting from rusting iron

Wrought iron and mild steel fixings have caused enormous amounts of damage to stone buildings. The splitting and spalling of stone caused by the rusting of ferrous fixings is a chemically induced expansion following access of air and water to the metal. All renewals of such fixings should be of stainless steel or non-ferrous metal.

11 Weathering of 'soft' seams or pockets

Some sedimentary stones are characterized by the presence of readily eroded pockets of clay or sand or poorly cemented material. The illustration shows the critical effect produced by the weathering out of such a pocket in a limestone parapet at Gloucester Cathedral.

12 Face bedding of limestone sculpture

Decay of this sculpture on Wells Cathedral, Somerset, could have been avoided by placing the stone on its natural bed or on its edge (edge bedding). In general, sedimentary stones should be placed in the building in the same position in which they were laid down. Failure to carry out this practice can result in unnecessary deterioration (see also 13 and 14).

13 Failure of stones in an arch construction

Decay of these stones at Crowland, Lincolnshire, could have been avoided by placing the bed of the stone at right angles to the thrust of the arch.

14 Edge bedding of sandstone dressing

Edge bedding of this window jamb lining at Mount Stewart, Northern Ireland, is also inducing face bedding failure. Decay could be avoided only by natural bedding.

15 Structural disruption caused by climbing plants

Masonry ruins can be substantially colonized by trees, climbers and creepers, which can attach weak points in the walls by seeking sources of moisture. The illustration shows the displacement of large ashlar blocks at Corfe Castle, Dorset, by climbing plants. Ivy is notoriously destructive. Creepers which cling to the walls without the assistance of deeply penetrating roots are much less harmful, but when luxuriant can obscure the true condition of a wall.

Index

Page numbers in *italic* indicate illustrations

Aberdeen, 37, 45, 48
Abrasion, 21, 23, 120
Access, influencing repairs, 12
Acetylene lamps, effects of, 132
Acid gases, 132, 155, 156–159, 176
Acid rocks, 23
Aesthetic errors, 171
Africa, 95
Agglestone Grit, 81
Aggregate, 63, 167
Ailsa Craig microgranite, 46
Air pollution, 1, 89, 159
Aislaby Sandstone, 77–78
Alabaster, 19, 125–127
Alabaster windows, 125
Albert Memorial, 45, 46, 47, 68
Algae, effect of, 168
Algal limestone, 88, 112
Alps Grey Granite (Switzerland), 136
Alta Quartzite (Altazite, Crystalite) (Norway), 136
Alteration, 42, 48, 50, 89
Alton Mottled Stone, 63
Alton Stone, *see* Hollington Stone
Alton Towers, 76
Alwalton 'Marble', 109
Amianthus, 52
Ampleforth Abbey Church, 100
Ancaster Stone, 103
Anchor bolts, resin, 9
Anderson, J.G.C., on naming stone, 32–33
Andes Black Granite, South America, 38, 50
Angkor Wat, Cambodia, 20
Anglesey Serpentine, 50
Anhydrite, 125
Annanlea Sandstone, 74
Anston Stone, 95–96
Anteaga limestone (Spain), 124
Antrim Plateau, 59
Apache Tears, 57
Apsley House, London, 106, 108
Arabescato Marble (Italy), 147
Arbroath Pavement, 64
Architect, judgement of, 13
Architectural sculpture, decaying, 11
Argillaceous sandstone, 62, 158, 169
Arkoses, 62, 63, 67, 70
Armagh Red 'Marble', 95
Arequipa ('White City'), Peru, 55
Asbestos, 51–52
Ashburton 'Marble' (Renfrew 'Marble'), 90
Ashdown House, Berkshire, *116*, 117
Ashdown Sand, 78
Ashford Black limestone, 93
Ashlar, *18*, 41
Associative decay, 129, *131*
Assyrian sculpture, 19
Auchinlea Stone, 70
Augite, 50, 54, 57
Aurisina limestone (Italy), 123
Australia and New Zealand, marble, 149
Availability of stone, 21
Avebury Circle, 84
Axminster Church, 117

Bacteria, effect of, 168–169
Ballachulish granite, 45–46
Ballachulish slate, 138
Balmoral Castle, 45
Baltic Brown Granite (Finland), 38, 48
Bank of Australia, Melbourne, 45
Barbary Plane (St Bees Sandstone), 75
Bardiglio Marble (Italy), 122, 146, 147
Bargate Stone, 80
Barge Quartzite (Italy), 136
Barnack Stone, 103
Basalt, 38, 57–59
Bath Stone, 106–109, *130*
Batholiths, 38, *39*
Battle Abbey, restoration, 78
Baveno granite (Italy), 48
Beachy Head Lighthouse, granite, 41
Beaumaris Castle, 93
Bedding, natural, 171
Bedding planes, 29, 30, 62, 129
Beds, 129
Beer Stone, 117, 121
Belgium,
  limestones, 122
  'marble', 38, 94
Bell Rock Lighthouse, Scottish granite, 45
Bembridge Formation (Limestone/Marls), 117
Bergen Hospital, Norway, 136
Bessbrook granite, 47
Bethersden Marble, 114
Bethesda-Nantlle slate belt, Wales, 139–140
Beverley Minster, 97, 106
Bianco Chiara (Blanc Clair) Marble (Italy), 146
Bianco Chiara Venato (Bianco Venato, Blanc Veine) Marble (Italy), 146
Big Flint Rock, 71
Billiard table beds, 144
Binstead Stone, 118
Bioclastic limestone, 102
Biotite, 38, 40, 44, 45, 46, 47, 135
Birchover Gritstone, 68
Birds, effect of, 169
Bird's eye diorite, 47
Bitumens, 127
Black Diamond 'Granite', S. Africa, 38, 50
'Black Granite', Herrestad, Sweden, 50
Black 'Marbles', Ireland, 94
Black Pasture Stone, 66
Black Swede H, 49
Blackfriars Bridge, *46*
Blaenau Ffestiniog, 140
Blandford Forum Church, 113
Blaxter Stone, 66
Bleu Turquin (Tarquin) marble (Italy), 122, 146, 147

Blister formation on limestone, 156, 164, 176–177
Blue Bahia, Brazil, 49
Blue Granite (Channel Islands), 38, 47
Blue Lias, 97, *99*
Blue Liver Rock, 66
'Blue Pearl Granite' (Norway), 32, 38
Blueys, 54
Bodiam Castle, Sussex, 78
Bodmin Church, Prior Vyvyan's tomb, 55
Bodmin Moor, 41
Bolsover Castle, Derbyshire, 73, 95, *96*
Bolsover Moor Stone, 95
Bolton Wood Stone, 68, 69
Bon Accord Black 'Granite' (Sweden), 49–50
Borrowdale Volcanic Series, 138
Box Ground Stone, 106, 108
Box pews, removal of, 5
Box stones, 80, 81
Boynton Stone, 115
Bracklesham Group, 81
Bradenham Puddingstone, 84
Bramley Fall Stone, 68
Brathay Slate (Brathay Flags), 138, 139
Brazilian onyx, 121
Breakdown, mechanical and chemical, 23
Breche Rose Marble (Norwegian Rose, Norwegian Pink), 148
Breedingstone, 85
Bricks, fired-clay, 155
Bridestones, 84
Brincliffe Edge Rock, 69
Bristol Cathedral, 13, *14*, 97
British Museum, granite, 40
Britton, John,
  Architectural Antiquities, 3
  Cathedral Antiquities, 3
Brocatella (Spain), 124
Brockley Down Stone (Bastard Downside), 99
Brown Clee Hill, 54
Brynteg Freestone, 71
Buckingham Palace, 108, 121
Building Freestone, 102
Burke, Edmund (philosopher), 2
Burlington Slate, 138–139, *140*
Burns Monument, Kilmarnock, 74
Burrell Collection, Glasgow, 74
Burrystone, 81
Burwell Stone (Rock), 117
Butterfield, William, Winchester College Chapel Tower, restoration of, 6

Caen Stone, 104–105, 121
Caerbwdi Sandstone, 63
Caithness Flagstone Series, 64
Calcareous Sandstone, 61, 64, 157
Calciferous sandstone, 157, 158
Calciferous Sandstone Series, Scotland, 66
Calcite, 50, 61, 118, 119, 144, 156, 157, 158, 164
  crystalline, 103, 104, 105, 106
Calcite cement, 157
Calcite crystals, 164
Calcite veins, 111
Calcite-mudstones, 97
Calcium carbonate, 86, 88, 115
Calcium sulphate, 156
Calcium sulphite, 156
Cambridge Camden Society, 4–5
Campan 'marbles' (Vert, Rouge and Mélange), French, 122, 148
Canford Magna Church, 81
Cannel coal, 127
Cannstatt Travertine (Germany), 119
Canterbury Cathedral, 11, 121
Canterbury City walls, 16, *17*, 18
Carboniferous Limestone, 65, 90–95
Carboniferous Limestone Series, Scotland, 66
Cardiff Castle, 91
Carnmenellis, 41
Carnsew granite, Penryn, 41
Carrara Marble, 122, 147
Carstone, 62, 80–81
Carter, John, cathedral drawings, 3
Cast iron gutters and pipes, 163
Casterton Stone (Stamford Stone), 103–104
Castle Drogo, Drewsteignton, Devon, 42
Castle Howard, restoration work, 70
Castles, destruction of in the Civil War, 2
Castlewellan granite, 47
Cataclews Stone, 55
Catacombs of Paris, 122
Catapult balls, 84
Caustic potash and caustic soda, 155–156
Cave Marble, 106
Cave onyx, 88
Cave Oolite, 103, 105–106
Cavernous decay, 157
Cefn Rock, 71
Cefn-y-fedu sandstone, 69
Cementation, 23, 25, 61
Cementing minerals, 23, 25
Central Post Office, Jerusalem, 59
Chalcedony, 86
Chalk, 37, 86, 89, 115–117
Chambers, Sir William, *Treatise on the Decorative Part of Civil Architecture*, 2
Chamosite, 89
Charterhouse School, 80
Chatsworth House, 92, 93
Cheesewring granite, Liskeard, 41
Cheltenham Stone, 102
Chert, 80, 86
Chichester Cathedral, 90, 116, 118
Chilmark Stone, 112, 113
Chilmark Trough Bed, 113
China Clay, 42, 155
China, Great Wall, 20
Chlorite, 54, 135, 137
Church of the Holy Sepulchre, Cambridge, restoration of, 4–5
Church of the Primacy, Sea of Galilee, 59
Churches, 2, 4, 40, 74, 86
Civil engineering work, 68, 70–71
Cladding, 48, 49, 120, *139*, 143
Clashach Stone, 74
Clay, 26, 100
Clay minerals, 23, 155
Cleavage, 136, 140, 142
  slaty, 137
Cleopatra's Needles, 48
Clifton-Taylor, Alec, *The Pattern of English Building*, 37
Clipsham Stone, 104
'Cliving', 101
Clunch, 117
Coal, 127
Coal Measures, 65, 69–71
Cobb, the, Lyme Regis, 112
Coccolite, 146
Cockeysville Marble (USA), 149
Coffins, 100, 114, 121
Colchester Castle Museum, 119
Collyhurst Stone, 71
Collyweston Slates, 101–102
Cologne Cathedral, 58
Colosseum, Rome, 120
Colossi, Easter Island, 19
Colour of rocks, 32
Columnar jointing, 27, 57, *58*
Concretions, 25, 62, 118–119
Condensation, 172–173
Conglomerate, 63, 84
Connemara Marble, 146
Contact metamorphism, *see* Thermal metamorphism
Contour scaling, 158–159, 164
Cooling, multi-directional, 159
Cooling rate, 22–23
Coombe Down Stone, 106, 108
Copper (and alloys), staining effects, 163
Copper lightning conductors, 163, 170
Coral limestone, 88, 90, 92
Coral sands, 61
Cork Red (Victoria Red) 'Marble', 95
Coronation Stone, 64–65
Corrennie granite, 45
Cotswold Slates, 106
Cotswold Stone, 37, 109–111
Country rock, 22
Coventry Cathedral, 76, 124, *139*
Craftsmen, 14
Craigleith Stone, 66, *67*, 69
Craigmillar Sandstone, 64
Cramps/dowels, inaccurate positioning, 171
Creetown granite, 46

Crinoidal limestone, 88, *92*, 93
Crosland Hill Stone, 68
Cross-bedding, 29, 76
Crushed rock, 54, 89
Crushing strength, 36
Cryptoflorescence, 154
Crysotile, 52
Crystallization cycles, 154–155
Cuillins, Skye, 50
Curling stones, 43, 46
Current-bedding, 29, 67, 68, 71, 73, *130*
'Cut out', 16

Dalbeattie granite, 38, 46
Dark Pearl 'Granite' (Norway), 38, 49
Darley Dale Stone, 67–68
De Lank granite, St Breward, 41
Decay, 1, 12, 13, 20, 129, *131*, 169
  by acidic gases in the air, 156–159
  by freezing, 159–162
  by salt crystallization, 153–156
  patina of, 6
Deepdale Fossil limestone, 93
Defects, diagnosis of, 9
Deformation, 48
Delabole Slate, 142–143
'Denmark (Red Denmark)' stone (Sweden), 123, 124
Derby Black limestone, uses of, 93–94
Derby Fossil limestone, 92–93
Derby inlay work (*pietra dura*), 93
Derbydene Fossil limestone, 92–93
Derbydene limestone, 92–93
Desert Roses, 125
Design errors, 169–171
Deterioration,
  caused by decay, 153–163
  caused by living organisms, 167–169
  effects of errors in design, specification or construction, 169–172
Devil's Post Pile, USA, 59
Devitrification, 57
Devon 'marble', 89–90
Diabase, *see* Dolerite
Diamant Quartzite (Diamantzite, Allied Quartzite) (S. Africa), 136
Dimension stone, 20, 69–71
Diorite, 49
Disruptive expansion, 166–167
Doddington Stone, 66
Doggers, 62, 79
Dolerite, 52, 54–55
Dolgelly Beds, 140
Dolomite, 89, 156, 158
Dolomite cement, 71, 157–158
Dolomitic Conglomerate, 76–77
Dolomitic limestone, 89
Dolomitic sandstone, 62, 71
Dolomitization, 89
Doulting Stone, two varieties, 102
Downside Stone, 99
Draycott Marble, 77, 89
Dressing, of stone, 13, 14
Dripstone, 88
Druid sandstones, 84
Dry stone walling, 20, 90, 91
Duke's Red (Rowsley, Derbyshire), 92
Dundry Stone, 102
Dune bedding, 29
Dunhouse Stone, 70
Duporth Stone, 51
Durability, 21, 67, 70–71, 90
Durham Cathedral, 70, 92
Dyce granites, 45
Dykes, 27, 42, 52

Eastbourne Stone (Eastbourne Green), 83–84
Eastlake, Charles, *History of the Gothic Revival*, 3
Ebony Black Granite, Sweden, 49
Ecclesiological Society (*formerly* Cambridge Camden Society), 5
Economist Building, London, 112
Eday Sandstone, 65
Eddystone Lighthouse, granite, 41
Efflorescence, 154, 162, 173
Egypt, 19
  porphyry, 52, 53–54
  Aswan (Suwan) granite, 48
Eifel basalt, 58
Elaterite, 127
Eleanor/Norman crosses, 96–97, *105*
Elland Flags, 69
Elvans, 42, 52–53
Ely Cathedral, 11, *37*, 81, 94, 103, 104, *109*, 113
Ematita Granite (Verde Ematita) (Argentina), 135
Empire State Building, 49
Environmental Museum, Llanberis, 140
Epidote, 49
Equilibrium humidity, 154
Erosion, 23, 62, 163–164
Ettringite expansion, 166
Euston Arch, London, 68
Euston Pavement, Mount Sorrel Granite, 43
Euston Railway Station, original, 68
Euston Tower, London, 148
Euville Stone, 122
Evaporites, 124–127
Exeter Cathedral, 97, 113–114, 117
Exeter Traps (Exeter Volcanic Series), 54
Expansion, chemically induced, 165–167

Face-bedding, 171
Faces and joints, finish of, 14
Facework, tying back *in situ*, 9
False bedding, 29, 65, 70, *130*
Farnham Castle, Surrey, 83
Fatigue failure, 158
Feldspar, 23, 38, 40, 44, 48, 52, 62, 155
Feldspar clotting, 47
Fell Sandstone, 65
Ferns, 168
Ferruginous limestone, 99–100
Ferruginous sandstone, 61–62, 81
Fetlar serpentinite, 50
Finland, granite, 48
Fire, effects of, 131–132, 165
Firestone, 81
Fissile rocks, 62, 67–69, 78, 101–102, 106
Flaggy sandstone, 63, 64
Flagstones, 62, 64, 65, 67, 68, 69
Flame-cutting, 30–32
Flame-texturing, 164
Flint, 21, 81, 84, 86, *87*
  knapped, 86, *87*, 121
Florescence, 154
Flow-stone, 88
Flow-structure, 47
Foggintor quarries, Dartmoor, 40
Foliation, 26, *27*, 30, 48, 136
Folkestone Beds, 80
Fonts, 3, 50, 51, 94, 124
Foreigners, *see* Xenoliths
Forêt des Brousses (French limestone), 122
Forum Romanum, arch of Titus restored, 7
Fossil 'Marble', 89
Fossils, 62, 93, 99, 109, 111, 113, 114, 117
Fouls, 64
Fowey Church, 53
Foyaite, 49
Fractures, 11, 21, 86
Fragmentation, large scale, 154
France, 95
  limestones (pierres marbrières), 121–122
  marbles (marbres), 122, 148
  slate, 143–144
Freestone, 71, 73, 75, 84, 102, 112, 117, 129
French Pummy, 119
Frost attack on stone, 159–162, 174–176
Frost shattering, 160–161
Frosterly 'Marble', 91–92
'Frosting', of Colleyweston Slates, 101–102
Fungi, effect of, 168
Furness Abbey, 75

Gabbro, 38, 50
Gaisby Rock, 68
Galleting, *see* Garnetting
Galliard Balls, 63
Galway Granite, 47
Galway 'Marble', 94
Galway Serpentine, 146
Garnet, 135

Garnetting (Galleting, Nailing), *80*, 81, 84
Gatton Stone, 81
Geodes, 62
Geological Museum, London, 90, 133, 138
George V Bridge, Glasgow, 46
Georgia marble (USA), 148
Giant's Causeway, N. Ireland, 27, *58*, 58–59
Gibraltar Stone (Onyx), 121
Giffnock Stone (Giffneuk), 67
Gingerbread stone, 81
Glauconite, 62, 80, 81, 89, 112, 114, 115, 117
Glen Tilt Marble, 146
Gloucester Cathedral, 119
Gneiss, 30, 136
Gneissose banding, 136
Godstone Stone, 81
Goodwood House, 86
Gothenburg Cathedral, Sweden, 67
Grains, smooth or angular, 62
Grandison tombs, Ottery St Mary, 117
Granit de Rocq (French limestone), 38
Granite, 23, 28, 33, 155, 161, 164
  Channel Islands, 47
  Cumbrian, 43–44
  imported, 47–48
  Irish, 47
  Scottish, 44–47
  south-west England, 40
  Welsh, 43
Granite railway, forgotten, 40
Granito Nero (Switzerland), 38
Granodiorite, 43, 45, 47, 49
Graphite, 135, 138
Great Whin Sill, 54
Greece, 19–20, 53, 95
  decorative serpentinite, 51
  marble, 147–148
Green Porphyry, Greece, 53
'Green-marble' (Italy), 122
Greenbrae Stone, 74
Greenmore Rock, 69
Greensand, 62
Greenstones, 54
Greetland Stone, 68
Grenoside Sandstone, 69
Grès de Vosges (France), 85
Grey-wethers, 84
Grinshill Stone (Red and White), 75–76
Gris d'Alesia (French), 122
Gritstone (Grit), 62, 67, 68
Ground waters, 86, 88
Growing Stone, 85
Guildhall, London, roofing, 102
Guiting Stone (Yellow and White), 102–103
Gypsum, 125, 126, 156, 158, 162, 167, 176
Gypsum skin, 156, 157

Hackness Stone, *78*
Haddon Hall, Derbyshire, 91
Hadene Stone, 93
Hadrian's Wall, 54
Haematite, 53, 66, 95, 137–138
Hag Stones, 84
Hailes Stone, 66, 69
Half-and-half repair technique, 11
Halite (rock salt), 124–125
Hall Dale Stone, 68
Ham Hill Stone (Yellow/Grey Beds), *87*, 100
Hamstone House, Weybridge, 100
Hantergantick granite, 41–42
Hardened (case-hardened) rock, 33
Hardness, 21, 33
Harlestone Stone, 77
Hassock, 114–115
Hatrurian Formation, 124
Hay Tor granite, Dartmoor, 40
Headstones, 50, 146
Healing stones, 80
Hearthstone, 81
Heathens, *see* Xenoliths
Heavitree Conglomerate, 74–75
Hereford Cathedral, restoration, 76
Hereford Stone, 63
Hertfordshire Puddingstone, 84
Hexagonal columns, *see* Columnar jointing
Historical material, preservation of, 8–9
History in stone, 19–20
Hoar Edge Grit, fissile, 63
Holborn Viaduct, Ross of Mull granite, 47
Holkham Hall, Norfolk, Marble Hall, 125
Hollington Stone, 76
Hopton Wood Stone, 93
Hornblende, 44, 46, 47, 48, 135
Hornstone, 86
Hornton Stone, 99–100
Horsham Stone, 78
Household cleaning powders/grits, 173
Huddersfield White Rock, 62–63
Huddlestone Stone, 96
Humidity, relative, 155, 172
Hydration, late, 166
Hydraulic cement, 56
Hydraulic lime, 163, 166
Hydraulic limestones, 97
Hydrogen sulphide, 89
Hythe Beds, 114, 119

Ice, growth of, 161
Ice lenses, 161
Iceland, Parliament Building, 59
Iceland Spar, 145
Ightham Stone, 80
Igneous intrusions, *28*
Igneous rocks, 22–23
  basalt, 57–59
Igneous rocks, (*cont.*)
  from Leicestershire, 43
  from minor intrusions, 52–55
  plutonic,
    acid, 38–48
    basic, 50
    intermediate, 48–50
  tuffs, 55–57
  ultrabasic, 50–51
  volcanic glass, 57
Imperial Mahogany granite (USA), 48
Imperial Pearl Granite (Norway), 38, 49
Imperial Porphyry (*Lapis porphyrites*) (Egypt), 52, 53–54
Indian Ebony Black, 50
Inferior Oolite, 77, 101–106
'Ingleton Granite', 32
Institut Français du Pétrole, France, 49
Iona Abbey, 47, 63, 138, 146
Iona Marble, 145–146
Irish Green and Irish White Marble, 146
Iron, in stonework, hazards of, 165
Iron Age Camps, 54
Iron Age granite structures, 40
Iron compound cements, 61
Iron cramps, 1, 163
Iron minerals, 89
Iron and steel, problems with, 163
Iron-bearing minerals, 50
Ironstones, 97
Israel,
  basalt, 59
  limestones, 124
Istrian Stone, 123
Italian Dove marble, 122, 146, 147
Italian Quartzite, 136
Italy,
  decorative serpentinite, 51
  granite, 47–48
  limestone and marble, 122–123
  marble, 122, 146–147
  schists, 136
  slate, 144
  travertine, 119–120
Ivy, 167, 173

Jasper, 86, *88*
Jet, 127, 129
John Dalton House, Manchester, 139, *140*
Joint sets, 27–28
Joint systems, 27, *29*
Joint-bedding, 171
Jointing, 27, 57, *58*
  and quarrying, 30–32
Joints in rock, 27–30
Jubilee Stone, 123

Kairuru Marble (New Zealand), 149
Kaolinite, 23, 155
Kaolinization, 42, 53, 155
Keene's cement, 167

Kemnay granite, 44, 45
Kentallenite, 50
Kentish Ragstone, *37*, 81, 85, 114–115
Kerbs, 47, 69, 77, 93, 97, 113
Ketton Rag, 104
Ketton Stone (Ketton Oolite), 104
Kildare Black 'Marble', 94
Kilkenny 'Marble', 94
Kilpeck Church, Hereford, 63, *64*
Kinderscout Grit, 67

Labradorita, 135
Labradorite, 50, 53
Lakeland Green Slate, 138
Landewednack Church, 50
Languedoc Marble, 122
Lapis Atracius (Italy), 51
Lapis Tiburtinus, 88
Larvikite, 49
Laughton Stone, 114
Laundry detergents, 173
Lava, 22, 57
Lazonby Grit, 73
Lazonby Stone (Red and White), 73, 74
Lead flashing, 11
Lead water channels, 173
'Leaning Tower', Pisa, 147
Ledbury 'Marble', 89
Lee Marble (USA), 149
Leyborne Castle, destruction of, 167
Liassic limestone, 97, 99–100
Lichens, 168, 173
Light Pearl Granite (Norway), 38, 49
Lime mud, 23
Limestone, 37, 89, 104, 156–157, 176
  Tertiary, 117–118
  Cretaceous, 89, 114–117
  Jurassic,
    Liassic, 89, 97–100
    Middle and Upper, 100–114
  Permian, 95–97
  Carboniferous, 90–95
  Devonian, 89–90
  Silurian and older, 89
  Belgian, 122
  chemical, 86, 88
  clastic/detrital, 88–89
  crystallization damage, 169
  fissile, 101–102, 106
  French, 121–122
  Israel, 124
  Italian, 122–123
  organic, 88
  salt crystallization, 153–155
  Swedish, 123–124
Limpsfield Church, 8, *10*
Lincoln Cathedral, 95, 103, 109
Lincolnshire Limestone, 101–102, 103–106, 119
Lissoughter Marble, 146
Lithification, 23, 61
Liverpool Anglican Cathedral, 75
Living organisms, and deterioration, 167–169
Llandaff Cathedral, 99, 102
Lochabriggs Stone, 74
London Bridge, granite, 40
London Clay, 118
Longchant Stone, 122
Lonnenstane (London Stone), 104
Lower Freestone, 102
Lower Greensand, 78, *79*, 80–81, 114
Lundy Island granite, 42
Luni Marble (*Mamor Lunense*), 147
Luxullianite, 42
Lychnites, 147
Lydian Stone, 58

Macduff Slates, 138
Madeira, 59
Madreperla (Argentina), 135
Madsen, Stephan Tschudi, ***Restoration and Anti-Restoration***, 5
Magma, 22
Magmatic fluids, 42
Magnesian Limestone, 89, 95, 156–157
Magnesite, 156
Magnesium, 89
Magnesium carbonate, burning of, 165–166
Magnesium sulphate, 157
Magnetite, 48, 57
Maintenance, 2, 7
Malachite, 151
Mallett, David, ***The Excursion***, 2
Malmstone (Malm Rock), 81, 83
Manchester Town Hall, 68, 93
Manganese, 142
Manganese minerals, 89
Manganite, 89
Mansfield Stone (Red or Yellow/White), 62, 71, 73, 96
Mansfield Woodhouse Stone, 73, 96
Marble, 25–26, 30, 144–149, 155, 156–157
Marble Arch, London, 147
Marble tops, 50
'Marbles', commercial, 88
Mare Balls, 63
Markfieldite, 43
Marmo di Castellina (alabaster), 127
Marmor Lacedaemonium Viride (Pliny), 52, 53
Marmor Proconnensus, 148
Mason bees, 1, 169
Masonry,
  deterioration of, 153–174
  distressed, 13, *14*
Masonry adhesive, 11
Master joints, 27, 30
Matlock Fossil limestone, 93
Mauchline Sandstone, 74
Mayan culture, 20
Meat preservation, and salt crystallization, 155
Mediaeval architectural styles, 3
Megacrysts, 40, 41, 43
Megalithic monuments, 84
Melanterite, 138
Menhir avenues, Carnac, 19
Merrivale granite, 40–41
Mersey Docks, Creetown granite, 46
Merstham Stone, 81
Metamorphic rocks/metamorphism, 25–26
  regional, 25, 26, 135–149
  thermal, 135, 144, 146
Mica, 23, 38, 40, 46, 62, 66, 69, 135, 136
Mica schists, 135
Micaceous sandstone, 62, 63–64, 70–71
Microgranite, 46, *52*
Millstone Edge, 67
Millstone Grit, *29*, 37, 65, 67–69, 91
Millstones, 58, 63, 67, 77
Milner, John, ***Treatise on the Ecclesiastic Architecture of England***, 3
Milton Keynes, Cornish granite, 41
Minerals, 20
Mohs' scale of hardness, 33
Moisture rhythm, 158
'Mona Marble', 50, 51
Monks Park Stone, 108
Monoliths, Callanish, 19
Monomineralic rocks, 145
Montacute House, Somerset, 100
Montparnasse Station, Paris, 140
Monyash 'Marble', 92–93
Moorstone, 40
Mortar, 162–163, 171, 172
Moss, effect of, 168
Mother Stone, 85
Mount Sorrel granite, 43
Mourne Mountains granite, 47
Muscovite, 38, 40, 45, 47, 48, 81
Museum of Practical Geology, London, 95, *96*

Nabresina limestone (Italy), 123
Nailing, *see* Garnetting
Nailsworth Stone, 103
Names of rocks, 32
Napoleon Stone (France), 122
National Gallery, London, 40, 51
National Library of Wales, 158
Nelson's Column, London, 40, 66, *67*
Nepheline-Syenite, 49
New Red Sandstone, 63, 71–77
New Scotland Yard, 1888–89 and 1967, 40–41
New Sessions House, London, 51
New York Central Railway Station, 122
Newbald Stone, 106
Newbigging Stone, 67
Newer Granites (Scotland), 44
Newry granite, 47
Niedermendig lava, 58

North Perrott Stone, 100
Northampton (Sand) Ironstone, 77
Norway,
  granite, 48
  marble, 148
  schists, 135–136
Norwich Cathedral, Losinga statue, 103
Norwich Union Building, London, 86, *88*, 148
Notes on the Cambridgeshire Churches, 3

Obsidian, 57
Øland limestone (Sweden), 123–124
Old Red Sandstone, 63–64
Older Granites, 48
Oligoclase, 38, 46
Olivine, 50
Olivine-dolerite, 54
Onyx, 32, 120
Onyx-marble, 88, 120–121
Oolites, 88, 111
Ooliths, 88
Oolitic ironstone, 77, 89
Oolitic limestone, 88, 89, 97, 101, 102, 104
Ophicalcite, 50, 51, 145, 148
Ornamental stone, 53
Orthoclase, 23, 38, 43, 45, 48, 49
Orton Scar limestone, 93
Otta slate (Norway), 135–136
Overloading, remedying effects of, 1
Oxidation, 165

Painswick Stone, 103
Palace of Versailles, France, 122
Palace of Westminster (Houses of Parliament), 95, 96, 104
'Paludina' limestone, Large- and Small-, 114
'Paludina' marble, Large- and Small-, 114
Parian Marble (Greece), 147
Parliament House, Melbourne, *60*
Parona Marble (Italy), 147
Parthenon, Acropolis, Athens, *20*, 147
Particulate pollution, 156, 162
Parys Granite (S. Africa), 136, *137*
Patina of age, 7, 8
  see also Decay, patina of
Patina formation, copper, 163
Paving, 47, 64, 69, 73, 75, 81, *90*, 97, 112, 114, 123, 136, 172
  non-slip, 78, 120
Pavonazetto, 148
Pearl 'Granite' (Norway), 32, 49
Pelastine granite, Mabe, 42
Pellet limestone, 121
Penmon Limestone, 93
Pennant Sandstone Series, 70–71
Penrhyn Slate, 140
Penrith Stone (Sandstone), 73, 75
Pentelic Marble (*Marmor Pentelicum*) (Greece), 147–148, 152
Pentewan (Pentuan) Stone, 53
Peparino Tufaceo (Peperino), 57
Peridotite migration, 51
Permeability, 91, 171
Peterborough Cathedral, 50, 92, 103, 117
  Abbot Benedict effigy, 109
Peterhead granite, 44–45
Petit Granit (Belgium), 38, 122
Petrifying springs, 119
Petworth House, 114
Petworth 'Marble', 114
Phenocrysts, 23, 52
Picrite, serpentinized, 51
Piles, bored rather than driven, 9
Pillaguri Slate (Norway), 135
Pisolites, 88, 103
Plagioclase, 23, 38, 43, 45, 46, 48, 54, 57
Planes of separation, *see* Bedding planes
Plaster of Paris, 126
'Plastic stone', 8, *10*, 13
Platey crystals, 137–138
Plymouth, post-war rebuilding, 90
Pointing, 14–16
Polish, 40, 49, 50, 93, 172
Polishing capability, 21
Polyphant Stone, 51
Pore size, and frost attack, 161, 162
Pore structure, 159, 174–177
Pores, fineness of, 174–175
Porfido Rosso Antico, *see* Red Porphyry, Egypt
Porfido Serpentino, *see Marmor Lacedaemonium Viride* (Pliny)
Porfido Verde Antico, 53
Porosity, 91, 155, 175–176
Porphyries, 52, 53–54
Porphyrites leptopsephos (Pliny), 52
Portland Beds, 111
Portland cement, 163, 166
Portland Limestone, *130*
Portland screws, 111
Portland Stone, *29*, 91, 101, *110*, 111–113, 158
Portmadoc Slate, 140
Portsoy 'Marble', 50
Portugal, 49, 124
Post-repair drawings, 16, 18
Powdering of surface, 154, 157, 162
Powys, A.R., *Repair of Ancient Buildings*, 8, *9*, *10*
Pozzolana (Pozzuolana), 56
Pozzolanic substances, 57
Presents, 106
Preservation without distortion, 18
Princetown granite, Dartmoor, 40
Prinknash Abbey, 103
Prior, E.S., on the shrine of St Alban, 6
Prison granite, Dartmoor, 40
Projecting features, microclimate of, 171
Prudham Stone, 65
Puddingstone, 84
Pugin, Augustus (father), *Specimens and Examples of Gothic Architecture*, 3
Pugin, Augustus (son), on Selby Abbey, 3
Purbeck 'Marble', 109, 113–114
Purbeck-Portland stone, 112
Pyramids, 19
Pyrite, 89, 138, 158, 164
Pyroxenes, 49

Quarr Stone, 117
Quarry sap, 33
Quartz, 23, 40, 45, 47, 48, 52, 89, 117
Quartz cement, 61
Quartz grains, millet-seed, 73
Quartz-diorite, 38, 45, 49
Quartz-dolerite, 54
Quartz-porphyry, 52–53
Quartzite, 61, 84, 135, 136
Querns, 58
Quicklime, 97, 165

Racephas Stone, 63
Rag beds, 102
Rain-washing, 156, 157, 162
Rain-water removal, 169
Rainhill Stone, 75
'Rake out', 15
Rapakivi texture, 38, 48
Raunds Marble, 111
Recess Marble, 146
Record drawings, 16, *17*, 18
Red Porphyry, Egypt, 53–54
Red Wilderness Stone, 63–64, 75
Reddening, by fire, 131
Reef limestones, 88
Reigate Stone, 81–83
Rembrandt Stone Quartzite (Norway), 135
Renaissance building, 20
Renewal, in context of whole building, 12
Renish Basalt columns, sea defences, 57
Repair, 1
  birth of conservative approach to, 2–8
Repen Classico (Italy), 123
Repen Zola (Italy), 123
Repointing, 2, 167
Restoration, 5–6
Rhodochrosite, 151
Rickman, Thomas, *Attempt to discriminate the Styles of Architecture in England*, 3
Riebeckite, 46
Ripple marks, 29, 62, 78
Rising damp, 162
Roach (Portland Stone), 111–112

Roadstone, 54
Roche Abbey Stone, 97
Rock (definition), 20
Rock-Color Chart, 32
Rockdale (Upholland) Flags, 69
Rocks, 32–33, 36
Roman Stone, 123
Roman Wall, London, 66, 86, 133
Romans, and building stone, 19–20, 112
Roofing,
  slate, 137–144
  see also Tilestones
Rora granite, 45
Rose Brae Stone, 75
Ross of Mull granite, 28, 46
Rossi di Levanto (Italy), 51
Rottenstone, 89
Rouge Royal Marble (Belgium), 122
Rougemont Castle, 74–75
Rough Rock, 67
Rough Rock Flags, 68
Rough Rock Grit Group, 68
Rowley Rag, melted, 59
Royal Blue 'Granite' (Norway), 49
Royal Festival Hall, 93
Rubislaw granite, Aberdeen, 45
Rufus Castle, Isle of Portland, 112
Ruins, aesthetic qualities of, 2
Running water, 23
Ruskin, John,
  Lamp of Memory (from *Seven Lamps of Architecture*), 5–6
  The Stones of Venice, 6, 37
Rust, 163

Saccharoidal weathering, 144
Safari Quartzite (S. Africa), 135, 136
St Ann's Cathedral, Belfast, 117
St Ann's Church, St Ann's Square, Manchester, 71
St Bees Sandstone, 74, 75
St Bene't's, Cambridge, removal of rough cast, 4
St David's Cathedral, 63
St Frideswide's shrine, Christ Church Cathedral, Oxford, reconstruction of, 7
St George's Chapel, Windsor, 92
St George's Hall, Liverpool, 68, 93, 123
St Germanus church, Cornwall, 53
St Giles' Church, Little Malvern, 2, 3
St John's Church, Wateringbury, repair of drip mould, 12
St John's College, Cambridge, 50, 92
St Magnus Cathedral, 65
St Margaret's Church, Horsmonden, *17*, 18
St Mary's Church, Northgate, Canterbury, 16, *17*
St Michael's Church, East Peckham, decayed masonry sound, 12
St Pancras Station, 44, 46, 73
St Paul's Cathedral, London, 11, 112
  Duke of Wellington's tomb, 41, 42
St Paul's Churchyard, London, xenoliths, 43, 44
St Peter's Church, Cambridge, 4
St Sennor Church, Land's End, *38*
St Sophia, Constantinople, 54
St Stephen Wallbrook Church, London, 109
St Vaast Stone, 122
Salisbury Cathedral, *112*, 113
Salt, harmful, 173–174
Salt crystallization, 153–156, 169
Salt crystallization attack, 158, 164, 176
Salterwath limestone, 93
Salting of roads, 155
Salts,
  hygroscopic, 154, 173
  known to damage masonry, 153–154
  soluble, 23
  sources of, 155–156
Samples, determination of, 150–152
San Grita granite, Poland, xenoliths, 44
Sandstone, 36, 61–86, 97, 153–155, 157–158
  Tertiary, 84–85
  Cretaceous, 78–84
  Jurassic, 77–78
  Permian and Triassic, 71–77
  Carboniferous, 65–71
  Devonian, 63–65
  Precambrian-Silurian, 63
  imported, 85
Sandy limestone, 89
Sanfront Stone (Italy), 136
Sapone, *see* Soapstone
Sardinian granite, 48
Sarsens, 61, 65, 84, *85*
Satin Spar, 125
Scarborough Museum, *78*
Schiller, 49
Schist, 25, 135–136
Schistosity, 30, 135, 144, *145*
Scoriaceous basalt, 57
Scott, George Gilbert, on the shrine of St Alban, 6
Scott, Sir Gilbert, 6, 113
  anastylosis of shrine of St Alban, 6
Scrabo Sandstone, 77
Screwstone, 93
Sculptures,
  Barbara Hepworth, *Image*, 93
  Henry Moore,
    Figure, 74
    Memorial Figure, Dartington Hall, *100*
    Mother and Child, 100
    Reclining Figure (1935), 74
    Reclining Figure (1947), 100
    Reclining Figure (1957–8), *119*, 120
    Reclining Nude, 93
Sculptures, (*cont.*)
  Henry Moore, (*cont.*)
    Square Form, 100
    Three Standing Figures, 68
  Jacob Epstein, *Consummatum Est*, 126
  Milles, eagle, 49
  Elephant and Calf, 49
  The Tetrarchs, Venice, *54*
Sea salt, 155
Seasoning of rocks, 33
Sedimentary rocks, 23, 25
  bitumens, 127
  coal and jet, 127, 129
  deposition of, 29
  flint, chert and jasper, 86
  gypsum (alabaster), 124–127
  limestone, 86–124
  sandstone, 61–85
  special considerations, 129–133
Sedimentary stones, placing of, *128*, 129
Selby Cathedral, 96
Selenite, 125
Septarian nodules, 118–119
Serpentine, 50
Serpentinite, 32, 50, 51, 122
Serpentinization, 50
Serpentinous marble, 50, 145
Setts, 43, 46, 47, 54, 77, 93, 113
Shantallow granite, 47
Shap granite (Dark and Light), 43
Shattering,
  fire, 165
  frost, 160–161
Shattering pressure, 160–161
Sheet jointing, 27–28, 42
Shelly Limestone, 88, 100
Shelly sands, 61
Sherborne Abbey, 100, 119
Shrewsbury Castle, 76
Shrinkage joints, 30
Shropshire 'Marble', 89
Sicilian Marble, *46*, 147
Siderite, 89
Sienna marbles, 122, 123
Silica, 23, 114, 115
Silica cement, 62, 73, 157
Silicates, 23
Sillar, 55
Sills, 27, 42, 54
Silsden Moor Grit, 67
Skye Marble, 146
Skyros Marble, 148
Slaked-lime, 165, 166
Slate, 26, 158
Slate, 158, 165
  Cornish, 142–143
  imported, 143–144
  Lake District, 137, 138–139
  Leicestershire, 141–142
  Scottish, 138
  Welsh, 137, 139–141
Slate Sills, 65

Slate sizing, 140–141
Slaty cleavage, 26, 137
Snail-creep (ribbon-creep), 15, 111
Soapstone, 50, 51
Society of Antiquaries, 2–3
Society for the Protection of Ancient Buildings, *Manifesto*, 6–7
Sodalite, 49
Soft seams, occurrence of, 171
South Africa, 50
  gneiss and quartzite, 136
  granite, 38, 50
Southwark Cathedral, 116
Southwell Minster, 73, 95
Spain,
  marbles, 124
  slate, 144
Spallability of rock, 30
Spalling, 1, *131*
Specification errors, 169–172
Sphene, 38, 46
Spinkwell Stone, 68
Spynie Sandstone, 75
Staining, 162–163, 169, 172
Stainton Stone, 70
Stalactites and stalagmites, 88
Stamford Grit, 103–104
Stamford 'Marble', 104
Stancliffe Stone, 67–68
Stanhope Black Marble, 92
Stanwick Ragstone, 111
Statuario (Statuary) Marble, 146
Steel, corrosion-resistant, 169
Stink Stone, 89
Stock Exchange, Manchester, granite, 48
Stone, 1, 13, 14, 20, 21, 158
  bruising of, 171
  classification, 22–26
    igneous rocks, 22–23
    metamorphic rocks, 25–26
    sedimentary rocks, 23, 25
  criteria for use, 21
  distribution of, 21–22
  extraction of, 30–32
  green, 33, 66, 74, 76
  incompatible, 129
  renewed to be distinguishable from old, 7
Stone facings, 20
Stonehenge, 19, 84
Stonesfield Slates, 106
Stonework,
  damaged, interest in retention of, 132–133
  historic, preservation of, 1
  mediaeval and modern, 13, 14
  present-day attitudes towards repair of, 8–18
Strasbourg Cathedral, 157
Strathclyde University, 45
Stratification, 29
Street, Edmund, rebuilding of Monkland church, Herefordshire, 6
Stress, 1
Structural concrete, collapse of, 167
Structural problems, resolution of, 9–10
Stylolites, 124
Sugaring, 157, 165
Sulphur-based acids and gases, 156, 157
Sulphurous acid, 156
Sun cracks, 62
Surface Granite, 40
Surveys, 9
Sussex 'Marble', 114
Sussex Sandstone, 78
Sutton Stone, 89, 99
Suwan granite, Egypt, 48
Swale Dale Fossil limestone, 93
Sweden,
  granite, 47
  limestone, 123–124
  marble, 148
Swedish Black Granite, 38
Swedish Green 'Granite', 49
Swedish Green marble, 148
'Swedish (Swedes)' Stone, 123, 124
Swithland Slates, 141–142
Syenite, 38, 43, 48–49
Syeno-gabbro, 38, 50

Tadcaster Stone, *96*, 97
Talc, 50, 135
Tarry pollutants, effects of, 162
Taynton Stone, 109
Temperature changes, 154, 155, 157, 164
Temple of Zeus, cracked lintel, 11
Tennessee marble (USA), 149
Texas marble (USA), 149
Thermal conductivity of rocks, 132
Thermal expansion, 131–132
  coefficients of, 158, 164, 165
Thermal metamorphism, 25–26
Throne Room of King of Siam, Bangkok, 123
Tiles, 13
  rendering of, 8, *9*, *10*
  replacement with, 7–8
Tilestones, 54, 63, 65, 67, 69, 78, 101–102, 106, 112, 113
Tilestones, The, 63
Tinos (Tenos, Vert Tinos) Marble, 51
Tiree Marble, 146
Tisbury Stone, 112
Titterstone Clee Hill, 54
Tobacco smoke, effects of, 172
Tombs, 54, 97, 102, 114
Tombstones, 113, 142
Torridonian Sandstone, 63
Totternhoe Stone, 117
Touchstone, 58
Toughness, 33, 36
Tourmaline, 40
Tourmalinization, 42
Tournai 'Marble' (Belgium), 94
Trachyte, 58
Trafalgar Square, paving, 73
Transport, 23
Trass, 56
Travertine, 56, 88, 119–120, 122
Trees, creepers and climbers, 167–169
Trilithons, Stonehenge, 19
Truro Cathedral, 50, 51, 103, 143
Tufa, 88, 119
Tuff, 55–57, 138
Tuffeau Stone, 122
Tulanto Marble, 147
Tunbridge Wells Sand, 78
Turkey, marble, 148
Tutbury Gypsum, 125
Tynemouth Priory, ruined character, 12–13

Ulster Bank, Belfast, Newry granite, 47
Ultra-basic rocks, 23
Unio Marble, 114
Unst serpentinite, 50
Upper Greensand, 81–84
Upper Limestone Group, Glasgow area, 66–67
USA,
  basalt, 59
  granite, 48
  marble, 148–149
Users and occupiers, effects of, 172–174

Valadier, Guiseppe, 7
Vale of Wardour Stone, 112–113
Valley Trains, sarsens, 84, *85*
Verde Antico, 50
Verde Antico (Greece), 51
Verde Antique, 53
Verona limestone (Red and Yellow), 122
Veseljie Stone (Italy), 123
Vesicles, 57
Victoria and Albert Museum, London, 112, 143, 148
Virginia Creeper, 167
Visitors, direct/indirect effects, 172–173
Vitis species, 167
Volcanic (extrusive) rocks, 22, 27
Volcanic glass, 57

Walker Gallery, Liverpool, 71
Walls,
  individual components, 10–14
  structural problems of, 9–10
Washing powders, contamination by, 163
Washington Monument, 149
Water marble, 88, 149
Water repellent, application of, 173
Waterholes Grit Stone, 69
Waterloo Bridge, Scottish granite, 45
Watermarks, 106

Waterstone, 88
Wax, soiling by, 129, 130
Weald Clay, 78, 114
Wealden 'Marbles', 114
Wealden Series, 78, 80
Wealden Sussex (sandstone), 78
Weathering, 10–11, 20, 23, 50, 89, 144, 153
Weir, William, 8
Weldon Stone, 96–97, 104–105
Wellfield (Johnsons Wellfield) Stone, 68–69
Wellington Monument, Phoenix Park, Dublin, 47
Wells Cathedral, 77, 94, 97, *99*, 102
Welsh Red Slate, 140
Wenlock Limestone, 89
Westminster Abbey, 54
  Henry VII's Chapel, 2, 108
Westminster Bridge, granite piers, 41
Westminster Cathedral, 54, 148
Westminster Hall, paving, 69
Westmorland Green Slate, 138
Wetting and drying, effects of, 164
Whatstandwell Stone, 68
Whitby Abbey, 77
'White City' (Arequipa), Peru, 55
White, Gilbert, on nailed walls, 81
White Lias, 97, *99*
White Limestone, N. Ireland, 115
Wicklow granite, 47
Wiltshire Greensand, 113
Winchester Cathedral, 118
Window glass, mediaeval, 172
Windsor Castle, 121
Winkle stone, 114
Wirral Peninsula, 75
Woburn Abbey, Bedfordshire, *116*, 117
Woe Stones, 84
Woodkirk Stone, 69–70
Woolten Stone, 75
Worcester Cathedral, Mona Marble, 51
Workmanship errors, 171–172
Worksop Giant, 148
Wrabness Church, Essex, 118–119
Wyatt, James, controversial approach to restoration, 4

Xenoliths, 43–44, 45

Yoredale Series, 65
York, Castle Walls, *130*
York City Art Gallery, paving, 69
York Minster, 96, 97
York Stone, *15*, 69, *70*

Zimbabwe, 20
Zircon, 61

Part 2

Contents

1 Methods of repairing and consolidating stone buildings 1
John Ashurst

2 Structural failure and repair 55
Ralph Mills

3 The selection of stone for repairs 71
David B. Honeyborne

4 Mortars for stone buildings 78
John Ashurst

5 Traditional handworking of stone: methods and recognition 97
Peter Hill

6 Earthquake damage to historic masonry structures 107
Alejandro Alva Balderrama

7 The repair and remedial treatment of the East Block Parliament buildings, Ottawa, Canada 114
Keith Blades and John Stewart

8 Cleaning masonry buildings 125
John Ashurst

9 Surface treatments 155
David B. Honeyborne, John Ashurst, Clifford Price and Keith Ross

10 The conservation of stone monuments in churches 185
John Larson

11 The conservation of stone sculpture in museums 197
John Larson

12 The museum display of architectural features 208
Deborah Carthy

13 The cleaning of painted stone 214
Clare Finn

14 The cleaning and consolidation of the stonework to the Annuciation Door, Chapter House, Westminster Abbey 219
Keith Taylor, Christopher Gradwell and Teresa McGrath

Appendix 1 Limewashing 229
John Ashurst

Appendix 2 Effects of large numbers of vistors on historic buildings 231
David Honeyborne

Appendix 3 The use of air-abrasive cleaning techniques for stone building surfaces 237
Peter Moss

Appendix 4 The analytical approach to stone, its cleaning, repair and treatment 240
Nicola Ashurst and John Kelly

Index 245

1

Methods of repairing and consolidating stone buildings

John Ashurst

Introduction

A stone building of any age and condition requires an experienced practitioner to assess its real state and its repair and maintenance requirements. The objective of this and subsequent chapters is to assist the general building practitioner to become more familiar with the problem of stone construction and the various repair and maintenance options, rather than to discuss matters of general survey and inspection.

There are as many dangers associated with unnecessary or incorrect interference with masonry structures and surfaces as there are associated with neglect. Whilst the interference problem is not new it is tending to take over from neglect as the prime enemy of historic stone buildings in the more affluent areas of the world. Typical examples of harmful intervention include:

1. Introduction of massive concrete stitching or beams into cracked but stable masonry
2. Introduction of large quantities of cement grouting
3. Introduction of large quantities of polyester or epoxy resin grout
4. Unnecessary replacement of worn and heavily weathered stones
5. Widening of original joint widths and spalling of arrises by the use of cutting disks and wedge-shaped chisels
6. Superficial pointing of joints with cement-rich or resin-based mortars
7. Alteration of original joint profiles
8. Damage by air-abrasive and disk cleaning
9. Residual damage associated with acid and alkali cleaners
10. Use of inappropriate surface treatments, such as water repellents, consolidants and anti-graffiti coating of the wrong type

In some cases the work carried out will not be physically harmful, but when stones are replaced unnecessarily or the original joint profiles are altered this will have a de-valuing effect on the building.

The keys to good masonry conservation are undoubtedly experience in problem recognition and diagnosis, competent specification, minimal physical intervention and maximum technical site skills. Clearly these desirable elements need the involvement of more than one discipline, but it is likely that the central co-ordinating discipline will be the architect's.

On pages 2–3 the architect's plan of approach to a masonry building is suggested in the form of various action options. Unless the problem is very simple, however, the architect should involve the archaeologist, art historian, specialist engineer, analytical chemist, masonry technician and stone or sculpture conservator at an early stage.

The need to examine minutely and to record before anything is altered or repaired is paramount. In some situations there may be no money available for any work for many years. In these cases recording should be given a high priority. Photography, photogrammetry and monitoring are all important, sometimes critically so, but so, still, is the making of drawings, the taking of moulds and casts and the making of accurate templates of original profiles. Although there are some highly sophisticated recording techniques, and in some parts of the conservation world there is so much specialized technical back-up that simple site observation becomes relegated, there will never be a substitute for close site observation based on long experience. All techniques must be subordinate to and supportive of personal site survey.

Sites with ruined masonry and roofed and occupied masonry buildings have various repair and maintenance requirements in common, but ruined

REMEDIAL WORK TO MASONRY : SCOPE AND OPTIONS

Inspection and diagnosis of condition can usefully be considered in the following categories :-

A : THE WALLS [structural condition] **B :** THE STONES [individually]

C : THE JOINTS

A : THE WALLS

Are they leaning, bulging, twisting, fracturing ? If so, the reasons must be known. Are the structural problems real and "live", or have they already been resolved ?

CAUSES OF PROBLEMS may be :

- UNEQUAL SETTLEMENT [inconsistency in the bearing capacity of the ground, mining subsidence, unequal loads from different building elements]
- COLLAPSE OF ARCHES VAULTS or BUTTRESSES [knock-on effects from destruction of essential supports or counter-thrust elements]
- GENERAL INSTABILITY [due to structural alterations, explosion, earthquake, robbing of stones, washing out of wall core and joints]
- INAPPROPRIATE STRUCTURAL INTERVENTION [stresses imposed by rigid restraints and ties, unecessary buttressing, strong resin-based or cementitious grouts]

REMEDIAL WORK TO WALLS

Must be preceded by detailed site investigation and survey, including accurate monitoring. Work should not be visually obtrusive and must not impose new problems on the fabric. Remedial work may include :-

- SECTIONAL UNDERPINNING
- PILING
- STITCHING ACROSS FRACTURES
- INSERTION OF HIDDEN WALL HEAD BEAMS, RING BEAMS, ANGLE BEAMS
- INSERTION OF HIDDEN LINTOLS AND HANGING SYSTEMS FOR ARCHES
- GROUTING BY GRAVITY OR LOW PRESSURE WITH LIME, FLY ASH, WHITE CEMENT

Full records of all structural interventions must be kept; some on-site monitoring may need to continue indefinitely

B: THE STONES

Are they spalling, scaling, splitting, powdering, disfigured by staining and pitting? If so, the reasons must be understood, using laboratory analysis if necessary.

CAUSES OF PROBLEMS may be :

- ACID ATTACK ON BINDING MATRIX OF STONE [especially calcareous, dolomitic, argillaceous and ferruginous sandstones and marble]
- SULPHATE SKIN FORMATION ON LIMESTONES [especially in sheltered zones]
- CONTOUR SCALE FORMATION ON SANDSTONES [especially in saturation zones]
- OTHER SALT CRYSTALLISATION [associated with rising damp, cement grout, incompatible stones]
- FREEZING
- FIRE DAMAGE
- WEATHERING OUT OF SOFT BEDS
- WEATHERING OUT OF VENTS AND SHAKES
- INCORRECT BEDDING
- RUSTING OF IRON CRAMPS
- COMPRESSION FRACTURES
- STAINING AND EFFLORESCENCE AFTER CLEANING

DISCOLOURATION, PITTING AND SPALLING ASSOCIATED WITH SURFACE TREATMENTS [especially traditional pore-blocking treatments]

REMEDIAL WORK TO STONES

Must be preceded by a comprehensive survey with adequate diagnosis completed on all damage and decay. Study of thin sections and salt analyses may be needed; identification of stone type and any treatment or unusual soiling must also be made. An elevational record with large-scale profile details is necessary on which each stone is identifiable and referenced. This record may be a measured survey, corrected photography or a photogrammetric survey. All work and treatment must be recorded.

Remedial work may include :-

- Modification of external environment [providing weather protection, re-routing water channels, introduction of damp-proof membranes, dirt removal]
- Modification of internal environment [humidity, temperature controls, restriction on visitor numbers]
- CUT OUT AND REPLACE OR RE-FACE WITH MATCHING STONE [to original profiles]
- CUT OUT AND PIECE-IN WITHIN EXISTING STONES, IN MATCHED STONE
- CUT OUT AND FILL WITH MORTAR [lime based fills for limestone, epoxy or acrylic based fills for sandstone etc., ensuring fills are permeable and impose no new stresses]
- DRILL, GROUT AND PIN FRACTURED STONES
- CUT OUT AND BUILD UP REPAIR IN TILE COURSING
- PROVIDE WEAK, PROTECTIVE PLASTER
- PROVIDE SACRIFICIAL PLASTER

  } the constituents and porosity of these plasters are designed to take up moisture and salts in solution without rapid failure
- CLEAN AND PARTIALLY DESALINATE [leaching packs of paper pulp, attapulgite or sepiolite clay, CMC and solvents]
- USE A WATER REPELLENT [silicone or stearate based repellents are only very rarely useful. Competent diagnosis of the cause of damp is essential]
- USE A CONSOLIDANT

  e.g. limewater for limestone. Alkoxysilanes are promising consolidants : TETRAETHOXYSILANE [TEOS - ethyl silicate] gives good penetration and consolidation without water repellence ETHYLTRIMETHOXYSILANE [ETEOS] consolidates and imparts water repellence. Acrylic resin may be added to both to impart surface hardness. METHYLTRIMETHOXYSILANE (MTMOS) is usually used in conjunction with a catalyst such as acrylic resin or lead soap Although primarily suitable for sandstones, alkoxysilane consolidants have been used successfully on siliceous and argillaceous limestones and even on magnesian limestones.

  NOTE : CONSOLIDANTS MUST NOT BE USED UNLESS THE CAUSE OF DECAY AND THE CONSTITUENTS OF THE STONE ARE FULLY UNDERSTOOD ALL OTHER OPTIONS SHOULD BE CONSIDERED FIRST

C: THE JOINTS

Are they partially or wholly open, deeply weathered, loose and powdery? Have they been re-pointed in unsuitable, impermeable mortar?

CAUSES OF PROBLEMS may be :-

- POOR CARBONATION OF MORTAR
- SATURATION AND FREEZING
- SOLUBLE SALT CRYSTALLISATION [from contaminated aggregates, marine environments, rising damp, flue gases]
- SHRINKAGE AND CRACKING [from wet mixes or use of strong hydraulic limes/cements or oil mastics]
- MASONRY BEE BURROWING AND BIRD ATTACK
- ESTABLISHED IVY GROWTH

REMEDIAL WORK TO JOINTS

Must only be carried out when the absence or failure of mortar is adversely affecting stones or walls, or where strong, sound mortar is causing decay or is visually destructive. Original mortar should be sieve-analysed and new mortar should incorporate matching aggregates and be designed to suit the condition of the stones first and the exposure of the wall second. Work may include :-

- RAKE OUT, TAMP AND POINT [open joints or inadequate mortar]
- CUT OUT, TAMP AND POINT [dense, unsuitable mortar]
- SAW OUT, PLUG AND POINT [fine joints - under 3mm]
- RAKE OUT, PLUG AND POINT [special joints with weathering problems]
- CLEAN OUT AND PLUG AND POINT [local damage by birds or bees]

masonry in particular requires a special approach and treatment which demands a close co-operation between archaeologists, architects, engineers and stone masons.

Treatment of monument sites

Ruined masonry buildings, especially those classified as ancient monuments, have special problems. They may be of considerable archaeological and historical importance, which would be lost in whole or part if neglect continued or demolition took place or, on the other hand, if clumsy, inappropriate repairs or ignorant restorations were carried out. Archaeologically important sites may consist of standing, partly ruined walls, or an open or wooded site with all surviving masonry below the modern ground level, or, most commonly, a combination of both.

Development of inner city areas frequently exposes even more problematical remains in the course of rescue archaeology. Usually, because of building programmes, nothing but recording and removal of finds can take place; exceptionally the value of an uncovered site is such that modifications to the proposed building are possible. These situations call for particular care in temporary reburial.

Walls below modern ground level

These walls may be exposed as the result of a planned archaeological investigation and the sole intention may be to record what is there and to backfill. Alternatively, the site may be discovered or opened fortuitously by road or drainage works or by building development, and 'rescue archaeology' will then be needed to record ahead of destruction. In neither situation will much maintenance of the masonry exposed be required.

Other circumstances, however, may require the excavated walls to remain exposed to view. In this case a programme of consolidation and repair, followed by some plan for maintenance, should be instituted as soon as possible. Stones and mortar which have lain for centuries in saturated ground or dry sand may have survived in excellent condition due to these stable environments. Once exposed, however, they may begin to show signs of deterioration fairly quickly as exposure to wind, sun and rain sets up wetting and drying cycles and the destructive crystallization of soluble salts begins to take its toll. Winter conditions bring the additional hazard of frost to walls saturated with water, and substantial losses may occur in one night.

Availability of finance, skilled labour and professional supervision will determine how quickly consolidation can begin. Delays will almost certainly be involved, and temporary protection must then be provided appropriate to the risks of exposure. Such protection may range from geotextile sheets and sand or 'duvets' of straw or polystyrene weighted down, to temporary boxing filled with polystyrene beads, to temporary scaffold frame structures that can double up as protection for the excavation or maintenance team and may even be heated.

Walls standing above ground level

Unroofed and often ruinous buildings which stand above ground level require the attention of an experienced team of specialists, not only to investigate, excavate and record, but also to strengthen and consolidate what survives. When funds and expertise are limited, it is essential that the necessary first-aid is carried out to ensure that further collapse, disintegration or vandalism are kept to a minimum. Emergency work may include the provision of secure fencing, formwork to support vaults and arches in danger of collapse, and strutting and shoring to support leaning and bulging walls. Wall head protection may also be necessary; see below. Features of particular value may need to be protected by temporary roofs.

Much of the final consolidation will consist of stabilizing double skin walls of ashlar, or the consolidation of exposed mortar and rubble fills. The latter are much more difficult to consolidate to a visually acceptable standard than walls with facework and head intact. Core filling may have become exposed by many years of neglect, by deliberate destruction, or by the robbing of dressed facework for use elsewhere. Common problems resulting from this neglect or destruction are:

1. The thickness of the original wall has been reduced and the wall may have become unstable.
2. The core filling is frequently of inferior stones and mortar, with a high percentage of mortar exposed. Such surfaces often have poor resistance to weathering and encourage the development of organic growth.

Considerable experience is needed to 'read' corework when a substantial quantity of the face is missing. The survey and recording of untouched core before any work commences is of great importance; even superficial treatment can obscure or destroy the last traces of, for instance, the size of an opening, the bearing of a beam or indications of alteration or rebuilding. The impressions made in the corework by the tails of missing stones will often yield much information, such as the pattern of previous coursing, or the existence of a former vault or line of corbels.

The initial survey should include the archaeological examination of the adjacent ground. Often this

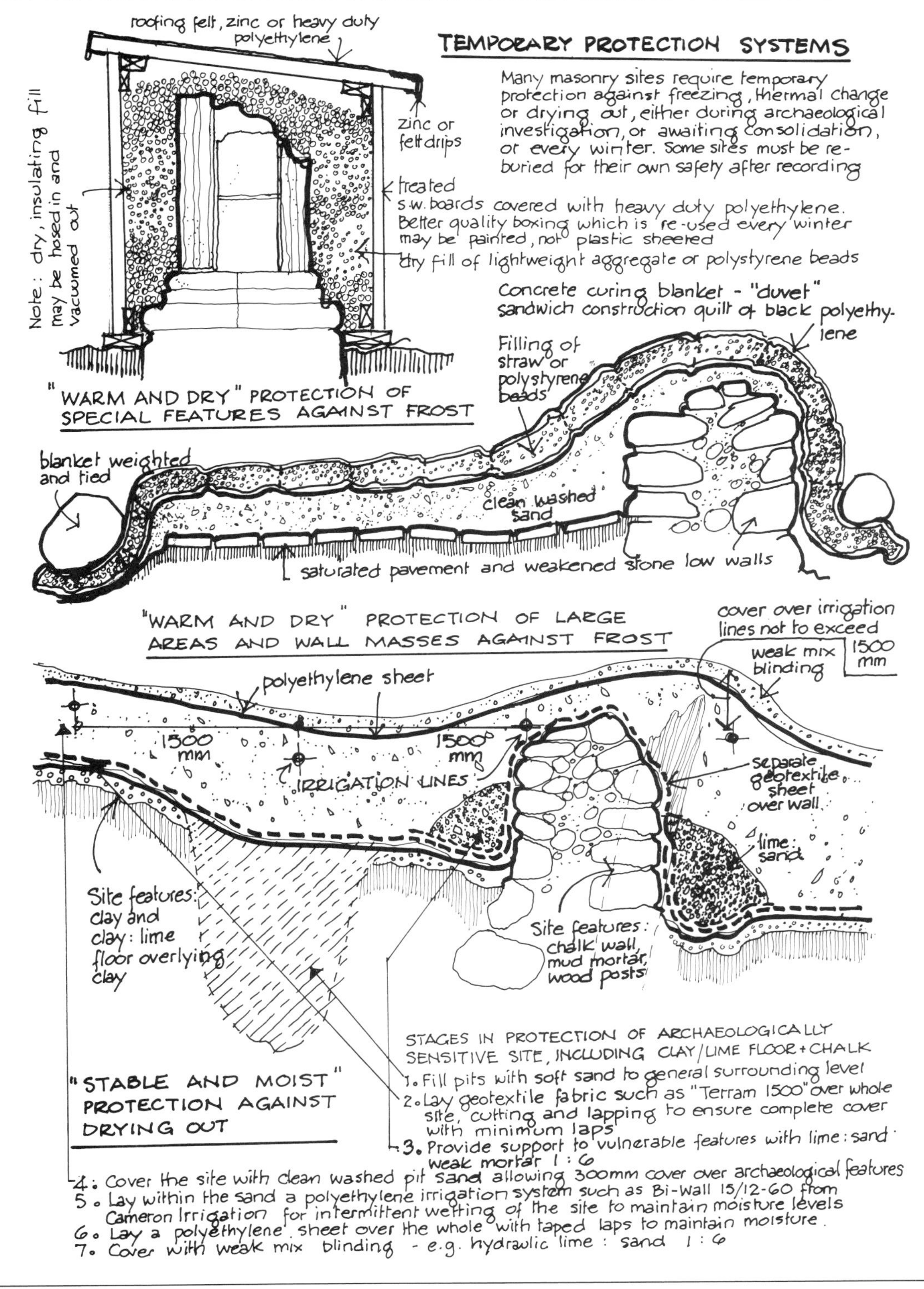
TEMPORARY PROTECTION SYSTEMS
Many masonry sites require temporary protection against freezing, thermal change or drying out, either during archaeological investigation, or awaiting consolidation, or every winter. Some sites must be re-buried for their own safety after recording
roofing felt, zinc or heavy duty polyethylene
zinc or felt drips
Note: dry, insulating fill may be hosed in and vacuumed out
treated s.w. boards covered with heavy duty polyethylene. Better quality boxing which is re-used every winter may be painted, not plastic sheeted
dry fill of lightweight aggregate or polystyrene beads
"WARM AND DRY" PROTECTION OF SPECIAL FEATURES AGAINST FROST
Concrete curing blanket - "duvet" sandwich construction quilt of black polyethylene
Filling of straw or polystyrene beads
blanket weighted and tied
clean washed sand
saturated pavement and weakened stone low walls
"WARM AND DRY" PROTECTION OF LARGE AREAS AND WALL MASSES AGAINST FROST
cover over irrigation lines not to exceed 1500 mm
weak mix blinding
polyethylene sheet
1500 mm
1500 mm
IRRIGATION LINES
separate geotextile sheet over wall
lime: sand
Site features: clay and clay: lime floor overlying clay
Site features: chalk wall, mud mortar, wood posts
"STABLE AND MOIST" PROTECTION AGAINST DRYING OUT
STAGES IN PROTECTION OF ARCHAEOLOGICALLY SENSITIVE SITE, INCLUDING CLAY/LIME FLOOR + CHALK
1. Fill pits with soft sand to general surrounding level
2. Lay geotextile fabric such as "Terram 1500" over whole site, cutting and lapping to ensure complete cover with minimum laps
3. Provide support to vulnerable features with lime: sand weak mortar 1 : 6
4. Cover the site with clean washed pit sand allowing 300mm cover over archaeological features
5. Lay within the sand a polyethylene irrigation system such as Bi-Wall 15/12-60 from Cameron Irrigation for intermittent wetting of the site to maintain moisture levels
6. Lay a polyethylene sheet over the whole with taped laps to maintain moisture.
7. Cover with weak mix blinding - e.g. hydraulic lime : sand 1 : 6

will reveal stones that have fallen from the wall and may be replaced. Sometimes quantities of stone tracery, vault ribs and tilestones will also be found. These can provide valuable information about the building. It is important to record them in the exact positions in which they have fallen.

Plants, shrubs, later buildings and insertions and heavy soiling may all obscure evicence surviving in the core. However, their incautious removal can destroy the evidence altogether.

Consolidation by taking down and rebuilding

Some core consists of loose stones and other aggregate in a largely disintegrated matrix of mortar, soil and the roots of weeds. After a photographic record has been made and dimensions and levels taken, the stones should be lifted off and cleaned. This operation should be carried out over a few metres at a time. The top of each stone should be numbered in its take-down sequence. In some cases, the arrangement of the stones may be traced through onto a sheet of untearable plastic film. The stones and film can then be given reference numbers to assist in the reassembly. The condition and type of core will determine whether this technique is practicable or not.

The cleaned stones must be rebedded in a mortar which is a good visual match with the original surviving core. The mortar must be resistant to weathering and not too dense or impermeable for the stones forming the filling. Where stones that have no weather resistance were used as fill in the past, a compromise must be made: replacement stones of at least similar appearance and size, but with a better resistance to wetting and drying cycles and to frost, should be used. The aim in rebuilding is to reproduce the same outlines as found, modifying only as necessary to avoid water traps and pockets. Results resembling a garden rockery or rubble facework can be avoided by technical expertise based on study and familiarity with the true appearance of untouched core.

Sometimes it is necessary to insert new core to support sections of the original wall or features that are in danger of collapse. Other methods of support have been used from time to time, including delta metal brackets and straps, which can be pre-formed to profiles of, for instance, traceried heads or lintels. Page 7 illustrates the insertion of a concrete stitch behind the facework to tie the masonry together across an open fracture. Page 8 shows methods of providing support to the damaged heads of arches.

Treatment of wall tops

The treatment of the wall tops of ruined buildings is of particular importance. These areas, which have become exposed to the weather through the loss of roofs, now have to take on the role of parapets. What is more, they must be parapets without copings, unless the visually disastrous and archaeologically confusing expedient of setting coping slabs on levelled wall-tops is followed. In the wall top consolidation, therefore, modifications must be made in lifting and re-setting to ensure that water is shed as rapidly as possible and that there is no risk of ponding. On very thick wall tops a lead-lined sump is sometimes formed with a lead downpipe carried through the core to some convenient outlet. This should only be considered in exceptional circumstances, and the sump must be fitted with a strong, secure wire balloon or grid of fine stainless steel or non-ferrous metal mesh, to avoid blocking with leaves or bird excrement.

Temporary wall coverings (accepting that 'temporary' may mean many years) may be provided by mortar 'blankets', isolated from the historic masonry by a thin sheet of polyethylene and include a reinforcing mesh of alkali-resistant fabric. Non-ferrous wire anchors may be used to secure this rendering into the wall top. Carefully designed and colour-matched mortar blankets provide good and usually acceptable protection for wall tops; if necessary they can be broken up and removed from the historic level at a later date. In less severe climates the mortar blanket may be of a weaker mix than the wall core and be used without an isolating membrane, as was done in the so-called Temple of Saturn in the Forum at Rome.

Where the climate permits, another form of wall capping suitable for low walls in rural situations is turf set, or allowed to grow, on a reinforcing net of synthetic land mesh pegged into the heart of the wall with glass-fibre or non-ferrous wire pegs. The use of mesh makes it easier to remove the turf if further examination of the wall is required at a future date. Mesh has sometimes been used on rough dry stone or on stones which were originally clay-mortared, to form a kind of gabion by stretching it from wall base to wall base and pegging it into the core. However, this is a first-aid procedure only and should not be seen as a permanent method of consolidation. Page 9 illustrates different types of wall topping.

Removal of woody weeds

Where sites are covered with woody species of weeds, the Building Research Establishment recommends control by spot spraying with glyphosate. This is a non-selective herbicide, so care must be taken to protect non-target species from drift. The spray equipment should also be kept for glyphosate

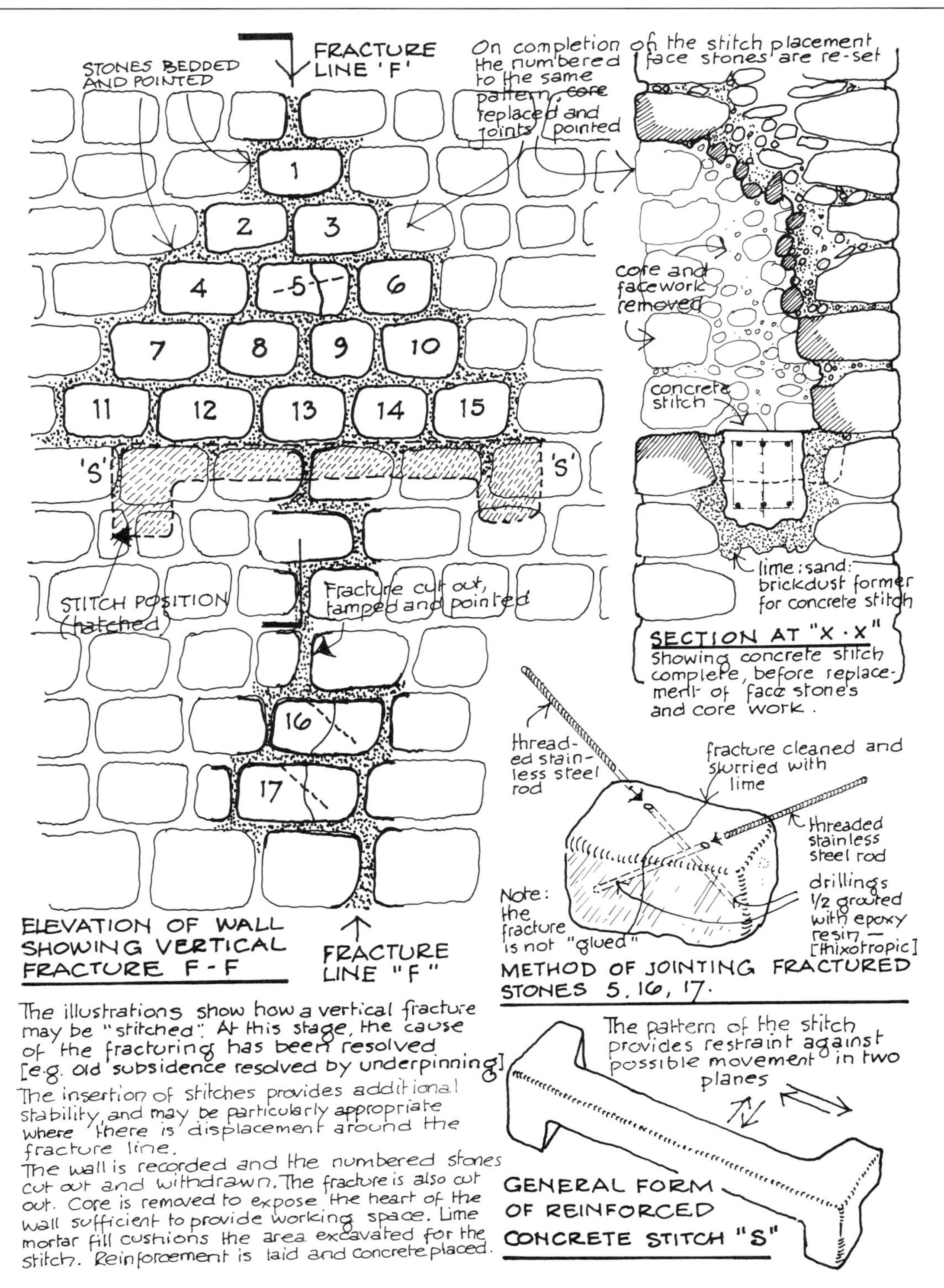
FRACTURE LINE 'F'
STONES BEDDED AND POINTED
On completion of the stitch placement the numbered face stones are re-set to the same pattern, core replaced and joints pointed
1
2
3
4
5
6
7
8
9
10
11
12
13
14
15
'S'
'S'
STITCH POSITION (hatched)
Fracture cut out, tamped and pointed
16
17
ELEVATION OF WALL SHOWING VERTICAL FRACTURE F-F
FRACTURE LINE "F"
core and facework removed
concrete stitch
lime: sand: brickdust former for concrete stitch
SECTION AT "X·X"
Showing concrete stitch complete, before replacement of face stones and core work.
threaded stainless steel rod
fracture cleaned and slurried with lime
threaded stainless steel rod
drillings 1/2 grouted with epoxy resin — [thixotropic]
Note: the fracture is not "glued"
METHOD OF JOINTING FRACTURED STONES 5, 16, 17.
The illustrations show how a vertical fracture may be "stitched". At this stage, the cause of the fracturing has been resolved [e.g. old subsidence resolved by underpinning]
The insertion of stitches provides additional stability, and may be particularly appropriate where there is displacement around the fracture line.
The wall is recorded and the numbered stones cut out and withdrawn. The fracture is also cut out. Core is removed to expose the heart of the wall sufficient to provide working space. Lime mortar fill cushions the area excavated for the stitch. Reinforcement is laid and concrete placed.
The pattern of the stitch provides restraint against possible movement in two planes
GENERAL FORM OF REINFORCED CONCRETE STITCH "S"

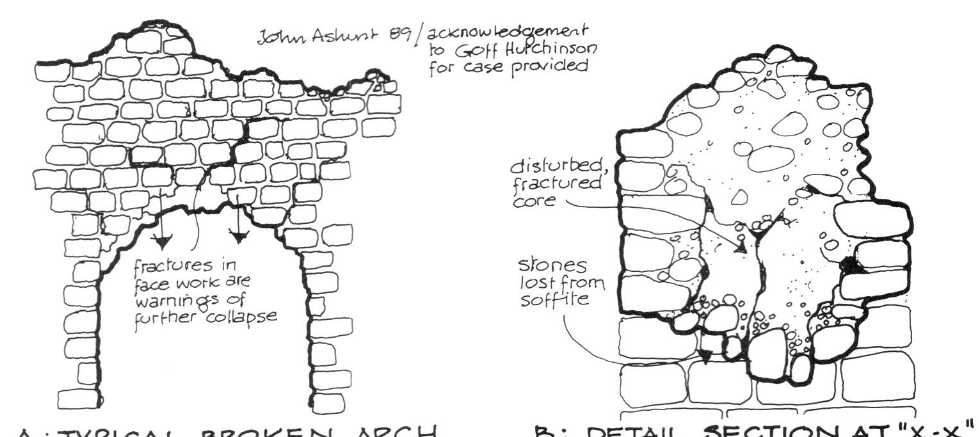

Broken heads of openings are a common feature of ruined masonry buildings. Further failure represents a major hazard and can constitute substantial losses of historic fabric

These situations are sometimes resolved by unsatisfactory permanent propping. A more acceptable solution is to form surface supports in phosphor bronze or stainless steel straps. These are profiled to the ruined soffite of the opening using a template. The straps act as permanent "false-work" when bedded under the arch. Unfortunately, they are usually obvious [Example 'E]

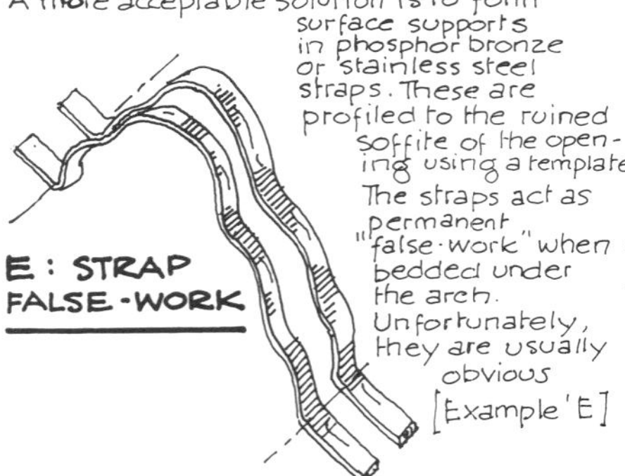

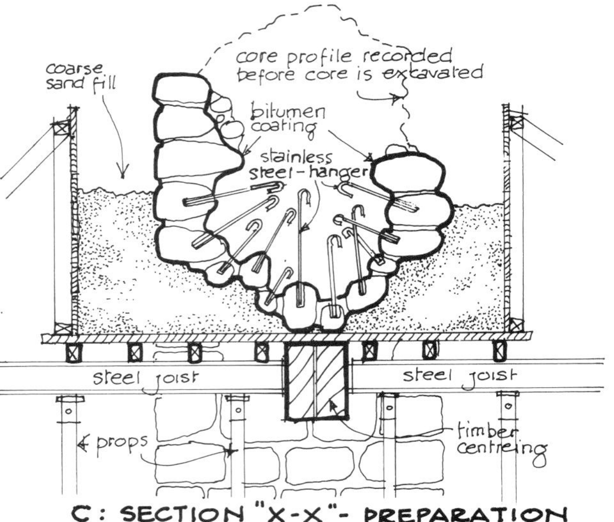

Details B-C-D illustrate a system of inserting a secret lintol

B: shows the condition as found Careful recording and numbering of all the stones takes place at this stage

C: full support for the broken arch head is provided in the form of temporary centreing. Steel joists, props and timber bearers support a platform and boarded, strutted timber sides form a sand-box. Coarse sand is packed in to provide full support for all the stones.

The core is carefully lifted out in sections to expose the back of the stones. Each stone is drilled to receive a threaded stainless steel hook bar set in epoxy resin. The stones are bitumen coated at the back. Reinforcement is placed and concrete is poured to form a lintol from which the stones are now hanging.

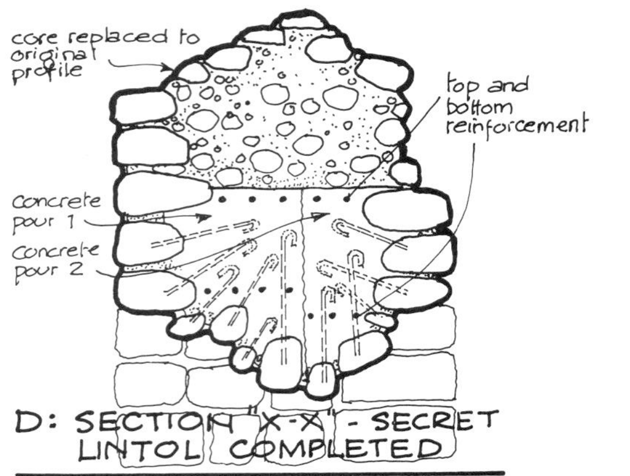

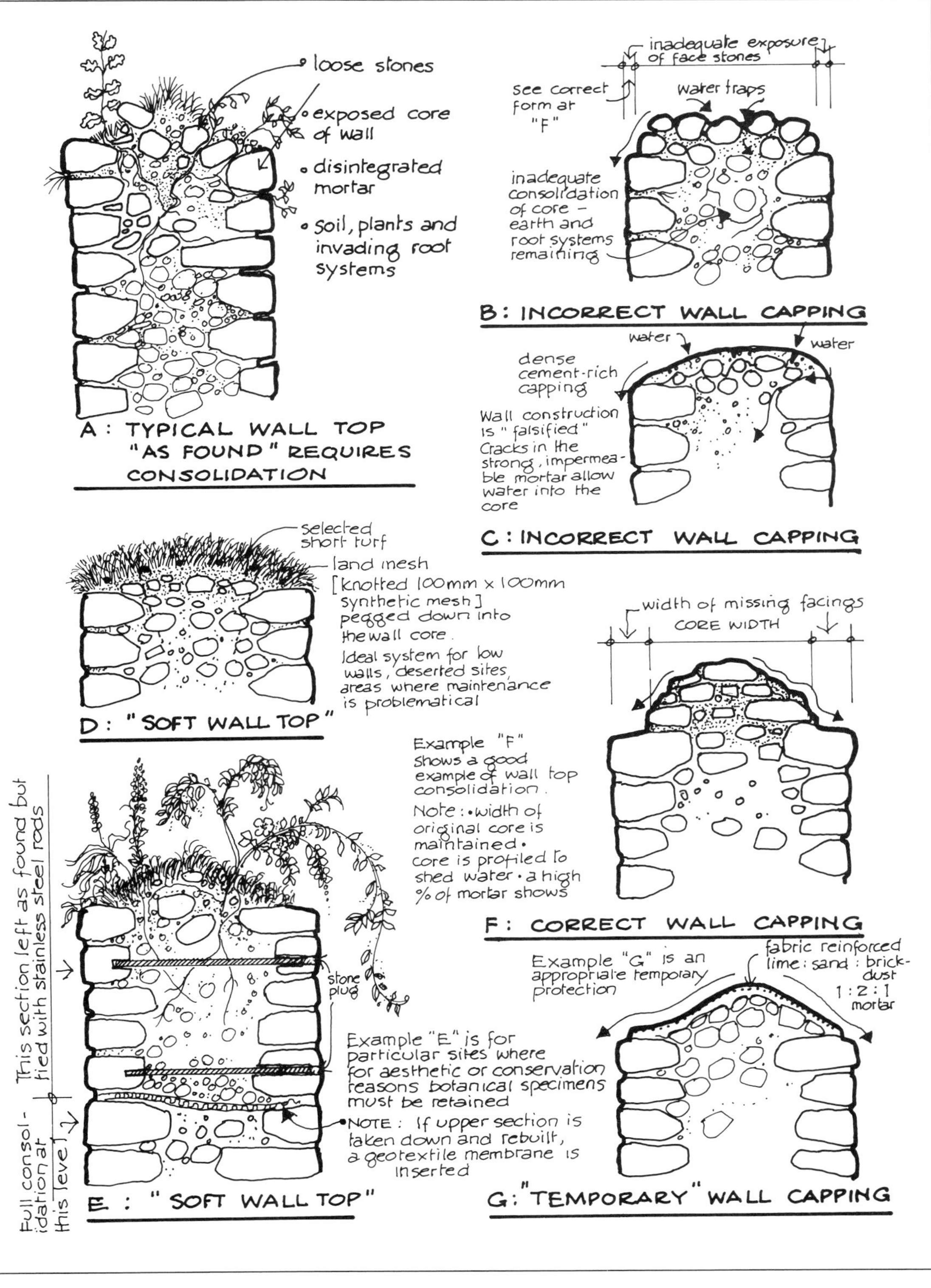
loose stones
exposed core of wall
disintegrated mortar
soil, plants and invading root systems
A : TYPICAL WALL TOP "AS FOUND" REQUIRES CONSOLIDATION
inadequate exposure of face stones
see correct form at "F"
water traps
inadequate consolidation of core – earth and root systems remaining
B : INCORRECT WALL CAPPING
water
water
dense cement-rich capping
Wall construction is "falsified" Cracks in the strong, impermeable mortar allow water into the core
C : INCORRECT WALL CAPPING
selected short turf
land mesh
[knotted 100mm x 100mm synthetic mesh] pegged down into the wall core.
Ideal system for low walls, deserted sites, areas where maintenance is problematical
D : "SOFT WALL TOP"
width of missing facings
CORE WIDTH
Example "F" shows a good example of wall top consolidation.
Note : • width of original core is maintained • core is profiled to shed water • a high % of mortar shows
F : CORRECT WALL CAPPING
This section left as found but tied with stainless steel rods
Full consolidation at this level
stone plug
Example "E" is for particular sites where for aesthetic or conservation reasons botanical specimens must be retained
• NOTE : If upper section is taken down and rebuilt, a geotextile membrane is inserted
E : "SOFT WALL TOP"
Example "G" is an appropriate temporary protection
fabric reinforced lime : sand : brick-dust 1 : 2 : 1 mortar
G : "TEMPORARY" WALL CAPPING

application only, in order to avoid accidental contamination. Site clearance for archaeological investigation may be facilitated and field sites may be kept accessible to visitors by these means. It is worth remembering, however, that the presence of undergrowth, especially brambles, sometimes forms the best and most economic protection of unexplored or only partly explored sites from inquisitive amateurs.

Where walls stand above ground, control of woody weeds may be more essential. Whilst there are many circumstances in which small flowering plants may enhance the appearance of masonry walls without adverse effect, some creepers (especially in maturity) and trees are obviously undesirable. This is because their root systems feed on the wall core and disrupt stones. In particular, ivy (*Hedera helix*) should not be left on walls, because of its rapid growth and the searching effect of its aerial roots. These intrude into joints and rubble fill, converting originally substantial walls into an unstable mass of loose stones and decomposed mortar. In occupied buildings, mature creepers may cut out light, inhibit drying out and obscure the condition of the walls.

Whatever means are employed to kill the disruptive growth, digging out the roots is laborious but inescapable. The survival of even small pockets of woody root may allow the plant to re-establish itself or may create a void in the wall as the organic matter decomposes. Stones will normally have to be lifted out and reset, following the general advice already given. If the plant has its main root system established in the ground (a large ivy, for instance), the following procedure should be adopted.

1. Cut out a 1 metre (3 ft) section of the main stem between 300 mm (1 ft) and 1 metre (3 ft) above ground level, taking care not to let the saw slip against the masonry.
2. Spray the plant with a herbicide such as an ester formulation 2, 4, 5-T, and leave it to die. After the cutting the plant would die of its own accord without the spray treatment, but a well-established specimen might survive between one and two years on the wall.
3. Cut a frill girdle around the parent stem and coat all the exposed surfaces with a paste made from ammonium sulphamate crystals. The root system may then be left to die. This method is preferable to the more traditional process of drilling the stump and pouring in a corrosive acid. If the acid process is used, the drillings must be securely plugged afterwards. Ammonium sulphamate should not be used on masonry surfaces, especially limestone, where, in association with lime, it would become a nitrogenous fertilizer.
4. The dead plant on the wall must be removed carefully. Attempts to pull off well-established plants with a rope are always hazardous and can result in the collapse of walls with weakened cores. Roots in the wall must be cut out and pursued, if necessary, deep into the core. If they are left to decay, voids will be created in the wall, threatening its later stability. Local grouting, wedging of blocks, tamping and resetting of stones must be anticipated in this kind of remedial work.

Coexistence of masonry and plant growth

In some situations botanical specimens, natural habitats and valuable, mature climbing plants of historical/horticultural importance have substantial claims on conservation and may well be valued more highly than the masonry against or on which they are growing. Cooperation between the conflicting interests is a necessary part of the solution. Whilst it is true that vegetation is not generally the friend of historic masonry, it is possible to contrive an acceptable co-existence by planning and control.

In no circumstances should plants be allowed to enter masonry joints, to interrupt the collection and discharge of rain-water or to take hold of a roof. Within this restriction, however, arrangements can be made by judicious cutting back of plants at the right season to introduce a climbing frame against a masonry wall. This should be a light grid of aluminium (painted with epoxide paint) or stainless steel, carefully fixed into joints or plugs in the stones with long expanding stainless steel bolts passing through sleeve spacers. The object of such a construction is to allow the climbing or spreading plant to grow against a screen. A useful gap of 50–100 mm (2–4 in) between the screen and the masonry face can usually be achieved, and the frame facilitates the 'disciplining' of the plant. Although such an installation can be seen as a considerable security risk on occupied historic buildings, it can be argued that mature plants on walls are also a security risk. Climbing grids can be linked to alarm systems.

On ruined sites the need to keep high-level wall tops clear of vegetation has already been made clear. An interesting experiment is currently in hand at Jervaulx Abbey in Yorkshire on lower ruined walls. The Jervaulx site is important botanically, and preservation of the masonry has consisted of consolidating the walls from ground level only up to within three or four courses of the broken wall tops. Consolidation consists of grouting, tamping and pointing to achieve a solid construction. There is a 'soft' wall top containing soil, grass and established flowering plants and small, wild shrubs. Although such wall tops are obviously moisture-holding and there is a frost-risk to the mortar, the experiment is promising. 'Soft' wall tops should not be left on walls over four metres (13 ft) high which are not readily accessible for maintenance.

Treatment of historic masonry

Good masonry practice is not always in harmony with the aims of stone conservation. The trained mason and the owner of an old stone building may be in agreement on the replacement of all heavily weathered, disfigured or damaged stones; the mason's approach may be in the best traditions of repair and maintenance, and the owner may want to see a complete and pristine building. Conservation, however, is about minimum replacement and minimum, or no, restoration.

Cutting out existing stones

In the context of conservation a moderate, sensible balance must be reached between the extensive, speculative restorations of the nineteenth century and the reaction-opinion that to insert any new stone at all in an ancient wall is debasement and dishonesty. The criteria for deciding which stones in an old masonry structure should be replaced include:

1. *The value of the stones.* The intrinsic value of any worked stone in a building varies considerable with the age of the building and the quality and condition of the detail. The approach to a decayed eighteenth century rusticated ashlar is usually, for not very well defined reasons, rather different to the approach to a twelfth century door moulding. The ashlar will certainly involve less speculation if it is replaced than will the medieval detail. The ashlar can usually be replaced with accuracy from well known matching examples.

It is difficult to determine 'value' and to make rules about it. Perhaps it is sufficient to say that copies should not usually be attempted of carving and sculpture too distant from us in time and culture, especially where the original work is characterized by subtle freedom of line and form. Sometimes the value of individual stones, especially in Renaissance and later work, is subordinate to the value of the architectural design of the building. The line of a string with its important, unbroken shadow may be considerable of far more importance than the preservation of a few decayed stones in its length.

2. *The function of the stones.* The function of any stone which is under consideration for replacement must be clearly understood. Decaying stones which have a structural role and on which the stability and survival of other stones or other elements of the structure depend have a clear priority for replacement, almost regardless of their intrinsic value. Typical stones in this category are quoin stones, arch and vault springers and decayed ribs.

Stones which have a protective role provide another essential function. Examples in this category include copings, buttress and plinth weatherings and label mouldings. The replacement of these stones if they are decayed is essential for the survival of the stones below them.

3. *The timing of the replacement.* The expense of a scaffolding is, in itself, an encouragement to replace 'border-line' stones which might or might not survive until the next scaffold access in twenty, fifty or one hundred years. No one in this situation likes to leave a doubtful situation which may require emergency scaffolding a few years after consolidation and repairs had, supposedly, been completed. A.D.R. and M.B. Caroe[1] suggest, in the context of the English parish church, that the life of the stones should be considered in relation to likely scaffold access intervals as follows:

- Low aisles: stones with 25–30 years estimated life should remain.
- Towers: stones with 50–70 years estimated life should remain.
- Spires: stones with at least one hundred years of estimated life should remain.

Estimated life depends entirely on the experience of the architect and his masons, who should use their knowledge to balance their concern for the building with the need to preserve for posterity as much original fabric as possible.

4. *Alternative remedial work.* Alternatives to removing stone must always be considered first. Such measures may simply involve attention to open joints or the provision of a lead flashing or discreet gutter over a label mould and stop. They may also include the removal of an impermeable cement pointing, or a surface treatment designed to protect with a sacrificial layer or deeply penetrating consolidant. In this category, too, may be the design and provision of a protection screen or roof over, for example, a rood or tympanum.

In the face of over-enthusiastic restorationists demanding a new building it should be remembered that it is replacement, not retention of original fabric, that has to be justified.

Once decisions have been made, based on the above criteria, on which stones are to be replaced, these will need to be indicated on a record drawing or photograph, or ideally on a photogrammetric survey drawing. They must also be clearly marked on site with an indelible marker. There is no satisfactory short-cut to on-site marking of individual stones, which is best carried out in the company of a stone mason who will understand the practical implications of cutting back the selected stones. Once a decision has been taken on replacement, the most economical and sensible way of carrying out the work must be determined. In general, new stones will need to be 100 mm (4 in) on bed, unless the stones are very small or only local piecing-in of a larger stone is taking place, but it is often cheaper to remove an old stone completely than to face it with a new 100 mm (4 in) skin. During the marking up procedure notes should also be prepared for the specification of necessary temporary supports which may simply be wooden plates and blocks or, when lintels, arches and vaults are involved, full centering.

The physical process of cutting out the old stone will vary according to the situation. The old stone may still retain some vestige of moulding or carving and it may be retained for a museum. Alternatively, it may be a faceless, scaling lump which is simply to be broken up and disposed of. In either case care is required to ensure that the adjacent surviving stones are not damaged. Cutting of perimeter joints may be carried out with a masonry saw or a diamond cutting disc mounted on a power tool. If the old stone is to be retained the cut will first be made by a diamond disc in the case of a fine joint and hard mortar, or with a plugging chisel in the case of a wide joint and lime mortar. In both cases the cut should be finished with the help of the saw. If the stone is to be wasted it may be drilled out after the initial cutting or broken up with a hammer and chisel.

Smaller-scale piecing in will involve cutting into an existing stone to remove a pocket of decay. Piecings may be very small in good quality work, for example 20 mm (0.8 in) square on face. The cut out must be made with small, sharp chisels and small saw blades to a neat, square profile.

Large stones may be 150 mm (6 in) on bed. Bonders whose tails are to be bedded into core work may be larger. If a large area is to be faced up with new stones it is essential that the new 'skin' should be cramped back with a staggered grid of stainless steel fishtail cramps.

Replacement stones

New stone should match the original as closely as possible. In Chapter 3 criteria relating to selection are discussed. In many cases a substitute stone will have to be found. In these cases some knowledge of the characteristics of original and new stones is necessary. In the UK, the Building Research Establishment has published books on the durability of French and British limestones and British sandstones and Magnesian Limestones.[2].

Stones must be carefully matched to original sizes

Piecing-in

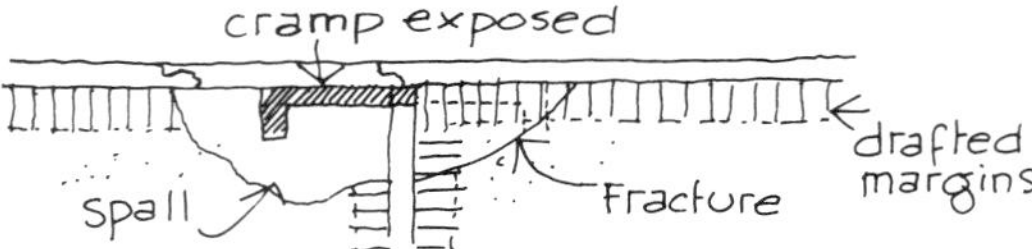

Typical problem Rusting iron cramps cause the splitting and spalling of ashlar faces

Typical solution The spalls, and incipient spalls, are cut out, the cramps removed and substituted and new, matching stone is pieced-in.

Note In a situation of this kind the whole wall should be examined for potential failures. The cramp failure may be isolated due to a positioning too near the wall face or due to a faulty joint which has allowed water to enter locally; alternatively, it may be the first sign of wholescale failures over the wall. The stages described represent the execution of the best quality work. Short cuts may be thought appropriate in any given similar situation, but it is important to remember that short cuts often involve an element of gambling and frequently lead to inaccuracies.

Specification and procedure

1. Determine the overall size of the stone pieces required to make good the damage. Each stone must be repaired independently with no bridging of joints.
2. Select a matching stone for the piecing-in. The stone must be as close as possible to the original in colour, grain size, shell content and other particular characteristics. The pieces must be geologically compatible with the host stones and placed in the same bed. Colour differences which will be corrected by natural weathering should be accepted.
3. Reduce the two pieces for the repair down to the required size with the joint and bed faces finished fine and true (see note 16).
4. Offer the prepared pieces up to the damaged wall and scribe the areas to be cut out using a tungsten tipped or hardened steel scribe and using the new pieces as a template.
5. Cut out the damaged stone with tungsten or fire-sharp tools to expose the cramp, providing a slight undercut to the joint faces. The scribe line should be removed by the cutting tools leaving a sharp, true, clean edge to the socket being formed. Cut round the old cramp with a sharp quirk, lift out the cramp, brush out all rust and scale and form new shoulders for a new cramp.
6. Fix locating pins into the back of the new pieces. The size and number of these pins is determined by the size of the piece to be fixed, but normally there should be a minimum of two. Drill the back of each piece to receive the pins (e.g. 25 mm in a 50 mm piece). Wash out the drill holes to ensure

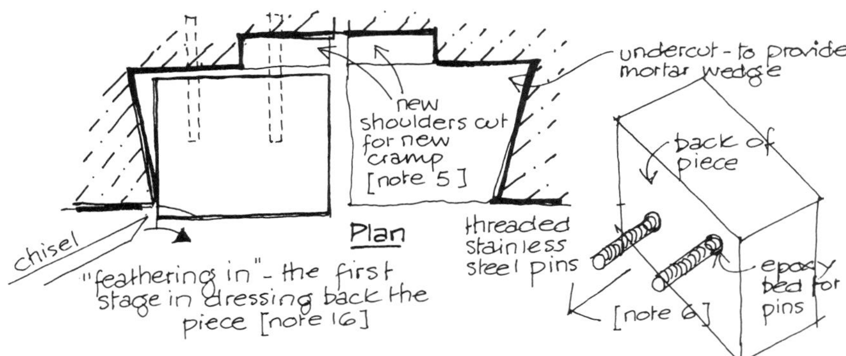

that they are free of dust and that no slurry remains in the holes. Form a template in zinc or hardboard to fit the back of the pieces and mark the position of the holes on the template.

Select and cut to size suitable pins (e.g. threaded stainless steel or ragged phosphor bronze 4–3 mm diameter). On no account should ordinary ferrous pins be used. When the stone pieces are dry, fill the drill holes no more than two-thirds full with a thixotropic epoxy grout such as SBD Epoxy Plus Anchor Grout. Place the template on the back of the piece so that the template holes overlie the holes in the piece, and drop in the pins. The purpose of the template is to hold the pins true and square while the resin cures (e.g. 2–4 hours). Ensure that no displaced resin is in contact with the template.

7. When the resin has cured, offer the pieces up to the socket again. Mark the ends of the newly fixed pins with wax chalk to enable corresponding marks to be transferred to the back of the socket.
8. Drill out the hole positions now marked to a suitable depth to receive the pins (e.g. for a 30 mm pin projection on the back of the piece, drill out 35 mm). Thoroughly remove all dust and slurry from the drill holes and the socket. A hand-held water spray with a fine pencil jet and an off-cut of threaded rod is a good combination to scrape out all the slurry from the holes. It is essential not to rely on washing out alone, as any remaining film of slurry will adversely affect the bond.
9. Offer up the pieces of the socket again to ensure that the fit is good and that the pins are properly aligned. At this stage, final trimming and sharpening of the arrises with a fire-sharp chisel may take place if required.
10. Thoroughly soak the new pieces in clean water.
11. Wet up the joint faces and surrounding faces of stone in the socket using a hand spray and clean water. Ensure, by temporary plugging or other means, that the holes formed for the pins remain dry.
12. Slurry the surfaces of the socket and the pieces which come into close contant with each other. The slurry should be a finely sieved paste of lime putty and white refractory brick dust (suitable for limestone) or hydraulic lime and stone dust (suitable for sandstone) and should, by the choice of fine, staining sands or dusts, endeavour to provide as close a match as possible to the host stone.
13. Fully fill the drill holes with thixotropic epoxy anchor grout.
14. Offer up the slurried piece and ease it into the socket with a sawing motion to ensure full contact of all surfaces until the piece is fully home.
15. Sponge off any slurry on the face of the work at once.
16. After an adequate curing time, which should be at least 24 hours, surface dressing or finishing of the piece may be undertaken. In general, most new pieces will require some dressing at this stage, which may range from simple carborundum rubbing to the full replication of the tooled surface of the host stone. The amount of stone left proud of the surface will be dicated by the finish required. To avoid damage to the edge of the new pieces during tooling back, the edges should first be feathered down flush.

Note Stones should not be bedded in resins. Resins such as the familiar epoxies, polyesters and acrylics set up impervious or relatively impervious barriers against which water in the wall will be checked. Staining and salt crystallization will almost inevitably follow. Quality piecing-in should, in time, be almost indistinguishable from the host stone. Note also that if the wall is to be cleaned, this cleaning should take place before the piecing-in is carried out, to avoid the risk of staining the new pieces.

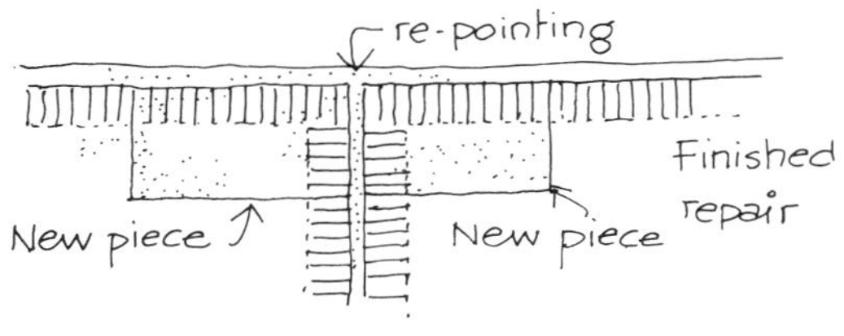

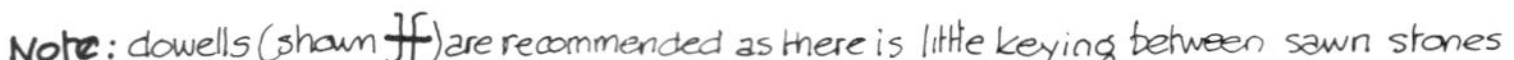

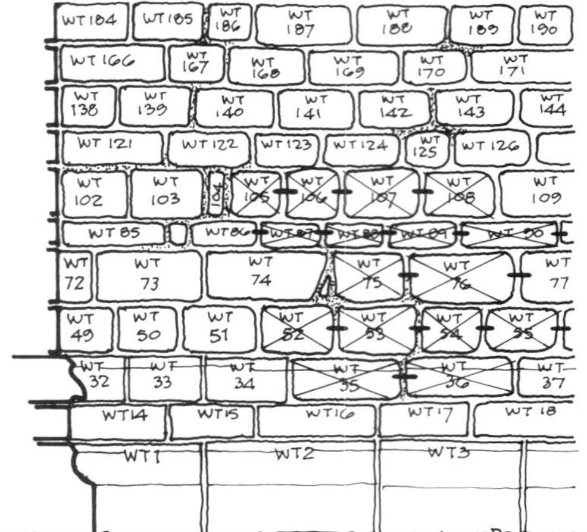

PART ELEVATION Showing all stones identified by a code number on a drawing or survey photograph. The condition of each stone is considered individually and as part of the wall. The crossed stones have decayed extensively and are to be replaced. Areas for pointing are hatched.

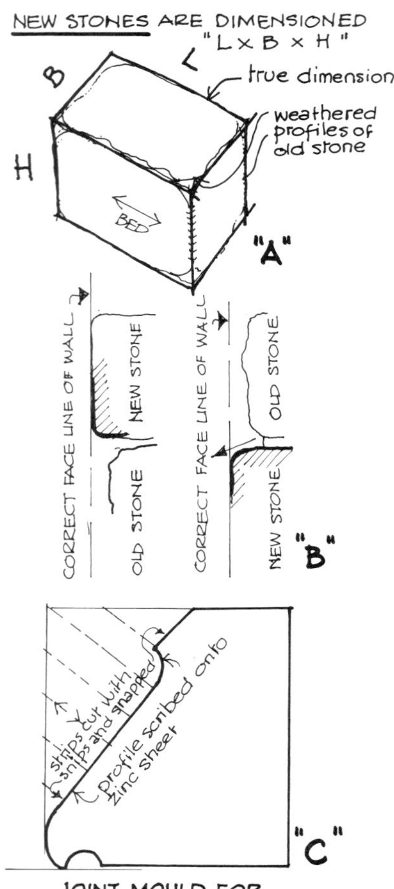

JOINT MOULD FOR WT 35 AND WT 36

STONES are marked insitu for removal with an indelible marker or incision. They are similarly recorded on a survey document. New stone for replacement must be geologically compatible and of similar grain size and colour. Dimensions are taken as "A" and "C". These must be the true dimensions and not weathered or restoration dimensions. Careful note should be made of any surviving tooling, which should be matched on the new stones. If no such evidence survives a fine, textured, rubbed finish is recommended. This is achieved with a hand-held block of the same stone and a uniform size coarse sand abrasive. This will "mellow" the face without artificiality or speculation about tooling patterns. At the very least, all saw marks must be removed. Sharp arrises off the saw can be translated into "pencil-rounds" in the same way to good effect. New stones will stand proud of the old if the correct face line is maintained. Where necessary, water traps in the form of ledges should be subtly weathered off, as at "B", not covered with thick mortar fillets.

CUTTING OUT is generally from the bottom up, a course or part of a course at a time. This will avoid major collapse if a separation between face and corework occurs. The sequence of cutting out, and indenting, is as follows:-

[WT] 35·36·53·55·54·52·76·75·89·87·86·88·70·107·105·106·108·

The method of cutting out is to work from the centre of the stones breaking them with points and chisels and working towards the edge. The cavities should be well-washed out and, if salt migration has been a problem it is recommended that the cavity is lime : sand slurried and bitumen coated.

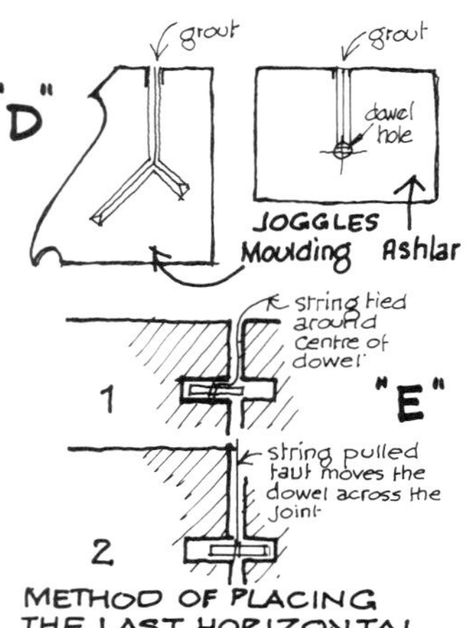

METHOD OF PLACING THE LAST HORIZONTAL DOWEL

JOGGLES AND DOWELS AND CRAMPS tie the stones into each other and to the wall core. Plain ashlars are cut in the joint beds with straight joggles and the moulded stones with Y-joggles. These correspond to horizontal dowell holes as shown at "D" and "E". The top beds of the stones are morticed to receive stainless steel fishtail cramps which are bedded into the core. It is vital not to form skins of consolidated masonry which are not properly bonded or tied back.

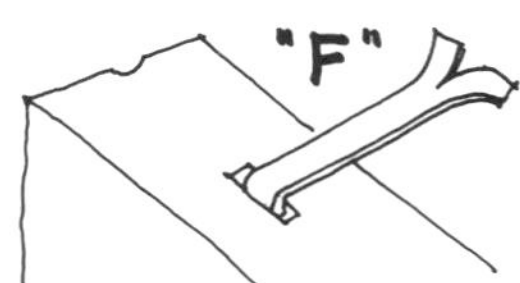

POINTING AND GROUTING are the last stage. The top joint is dry packed while grouting takes place of the final course.

and profiles. Where possible the original finish should be matched, except when, for reasons of historical accuracy, the repair stone is deliberately left to a simpler profile or with a distinctive finish. Sometimes the original profile may not be readily determined, especially when there has been extensive weathering or where there has been a succession of repairs and replacements perhaps over several hundred years. To make a copy of a copy is almost always a mistake, because details can become less and less accurate. In such cases the advice of a competent archaeologist must be sought, so that profiles can be taken from the original stones where possible. Such information may only survive in one small, sheltered area; if so, its value is extremely high and the making of an accurate copy is essential. A profile may be drawn *in situ* directly onto a zinc or tough plastic insert where this can be slipped into a joint carefully sawn out with a small masonry saw. If a joint does not occur in the run of desired moulding a fine saw cut may be made through the moulding itself. In exceptional circumstances it may be necessary to take a squeeze mould in clay and to produce a good cast from which the profile may be taken. From these and from face measurements the bed moulds (plans of the stones) and joint moulds (profiles) can be prepared as drawings and as zinc or acrylic sheet templates. These drawings and templates must be carefully and indelibly marked so that their identity and location are in no doubt. They should be kept safely after the work is complete as part of the building records, and hung or pinned up, not left lying.

Today the replacement stones are sawn to size and may be partly machined to reduce the time which must be spent on hand working. The moulds and templates are then used to mark out the stone in pencil. Further reduction takes place with hammer and punch, mallet and claw tool, mallet and chisel and perhaps drag. As much use as possible may be made of compressed air tools to reduce the time involved. When the stone has progressed with its job card through the production line it should be clearly marked with its job reference and location and packed in polystyrene and straw to protect it from damage during transit and handling. Limestone and marble may receive a temporary protective slurry of lime and stone dust which can easily be cleaned down on completion of fixing. Although straw is a cheap and traditional packing, when wet it can stain light coloured stones. Synthetic packaging is increasingly used, and in many ways is preferable but it must be effective. To spoil expensively produced stones through carelessness is an unforgivable waste of money and shows scant regard for the work which has gone into their production. On arrival at the site the new stones must be stored off the ground (with air spaces between them) to prevent absorption of water and salts from the ground, and with heavy-duty polyethylene sheets over them to avoid saturation from rain.

Placing the new stones

The stones can be raised into position by hand, hoist, or hand winch depending on their weight and location in the building. The cavity or open bed to receive them should be carefully cleaned out and a mortar bed spread onto the wetted old stone. The new stone must also be dampened to avoid the risk of dewatering the mortar. The mortar may be a 12 mm (0.5 in) thick bed with coarse sand and grit to match the original mortar, or no more than a fine buttering with masons' putty. The stone should be handled into position and eased into the correct alignment with the aid of the lubrication provided by the wet mortar. Very heavy stones may have temporary additional support in the form of lead or slate packs. The top bed joint and the perpendicular joints may then be stopped up on the surface with clay ready for grouting. Grout pouring holes and proving holes (exit points to indicate the grout flow) are left in the joints. The grout should be lime with a low sulphate fly ash or lime and a pozzolanic additive such as HTI powder; it must *not* be a cement grout, which is brittle when set, extremely hard and notorious for staining from alkali salts. Mortar staining of new light coloured limestones is a constant problem; the recommended grouts and the protective slurry left on until completion of the work should avoid the worst risks.

Where a background of core or brick cannot, for some reason, be treated with an isolating paint such as sanded bitumen the new stone may itself be painted on all but its face to avoid contamination from salt laden moisture in the old wall. Such a treatment must stop 25 mm (1 in) short of the face to avoid any risk of discoloration from the paint. The condition of the wall, the reason for the decay and likely moisture movements will influence the decision on painting, but it is generally considered to be a sensible procedure.

New stones, when not to be grouted up as described above, must be bedded but not pointed until the work has settled in. If the stone is a sill or lintel the bedding mortar may initially be placed under bearing points only and subsequently tamped and pointed, but this procedure relates principally to new work rather than replacement. Even so, pointing of the outer 25 mm (1 in) should be left until all the bedding work has settled.

Sometimes new stones, or new stone faces, may be spot-secured with an epoxy adhesive. A typical example of this is the halving of decayed mullions in traceried windows, where the decayed stone is cut back to the glass line and half mullions are glued to the face of the surviving internal half. Excellent as modern resin adhesives may be, it is always unwise to rely on the interface bond alone. The halving technique relies, therefore, on dowell pins of stainless steel, phosphor bronze or even glass fibre.

In some situations the use of pins and epoxy mortars has enabled valuable masonry features to be saved which otherwise would have been lost. An illustration of this is the securing of the traceried windows of the Temple Church in Bristol. They were shattered during the blitz of World War II when the roof burnt off as incendiary bombs dropped into the nave and the use of fire hoses produced a thermal shock. Thirty years later the tracery was a fragile jigsaw of pieces retained in position only by rusting ferramenta and softwood corsets bolted together. The alternatives were total replacement or *in situ* stitching together of the pieces. Careful drilling down the length of the mullions and through the tracery bars enabled grouping with an epoxy mortar and stitching with pins of glass fibre to take place. The spalls and lacunae were then built up in phosphor bronze wire and matching mortar. A similar technique was used to hold back the fire-shattered external face of the Norman masonry in Westminster Hall.

The drilling and injection of holes to receive resin and reinforcement requires great care and thoughtful preparation of the site. The viscosity of the resin should permit the drill hole to be filled adequately under the pressure from a gun or a hypodermic syringe. Fine fissures may be grouted with a very thin, low viscosity resin, but the useful mobility of such materials is also a risk; it is not possible to control or to 'pull back' the grout once injected, so adequate precautions must be available in the form of latex paint 'facing', modelling clay for plugging runs, and swabs and solvents. Latex paint can be brushed onto the surface in one or preferably two applications, and can be peeled off on completion of the work.

After holes have been drilled, they must be flushed out with a solvent, or, if drying time is available, with water. Flushing out is best achieved with the same apparatus used to inject the resin. Small holes may sometimes be cleared of dust by blowing out with a small tube. One of the problems especially associated with smaller holes is the entrapment of air when the resin is injected. If a hypodermic syringe is used, a length of tube or plastic drinking straw, cut to the depth of the drilling, can be attached to the end of the hypodermic and filled with resin before insertion into the hole. In this way, the hole will be filled from the deepest point back to the surface. The amount of resin injected into the hole must take account of the displacement that will occur when the reinforcement is inserted. Unless the hole is very small in diameter, the resin should not come too close to the surface. For a hole 6 mm (0.25 in) in diameter, prepared to take a 3 mm (0.125 in) rod, the hole should be injected for approximately two-thirds of its depth. Pins should be sized before injecting resin. The heads of the pins should not be closer to the surface than 6 mm (0.25 in) for small diameters, or 12 mm (0.5 in) for large diameters, allowing the outer 6–12 mm (0.25–0.5 in) to be filled with a fine matching mortar.

Redressing stone

The removal of the original face from the surface of an old stone wall is a drastic process and one that is quite alien to the normal principles of conservation. Although the practice should be resisted while there is any hope of conserving the original face, there are some circumstances when it may be justified—for instance, where the face of the stones has become badly disfigured by blistering, splitting or spalling, or by poor quality, superficial repairs. There are many examples where redressing has taken place on a large scale, especially in the English cities of London and Oxford, where there was no satisfactory alternative. However, there are many other examples where redressing has been used as a cosmetic treatment, with the object of re-introducing uniformity and creating a 'new' appearance. Destruction of an original face for such reasons is always to be discouraged.

Successful redressing demands a high level of expertise, especially where mouldings and columns with entasis are involved. Recent examples of successful redressing can be seen at All Souls College, Oxford, and at Woburn Abbey, England, where the decayed, original clunch face has been taken back with compressed air chisels and hand rubbing. Other redressing tools include combs and drags.

A more sophisticated system for putting a new surface on badly decayed and disfigured limestone was employed recently on a Palladian-style building in Cirenester, England. Ian Constantides (St Blaise Ltd) developed a system with Diamant Boart Ltd based on the latter's standard drilling rig. The system was modified to lock into the scaffold. A two-speed 2.1 kW motor powered the machine which 'dressed' the surface with an electro-plated, diamond-faced grinding disc. Approximately 6 mm of stone was removed from the surface and approximately 12 square metres could be redressed from one position of the rig. Clearly, the use of such a system is limited to simple, flat surfaces and does not eliminate the need to work by hand, but it can produce a very accurate, close finish compatible with the original fine rubbed surface.

There is no technical reason why redressing should not take place, although many masons are opposed to it and E.G. Warland, in his *Modern Practical Masonry*,[3] claims that the quarry sap drying from the freshly quarried block leaves 'a deposit of crystals which fills, or partly fills, the pores of the stone, thus forming a film on the surface. The removal of this film greatly reduces the weathering properties of the stone'. The long history of reworked and redressed stone does not bear out this claim, and Schaffer[4] discounts it altogether. What is certainly true is that weathered stone is usually very tough to work and very demanding on the tools.

The hardening of a freshly quarried stone from the face is a well known phenomenon. The moisture present in the stone contains some of its natural cementing matrix in solution. (This is discussed more fully in Volume 1, page 33.) Traditionally, the more the stone could be worked in its 'green' state, the more receptive it was to cutting and carving. The finished stone would then be seen to harden in a very satisfactory way. If the finished faces of sculpture received a thin plaster of lime gesso while the stone was still drying out, the plaster hardened onto the face and became a superb and very durable ground for polychrome. Traditional practices of this kind, coupled with the failure of thin sulphate skins after exposure to a polluted environment and the observation of powdery stone and small crystals immediately below the skin, are likely to have reinforced the 'essential surface' idea. It would be an easy step to link the relatively tough sulphated surface on a weak limestone with a protective skin provided centuries before.

Redressing of the arrises of sandstone blocks is a common solution to the problems of contour scaling exacerbated by lime leaching from core work through the masonry joints. This situation is typically identifiable by a margin of decay around each stone, sometimes accompanied by efflorescences and splitting parallel with the arrises. Redressing is commonly carried out to improve the appearance and to reduce the occurrence of water traps. However, a curious rusticated appearance may result, or a rough surface patterned with claw or drag marks may be left if the work is carried out by an inexperienced operative. Limited redressing coupled with piecing in with new stone is often a satisfactory compromise.

Wholescale redressing should not be attempted where the stone is weak or of poor quality. There are nearly always alternatives to redressing even in the most problematical situations.

Repairing with tiles

The use of clay tiles as an alternative to piecing in with new stone is of some antiquity but was adopted and developed for philosophical reasons under the influence of the Society for the Protection of Ancient Buildings. The insertion of tiles, bedded in lime mortar and limewashed or left exposed or sometimes rendered, was seen as a way of carrying out an 'honest' and readily identifiable repair which could not be confused with original work. The technique has some specific technical advantages, too.

Powys[5] says: 'The material [tile] is very durable, the surface is plastic and can be modelled to fit adjoining stones, it is so keyed to the stone backing as to become part of it, and the finished texture and colour are not objectionable, and "weather" pleasantly.' In the absence of appropriate stone for repair or the appropriate masonry skills, a further advantage may be claimed in that cutting away and building up in tiles may be carried out with a readily available material using relatively unskilled labour.

Repairs of this kind can be structural or only cosmetic. Complete mullions may be built up in tile, or jambs or quoins may be rebuilt by blockbounding courses of tiles into the stone behind. Alternatively, minor damages or lost faces may simply be covered in tile pieces and rendered. The informal line which Powys describes as the 'plastic surface' and which can be drawn between the heavily weathered faces of adjacent surviving and remaining stones overcomes one of the problems of attempting to marry in a new piece of stone.

Understandably, this repair method does not often appeal to stonemasons nor to many architects and building owners. It may be seen as the thin end of an unattractive wedge, leading to a ridiculous hotch potch of materials which will finally rob a building of its dignity and interest. There is no doubt, however, that tile repairs have saved stones in the past and will continue to do so. The technique has an established place in masonry conservation.

Rendering external masonry surfaces

If there is sound evidence for the existence of external rendering at the period of building then re-rendering in a suitable material may be justified on historical, visual and maintenance grounds. The wall construction of much church building in Britain, for instance, consists of dressed stone quoins, jambs and arches, and areas of random coursed or uncoursed stones which were rendered to keep walls weatherproof. The rendering may have failed and not been replaced, or it may have been deliberately stripped off and all the joints laboriously pointed in ignorance of the original design and intent or merely for visual preference. There is often a temptation to remove rendering from old walls, especially when extensive, ugly patching up has been carried out in a dense mortar; indeed if an old wall has been re-rendered with an impermeable cement-rich mortar it is often good sense to remove it and replace it with a more permeable lime render. Dense renders always crack and admit water into the body of the wall. The water cannot escape except, perhaps, through the inside face. Successful rendering must inhibit the direct penetration of water through the joints but be capable of absorbing and then yielding moisture through evaporation without detaching from the wall surface.

Matching the rendering

Careful study should be made of what original, or likely original, plaster survives. If the evidence is slight it may be difficult to tell if a thin or a thick rendering existed or if, as is so often the case with undressed or roughly dressed stones, the thick mortar joints were simply extended as a slurry over most of the stone face. In these cases the line of any dressed quoin or jamb stones in relation to the infill masonry may be some guide, as may be other buildings of similar age and construction in the area. In some cases the rendering may have extended over dressed stones as well as infill, although not usually over mouldings. Some help may be found from old paintings or prints.

Surviving areas of render may be analysed to determine binder:aggregate ratios and to assist in the identification of aggregates for matching purposes. The design of new rendering, however, although seeking to be a good visual match for the old, should be based more on known good practice than on results of analysis. Samples of the new rendering should be laid on the wall and approved when dry for colour and texture.

Preparing the wall

Preparation procedures for most situations tend to follow the same principles. They may be summarized as follows:

1. Brush down all wall surfaces with a stiff bristle or non-ferrous wire brush to remove scales, loose mortar and algae and lichen. Wash off with mains-pressure water through a hose, or high-pressure water through a lance. When dry, treat with a biocide.
   Or de-scale walls with a high-pressure, low-volume water lance at 500 psi to remove all loose scale and loose mortar. When dry, treat with a biocide.
   Or clean all wall surfaces with a wet-head system compressed air and abrasive to remove all loose scale and loose mortar. Finish the work by flushing with water alone. When dry, treat with a biocide.
2. Deep tamp all open joints with lime mortar. Dub out cavities in lime mortar and small stones or pieces of clay tile, leaving a rough surface for keying to the render.
3. Form a bridging over wood, metal, concrete (or other material which is significantly dissimilar in porosity to the general background) with stainless steel expanded metal secured with stainless steel screws and washers, *or* with a spatterdash coat of hydraulic lime aggregate; 50% of the material should be of approximately 5 mm (0.2 in) size, the remainder graded down.
4. Thoroughly dampen the substrate immediately before applying the undercoat and all subsequent coats with water from a hose or lance to cut down the risks of suction and de-watering the rendering mix.

Mixes for rendering

Although the variations on substrate and exposure combinations are endless, some typical situations which involve rendering stone surfaces include:

1. Thick, rough textured rendering on sound stone rubble.
2. Thin, smooth textured rendering on sound stone rubble.
3. Rendering on weak, friable backgrounds.
4. Rendering on strong, impermeable backgrounds.

Thick, rough textured renderings have the best chance of survival when correctly specified. They have good drying-out characteristics and are least susceptible to shrink crazing and cracking. Two or three coats are usual for masonry.

Thin, smooth textured rendering on sound stone rubble may be carried out in the same mixes but in one or two coats only and omitting the stones and some of the hair. The principal differences are in some of the application techniques, described below. The render coat thickness and finishing coat should be in the order of 6–9 mm and 4–6 mm respectively.

Rendering on weak, friable backgrounds presents particular problems of adhesion which can only satisfactorily be overcome with the aid of fabric reinforcement and anchors. Mixes should be of the lime type only, as above, but if the exposure is moderate to severe the HTI proportion may be doubled and the lime:aggregate ratio kept at 1:2.5 for render and finishing coats. Reinforcement in the form of stainless steel or other expanded metal is possible but will necessitate a greater thickness of rendering than may be desirable. An alkali-resistant glass fibre woven fabric, with anchors into masonry joints, is therefore recommended.

Table 1.1 Mixes for thick, rough textured renderings

Type one: Cement compo. These may be used on sound backings in quite severe exposures.

		Cement	*Lime*	*Aggregates (sharp sand, pebbles and small stones) Sand:stones*
Render coat (up to 9 mm (3/8 in) thick)		1	1	6:0
Floating coat (up to 9 mm (3/8 in) thick)		1	1	6:0
Butter coat	*either*	1	1	6:0
	or	1	2	9:0
Finishing coat	*either*	1	1	3:3
	or	1	2	5:4

The butter and finishing coats combined can be up to 12 mm (1/2 in) thick.

Type two: Hydraulic lime. These mixes may be used on slightly weaker backgrounds in moderate to severe exposures.

	Cement	*Hydraulic lime*	*Aggregates Sand:stones*
Render coat (up to 9 mm (3/8 in) thick)	0.5	2	5:0
Floating coat (up to 9 mm (3/8 in) thick)	–	2	5:0
Butter coat	–	2	5:0
Finishing coat	–	2	3:3

The butter and finishing coats combined can be up to 12 mm (1/2 in) thick.

Type three. Lime. These mixes may be used on weak to moderately strong backgrounds in sheltered to moderate exposures.

	Lime	*Pozzolanic additive (HTI)*	*Aggregate Sand:stones*
Render coat (up to 9 mm (3/8 in) thick)	1	0.1	2.5:0

A hair or synthetic alkali resistant fibre reinforcement is often to be recommended, beaten in to the render coat at 5 kg/m^3 of coarse stuff (lime:sand). The hair must be clean, well combed (natural hair) and chopped to 50 mm to 150 mm lengths.

	Lime	*Pozzolanic additive (HTI)*	*Aggregate Sand:stones*
Floating coat (up to 9 mm (3/8 in) thick)	1	0.1	3:0
Finishing coat	1	–	2:1

The lime rendering would traditionally be limewashed (see Appendix 1).

Table 1.2 Mixes for thin, smoother renderings

Type one: Two coat

	Pozzolanic additive (HTI)	*Lime*	*Aggregates (fine sharp sand and stone dust)*
Render coat	1/2	1	2
Finish coat	1/4	1	2

Type two : One coat

	Pozzolanic additive (buff coloured brick dust	*Lime*	*Aggregates (fine sharp sand and stone dust)*
	1/2	1	1 1/2

Rendering on strong, rather impermeable backgrounds such as granite, basalt or flint is often, mistakenly, carried out in dense, cement-rich mixes. In these cases, although the strong mortar will not damage the background, an inefficient rendering results which lets water in through shrinkage and movement cracks and traps it in the wall. Adhesion is often poor initially and these dense renderings tend to detach in large areas. Unless an overall backing of stainless steel expanded metal is used, a haired or fibre reinforced undercoat is recommended on a spatterdash render coat. PVA (polyvinyl acetate) bonding agents are often used to overcome the natural bonding problem, but bonding agents based on SBR (styrene butadiene rubber) are preferred in conditions which are likely to remain permanently damp. Type one, two or three mixes may be used as appropriate to the exposure, but types two or three are preferable. Suitable mixes are given in Tables 1.1 and 1.2.

Techniques of mixing and application

Storage of lime putty and aggregates in wet, air-tight conditions is strongly recommended, unless hydraulic lime is used. Hydraulic lime and sand must be mixed together dry before water is added. Cement or HTI powder must only be added to wet lime putty and sand mixtures just before use. Hair or fibre should be beaten into the wet mix when appropriate, chopped to lengths and added to quantities as specified above. Water ratios must be kept as low as possible.

Typical procedures are described below for the thick, rough textured rendering and the thin, comparatively smooth textured rendering which are likely to be found covering rubble masonry.

Rough textured rendering

This is also known as rough-cast, wet-dash or harling.

1. Prepare the wall.
2. *For patch repairs*. Cut out detached and bulging areas to regular, square-edged shapes, preferably between architectural elements before preparing the wall.
3. Apply a rendering coat with a laying-on trowel on to a damp substrate to the general levels required but not exceeding a 9 mm (3/8 in) thickness. Iron the coat hard on to the wall and finish with a comb scratcher to provide a key.
4. Protect the rendering coat from rain and hot sunshine or direct draughts. Allow to dry as slowly as possible and ensure that the coat has completely dried out before the next stage.
5. Wet up the rendering coat with a hose and spray attachment sufficient to ensure a damp substrate.
6. Apply a floating coat with a laying-on trowel to the damp substrate and finish with a comb scratcher to provide a key.
7. Repeat stage 4.
8. Repeat stage 5 on the floating coat.
9. Apply a butter coat to aid the adhesion of dashed material to the damp substrate with a laying-on trowel. While the butter coat is still soft and sticky, throw on the finishing material from a board or shallow box using a dashing trowel with a wrist flicking action. As large an area as possible should be covered in one operation. If a wall must be divided up by day working limitations, every attempt must be made to work between plinth and eaves, or between windows. Accidental bunching up of aggregates should not be corrected by attempting to spread the stones out with a trowel but by taking off, re-buttering and re-dashing.
10. Repeat stage 4.
11. Limewash if required.

A different finishing coat, which is simply a coarse textured version of the render and float coats, can be substituted for the butter coat. The finishing coat should be about 6 mm (1/4 in thick, finished either with a cross-grained wood float or about 10 mm (3/8–1/2 in) and scraped down with a fine-toothed saw blade after a slight stiffening of the rendering has begun to take place. The latter technique is a common continental practice which has the advantage of removing any slight surface shrink crazing and any patchiness in the form of laitence, leaving a uniform, slightly rough textured face.

Smooth textured, thin rendering

Whereas the thick rendering may cover all but the most prominent irregularities, thin renderings spread over rubble between dressed stones will show much of the form of the stones underneath.

1. Prepare the wall.
2. For patch repairs follow stage 2.
3. Ensure that the substrate is damp enough not to de-water the thin render. Iron on one thin coat of lime and sand gauged with HTI powder (see Table 1.1) with a small trowel, pressing hard into all contours of the wall. Compaction is absolutely essential to the success of the render. Work is necessarily slow, and re-wetting of the substrate may be necessary. Protect the work area from strong sunlight.
4. Press on with pads of damp sacking or other coarse, absorbent cloth. This technique leaves a slightly rough texture.

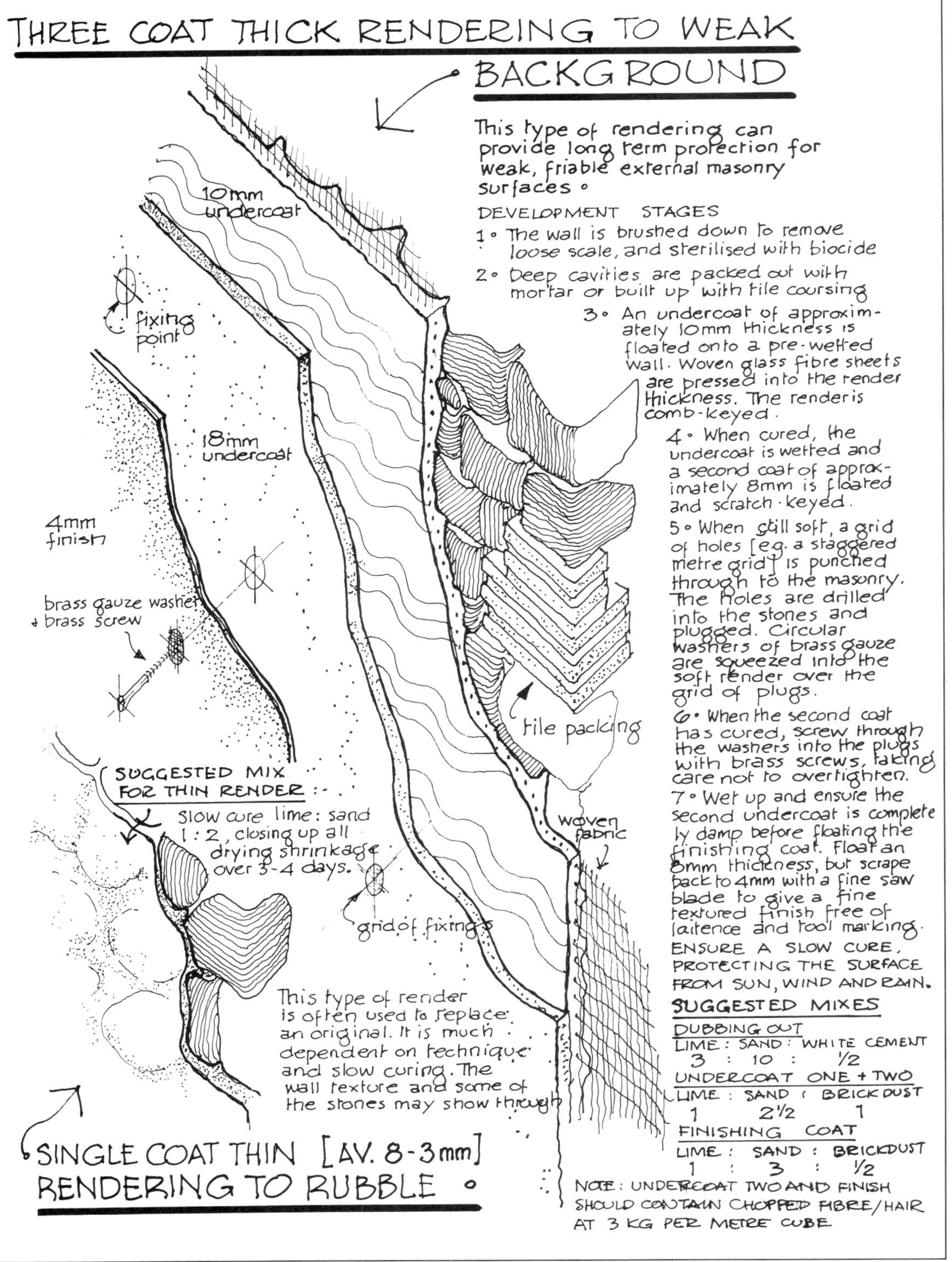

THREE COAT THICK RENDERING TO WEAK BACKGROUND
This type of rendering can provide long term protection for weak, friable external masonry surfaces.
DEVELOPMENT STAGES
1. The wall is brushed down to remove loose scale, and sterilised with biocide
2. Deep cavities are packed out with mortar or built up with tile coursing
3. An undercoat of approximately 10mm thickness is floated onto a pre-wetted wall. Woven glass fibre sheets are pressed into the render thickness. The render is comb-keyed.
4. When cured, the undercoat is wetted and a second coat of approximately 8mm is floated and scratch-keyed.
5. When still soft, a grid of holes [eg. a staggered metre grid] is punched through to the masonry. The holes are drilled into the stones and plugged. Circular washers of brass gauze are squeezed into the soft render over the grid of plugs.
6. When the second coat has cured, screw through the washers into the plugs with brass screws, taking care not to overtighten.
7. Wet up and ensure the second undercoat is completely damp before floating the finishing coat. Float an 8mm thickness, but scrape back to 4mm with a fine saw blade to give a fine textured finish free of laitence and tool marking.
ENSURE A SLOW CURE, PROTECTING THE SURFACE FROM SUN, WIND AND RAIN.
SUGGESTED MIXES
DUBBING OUT
LIME : SAND : WHITE CEMENT
3 : 10 : 1/2
UNDERCOAT ONE + TWO
LIME : SAND : BRICKDUST
1 : 2 1/2 : 1
FINISHING COAT
LIME : SAND : BRICKDUST
1 : 3 : 1/2
NOTE: UNDERCOAT TWO AND FINISH SHOULD CONTAIN CHOPPED FIBRE/HAIR AT 3 KG PER METRE CUBE
10mm undercoat
18mm undercoat
4mm finish
fixing point
brass gauze washer + brass screw
tile packing
woven fabric
grid of fixings
SUGGESTED MIX FOR THIN RENDER:
slow cure lime : sand 1 : 2, closing up all drying shrinkage over 3-4 days.
This type of render is often used to replace an original. It is much dependent on technique and slow curing. The wall texture and some of the stones may show through
SINGLE COAT THIN [AV. 8-3mm] RENDERING TO RUBBLE.

5. Ensure that the work is protected from rapid drying, if necessary by laying on thin, damp cloths or cotton wool. See also description of the lime method in Chapter 9.

Painting rendering

If the colour of a rendering can be satisfactorily achieved as the result of selection of aggregates, this is obviously preferable to introducing any form of paint. Where applied colour is necessary to follow existing conditions, the new rendering must be dried out completely before application. In average drying conditions, protecting the work from rain and direct sunlight, a 25 mm (1 in) thickness of rendering will take about four weeks to dry. Paint systems which can be applied to new rendering soon after this period are:

Limewashes
Lime casein paints
Distemper (size-bound)
Distemper (oil-bound)
Cement paints
Emulsions
Silicate paints

These paints are also likely to be the most suitable for matching early surviving examples. Paints which provide a tough, impervious envelope, especially those which are sprayed on, should always be avoided for historic buildings both on grounds of appearance and because no envelope can ever be complete. Water and salt trapped behind a tough paint film will result in loss of adhesion and can increase dampness in a building and the risk of persistent deterioration behind the paint.

Painting stone direct

If the stone is to be painted or limewashed directly, the substrate should be prepared in the same way as for rendering. Similarly the paint system used should be from the list given above. Limewash is likely to be the most usual finish (see Appendix 1). Paint systems on masonry must, as an absolute minimum requirement, be vapour permeable. In the past, soiled or disfigured masonry has sometimes been painted to improve the appearance, and the same temptation will sometimes persuade building owners to cover up a problem, especially where cleaning has failed. Whilst this is not a course of action to be recommended, if there is no acceptable alternative a system must be selected which can be removed without abrasion or caustic strippers.

Repair with mortars

Repair of stone with mortars, or plastic repair as it is traditionally known, is useful to conservators of stone as an alternative to cutting out and piecing in with new stone. Unfortunately the reputation of such repairs has suffered from inadequate specification, misuse and inexpert handling. Plastic repair is thought of as a cheap option to repairing with stone, but the cheapness relates very often to poor quality workmanship. Properly prepared and placed plastic repair is not cheap, except that its use may sometimes mean the avoidance of such expensive items as temporary supports for vault and arch stone replacements or reduce the amount of cutting out required.

Plastic repairs are of particular interest and importance to conservators because the technique frequently permits the retention of more original material with much less disturbance than would be possible for the execution of conventional masonry repairs. In this respect the familiar description of the method as 'dentistry repair' is very apt. The careful removal of decayed material, the cleaning and sterilization of the cavity and the placing, compaction and finishing of the amalgam are common to the repair of both teeth and stone. The analogy may be extended further; if careless filling of imperfectly prepared cavities is carried out much energy and expenditure will have been wasted and failure will occur in a predictably short time.

Failure of plastic repairs may be both cosmetic and mechanical. In particular, mortar repair material coloured with pigments, or feather-edged to ragged areas of decay or finished with steel trowels, is often visually disastrous. Over-strong mortars, mortars relying on bonding agents instead of mechanical keying, or large surface areas in exposed positions, will be mechanical failures.

Although there are exceptions, plastic repair should always be carried out by a stone mason or a stone conservator, because their familiarity with the material should give them a feeling for the repair which other trades and disciplines will not necessarily have.

The following criteria will affect the decision to use a plastic repair.

1. Will the use of mortar enable more original material to be retained than if stone is used?
2. Will the use of mortar avoid disturbing critically fragile areas?
3. Will the use of mortar avoid the removal of structural elements such as vault or other arch voussoirs?
4. Will mortar perform satisfactorily in the intended context, i.e. is it capable of weathering adequately? Would cast stone be more appropriate?

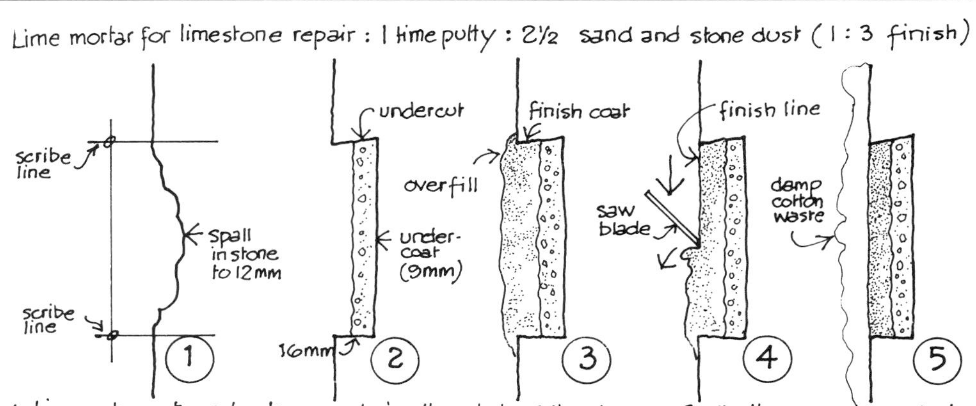

1 Line out a rectangular shape enclosing the whole of the damage. Scribe the area using a steel rule.
2 Using fire-sharp small chisels, cut back to a uniform sinking of 16mm, undercutting at the top and sides. Wet up the cavity and fill to 9mm with backing mortar. Iron in hard, cover and allow to cure slowly.
3 Wet up the remaining cavity and overfill with finishing mortar, ironing in hard until no shrinkage appears. Ironing may be repeated over 2-3 days with non-setting (non-hydraulic) lime
4 Scrape back with a fine hacksaw blade to finished line, leaving a laitence-free, uniform texture
5 Cover with damp cotton waste and allow to cure slowly.

PATCH REPAIR OF STONE USING MORTAR

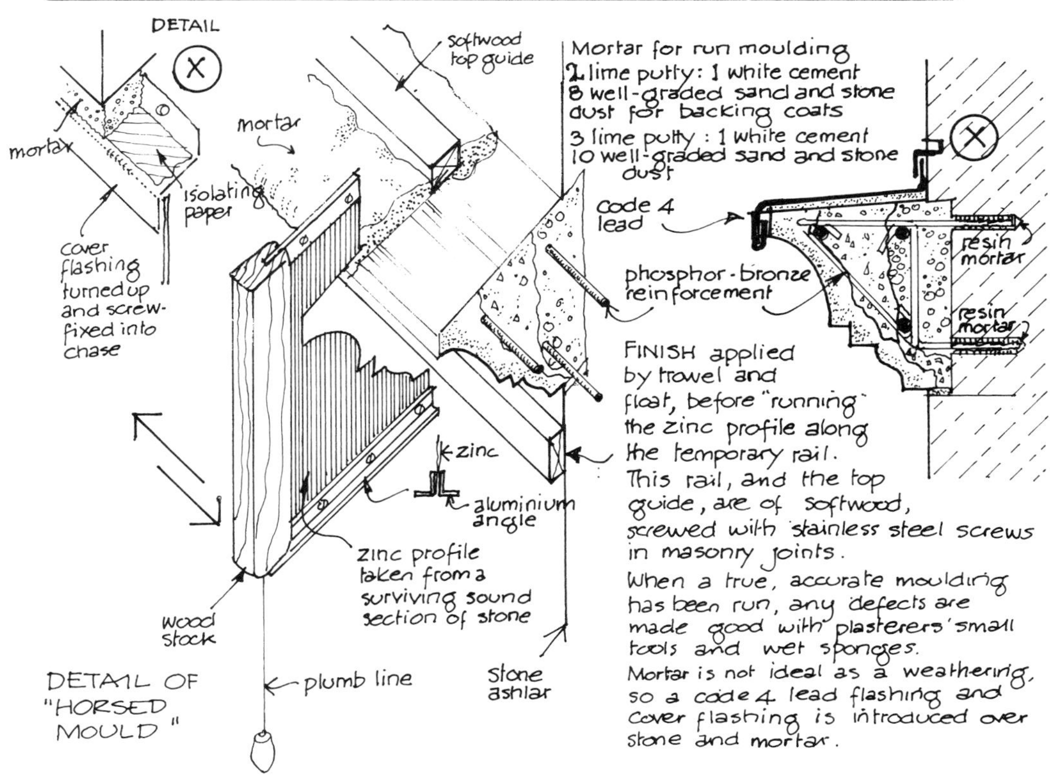

REPAIR OF MOULDING USING MORTAR

5. Are the areas to be repaired small enough to be repaired with mortar? Would rendering be more appropriate or should a large replacement of stone with matching stone be accepted?
6. Will mortar provide a visually better repair than new stone in the context of heavily weathered, softened outlines?
7. Are the appropriate skills available to produce high quality mortar repairs?

If, after consideration of these factors, it is decided to proceed with mortar repairs, wholly or partially, the following procedures should be put into operation.

1. Prepare a schedule of stones to be repaired with mortar or with stone.
2. Prepare samples of mortar to match the various conditions of weathering on the building. Weathered stones exhibit a subtle variety of colour which must be matched in the repairs. Much plastic repair suffers from an unnatural uniformity. The repairs must be prepared as samples on a piece of stone or tile, not in a wooden mould.
3. Cut out the decayed areas.
4. Wash and sterilize the cavity with water and formalin.
5. Saturate the cavity with water using handsprays to prevent dewatering of the repair mortar.
6. Place the selected repair mortar, compacting in layers not exceeding 9 mm (3/8 in) in thickness in any one application. Allow each layer to dry out before rewetting and placing the next layer.
7. In cavities exceeding 50 mm (2 in) in depth and extending over 50 mm (2 in) square surface area, drill and fix non-ferrous or stainless steel reinforcements. These may vary between simple pins and armatures. The most common materials are copper, phosphor bronze and stainless steel wire. After drilling to receive the reinforcement the holes are filled with an epoxy mortar before embedding the wire; 18 mm (0.7 in) of cover should be allowed for any reinforcement.
8. The repair may be finished directly to the required profile using a wood or felt-covered float, or with a damp sponge or coarse cloth. Ingenuity will provide other finishing tools appropriate to the texture of the finish required. Unsuitable tools to be avoided are steel trowels or dry, absorbent pads. Steel trowels will leave an undesirable and unnatural laitence on the surface, and absorbent pads will risk the removal of water from the repair too soon. An alternative repair finishing method is to build the repair up proud of the required profile and then to work it back after an initial set has commenced on the surface with a fine saw blade or purpose-made scrapers.

Mortar repairs must be protected from direct sun or other rapid drying conditions. This may be achieved with damp cotton wool pads on small-scale repairs or with damp sacks on larger areas. Care taken during preparation and after placing of the repair will avoid one of the most common problems associated with this kind of work, the appearance of fine shrinkage cracks during drying.

Different mixes may not always provide quite the variation in colour required. In this situation, stone dusts may be added to the face of the repair before a set commences. This is very skilled work and is best avoided unless the repairer is particularly skilled. This and other aspects of high quality mortar repair, especially of limestone, are described in detail in Chapter 4.

A number of proprietary mortar repairs are available. Some of these have proved to behave well on weathering and they may be useful where on-site matching expertise is questionable. Unfortunately, to be successful, the repair mix has to be matched in a laboratory to samples of stone provided by the client, and it is difficult to vary the potential strength of the repair. A match which involved a number of site visits from a laboratory would become very costly. There is no doubt that the most desirable way of forming mortar repairs is to use on-site expertise throughout.

It should be noted that while most of the plastic repair mortars are based on a lime binder, repairs to sandstones may be better carried out using a cement binder and a plasticizer, or a masonry cement. This is because sandstone which is already decaying may further deteriorate in the presence of lime washing into the edges of the prepared cavities. This problem is described in Volume 1, Chapter 7, in the context of incompatibility of sandstones and limestones. A comparison of mortars of equivalent strengths is given below, using a variety of binders.

Plasticizer	*Portland cement*	*Lime*	*Masonry cement*	*Aggregates*
–	1	3	–	10
yes	1	–	–	8
–	–	–	1	7

The high proportion of aggregate to binder in the cement:aggregate mixes is a further advantage when matching a strong coloured sandstone. The mortar mixes need not be as strong as shown above for many small-scale repairs, but preparation must always ensure that the grains of sand and stone dust are adequately coated with the binder paste.

Although plastic repairs should not be used for areas of extreme exposure it may be possible to use them in strings and cornices if a lead flashing is provided as well. A limited amount of experience indicates that plastic repairs of exposed elements such as balustraded parapets may perform well if they are subsequently treated with a catalysed silane consolidant.

Plastic repair using resin binders

Whilst it is true that some of the worst mortar repairs in the last decade have been those based on epoxy mortars, there is an important potential in the use of resin binders, especially for the dentistry repair of sandstones. In particular, Mr Jack Heiman of the former Commonwealth Experimental Building Station in Sydney, Australia, has carried out preliminary studies on epoxy/quartz sand blends using very small proportions of epoxy (for example 1:12, 1:16 resin:sand by weight). The performance of these mortars in Australia and in Britain is currently being compared with the performance of sandstone originals, especially in conditions of wetting and drying, heating and cooling and during salt crystallization cycling. In general, behaviour of the resin-bound sandstone mimics is much closer to original sandstone than mimics with cementitious paste binders. The appearance, too, is much better than traditional lime/cement based repairs, as the full colour potential of the aggregate can be exploited. The permeable resin mortar, carefully matched and properly cut in, avoiding feathering, has an undoubted role to play in dentistry repair.

Replacement with cast stone

The British Standard (BS 1217:1975) specification for cast stone defines it as 'any product manufactured from aggregate and cement and intended to resemble in appearance and be used in a similar way to natural stone.' Although there are no savings on on-site labour or on disruption for fixing when cast stone is used in place of natural stone, economies are achieved when repetitive elements need to be produced. In some situations, cast stone may be preferable to natural stone for the replacement of copings, ridges and chimney caps where the environment is particularly demanding and aggressive. Cast stone has also been used extensively in England as a substitute for some forms of stone slate. Casts of varying quality have also been used extensively as *in situ* replacements for sculpture which has been removed to some place of safety.

Cast stone used as a building element may either be homogeneous or may consist of a facing material and a backing concrete. Where reinforcement is included for structural or handling purposes it is recommended that this is stainless steel or bronze alloy with a minimum 10 mm (0.4 in) of cover. If untreated mild steel or even galvanised steel is used, a cover of 30 mm (1.2 in) is recommended.

Good cast stone can be immensely durable but it is subject to the same weathering processes and, eventually, to similar forms of decay as natural stone. Unfortunately its appearance is liable to become less and less stone-like with passing years and its very durability will count against it visually unless the surface is masked by organic growth. The repetitive precision of replacement mullions or balusters in cast stone can be very detrimental aesthetically in a weathered stone facade. Cast replacements of sculptural elements are sometimes desirable for architectural completeness or as landscape features; in such cases the most important point is that the original is not stained or damaged by the moulding process, and a careful inspection must determine how safe the operation will be. It may be necessary to consolidate the original to enable it to be used in this way (see Chapter 9). A silicone rubber is recommended as the moulding medium. Individual moulds should be kept to as small as sensibly possible, especially where there is undercut detail, and the surface should be treated with a barrier which will not stain. Liquid detergent has been found safer in this respect than many proprietary barrier treatments. A good quality cast should always be made and retained for further moulding processes, because the moulds themselves will deteriorate with age and use, even when kept in rigid 'mother mould' casing. The original should not need to be subjected to the hazards, however small, of moulding more than once. Some cast replacements are, of themselves, of considerable interest beause of their age or originality.

Providing protection

Providing protection on the building should always be considered as an alternative to repair or replacement. Protection may be in the form of a new architectural element such as a small roof over a piece of sculpture or a complete porch over a door. Care must be taken that the new element does not create additional problems, such as run-off from new roofs creating drip and splash patterns, or undesirable changes in relative humidity at different times of the year, especially under glass, polycarbonate or other plastic sheet. Occasionally the cover may be a complete new structure in itself, such as that proposed for Sueno's stone in Aberdeenshire, or in a ruined building a new roof may be put back on the line of the old, as at Howden Minster Chapter House with long term beneficial results for the carved and sculpted stones inside. These are, of course, important architectural decisions as well as protective measures and must be fully and professionally assessed.

Protection in the form of lead dressings is a much simpler expedient which may be introduced discreetly to assist stone elements with a particularly difficult weathering job to do. Thus a Code 4 flashing may be dressed over a small string, label mould or transom neatly fixed into a carefully prepared chase, or in ruined buildings a Code 5 lead cap may, for instance, be dressed over the exposed top of a tas-de-charge. The unique ability of lead to take up, through careful bossing, the informal, soft outlines of weathered or damaged stone is particularly useful. Modest expenditure on protective flashing and capping may secure much valuable detail if thoughtfully placed and skilfully executed. Partially damaged strings or other projections may sometimes be built up in mortar with minimum disturbance if a lead flashing is subsequently run along the top. Fixing and detailing is, however, critical to performance and appearance.

Grouting

Grouting is the introduction of a binding agent in the form of liquid into masonry or soil. The first recorded use of grouting in the UK was in 1876. Previously, sand-lime slurries were used in France (by Bengay, in 1802) and in Germany (Hamburg, *circa* 1840). Pressure grouting was used in mining activity in France in 1886. In 1896, the Belgian, Albert François, developed a method of drilling and injecting from within a shaft, the process which became known as the François Cementation process, subsequently introduced into the UK in 1909.

Grouting by hand or machine has been a traditional method of consolidating the fabric of monuments since the 1920s. In the early years, liquid Portland cement with a fine sand filler was used, but this has a number of disadvantages. Portland cement grouts do not have good flow properties, shrink on setting and are brittle when set. Wet cement grouts will also introduce undesirable amounts of sodium salts in masonry and should never be used in the vicinity of wall paintings or sculpture. Low sulphate fly ash and lime, sometimes combined with wetting agents and penetration aids, have much better characteristics with fewer risks, and are now in common use.

Grouting masonry walls

The consolidation of historic masonry often involves the need to stabilize walls by filling voids within their thickness. This operation is most commonly needed when thick walls of double skin construction, with rubble core filling, have been subjected to the percolation of water for many years. The tendency of this washing action is to cause the mortar (often of poor quality in fills) to disintegrate and either to wash out of open joints, or to accumulate as loose fill at the base of the wall or pier. This sometimes causes bulging, cracking and displacement of stones. The absence of such evidence on the face, however, should not be taken to indicate a solid and stable condition within. Disintegrated joints must always be raked out and probed for voids. 'Sounding' with a hammer can be carried out to test for hollows. The removal of selected face stones and the drilling behind of deep cores of, say, 100 mm (4 in) diameter are other ways of testing for voids. Hole fillers can often be conveniently removed to allow for exploratory coring.

Detailed investigations

In special circumstances, especially where large areas are involved, it may be advisable to commission a detailed specialist investigation of some typical areas where voids, or internal fractures, are suspected. Examination may be by gamma radiography (X-ray), or by ultrasonic measurements. Both methods of investigation require scaffolding for measurements above ground level. X-rays penetrate about 450 mm (6 in) through masonry, but this range can be extended by drilling pilot holes or by removing some of the face stones. During the working period, the site must be properly roped off, with warning signs displayed, and the Local Authority informed. Night working may be necessary.

Ultrasonic methods of testing for voids and moisture are more versatile than X-ray, but require interpretation. Once a datum signal has been established through a known solid section of the wall, such as a door or window jamb, other measurements may be taken through the wall on, say, a 200 mm (8in) grid. In this way the pattern of void can be established over the elevation.

Grouting techniques

The use of liquid grout avoids dismantling and rebuilding defective masonry in many cases. In its simplest form, grouting may be carried out by hand by pouring liquid grout into clay grout cups on the face of a wall. However, this method is only applicable to small, local voids. There is a choice of three basic methods:

1. Gravity systems
2. Hand or mechanical pumped systems
3. Vacuum systems

The choice of system is dictated by the nature and condition of the masonry. Gravity grouting is particularly suitable where the masonry is very vulnerable to movement under pressure. Pumped systems of various kinds may be used to deal with most grouting problems. Vacuum systems may be useful where fine fractures and small-scale voids are suspected.

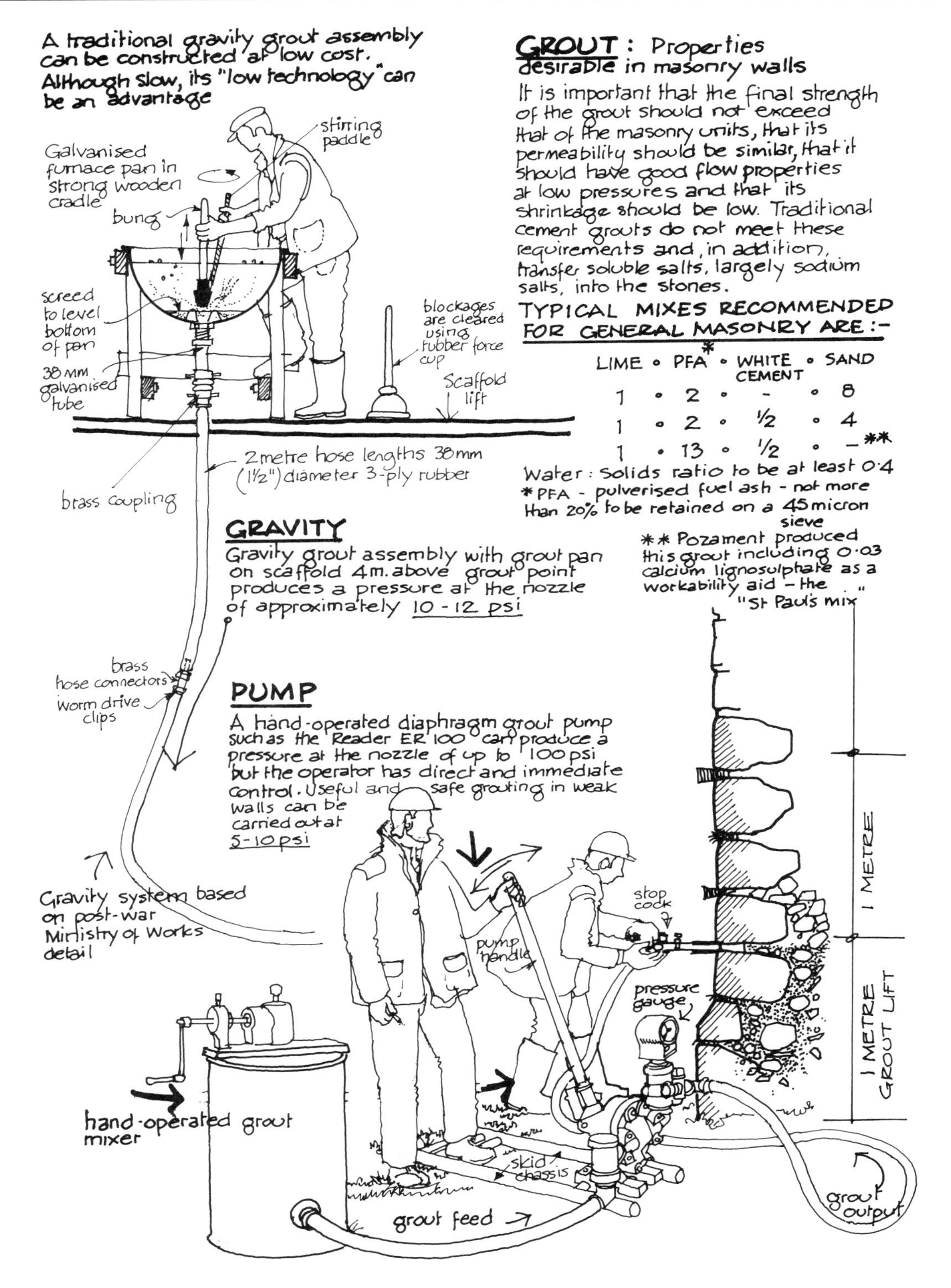

A traditional gravity grout assembly can be constructed at low cost. Although slow, its "low technology" can be an advantage
stirring paddle
Galvanised furnace pan in strong wooden cradle
bung
screed to level bottom of pan
38 mm galvanised tube
blockages are cleared using rubber force cup
Scaffold lift
2 metre hose lengths 38 mm (1½") diameter 3-ply rubber
brass coupling
GROUT: Properties desirable in masonry walls
It is important that the final strength of the grout should not exceed that of the masonry units, that its permeability should be similar, that it should have good flow properties at low pressures and that its shrinkage should be low. Traditional cement grouts do not meet these requirements and, in addition, transfer soluble salts, largely sodium salts, into the stones.
TYPICAL MIXES RECOMMENDED FOR GENERAL MASONRY ARE:-
LIME • PFA* • WHITE CEMENT • SAND
1 • 2 • - • 8
1 • 2 • ½ • 4
1 • 13 • ½ • -**
Water : Solids ratio to be at least 0·4
* PFA - pulverised fuel ash - not more than 20% to be retained on a 45 micron sieve
** Pozament produced this grout including 0·03 calcium lignosulphate as a workability aid - the "St Paul's mix"
GRAVITY
Gravity grout assembly with grout pan on scaffold 4m. above grout point produces a pressure at the nozzle of approximately 10 - 12 psi
brass hose connectors
worm drive clips
PUMP
A hand-operated diaphragm grout pump such as the Reader ER 100 can produce a pressure at the nozzle of up to 100 psi but the operator has direct and immediate control. Useful and safe grouting in weak walls can be carried out at 5-10 psi
Gravity system based on post-war Ministry of Works detail
stop cock
pump handle
pressure gauge
1 METRE
1 METRE GROUT LIFT
hand-operated grout mixer
skid chassis
grout feed
grout output

Gravity system

The grouting apparatus required for filling large voids consists of one or two open galvanized iron pans with outlets in the bottoms. A union with 38 mm (1.5 in) diameter galvanized pipe is fitted to the outlet, which in turn is connected by means of couplings to several lengths of 38 mm (1.5 in) diameter rubber hose, terminating in a galvanized iron nozzle 19 mm (0.75 in) in diameter and fitted with a stopcock. Each grout pan is provided with a wooden plug about 460 mm (18 in) long to fit into the hole in the pan bottom and with a plunger in the form of a rubber cup on a wooden handle. This plunger is used when the grout is flowing, to give an added impetus to the flow in the event of an airlock or other stoppage in the tube.

Preparation

Small holes are drilled into the wall where voids have been located, or are anticipated. They should be about one metre (3ft 3in) apart horizontally and 500 mm (1ft 8in) vertically on a staggered pattern. As the holes are drilled, they should be washed out thoroughly with clean water, by pouring in at the top holes and continuing to pour until the water runs out clean at the bottom. During this process, note should be taken of the joints through which the water runs out. Before grouting begins these joints must be tightly filled with tow or clay, pressed well into the joint to a depth of 38–50 mm (1.5–2 in). The nozzle of the delivery hose is then inserted into the lowest hole and plugged round with tow.

Operation

The assembly of this simple equipment is shown on page 27. To operate it, two men are stationed at the upper level with the grout pans. They regulate the flow of grout into the delivery hose from one pan and mix the grout in the second pan ready for use, so that a continuous operation can be carried out. A third man is stationed at the lower level, to open and close the stopcock on the nozzle as required. Ample supplies of water and grout components must be kept on the scaffold.

When the grout has been mixed to the right flow consistency in the pan, the wooden plug is withdrawn and the grout flows down the delivery hose. The stopcock on the nozzle is then opened, allowing the grout to flow into the wall, until the grout level in the wall has risen sufficiently to begin to flow out of the series of holes immediately above. These holes may then be stopped up, the grout cut off and another section of wall prepared, or grouted, while the first begins to set. After the initial set, the tow or clay can be stripped out of the joints in readiness for pointing at a later stage. The next lift can then be grouted in the same way. One metre should be taken as the maximum lift at a time, to avoid the build-up of pressure from liquid grout behind loose face stones. A pressure of about 0.98–1.28 kgf/cm^2 (14–18 lbf/in^2) (10–12 ft) is obtained in the hose when the pan is placed about 3.5–4.5 m (11.5–15 ft) above the point of inlet.

Pumped systems

Hand and power operated pumps usually consist of a mixer, diaphragm pump, suction and delivery hoses and metal nozzles fitted with stopcocks. Hand-operated pumps are recommended for ancient masonry in unstable conditions. The compact nature of these assemblies usually permits the equipment to be located adjacent to the work in progress and cuts down on the hose lengths required.

Preparation

Preparation is similar to that needed for the gravity system. The nozzles are fitted into the holes and plugged around with tow. The lowest nozzle is usually then coupled up to the delivery hose.

Operation

One man will be required to operate the mixer, one to operate the pump and one to open and close the stopcock as required. When all is ready, the stopcock is opened on the nozzle and the pump started. The level of the grout rising up the wall is indicated by the seepage of grout from weep holes, which can then be plugged with clay. Hidden grout flows may sometimes be identified by sweating of the wall surface as water is forced through under pressure.

When the grout reaches the next line of nozzles, the lower stopcock can be closed and the delivery hose can be removed and coupled to the nozzle above. The lower nozzle can be left in position until the grout has set.

The maximum pressure obtained depends upon the model being used, but a range of 10–15 kg/cm^2 (140–210 lbf/in^2) is usual. Much lower pressures are obtained with hand-operated pumps. Hand-operated pumps have a capacity of 18–45 litres/minute (4–10 gal/min). Power-operated pumps have a capacity of 1400–1800 litres/hour (300–400 gal/h).

The aerated pressure system (Aerocem) is useful in large scale grouting, especially where tunnels and vaults are involved. The apparatus consists of a compressor, mixer, pressure vessel, air lines and delivery hose, with a wide variety of nozzle designs suitable both for pointing and grouting. The pointing finish is unsatisfactory and messy if left from the nozzle, but can be acceptable if followed up with pointing tools.

The preparation of the walls for grouting is the same as that used in the gravity system. Metal nozzles are fitted into drilled holes and plugged round with tow. The spacing of the holes will vary with the condition of the masonry, but could be set, for example, 0.5 m (18 in) apart vertically and 1.25 m

(4ft 6in) apart horizontally. The point positions should be staggered as before.

During operation, one man is stationed at the nozzles to open and close the stopcocks, one man at the pressure vessel to ensure that the correct pressure is maintained, and one man at the mixer to prepare the next grout batch.

Vacuum grouting

Vacuum grouting is a relatively recent development which has considerable potential for structural consolidation and for the conservation of architectural detail and sculpture.

During the electrification of the Dacca-Chittagong railway in 1972, the late Mr Jimmy Milne evolved a system of applying resins to brick and stone bridges under vacuum. As so often, an emergency situation, in this case the transport of vital supplies by rail and the need to adept bridges to carry high speed trains, provided the stimulus for the idea. Patent applications were registered world-wide and the system is now known as the Balvac process (Balfour-Beatty).

In the United Kingdom the system was used on another railway bridge, the eighteenth century Causey Arch at Tanfield, County Durham. In this case, the traffic across the bridge was originally horse-drawn on rails, and carried coal to the River Tyne. Water percolation, open joints, salt crystallization damage and freezing of saturated masonry was causing considerable damage, especially to the inner ring of the single-span, three-ring arch. Vacuum sealing of a complete structure of this kind would have involved enormous practical problems. The sandstone arch was therefore prepared for local vacuum application and injection by tamping the open joints with conventional mortar, sealing the mortar face with resin and by drilling holes into the inner ring, which were then capped with nipples. A vacuum pump was applied to the nipples in turn, to remove air and water. This was followed by resin injection under low pressure. Structural grouting under vacuum is fraught with problems, but there is no doubt that it can sometimes provide an answer where straightforward injection under pressure will not work, or is too hazardous.

The application of vacuum techniques to smaller, freestanding objects is a subject which has now been quite extensively explored, especially by Kenneth Hempel. In the early 1970s, Mr Hempel, then of the Victoria and Albert Museum, London, began to use the Balvac system. He subsequently introduced various modifications which enabled it to be applied to valuable and, in some cases, fragile pieces of sculpture.

For eight years before the Balvac process was patented, the Victoria and Albert Museum had been brush applying silane monomers to decaying sculpture, on some occasions with considerable success. Before the silane monomers were applied the sculpture was dried out as much as possible, sometimes under ventilated black polyethylene shrouds, during the summer. Before treatment, the dry stone was painted with cellosolve and left overnight in preparation for the silane monomer, which was applied by brush, mixed with equal parts of cellosolve and two to eight parts of water. Brush application was continued until no more silane was absorbed. Up to 80 mm (3.25 in) penetration was achieved in this way. Application under vacuum presented a way of improving the consolidation by increasing the depth of impregnation and extending the absorption time by omitting the solvent and water and thus delaying polymerization.

In the procedure developed by Hempel, which is still sometimes used, the sculpture is placed on a non-porous base which extends well outside the surface area of the base of the stone to be treated. A fine polypropylene mesh is cut and fitted over the sculpture, followed by a clear polyethylene shroud, which is cut and sealed to form an envelope. The shroud is sealed at the top around a vacuum head and at the bottom to the non-porous base with a mastic cement. The polyethylene shroud is turned up all round the base to form a trough. When the vacuum is applied, the shroud clings tightly to the surface of the sculpture as the air is removed. At this stage, the consolidant is poured into the trough at the base and the shroud is pierced below the surface of the liquid. The consolidant can then be seen to move up the sculpture within the vacuated shroud, until it reaches the vacuum head. The vacuum is then switched off, allowing any consolidant which is not absorbed to flow back to the base. The vacuum is applied a second time to cover any area which has been missed. Impressive depths of impregnation of up to 300 mm (1 ft) have been achieved in this manner.

One of the hazards to fragile sculpture is the pull exerted by the shroud under vacuum, which can cause damage. Hempel modified his system to overcome this problem by carefully wrapping the sculpture in cotton flannelette, secured to sound surface with very small spots of latex. At the base, the flannelette is secured to the non-porous base with polyester cement. Instead of being enveloped in a polyethylene shroud, the flannelette is painted with a rubber latex, which cures to form a continuous skin. A vacuum head is sealed into the latex skin at the highest point, but the consolidant is introduced through a perforated polyethylene tube at the base. This is linked by a supply line to a polyethylene reservoir, which is fitted with a tap. When the vacuum is applied, its meter will register at once if the seal is successful. Any holes must be sealed with a puncture repair kit, consisting of small squares of polyethylene painted with latex. When pressed over a hole, the polyethylene can be peeled off the patch. After the vacuum has been held successfully for about an hour, the reservoir tap is turned on and the advance of the consolidant up the surface of the sculpture can be seen through the latex skin. The vacuum is maintained for ten minutes after the consolidant has reached the head, after which it is switched off and reapplied as before. On the following day, the latex and flannelette 'suit' can be cut away with a sharp scalpel. Impregnations of between 25–150 mm (1–6 in) have been achieved in this manner.

Some of the successful consolidations carried out by this process can be seen on the fifteenth century Porta della Carta in Venice, which was restored (1976–1979) by K. and G. Hempel, as part of a complex and delicate overall cleaning and consolidation programme. The Carrara marble sculptures of Prudence, Fortitude and Temperance were consolidated under vacuum in the laboratory. The figures of Justice, Charity, the Doge Foscari and two angels were treated *in situ*.

Repair of stone roofs

Stone slates, properly called 'tilestones', are perhaps the most distinctive of the many forms of roof covering found on traditional buildings. In *The Pattern of English Building*, Alec Clifton-Taylor defines their special quality by describing the effect of stone slates on a roof as 'complete visual harmony, both with the architecture of the buildings of which they form a part and with the landscape in which they are placed'. This harmony is due largely to the fact that both the tilestones and the stones from which the buildings are constructed were obtained from the same geological formations, so that, in composition and colour, there is often a close similarity.

Since the early nineteenth century, when mechanical means of producing roof coverings were developed, both thatch and stone roofs have been replaced by lighter, more regular roofing materials. Welsh slates, pantiles, plain tiles and, more recently, concrete and asbestos roof coverings have replaced traditional stone roofs. This often has a damaging effect on the character and appearance of the building. The decline of stone roofing undoubtedly also relates to the practical difficulties of maintenance and repair, the decreasing number of craftsmen capable of laying a stone roof and the steadily declining availability of both new and good quality secondhand stone slates. Surviving stone roofs are often important visual components in many urban and rural settings and their loss would seriously affect the appearance of numerous towns and villages throughout the country.

The laying of stone slates is a craft tradition of considerable importance, which demands not only a high standard of workmanship, but also an understanding of the variable characteristics of the material with which the roofer is working. Stone slates are obtained from stone deposits which allow the splitting of the stone along the bedding planes into thin sheets, capable of being used for roof coverings. These stones, generally sandstones, split or laminate quite easily along straight lines, giving a fairly smooth-faced finish which allows one slate to be bedded upon another quite evenly. The slates are laid in diminishing courses. The large eaves slates are several feet wide. The slates decrease in size up to the courses near the ridge, where the slates are considerably smaller. Traditionally, the slates are hung with oak pegs, which are driven into holes in the heads of the slates made with a pointed pick-end. The slates are fixed to riven oak laths, except where a peg hole coincides with a rafter position. In that case the slate is nailed with a large round-headed, non-ferrous nail. At the eaves, under-eaves slates are bedded directly onto the wall and the first course of slates laid over these, with the tails meeting. At the ridge, the roof is finished with ridge stones cut from the solid, either laid dry or bedded on mortar. Ridge stones vary in size and angle, according to the pitch of the roof.

In the past, before waterproof felting was available, various devices were adopted to make the stone slates, which were laid on open battened roofs, more weatherproof. One of the earliest methods was to drive moss into the joints, known as 'mossing'. Another method was called 'torching' or 'tiering'. Torching was a mixture of sand and slaked lime, to which beaten cow hair was added. This mixture was applied to the underside of the slated roof, either at the top of the laths (single torched), at the top and the bottom (double torched), or entirely filling the space between the laths (fully torched). The torching not only acted as a means of preventing rain and snow from penetrating the roof, but also cemented the wooden pegs firmly in position, preventing them from twisting and moving. Torching has been replaced, in recent years, by the use of bituminous roofing felt.

Many of the defects which develop in old stone roofs are attributable to the method in which the roof is laid, rather than to the deterioration of the roofing material. The most common failures occur in the wooden pegs, which shrink and dry out with age, allowing the slates to slip. Another common failure is in the laths, which tend to deflect under the weight of the stone slates. Often, the roof timbers themselves may have bent under the weight of the covering early in the life of the roof, but unless the timbers are cracked, or are badly infested with deathwatch beetle or dry rot, this is not necessarily a cause for concern. In many older buildings there is a considerable margin of safety provided by timbers whose scantlings are far in excess of the structural requirements. If, however, the laths and pegs have generally failed throughout the roof, then there is no alternative to re-roofing.

Signs of a defective roof covering include areas of bitumen painted over the stone slates, the presence of bitumen impregnated fabric covering the entire roof, or the external pointing of the stone slates with cement mortar. These signs indicate water penetration and imply that the original mossing or torching has failed. The bituminous covering is the most unfortunate, as it blurs the outline of the stone slates and renders their re-use impossible in all but hidden locations. Also, like external rendering, a damaged bituminous covering can help to trap water inside the roof covering, increasing the effect of even a small fault, which cannot be seen. The result will only be apparent when serious damage occurs.

If a stone roof needs attention, it is essential to consult a specialist roofing contractor who is familiar with stone roofing techniques. The principles which apply to Welsh slating and plain tiling do not necessarily apply to stone roofing. A suggested specification for stone roofing is outlined below.[7]

1. The existing roof covering should be carefully removed and the slates carefully stacked in preparation for sorting for re-use. All badly laminated and spalled slates should be rejected, but those which are damaged by fractures should be stacked separately, for possible re-use after re-dressing. Ridges should be carefully lowered and stacked. They should never be dropped to the ground.
2. All leadwork should be removed from the roof and only re-used if it is in good condition. The leadwork should be renewed in lead of adequate weights, for example, in BS 1178 Code 4 (1.80 mm) for flashings and minimum Code 5 (2.28 mm) for gutter linings.
3. Roof timbers should be cleaned down and all loose debris and accumulated material removed from the roof space. The timbers should then be repaired and treated as required. The replacement of original roof timbers should be kept to a minimum.
4. Sound salvaged slates should be carefully cleaned down, sorted to length and thickness and arranged in stacks corresponding to the various lengths. The slates should be stacked vertically, standing on their heads (with the peg holes to the ground). The length of each slate should be measured from the peg hole to the tail and sorting to length should precede sorting to thickness. Each stack of sorted slates will then constitute one course of stone slates. The number of slates required for the eaves course should be established by measuring the length of the building and then by checking this dimension against the combined widths of the longest slates. If there are insufficient large slates of one size, then the slates can be dressed to the length of the next largest size, which will then become the eaves course.
5. When sorting has been completed, the roof should be covered with reinforced untearable roofing felt to BS 747 (type IF), with a minimum vertical lap of 150 mm (6 in) and, where lengths are joined, a minimum horizontal lap of two spars width, fixed with 25 mm (1 in) galvanized clout nails.
6. New battens treated with preservative should be fixed as required to replace missing or defective material. Typical sizes are 38 × 19 mm (1.5 × 0.75 in) secured with 50 × 25 mm (2 × 1 in) eaves course battens and fixed with 63 mm (2.5 in) nails. For pegged slates counter battens will be required under the slating battens. Double battens are recommended for pegging to prevent the peg moving due to shrinkage or twisting. Pegs should be of seasoned oak, treated with a suitable preservative. Sometimes a tough plastic peg is used, especially in conjunction with a combined plastic sleeve and double washer where the nail/peg hole has become enlarged.
7. Re-slating should proceed using the sound slates previously removed, with deficiencies made up with sound, second-hand slates of matching type, thickness and, where possible, colour. The slates should be fixed in regularly diminishing courses. A double course should be laid to the eaves, fixed and positioned to give a minimum of 75 mm (3 in) overhang beyond the outer face of the wall. Each course of slates should overlap the second course below by 75 mm (3 in) and each horizontal joint below should be similarly lapped by a minimum 75 mm (3 in). The slates should be pegged, or nailed with 63–75 mm (2.5–3 in) heavy gauge copper nails, driven into the centre of the batten. The largest slates should be double nailed. No nails should penetrate the thickness of the batten.
8. The stone ridges should be re-bedded on a cement:lime:sand mortar (in the proportions 1:1:6) and supported at the joints with small wedges of stone. This traditional mix may be improved by using a styrene butadiene rubber additive with the gauging water. This additive should also be used to point up the ridge. The junction of roof and abutments should be finished with lead soakers and flashings and pointed in SBR modified mortar. Traditionally this lead was pointed into stone with an oil

mastic based on linseed oil and sand with litharge.

9. The gutters should be re-fixed with the roofing felt carried over into them.
10. The contractor should, wherever possible, leave on the site an assortment of sound slates to enable localized repairs to be carried out when necessary.

Repair of slate roofs

True slates provide a much lighter roof covering than tilestones. They form a good waterproof roof when properly laid, close butted and accurately lapped vertically and horizontally. The failure of slate roofs is generally as a result of the deterioration of fixings, although the slates themselves are brittle and vulnerable to impact. They may be lifted and detached in gale-force winds.

As with any other stone there is a range of durability. Slates containing significant amounts of calcium carbonate, which is attacked by acids present in the atmosphere, are likely to be of poor durability. However, calcium sulphate can be formed from calcite and pyrite present in the slate by regular wetting and drying, and atmospheric sulphate is not necessarily the sole cause of decay.

Deterioration often occurs under the laps where moisture is held by capillarity. Replacement or refixing of even single damaged or slipped slates is important. If left unattended, damage may result to the roof structure. Unfortunately the expense of access in order to refix a few roof slates is frequently well in excess of the cost of the repair, and neglect is all too common.

Slates are often pegged with wood or nailed direct to close boarding, or to battens, with copper or iron nails. Commonly a slate roof which was intended to be wholly copper nailed was fixed with iron as the work progressed. Replacement nails should be of copper, or tin alloy. Where oak pegs were used to hang the slates on battens these nails can be used as substitutes. Enlarged holes can be reduced by making an epoxy-slate powder amalgam filler and drilling to form the desired size of hole. New holes in old slates should always be drilled and not punched through, to avoid the risk of shattering.

Original, hardwood pegs were frequently trimmed from green, unseasoned wood. They did not endanger the slate when driven through, but lost their wedging effect as they dried out. For this reason the re-use of unseasoned hardwood pegs is undesirable. On the other hand, seasoned hardwood may damage the slates during driving in. For these reasons, seasoned, good quality softwood pegs, treated by immersion in timber preservative so that they will be rot-resistant and retain their tight hold on the slate, are often substituted.

Individual slates which have slipped may be secured with slating hooks. New slates may be fixed in the same manner without cutting nails. Although hooks may be visible they allow minimum interference with the roof and avoid some of the risks to good slates when cutting nails with a ripper.

Large-scale failure of fixing almost inevitably means the stripping and relaying of the roof using as many new slates as necessary. It is important that the coursing pattern is maintained and that any polychromatic designs or special shaped slates are retained.

Another method of securing stone slate on slate roofs which has been used in a limited way over the past two decades is to fix a resin-impregnated glass-fibre membrane to the back of the slates or, alternatively, to attach a resin block to the back of the slate to act as a hanging nib. The first system involves the slating battens, and it is claimed that they remain sufficiently flexible to accommodate normal roof movements. The second is less of a commitment in that each slate remains free to move or to be replaced. Both systems rely on adhesion to the underside of a laminated slab, which may be seen as an inherent weakness, but both allow relatively inexpensive repairs to be carried out without access to the external slopes.

A number of Local Authorities in the UK have accepted a patented process, the 'Roof-Bond' system, for inclusion under House Improvement Grant schemes.

A third system secures slipped slates and provides insulation by covering the underside of the slates with an adhesive polyurethane foam. Like the glass-fibre sheet method this is a major commitment which, however successful initially, is likely to make future replacement of damaged slates very difficult. The foam and glass-fibre systems are visually undesirable, increase the fire loading, and can encourage the retention of moisture in encapsulated wood and in stone slates, which may subsequently become more frost vulnerable. Although some foams are reversible in theory, the likelihood of their removal is very small until a problem has been well established.

Stone paving

Stone has been used extensively as an external and internal paving material since prehistoric times. As paving it is subjected to some of the most severe deterioration processes. In addition, it may have to withstand the effects of pedestrian and/or vehicular traffic concentrated in specific zones. Street paving, including kerbs, roads and pavements (sidewalks) is very vulnerable to damage and liable to loss through replacement with substitute materials. Internal paving is primarily at risk on stairs and thresholds. All paving can be damaged by poorly prepared or carelessly disturbed substrates.

One of the most troublesome modern aspects of maintaining external stone paving is the constant need for access to services below the paved surface and the problems associated with heavy vehicles. For example, small basalt or granite setts are often lifted with a pick and shovel to expose a defective drain. The surface is then back-filled with poorly compacted material and the setts are relaid by road-gangs or service maintenance engineers with no appropriate skills and, in some cases, no interest beyond the service repair they have completed. These repaired areas are frequently disfigured by slurrying the joints with cement mortar. They soon show signs of subsidence, creating hazards for vehicles and pedestrians. Paved footways which are similarly disturbed are especially vulnerable to cracking after poor rebedding and rocking under the wheels of vehicles mounting the pavement, especially when large slabs are involved. Slabs are commonly broken or have their edges damaged during careless lifting. The attractions of tarmacadam, asphalt and cheap concrete paving slabs in terms of economy and fast servicing are obvious enough, but these materials are visually disastrous and their use causes an enormous loss of the historic characteristics of a street or area of old buildings.

An ideal arrangement to avoid disturbance during repairs would be to contain all services below roads and pavings in adequately sized ducts spanned by slabs or tray-profiled covers in which units of setts or cobbles or some lighter and sympathetic material can be bedded. Large slabs covering services should be fitted with slots for lewis pins so that they can be lifted mechanically without recourse to leverage. Unfortunately this ideal can only rarely be achieved. Sewers, gas lines, water mains and later electrical and telephone services have arrived at different periods and their maintenance is the responsibility of different authorities. The best solution is for long-term plans to be made to phase the grouping of services when possible. In the meantime, careful excavation and reinstatement remains the responsibility of road crews. In areas where there are still considerable areas of original or early and interesting paving, a plea must be made for at least one competent supervisor to oversee all disturbance and reinstatement work with the support of a small gang who carry out all the re-setting work. Protests about the increased time of operation with added inconvenience to traffic and increased costs to the ratepayer must be balanced, against the value of the conservation approach and the preservation of the original environment.

Paving specifications

Backfilling normally provides an unstable base for paving and is frequently followed by subsidence, displacement or cracking of units. A well-compacted sub-base of broken stone or brick of 100 mm (4 in) gauge topped with similar material of 25–50 mm gauge should be laid first and blinded with fine, well-graded stone aggregate to correct contours and profiles. The compacted thickness of the sub-base should be at least 150 mm (6 in). The sub-base should be covered with a 75 mm (3 in) thickness of 50 mm hoggin topped off with 13 mm (0.5 in) of fine hoggin well rolled or otherwise compacted.

Typical specifications for surface finishes

Granite or basalt setts. These vary in size, but 100 mm cubes or wedge-shaped square or rectangular sizes such as 100 mm × 125 mm × 180–250 mm (4 × 5 × 7–10 in) are common. Setts may be laid in regular lines or in concentric rings (fans) for decorative effect. The setts are trimmed to shape and laid tight-butted or sometimes with 6 mm wide joints. They are rammed home with wooden rammers or laid out on the compacted sub-base into sand or onto a 25 mm bed of cement:sand mortar in the proportion 1:3. The setts which are jointed should then be vigorously brushed over with a dry 1:6 cement:sand mortar, or 1:3 hydraulic lime:sand mortar. All the surplus should be swept away and the paving watered with a fine mist spray.

Limestone and sandstone setts. These are usually laid in the same way as granite but should be edge bedded and jointed in hydraulic lime:sand 1:3. Only very tough stones are suitable for paving.

Cobble stones. Cobbles are traditionally made of a very durable sandstone and have been water-worn into approximately spherical or flat shapes with well-rounded edges. Approximately even sizes graded between 40–50 mm (1.6–2 in) and up to 100–120 mm (4–5 in) are common. Split cobbles are also used. Cobbles are typically laid on a 100 mm (4 in) bed of 1:2:4 semi-dry concrete using 19 mm (0.7 in) nominal aggregate. The cobbles are set, as tightly butted as possible, into the base to no more than 14 mm of their depth and compacted with a heavy wooden mallet. A dry grout of cement:sand in the proportions 1:2 is then brushed in around the cobbles to achieve the desired level, which is often determined by adjacent paving. The surface is then watered with a fine mist spray. Rapid-hardening cement is sometimes used. Although the mortar bed is important to grip the cobbles, a more visually pleasing mortar will be obtained using hydraulic lime:sand 1:2.

Stone flags. Limestone, sandstone or slate flag stones of specified size, thickness and finish, with edges sawn at right angles unless otherwise described, are usually laid on a 25 mm (1 in) thick bed of semi-dry lime-sand mortar which is well compacted to a true and level surface. Old slabs are usually only worked level on one face (and four edges), so the base must be thick enough and accommodating enough to take the irregularities and provide support at all points. Modern replacements are six sides sawn. Lime:sand mortar 1:2.5 should be brushed dry into all the joints, sprinkled with water and protected from rain and hot sun under ventilated covers, such as sheet material laid on bricks. For tough, durable stones hydraulic lime:sand 1:3 is recommended. Cement is not necessary and should be avoided.

When pavements are repaired, flags of a similar size and pattern to the old flag should be used. For new infills a general recommendation is that no less than 25 slabs should be used to cover 10 m^2 (100 ft^2) of surface area. If precedent demands very large slabs some form of perimeter sleeper wall will be advisable. Slabs of large size, say 2 m (6.5 ft) square, will be 100–150 mm (4–6 in) thick and extremely heavy, so that lewis holes must be left for mechanical lifting.

Paving in light traffic areas

Much paving was traditionally bedded direct on the soil or a levelling base of sand. If there is only to be light pedestrian traffic there is no need to change this. Even joints may be simply filled with sand, although from a mainenance point of view a weak binder of lime is advisable (say lime:sand 1:4 or 1:5).

Marble and decorative limestone paving

Marble and decorative limestone paving, whether used internally or externally, should not be bedded on cement mortar. A white cement:white lime:silver sand base and jointing of 1:1:8 is typical good practice and will avoid the staining and possible damage arising from alkali salt migration. A reliable damp-proof membrane is also required. Internal marble should never be cleaned with powdered detergents or abrasive scouring methods.

A peculiarity of marble paving (or any thin marble slabs) is the phenomenon of stress-release where there has been inadequate seasoning of the stone. A number of examples are known where thin (20 mm (0.8 in) thick) marble slabs have distorted and cracked, producing either humped or dished profiles. The removal of confining stresses during the quarrying operation may lead, gradually, to expansion towards the marble's original condition. Extremes of cold and heat can accelerate the process of de-stressing. Micro-cracking from stress relief can largely be avoided by the storage of the block for a few months.

Deformation may also be linked to weathering in damp, polluted environments. Recrystallization phenomena associated with acidic solutions washing the crystals of calcite in the marble may bring about upward buckling as well as dishing effects. Unfortunately, the distortion of thin slabs cannot be remedied and they must be replaced with seasoned stone. This problem is a relatively modern one, linked to fast delivery and laying times and the sophisticated sawing which produces very thin slabs economically.

Wear problems

Problems of wear associated with the modern tourist industry must inevitably lead to restricted circulation and covering of valuable areas, however unpopular this may be. The seriousness of the problem may be seen externally at such important sites as Pompeii and the Acropolis at Athens, which have to contend with a phenomenal amount of foot traffic. At such sites as S. Maria Maggiore in Rome the resistance to constant wear of the constituent stones in a polychromatic scheme varies, so that the red and green porphyries stand proud of marble and travertine. In these situations decks, raised walkways externally and carpets with thick, absorbent underlay which are turned and vacuum-cleaned regularly internally must be tolerated. Our increasingly conservation-conscious society will not, in the end, thank us for allowing our monuments to be 'visited to destruction'.

References

1. Caroe, A.D.R. and Caroe, M.B., *Stonework: Maintenance and Surface Repair*, Council for the Care of Churches, London, 1984
2. BRE Digest 269, *The Selection of Natural Building Stone*, Building Research Establishment, 1983; D.B. Honeyborne, *The Building Limestones of France*, Building Research Establishment Report, HMSO, London, 1982
3. Warland, E.G., *Modern Practical Masonry*, reprinted by the Stone Federation, London. 1984
4. Schaffer, R.J., *The Weathering of Natural Building Stones*, Department of Scientific and Industrial Research Special Report 18, HMSO, London, 1932 (available from Building Research Establishment, Watford WD2 7JR, England)
5. Powys, A.R., *Repair of Ancient Buildings*, reissued by the Society for the Protection of Ancient Buildings, London, 1981
6. Clifton-Taylor, A., *The Pattern of English Building*, 2nd edition, Faber, London, 1977
7. Derbyshire County Council, *Traditional Stone Roofing*, Design and Conservation Section, County Planning Department, Derbyshire County Council

Figure 1.1 Corfe Castle, Dorset, is constructed of some of the finest quality masonry found in medieval castle building in England. Although deliberately slighted by the Parliamentary army in the civil war of the seventeenth century it remains a testimony to the technique of double skin core-filled construction carried out by master builders

Figure 1.4 Vertical fractures, split and exposed wall core and broken wall heads require possible stitching, grouting and wall-top weathering. The first essential is to record the condition and the position of all the stones, including those which have fallen (Jervaulx Abbey)

Figure 1.2 Castle Acre Priory is a good example of a ruined building consolidated 'as found' with very little added or taken away but with corework and wall tops consolidated and internally reinforced. Decorated stones and stones with tooling survive in a good state of preservation. Each stone has an intrinsic value in its original position

Figure 1.3 Jervaulx Abbey in Yorkshire is typical of roofless and otherwise depleted construction where survival is dependent on structural intervention and weatherproofing. The failure of one structural element at this stage in the building's deterioration can have a knock-on effect of considerable magnitude

Figure 1.5 Developing fractures may take decades to become serious, but may also fail with surprising rapidity, especially when temperature extremes, such as a long dry summer or severe freeze-thaw cycling at the end of the winter, interfere with the normal equilibrium. Recording and monitoring of fractures, and temporary support, are desirable if not essential

Figure 1.6 Successful consolidation of ruined masonry requires an understanding of the roles of facework and corework. At Goodrich Castle, on the Welsh border of England, core has been accurately consolidated with a high ratio of mortar visible and with water traps eliminated. The facing stones have been tamped and pointed where necessary

Figure 1.8 Occasionally it is necessary to introduce new stone into ruined buildings. In this illustration of Cleeve Abbey in Somerset, three new stones have been corbelled out to provide a discreet support for the arch. They have been carefully selected and professionally bonded in

Figure 1.7 An exposed wall head at Corfe Castle in Dorset illustrates the proper treatment of corework. The main points to note are: (1) the core does not extend over the area which was once occupied by face stones, (2) the impression of the tails of missing stones has been made in the core profile, (3) the core shows stepped 'course lines' reflecting the coursing of missing facings and (4) the mortar to stone ratio is high and the stones themselves have been slurried in lime mortar (work of St Blaise, Evershot)

Figure 1.9 Falsework provides temporary support for this archway at Jervaulx Abbey, Yorkshire. To the left of the arch, masonry is missing, with the result that the arch has become distorted by an unequal thrust from the right. To counteract this, corework will be rebuilt on the left-hand side to provide an opposing thrust. No attempt to rebuild or alter the arch is made

Figure 1.10 Masonry elements, once properly consolidated, can be re-aligned if necessary. This shored-up section of wall at Fountains Abbey, Yorkshire, was leaning due to settlement. It was supported as shown (left), grouted, tamped and pointed until fully consolidated. After archaeologically supervised excavation under the footings the leaning wall was jacked up into a vertical position and underpinned with masonry and concrete

Figure 1.11 The nave arcade of Fountains Abbey in Yorkshire illustrates the effects of water washing through the mortar core of the drum piers. Unprotected wall heads allow the ingress of water which carries calcium carbonate and sulphate into the sandstone ashlars and mouldings. Apart from the encouragement of decay in the sandstone, the major risk is that progressive washing out of the core will threaten the stability of the piers and walls

Figure 1.12 Replacement of mortar in wall cores to achieve structural integrity of double skin, core-filled walls is achieved by grouting. In this illustration a wall which has lost core and bedding mortar is being prepared for grouting. The blocks are being levelled and secured by oak wedges driven into the joints. The bottom four courses have been plugged with tarred hemp, pushed in with a pointing key as a temporary seal

Figure 1.13 The grout (liquid mortar) is being introduced by a gravity system. The grout pan, hung in a timber cradle, is located on a scaffold about four metres above the grout points. A hose conducts the grout from the bottom of the pan to the grout point. A wooden plug closes and opens the grouting line. The solids in the grout are kept in suspension by continuous stirring. The force cup standing on the cradle is used to clear any blocking in the line

Figure 1.14 Below the grout pan at the base of the wall the hose delivers the grout into the wall through a galvanised feed pipe fitted with a stop cock. When the pan plug is lifted and the stop cock opens the grout flows into the wall and rises up to proving holes left at one half metre height. The dark patch is left by escape of water during the preliminary flushing out process which must always precede the introduction of grout

Figure 1.15 The grout has filled the voids of the first lift of masonry and is escaping from the proving holes, which are immediately stopped up with tarred hemp

Figure 1.16 Grouting proceeds in lifts of between one half metre and one metre height. When grouting is complete, the tarred hemp is pulled out and the joints pointed up back to the grout line. This illustration (left) shows the bottom section grouted and pointed

Figure 1.17 When structural intervention is necessary, the aim should be to provide the assistance to the wall in as unobtrusive a manner as possible and without imposing new stresses on the wall being repaired or on associated masonry elements. The wall in the illustration above shows distinct bowing at its head, as indicated by the vertical line of the scaffolding. To prevent further movement, a wall head beam is inserted into the wall, spanning between two cross walls

Figure 1.18 A view of the top of the wall shows several stages in the process of installation of the beam. First, all vegetation must be cleared from the wall top. Second, the wall is photographed and the stones numbered as found. Third, the stones are lifted off the top of the wall and the core work between the two lines of facing stones is excavated under archaeological supervision. Fourth, a lime mortar 'cushion' is placed to isolate the tails of the stones from the new concrete. Fifth, the reinforcement cage is placed, section by section. Sixth, concrete is tamped around the reinforcement. Finally, the wall head stones are replaced, from the records, exactly as found. The wall head beam reinforcement is turned into the heart of the cross walls to provide anchorage and restraint

Figure 1.19 Although organic growth on ruined masonry is rightly acknowledged as a problem, there are sometimes situations where plants are also important. Some species thrive on lime-rich substrates and may be considered proper subjects for conservation in their own right. The ruins of Jervaulx are of considerable interest to botanists and the total clearance of the wall tops would be unacceptable

Figure 1.21 Similar problems to those at Jervaulx can exist in the context of occupied buildings, where the garden encroaches on the masonry in the form of ornamental climbing plants. Some decorative climbers can be of considerable age and beauty. A satisfactory compromise can be reached if work is planned to allow pruning at the correct season by the correct personnel. Sometimes a stainless steel grid on 100 mm spacer bolts can provide a discreet climbing frame which allows some maintenance. Climbing plants should not be allowed to invade gutters and roof coverings

Figure 1.20 This illustration shows an experimental section of wall at Jervaulx where the masonry has been consolidated (deep-tamped and pointed up from the ground to within two or three courses of the broken wall head). The wall head zone is left untouched, unless individual stones are loose, to allow the flowering plants to remain in their natural habitat. Whilst this would be a dangerous practice on high walls where access was difficult, it is an acceptable compromise on walls up to about five metres in height

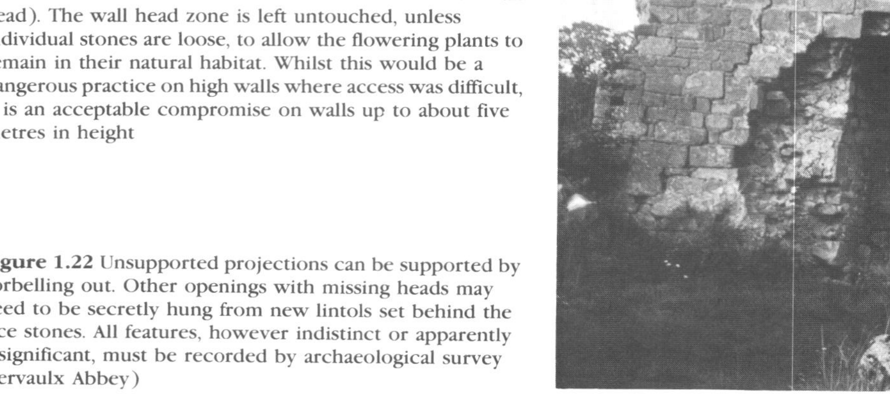

Figure 1.22 Unsupported projections can be supported by corbelling out. Other openings with missing heads may need to be secretly hung from new lintols set behind the face stones. All features, however indistinct or apparently insignificant, must be recorded by archaeological survey (Jervaulx Abbey)

Figure 1.23 The 'Achilles Heel' of the ruined masonry structure is the exposed and weathered-out core, whose disintegration is brought about by water, frost and plant growth. The wall head protection is critical

Figure 1.24 Tintern Abbey, in Monmouthshire, after wall head consolidation. The core is recorded, lifted and reset as found after consolidation, with one modification: the stones are so placed to shed water off the wall and to eliminate any pockets where water could be trapped or organic debris could accumulate

Figure 1.25 The wall enclosing the Roman city of Silchester has fallen prey to stone robbing, especially at the base of the wall, to exposure to weather and to colonisation by plants. Construction of this kind, small stones with lacing and bonding courses, contains a high ratio of mortar to stone. As such, it is relatively easy for major growths to establish themselves and for root systems to penetrate deep into the wall. This tree has been cut back but must now be carefully excavated from the fragile masonry. The voids left by its removal are packed with lime mortar, tile and stones. The wall section in the second illustration shows the consolidated work, including underpinning with stones which had fallen out at the wall base

Figure 1.26 Thousands of metres of exposed wall top at Bolsover Castle, Derbyshire, present a major and ongoing maintenance problem which only re-roofing would solve permanently. Even so, false detail such as coping stones is not introduced and the work is achieved by core consolidation

Figure 1.27 Wall head maintenance is just as critical in an occupied building but the situation is less of a philosophical problem. This building complex in the university city of Oxford has had a long history of repair and maintenance which includes essential replacement of copings and weatherings when they fail but also preserves the architectural integrity by replacement of decayed pinnacles

Figure 1.28 Not all decorative elements are non-functional. These buttress caps on the nave buttresses at Westminster Abbey are both weathering and structural elements, providing the necessary load on the buttress to withstand the thrust of the flying arches

Figure 1.29 The Treasurer's House in York shows how new stone should be introduced into an old facade. The most important weathering element, the cornice, has been substantially replaced and has had a lead flashing installed. Elsewhere, minimum replacement has been carried out, leaving every original stone where possible. New detail is an exact replica of the old and stones are replaced on the same line. The stone is geologically compatible with the original Magnesian Limestone

Figure 1.30 Depending on the type of construction and the bed depth of the original stones it is sometimes expedient and economic to replace only the front face of a stone block, usually between 75 mm and 100 mm on bed. The rusticated sandstone ashlar in the illustration has been faced in this way where the lighter tone can be seen. Facings such as this are sometimes bedded in epoxy or polyester resin, but this is not good practice, since moisture movement is checked against the resin barrier. Fixing should be in the form of threaded stainless steel dowels set in resin, the rest of the interface between new and old stone being coated in lime and white cement

Figure 1.31 Replacement stone of the right kind may be much lighter in colour than the weathered original. The weathered colour can be anticipated by an iron oxide wash if considered essential

Figure 1.32 Minimum piecing-in or minimum replacement can result in an initially startling patchwork. This replacement stone at Durham Cathedral is, however, technically and philosophically absolutely correct. New stone weathers over a period of decades. Owners of historic buildings, and sometimes their architects, must be dissuaded from replacing too much for the sake of uniformity

Figure 1.33 A detail of the original stone at Durham shows a heavily weathered, textured surface which is, nevertheless, perfectly sound and not in need of replacement. Any water traps can be rubbed back using a hand-held carborundum stone. Discreet mortar fillets and fills may be used in deep pockets or ledges provided they are well matched to the stone in colour and are not gauged with water-repellent adhesives

Figure 1.34 The medieval market cross at Chichester in Sussex, largely constructed in Caen stone, has suffered extensively from pollution and crude repairs in dense, hydraulic mortars. The two pairs of trefoils in the illustration were largely reconstructed in Portland cement mortar. The mortar was cut out to a square line on the springing point of the trefoil heads and a limestone insertion secured in its place with stainless steel dowels and a restraint fixing back into the core. White cement and lime were used to grout behind the new piece. Slightly weathered Caen stone below the springing line was repaired in lime mortar (Cathedral Works Organization, Chichester)

Figure 1.35 The replacement of a damaged course of stone above a plinth weathering has been completed, except for the last stone. Because the damage was partly due to water leaching through the contaminated corework, the back of the cavity has been mortar slurried and coated with sanded bitumen. Note that the bitumen is stopped 25 mm back from the face (right of illustration) to prevent staining. The object of the bitumen is to prevent any salt contamination of the new stone

Figure 1.36 The stone is here in place, on bedding mortar with vertical joints filled. Grouting takes place through holes left in the vertical joints until it appears at the hole shown in the top bed (the proving hole)

Figure 1.37 Poor quality finishing of indented stones defaces and devalues the building into which they are placed. These quoin stones have been set in, six sides sawn but over-sized. A grinding disc has been applied to the face to achieve the correct line. Because of incorrect tools being used by an operative with no masonry skills the exercise is a waste of money. The stones are misshapen and scoured with disc marks

Figure 1.38 Hand-dressing on site is a skilled operation. In this illustration a mason is putting the final tooled finish on the stone. Note that the new stone is not being dressed back to 'fit' the weathered profile, but is maintaining the correct original line

Figure 1.39 Good quality quoin indents contrast with the work of the non-mason. These stones at Fort George, Scotland, are correctly and accurately sized and neatly tooled to match surviving original stones. The edges of the blocks have a subtle 'pencil-round' to take off the sharpness of sawn arrises

Figure 1.40 Rebuild of a limestone parapet wall, Richmond Terrace, London. The illustration shows the use of joggles in the joint beds of cornice, blocking course, die stone and coping. With sawn stones the importance of these joggles, into which liquid grout will be run, is paramount. Note the damp proof membrane inserted under the coping, and the chase cut into the face of the blocking course to receive the edge of the lead flashing to the cornice

Figure 1.41 There is no technical or practical reason for not redressing stone and it has often been used as an economic way of producing a 'new' facade. In construction terms it represent a major loss of original worked surface (if any survived) and can create curious details, such as projecting window dressings at Oxford, which are replacement stones on the original line

Figure 1.42 Sometimes uniform-depth redressing will still leave cavities which cannot be left. In fact, redressing tends to accentuate remaining damage, so that mortar filling or limited piecing-in with new stone becomes almost essential

Figure 1.43 Mortar filling in a redressed surface is one of the most difficult cosmetic activities to achieve successfully and requires considerable skill and investment of time in mortar matching. In this illustration a mortar consisting of one part buff hydraulic lime to five parts stonedust and sand graded down from 600 μm has been designed to match the stone in wet and dry conditions. It is ironed in with small wooden floats and is here being finished with a small float faced with felt. Protection from the weather during curing is essential

Figure 1.44 Contrasting textures of weathered and redressed clunch [limestone] at Woburn Abbey illustrate why, architecturally, the technique of redressing can be attractive. Nevertheless, the first consideration should always be the retention of as much as possible of the original worked face

Figure 1.45 Experimental treatment to save the weathered faces at Woburn included cleaning with hot lime poultices, treating the friable areas over two to three days with limewater, grouting behind scales with lime, brickdust and acrylic emulsion and closing up water traps with weak lime, stonedust and brickdust mortar. The brickdust was from white, refractory bricks and graded down from 150 μm

Figure 1.46 Redressing is seen here at Lichfield not for architectural reasons but to remove contour scaling around joints. This is very much an intermediate treatment to exclude water and prevent large scales falling from the walls. It may also 'buy time', before indenting with new stone takes place

Figure 1.49 A major weathering element such as a cornice cannot be repaired in reinforced mortar unless it is to be covered with a lead flashing. Frost has removed this mortar repair within one year

Figure 1.47 Mortar repair or 'plastic' repair has a poor reputation largely because it is too often used as a cheap option to be carried out by operatives with limited expertise and because it is used on too large a scale. Three periods of plastic repair are shown here in different stages of disintegration. All are feather-edged and two are relying on bonding agents to keep them in position

Figure 1.48 Plastic repair is never satisfactory, except on a very minor scale, as a weathering. The mouldings on this buttress have been repaired with a coloured mortar with little preparation or mechanical key. Failure is commencing within two years of completion

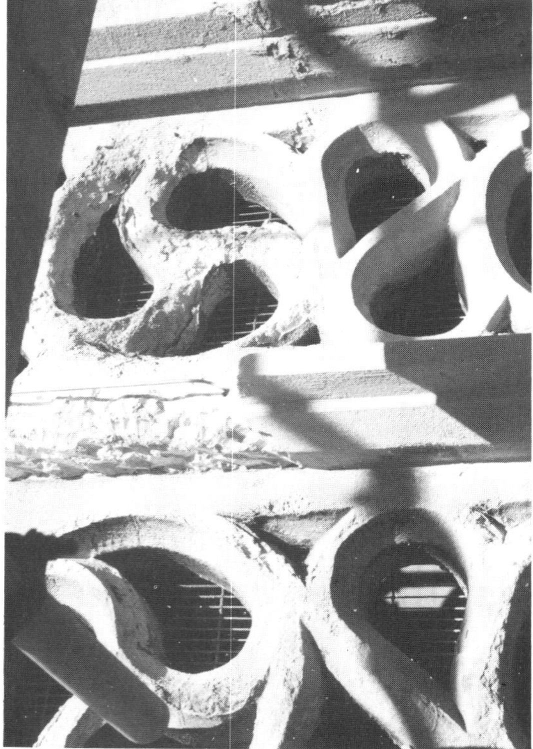

Figure 1.50 Good quality mortar repair is not cheap, because the amount of preparation can be as great as for stone replacement. This pierced work at Bristol is being very professionally carried out using a well matched mortar, phosphor bronze wire armatures and considerable practical expertise. In this case, the use of mortar enables more of the original stone to be retained than if a stone replacement was selected

Figure 1.51 Mortar is most often applicable as a 'dental' repair i.e. the filling of small lacunae in such a way that the maximum amount of the stone under repair is retained. The work involves dental tools and plasterers' small tools and requires experience to be successful

Figure 1.52 Mortar repair in association with surgical techniques sometimes makes it possible to save masonry which otherwise could only be recorded and replaced. During World War II the Bristol Temple Church was burnt out by incendiary bombs. Rapid cooling promoted a shattering of much of the stone, especially the tracery. Subsequent weathering of the roofless building brought the windows to a dangerous condition. Many of them were kept in place only by timber corsets, bolted together

Figure 1.53 Colour-matched mortar was built up round the wire armatures and glass fibre rods until the full profile was re-created. The final stage was to dress and rub the cured mortar with masonry chisels and carborundum blocks until an acceptable finish was produced

Figure 1.54 The tracery was drilled horizontally and vertically whilst clamping the stone with timber splices. These drillings, after flushing out dust, were grouted with epoxy mortar and glass fibre rods were inserted as a complex stitching system. The ends of all rods were kept within the general line of the tracery. When the resin had cured, a cage of phosphor bronze wire was built up around the rods as an armature for mortar repair

Figure 1.55 This illustration is of a completely reinforced, stitched and repaired window after the removal of the corsets. The repairs are all concealed and the tracery has regained full structural integrity

Figure 1.56 Fire damage and the rapid cooling of masonry by fire hoses created typical fracturing of the Norman period masonry of Westminster Hall in London. The fractures run parallel with the face of the stone at (typically) 5, 10 and 15 mm depths. To secure the stones, all of which bore marks of axe-work and some of which had mason's marks, it was decided to pin the 'plates' of stone back into position. The stones were covered with a temporary, protective latex coating and supported with padded shuttering. A small, diamond disc was used to open the weakened joints, because any impact tools would have destroyed the fragile bond between the 'plates'

Figure 1.57 Drillings were made into the joint thicknesses to a depth of 75 mm, beyond the deepest of the fractures. An average of five drillings were made, each 12 mm in diameter, round the perimeter of each stone. The holes were blown free of dust

Figure 1.58 The drillings were grouted with a thixotropic epoxy placed with a mastic gun fitted with an extension tube, so that the holes could be filled from the back. Each hole was grouted two-thirds full

Figure 1.59 Glass fibre rods, 8 mm in diameter and constructed of continuous glass roving set in polyester resin, were sandpapered to clean and roughen the surface before being pushed fully home. As the rods are squeezed forward, the resin mortar is displaced into the fracture lines wherever they have been intersected by the drilling. When cured, each 'plate' of stone has four to five squeezed resin keys anchoring it to the rest of the block. The drill holes and joints are finally pointed up in lime mortar

Figure 1.60 Horizontal projections such as cornices can act as water catchments, especially when there is inadequate fall and when joints begin to fail. Breakdown of such a major weathering element as this can lead to accelerated deterioration of the stones below. The introduction of a lead flashing to this detail, even if slightly obtrusive visually, would play a major role in extending the life of the building

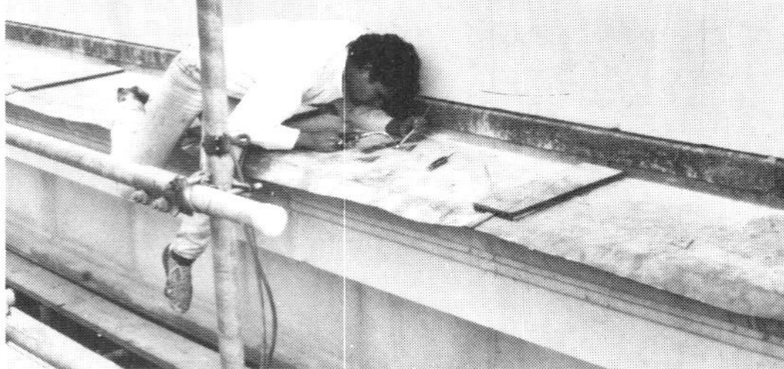

Figure 1.61 The installation of a lead flashing to a wide cornice in progress. Code 6 lead is used for a major projection and sheets are limited to 1.5 m in length. The sheets are welted together, the welts incorporating copper clips. The front edge is also secured with copper clips and intermediate fixings are made into the cornice with lead-capped brass screws

Figure 1.62 The versatility of lead as a protection is illustrated by its use on the chapter house of Howden Minster in Yorkshire. Vulnerable wall heads and decorative detail are covered in Code 6 and Code 4 lead, welt jointed and secured with copper clips and brass screws and washers

Figure 1.63 At Drumlanrig Castle in Scotland it was necessary to take the lead flashing up over the blocking courses of the parapet. Because the detailing of the parapet required each stone baluster to be fixed through the lead, separate cover flashings were provided to each baluster, welt jointed together. This ensured that the lead would not be 'over-fixed' and unable to accommodate thermal movements

Figure 1.64 At Tintern Abbey in Monmouthshire the malleability of lead has been put to good use by bossing over the mouldings of a damaged roundel in the traceried window. This lead dressing, turned down into masonry joints, lead wedged and pointed in, sheds water off a natural collection point and protects the tracery below

Figure 1.65 The splendid tympanum at Kilpeck is in such good condition that it needs little attention other than deflection of water. A Code 4 lead flashing has been dressed carefully over the hood moulding and fixed back into the joint with lead wedges to prevent water running off the wall into the sculpture

Figure 1.66 The church of St Mary the Virgin (1154–1189) at Iffley, Oxford, has an external rubble construction which was once plastered. Evidences of the plaster remained on the face of the stones in sheltered areas. Stripping of external plaster is quite unacceptable in conservation terms but also creates weathering problems because of the difficulty in pointing round rubble which was not intended to be exposed. The rubble can be seen on the south wall

Figure 1.67 The west front at Iffley contains a superb portal of six orders with chevron and beakhead enrichment, as well as circular and circular headed window dressings, all moulded. It was decided to replaster for aesthetic and sound maintenance reasons, to provide a weathercoat which would act as blotting paper, absorbing water and releasing it by evaporation but denying it access to the heart of the wall. The plaster had the considerable additional benefit of providing a simple background against which the enrichment could be enjoyed. The decorative stones were cleaned by lime/poultice, consolidated with limewater and given a lime shelter coat

Figure 1.68 The plaster was a single coat of lime putty, sand and stonedust with a light refractory brickdust gauging. It was applied using small purpose made wood floats and standard small tools, pressing and ironing hard into the profile of the rubble. The result is a pleasing and functional weathering coat with a warm limestone colour which follows the texture of the wall underneath

Figure 1.69 The parapet, buttress caps and finials, distinguished by the lighter (cleaner) colour, are a combination of synthetic mortar and cast stones. Cast stone tends to weather differently from natural stone and its quality varies with the expertise of the manufacturers. Although replacement of 'like with like' should always be the objective in the repair of historic buildings, there are sometimes justifications for using limited casting on selected areas. For instance, if there is genuinely no compatible stone available, parapets and other essential weatherings are better replaced in good quality casts than left at risk

Figure 1.70 The danger of accepting casts in place of natural stone is that it may be seen as a quick and easy option. Larger scale production of these cornice sections in concrete with one 'artificial stone' face is likely to encourage unnecessary replacement. Note that even casts should not be stored on the ground in this haphazard manner. They are liable to damage and staining

Figure 1.71 Some cast stone is of some antiquity and should be conserved. This wall contains about 30% of cast stones made up of hydraulic lime and coloured sands. These casts, placed in late medieval construction, are believed to be of very early nineteenth century date and have performed well without damage to the surviving stones

Figure 1.72 Stone paving is often remarkably durable, having been selected for its resistance to impact and abrasion. The largely undisturbed eighteenth century roadway in Italy is formed of basalt setts. The long dimension embedded in sand or lime sand and pozzolana is 200–250 mm to a surface dimension of 100 × 100 mm. The shape is like a wedge or 'nail', enabling it to be driven into the substrate. This is an efficient unit which takes considerable punishment

Figure 1.73 Limestone setts at Eton, England, in a geometric pattern. Pavings of this kind, or in the more familiar granite, are effective as long as they are thoroughly compacted into the substrate. Eighteenth and nineteenth century pavings of this kind, typically 70 × 160 × 160 mm deep will take heavy traffic if the tails are securely in a well packed base of hydraulic lime and sand or cement:lime: sand (1:3 or 1:2:8)

Figure 1.74 Cobble (water washed sandstone) paving in the process of laying at Richmond, Yorkshire. Note the intermediate bay construction to assist laying to falls. Bedding and tamping are the secret of successful laying. Shallow units of this kind need to be bedded in a strong cement:lime:sand base such as 1:1:6, but they should not be pointed in hard, dense mortar. Hydraulic lime:sand 1:4 would be suitable for pointing, leaving the top and shoulder of the cobble exposed

Figure 1.75 The architect Street's paving at Kingston Church, Dorset. This is a good example of stone texture being used in a functional way to assist pedestrian traffic in the ascent of a steep hill. The kerbs and setts are in Purbeck limestone. Note the importance of not flush-pointing. These random size setts are on average 100 mm deep

Figure 1.76 The process of removing soluble salts from masonry is difficult and can never be totally effective. The concentration of salts can sometimes be reduced by irrigation and poulticing to the extent that lime plastering, limewashing or the local use of a consolidant is successful; or the surface may become more stable without further treatment. This picture shows the effects of storing de-icing salt in a single-skin masonry building. The light coloured zones are evidence of active decay on the external wall surface

Figure 1.77 The first stage in the poulticing process involves the preparation of the wall. Not every wall can be treated by this process and it should never be used where valuable plaster or any timber is associated with the wall surfaces. This picture shows the light coloured area of decay, a temporary gutter secured at the bottom of the wall to receive run-off, and an assembly of water sprays playing on the wall surface

Figure 1.78 Moisture measurements are taken from the centre of the wall. When the joints show that the wall is well penetrated by water (up to seven days on a 450 mm [18 in] wall) the poultice medium is prepared. This picture shows the correct consistency of an attapulgite clay which has been added as a dry powder to clean, fresh water. At this stage the clay can be applied to the wet wall surfaces and will cling to the wall when pressed on with a plastering float

Figure 1.79 This shows the attapulgite clay covering the area of decay. To assist in the support of the clay and to ensure good adhesion is maintained for as long as possible, a galvanized wire mesh is pushed into the wet clay and secured with galvanized staples into the masonry joints. A final working over of the surface with a float assists the embedding of the wire, giving a finished thickness of approximately 20 mm

Figure 1.80 An external clay application must be protected from rain, direct sunlight and strong draughts of air. Here, a simple tarpaulin sheet, securely anchored at the eaves and at the base of the wall, provides adequate protection for the poulticed wall. At this stage, the irrigated wall begins the drying out process. The clay is the drying face and will receive salts in solution from the wall

Figure 1.81 As the wall dries the clay poultice also dries and begins to shrink and crack, pulling away from the wall. Salt growths can be seen on the clay face and the reinforcement. With care, by gently pulling out the staples, the clay and wire 'curtain' can be lifted off the wall as shown here. The dry poultice must be removed from site and not allowed to recontaminate any other surface. The wetting and poulticing cycle is normally repeated three or four times to achieve any useful reduction in salt concentration

Figure 1.82 Desalination attempts are little use if the source of soluble salts remains. At Muchelney Abbey, Somerset, the internal cloister wall had suffered from rising groundwater during marine flooding. Since irrigation and poulticing of these walls would only serve to draw up further salts in solution a barrier needed to be introduced. This picture shows the external face of a wall which is approximately 1.5 m thick at base and is of double skin construction with a core filling

Figure 1.83 A stage in the introduction of a water barrier. Drillings are made through the wall from both sides using the 25 mm diameter, 1.25 m long drill bits seen in the foreground. The wall core is then grouted with a lime:pulverized fuel ash grout to provide continuity through the wall at this level, eliminating any large voids. When the grout has cured, the drill holes are opened again to sufficient depth to insert the feed lines for a pumped silicone resin in solvent. The resin is pumped in from both sides of the wall to establish a damp proof zone against further salt migration

Figure 1.84 The internal face of the same wall, after fresh water irrigation and clay poulticing. At floor level is a bitumenous felt-lined temporary gutter to collect the water during the spraying process. Between the floor and the horizontal string course is the attapulgite clay during the drying-out stage. The light coloured areas show the deposition of soluble salt in the clay. Four wetting and poulticing cycles were needed to stabilize the surface for plastering

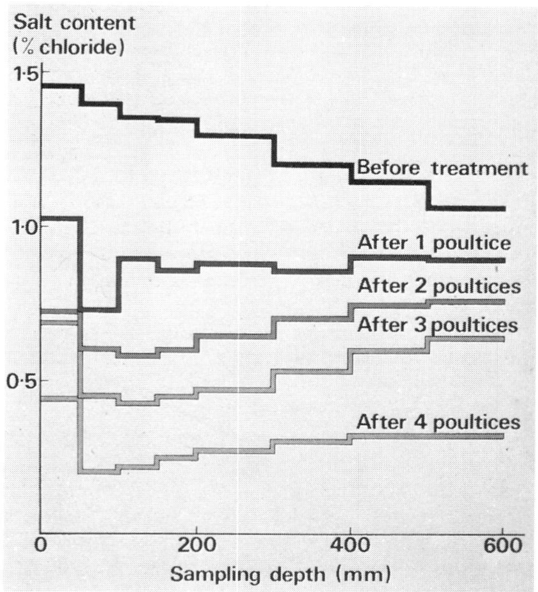

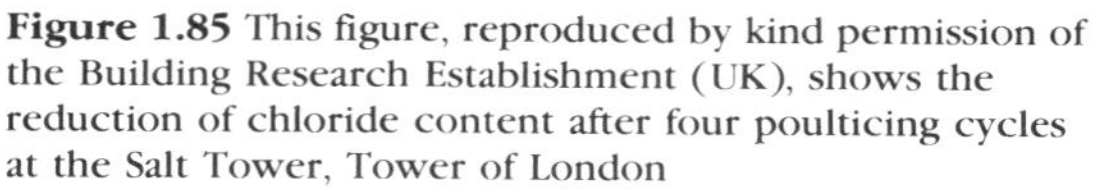

Figure 1.85 This figure, reproduced by kind permission of the Building Research Establishment (UK), shows the reduction of chloride content after four poulticing cycles at the Salt Tower, Tower of London

2

Structural failure and repair

Ralph Mills

Introduction

Before attempting to carry out remedial works to masonry structures, the cause of failure must be determined, bearing in mind that some of the faults may have their origin in the basic form of the construction. Such built-in weaknesses can develop during the life of the structure and may lead to structural failure at a much later date. It is essential, therefore, to diagnose the reasons for failure accurately, in order to avoid unnecessary remedial work.

Foundation failure

Many historic masonry structures have foundations which would be considered inadequate by present-day design standards. However, if such a structure shows no signs of distress and there are no proposals for change of use or for an alteration in the loading pattern, it is unnecessary to improve the bearing capacity. The foundations have proved their ability to transfer safely the loads placed upon them throughout the lifetime of the building. Generally foundations which are satisfactory in an existing situation will only need to be improved if the loading is increased by more than 10%.

Signs of foundation failure can be found by examining the plinth line for differential settlement, or by checking the alignment of masonry joints at wall junctions. The development of cracking in the superstructure should also be assessed, as this may provide further evidence of foundation failure.

The problems caused by shrinkable clays have been widely publicized, particularly the cracking of foundations which can occur in periods of drought. Foundation cracking can also be caused by the removal of nearby trees and shrubs because this will increase the moisture content of the clay and result in local ground heave.

When considering the repair of a masonry structure, the design team is faced with the dilemma of balancing the need to ensure that sufficient remedial work is carried out to secure the safety of the structure against the temptation of trying to achieve too high a safety margin at unnecessary expense.

Structures settle as they are being built and continue to settle thereafter. The rate depends upon the nature of the ground, the speed of the construction and the dead and live loads imposed. This settlement consolidates the ground beneath the foundations, which may eventually provide an adequate load-bearing medium. It would be imprudent to disturb this consolidated ground unnecessarily. If it can be established that differential movement is due to seasonal or moisture variations or shallow foundations, or that only a small increase in bearing capacity is required, then underpinning of the type shown in *Figure 2.1* is likely to be the most appropriate. The base of the masonry must be consolidated to ensure adequate stress distribution, and the excavation and the underpinning should be carried out in the order shown in *Figure 2.2.* This system has the advantage of retaining a large proportion of the existing compacted ground, whilst providing additional depth and bearing capacity to the foundations, thereby minimizing differential settlements. Any further settlement will be resisted by the joint reaction of the consolidated ground and the concrete underpinning.

Chemical grouts can be injected to increase the loadbearing capacity of granular soils, but this method is ineffective for clay or silty soils, because the impermeability of these materials prevents the flow of the grout.

Proprietary piling systems, composed of 'pre-bored' or 'jacked' piles, have been developed for

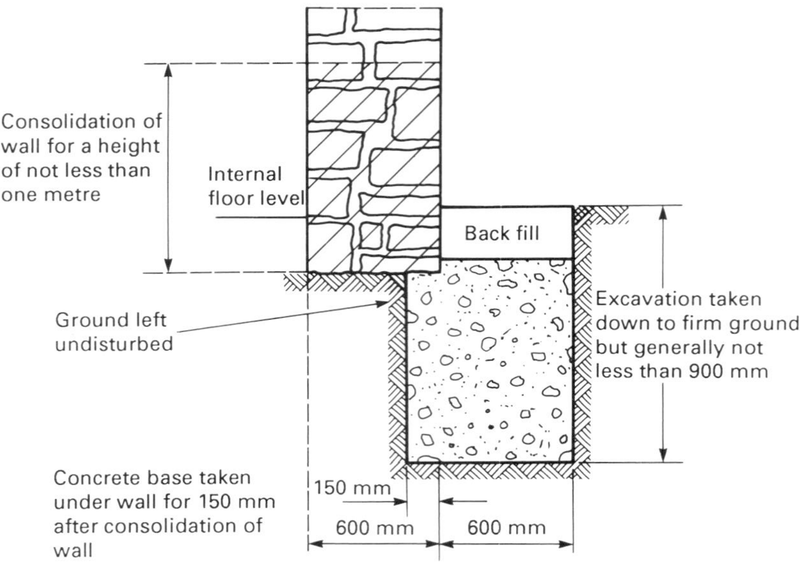

Figure 2.1 Underpinning to walls on shallow foundations

3	1	6	4	2	5	7

Figure 2.2 Order in which foundation underpinning should be carried out

underpinning structures with a minimum of vibration or shock to the surrounding strata. These systems have the added advantage of enabling underpinning to be carried out without the need for dewatering.

Lowering the water table near an existing structure can cause settlement. Therefore piling systems are particularly useful when the water level is above the existing foundation line. Examples of some of the more commonly used types of traditional piling are shown in *Figures 2.3* and *2.4*. A relatively recent development is the introduction of micropiles. These can be either of *in situ* concrete, with external reinforcement in the form of a permanent steel tube, or the well known, friction pile type, with reinforcement embedded in the *in situ* concrete. Pile diameters can be as small as 100 mm and the length can be in excess of ten metres. These piles are usually installed by drilling holes into the ground through the bottom section of the walls as shown in *Figure 2.5*. Installation can be carried out with a minimum of vibration or disturbance to the existing structure. The piles provide good load distribution, whilst ensuring a physical link between the structure and the ground.

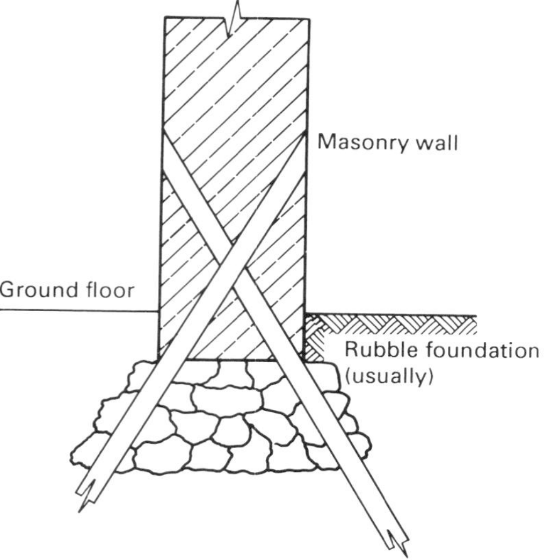

Figure 2.3 Piles through walls of building

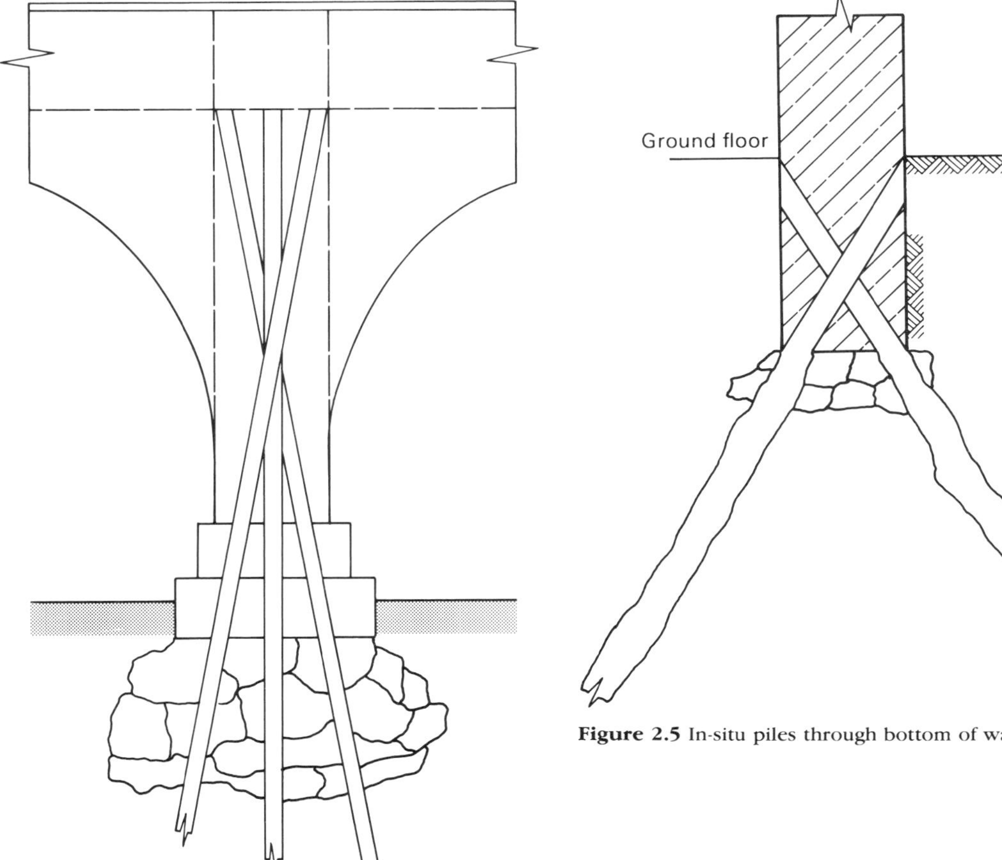

Figure 2.5 In-situ piles through bottom of wall

Figure 2.4 Piles through bridge pier

Structural failure in the superstructure

Factors affecting the strength of masonry struts or compressional members are:

1. *The compressive and shear strength of the masonry units.* In masonry structures, loads are often supported by stone lintels. Whilst these may be relieved to some extent by the arching effect of the masonry above, depending upon the size of unit and the bonding, overloading can occur due to disturbance of the fabric or to differential settlement. Axial compressive forces do not usually present a problem.
2. *The strength of the mortar.* This is usually less than the strength of the stone. However, a mortar of excessive strength can have an adverse effect on the masonry.
3. *The slenderness ratio of the component.* This ratio is determined by the length, form of restraint and cross-sectional shape. A long unit will support a smaller compressive load than a short unit of the same cross-sectional dimensions. A unit which is square or circular in cross-section will support a larger compressive force than a rectangular unit of the same length. The provision of additional end or intermediate restraints will increase the load-bearing capacity of a compressive member. The combination of these properties is expressed as the slenderness ratio, which must be taken into account when designing compression units. Although analytical work is sometimes essential,

it is usually sufficient to have a general understanding of the importance of the slenderness ratio when proposing measures to strengthen or repair masonry structures. Methods used to reduce the slenderness ratio of masonry elements are described later.

4. *Eccentricity of loading.* A force which is not applied uniformly across the section of a compression member, or along its axis, will cause a redistribution of the stresses within the member and will lead to failure either by crushing or by buckling. Horizontal forces due to wind or earth pressures can also produce the same effect. The stresses in masonry structures can, therefore, sometimes be reduced by removing eccentric or horizontal forces. Two simple examples are the provision of a padstone in a wall under a heavily loaded beam, to obtain a more uniform distribution of stresses along the wall, and the support of a beam on a padstone rather than on a corbel.

Tensile members, or ties, are dependent only on the tensile strength of the material and on their cross-sectional area. The slenderness of the component will not affect the strength, although unsightly deflection may need to be prevented. Masonry structures which incorporate large openings or colonnades can sometimes lack lateral stability. Structural integrity can be provided by introducing diagonal bracing, a structural frame, or cross walls.

Failure of arches

The other important structural form which is often used in masonry construction is the arch. Arches can be used in a simple form to support masonry above an opening in a wall, or in a complex arrangement, such as in a vaulted floor or roof.

The two important properties of an arch are the span and the rise. Although the shape of an arch affects the horizontal forces to some extent, these forces reduce as the rise increases in relation to a given span. Therefore, care must be taken to provide adequate lateral restraint to an arch, particularly one which has a small rise. Where distress indicates horizontal movement of the supports, either the load on the arch must be reduced, or remedial measures (in the form of ties, buttressing or corsetting) must be provided in order to resist further horizontal movement. A corset is usually formed of *in situ* reinforced concrete, placed over the extrados of the arch and keyed into the voussoirs. It is designed to resist the horizontal forces by developing a beam action over the span of the arch. In arches constructed of voussoir rings of shallow depth, especially where the mortar joints have deteriorated, there is a risk that buckling will develop.

Compression failure

This type of failure is relatively rare and can be recognized by the spalling face of the masonry. However, care must be taken to ensure a proper interpretation of the symptoms. For instance, where a thin joint was required on the face for architectural reasons or for weatherproofing, it was common practice amongst masons to form rough dressed 'hollow beds' in the stones. This meant that only the outer 15–25 mm (0.6–1 in) needed to be finely and accurately dressed. Similarly, stones with a small bed dimension (front to back) were often dressed off behind the face, to enlarge the mortar joint where it would not be seen. In both cases, as minor settlement, mortar shrinkage or mortar deterioration takes place, an increasing pressure is placed on the vulnerable front edge of each unit, resulting in spalling. This can appear very similar to spalling caused by a compression failure in the structure. Sometimes, damaged stones which were repaired at the time of construction, especially on the arrises, by glueing pieces together with casein, animal glue, or shellac and stonedust, appear to be suffering from compression damage when spalls are lost as a result of the breaking down of the adhesive bond by weathering. Examination of the surface of the break usually indicates the true reason for the failure.

Masonry defects and weaknesses

It has been common knowledge from the earliest times that sedimentary stone should be set on its natural bed, that is, in the way in which it was originally deposited. However, such stones are still sometimes bedded incorrectly, which eventually results in a tendency to delaminate. In these circumstances, the damaged stone may have to be replaced, although consolidation and injection with a resin system, sometimes coupled with stainless steel pins, may significantly slow down the deterioration and avoid disturbance of the original structure.

Built-in ferrous metal cramps and ties were often bedded in lead. However, they were sometimes not given such protection, and as a result corrosion has caused the metal to laminate and to split the surrounding stones. If this has happened, the corroded metal must be cut or drilled out and the damaged stonework repaired. This can be done with a conventional 'plastic stone' or a resin-based filler, although there will be circumstances where the scale of the deterioration, or architectural requirements, will demand replacement in matching natural stone.

Pointing with a cement-rich mortar can produce the same effect as that caused by forming a hollow bed in the stone. The rich mortar provides a very strong wedge, which causes the face of the stone to spall off under compression.

The role of atmospheric pollution and other agencies of decay and weathering (see Volume 1, Chapter 7) can be responsible for symptoms which may be misinterpreted by the uninformed. For instance, the small cracks naturally present in stone, and referred to as 'vents', can open up after weathering has removed superficial natural bonding. They can look remarkably like fine cracks caused by differential movement of the structure.

The failure patterns caused by some methods of cleaning, the proximity of sandstone to limestone, efflorescence, vegetation and fire must be diagnosed correctly in order to avoid unnecessary remedial work.

Investigation of cracking

Examination of cracking in the internal plaster or external rendering, without cutting chases to expose the basic structure, is a common mistake. Plaster or rendering can conceal built-up doorways or window openings where the infill has not been bonded or toothed into the original work, with the result that cracking can occur along the straight joints. It is a relatively simple operation either to stitch across these straight joints, or to fix one of the proprietary light, expanded metal strips over the joint before replastering or rendering. There will be occasions, both when the masonry is exposed and when it is covered by rendering or plaster, when it may be necessary not to disturb the form of an opening and when stitching will not be appropriate for historical reasons. If the masonry is exposed, the plane of weakness formed by the straight joint can be strengthened by distributing the loads over the opening by inserting spreaders or ring beams, or, in some cases, by resin injection and pins.

Cracks can also be caused by the differential settlement of adjacent parts of the structure which have been built at different periods. In these circumstances, quite large cracks may be apparent, but, if the structure has reached a state of equilibrium, it will not be necessary to install underpinning. If continuing movement is suspected, accurate monitoring over a period of up to two years will indicate whether or not remedial work is necessary (see below). There can also be variations in ground conditions across the building which may have caused differential movement in the past, but which have reached a state of stability during the lifetime of the building.

Bomb damage, or nearby explosions, can develop planes of weakness in the structure or aggravate an already weakened situation. Most masonry structures have been subject to alterations during their life and the structural implications of their movements have not always been recognized or understood by those carrying out remedial work. For example, bowing and bulging of face walls may have been caused by the removal of cross walls, or the insertion of large openings in cross walls, rendering them ineffective as lateral supports. The reason for the failure must be established. In such cases, suspended floors might, for instance, be used to provide the necessary support, as shown in *Figures 2.6* and *2.7*.

Thick masonry walls are often constructed of two skins with an unbonded rubble core between. If there are sufficient voids within the core, the effective thickness and, therefore, the strength of the wall can be increased by a cementitious grout injection, provided care is taken to avoid a high hydrostatic pressure developing within the wall due to an excessive head of grout. Grouting will be of very little value if the core has been filled, or almost

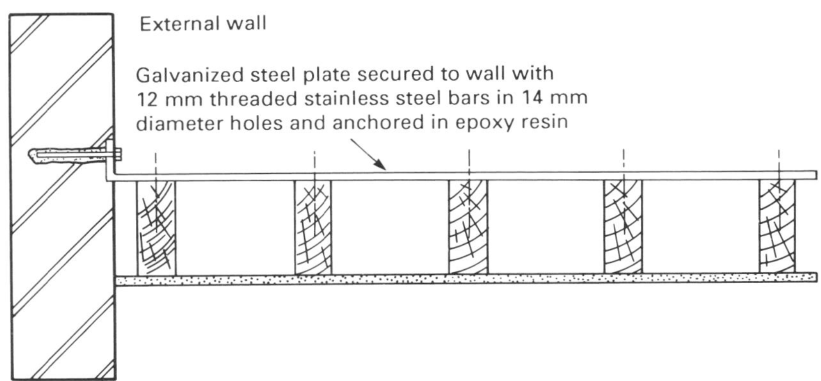

Figure 2.6 Suspended floor providing lateral support to external wall (1)

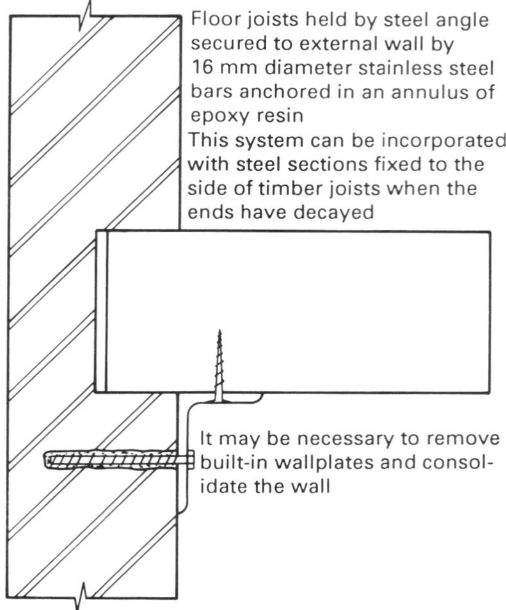

Figure 2.7 Suspended floor providing lateral support to external wall (2)

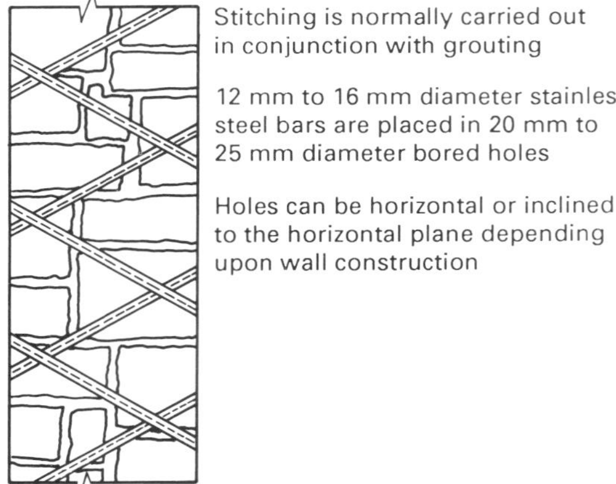

Figure 2.8 Stitching masonry wall

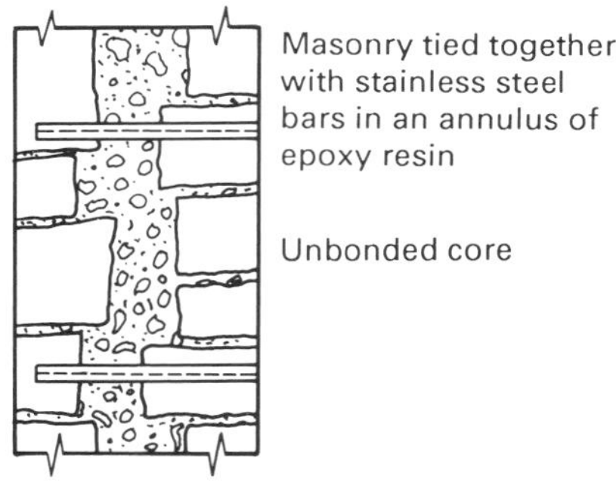

Figure 2.9 Masonry tied together with stainless steel bars in an annulus of epoxy resin; unbonded core

filled, with a very soft lime mortar. It is wise, therefore, to drill a number of exploratory holes through the wall in order to properly examine the composition of the core.

Alternative methods of increasing the effective thickness of masonry walls are to stitch, as shown in *Figure 2.8*, or to tie the two skins together. *Figures 2.9* and *2.10* show a number of techniques which are now used to form a tie between two skins of masonry. There are several proprietary systems now being offered by specialist firms, but the technique was originally developed in the UK by the Building Research Establishment in conjunction with the Directorate of Ancient Monuments and Historic Buildings.

There are many masonry structures where the cross walls are not bonded into the external walls and, as a result, the external walls can become unstable. *Figures 2.11* and *2.12* show a number of ways in which to restore stability to such walls.

Where conservation work has been carried out, ties have sometimes been installed because of a misinterpretation of the visible symptoms. For example, walls with a batter have not necessarily moved, and a measurement of both faces for out-of-plumbness, with careful examination at the junctions with any cross walls, will often show that the walls are structurally adequate. The chancel and nave walls of churches are good examples of walls which are often out of plumb and where unsightly ties have been installed unnecessarily in the past. These ties must not, of course, be removed without very careful study of the structure. If removal is being considered, it is prudent to dismantle the ties gradually, after first installing an accurate system of monitoring and establishing a record of any movement before the ties are disturbed.

Bonding timbers are often found in masonry walls, particularly in walls of random rubble, and it is a great temptation to remove them on discovery. Removal of these timbers, however, can cause a great deal of disturbance to the masonry and, if the timbers are free from decay, it will often be more economic and less disruptive to inject them with a fungicide and leave them in place.

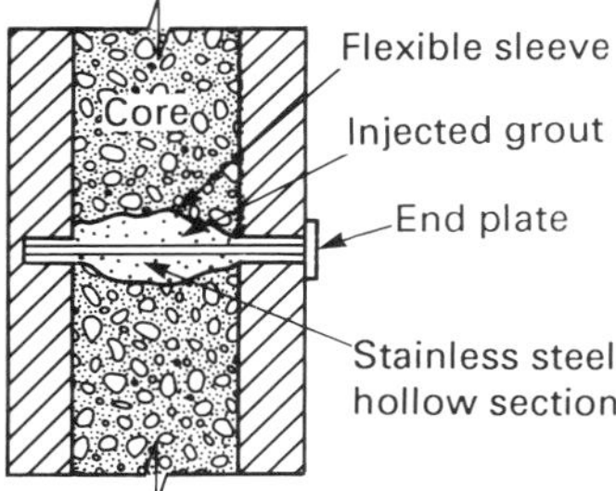

Resin cartridge pushed to the end of the drilled hole. Cartridge broken and resin mixed when bolt is inserted

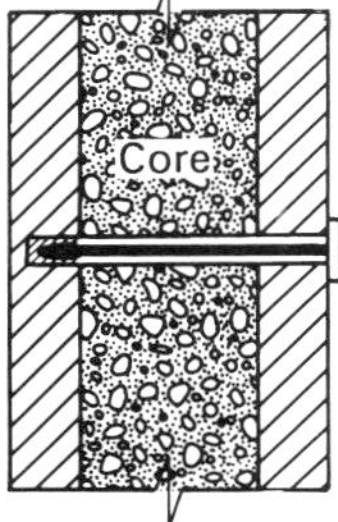

Figure 2.10 Proprietary systems of wall ties

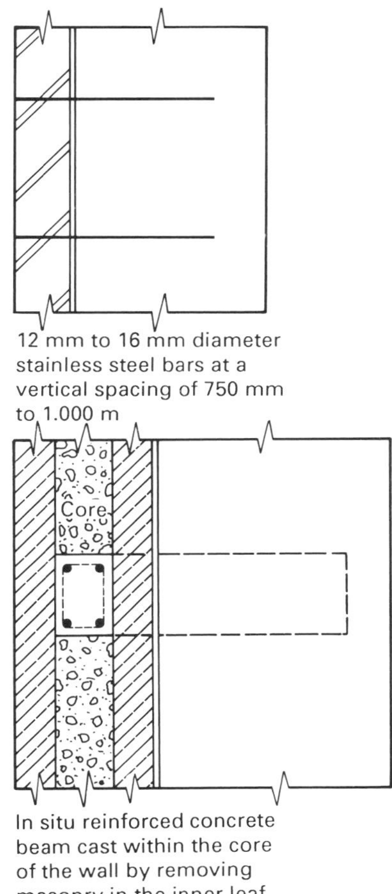

Figure 2.11 Reinstating the bond between external and cross walls (1)

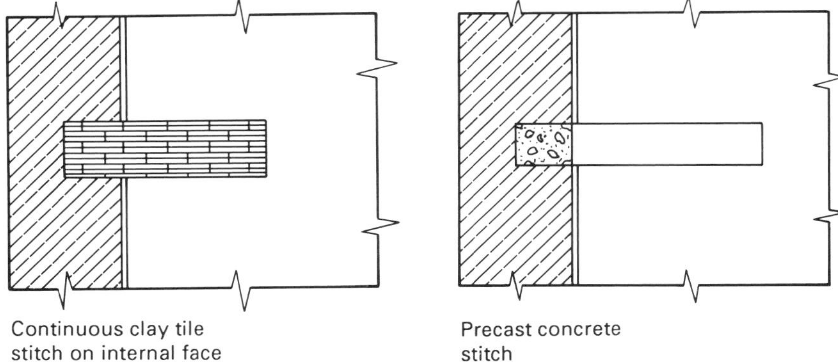

Figure 2.12 Reinstating the bond between external and cross walls (2)

Monitoring

The implications of cracks in historic masonry structures should not be judged on appearances. Such structures can have cracks of 25 mm or more in width and still be considered structurally adequate. However, assessment of the importance of large established cracks, or the possibility of continuing differential movement, should not be based on visual memory, but on a proper system of monitoring.

Significant results from an accurate monitoring system may take up to two years to obtain, but there can be occasions when such a system is of almost immediate value. For instance, a monitoring system may be able to demonstrate quite quickly that an anticipated structural repair is not required, thus saving money and avoiding unnecessary disturbance of the building. Unfortunately, there have been many examples of the collapse of masonry structures during repair works of questionable necessity where insufficient attention was paid to existing places of weakness. Sensible examination, supported by evidence obtained from monitoring, could have prevented these problems.

The choice of monitoring system will depend upon the location, the defect to be monitored and the nature of the material to which the system is to be fixed. Accuracy is essential and expenditure on labour and materials may vary only marginally between relatively crude and sophisticated systems. However, the possibility of vandalism or accidental damage can be a serious problem in locations where the general public has access. For this reason and in order to avoid disfigurement of a building, monitoring systems should be unobtrusive. Glass and cement tell-tales, which are still sometimes seen on masonry structures despite their ugly appearance and their unreliability, should not be used.

Proposals to carry out work on masonry structures which are scheduled or statutorily listed will need to be approved either by the Secretary of State or by the local authority. Approval can be refused if it is considered that the historic structure would be damaged or significantly altered. An accurate system of monitoring can be invaluable in such circumstances, because it can provide information on the exact extent of the repairs required.

Measuring differential movement

One of the most effective, inexpensive and inconspicuous systems of monitoring differential movement over cracks and planes of weakness is the Demec mechanical demountable strain gauge, which was developed in the UK by the Cement and Concrete Association and is shown in *Figure 2.13*. However, for friable surfaces and for areas where the public has free access, it will generally be necessary to use pins fixed into pre-drilled holes, as shown in *Figure 2.14*. The pins are normally driven flush with the surface and a small hole is then drilled in the head of each pin, as a locating point for the demountable gauge.

Whatever system is used, locating points should not be fixed across cracks in plaster or rendering. These cracks often follow straight joints, or places of weakness in the load-bearing structure, which can be easily revealed by cutting small, neat chases across the line of the crack as shown in *Figure 2.15*. Remedial work can then often be proposed in the form of stitching or grouting, based on the evidence uncovered. Moreover, plaster can move independently from the basic structure, owing to variations

Figure 2.13 Demec demountable strain gauge

Figure 2.14 Preparing locating point for demountable strain gauge

in temperature. More reliable information, therefore, will be obtained by fixing the locating points or pins to the main load-bearing elements.

Movements of 0.025 mm (0.001 in) are easily detected by the mechanical strain gauge, but it should be remembered that the readings obtained are strain and not absolute movements. In order to obtain the actual movement, the following calculation is necessary;

$$\text{Strain} = \frac{\text{displacement}}{\text{original length}}$$

For the imperial gauge, one division represents a strain of 1×10^{-5} and a movement of 1×10^{-4} in. The corresponding values for the metric gauge are 0.53×10^{-5} strain and 2×10^{-3}mm movement. The pivot on the moving arm is off-centre and the lengths on each side of the pivot have a ratio of 10:8. Therefore, using the metric gauge one division is equal to a displacement of $2 \times 10^{-3} \times 0.8 = 1.6 \times 10^{-3}$ mm. Checking the values,

$$\text{Strain} = \frac{2 \times 10^{-3} \times 0.8}{300}$$

$$= 0.53 \times 10^{-5}$$

An Invar bar is provided, so that a correction can also be made for changes in temperature.

An alternative and less expensive system is to allow the locating pins to project from the surface and to measure the distance between the external faces, using vernier callipers as shown in *Figure 2.16*.

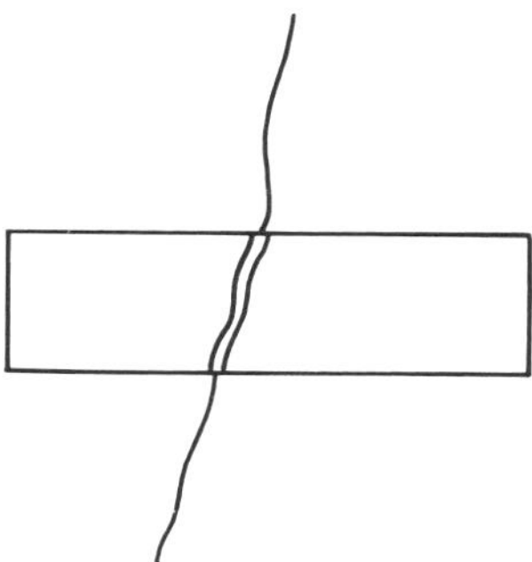

Figure 2.15 Chase cut through plaster across line of crack exposed in basic structure

Figure 2.16 Alternative method of measuring differential movement

Measuring vertical movement

Vertical movement will only damage a structure if differential displacement takes place. However, in order to provide a reliable record and to avoid misinterpretation, it is necessary, especially for the more important projects, to record absolute movements.

The greatest structural problems in masonry buildings usually occur in areas where coal or salt mining operations have caused subsidence. In these areas a great deal of useful information can be obtained by examining the recorded heights of the Ordnance Survey bench marks. These marks are found on substantial structures, as illustrated in *Figure 2.17*, and the locations are shown on large-scale maps of the area. Bench mark lists, containing fuller and possibly later levelling information, are obtainable from the Director General of the Ordnance Survey in Southampton, England.

Because of the likely distance between the Ordnance Survey bench mark and the structure to be monitored, and also to obtain initial support for the levelling staff, it will usually be necessary to establish an independent datum. Where independent datums are set up, a minimum of three reference points should be provided in order to confirm the stability of the datum being used.

When a satisfactory datum is established, levelling stations can be provided most efficiently by the use of Building Research Establishment levelling sockets. Care must be taken to ensure that the sockets are securely fixed into masonry which is firmly bonded into the wall. This will provide reliable stations, which will indicate accurately any vertical movement which has occurred in the structure. The vertical movements recorded will generally be of such small magnitude that the use of a precise level of the type shown in *Figure 2.18* will be required, combined with a levelling staff equipped with a device to ensure its verticality.

Figure 2.17 Ordnance Survey bench mark

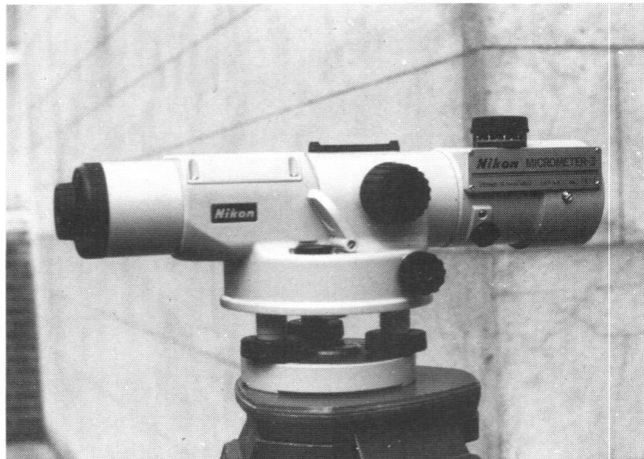

Figure 2.18 Precision level

Measuring movement out of the vertical plane

Plumb bobs are still used to measure movement out of the vertical plane. They can be quite accurate if a plumb bob of sufficient weight is used and it is suspended from a high tensile wire.

There are two main problems in the use of plumb bobs;

1. The readings will generally need to be taken over a relatively long period and there are very few locations where fixed gauging wires can be tolerated. The use of demountable plumb bobs requires an accurate means of location, which will ensure that repeated measurements within the permissible range of variation can be made.
2. The plumb bob will oscillate in the wind, although this can sometimes be prevented by suspending it in a container of oil or water.

Alternatively, a theodolite can be used by sighting on to installed targets or architectural features; this overcomes the various disadvantages of the plumb bob. A five-second variation in the subtended angle will result in an error of approximately 20 mm over a distance of 10.000 mm, which is within the acceptable tolerance limits for this type of work.

The autoplumb is a sophisticated form of plumb bob and is shown in *Figure 2.19*. A target is required at a high level and a station at ground level. The height of the target above ground level should be recorded accurately at the time of installation. The procedure for recording movements is described below.

The autoplumb is levelled in all directions and sited over the ground station, as shown in *Figure 2.20*. Compass readings in all directions are then taken on the high level target. A reading of 10.00 represents a truly vertical line and the rotation of the micrometer drum tilts the line of site away or towards the observer, depending upon the direction of rotation. One revolution of the drum displaces the line of site by an angle having a natural tangent of 0.001. As shown in *Figure 2.21*, b_1 is recorded and deducted from H to give b_2.

In *Figure 2.21:*

H = height of target from ground station
b_1 = height from ground station to centre of focusing control (top telescope)
b_2 = height from the centre of the focusing control (top telescope) to target
d = displacement recorded on micrometer drum

Therefore, $\tan \theta = 0.001 = d/b_2$ for one revolution. Assuming a value of 10.50 m for H and 1.50 m for b_1, $b_2 = 9.00$ m.

A reading of 9.560 with the instrument pointed in a southerly direction represents a displacement of $10.00 - 9.560 = 0.440$ in a northerly direction. Reversing the line of sights and taking another reading of, say, 10.436 represents a displacement of 0.436 in the northerly direction. For absolute accuracy and with the instrument in perfect adjustment, the two readings should total 20.000. In the example in *Figure 2.21*, the readings total 19.996.

Figure 2.19 Autoplumb

Figure 2.20 Autoplumb positioned over ground station

$$\text{The actual value of } d = \frac{0.440 + 0.436}{2} = 0.438$$

$$\text{From } 0.438 \times 0.001 = \frac{\text{displacement}}{9.000}$$

$$\text{displacement} = 0.438 \times 0.001 \times 9000 = 3.94\text{mm}$$

By repeating this procedure in an easterly and a westerly direction, the centre of the target can be located in relation to the ground station. The actual positions can then be recorded and the movement plotted on a graph.

Recording the results of monitoring

The recording of monitoring on site is best carried out in tabular form. A proper interpretation can only be made, however, if the results are presented in a graphical form. Typical examples are shown in *Figures 2.22* and *2.23*.

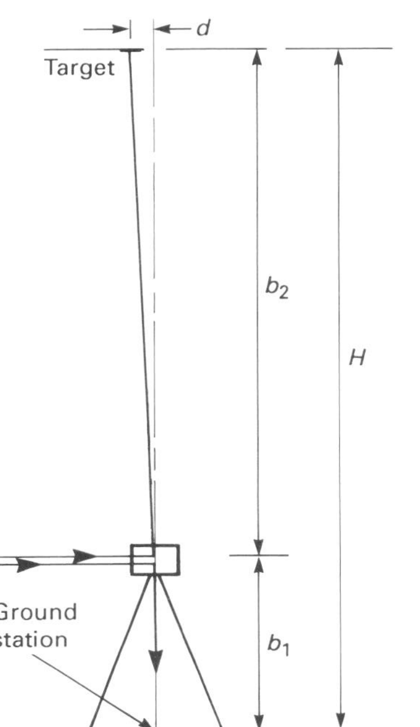

Figure 2.21 Measuring movement out of vertical

Lasers

The very narrow monochromatic beam from a laser, used in conjunction with one or more targets, is a very reliable way in which to measure deflection or differential movement over a structure, where access can be provided to the laser and to the targets. In most situations, the laser will have to be demountable, but fixed in such a way that it can be repositioned accurately. The possibility of the targets being accidentally damaged or vandalized should also be considered.

Repair techniques using polyester and epoxy resins

Resins and polymers have been used increasingly over the past twenty to thirty years, but there is no doubt that their full potential has yet to be exploited. Unfortunately, the reputation of these materials has probably suffered because of their use by inexperienced operatives, with disappointing results. Nevertheless, resins and polymers have a valuable role to

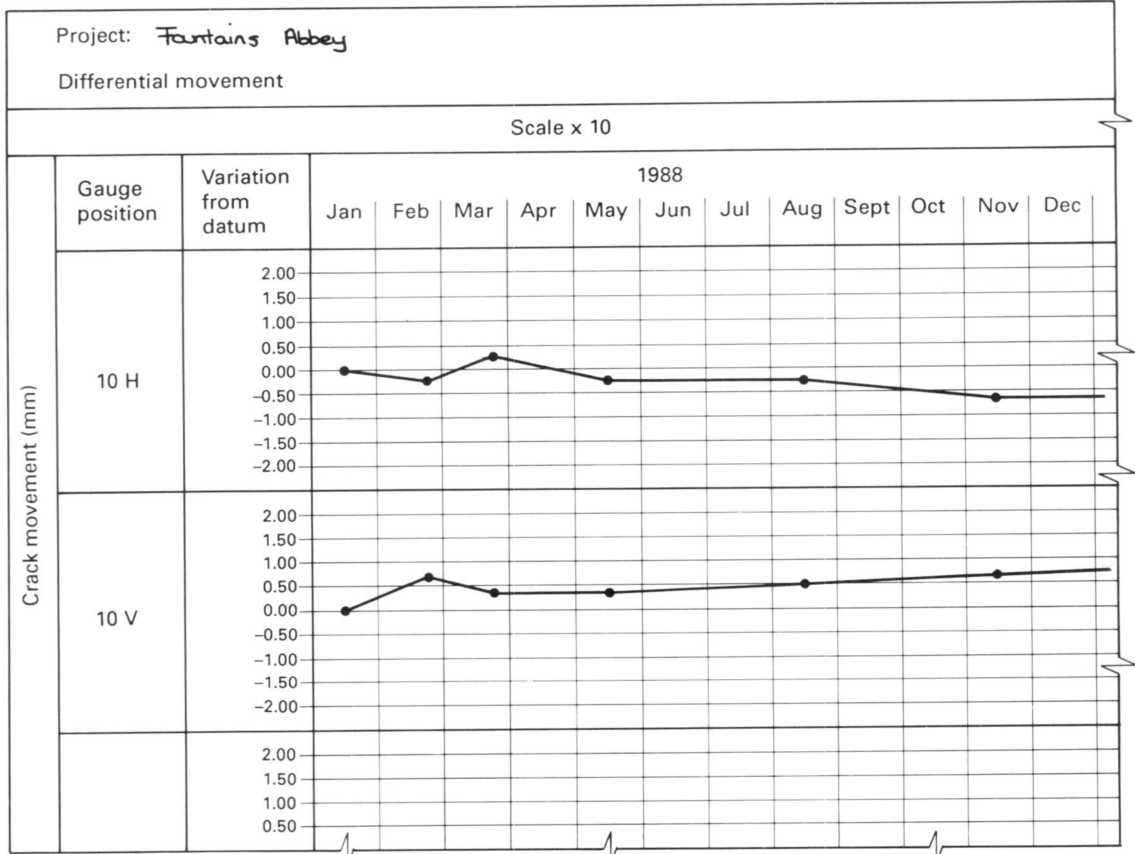

Figure 2.22 Record of differential movement

play in the repair of historic structures, provided that the manufacturer's instructions are followed carefully.

The chemistry of epoxy and polyester resins

Polymerization is the linking together of small, simple molecules to form large units called polymers. It was first developed in Britain during the 1930s. Polymers can be either thermosetting or thermoplastic. A thermosetting polymer is one that can be moulded into the required shape whilst hot, but becomes hard and brittle when cool. It cannot be melted again once solidified. A thermoplastic polymer may be softened and hardened alternatively.

Epoxy and polyester resins are both classed as thermosetting unsaturated polymers because, when cured, the molecular chains are locked permanently together. Unlike thermoplastics, unsaturated polymers do not melt or flow when heated, although they do become more rubbery and gradually lose strength with the increase in temperature. For cured epoxy systems, the heat distortion temperature is in the region of 50 °C (122 °F). If the temperature is allowed to exceed this level, thermosetting polymers will decompose. Unsaturated polymers are composed of organic compounds containing double or triple bonds. Polymers generally have good electrical insulating properties, excellent adhesion and high strength. They are resistant to a large range of chemicals and are impermeable. However, there are chemical differences between epoxy and polyester resins, which give them different properties.

Epoxy resin

Epoxy resin consists of a reactive resin, which cures by the addition of a hardener. It is essential to comply strictly with the manufacturer's recommendation for the proportions of hardener and resin, in order to achieve the required chemical bond and optimum strength. Part packs of the materials should

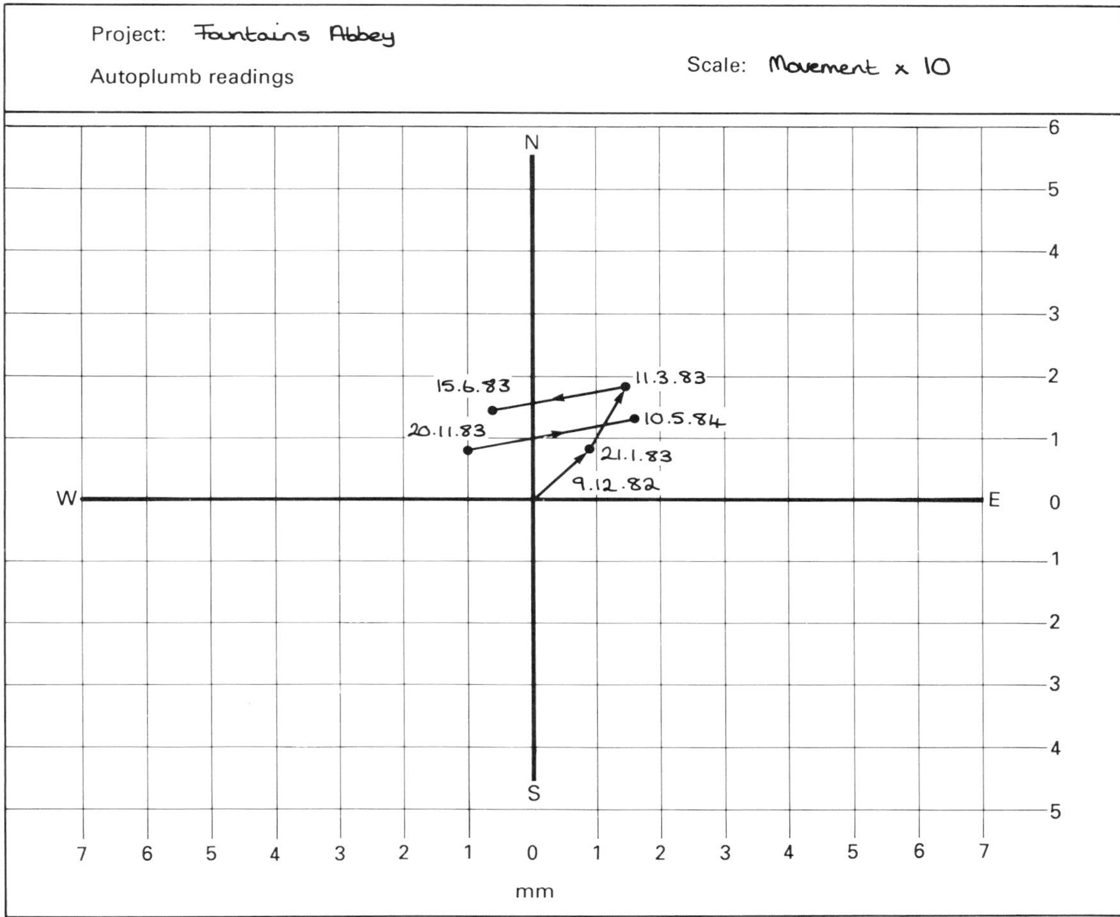

Figure 2.23 Record of autoplumb readings

never be used. If the recommended proportion of hardener is increased, in an attempt to produce a high strength resin, the opposite result will be achieved. Because the curing of epoxy resins is an exothermic reaction, during which heat is given off, the rate of cure is temperature dependent and can be assumed to double with an increase of temperature of about 10 °C. Because epoxy resins are poor heat conductors, the rate of cure also depends upon the volume of material used. Although special formulations will cure down to 0 °C, curing will generally stop at temperatures below 5 °C.

Maximum heat evolution usually occurs when the epoxy resin is in a fluid state, although there can be a considerable temperature differential between the set resin and the surrounding structure. Although the volume change between the freshly mixed and the cured resin is small, the subsequent thermal contraction can result in a build-up of stresses between the resin and the adjacent materials. Therefore, the volume of resin to be placed or injected, the size of the fissure to be filled and the ambient temperature all need to be taken into consideration.

Polyester resins

Polyester resins are generally much cheaper than epoxy resin systems and chemically more simple. The hardener acts only as a catalyst and does not combine chemically, as in epoxy resin systems. The proportioning is therefore not so critical, but this slight flexibility should not be abused.

The curing of polyester is also exothermic, but it differs from the curing of epoxy resin in two significant aspects:

1. The maximum heat evolution occurs after the resin has set.

2. The change in volume between the freshly mixed and the cured polyester is greater than for epoxy resins.

The effect of these two characteristics is dependent upon the volume of resin injected. They increase the possibility of differential stresses between the resin and the surrounding material and can also be responsible for the development of shrinkage cracking. Specialist contractors, therefore, usually have an understandable preference for using epoxy resins, rather than the cheaper polyester resin. Additionally, polyester resin is not as reliable in damp conditions as epoxy resin.

Application

The proportion of filler for both epoxy and polyester resins can be varied by experienced operatives, but as a general rule the two or three balanced pack systems, which are normally supplied by the manufacturers to suit the requirements of a particular set of conditions, should not be altered. As well as correct proportioning of the constituents, particularly for epoxy resins, adequate preparation of surfaces and proper application of the material is also important in order to obtain optimum bonding. Care should be taken to prevent the material from marking or damaging surrounding surfaces, although new manufacturing techniques have recently produced epoxy resins which can be removed from plain surfaces with a moistened sponge or rag, provided that the resin has not yet cured and there has been no absorption into the surface.

Safety precautions

The need for adequate precautions to be taken to prevent personal injury cannot be overstressed. Some materials present a fire hazard and it may be necessary to enforce regulations governing the storage of highly flammable and liquefied petroleum gases and to prohibit smoking during the handling of these materials. The raw materials should be kept dry and protected from extremes of temperature.

Some materials can cause skin irritation which may, in some cases, accelerate the onset of dermatitis. Therefore, handling precautions should be observed to prevent uncured epoxy resin, or polyester resins and their solvents, from coming into contact with the skin or eyes and from being inhaled. An adequate supply of warm water, mild soaps, disposable hand towels, protective clothing, breathing apparatus and special barrier and removing creams should be provided for the use of the operatives, as appropriate. The provision of proper ventilation is also essential. Solvents must not be used to remove any material which may have come in contact with the skin, as this may increase penetration into the pores and remove essential oils from the skin.

Masonry repairs

Small cracks of less than 0.1 mm can be filled with epoxy or polyester resin using gravity, pressure or vacuum techniques. The method chosen will depend upon the size, nature and location of the repair to be carried out and, also, on whether a specialist or general contractor is to be responsible for the work. Vacuum injection is usually carried out by developing a negative pressure between an enclosing polythene membrane and the masonry to be treated. The negative pressure enables the resin to be conducted from tanks around the masonry into the fissures or cracks which may be present. A vacuum process should only be adopted when the section of masonry under repair can be isolated, because any inflow of air from an adjoining unprotected section can prevent the maintenance of an adequate negative pressure, which is necessary to ensure proper impregnation. The choice between gravity or pressure techniques will usually be dictated by the nature of the work and the size of the fissure or crack to be filled. Specialist contractors will usually recommend some form of pressure impregnation, by using the type of gun shown in *Figure 2.24*, or the simple pump shown in *Figure 2.25*. Grease guns were used in the early days, but they have been superseded by more sophisticated equipment. This has largely overcome the difficulty of controlling the pressures applied and the problems arising from intermittent injection. Pressure guns should be fitted with gauges to ensure accurate use.

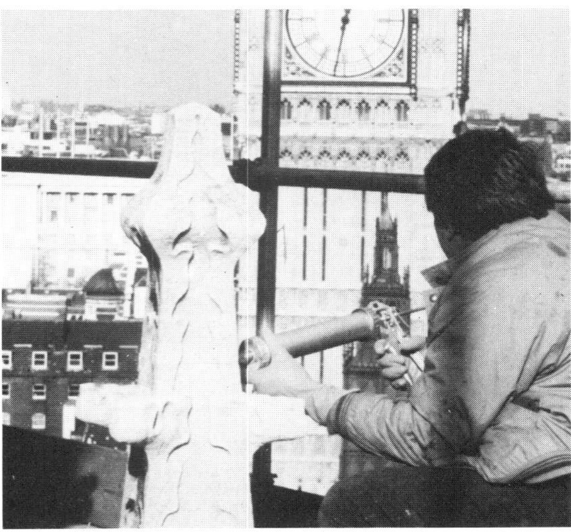

Figure 2.24 Pressure impregnation using gun

Figure 2.25 Pressure impregnation using pump

Pressure pots can be used, but these need to be quite large and it can be difficult to determine when the pots are empty and whether the resin is flowing freely, especially at low flow rates.

Whatever equipment is being used, it needs to be mobile in order to avoid long delivery lines. There are obvious advantages in having equipment which allows the continual supply of freshly mixed resin on demand.

Cracking, due to differential movement of the structure caused by foundation settlement or failure of the superstructure, by expansion of embedded and corroding ferrous metal, or by mortar under sulphate attack, can result in the disintegration of joints, the core filling and the masonry units themselves. The repair of mortar joints should be made by raking out, followed by packing and pointing in lime mortar. The integrity of the masonry units can often be restored *in situ* by the injection of epoxy resin. In some cases, the original profile of the unit also can be restored, if required, by using special epoxy mortars. However, this may be inappropriate because of the variation in weathering between surviving stones and the relatively impermeable resin-faced repairs. Embedded and corroding metal should be removed before any masonry repairs are attempted. Once disruptive metal has been removed, epoxy resin repairs can prevent further deterioration of the masonry caused by the ingress of water and subsequent frost action. Cramps can be replaced by using epoxy resins and, where additional strength is required, stainless steel dowels set within an annulus of epoxy resin can prove an effective tie. Repairs of this kind may enable more original material to be retained than would be possible by conventional cutting out and piecing in with replacement stone. They may also be more economic.

The cause of the masonry failure should always be established before repairs are attempted. The rectification of foundation settlements is beyond the scope of this book, but the strength of the superstructure can often be restored by re-establishing the bond between external and cross walls, or between floors and walls, by using stainless steel ties set in epoxy resin. Some typical examples are given in *Figures 2.9* and *2.10*.

Should there be any suggestion that differential movement in the structure has not stopped, it may be better to seal the cracks with a low modulus sealant in order to prevent the ingress of water, rather than to form a rigid area of repair, which may encourage cracking to develop in another part of the structure. If this course of action is followed, it is essential that an accurate system of monitoring is installed.

Separating skins of masonry can be tied together by stainless steel rods set in epoxy resin. This system was first developed in the UK at the Building Research Station, working in conjunction with the Directorate of Ancient Monuments and Historic Buidings. Several proprietary systems have been evolved subsequently. Anchor bolts can also be set in epoxy resin. These have an advantage over expansive mechanical systems because there is no danger of cracking the stone by overtightening.

Repairing cracks in masonry

The cracks should first be examined to determine whether any cleaning is necessary and any loose material present should be removed by flushing out with water or compressed air. Care should be taken to see that small pieces of stone are not displaced, which could cause an unsightly appearance after the injection has been completed. If there are many small fragments of stone in the area of the repair, it will be more difficult to seal the joints effectively in preparation for injection. Sealing can be carried out by one of the following methods:

1. Packing and pointing the vertical and bed joints with lime mortar.
2. Packing and pointing with a polymer modified cementitious stonedust and sand mortar.
3. Adhesive taping of cracks. Taping is unreliable on friable, dusty surfaces and there is a high risk of resin bleeding. This method leaves the cured resin flush with the exposed masonry face.
4. The cracks can be plugged with a material which can be stripped or melted out after completion of the injection. This method enables conventional mortar pointing, matching the face of the stone, to conceal the repair. This is usually the most satisfactory method, allowing a visual check to be made on the effectiveness of the grouting and for the work then to be concealed.

Injection points can then be formed through the seal at a spacing which depends upon the width, depth and length of the cracks (see *Figure 2.26*).

Injection should be carried out systematically in order to dispel air and water in the voids, starting

Figure 2.26 Injecting resin to repair masonry cracks

from the lowest point and maintaining pressure until the resin exudes from one of the injection points at a higher level. Any resin which runs on the face of the masonry must be removed immediately. The danger of runs staining the masonry or curing on the face can be minimized by the application of a synthetic latex skin around the area of repair before injection is carried out. Once the resin has reached the level of a higher injection point, the lower entry point is plugged and injection continued upwards. Injection pressures can be varied over a wide range and can be as high as 2 N/mm^2. The viscosity of the resin can be adjusted, in order to prevent loss through internal voids.

Surface repairs in epoxy resin

The success of surface repairs depends to a great extent on the surface preparation and on the choice of formulation related to the performance required. Resin mortars can, if necessary, be made relatively weak and porous. Proprietary materials are available for cleaning the surface of the substrate before the application of epoxy resin. This is necessary if a high bond is to be achieved. Alternatively, an acid cleaning solution for limestone can be prepared by adding commercial grade concentrated hydrochloric acid to clean water, in the proportion of 1 to 4. This acid solution is brushed on to the surface of the substrate with a stiff brush and then washed off with water. Care must be taken not to spill cleaning solutions on surrounding work, or to leave residues in the stone. Pre-wetting the area before the use of acid, in order to reduce absorption, is important.

Metals can usually be cleaned of traces of oil and grease by washing with a detergent, followed by rinsing with clean water. Mill scale or rust should be removed by grit blasting, if possible, but vigorous wire brushing can be a satisfactory alternative.

The future

Development work is being carried out in the UK, the USA and Japan which is principally concerned with the addition of external reinforcement to structures, such as the strengthening of bridges by bonding steel plates on to existing concrete beams with epoxy resin. Experimental work is also being carried out concerning the effects of curing temperatures, thickness of adhesive layers, fatigue loading and contact with water on the shear and bonding stresses of epoxy resin. The results are awaited eagerly by conservationists and the building profession generally, who perhaps still need to be convinced of the long term effectiveness of these new repair techniques.

The physical properties of epoxy and polyester resin systems

The precise physical properties of epoxy and polyester resin systems are indefinable. However, the following values given in Table 2.1 can be used as a guide when considering the use of these materials.

Table 2.1 Physical properties of epoxy and polyester resin systems

Physical property	*Epoxy resin*	*Polyester resin*
Compressive strength (N/mm^2)	40–100	60–100
Tensile strength (N/mm^2)	10–50	10–40
Flexural strength (N/mm^2)	25–60	25–30
Young's modulus *E*, in compression (N/mm^2)	1000–20 000	2000–10 000
Percentage elongation to break	0–15	0–5
Linear coefficient of thermal expansion per degree Celsius	$25–30 \times 10^{-6}$	$25–30 \times 10^{-6}$
Linear shrinkage (per cent)	~0.15	–
Rate of strength development	6–8 hours	2–6 hours
Heat distortion per degree Celsius	50–70	60–100

3

The selection of stone for repairs

David B. Honeyborne

Introduction

No doubt any architect responsible for selecting stone for repairing a building of historic or artistic merit would prefer to employ stone from the same quarry and even from the same bed that provided the stone originally, and to ensure that the new stone has reasonably high resistance to weathering.

In many circumstances the origin of the stone is not sufficiently well established for the bed or quarry to be identified. Even if the quarry is known, the working face may have retreated so far that the exposed stone differs significantly from the stone in the building. A change in land-ownership or some other factor may also prevent any further extraction of the stone. The architect is then faced with the task of finding a stone which is a reasonable match with the original, and possesses workability, durability and other properties appropriate for the circumstances.

Selecting new stone to match the original in appearance

To provide a good match, a cut surface of the new stone must be similar in texture and colour to the cut surfaces of its prospective neighbours, both wet and dry. Its appearance must also merge well with the weathered surfaces of its neighbours after long exposure. Unless the architect knows of suitable types of stone from past experience, the best way to make a choice is to look for a good match in other buildings of similar age which are constructed of stone from known quarries that are still in business or could easily be re-opened.

In the rather rare circumstances where the need for repair is foreseen, but the repair is not to be effected for a number of years, it can sometimes be helpful to expose blocks of possible substitutes near the building and observe the appearance they develop. Stone required for very exposed features such as copings, string-courses and sills, should be exposed free from shelter and facing the same direction as those features. Stone that is intended for more sheltered features should be exposed facing the same direction as those features, but comparably sheltered. In all circumstances, the proposed substitute stone should be of the same lithology as the stone it is required to match; that is, limestone should be used to match limestone, sandstone to match sandstone and so on. The use of Magnesian Limestone to match limestone should be avoided as far as possible. The options rationally open to the architect are summarized in the logic flow chart given in *Figure 3.1*.

Organizations such as the British Geological Survey[1] and the Building Research Establishment[2] might be able to help locate appropriate quarries and buildings in the United Kingdom. The Building Research Establishment, the Sedgwick Museum[3] and the British Museum (Natural History) also hold collections of a wide range of building stones, including some foreign stones. However, many of these stones are no longer commercially available. Some commercial organizations, such as the Cathedral Works Organization,[4] have specimens of some currently available foreign stones, particularly from France and Germany. The *Natural Stone Directory*[5] gives addresses of currently operating quarries in the United Kingdom.

Selection for durability

After tentatively choosing a type of stone that will match the existing stonework, consideration should

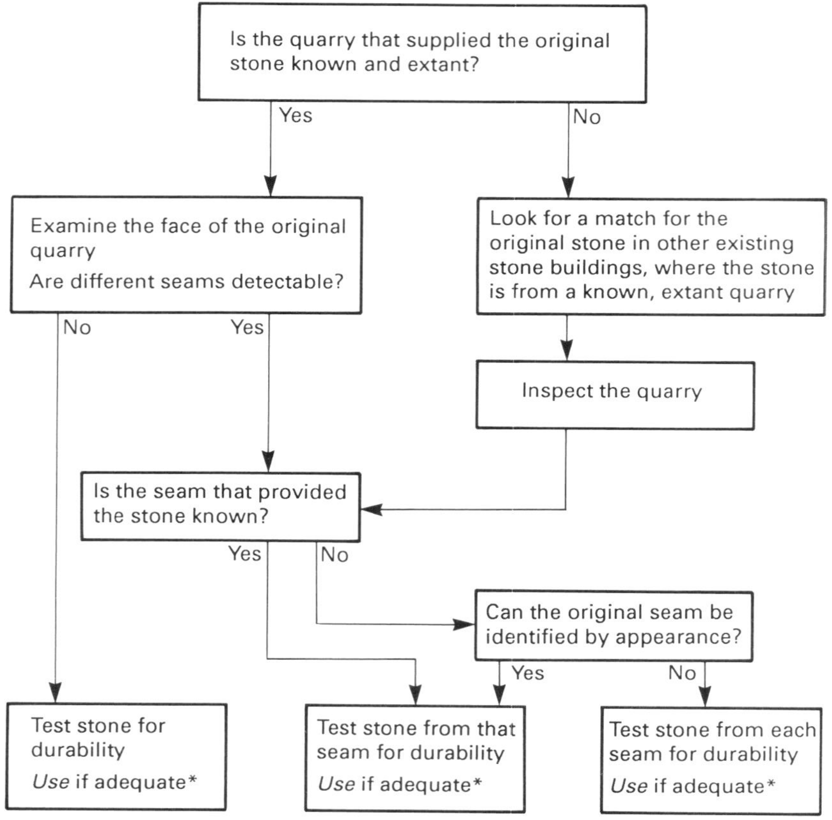

Figure 3.1 Guide for selection of stone for repair of an existing building

be given to the life that might be expected of it once it forms part of the building in question. If the substitute is too short-lived, clearly it should not be used.

The life of a stone depends equally on the aggressiveness of its environment and the intrinsic durability of the stone. This is normally dependent on a combination of chemical, mineralogical and physical factors which cannot be judged from the initial appearance of the stone. Unless wide experience of a particular type of stone leaves no room for doubt about its suitability for use in a particular environment, the architect would be wise to consult a reputable testing organization. However, it should be noted that durability assessment is currently less reliable with magnesian limestones than with other types of building stone.

Determination of the weathering characteristics of a stone is not straightforward. In fact, attempts to devise satisfactory artificial weathering machines for inorganic materials have so far failed. Instead, testing laboratories in many parts of the world now apply a test system that is appropriate for assessing the particular vulnerability of a stone to the weathering agencies present in the environment in which it is to be exposed. The system has been developed in Britain at the Building Research Establishment and is briefly described in a BRE Digest.[6] Other systems have been developed in the USA, France, Belgium and elsewhere. These systems may be adequate in the countries where they were developed, but are probably not suitable for conditions in Britain, because they do not give enough weight to the hazards of coastal exposure.[7] The British system applies particularly to porous limestones and sandstones, the classes of stone most commonly used in the British Isles. There are special difficulties in applying it to Magnesian Limestones.

Limestones are tested to determine their resistance to the destructive forces associated with the crystallization of soluble salts. Limestones that resist salt crystallization well also exhibit considerable resistance to frost attack and to the secondary destructive processes caused by exposure to acid gases in the air. Descriptions of the test method are given in references 6 and 7. Susceptibility is measured by the mean weight loss of the test pieces after fifteen cycles, or the number of cycles required to reduce the stone to incoherent pieces, if this occurs before completion of the fifteenth cycle. The test conditions must be extremely carefully controlled to ensure that the test results are reproducible. For this reason, at least one set of test pieces of well established durability are included in each test as calibrators. A test specifically carried out to determine whether a limestone is suitable for use in a particular environment should ideally include a calibrator that would fail on exposure to that environment and a calibrator that would survive.

It is important to have some means of defining the different levels of aggressiveness likely to be encountered. In this system, the general environment is divided into four levels of aggressiveness:

1. Low acidic air pollution (rural)—inland.
2. High acidic air pollution (urban)—inland.
3. Low acidic air pollution (rural)—exposed coastal.
4. High acidic air pollution (urban)—exposed coastal.

The *microclimate* is the environment that acts on a block of stone in a building. This depends not only on the general environment, but also on local sheltering and other effects caused by the building itself. The concept of building zones as defined in the French standard for limestones[8] takes this into account. In the French standard, four distinct zones are recognized:

Zone 1 Exterior pavings, where salts from the soil often add a further aggressive element to the environment.

Zone 2 Plinths. Even when there is a damp-proof course, splashes tend to raise the salt content of the stone. However, wetting is less frequent than in Zone 1.

Zone 3 Projecting features such as cornices, sills, string courses and splash courses. These features are substantially wetted more often than in Zone 4.

Zone 4 Elevations under projections.

The micro-climate decreases in severity from Zone 1 to Zone 4.

The ideas of general environment and building zones have been incorporated in *Table 3.1*, which has been taken from reference 7. Limestones are divided into six categories, A to F; the crystallization test is used to determine the appropriate category for each limestone tested. This allows a prospective user to decide where the stone in question may be used. A special case arises when sporadic replacement of blocks in an old building is contemplated and the surrounding stone is already contaminated with salts. The table may still be used in these circumstances, but instead of using the building zone that would normally be applicable, the next lower zone should be used. An exception must be made if the appropriate building zone is 1, because limestone that will survive in Zone 1 must be the best available anywhere. At the other end of the scale, a limestone that is in durability class C or D and is suitable for no better than Zone 4 can be upgraded to Zone 3, if it is covered by an effective flashing. The use of a

Table 3.1 Effects of change of environment on suitability of limestone for various building zones* (from reference 7, reproduced by permission of the Controller, HMSO; Crown copyright)

	Suitability zones for various limestones in a range of climatic conditions							
	Inland				*Exposed*			
	Low pollution		*High pollution*		*Low pollution*		*High pollution*	
Limestone type	*No frost*	*Frost*	*No frost*	*Frost*	*No frost*	*Frost*	*No frost*	*Frost*
A	Z 1–4	Z 1–4	Z 1–4	Z 1–4	Z 1–4	Z 1–4	Z 1 –4	Z 1 –4
B	Z 2–4	Z 2–4	Z 2–4	Z 2–4	Z 2–4	Z 2–4	Z 2†–4	Z 2†–4
C	Z 2–4	Z 2–4	Z 3–4	Z 3–4	Z 3†–4	Z 4	—	—
D	Z 3–4	Z 4	Z 3–4	Z 4	—	—	—	—
E	Z 4	Zone 4	Z 4†	—	—	—	—	—
F	Z 4	Zone 4	—	—	—	—	—	—

* Zones referred to are those in French Standard for Limestone
† Probably limited to 50 years' life

flashing will similarly upgrade limestones in durability classes E and F where they are to be used in inland, rural areas, but there must be doubt about the wisdom of permitting their use in Zone 3 positions under other conditions, if long trouble-free life is required of them.

There are two serious problems with the crystallization test: it is often difficult to obtain reference stones of the desired proven durability, and the test takes an irreducibly long time to carry out.

Use of interpolative methods when the available reference samples represent only a few of the six limestone classes has been suggested in the literature.[6,7] This would be fairly satisfactory if the classes represented were, say, three steps apart and the crystallization loss rose by approximately equal increments from class A through to class F. Unfortunately, the crystallization loss increases more than linearly as the durability classes are traversed. Even with these disadvantages, this test is still of vital importance, though not so useful as it might be.

Assessment of the durability of *sandstones* is simplified by first eliminating those types where the quartz particles are cemented together by crystals of calcite. These calcareous sandstones are unsatisfactory for long service in urban areas, because even slight attack by acidic gases on the calcite releases many grains of quartz. Immersion of a specimen of sandstone in a solution of sulphuric acid of specific gravity 1.145 for 10 days at a temperature of 16–21°C is sufficient to eliminate susceptible sandstones which are reduced to residual sand grains. Sandstones that survive this test are then normally assessed using the same crystallization test that is used for limestones. If, however, the sandstone is required for long use in an urban coastal district that is exceptionally exposed, or for piecemeal insertions into stone that is already heavily contaminated with soluble salts, the saturated crystallization test—which employs a saturated solution of sodium sulphate instead of the normal 14 per cent solution (specific gravity 1.055)—is more useful. The test is a comparative one and samples of sandstone of well-established durability must be available. The procedure is summarized in *Figure 3.2*.

A suitability-zone table analogous with that shown for limestones can be drawn up for sandstones (*Table 3.2*), but the principles involved are rather different. This is because sandstones are less affected by frost and acidic atmospheric gases, except where the masonry has unusually wide mortar joints or underlies limestone, and are relatively more affected by soluble salts. It should be noted that *Table 3.2* is based on the author's views alone and is backed by less experience than *Table 3.1*. The sandstones are assumed to fit into five durability classes, and the four building zones are defined as in *Table 3.1*. A flashing over a projecting feature will increase the

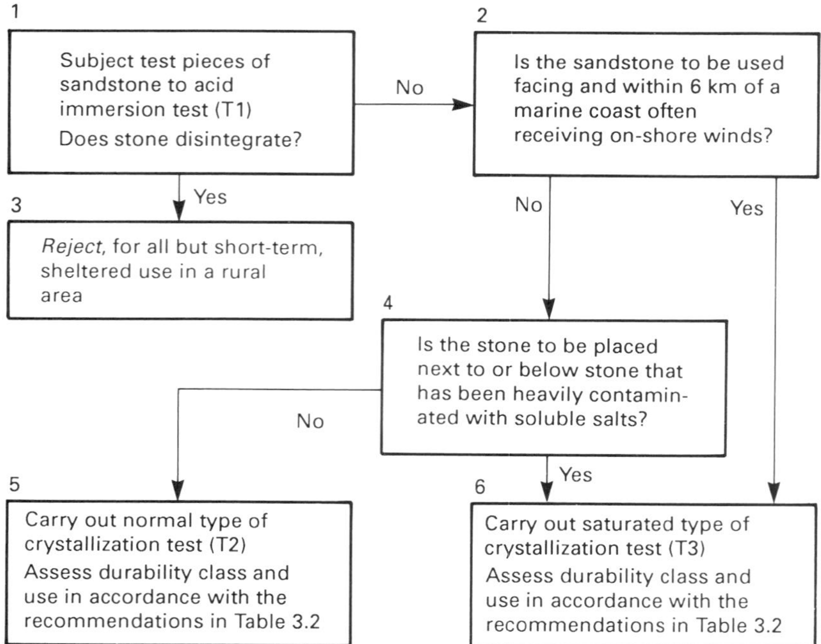

Figure 3.2 Guide for selection of sandstone for repair of an existing building

Table 3.2 Effect of change of environment on suitability of sandstones for various building zones

Sandstone class	*Suitability zones for various sandstones in a range of climatic conditions*							
	Inland				*Exposed coastal*			
	Normal joints		*Very wide joints or below limestone*		*Normal joints*		*Very wide joints or below limestone*	
	Rural	*Urban*	*Rural*	*Urban*	*Rural*	*Urban*	*Rural*	*Urban*
A	Z 1–4	Z 1–4	Z 1–4	Z 1–4	Z 1–4	Z 1–4	Z 1–4	Z 1–4
B	Z 1–4	Z 1–4	Z 2–4	Z 3–4	Z 3–4	Z 3–4	Z 3–4	Z 3–4
C	Z 2–4	Z 2–4	Z 3–4	Z 4	Z 4	Z 4	—	—
D	Z 3–4	Z 3–4	Z 4	—	—	—	—	—
E	Z 3–4	Z 4	—	—	—	—	—	—

1. Z indicates building zone as defined in French Standard.[8]
2. When the sandstone is below 'very wide joints' or 'limestone' it is assumed to be in such a position that it will receive rain drips or runs from the joint or limestone.
3. — indicates that the sandstone is not suitable for use in any zone under the climatic conditions indicated.
4. None of the five sandstone classes (A to E) includes calcareous sandstones.
5. For effect of flashings, see text.

effective life of a sandstone when it underlies limestone in an urban region, or is subject to onshore storms but sheltered from direct, driving rain.

Assessing the durability of *Magnesian Limestones* is much more difficult. This class of stone varies significantly in mineralogical composition as well as in pore structure. Therefore there is no one adverse composition that can be simply tested for and eliminated, as with sandstones and calcareous sandstones. Where the main aggressive element is soluble salt attack, a crystallization test may be enough to assess the service life of a magnesian limestone correctly, but where other factors are involved this test is not sufficient. Assessing the durability of a magnesian limestone is an art rather than a science. In the past it was thought that Magnesian Limestones with a composition approaching that of dolomite (45.7% magnesium carbonate; 54.3% calcium carbonate) had the highest durability. Study of the correlation between observed durability, magnesium/calcium ratio and pore structure in magnesian limestones may be useful.

The very low porosity of *slate* ensures that it will not suffer significant attack by frost or soluble salt crystallization. Some slates, however, contain constituents that will be attacked by acidic gases, such as those in urban air. If slate of this kind is used as a roof or mansard roof covering, acidic gas attack can be very serious: the acidic gases dissolve in the rainwater held by capillarity between the overlaps and this acid solution remains in contact with the slate for a long time. A British Standard test system, BS 680,[9] may be used to identify slates that are immune to acid attack. An acid immersion test, a wetting and drying test and a water absorption test are involved. It should be noted that it is widely considered that the acid immersion test deals unduly harshly with the rather thick, slightly calcareous slates from the English counties of Lancashire and Cumbria, and a dispensation clause is given in a footnote to this Standard. Where slate is to be used in block form, as drums for columns or shafts or in thick slabs, no water will be held between overlaps and only the wetting and drying test need be applied. This will eliminate those slates that contain both calcium carbonate and pyrite (iron disulphide). The oxidation of pyrite produces sulphuric acid which attacks the calcium carbonate and causes general loss of strength of the material.

The very low porosity of *marble* ensures that it will also be unaffected by salt or frost attack as long as it retains its original cohesion. However, if marble is subjected to large variations in temperature minute cracks can occur at the boundaries of the calcite crystals. These cracks make the marble more susceptible to acidic gas attack. In severe cases the marble loses cohesion and is said to 'sugar'. In the absence of these minute cracks, acidic gases attack only the external surfaces of the marble. This causes loss of polish but the rate of attack is normally very slow even in urban areas. There is no standard or generally accepted test of a marble's propensity to 'sugar'. It is very difficult to forecast the service life of a marble unless its environment precludes any undue heating and cooling. *Dense limestones* will generally be as durable as marble without any risk of 'sugaring'.

Granites and closely related igneous rocks of good quality are unaffected by any of the three main weathering agencies. However, if they are exposed to frequent large changes in temperature they may well develop micro-cracks. Unlike marbles, they will not become susceptible to acidic gases, but they may become susceptible to salt crystallization attack. There is no standard test, but the experiments done by Hochman and Kessler[11] discussed in Volume 1, Chapter 7, could be used by a competent testing laboratory as a basis for making some assessment of the risk with any particular igneous stone.

Occasionally granites that have undergone some kaolinization have been used for buildings of importance and have weathered rather poorly. Competent mineralogists can recognize such defects if they inspect a potential consignment. These granites usually have greater than normal porosity.

Alternatives to the crystallization test

Because of the difficulties that arise with the crystallization test there have been many attempts to assess the durability of stone based on the values of properties that are more easily measured. Since pore structure plays such an important part in determining durability, properties that are closely related to pore structure seem to offer the best hope of solving the problem. In fact, some successes have been achieved using such parameters. *Table 3.3* gives a list of some of these properties and some notes about their usefulness. Although very good results can be obtained with a limited number of types of stone, for example Portland stone using microporosity and saturation coefficient, there is not yet any generally applicable system. More research is needed to refine the crystallization test with the aim of developing a test which is not dependent on testing a range of reference samples.

Selection for workability

To ensure that a type of stone is of adequate workability for its intended use it is probably best to ask the opinion of an experienced mason. The French Standard for limestone[8] classifies limestone into hardness groups on the basis of laboratory measurements. The groups are numbered from 1 to 14 on a scale of increasing hardness. These numbers

Table 3.3 Some structural parameters and the durability of stone

Parameter	*Description*	*Comment*
1. Porosity	Accessible pore volume expressed as a fraction of apparent volume of stone.	Generally a poor guide to durability but, used in conjunction with (2) it is helpful for indicating the durability of Bath stone. This combination also forms part of the French Standard for Limestones.
2. Saturation coefficient	Volume of water absorbed under some specific conditions (usually 24 hours complete immersion in water at room temperature) expressed as a decimal fraction of the accessible pore volume.	This is a complex function of the pore structure. With (1) it occurs in the French Standard for Limestones and is useful for assessing the durability of Bath stones. With (3) it is very effective in assessing the durability of Portland stones.
3. Microporosity	(a) The fraction of the pore volume that is accessible only via pores less than 0.5 μm in diameter. (b) Alternatively, the fraction of water retained by an initially water-saturated stone after application of a negative pressure of 62.6 kPa.	Very useful in conjunction with (2) for assessing the durability of Portland stones.
4. Capillarity	Defined in the French Standard by $\frac{100\,M}{S\sqrt{t}}$ where M is the mass of water absorbed from the beginning of a test in which a cube of cross section area S stands in water. The elapsed time is t.	The constant obtained is a measure of the pore structure. For example, the lower the value, the less water will rise in the stone when standing on wet soil. While the Belgians propose to use it as part of a durability assessment, recent research has suggested that it has no advantage over (2) for British stone and conditions[10].
5. d_{10}	The maximum pore diameter still filled with water when 10% of the water from an initially saturated piece of stone has been removed by suction.	This is clearly related to (3). It forms part of the Belgian selection procedure. Stone with d_{10} less than 2.5 μm is considered susceptible to frost. Trials of this parameter under British conditions have not been undertaken.

have become known as AFNOR numbers. If the stone chosen is a French Limestone its AFNOR number may be sufficient indication of its workability.

Selection for plinth courses

Stone that has adequate durability for a plinth course will not necessarily have the desirable property of discouraging the upflow of soil water. Stone of very low porosity usually remains apparently dry, but so will some stone of very low suction. The capillarity test in the French Standard is useful for distinguishing such stone.

References

1. British Geological Survey, Keyworth, Nottingham NG12 5GG, England
2. Building Research Establishment, Garston, Watford, Herts WD2 7JR, England
3. Sedgwick Museum of Geology, Downing Street, Cambridge, England
4. Cathedral Works Organization, The Cathedral, Chichester, West Sussex, England
5. Anon, *The Natural Stone Directory*, 7th edn, Ealing Publications Limited, Maidenhead, 1987
6. *Building Research Establishment Digest No 269,* HMSO, London, January 1983
7. Honeyborne, D.B., *The Building Limestones of France*, Building Research Establishment Report, HMSO, London, 1982
8. Association Française de Normalisation, *Matériaux Pierres calcaires*, Paris, 1945
9. BS 680, *Roofing slates*, British Standards Institution, Milton Keynes, 1971
10. Leary, E.A., 'A preliminary assessment of capillary tests as indicators of the durability of British limestones' *Proc. Int. Symp. on Stone Conservation*, p.73, Bologna, 1981
11. Hochman, A. and Kessler, D.W., 'Thermal and moisture expansion studies of some domestic granites', *US Bureau of Standards, Journal of Research*, **44**, 395–410, 1950

4

Mortars for stone buildings

John Ashurst

Introduction

The consideration of historic masonry must necessarily include the mortar on which its unity and stability, to a greater or lesser degree, depends. True, there are unmortared walls of all periods, from the spectacular polygonal masonry of Peru to the dry-stone walls of Europe, and others which were packed with earth; but for the most part masonry involves a mortar based on lime or gypsum. Generally speaking, gypsum mortars are most likely to occur in those countries where trees are scarce and sources of gypsum are plentiful. They are found in Mesopotamia, Egypt and other countries of the African continent and Greece. Gypsum for mortar and plaster is prepared by heating selenitic rock (composed of hydrated calcium sulphate) to temperatures in the 150–160°C range. The resultant hemi-hydrate ('plaster of Paris') sets rapidly when mixed with water. The set is accompanied by a slight expansion. In wet climates, even when raw materials are plentiful, gypsum is rarely used on external, exposed surfaces because of its slight solubility in water. There are, however surprising examples in the fifteenth and sixteenth centuries of external gypsum plastering in England, and combinations of lime and gypsum are not unknown. It is wise, therefore, to eliminate all assumptions in the investigation of historic mortar.

Materials

Lime (non-hydraulic)

Lime is the ubiquitous constituent of the greatest percentage of ancient mortars. Almost any source of calcium carbonate will provide lime, the most obvious being a very wide range of limestones; but lime produced from burning sea shells and coral and from marble is also common.

Richard Neve[1] and other writers of his time in England drew attention to differences in limes prepared from 'Chalk' and from 'Stone'. The 'Chalk' lime was considered suitable for internal use only, whilst the 'Stone' lime (that is lime burnt from limestone other than Chalk) was suitable for external mortar and plaster. Regional differences affecting the quality of the lime were also recognised to be important by these early observers, as were the firing techniques.

It is as well to remember the contexts in which lime was produced historically and to be careful about simple assumptions arising from, say, analysis of ancient mortars. We have as much to learn about production and preparation as about constituent parts; in particular we must remember that there are significant differences between a modern, commercially produced lime and a lime, full of impurities such as slag and ash, produced in a clamp in the fourteenth century.

Lime is produced by breaking the stone into lumps and heating the raw material in a kiln. Early kilns were sometimes very crude, being no more than simple clamps of alternate layers of stone and fuel, covered with a clay skin ventilated through stoke holes. Traditional kilns, however, are normally flare kilns, in which intermittent burning takes place, or draw kilns, in which loading and burning are continuous. Modern rotary kilns are fuelled by oil or gas, and burn the limestone at temperatures between 900 °C and 1200 °C (1650–2200 °F). The minimum effective temperature for burning limestone for lime is 880 °C (1616 °F), but for this temperature to be reached in the centre of the stone lumps, an overall temperature at the surface of 1000 °C (1800 °F) is necessary.

During burning, carbon dioxide (and any water) is driven off. The chemical process consists in the dissociation by heat of calcium (and sometimes magnesium) carbonate, in an atmosphere relatively free of carbon dioxide, to prevent recombination. The end product is calcium oxide, 'quicklime', sometimes described as 'unslaked lime' or, rather misleadingly, as 'lump lime'.

Slaking

Most lime is slaked as part of a production process and sold either as a dry powder (hydrated lime), or, rarely, as lime putty.

If calcium oxide (quicklime) is left exposed to the air, it will air-slake, or wind-slake. The calcined lumps will gradually reduce to powder, with an increase in volume. For site slaking, the lime should be delivered as fresh as possible and kept in dry conditions.

Slaking is the reaction of the quicklime with water. During the process, hydroxides of calcium (and magnesium) are formed by the action of water on the oxides. Traditionally, this process was carried out in pits and the slaked lime was left to mature for several months, or even years. Slaking on site for repair work is most conveniently carried out in a galvanized steel cold water storage cistern.

Clean, potable water is run into the tank to a depth of approximately 300 mm (12 in) and the quicklime is added by shovel. Because of the violent reaction which occurs between the water and the quicklime, which frequently raises the water temperature to boiling point, this operation must be carried out slowly and carefully. Eyes must be protected by goggles and hands by suitable gloves. Anyone who is unprotected must be kept away from the slaking tank. The initial slaking process may be carried out more quickly and safely by first breaking the lumps of quicklime down to a large aggregate size and then by using hot water in the tank. The slaking lime must be hoed and raked and stirred until the visible reaction has ceased. Enough water must be used to avoid the coagulation of particles together, which significantly reduces the plasticity of the lime. Experience will dictate the correct amount of water required, which can be adjusted as the process demands. It is always better to have an excess of water than not enough. The addition of water and quicklime continues until the desired quantity has been slaked. Using an excess of water without 'drowning' the lime results in the formation of a soft, rather greasy mass of material, described as lime putty. Sieving the putty through a 5 mm (0.2 in) screen will remove unburnt lumps and the larger coagulations. The screened putty should be left under a few centimetres of slaking water. This lime water may be siphoned off when required for use. It contains small quantities of calcium hydroxide (0.14 g in 100 ml of water at 15 °C)[2] which can be useful in hardening up lime plaster. A thin skin will form on the surface, which should be left unbroken until the insertion of a small siphon tube to remove the water.

The lime putty, with a shallow covering of water, should be kept for a minimum period of two weeks before use. It is better to keep it for two months if practicable and there is no upper limit of time. The minimum period is to ensure that the entire mass is thoroughly slaked. After this time, plasticity and workability go on increasing. Pliny's well known and much quoted view that '. . . the older the mortar . . . the better it is in quality . . .', supported by Vitruvius and Alberti and by rather more recent experience, is based on observations of this increasing plasticity. Old lime putty, which is protected from the air in a pit or bin, acquires a rigidity which is rather like that of gelatin. When the rigid mass is worked through and 'knocked up', it becomes workable and plastic again. This property is peculiar to non-hydraulic lime putty. Any material which has a hydraulic set (see below) must not be 'knocked up' after it begins to stiffen.

A variation on the slaking procedure, which has a long tradition behind it, is to slake the quicklime in a pit, already mixed with the sand with which it is to be combined as mortar, or plaster. This process requires time and space and is really only practicable in long programmes of repair or restoration, where it is intended to lay up quantities of lime putty and sand for a long time. The technique has, however, a distinct advantage over more familiar mixing procedures, in that this early marriage between binder material and aggregate encourages the covering of all the aggregate particles with a lime paste, in a way and to a degree which can never be matched by conventional modern mixing.

A recommended compromise between slaking the lime and sand mixture and turning over dry constituents later, is to mix the slaked putty with the sand and other aggregates and to store the constituents together, protected from the air, as wet 'coarse stuff', for as long as possible to mature. This 'coarse stuff' is the best possible base for mortar and lime plaster, whether or not it is to be gauged later with any pozzolanic additives. Storage is best arranged in plastic bins with an additional covering inside the bin, of wet underlay felt, or wet sacks. (Slaking must not, of course, be carried out in a plastic bin!) Another advantage of storing wet 'coarse stuff' is that all the mixing for a large job can be carried out in one or two operations and a consistent mortar, or plaster, will be available for use as required.

Mixing

Initial mixing of the 'coarse stuff' and final mixing, or 'knocking up', must be thorough. But mixing, in the familiar sense of turning over with a shovel, was not considered sufficient in ancient times, nor is it sufficient now, if the best possible performance is to be obtained from the lime mortar. The old practice of chopping, beating and ramming the mortar has largely been forgotten and seems to have acquired the status of a quaint superstition. It requires additional labour and is, therefore, unwelcome in terms of cost and effort. Therefore it can only be justified by proven returns. Recent field work has confirmed that 'coarse stuff', rammed and beaten with a simply made wooden rammer and paddle, interspersed with chopping with a shovel, does improve workability and performance. The value of impact is to increase the overall lime-aggregate contact and to remove surplus water by compaction of the mass.

Much of this labour can be avoided by making use of a mortar mill which blends and squeezes the lime putty and aggregates very efficiently. Although initially expensive, a mill soon pays for itself in terms of labour saved.

Hardening of lime mortar

When the coarse stuff is left exposed to air, it stiffens and hardens, with a contraction in volume. There is a much greater contraction in volume of the lime putty alone as it loses water. This is why it is always used with sand, except in very fine joints, where no more than a buttering of lime is used in the work. This hardening is not to be confused with the setting of hydraulic limes and cements. Hardening will only take place through contact with air, by reaction with atmospheric carbon dioxide and evaporation of water. Preliminary hardening takes place fairly rapidly, both as water in the mix is lost to the porous surface of the masonry and by evaporation. Water renders the mix plastic, but has no chemical effect on ordinary lime mortar, except as a carrier. Only the minimum additional water should be added to wet coarse stuff, to achieve the necessary workability, so that the volume changes during drying out can be kept to a minimum. Further evaporation takes place over a very long period of time and the carbonation process may continue for many years. Soft mortar, which is isolated in pockets of construction from contact with the air, will remain soft indefinitely.

Studies carried out by ICCROM[3] on mortar cubes showed that only a superficial external carbonation of a few millimetres occurred after standard curing periods (i.e. 60 days for lime:sand mortars and 28 days for cement-gauged lime:sand mortars). Evidence suggests that complete carbonation of 50 mm cubes could take place in three to six months. The carbonation process is, in practice, difficult to control or to predict since it is affected by temperature, moisture presence, pore structure (access of carbon dioxide) and bulk of material.

Various experiments have indicated that the carbonation process may be significantly accelerated by periodic wetting of the work. Rapid drying out, which sometimes takes place in hot weather on unprotected work, retards the carbonation process and results in poor ultimate strength. Direct heat and local draughts should be avoided and good general circulation of air encouraged. The periodic wetting is most conveniently carried out using a hand spray with a fine nozzle, sufficient to create a fine mist. (Jets of water will disrupt the surface of the mortar and cause staining of the masonry and must be avoided.) This process is a refinement which has rather a limited application, but it is simple enough to execute for a day or two after the mortar has been placed. Local conditions will dictate the frequency of wetting, but it may be as often as every hour initially, if drying-out of the face is likely to be rapid, and eventually decreasing to every three or four hours. Current experiments are comparing the effects of using water containing carbon dioxide (soda water), or lime water, with ordinary tap water.

A summary of procedures to obtain optimum performance from mortars based on non-hydraulic lime is as follows:

1. Slake freshly burnt lime on site with enough water to obtain a soft mass of putty. Continue stirring during the slaking process. Sieve to remove lumps. Keep the putty under a water layer for at least one week to ensure thorough slaking.
2. Mix putty thoroughly with chosen aggregates in the desired ratio (1:3 or similar) mechanically, or by hand, turning, beating and chopping the coarse stuff. Alternatively, blend the putty and aggregates in a mill.
3. Store wet coarse stuff under wet underlay felt, or wet sacks, preferably in bins with air-tight lids, for a minimum period of one week, but for as long as possible.
4. Remove the required quantity for one day's work on to a clean, boarded platform. Mix again, chopping, beating and ramming. If the coarse stuff is too crumbly, add a little water to increase plasticity, but keep additional water to an absolute minimum. Remember that chopping and beating coarse stuff based on lime putty will render it more plastic and workable without more water.
5. Keep the finished work protected from rain, strong heat and local draughts. Encourage good general air circulation. In special cases, where justified, carry out intermittent mist spraying of the mortar surfaces, to retard the drying out and to encourage carbonation.

Alternative sources of lime putty

If there is no supply of lime putty available and site slaking is impossible, use hydrated lime and soak it in enough clean water to produce a thick cream, for a minimum period of twenty-four hours. Proceed from stage 2 after soaking.

Another method is to buy ready-mixed lime and sand. Ready-mixed coarse stuff should be kept from drying out and used as soon as possible. It is better restricted to work where the mix is to be gauged with cement, and will always benefit from beating or milling.

Gauging with pozzolanic additives

Certain materials will react with lime in the presence of water, to enable a lime mortar, or rendering, to set hydraulically. This phenomenon seems to have been appreciated first in Mediterranean countries under Roman influence, where there was an abundance of natural materials ejected from volcanoes. These materials were in the form of rocks such as tuff, trachyte and pumice, or deposits of volcanic ash or earth, such as pozzolana or trass. Large deposits of ash in the region of Pozzuoli near Naples, used from early times with lime for mortar and Roman concrete and described as *pozzolana*, are still used extensively in Italian and other Mediterranean building industries. (Another well-known source, used by the Romans, was the great caldera of Thera (Santorini), situated on the southern periphery of the Cyclades. 'Therian Earth' is still quarried from this active volcanic site for the building industry.) *Pozzolana* has become a generic name for any additive which will react with lime to produce a hydraulic set; however, unless *pozzolana* is specifically meant, other similar materials should simply be described as 'pozzolanic additives'.

These volcanic materials contain reactive silicates, from the rapid cooling of bubbling, molten material. Their structure typically is vitreous, amorphous and unstable. Their reaction with lime and water produces calcium aluminate hydrate and calcium silicate hydrate. The process is observed as relatively rapid hardening of the material.[4]

One of the interesting pozzolanic additives used in Roman times, and again from the seventeenth century in Europe, is trass, variously described in historical texts as 'terrace', 'tarrace' or 'tarras'. The principal source appears to have been the region of Andernach on the Rhine. Trass was imported to England via Holland (hence the occasional reference to 'Dutch tarras') for engineering and dock works, mixed 1:2 or 1:1 with lime. Roman builders also used bricks, tiles and pottery crushed to dust and ground iron slag as pozzolanic additives.

Modern practice in Britain makes use of low-fired brick powders (typically fired at < 1000 degrees Celsius and of fine particle size (< 100 microns), metakaolin (from china clay) and low sulphate pulverized fuel ash. These materials, gauging lime: sand coarse stuff with between 10% and 75% reactive powder are useful where strong and fast sets are not required.

Hydraulic limes and natural cements

Hydraulic limes

The technology of hydraulic mortars, developed during the Roman period, survived in texts, but seems to have almost completely disappeared from use until the seventeenth century.

The source of hydraulic limes is also limestone, but limestone which contains a proportion of clay, in addition to calcium and magnesium carbonates. Such limestones will yield 'hydraulic' lime after calcination, i.e. limes which will set by reaction of hydraulic compounds with water, even without the present of air. Other impurities, such as iron and sulphur, may also be present in these limestones.

Kilning procedures are the same as those for high calcium lime, but the chemical actions are much more complex during the calcination process. As the temperature reaches 900 °C (1650 °F), pozzolanic compounds are formed while decomposition of the carbonates and reaction with clay materials proceeds. Over 1000 °C (1800 °F), calcium aluminates and silicates are formed and sintering takes place. This produces a clinker which is somewhat inactive until finely ground. Changes in the firing temperature, as well as in the constituents, can produce hydraulic limes of very different characteristics. Although many famous hydraulic limes were produced in the UK until World War II, such as those from Arden, Aberthaw, and Watchet, only one is currently in production. This is a 'feebly hydraulic' lime from the Blue Lias in Somerset. Moderately to eminently hydraulic limes are increasingly imported from France, Italy and Switzerland.

Hydraulic limes range in colour from pale grey to buff, and are delivered in sacks as a ground, dry hydrate. Sacks of hydraulic lime must be delivered sealed and must be kept dry. The lime must be mixed very thoroughly with the selected aggregates and with the minimum amount of water to make the coarse stuff workable. The mixed material should be able to take a 'polish' from the back of a shovel. Mixing should take place on a clean, boarded platform before any water is added and then again after watering. This coarse stuff must be used within four hours and must not be knocked up after stiffening has taken place. Correct judgement on the quantity required for each working phase is, therefore, important, and manufacturer's instructions must be rigorously followed.

Natural ('Roman') cements

Natural cements are really eminently hyraulic limes. In the eighteenth century various experiments were taking place, mixing different limes with volcanic earths. John Smeaton found that Aberthaw (Glamorgan) lime gave better results than others and concluded that the best limes for mortar were those fired from limestones containing a considerable quantity of clayey matter. The discovery that a useful, quick-setting hydraulic cement could be made by calcining nodules of argillaceous limestone (septarian nodules) resulted in a patent being taken out in 1796 by James Parker of Northfleet. Similar, brown coloured natural cements were made from the septaria of Harwich and the Solent ('Sheppey' and 'Medina' cements) and Weymouth, Calderwood, Rugby and Whitby. At about the same time, similar natural cements were being used near Boulogne and at Rosendale and Louisville in America.

These cements were characterized by their colour and their quick set, which might be as little as half an hour. They were mixed with sand in a 1:1 proportion, sometimes 1:2 and sometimes, for fine moulded work, almost neat. The name 'Roman Cement' seems to have been acquired about 1800 and arose from the distinctive colour and hydraulic properties.

It is a strong durable material, and was welcomed as an external rendering. It is in this form that Roman Cement is usually found, lined out in the imitation of masonry, sometimes coloured with ('green') copperas in lime, sometimes painted, sometimes left uncoloured. Peter Nicholson[5] commented in 1823: '... when the works are finished, they should be frescoed, or coloured, with washes, composed of five ounces of copperas to every gallon of water, and as much fresh lime and cement as will produce the colours required ... these sorts of works ... are drawn and jointed to imitate well-bonded masonry, and the divisions promiscuously touched with rich tints of umber, and occasionally with vitriol ...'. Unfortunately, it was also used extensively for plastic repairs of masonry and for pointing, roles for which it is too impermeable and too strong. The removal of Roman Cement from mediaeval masonry, especially architectural detail and carving, is one of the most familiar and taxing jobs for the conservator.

A form of Roman cement was available until the 1960s, but is no longer made. Cement:lime:sand mixes of 1:2:8 (flat work) and 1:1:6 (mouldings) were recommended by the Building Research Station in the late 1940s as repair mixes. Better results can now be obtained using moderately to eminently hydraulic limes with not more than 10% lime putty added to improve workability. The lime is typically gauged with 2-3 parts sharp, washed, coloured sand.

Portland cement

In 1811, James Frost took out a patent for an artificial cement obtained by lightly calcinating ground chalk and clay together, anticipating the principle which later led to the establishment of many similar artificial hydraulic cements. The most famous of these became known as Portland cement, from its supposed appearance and similarity to Portland limestone. The beginning of the nineteenth century saw much experiment and investigation into these materials.

The first Portland cement type in the UK was patented by Joseph Aspdin of Leeds, whose plant at Wakefield crushed and calcined a 'hard limestone', mixed the lime with clay and ground the mix into a fine slurry with water. The mixture was fired, broken into lumps and fired a second time, until the carbonic acid is expelled (*sic*). Because low temperatures were used, the quality of the cement cannot have been high. By 1838, however, Aspdin's son, William, was producing the cement at Gateshead and on the Thames. Brunel used it for his Thames Tunnel, in spite of the fact that the price was twice that of Roman Cement. Therefore it may be assumed that results were satisfactory and, perhaps, the calcination was taking place at higher temperatures. To Isaac Johnson belongs the credit, however, of observing that overburnt lumps in the old Aspdin kilns at Gateshead, which he had taken over, made a better final product and were slower setting. At Johnson's works at Rochester, the results of his observations were produced as Johnson's Cement. Along the Thames and Medway a number of cement works opened up, making use of the Chalk and the Thames mud and firing at a temperature high enough to produce vitrification.

The cements produced by the late 1850s were close to those produced by modern methods. They were made by grinding Chalk and clay together in a wet mill and firing the screened slurry at temperatures of 1300–1500 °C (2400–2700 °F). The Chalk is converted into quicklime, which unites chemically with the clay to form a clinker of Portland cement. After regrinding and firing, the white hot clinker is allowed to cool and a small amount of gypsum is added to lengthen the setting time.

Objections to the use of hydraulic limes, natural cements and especially Portland cement are based on their high strength, their rather impermeable character and the risk of transferring soluble salts, especially sodium salts, to vulnerable masonry materials.

Other modern cements

White Portland cement

This cement is produced from Chalk and china clay and is burnt, using oil fuel instead of coal. Although the strength of white cement manufactured in the UK used to be rather less than that of ordinary Portland cement (OPC), the only currently available sources are now imported and are equal or superior in strength to OPC. White cement is useful in gauging white lime mortars and pale mortar repairs and, occasionally, in rendering, where the colour of OPC would be wrong. The cement should comply with the requirements of BS 12: 1971. It is about twice the cost of OPC. Some practitioners object to its use on the grounds that the surface is liable to craze. This problem can be overcome by keeping the water content low, using water-reducing agents, and avoiding overworking of surfaces.

Masonry cement

Masonry cements have the advantage over unplasticized OPC of greater plasticity and greater water retention. They are based on OPC, but have fine, inert fillers and plasticizers added, which do not present any additional hazards to porous masonry. However, properly slaked lime is preferable for historic building work. Their principal use is in rendering, where lime would kill the colour of natural aggregates, or in sandstone masonry repairs, especially 'plastic repairs', where lime has played a role in the decay of the sandstone. Masonry cements are useful in sites liable to be attacked by frost because of the air-entraining property of the plasticizer. The cement should comply with the requirements of BS 5224.

Sulphate-resisting cement

Some situations require the use of a cement which will resist sulphate attack. Industrial monuments, such as kilns and masonry associated with flue condensates or sulphate concentration in ground water, are common examples. Sulphate-resisting cement has a reduced tricalcium aluminate content (about 5% C_3A compared with 11% C_3A in OPC) and has good resistance to chemical attack from sulphates in these typical conditions. Mixes for mortars and renderings are the same as those based on OPC. Sulphate-resisting cement should comply with the requirements of BS 4027: 1972.

High alumina cement

This cement (HAC) is produced by fusing limestone and bauxite together. It is grey-black in colour and has different properties to OPC. Setting is slow (up to six hours for the initial set, as against 45 minutes for OPC), workability is good and rapid heat evolution, coupled with early strength development at low temperatures, makes cold weather working less hazardous. Resistance to sulphate attack is good, but resistance to caustic alkalis is poor. The use of antifreeze additives, lime and waterproofers should be avoided. Crushed Chalk may be added in place of lime.

This cement is sometimes recommended for repairing Roman or Portland cement stuccos, because, it is claimed, such repairs can be painted at an early stage without the use of special primers, unlike repairs based on OPC, which require special alkali-resistant primers and a long period of waiting to avoid alkali attack on paint. However, it should be realized that the early alkalinity of HAC is not likely to be much less than the alkalinity of OPC (HAC pH12: OPC pH12–13), so that special primers are still recommended, if early painting is necessary.

The distinctive colour can be useful in matching black ash mortar. HAC should comply with the requirements of BS 915: 1972. HAC is about three times the cost of OPC. Loss of strength and increased porosity due to conversion of calcium aluminate hydrates in conditions of prolonged warmth and humidity, which are critical in concrete construction, are not relevant in the context of renderings and mortars.

Pozzolanic cements

Pozzolanic cements in Britain are principally mixtures of OPC and pulverized fuel ash. The PFA reacts with lime liberated during the hydration of OPC, to give a slow hardening, low heat cement, with good resistance to sulphates.

Additives

One of the most interesting aspects of the study of old mortars is the identification of additives included to improve the workability or to induce hardening of lime:sand mixtures. Lauren-Brook Sickels[6] has carried out work on organic additives and on possible synthetic substitutes in mortars for conservation work, which provides a useful reference.

Typical of organic additives are materials such as urine, beer, milk, egg white, animal fats and beeswax. Not all these materials are readily identifiable, but a current programme of investigation by English Heritage and ICCROM is seeking to establish patterns of use in historic mortars. Nicola Ashurst, in an unpublished work, has identified animal fats and beeswax in mortars where waterproofing and/or adhesion to impermeable meterial such as flint was necessary. The English Heritage/ICCROM programme is recreating Roman mortars incorporating pozzolanic additives and fats as a contribution to the correct ongoing maintenance of historic sites.

Antifreeze additives

Although cold weather working should be discouraged, because of the hazard of exposing fresh mortar and rendering to freezing, there are situations when work must continue in undesirable conditions. The principle of the antifreeze additive is to increase the rate of heat evolution by accelerating the set. In most proprietary products the accelerator is calcium chloride; this should be specified as 1.5% anhydrous calcium chloride, dissolved in the gauging water. The introduction of chlorides into porous masonry is obviously undesirable. This practice must be kept to an absolute minimum generally and never extended to work of high intrinsic value.

'Waterproofers'

'Waterproofed' Portland cement is OPC mixed with small percentages of calcium stearate, or mineral oil, with the object of either preventing water movement or reducing permeability. The term 'waterproof', in the present context, is very misleading. 'Waterproof' should not be relied upon for rendering historic buildings. A thick, porous rendering, for instance, is usually likely to be much more efficient in keeping water out than a thin, 'waterproofed' one.

Air-entraining agents

A macro-porous mortar or rendering will tend to be resistant to frost and to stresses caused by the cystallization of soluble salts. Air-entrained OPC contains agents, such as calcium lignosulphate, which entrain 4–5% minute, discontinuous, uniformly distributed air bubbles. The density reduction may mean a decrease in strength of up to 15%. Experiments carried out in North America and in the UK have shown that up to 16–18% entrained air is a desirable percentage for aggressive freeze-thaw conditions.

Surfactants (surface active agents) improve the workability of mixes, by entraining small air bubbles and by reducing the surface tension of water, so that surfaces are wetted more easily. Experiments are in hand to determine how well air-entrained, thick renderings are able to withstand the problems associated with rising damp.

Water-reducing agents

The mechanical properties of mortars are significantly improved by water-reducing agents such as those based on naphto-sulphonates or sodium gluconate. The quantification of the effects is part of the current English Heritage/ICCROM study.

Pigments

Wherever possible, aggregates should be chosen to provide the necessary colour for a joint or rendering repair, in preference to colouring the cement or lime with pigments. However, it is not always easy to find the right constituents.

Where pigments are to be employed, they should be specified to conform to BS 1014:1961 and should ideally be incorporated in ready-mixed lime:sand coarse stuff. Controlled mixing is essential for consistency and site conditions are often against careful batching of the small quantities of pigment powder necessary to avoid colour changes.

PFA

To produce PFA, pulverized coal is blown into combustion in a stream of air and burnt. A high percentage of the resultant ash is in the form of minute, separate spheres. Seventy-five per cent of this ash is carried away in fine gases and is extracted as pulverized fuel ash ('fly ash' or PFA). Some PFA will react with lime in the presence of water, to form a cement-like material (pozzolanic PFA). Mixed with cement, PFA will react with the lime liberated during hydration. Colour, grading and pozzolanicity vary between power stations producing ash. Even the same station will produce different ash from time to time. Some of the ash is mixed with cement, or lime, with various other additives for grouting. Always specify what the ash is to be used for and ensure that a low sulphate ash is supplied. A typical sulphate content (as SO_3) is 1.2%, but the amount can be as low as 0.5%.

Brick powders

Fireclays are used in the production of ceramic products required to withstand high temperatures. During the 1970s and 1980s finely ground refractory material of this kind ('HTI powder') was used as a pozzolan with lime in repairs to stone. These tend to be replaced now by low fired brick or tile powders or metakaolin. One of the most important recent observations is that all reactive brick powders improve the frost resistance of lime:sand and cement:lime:sand mortars.

Aggregates

Materials

Limes and cements are used with fillers in the form of aggregates to make mortars and renderings. The proportion of binder to filler is normally 1:3. The binder paste occupies the 30% void likely to be present in the volume of aggregate.

Aggregates are commonly sand or grit, and may be rounded or angular. Old mortars may contain a wide variety of other materials, such as crushed brick, small lumps of old mortar, chalk, sea shell, kiln slag and ash. The performance of a mortar, plaster or rendering is affected by the size and condition of these fillers, as well as the quantity.

Washing

In general, a selection of clean, well-washed aggregate, which shows as small a volume of voids as possible and is well graded, will give the best service.

Washing is necessary to remove silt, sea salt and organic matter, which will weaken the mix, affect porous masonry and cause efflorescence. A useful on-site test for silt and clay is to add some salt solution (one teaspoonful of table salt to one half litre of cold tap water) to a sample of the aggregate in a clean jam jar. The contents should be shaken up together and left to stand for half an hour. The layer of silt which will settle on top of the sand should not exceed one tenth of the depth of sand in the jar. If it does, it is too dirty to use. Sand which stains excessively, or balls up in the fingers when rubbed, should also be avoided.

Grading

Uniform aggregate size creates problems in mixing and in performance. If a uniform coarse sand is used, the large voids between the grains will not be filled if the right proportion of binder paste is used. As a result the mix will be very harsh to work and will produce a weak, porous material. A uniform, fine sand is difficult to distribute evenly in a binder paste and is liable to produce a mortar or rendering which shrinks and cracks as it dries out and is of low strength. In particular, large percentages of limestone dust should be avoided, as these will always cause shrinkage cracking, with weakness and poor adhesion.

Allowance for 'bulking' should be made when gauging with damp sand. When dry sand is moistened, an expansion takes place, which Schaffer[7] suggests is due to the entrance of water into capillaries. This bulking reaches a maximum point, after which, as the sand becomes very wet, shrinkage back to the original volume occurs. The phenomenon of bulking is most apparent in very fine sands.

Poor workability, due to the use of a uniform, coarse sand, will sometimes lead to the use of increased amounts of water to try to counter the harsh working. However, high water contents cause excessive drying shrinkage. Additional water must not be used to achieve plasticity and wet, sloppy mixes must be avoided.

Summary of requirements for aggregates

1. Select a well graded sand, ranging from fine to coarse.
2. Avoid high percentages of clay and limestone.
3. Wash the aggregates thoroughly with clean water.
4. Keep the water:binder ratio low. Use only enough water to achieve stiff working.

To obtain a well graded sand, it may be necessary to mix aggregates from different sources together. Adding rounded grains to a predominantly angular grained sand improves workability.

Maintenance and repair

Mortar joints

Pointing

If the surface of mortar joints has weathered out to the extent that the face of the stones is vulnerable to damage, so that water can lodge and penetrate and support is inadequate, then a matching mortar must be introduced. The process of filling the joints from the face is known as pointing. In general, the original mortar joints of historic work were not bedded and pointed in separate operations (with notable decorative exceptions) but were filled full and struck off flush as the work was raised. If the stones have retained their sharp arrises, then the joints should be filled flush again, unless there is specific evidence that the joint face was profiled in some other way. Long years of weathering, however, will normally have blunted these arrises and, sometimes, all the original face of some stones will have spalled off. Flush filling in such a situation will greatly increase the apparent width of the joint, and therefore great care must be taken to keep the face of the new mortar within the original width, however far back that may be.

The correct procedure of cleaning out and refilling is well known, but, unfortunately, not widely practised. As a general rule, joints should be cleaned out to a minimum depth of 25 mm (1 in) and never to a depth less than their width. However, wide joints, especially those liable to exposure to extreme weathering, should be cut out to a minimum 38 mm (1.5 in), or even 50 mm (2 in). Sometimes the mortar has disintegrated to such an extent that the joints are largely empty. In this case they must first be deep tamped and, if necessary, hand grouted to fill the joint to the required depth for pointing. If tamped or grouted mortar comes closer to the face than 25–38 mm (1–1.5 in), it must be cut back to the proper depth and to a square face before pointing.

Raking out may be a simple operation, without risk to the fabric, where mortar is substantially decayed, but it is over-simplifying the situation to say that the joint does not need attention if it requires cutting out. Not infrequently, the face of a lime joint has been lost early in its lifetime, before sufficient drying out and carbonation had taken place to enable it to resist the winter. Meanwhile the more protected mortar has survived to become extremely hard. The empty joint at the face may be too much of a risk to leave alone, and additional cutting out may be necessary to achieve enough depth for pointing. More commonly, cutting out (as distinct from raking out with a knife blade or bent spike) is necessary to remove dense repointing of an earlier period, especially where this mortar (fortunately usually shallow in depth) is causing problems because of its high strength, impermeability and tendency to trap water behind it and accelerate the decay of the stones.

Cutting out should be carried out using plugging chisels, long-necked jointing chisels and toothed masonry chisels with a 2½lb club hammer. Wedge chisels should never be used because they may tend to stress the joints and cause spalling. Impact should be at an oblique angle to the joint face, not directly into it. Drilling with masonry drills is a useful way of creating an initial breach into a strong mortar. In exceptional cases, small carborundum disks may be used in cutting out, but usually only on regularly coursed work, with level beds, where running rules can be fixed to the wall as guides for the power tool. The risks of over-running are obvious, and extreme caution must be used in order not to cut into the masonry or increase the width of the joint.

All cutting out should leave a clean, square face at the back of the joint to provide maximum contact with the new mortar. Time for cutting out, which may be considerable, must be properly programmed.

Cleaning the joint

The prepared face should be carefully cleaned out with a soft or stiff bristle brush and flushed out with clean water, avoiding unnecessary saturation. All dust and loose material must be removed, working from top to bottom of the wall. If old, weathered-out joints have been colonized with algae or lichens, a biocide must be used on the dry surface as part of the cleaning out.

Filling the joint

If the joints have dried out after cleaning, they must be re-wetted before placing the new mortar, to avoid undue suction taking too much water too soon from the mortar. The mortar should be pushed into the joint from a board and ironed in with the maximum possible pressure. Pointing trowels are in common use, but it is regrettably unusual to see pointing irons, which can be improvised to suit the particular work in hand. These may be made of cranked iron, steel, flat or beaten out rod, or even wood. The function of these simple tools is to push the mortar evenly into the joint for the full joint width. They can do this because they fit into the joint and do not try to achieve compaction from the surface alone. In irregular work, this is particularly important.

The mortar face should be fitted flush, or slightly recessed, to avoid spreading the mortar over the face of the masonry. It should be struck and lined out as required.

If a weathered appearance is desired to match existing surviving work, a roughened texture can be produced after the initial set of the mortar has taken place, by light spraying, stiff bristle stippling, or rubbing with coarse sacking. Experience, but above all an understanding of what is required, on the part of the mason is essential. Of the above techniques, stippling with the ends of the stiff bristles in the brush is probably the most universally successful. The bristles should not be dragged across the face, but tapped against it. Timing is critical and no specification can substitute for experience. If this technique is applied too soon, mortar will be removed too easily and the bond forming between mortar and stone will be disrupted. If it is done too late, it will be difficult to make an impression and too vigorous efforts may be made with wire brushes, or masons' drags, to achieve the effect.

Apart from leaving a pleasant, weathered appearance, the rough textured joint tends to assist the wall to dry out and to concentrate wetting and drying activity in the joints, provided the right mortar is used.

There is a danger with this type of weathered finish that the joints may take on too distinctive a character. The old style of washed grit pointing, which used to be carried out by the Ministry of Public Building and Works (UK) on ancient monuments, was often a work of art, but tended to become an end in itself.

Over-pretty work, with mortar kept back to emphasize the outline of every stone, can look very self-conscious and rather odd in an area where the tradition is to slurry over joints in rough rubble masonry, to produce a flush face. A study should be made of surviving masonry to avoid the worst mistakes of this kind. More serious and more common is the error at the opposite end of the scale. Thick, strap pointing, raised proud of the wall, will positively shorten the life of much masonry, especially when the surface is already weakened with decay.

Cleaning off

Keeping the work clean is part of the skill of the mason, but occasionally staining from mortar is an inevitable hazard. Sometimes washing and brushing down is sufficient to remove recent material. However, if the traditional 10% concentration of hydrochloric acid is used (or a proprietary product based on this acid and a surfactant), the masonry surfaces must be pre-wetted to limit absorption and the acid must be thoroughly washed off afterwards. The biggest problem is keeping gauged brickwork clean. Every effort must be made to protect the vulnerable surface of these bricks from mortar spread and droppings when filling the joints.

Special joint treatment

Common historic variations on the flush joint were the beak, or double struck, joint and, later, in the eighteenth century especially, 'joints jointed' and

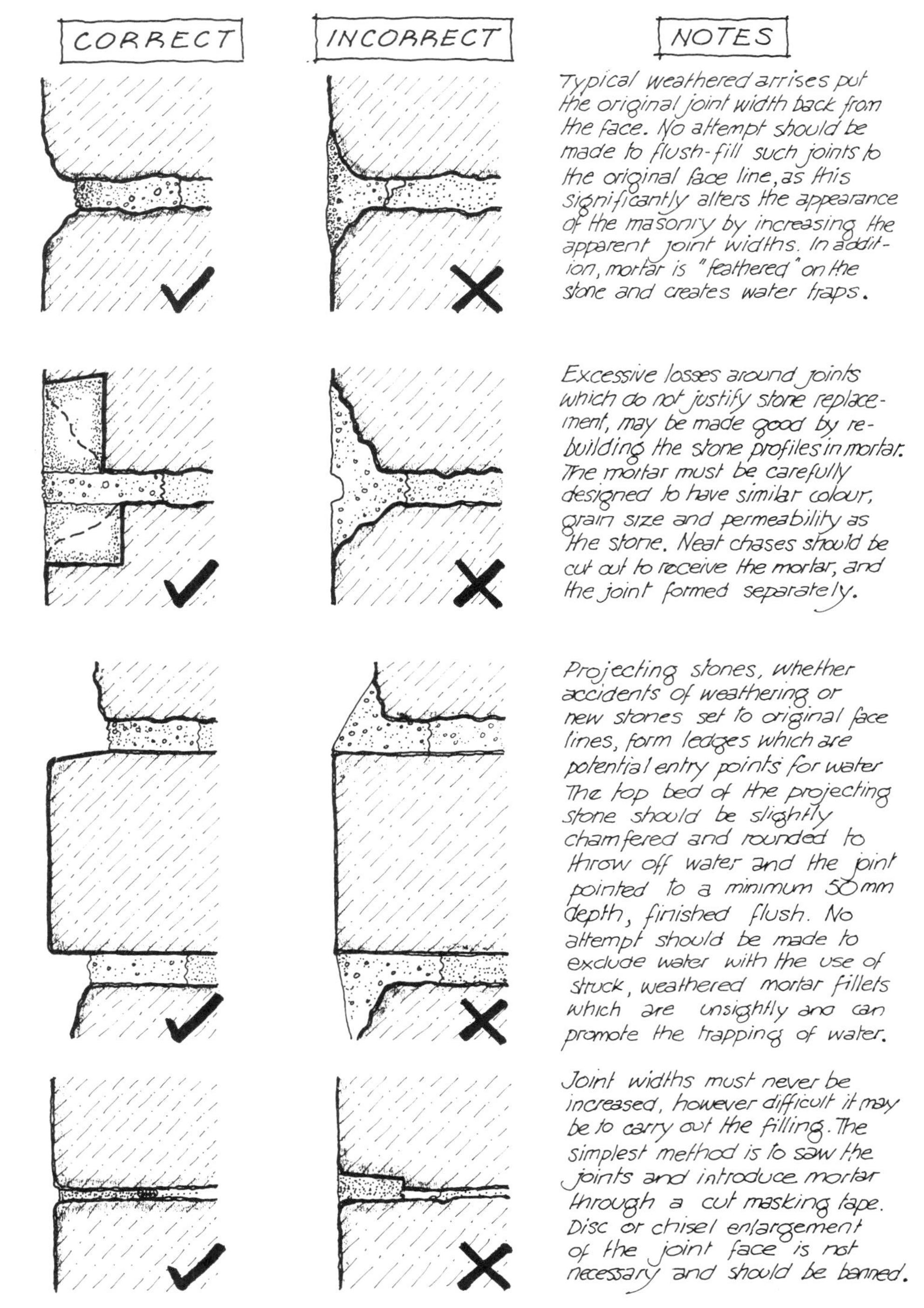

REMEDIAL TREATMENT OF JOINTS

tuck pointing. Where evidence of these survives it should be the pattern for the remedial work, unless the face of the masonry has decayed to the extent of making a finished joint of this kind appear nonsensical. Page 87 shows a method of filling very fine joints.

Damage to joints by 'masonry bees'

Some wild bees species (notably *Osmia rufa*) will burrow into soft mortar joints and even into some weak stones, in lieu of their normal habitat of easily eroded rock and earth banks. Raking out and filling of joints destroyed by these solitary bees may need to be accompanied by spraying or hole injection with a suitable insecticide (general-purpose sprays for garden pests approved under the Pesticide Safety Precautions Scheme). One of the most effective means of control, established by the Research, Technical and Advisory Service of English Heritage, is to place a plug of paste made up from water and the synthetic pyrethroid Permethrin in the hole and then to seal it over with lime:sand mortar. If many bees are present, the safest period for working is late summer or autumn.

Mortar mixes

Table 4.1 shows a range of mixes widely used in joint filling, but reference should also be made to the standard recommendations and codes, especially BS 6270: Part 1 1982, *Cleaning and Surface Repair of Buildings.*

Mortar analysis

Limitations

The choice of a mortar must relate firstly to the type and condition of the masonry and secondly to the degree of exposure. This choice is primarily based on a knowledge of the properties of various mortars and is not arrived at by analysis of the existing mortar alone. There may be good archaeological reasons for wanting to establish the identity and proportions of constituents in an old mortar, and simple separation of aggregates may be useful in identifying likely sources of aggregates for matching purposes. There are, however, limitations which should be understood and mortar specifications should not be based on the simple breakdown analysis of a sample. Analysis requires interpretation and there are important factors which affected the condition and performance of the mortar that is being sampled which analysis will not reveal. Examples of such factors are the original water:binder ratio, the rate of drying out, the method of mixing and placing, and the cleanliness and conditions of the aggregates.

There are also practical difficulties in isolating and identifying constituents. For instance, calcareous aggregates will be digested with the calcareous binder material in acid and present a misleading binder:aggregate proportion. The occurrence of old mortar crushed down and re-used as aggregate is a notorious problem of this kind. Clay minerals, present as impurities, may not be readily distinguishable from the silicates present in an hydraulic cement. An additional difficulty is accurate matching of an old clamp-fired lime, well mixed with fuel and kiln slag, with a modern lime produced in closely controlled conditions and delivered as a very pure hydrate.

The method of mortar analysis selected depends on the information required. Sufficient data may be provided by *in situ* visual analysis or simple on-site visual, physical and/or chemical testing. Laboratory analysis can provide additional information which may not be necessary for the task at hand.

The analysis of mortars is a specialized field. Even for the simplest method, experience is required for the identification of materials and the correct interpretation of evidence.

Mortar analysis and dating of structures

The analysis of old mortar is the analysis of changing technology. Only rarely can it be used to provide a specific date of construction. Laboratory analysis and expert interpretation will provide the most detailed and accurate results, but by themselves they are unlikely to give much indication of the dates when a mortar was prepared. The dating of masonry walls should not be attempted or expected from mortar analysis alone. A combination of evidence is necessary. A thorough examination of documentary sources relating to a structure and its site should be carried out by an experienced person with training in historical research. This should be correlated with analysis of the fabric, one aspect of which is mortar analysis. Further examination of the fabric should include interpretation of the method of construction and the manufacturer of its bricks and/or preparation of its stone.

Methods of analysis

On-site analysis

On-site visual analysis by an experienced person will provide a good indication of the general components of a mortar, particularly where a hand-held ×10 magnifying glass is used. The binder, aggregate and other large particle inclusions can usually be identified. Gentle scraping of a weathered surface may be necessary to reveal the unweathered mortar. This

Table 4.1 Mortars for remedial work on historic buildings based on cement, non-hydraulic lime and aggregates

Increase in strength and resistance to frost and salt damage (↑, from D7 up to A1)

Increase in workability and ability to accommodate movement (↓, from A1 down to D7)

Mortar designation	*Mortar mixes*							*Recommended uses (In selecting a suitable mortar the first consideration must be the condition and type of masonry unit; mortar function and degree of exposure are the next considerations)*	
	Cement	*Brick dust*	*Lime*	*'Sharp sand'*	*'Soft sand'*	*'Stone dust'*	*Air entrainer*		
A1	1	1	1	5–6	–	–	√	Dense, impermeable, durable material such as granite, basalt, flint or well-vitrified brick. Severe exposure situations such as sea and river walls, retaining walls, and demanding locations such as paving, plinths and copings.	**1**
A2	1	1	1	4	1–2	–	√		
A3	1	1	1	3	2–3	1	√		
A4	1	1	1	5–6	–	–	–		
A5	1	–	1	5–6	–	–	–		
A6	1	–	1	4	1–2	–	–		
A7	1	–	1	3	1–2	1	–		
B1	1	1	2	8–9	–	–	√	Durable, moderately permeable material such as many compact limestones and sandstones or semi-vitrified brick. All exposures and demanding situations such as cornices, quoins and other weatherings. Also recommended for Group 1 material in less severe situations.	**2**
B2	1	1	2	6	2–3	–	√		
B3	1	1	2	4	3	1–2	√		
B4	1	1	2	8–9	–	–	–		
B5	1	–	2	8–9	–	–	–		
B6	1	–	2	6	2–3	–	–		
B7	1	–	2	4	3–4	1	–		
C1	1	1	3	10–12	–	–	√	Weathered examples of Groups 1 and 2 which are tending to scale and powder, in all exposures and locations. Also recommended for less durable limestones, sandstones and bricks in all locations. Designations C1, C2, C3 recommended for more severe exposures.	**3**
C2	1	1	3	7	3–5	–	√		
C3	1	1	3	7	2–4	1	√		
C4	1	1	3	10–12	–	–	–		
C5	1	–	3	10–12	–	–	–		
C6	1	–	3	8–10	2	–	–		
C7	1	–	3	7–9	2	1	–		
D1	–	1	1	2½–3	–	–	√	Poorly durable material such as some calcareous sandstones, microporous limestones or gauged 'rubbing' bricks. Also recommended for Groups 2 and 3 in sheltered environments and locations other than paving and major weatherings. Reduced aggregate loadings on D7 suitable for fine joints.	**4**
D2	–	1	1	2	½–1	–	√		
D3	–	1	1	1	1	½–1	√		
D4	–	1	1	2½–3	–	–	–		
D5	–	–	1	2½–3	–	–	–		
D6	–	–	1	2	½–1	–	–		
D7	–	–	1	1	1	½–1	–		

Cement	In this table 'cement' refers to white cement. Cement to be slurried before adding to wet lime:sand mixes.
Brick dust	To be ground dust <150 μm.
Lime	To be non-hydraulic white lime—high calcium or dolomitic.
'Sharp sand'	To consist of angular, well graded sand, ranging evenly from 2.36 mm to 150 μm.
'Soft sand'	To consist of rounded aggregate with some silt but not more than 15% below 150 μm.
'Stone dust'	To consist of limestone powder graded between 600 μm and 150 μm.
Air entrainer	To be proprietary entrainer added to achieve 15% entrapped air.

inspection will also provide useful information about the construction of the masonry, such as the original joint profile, the condition of the original mortar and whether the joints have been repointed. It is usually advisable to remove a representative unweathered sample of mortar and inspect it with a × 10 magnifying glass in good lighting conditions. This sample should be inspected further after it has been disaggregated (crushed, but not ground).

At the completion of these inspections it should be possible to know whether the binder is predominantly lime-based or cement-based (Roman or Portland) or whether it contains a substantial proportion of clay or loam. The type and general characteristics of the aggregate as, for example, rounded or angular sand grains, crushed stone and brick dust should be revealed. Larger inclusions such as gravel, unburnt shell lime, shell aggregate and kiln slag will also be identified. The ease with which the mortar is scored with a fingernail and knife and the removed sample broken will help to identify the presence of any hydraulic constituent.

Simple chemical analysis

Chemical analysis is usually required to determine the proportions of mortar constituents. Several professional mortar analysis services are available in the UK. The basic principle of this analysis is first to dissolve the lime binder in acid, then to separate the aggregate (sand, brick dust, crushed stone) and the fines (cements, fine brick dust and crushed stone), and thereby determine their proportions. Only simple laboratory facilities are required to undertake the procedure which is as follows:

Examination and dissolution of the binder

1. Collect a sample of about 40–50 grams (2 oz). Examine it and record characteristics such as colour, texture, aggregates, inclusions and hardness (scratch resistance).
2. Powder half the sample with a mortar and pestle. Dry at 110 °C for 24 hours and then weigh it with a balance (to an accuracy of 0.1 g).
3. Place the sample in a glass beaker and moisten it with deionized water. Then immerse the moistened sample in a 10% solution of hydrochloric acid to dissolve the binder. The mixture will effervesce as CO_2 is given off (safety glasses should be worn). The mixture should then be stirred with a glass rod to make sure the reaction is complete.

Separation, filtration and sieving

4. Weigh a piece of filter paper, place it in a funnel positioned over a large flask.
5. Add a few drops of hydrochloric acid to the sample to ensure complete acid digestion of the binder and stir. Add water to it slowly and swirl with a glass rod to suspend the fines.
6. Pour the liquid with the suspended material through the filter, being careful to keep the solid particles at the bottom of the beaker. Add more water and repeat the swirling and pouring until the water added to the beaker remains clear.
7. Dry the fines collected on the filter paper and weigh. Determine the weight of the fines.
8. Wash the sand with water several times and leave to dry for 24 hours. Weigh the dry sand.
9. Express the amounts of sand and fines as a percentage of the whole sample. The amount of dissolved binder is calculated by subtracting the sand and fines weights from the weight of the original sample. The weights determined will give the proportions of binder, fines and aggregate of the original mix. Allowances must be made for the loss of any calcareous aggregates dissolved with the binder. The results of the analysis can be recorded on a sheet such as the one on pages 91–92.

Further sand and fines analysis

10. Inspect the colour of the dried fines. Simple inspection of this kind is normally sufficient to identify clay (yellow, plastic when wetted), brick (red/brown), cement (grey), sand (almost any colour, gritty to touch).
11. More accurate examination must be made with a binocular microscope to determine colour, particle shape and material types. Sieve through standard sieves to determine particle size distribution, expressing the amount of each particle size as a percentage of the whole. Note that the acid may have changed the colours of the sand.

X-ray diffraction

Sometimes more sophisticated techniques are needed, mainly for historic mortars research to provide more specific information than separation and sieving of constituents. In this case a sample is submitted to a laboratory where a portion of it is ground to a homogeneous powder and a mineral analysis conducted by X-ray diffraction (XRD). The sample is irradiated and the crystal planes of the material in it reflect the rays.

Lime, sand, Roman Cement, Portland cement and pozzolanic additives such as trass are all clearly identified by this method of analysis because each has a different crystal diffraction pattern. Most importantly, XRD provides conclusive evidence of clay in a mortar and is able to identify the type of clay present.

The XRD results can be expressed in the form of a graph with several prominent peaks. The position of these peaks on the scale indicates the type of material present. To positively identify a material it is usually sufficient to match its three most intense peaks. The approximate proportions of the constituent materials can be gauged from the height of the major peak of each mineral.

Sampling procedure

Particularly where mortar analysis is part of a programme of archaeological and historical research, a thorough sampling procedure is required. The objectives of the sampling should be defined well in advance. The number and size of the samples should

Table 4.2 Mortars for remedial work on historic buildings based on hydraulic limes

	Eminently hydraulic lime	*Moderately hydraulic lime*	*Feebly hydraulic lime*	*Non-hydraulic lime [as putty]*	*Brick powder (reactive)*	*Sharp sand*	*Soft sand*	*Porous limestone aggregate*	*Mix (by volume)*
M10	1	-	-	1/10	-	2½	-	-	1:2½
M11	1	-	-	1/10	-	2	-	1	1:3
M12	1	-	-	1/10	1/2	2	1/2	1	1:4
M13	-	1	-	1/10	-	2½	-	-	1:2½
M14	-	1	-	1/10	-	2	1/2	1	1:3
M15	-	1	-	1/10	1/2	2	1/2	1	1/4
M16	-	-	1	1/10	-	2½	-	-	1:2½
M17	-	-	1	1/10	-	2	-	1	1:3
M18	-	-	1	1/10	1/2	2	1/2	1	1:4
M19	-	-	1	-	-	-	-	1	1:1

Notes

- M10, 11 and 12 are based on 'eminently' hydraulic lime, which commercially would be identified as NHL 5 in the new European standard for lime classification. These mortars, especially M10, are suitable for severe exposures.
- M13, 14 and 15 are based on 'moderately' hydraulic lime, with a European classification of NHL 3.5. These mortars have a wide application for weathered historic masonry in moderate to severe exposures.
- M16, 17 and 18 are based on 'feebly' hydraulic lime with a European classification of NHL2. These mortars are suitable for historic masonry in sheltered to moderate exposures.
- Lime putty. The addition of 1/10 part of lime putty is not included in the final mix proportion and is added to improve the workability of the mortar. The proportion is 1/10 of the coarse stuff. This quantity must not be exceeded, or the setting properties and final strengths of the mixes may be significantly affected.
- Hydraulic limes are the traditional limes used for building, with good setting times, moderate strengths and good permeability. They are in all ways more compatible with traditional masonry than cement based mortars, and more enduring than mortars based on non-hydraulic lime.

MORTAR ANALYSIS SHEET

SITE:	SAMPLE LOCATION:
Cardray Castle	South Wall

VISUAL DESCRIPTION:

A soft white mortar which is easy to crumble by hand.

WEIGHT OF SAMPLE: 96.91g WEIGHT AFTER DRYING: 95.74g LOSS ON DRYING %: 1.2%

BS SIEVE REFERENCE	WEIGHT OF SAMPLE RETAINED	PERCENTAGE %	RATIO	REMARKS
A 5.0 mm	0.21g	0.2)		Single large aggregate
B 2.36 mm	0.10g	0.1)		Mixed aggregate plus burnt wood.
C 1.18 mm	0.13g	0.1)	¼	As above. Ratio total of A, B, C.
D 600μm	1.17g	1.2	1	Silvery sand mixed aggregate
E 300μm	25.11g	26.2	21 3/4	As above.
F 150μm	18.89g	19.7	16½	As above.
G finer than F	6.54g	6.8	5½	As above.
H other				
Lime by difference	43.59g	45.5	1:1	Strongish mix.
TOTAL	95.74g	99.8		

be the minimum necessary to gain the required information without doing damage to the historic structure. The sampling procedure should include the following guidelines:

1. Sampling should be done by persons well acquainted with a building or its remains, to ensure that a proper programme of sampling is prepared and the samples receive proper interpretation. It is essential to involve the analyst in the sampling operations.
2. The sample should preferably be in the form of lumps, not crumbled or powdered. The quantity usually required for comparative analysis and for reference material is about 40–50 g (2 oz), preferably in one or a few compact fragments (half for analysis, half for reference).
3. The exact position (not just the location) from which the sample was taken must be accurately recorded.
4. To make certain that a particular kind of mortar is typical for a certain wall, at least three samples should be taken from different parts of that wall and analysed separately. If they prove to be identical within limits of practical deviations, their composition and properties can be considered as typical.
5. The sample must be clearly and thoroughly labelled.

Recording

Pages 91–92 show a typical mortar analysis sheet on which the analysis of a lime render sample has been recorded. The sheet shows the kind of information which would be received from a laboratory after examining a mortar by chemical analysis and grading of aggregates. In this case the most useful contribution made by the analysis to work on site was the identification of aggregates which enabled them to be matched with some accuracy. Five per cent HTI powder was added to the repair mix because the wall surface, which was originally internal, was to remain exposed.

References

1. Neve, R., *The City and Country Purchaser and Builder's Dictionary*, 1726, reprinted 1969 by David and Charles, Newton Abbot, England
2. Peterson, S., 'Lime water consolidation', in *Mortars, Cements and Grouts used in the Conservation of Historic Buildings*, Proceedings of ICCROM Symposium, November 1981
3. Peroni, S. *et al.*, 'Lime-based mortars for the repair of ancient masonry and possible substitutes', in *Mortars, Cements and Grouts used in the Conservation of Historic Buildings*, Proceedings of ICCROM Symposium, November 1981
4. Torraca, G., *Porous Building Materials—Materials Science for Architectural Conservation*, ICCROM, 1982
5. Nicholson, P., *The New Practical Builder and Workman's Companion*, 1823
6. Sickels, Lauren-Brook, 'Organics vs. synthetics: their use as additives in mortars', in *Mortars, Cements and Grouts used in the Conservation of Historic Buildings*, Proceedings of ICCROM Symposium, November 1981
7. Schaffer, R.J., *The Weathering of Natural Building Stones*, Department of Scientific and Industrial Research Special Report 18, HMSO, London, 1932 (available from Building Research Establishment, Watford WD2 7JR, England)

Figure 4.1 The pointing key, a cranked bar or flat rod designed to fit into the width of the joint, is essential to the efficient packing of mortar from the back of the joint. Packing cannot effectively be carried out using a trowel

Figure 4.2 Tamping the packed joint with the ends of a flat bristle brush raises the joint texture and provides a good evaporation face. The textured mortar also matches old, weathered mortar. The brush should not be dragged on the surface or leave any marks

Figure 4.3 Joints should be cut out with sharp, flat-bladed quirks and a light hammer, as shown in this illustration. Quirks are satisfactory for joints down to 5 mm thickness

Figure 4.4 Below 5 mm thickness joints need to be sawn out with hacksaw blades set in purpose-made two-piece handles. Impact tools should not be used

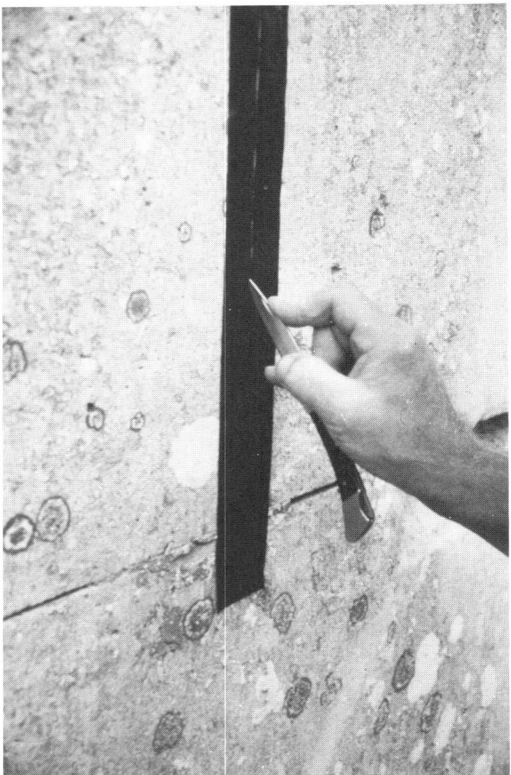

Figure 4.5 To place mortar in fine joints effectively, a heavy-duty canvas-backed adhesive tape is placed over the centre-line of the cut joint, and pressed firmly onto the surface. A sharp knife is used to slit the tape through to the joint, and the edges of the tape are pressed down

Figure 4.6 The open joint is flushed out with a fine water jet. In the final stage, a lime putty:stone dust mortar (1:1) is firmly pressed into the joint using a filling knife

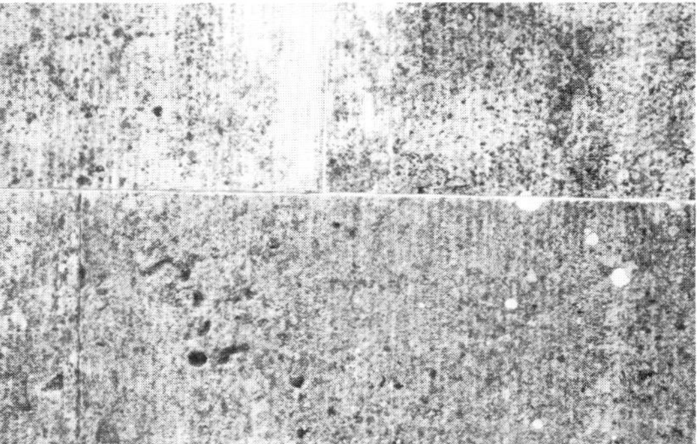

Figure 4.7 The tape is removed and any further packing of the mortar face takes place with a small iron or copper flat. The mortar is contained neatly in the joint and is well compacted, and the joint has not been widened to achieve success

Figure 4.8 Dense, impermeable walling stones such as granite provide good resistance to weather but make great demands on the mortar in the joints. Traditionally, quite strong mortars have been used with granite; Lutyens' mortar at Castle Drogo is 1:1:6, cement:lime:sand. Unfortunately, such mortars often exhibit shrinkage cracking at the mortar:stone interface. When water is consistently allowed access the inevitable result is wet conditions internally and lime leaching out onto the surface

Figure 4.9 Superficial repointing in similar strength mortar gauged with a PVA bonding agent has only exacerbated the problem in this early repointing, exhibiting substantial shrinkage cracking

Figure 4.10 There are no short cuts to resolving the problem. This illustration shows joints cut out to 50 mm depth, carefully removing all old mortar with plugging chisels. To the left and right is new mortar consisting of a 1:1:6 mortar which has been firmly packed to the full depth of cut and allowed to cure slowly. Success depends on a low water ratio in the fresh mortar and on slow drying

Figure 4.11 Joints which are particularly vulnerable to penetration may receive a different treatment. Such joints may be ledges, copings or the top bed joint of weatherings. Into a 50 mm cut a foam backing rod is inserted to the back of the joint

Figure 4.12 A two-part polysulphide mastic plug is placed against the backing rod, using a mastic gun with an extended nozzle

Figure 4.13 The mastic plug is firmly ironed into place using a spatula dipped into white spirit

Figure 4.14 A 40 mm depth of 1:1:6 mortar masks the plug

5

Traditional handworking of stone: methods and recognition

Peter Hill

Introduction

The faces of stones which bear the weathered marks of the tools used by the masons in their preparation are always of considerable interest to archaeologists and conservators and well worth study. How much may be safely deduced from such evidence, however, is a subject fraught with pitfalls. It seems reasonable that opinions on technical subjects should be based on a sound working knowledge of the principles involved. Some scholars, however, seem to have no inhibitions when discussing stonework in archaeological contexts, whether it be a discussion of excavated masonry, or papers and books on the techniques of the mason. A few examples will serve to illustrate the dangers involved. By one authority we are told that 'to cut long straight lines over a metre in length by means of a chisel alone is an almost impossible task'. This is a denial of the basic training of a mason in any age, the ability to dress stone against a straight edge being one of the more important indicators separating the skilled workman from the amateur. A deviation from the mean of under 1 mm can readily be achieved without recourse to any secondary work with abrasives.

Elsewhere, the gouge is variously referred to as 'unsuitable for stonework' and 'useless for working stone', statements readily refuted by a visit to the nearest mason's workshop, where any number of these tools may be found in use on both hard and soft stones.

A discussion of the 'drove', more properly called a 'boaster', contains the assertion that 'its size would have made it difficult to push evenly along the stone and, anyway, if this had been done, the resulting surface would have been very patchy and unpleasant'. It need only be said that it is used in precisely this way with excellent results and is, in fact, the basic tool used in finishing a clean, flat surface.

These few examples from a very rich field are of necessity selective in a partial approach and are perhaps somewhat extreme, yet it remains true that almost all writers on this subject perpetrate similar inaccuracies and tend to rely too heavily on work of other authors who are themselves working at second-hand. The Latin scholar will as a matter of course recognize gaps in his experience and consult an epigraphist about an unusual inscription, yet is quite prepared to perpetuate this almost circular transfer of what is, in some cases, little better than a collation of imperfectly grasped hearsay evidence.

The purpose of this chapter is to give sufficient, accurate information to enable the archaeologist or conservator to identify the tools used in the production of masonry on sites of any period and to assess the quality of the work on a common basis.

Identification of stone types

The starting point in any examination of masonry must be to identify the type and, as closely as possible, the source of the stone. (All excavated worked stone should be fully reported.) It is not sufficient, for example, to refer to limestone, or even oolitic limestone. The distance the stone has travelled has an obvious bearing on the difficulty and cost of the construction. For example, when Tutbury Castle was repaired in 1314 the cost of transport over 5–6 miles (8–9 km) came to nearly twice the cost of the quarried stone.[1] Information on the nature of the stone gives some guidance on the degree of labour expended to achieve a given finish. It should be the aim where possible to give at least a narrow geographical area, if not the precise quarry of origin. To this end, a petrographical analysis is clearly desirable, although a local stonemason may be able to give an accurate indication. As a general rule, sandstones tend to be uniform within a given quarry, whereas limestones may vary markedly in colour, texture and hardness within a 300 mm cube (approximately 65 kg or 150 lb).

Once the stone is known, some indication of its hardness and ease of working (not always the same thing) should be attempted. To determine this, a banker-mason trying a chisel on an unimportant part of the work is indispensable. It will be very difficult to relate the nature of the stone to a fixed standard, but an experienced subjective opinion should have some value.

A common misconception is that limestone is 'softer' (i.e. easier to work) than sandstone. However, the proportion of 'hard' to 'soft' stones commonly used in building is probably about equal between the two types, and apart from the problems of silicosis many sandstones are much more pleasant to work than limestones.

Types and descriptions of masonry

Stones appearing on the face of a wall should be referred to in general terms as facing stones. A more detailed description of stonework should be on the lines of the categories set out below. The term 'ashlar' must never, contrary to popular practice, be used as a synonym for 'facing stone', unless it is strictly appropriate.

The following categories are given in descending order of the degree of labour required.

1. *Ashlar*. This term should be confined to masonry that meets the following criteria. The stones should have carefully worked beds and joints, and be finely jointed (generally under 6 mm (0.2 in)) and set in horizontal courses. Stones within each course should be of the same height, although successive courses may be of different heights. Where the centre of the face, however it is finished, intentionally projects beyond the wall line, it should be bounded by a well chiselled margin, 20–25 mm (0.8–1 in) wide, worked straight and square to the beds. This allows accurate setting both to adjacent stones and to the general line of the wall. These drafts (strips of surface worked to the width of the chisel) should twist in reasonably well and, ideally, the stone should be perfectly rectangular in elevation. Ashlar should be described according to the surface finish. The more common finishes are listed below.

(a) *Plain or rubbed ashlar* is ashlar where the surface has been rubbed, usually with a piece of sandstone or carborundum, to remove all toolmarks, leaving a perfectly smooth surface.

(b) *Boasted or axed ashlar* is left finished with toolmarks visible. The regularity and form of the toolmarks will vary according to the style of the mason. They will in general show a row of diagonal grooves set in a series of drafts, although the individual drafts may not be distinguishable.

(c) *Punched ashlar*. The surface is left from the punch after the marginal drafts have been worked. The marks may be random or regular, the latter being the most likely on stone worked carefully enough to be called ashlar. A very finely worked surface, with very small and even indentations, is referred to as being *pecked*.

(d) *Rock-faced ashlar*. The centre of the stone is left boldly projecting in its natural state, or with a little assistance from a pitching tool within the chiselled margins.

(e) *Tooled or batted ashlar*. This is left with regularly spaced chisel marks set vertically on a rubbed surface. It represents not so much a stage of work, but rather a deliberately applied design introduced within the last 150 years or so. It is thus one of the few surface finishes to give any definite indication of date. It is sometimes seen today, often with diagonal toolmarks on a sawn surface, in a vain attempt to simulate non-mechanical work.

(f) *Rusticated ashlar*. The face projects from the wall line in a distinct step. The simplest indication is that the joints are set in a rebate behind the marginal drafts around the face, which may be finished in any fashion. The term is not a synonym for rock-faced work.

2. *Block-in-course*. This is a class of masonry, nowadays seen largely in railway and dock engineering, in which the stones are squared and brought to fair joints. The faces are usually dressed with the walling hammer or punch. It may resemble ashlar or coursed rubble according to the degree and quality of work applied to it, although the stones will usually be larger than coursed rubble. The distinction may be difficult at times, but measurement of the dressed stonework should assist. Joints may be wider than in ashlar work, and there will not necessarily be a good chiselled margin. The tools used for dressing the face should be specified where possible.

3. *Coursed rubble*. The term rubble is not a derogatory term. The majority of ancient stone buildings in Britain are in coursed or random rubble. Many have stood for centuries without any regular maintenance. Rubble is more cost effective than ashlar. In coursed rubble the stones are squared up, more or less roughly according to the quality, to about the same height within each course, usually not above 250–300 mm (8–12 in). The faces may be left rough, or dressed with walling hammer or punch. The joints and beds will tend to be in excess of 15 mm (0.6 in) and, on elevation, the corners of the

stones will tend to exhibit roundness rather than angularity. It is normal for the joints to be worked to something of a taper. This increases the hold of the mortar and makes accuracy in working (and thus cost) less important. Where the stones, although often small, appear to be particularly uniform in height and rectangularity, the style may be referred to as *coursed squared rubble*.

4. *Random rubble*. This is walling in which the stones have received little attention beyond knocking off the sharpest angles. Only minimum attention is paid to coursing, although the stones are laid horizontally as far as possible. Generally, this work occurs where stone of a highly stratified or fissile nature is available, because the resultant thin flat slabs, usually 100–200 mm (4–8 in) thick, are easily broken into a suitable size and can be bedded with a minimum of labour. When the stones are placed so as to level up to a horizontal course at intervals, the work is known as *random rubble built to courses*.

5. *Polygonal or rag walling*. In this work, the stones are of any shape as they come from the quarry. They are placed so as to fit best with their neighbours after a minimum of hammer-dressing. The effect is similar to that of crazy paving set vertically.

An approach to the measurement of dressed stonework

This section is relevant largely to the assessment of ashlar and block-in-course work. The principal indicators of the quality of work are the truth of the surface against a straight edge and the squareness of the stone on both elevation and plan. It is essential that physical checks of these factors be taken; the eye alone will not give the necessary objective evaluation. These indicators are not new. The ancient Egyptians also used these to check the quality of their stonework.[2]

To test the straightness, an edge is held so that it lies parallel to the notional face of the stone. Where the distance at point 'a' in *Figure 5.1(a)* is no more than 2 mm in 300 mm, the surface may in general be regarded as straight. Greater deviations should be recorded in steps as suggested in *Table 5.1*, to assist in comparative studies. The amount of acceptable deviation will depend to an extent on the nature of the work and the type of surface finish. On good, finely chiselled or rubbed ashlar or mouldings, the deviation should not be more than 1 mm. On run-of-the-mill ashlar walling, up to 3 mm in 300 mm would not necessarily be out of place, depending on the date and class of building.

The same test should, where possible, be applied to the beds and joints. The joints are relatively unimportant and need only to be examined closely to confirm the excellence of first-class work. For both ashlar and block-in-course work, they should be reasonably parallel as they run back into the wall. Bedding surfaces should be checked with some care. Although they will often not be worked particularly cleanly, the deviation should not exceed 2 mm. The principle to follow is that the stones should rest on one another with minimum use of mortar to give stability. On the other hand, beds should never be worked concave, as this causes pressure to fall on the arrises, with consequent spalling of the face.

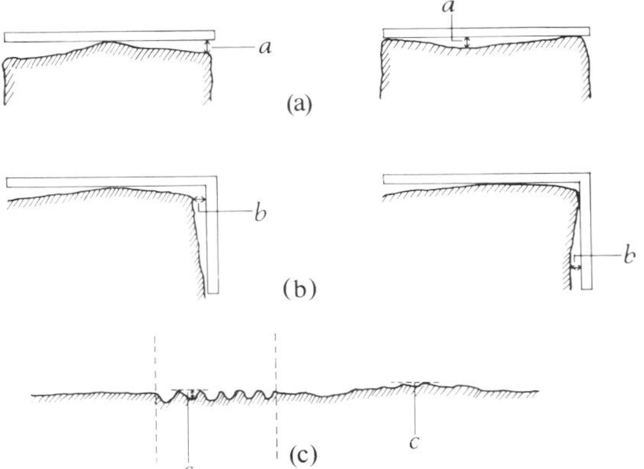

Figure 5.1 Measurement of dressed stonework (see text)

It is an axiom in masonry that mortar is used to keep the stones apart rather than to hold them together. Structures in ashlar and block-in-course depend for their stability on the large size of the stones, the well fitting beds and joints and the arrangement of the bonding. Where the strength depends largely on the mortar, the classification is more appropriately some type of rubble work.

To test for squareness, the square should be held with one arm parallel to the notional line of one face and any discrepancy measured on the other arm (*Figure 5.1(b)*). Anything under 2 mm in 300 mm may be regarded as square. As before, any greater deviations should be recorded as in *Table 5.1*.

Table 5.1 Recording data

Deviation per 300 mm (mm)			*Possible description*
(a) *Straight*	(b) *Square*	(c) *Range*	
under 2	under 2	under 1	Ashlar
2–4	2–4	1–2	
5–12	5–6	3–5	
over 12	7–12	7–12	Block-in-course

The angles to be checked are the quoins, the corners on the elevation of the faces and, where possible, the beds and joints against the face. The beds should always be square to the face, but the joints are not as important and up to 6 mm in 300 mm under square is not out of place in good work.

Note should be taken next of the surface finish, which should be accurately described according to the tools used and the regularity of the tooling. The profile of typical portions of the surface should be taken, especially on the better finishes, as an aid to identifying the general standard of the work. On good, straight, finely chiselled work, the range may well be less than 0.5 mm, although this will vary according to the heaviness of the chiselling. The key lies largely in the regularity of the surface. Punched work in which the peaks and troughs are all at similar levels will clearly have been worked with more care, or ability, than roughly chiselled work in which the range is perhaps less, but where much unevenness is apparent, although the labour on the punched work is likely to have been less. Examples are given in *Figure 5.1(c)*.

Where the maximum of more than one column of *Table 5.1* is exceeded, the work is tending towards coursed rubble. Measurements taken on the margins are the best guides to nomenclature, especially where (c) approaches the maximum when measured across the face. Isolated holes in an otherwise good face may be disregarded for measurement, but should be noted as detracting from the quality. It is important to remember that, in any period from Roman to modern, the *skilled* mason can achieve a deviation from both straight and square of under 0.5 mm, without excessive lack of skill, or a relatively low specification. The figures shown in *Table 5.1* reflect human frailty, rather than the achievable.

An indication of the size of stones used should be given. The dimensions should always be quoted in the order length of face, depth into the wall and bed height.

The overall assessment of stonework must be based on a combination of the above factors. Because of the infinite variety possible in stone dressing, it is difficult to establish a coherent system of grading. An experienced eye must take precedence over rigid rules, but it must be backed by physical measurement. Some of the standards given may seem over exacting, but they are no more than may readily be achieved, as required, by a skilled mason. It is only by using the best as a base that a common standard of appreciation, which is lacking at present, may be established.

It is worth noting in passing that, especially in regard to medieval work, the final position of a stone in the building should have relatively little bearing on the quality of workmanship. When the stone is being worked, it is only a few inches from the eye of the mason, who will be satisfying a fixed standard with small regard to its destination.

To assist the archaeologist with stonework, it may be well at times to take direct advice from a stonemason, but care is necessary here. 'Stonemason' can cover a number of different trades. The one to choose is the person who has been trained as a banker-mason and who spends the greater part of his time dressing stone with a mallet and chisel to a high standard. It is important to appreciate the distinction. Someone who has spent his life pointing or building rubble walls is no more competent to judge the dressing of ashlar than a banker-mason is to assess a dry-stone wall. An attempt may be made in each case, but this is hardly the approach for the professional archaeologist. No matter who finally judges the work, it must be within the framework of this or some other common standard of approach.

Tools, toolmarks and methods

The tools discussed below are, with a few specified exceptions, known to have been in use in one form or another from Roman times to the present day. When considering dating of stonework, it is of prime importance to bear in mind that the majority of modern masons' handtools are very similar in number, style and use to those of the medieval and Roman mason. Tomb drawings dating from *c.* 2600 BC to *c* 1100 BC found at Saqqara and Thebes[3] show tools indistinguishable from those in daily use today.

The marks left from the use of the tools are described and differentiated as far as possible below. However, in some cases it is quite impossible to differentiate between work done by different tools. This may be disappointing for the archaeologist, but it is a matter of simple fact which can be demonstrated by any competent banker-mason. Also, it is often the case that there will be a greater difference between the work of two contemporary masons than between works of two different millennia. As a general principle, it is not possible to use toolmarks to provide absolute dating evidence; even relative dating can be extremely hazardous and is best avoided.

The illustrations do not relate to any specific period. They are representative types showing the general form of the tools. They are described in approximate sequence of use.

Axe/adze (*Figure 5.2a,b*). These tools occur in a number of variations, including both tools combined in one.[4] They may, in their different forms, be used for either initial roughing out, or in final dressing. For rough dressing of rubble, an acceptable result can readily be achieved, particularly where the tool

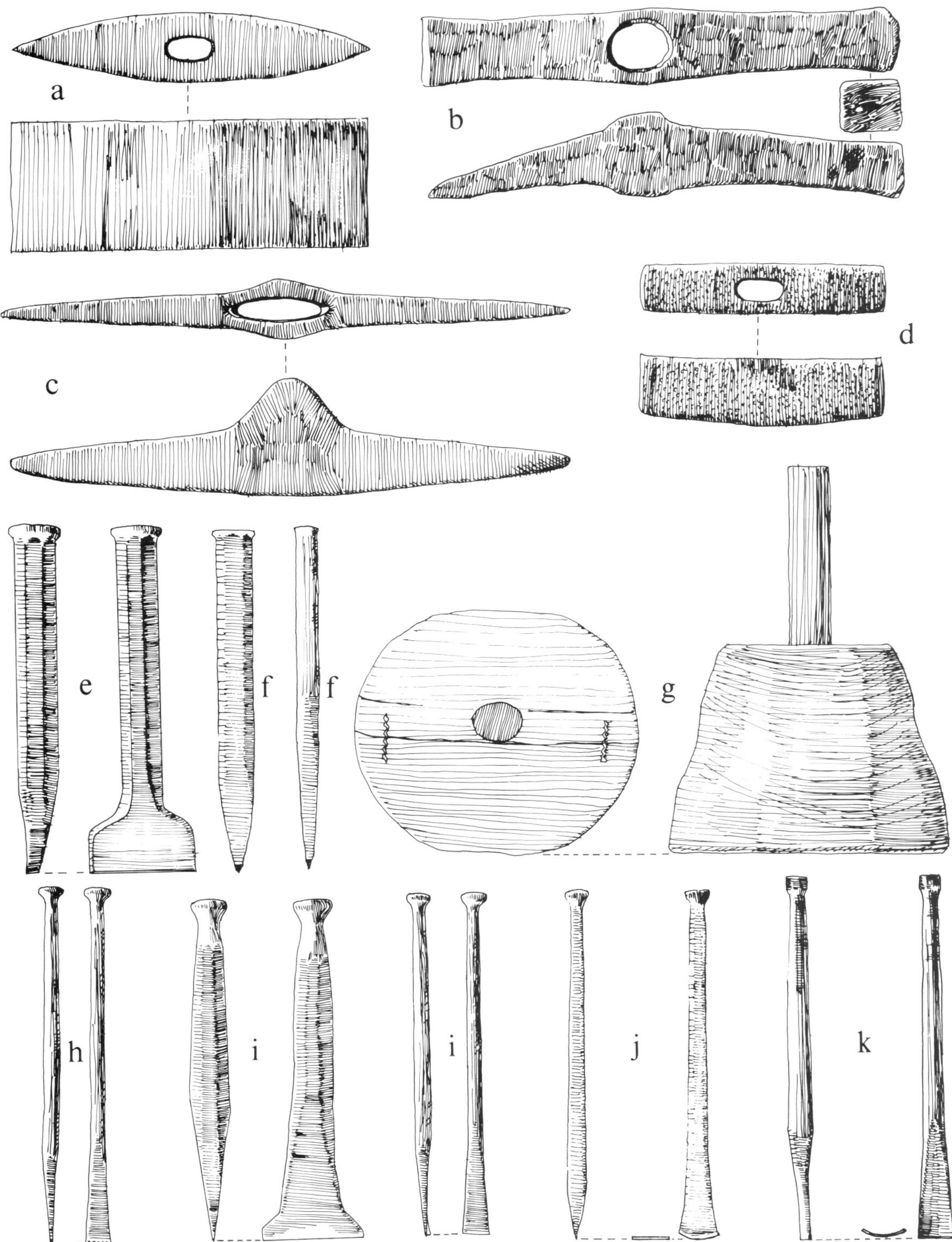

Figure 5.2 Representative types of stoneworking tools (see text)

consists of a vertical axe blade, and a hammer head,[5] which resembles one type of modern walling hammer. Other versions of the axe have two vertical blades. The adze has a horizontal blade, which may be combined with a hammer head,[6] pick[7] or axe.[4] The adze does not seem to figure in medieval records, but it may not have been distinguished by name from the varieties of axe. Neither of these tools is in general use today in England.

Pick (*Figure 5.2c*). This tool may have a point at each end, or it may have a hammer head at one end. It may also have an axe or adze blade—indeed axe, adze and pick may on occasions be the same tool. They are all referred to here according to which working surface is being used; in this form it is in effect a scappling hammer, which is a quarryman's tool.

The pick is mainly used for rough working of the stone, either for rubble work or in the early stages of ashlar. Use of a heavy pick, especially the type weighted with the hammer head on the back, will show a relatively long striation according to the softness of the stone. This may be V-shaped or U-shaped in section, depending on the form to which the tool has been sharpened and how blunt the edge has become. A small pick will leave marks largely indistinguishable from the use of a punch struck by a hammer. However, the finer dressed or smaller work will be more likely to have involved the punch. The effects of both will be treated together.

Hammer (*Figure 5.2d*). This tool is for driving other cutting tools. It is generally several centimetres long, hafted centrally and weighs 1–3 kg with a relatively small striking face. (Roman examples may be seen in the museum in Chester, England.) Tools designed to be used with the hammer have the struck end of about the same diameter as the shank.

Pitcher or pitching tool (*Figure 5.2c*). The antiquity of this tool is uncertain. It has never been positively identified in an archaeological context and its use leaves no trace. It is included for the sake of completeness. It resembles a very heavy chisel, with a blade from 40 mm to 75 mm (1.5–3 in) wide. Instead of a cutting edge, the end is up to 8 mm (0.3 in) thick and almost flat. It is used with a heavy hammer blow to remove surplus stone by fracture. One good blow may detach a piece weighing 2–3 kg. The only trace of its use is a slight bruising where the blade has been in contact. This mark is usually removed by further working and will, in any case, disappear after only slight weathering.

Punch (*Figure 5.2d*). This is an extremely versatile tool which is normally used with a hammer for removing either large or small amounts of waste. The amounts removed depend on the size of the punch, the hammer and the weight of the blow. The softer stones are not always quicker to rough-off with a punch than are the harder stones. Soft stone will often largely absorb the blow with only small effect and it may be easier to dispense with this tool in favour of a claw-tool or chisel. A good example of the variety of punched work is afforded by the east-central pier of the east gate of Chester Fort. There the upper right-hand side has been roughly worked-off with a punch to give a very irregular surface. The lower-right hand side has been more neatly worked over with the same tool to give a rather flatter finish. The left-hand side has been punched (or picked) to give an intermittently furrowed effect.

With both the pick and the punch, a single heavy blow in the right place will detach a large flake of stone, perhaps as big as a fist, by fracture alone, with only slight trace of abrasion at the point of contact. Repeated use of the tool over the surface will show as a number of pock-marks, whilst repeated blows of the hammer without removing the punch from the stone between each blow will result in furrows which may be a few millimetres long, or may extend across the face of the stone. Careful use of the pick can give the latter effect, but more irregularity will be likely. The variety of different effects to be obtained from the punch is almost infinite and the quality of finish depends largely on the skill and effort put into the work.

The cutting edge of a punch may be around 6 mm (0.2 in) wide for use on softer stones, but is normally drawn out to a point for harder stone. Where the tool has a head suitable for use with a mallet it is generally known as a point, as is the more delicate, hammer-headed tool of the carver.

Mallet (*Figure 5.2g*). A modern mason's mallet is circular or oval in plan, about 150 mm (6 in) across, and tapering in towards the handle. This is precisely the shape shown in Egyptian tomb drawings. However, medieval illustrations show a type more akin to a joiner's mallet, which is rectangular in plan and elevation. The Roman mallet is shown on tombstones, but its precise form is not discernible.

Chisels intended for use with a mallet nowadays have their heads mushroomed out above a narrow neck to present a large area to the mallet. The previous practice is not known, because no chisels have survived in this form and contemporary illustrations are not clear on the point.

Claw-tool (*Figure 5.2h*). This is basically a chisel, for use either as a finish in itself, or to bring the stone to within 2–3 mm of the finished surface prior to chiselling. Its use is optional on the softer stones, but it is of great value on the harder stones and on those stones which have a tendency to pluck into holes when equivalent amounts are removed with an ordinary chisel of the same width. Because of the reduced length of the working edge, it requires less effort to drive than the equivalent full-bladed chisel.

The effect of the claw-tool is to leave an irregularly 'combed' surface in which the tooth marks may easily be seen. Where the stone has been further chiselled or rubbed, the indentations may be very short and shallow, looking more like pin-pricks. The variety of claw-tools is endless. The teeth of the tool may have been close set, 2–3 mm long and sharply pointed, or the tool may have more nearly resembled a plain chisel, with the cutting edge interrupted by a series of nicks, 3–4 mm apart. The effect should be closely observed. No examples of the claw-tool are known to have survived in archaeological contexts in Britain, but its use is known at many Roman sites and on the majority of medieval churches. The date of the re-introduction of this tool some time in the early medieval period is uncertain, but it would be very surprising if such a useful tool, used by the Ancient Greeks and perhaps earlier, went completely out of use for a period of several centuries.

Chisels (*Figure 5.2i*). The term is used to cover all cutting tools driven by mallet or hammer, whose edge forms a straight line when viewed from the cutting end. Chisels are generally classified according to the width of the cutting edge, those of over 50 mm (2 in) also being referred to as boasters and used for final dressing of the stone to give a true surface. When the tool has, in elevation, a rounded edge, it is known as a bull-nose chisel (*Figure 5.2j*) and is used for working concave surfaces. The gouge, with a cutting edge curved on end view (*Figure 5.2k*), is used for largely the same purposes as the bull-nose.

The smaller chisels, from 20 mm down to 3 mm (0.8–0.1 in), tend to be used for working mouldings and for carving. As Blagg[8] points out, small chisels can be as finely drawn out as wood-chisels, making recognition difficult after years in the ground. A chisel of about 25 mm (1 in) is usually used for cutting-in marginal drafts, but this may vary according to the type of stone and the whim of the mason. No two masons today work in exactly the same way and there is no reason to suppose that they have ever done so. The chisel is also often used, especially on the harder stones, in sequence after the claw-tool to clear successive parallel drafts across the face which may then be left or finished off with a boaster, according to the quality of the work in hand.

The most commonly used chisels for work not going beyond simple, bold mouldings are probably 12 mm, 25 mm and 50 mm (0.5, 1 and 2 in) wide. With these three, plus appropriate roughing-out tools, a surprising variety of work can be undertaken.

The identification of marks left by the chisel is not always easy, owing to weathering, further finishing by abrasion and interference with the surface due to careless roughing out. A plain chisel, used with a little vigour on a hard, close-grained stone, will leave a series of contiguous, straight grooves.

The length of the grooves will correspond to the size of the chisel, except where successive drafts have overlapped (which is the norm). On coarse-grained or soft stone there may be no clear evidence of the tools used, even immediately after working. Where flat surfaces are being cleared, the grooves are at an angle to the line of approach, which is normally across the body of the mason. The right-handed mason holds the chisel in the left hand and works from right to left. If the mason stands square to the job, the chisel marks will slope from bottom left to top right, at an angle of about 60°–70° to the lower edge of the stone. The opposite slope will result from left-handed work. Holding the chisel at an angle is not done for any particular effect, but because it is the easier and most natural way to dress ashlar, whether chisel or axe is being used. The belief that diagonal tooling is a mark of axed work does not stand the test of close examination. Comparative studies have shown that, providing all the work is carried out to the same standard, it can be impossible to tell which portions of a surface have been worked with a boaster and which with an axe of similar-sized cutting edge. Even on occasions where differences were apparent, it was not possible to say which tool had worked which part.

The use of the adze can also be difficult to distinguish because it does its work with a paring action, cutting the stone in precisely the same way as a chisel used with a good swing of the mallet. Moreover, marks from the boaster may, depending on the coarseness of the surface, be as much as 5–6 mm (0.2–0.24 in) apart and 3–4 mm (0.12–0.16 in) deep. In contrast, the axe or adze can be used, as can the boaster if desired, to give a finer, shallower effect. Like the axe/adze, in heavily boasted work one corner of the chisel tends to dig in with depressing ease and frequency. The slightly radiating marks sometimes claimed as axed work can also readily be achieved in boasted work with only minimum carelessness.

The problem of differentiating the different tools applied equally to the work of all periods. All edged tools used on stone tend to wear first at the corners, both by abrasion in use and by the action of sharpening. This can lead to some confusion; for example, a pick which has suffered heavy use can leave a mark not dissimilar to that made by some indeterminate type of curved chisel.

Given the survival of individual marks, the work of the bull-nose chisel is readily identified and distinguished from that of the gouge. Although the grooves from both tools are curved on plan, those of the bull-nose chisel have the centre of the curve ahead of the sides. The opposite effects shown by the gouge. The direction of movement is usually easily determined, as the groove tends to show a slow descent and a sharper step up in a forward movement.

On the general question of toolmarks, it should be noted that on all but the hardest stones they are easily removed, or at least softened, by rubbing with a piece of sandstone or other abrasive. This is particularly true following use of the smaller chisels, whch tend to be used with a light blow and where, in careful finishing with the larger chisels, the tool is not removed from the job between strokes. this technique may leave a surface devoid of all but the faintest of marks.

Basic stone dressing

In both the initial reduction of the surface with the punch and in the final dressing of the plane surface, the archaeologist may care to substitute the use of an axe or adze. Whatever tool is used, the basic principle is the same.

To produce a piece of ashlar from the quarried block, a 25 mm (1 in) chisel is used in conjunction with a straight-edge to cut two rebates at opposite sides of the stone. These are checked for twist (the failure of a surface to lie in a straight plane) and adjusted as required. They are joined by similar rebates on the two remaining sides. These marginal drafts (drafts worked along the edge of a stone) should now be straight and lie in the same plane. The quality of the finished work depends to a large extent on their completeness and accuracy.

For rock-faced ashlar, the stone in the centre is left standing or perhaps reduced a little with the walling hammer. For better class work, the waste is removed with the axe/adze, pick or punch followed by the claw-tool, 25 mm (1 in) chisel or boaster according

Figure 5.3 Examples of toolmarks on newly dressed stone:
(a) Variations in axed work

(b) Pitched face with random punch marks

to the nature of the stone. These three tools are all used in a similar manner: successive drafts are worked across the face, moving away from the mason, the accuracy is judged by laying the straight edge between the marginal drafts. The other four surfaces (the back is normally left rough) are squared off from the marginal drafts, and are worked with a care appropriate to their function.

Where convex profiles are required, the surface is normally worked in a series of successively smaller drafts at a tangent to the curve, using whichever tool best suits the nature of the job. Curved work is normally finished by chiselling around the circumference, with the chisel held parallel to the axis.

Since at least the early medieval period the profiles of mouldings have been transferred to the stone with the aid of a wooden templet, or profile of the design. Surprisingly, the Roman masons seem not to have used the technique, as examination of the West Range of Site XI at Corbridge, England, makes clear. The stones there seem to have been cut roughly to size in the workshop and finally dressed when set in position. This method is exceedingly laborious and time consuming. This may account for the generally poor finish of the work, but it is certainly remarkable that so simple a device was not developed by such practical engineers.

The basic method of using templets is first to square the stone to the overall size demanded by the mouldings and then to apply the templet to each end of the stone in turn. The profile is marked on with a sharp point and the shape is worked through between the two ends, using a straight edge for straight mouldings and an edge cut to the correct radius for voussoirs, tracery and other curved work.

Columns, other than those cut on a lathe, are produced by the application of the same principle. If one long side is dressed flat and the two ends

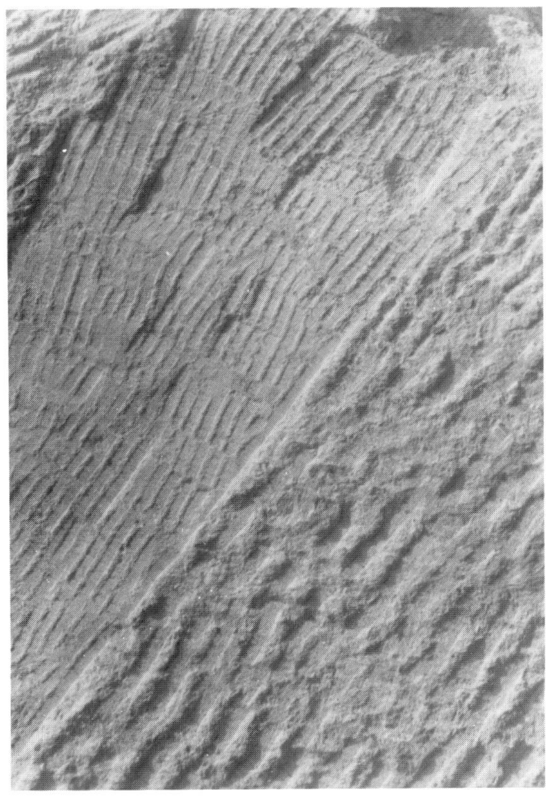

(c) Fine and coarse claw tooling

(d) Boasted ashlar

squared off from it and made parallel to each other, the centre point of the column may be marked on at each end. Circles of an appropriate size, depending on whether the column is to be a true cylinder or is to have an entasis, are scribed and the stone is worked in the manner described above.

If complex, stepped circular mouldings are to be worked, the basic method is the same, but the successive diameters are marked on the top bed of the stone, transferred to the appropriate point by squaring and worked in a series of sinkings.

Conclusion

There is much relevant information to be gained from close examination of the method of construction and the method of working and finishing the surfaces of building stones. However, unless the evidence is correctly understood and interpreted and unless it is accurately recorded and described, gross errors can be made and perpetuated by constant reference to the original mistake.

An appreciation of the methods of working stone will do much to avoid the use of meaningless generalizations and the over-confident assumptions sometimes made through ignorance and misconceptions.

Acknowledgements

Grateful thanks are due to Dr B. Dobson and Dr D.J. Breeze for their advice and encouragement over a long period. Chief amongst others who read early drafts, Mr A.D. Phillips and Dr B. Heywood made a number of valuable suggestions. Two colleagues, Messrs G. Butler and M.C. O'Connor, gave invaluable advice on certain technical aspects. The drawings were prepared by Mr P. Schofield of the York Minster Archaeology Office. Much of this chapter was first published in *Archaeologia Aeliana*,[9] hence the emphasis on Roman examples. All opinions are the author's and are not necessarily shared by those mentioned above.

References

1. Salzman, L.F., *Building in England*, p. 119, Oxford, 1952
2. Petrie, W.F.M., *Ancient Egypt*, pt. 2, pp. 33–39, 1930
3. Richter, G.M.A., *AJA*, xlvii, figure 8, 1943
4. Proceedings of the Society of Antiquaries of Scotland, 1952–1953 fig 6 E16
5. Bushe-Fox *Richborough iv*, plate lxi, no. 341, Oxford 1949
6. *Archaeologia*, lxxviii, Plate xxxii no. 50.
7. Collingwood, R.G. and Richmond, I.A., *Archaeology of Roman Britain*, Plate xx(u), Methuen, 1969
8. Blagg, T.F.C., 'The Roman stonemason', Britannia, **X**, 109–120
9. Hill, P.R., 'Stonework and the Archaeologist', *Archaeologia Aeliana*, **51X**

6

Earthquake damage to historic masonry structures

Alejandro Alva Balderrama

Introduction

It would be pretentious to try to summarize in a few pages the vast and complex problems created by earthquake damage to historic buildings. This chapter, therefore, will deal only with the broad aspects of these problems and with the concerns of the experts who are responsible for the protection of the built architectural heritage. It is hoped that the following considerations will be helpful in identifying current lines of action and research in soil dynamics and earthquake engineering, which are specifically related to the problems of earthquake damage to historic buildings.

Earthquakes

During earthquakes rocks will suddenly rupture and move, often violently, when stressed. Frequently rocks on one side of the rupture move relative to the rocks on the other side. As the rocks move the earth is shaken. Slight movements may give rise to disastrous earthquakes.

If the seismically active regions of the world are considered, it can be seen that much of the property susceptible to earthquake damage, or that which has already suffered damage, is of historic importance. The disasters of Buyin-Zava (Iran) 1962, Skopje (Yugoslavia) 1963, Varto (Turkey) and Lima (Peru) 1966, Mudurnu (Turkey) and Koyna (India) 1967, Dasht-e Bayaz (Iran) 1968, Banja Luka (Yugoslavia) 1969, Gediz (Turkey), Luzon (Philippines), Ancash (Peru) and Karnaveh (Iran) 1970, Ghir (Iran) and Managua (Nicaragua) 1972, Pattan (Pakistan) 1974, Friuli (Italy) and Antigua (Guatemala) 1976, Montenegro (Yugoslavia) 1979, Alta Irpinia (Italy) 1980 and El Asnam (Algeria) 1981, all affected historic structures.

Earthquake risk and historic buildings

In the conservation field, earthquake risk is one of the many decay factors encountered. It is, however, one of the least understood, perhaps because most of the related research is carried out on the performance of current or future construction, neglecting the world-wide problem of the existing building stock, which includes millions of historic properties in which people live and work.[1] The efforts put into the study and improvement of masonry construction are very limited, since this method of building tends to be regarded as out of date. Such an attitude, however, fails to consider the existing building stock and the very large number of structures which continue to be build of adobe, brick, or stone masonry. As little dynamic testing of masonry has been carried out so far, knowledge of the seismic response of this form of construction is based largely on field observations made after earthquakes. Such information does not provide satisfactory guidelines for strengthening unframed existing buildings (historic buildings are predominantly of this type), especially since so many different types of masonry exist. Much more dynamic testing is needed, in order to establish the principles of the seismic response of masonry structures in their various forms.[2]

Structural characteristics of historic buildings

The structural characteristics of historic buildings have great significance when considering their response to earthquake excitation. A primary and serious drawback in identifying the distinctive structural characteristics of historic buildings is the extremely variable quality of the materials and construction methods used. Except for timber, or timber-framed, buildings, most historic structures are in unframed masonry. They are built of a very wide range of materials including unburnt earths, bricks and stones, which are assembled with mud, or set in lime mortar or gypsum. Each of these materials varies widely in form and physical properties and is often used in combination with other materials, or in composite assemblies.

Masonry is brittle. It has a high mass and, therefore, a high inertial response to earthquakes. It is rigid and has low tensile and shear strengths, little ductility and a low capacity for bearing reversal loads and the redistribution of stresses.[2,3] In general, masonry structures are designed for static conditions and do not conform to the elastic theory.

From a limited viewpoint, the characteristics of historic buildings are disadvantageous to earthquake resistance. The poor performance of some forms of masonry has resulted in cautious attitudes that presume the inferiority of masonry materials and forms of construction. There are, however, several observations that contradict such a presumption.

Firstly, very little research has been done into the seismic response of masonry structures, whether reinforced or unreinforced, with or without a built-in frame. Most of the available knowledge is based largely on inferences from static loading tests.[2]

Secondly, field observations seldom mention the relationship between construction quality and the seismic structural performance of masonry buildings. Evidence has shown that there is a direct link between good quality construction and minimum damage. If properly used, masonry construction can have a reasonable resistance to earthquake movements. A common fallacy in field observations after earthquakes is the assumption that the performance of materials and structures is due to their inherent qualities.[4] It is often assumed that certain materials are, in themselves, either good or bad, durable or non-durable, resistant or non-resistant, strong or weak. In reality, these properties are relative and vary according to the conditions of exposure of the structure, the level of its loading and its capacity to re-distribute stresses, amongst other factors.

Historic buildings are not necessarily weak because they are old, or have been built with masonry. Some historic buildings, like some modern buidings, are weak because they are poorly constructed, or are subjected to abnormal stresses. From the engineering viewpoint, historic buildings have the useful characteristic of demonstrating all the inaccuracies in their construction, the possible mistakes made in assuming tolerances, and the unknown differences between the strengths of materials and structures.[5] All of these adverse factors can be identified and eliminated, one by one.

Strenghening historic buildings in earthquake areas

There are two main reasons for strengthening historic buildings in earthquake areas. The first and most important reason is the thousands of human lives at risk in these areas. The second reason is based on the recognition that architectural heritage is one of mankind's priceless and irreplaceable possessions and that its loss, through deterioration or disappearance, impoverishes the heritage of all the people of the world.[6] The first reason is incontestable. Fortunately the need to safeguard the world's architectural heritage is also becoming more and more widely recognized.[7]

For the strengthening of earthquake-damaged structures, however, new forms of earthquake engineering must still be developed. Buildings of this type have so rarely been strengthened after an earthquake that very few engineers, architects, or builders have any experience of how, or where, to begin.[1] As a consequence, strengthening is often carried out by using large masses of material and overdesigned structural members, which are, in most cases, incompatible with the character of the existing building. An historic building, as opposed to any other building, has values which go beyond the accommodation and facilities which it provides. In many cases these values derive from the physical characteristics of the historic building, including those of its structure. It is unfortunate that so often these structural characteristics are altered, destroying part of the value of the building.

Based on the previous considerations, certain conclusions can be drawn relating to the strengthening and repair of earthquake-damaged historic structures. These are:

1. The problems of strengthening, or repairing, historic buildings which have been damaged by earthquakes differ from those of new seismic design.
2. A plan for the strengthening or repair of this type of building should aim to alter the existing structure as little as possible, whilst enabling it to respond satisfactorily to seismic excitation. Satisfactory response does *not* go beyond obtaining reasonable security against damage in the event of an intense earthquake. The plan should consider traditional materials and techniques, as well as compatible modern technology.
3. There is an important body of reliable, observational data[8–10] concerning earthquake damaged masonry structures, making it possible, by informed comparisons of damage in various locations, to reach simple and logical generalizations about the causes and types of earthquake damage and to choose rational courses of action.

Figure 6.1 Kotor, Yugoslavia. Two historic masonry structures on the same site; one seriously damaged, the other virtually unaltered after the earthquake of 1979. Differing performance is related to the construction quality of each building

Figure 6.3 Ancona, Italy. A house in the historic centre of the city where reinforcement has been carried out by encasing the structure in a metal grid and spraying it with cement

Figure 6.2 Budva, Yugoslavia. A basically sound building which shows damage in one of its weakest points: a curved surface, insufficiently bonded and punctured by the apse window

4. Experience of earthquakes has shown that there is a direct relationship between the extent of the damage and the condition of the structural components and the quality of the construction of the damaged building.[11]

The building's original capacity to absorb seismic stresses is related to the condition of its structural components. This should be established. The quality of the construction of the damaged building is an important factor. Records of earthquake damage[8] provide evidence relating the extent of damage to such construction factors as the quality of the building's masonry units, the proportions of the single units, the bond between assembly elements, the connection of orthogonal walls, the quality of workmanship in the laying of the masonry courses, the ratio of height to base of the structure, the distribution and position of openings in the masonry walls, the connection between structural elements which should function as a complete unit, the characteristics of embedded structural elements, the appropriate use of partition walls, the characteristics

Figure 6.4 Kotor, Yugoslavia. Details of the masonry structures illustrated in Figure 6.1 showing the relationship between quality of construction and earthquake damage

Figure 6.5 Tito, Southern Italy. Interior and exterior view of a stone masonry house where poor connection between orthogonal walls has led to the damage illustrated

Figure 6.6 Budva, Yugoslavia. A situation in which the placements of apertures combined with the complete lack of lintels has led to collapse

Figure 6.7 Tito, Southern Italy. A situation in which a properly embedded lintel of adequate length has prevented earthquake damage

Figure 6.8 Tito, Southern Italy. A section of a damaged wall where collapse has resulted from the poor quality of the mortar

and condition of foundations, the soil–structure interaction, the quality of the mortar used, the quality of past repair works and the effects of these factors upon each other. The observation of inaccuracies in any of these factors can lead to the identification of potentially weak points in the structure, or, where some failure has occurred, to a reliable interpretation of the exposed earthquake damage. The progressive and careful elimination of the identified weaknesses, without elaborate strengthening procedures, will certainly provide the structure with an improved capacity to withstand future seismic events.

The approach proposed to repairs or strengthening is not a new one. Traditional principles of analysis are frequently overlooked by those seeking new techniques in the repair of earthquake-damaged historic structures. However, such an oversight seriously limits the validity of any diagnosis and any solution proposed

Figure 6.9 Kotor, Yugoslavia. Failure resulting from the quality of past repair and modifications, in this case the introduction of a large opening on the second floor

Figure 6.10 Arequipa, Peru. Buildings of traditional technique and materials which respond, in their architectural form and structure, to an understanding of seismic disturbance (lowered bell towers, self-buttressed walls, small and limited apertures, solid masonry assembly)

Figure 6.11 Tito, Southern Italy. The demolition of the Cathedral after the earthquake of 1980

Conclusions

In recent years historic monuments, or whole groups of old houses, have been completely and systematically demolished, or seriously altered, after earthquake. This destruction of the architectural heritage could be avoided with a better understanding of the performance of historic structures by those who are responsible for them.

Decisions regarding the strengthening or repair of historic structures should result from an informed analysis of earthquake risk and damage. Each type of damage should determine the selection of repair methods, based on the consideration of the condition of the building, the resources available (funds, materials and craft skills, for example), the value of the building and the prevailing conservation philosophy.

Completed repair work should be monitored, to assess its performance under any further seismic stresses. It is equally important to co-ordinate all the available experience and observational data concerning earthquake damage to historic structures.

Priority should be given to special research on aspects of the design and construction of existing buildings, related to their pre-earthquake and post-earthquake condition. In the same way, efforts should be made to promote special research in related fields, such as soil dynamics and earthquake engineering, which is specifically relevant to the problems of earthquake damage to historic structures.

Acknowledgements

The author wishes to thank Professor Eiichi Kuribayashi (Toyohashi University of Technology), and Professor Eng. Fabio Casciati (University of Pavia). He is also indebted to his colleagues Ms Cathleen Malmström and Ms Jeanne Marie Teutonico for their suggestions and criticism, and most grateful for the invaluable help of Mme Marie Christine Uginet, Head of the Documentation Centre of the ICCROM.

References

1. Moran, T. 'Strengthening earthquake-damaged structures', p. 234, in *The assessment and mitigation of earthquake risk*, Unesco, Paris, 1978
2. Dowrick, D.J., *Earthquake resistant design. A manual for engineers and architects*, p. 253, Wiley, London, 1977
3. Sachanski, S., 'Buildings: codes, materials, design', p. 158, in *The assessment and mitigation of earthquake risk*. Unesco, Paris, 1978
4. Baker, M.C., 'Introduction to the problem of cracks, movements and joints in buildings', p. 1, in *Cracks, Movements and Joints in Buildings*, Record of the DBR Building Science Seminar, National Research Council of Canada, Ottawa, 1972
5. Beckmann, P., *Third Mission to Kotor, Montenegro (YU)*, p.2, ICCROM/Unesco, Rome, 1982
6. Unesco, *Operational Guidelines for the Implementation of the World Heritage Convention*, p.1, Unesco-Intergovernmental Committee for the Protection of the World Cultural and Natural Heritage, Paris, 1977
7. Unesco, 'The Cultural Heritage and Natural Disasters', in *World Cultural Heritage Information Bulletin*, **15**, 5, Division of Cultural Heritage, Paris, 1980
8. CRYRZA, 'Peru: practical adobe construction with emphasis on earthquake resistant techniques', in *Adobe News*, **12**, 5–11; **13**, 10–11; **15**, 10–13, 1977
9. Benedetti, D., 'Riparazione e consolidamento degli edifici in muratura', in *Costruzioni in Zona Sismica*, Masson Italia, Milano, 1981
10. University of New Mexico (ed.), *Proceedings of the International Workshop, Earthen Buildings in Seismic Areas*, The National Science Foundation, New Mexico, 1981
11. Ambraseys, N.N., *Engineering Seismology*, p. 59, Imperial College of Science and Technology, London, 1975
12. Feilden, B.M., *Conservation of Historic Buildings*, Ch. 8, Butterworths, London, 1982

7

The repair and remedial treatment of the East Block Parliament Buildings, Ottawa, Canada

Keith Blades and John Stewart

Introduction

The East Block of the Parliament Buildings occupies a unique position in Canada's history. Built between 1859 and 1867, it has housed the offices of the Governor General and fifteen of seventeen Prime Ministers. Until recently, the Privy Council and Cabinet met periodically in the building. In 1974, the East Block was vacated to allow the Department of Public Works to start an ambitious programme of repair and restoration to the building. In April 1982, with the interior work completed, Her Majesty Queen Elizabeth II re-opened the building to serve once again as offices for Parliamentarians from the House of Commons and the Senate.

Following the Act of Union of 1840, Kingston, on Lake Ontario, was named the capital of Upper and Lower Canada. However, within three years, the capital had moved to Montreal. After riots and burning of the legislative buildings in 1849, the government resorted to a system of rotation, whereby the capital alternated every four years between Toronto and Quebec City. When Queen Victoria announced in 1858 that Ottawa was to be the permanent seat of government for the Province of Canada, the decision was met with considerable surprise because at that time Ottawa was little more than a frontier lumber town.

The Department of Public Works moved quickly to announce a competition, with designs to be submitted by architects for three public buildings: a parliamentary building, where the Provincial Parliament would sit, a library and two departmental buildings, to house various principal offices and all the civil service of the time, consisting of fifteen government departments.

The buildings were constructed between 1859 and 1867, in accordance with the competition requirements, 'in a plain, substantial style of architecture, the masonry to be coursed hammer dressed, with neatly pointed joints, cut stone quoins, window dressings and entablatures'[1], in a style referred to as 'Civil gothic' by Augustus Stent and Thomas Laver, the architects whose design was selected for the Departmental Buildings.

Of the three parliamental buildings, only the East Block remains in a form similar to that of the 1870s. The Centre Block, the Houses of Parliament, was destroyed by fire in 1916. It was subsequently rebuilt, although the octagonal library to the rear of the building was saved. The West Block was damaged by fire in 1899 and, while the original fabric remains, the interior has undergone extensive modernization. The East Block programme, begun in 1974, has restored the interior of the building as it was in 1880. Externally the consolidation and repair of the masonry is being carried out under a phased programme. This chapter deals with the first phase of that masonry programme, which was completed as part of the overall restoration project.

Construction

The construction of the East Block reflects the changing technology and materials available at the time. The building incorporated a trussed roof of heavy timbers, under a slate covering, with iron cresting. The present copper roof was installed in 1948. 'Fox and Barret' fireproof floors, consisting of wrought iron joists with a lightweight concrete infill, replaced the log floors of the original design and bear on solid masonry walls. Foundation walls 1200 mm (4 ft) thick, formed of an inner and outer skin of squared rubble masonry, with a rubble filled core, bear directly on bedrock. Above basement level, the external masonry, approximately 525 mm (20 in) thick, is tied through a dry, ventilated cavity to a one brick thick inner skin with iron straps and bond-stones.

Exterior stonework is a combination of rock-faced, squared rubble walling, known locally as 'Scotch work' because many of the stonemasons had emigrated from Scotland. Dressed ashlar was selected for the quoins, surrounds to openings and decorative features. The rubble stone is a local sandstone and the ashlar is a fine to medium grained siliceous sandstone from the Berea Formation in Ohio, USA. Interior walls and the core material of the basement walls are a compact, crystalline limestone, local to the Ottawa area.

Programme of repairs

Initial surveys indicated that there were three areas of concern which would require more detailed study: the third floor roof space, where many truss members were missing; the basement walls, which appeared in poor condition because of deteriorated or missing pointing; and the southwest tower, where large cracks and movement of the stonework suggested a serious problem might exist.

Repairs at roof level

In the 1890s previously unoccupied space was converted to offices, in response to the demand for accommodation for the ever expanding civil service. Dormer windows were inserted in the roof and numerous roof truss diagonals, columns and bottom chord members were cut, or removed, from the mansard roof trusses, resulting in fractures through the eaves masonry caused by thrust from the spreading roof. Selected replacements and reinforcement of members has restored the integrity of the structural system, which is now tied into a reinforced concrete ring beam, dowelled into the eaves masonry.

Masonry repairs

A detailed examination of the fabric of the East Block revealed that, at ground level, the exposed foundation walls below the plinth course were in poor condition. Open joints could be seen in many areas where the hard, cement-rich, projecting ribbon pointing had either failed through shrinkage, or had been lost through frost action after moisture had penetrated the joint. It was found that maintenance of the pointing had been a constant problem since completion of the building. John Page, Chief Engineer for the Department of Public Works, wrote in 1867 in his report on the buildings, 'the roof projections are so small, and there being no eaves-troughs, the water falls directly on the basement walls, and the alternate action of wet and frost takes out the pointing, which must be renewed from time to time'. Ottawa winter temperatures often dip below −20 °C (−4 °F) and sometimes reach −30 °C (−22 °F). Many winter days are clear with bright sun and on such occasions many freeze/thaw cycles occur, particularly in south and west facing masonry walls.

Internally, moisture staining and rusting of the iron floor joists where they bear into the foundation wall suggested that water was passing through the full thickness of the walls. Trial opening up revealed that the rubble core was a poorly consolidated mixture of stone rubble and a weak lime:sand grout. As a result, voids were present from the time of construction. Water penetrating the wall through defective pointing had leached out some of the grout, and in certain places settlements of the core material, in conjunction with frost action, had caused bulging of the outer skin of stonework. In many areas the facework was found to be bedded in wet sand, indicating that repointing contracts over the years had specified only replacement of a superficial bead of pointing, without any attention to the consolidation of the bedding material (*Figure 7.1*).

Trial excavations revealed a stable foundation below ground level, with stepped footings bearing directly on bedrock, but confirmed the absence of a drainage system. In periods of heavy rain and particularly during the spring thaw, a build-up of ground water against the foundation walls led to a rising damp problem in basement rooms.

It was proposed that the foundation walls should be grouted to fill the voids in the core material and to restore the structural integrity of the walls. This involved completing the repairs and the repointing before starting the grouting operation. It was also proposed to install a drainage system at the level of the footings. The excavation necessary for the installation of weeping tiles meant that the foundation walls were to be exposed right down to the bedrock. With the walls accessible externally, the difficulty of having to grout down to the footings from inside the building was removed. Accordingly, contracts for the masonry repairs and grouting ran concurrently with the installation of the drainage system, enabling grouting of the footings to take place from the exterior (*Figure 7.2*).

The mix found to have the best flow characteristics, a cement:pulverized fuel ash (PFA):expansive admixture combination, was injected through plastic tubing set in 25 mm (1 in) diameter holes, drilled approximately 750 mm (30 in) into the 1200 mm (4 ft) thick wall on a 450 mm (18 in) staggered grid.

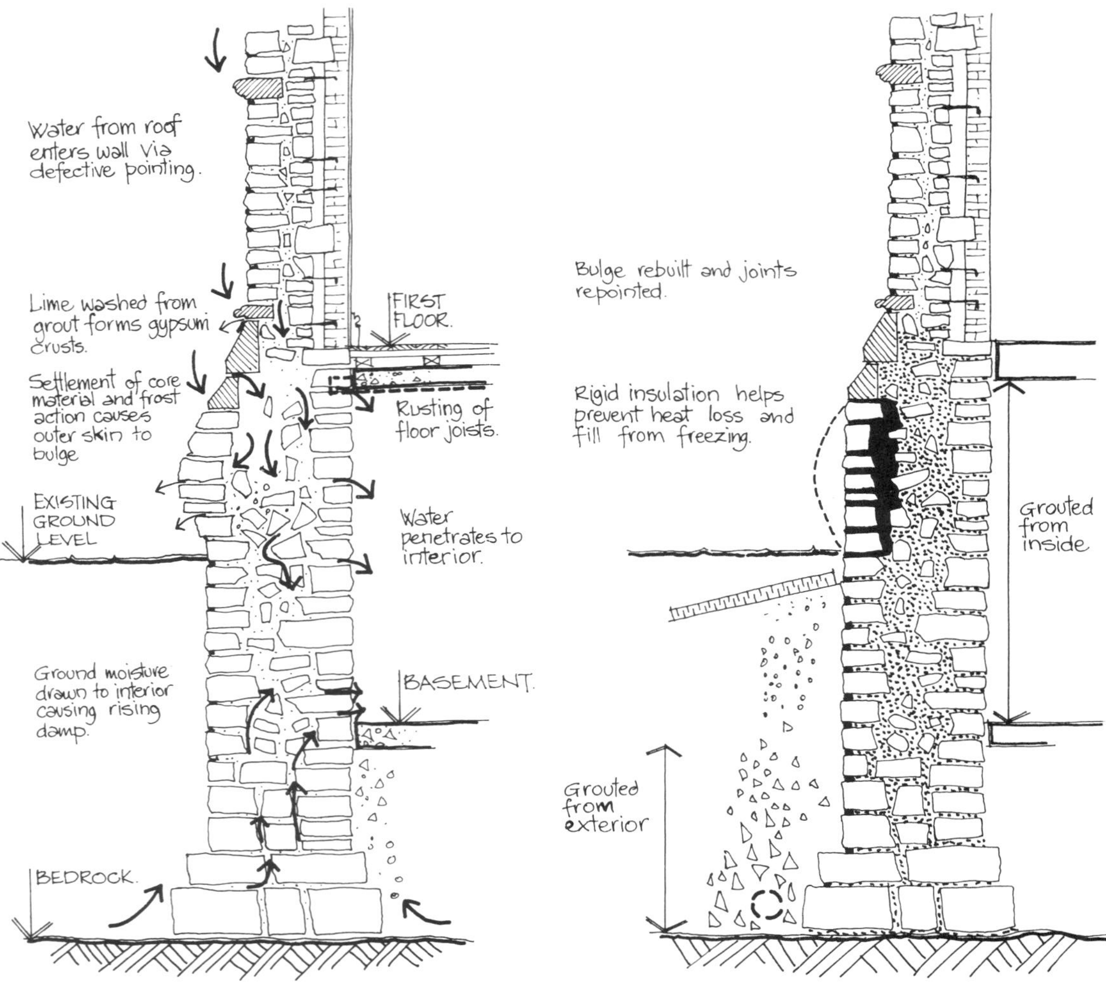

Figure 7.1 Typical section through basement walls before repair

Figure 7.2 Section through basement walls following repair

The initial pumping pressure was quite low (69 kPa), but following careful monitoring this was increased to 276 kPa without any problem and was adopted for the whole programme. In total, some 30 cubic metres (39 cubic yards) of grout was placed in the foundation walls, representing an actual grout take of 8% compared to the initial estimate of 10%. For sample cores taken, it is estimated that only 0.5% voiding remains in the walls.

The areas scheduled for rebuilding were carefully taken down, the position of all stones recorded on survey drawings and the rear face of each block identified with a water-based paint, to ensure the same pattern of bonding on rebuilding. The core material was raked back until sound mortar was encountered. It was filled solid in the traditional manner on rebuilding, with the addition of 12 mm (0.5 in) diameter brass dowels, randomly placed.

All the joints to the exposed foundation wall were raked out to a minimum of 50 mm (2 in) and repointed with a 1:1:6 cement:lime:sand mix, with the addition of a small amount of latex to the mixing water, to provide additional frost resistance. Where the bedding material was found to be in poor condition, deep tamping was carried out or individual blocks were reset.

The replacement of damaged stone was limited, because of the difficulty in obtaining suitable material at the time. The Ohio quarries are still operative, but only small quantities of the sandstone could be

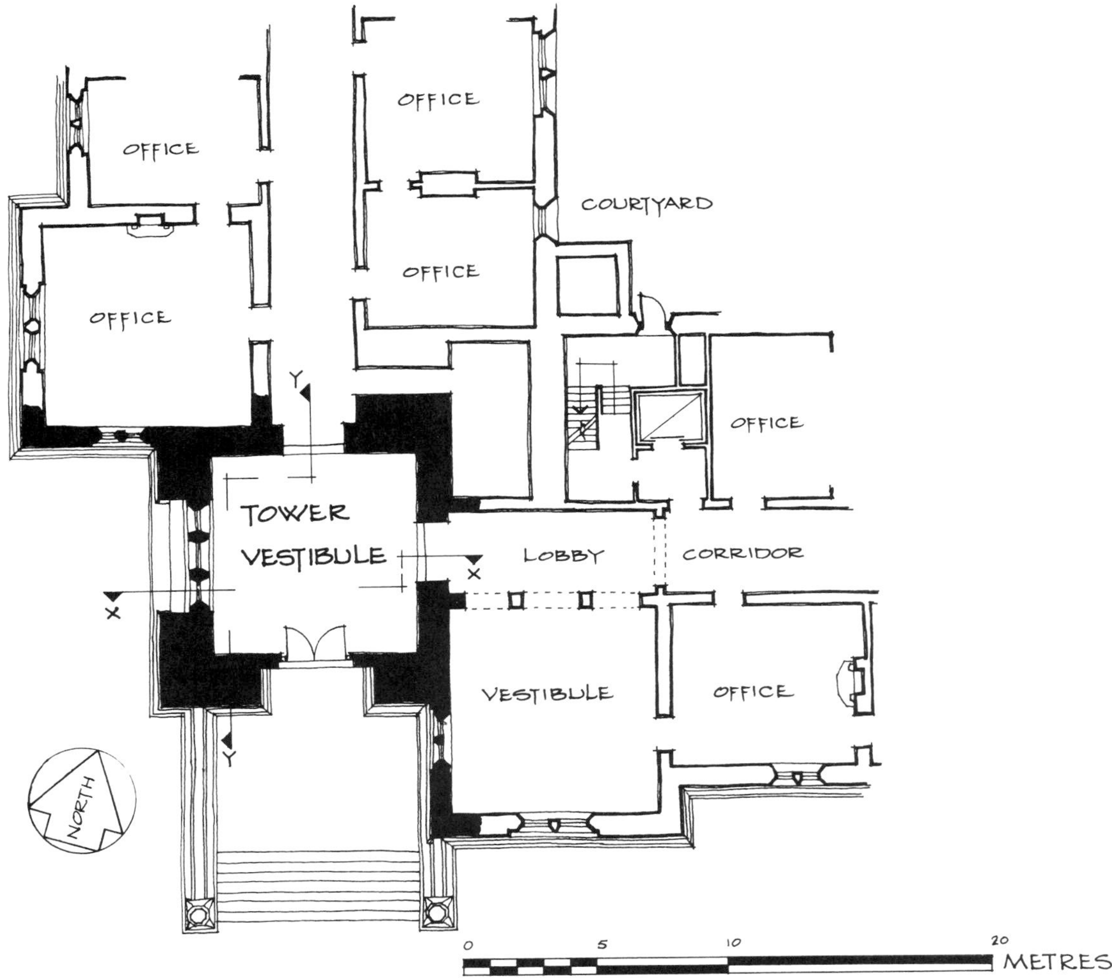

Figure 7.3 Part first floor plan at south-west corner of East Block Parliment Buildings, Ottawa

obtained for repairs to the window surrounds. The local Nepean sandstone quarries, which have supplied stone for many public buildings in the Ottawa area, have been inoperative for many years. It is hoped to re-open some faces in order to obtain the bed depths required for repairs to the plinth courses.

The south-west tower

The south-west tower is the dominant architectural feature of the East Block and, until the completion of the Centre Block in the 1920s, was the tallest structure on Parliament Hill. Movement, large crack patterns and spalling of stonework, not apparent elsewhere on the building, gave rise to some concern. A separate study was therefore commissioned to determine the causes and effects of the damage to the tower masonry.

Construction

The tower is constructed of massive load-bearing masonry walls, which support a first floor entrance vestibule, a balcony at the second floor level, a masonry vaulted ceiling, three intermediate floors, a copper-clad timber roof and decorative wrought-iron cresting (*Figures 7.3, 7.4* and *7.5*). The masonry rises some 50 metres (160 ft) above ground and it is a further 20 metres (65 ft) to the top of the

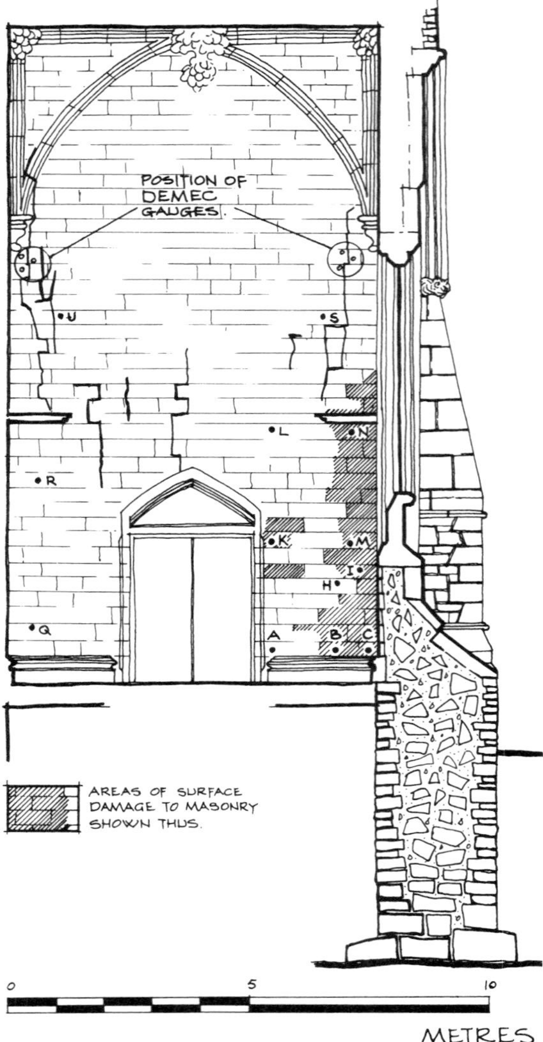

Figure 7.4 Section on X–X in Figure 7.3: elevation of south wall

decorative cresting. The foundation walls are 2.4 metres (8 ft) thick and bear directly on bedrock. The total weight of the tower is estimated to exceed 5500 tonnes.

Externally on the west and south faces, between the first and third floor levels, arches spring from buttresses, tapering from 2.4 to 1.5 metres (8–5 ft) thick, to enclose infill panels 750 mm (30 in) thick. Window and door openings, framed with secondary arches, penetrate these panels. The interior ashlar is Ohio sandstone, varying in thickness from 150 to 300 mm (6–12 in).

Structural problems

Surveys of the tower masonry identified movement and cracking in the large blocks of the raking buttresses externally, and extensive cracking to the interior walls between the second floor balcony and the top of the vaulted ceiling. These internal crack patterns to both the south and west walls closely followed the lines of the junctions between the exterior buttresses and the infill panels. To record movements, a two stage programme of monitoring was set up, using glass tell-tales to act as a visual indication of movement and 'Demec' studs to provide accurate measurements. Recordings were taken over an eighteen month period to ensure that seasonal variations were covered.

Results from the monitoring showed that the cracks were continuing to open at a rate of 0.25 mm (0.01 in) per annum. Comparing this rate of movement to the total widths of cracks suggests that movement had been taking place for at least 20 years. Due to the construction of the tower, differential settlement was to be expected since stress levels from concentrations of loading in the tower buttresses and infill panels varied considerably. It was assumed that voiding and settlement of the core material had also occurred and that this, coupled with moisture penetration and freeze-thaw action, was the primary factor responsible for the movement of the blocks. As for the remainder of the building, repointing of external masonry and grouting of the interior of the wall was recommended to stabilize the tower, with a note of caution that the condition would be improved, but not eliminated. Grouting of the two outer buttresses was carried out from within the adjacent offices, but for the central buttress it was necessary to core the ashlar wall to provide grouting points.

When the structural repairs were completed, attention was turned to the spalling ashlar of the internal masonry of the tower. Earlier analysis work had identified the presence of soluble salts on the building. Under protective mouldings (that is, areas not regularly washed by rain) gypsum crusts had formed on the surface of the sandstone and eventually caused spalling as crystallization and ice lensing detached the crust. These salts most likely were formed from leached calcium carbonate from the lime:sand mortar, in reaction with dilute sulphuric acid carried in rain and snow. For many years, Ottawa suffered from sulphate pollution from a pulp mill situated within one kilometre of Parliament Hill.

In the south-west tower the pattern of spalling was different. The decay of blocks around the entrance could be attributed to the practice of heavy winter salting, but not the efflorescence on the walls above the second floor balcony. The original intention was to repaint the interior of the south-west tower, in

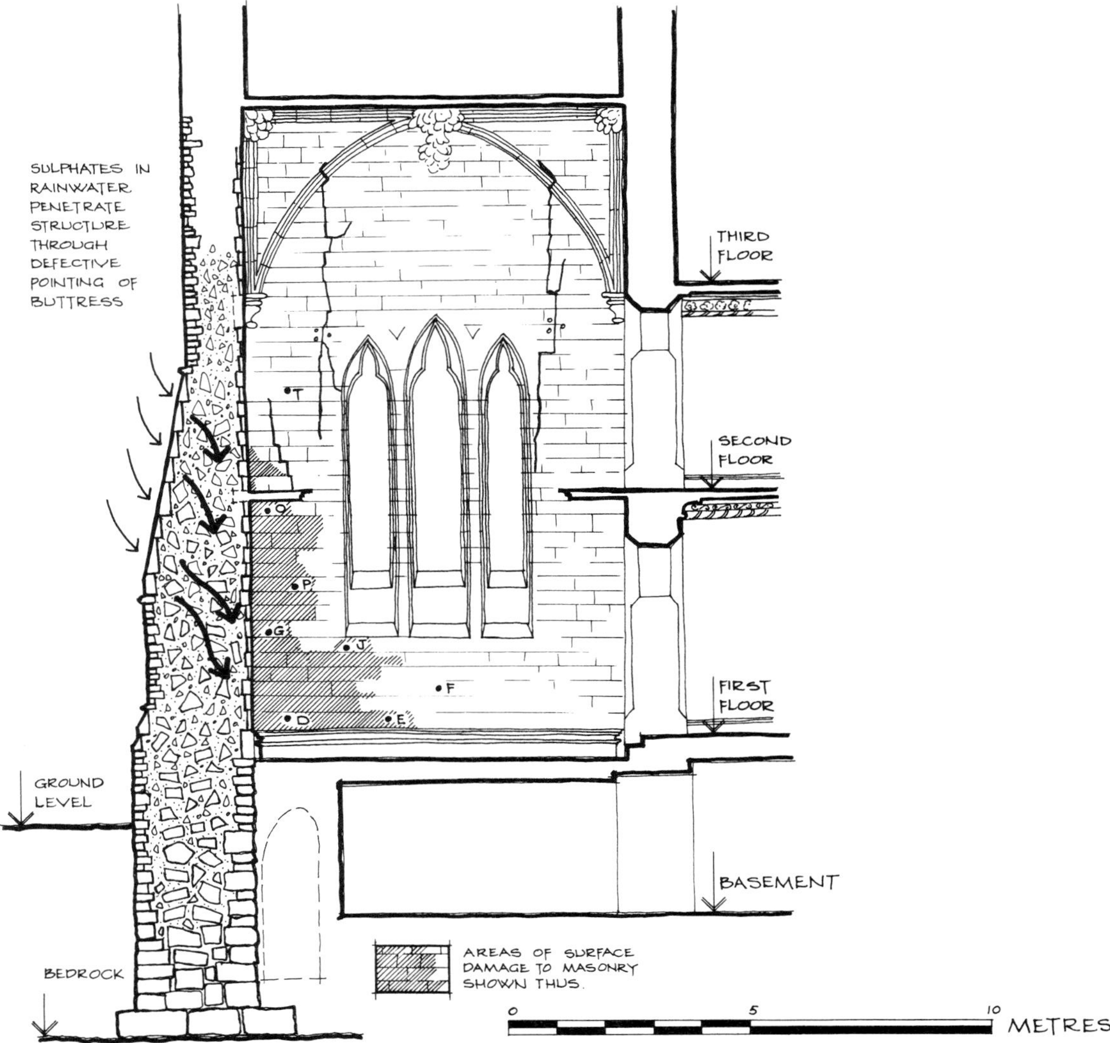

Figure 7.5 Section on Y–Y in Figure 7.3: elevation of west wall

order to link the colour schemes of the adjoining corridors. However, the continuous spalling and efflorescence determined that the original ashlar and ribbed vaulting should be exposed while a more detailed study of the nature and extent of the problem and methods for removing the salts was undertaken.

This involved a general examination of the structure to see if the damage was related to any specific architectural feature; the sampling and identification of the efflorescence and subflorescence to determine the salt responsible for the damage; the core sampling of the walls and the analysis of the cores to find the depth and location of the salt in the walls; and the monitoring of the relative humidity in the walls to determine their dampness. This study provided information on the cause of the damage and should now allow a rational restoration scheme to be planned.

General examination

Internally, the damaged stone (*Figure 7.6*) was spalled and covered with efflorescence. As much as 25 mm (1 in) of surface had been lost, and in general the surface was weak and friable. This was consistent

Figure 7.6 Area of damage inside south-west tower

with salt damage resulting from subflorescence. The damaged areas were localized on the two walls of the south-west corner (*Figures 7.4* and *7.5*). In all other areas, the ashlar appeared to be in good condition.

Examination of the outside of the tower revealed only a minor amount of salt damage to the stone, with some black crust and efflorescence evident. There was, however, obvious physical damage due to cracking of the stone and missing pointing. This was particularly apparent on the sloping portion of the buttress at the south-west corner. These open joints in the masonry allowed direct penetration of water into areas of wall associated with internal damage.

The general examination indicated that the internal ashlar had been damaged by salt and that this was localized in areas associated with the easy ingress of water through open joints and cracks in the external masonry (*Figures 7.4* and *7.5*). The association of these two factors indicated that deterioration of the interior resulted from the exterior conditions. The localization of the problem in one corner also tended to rule out rising damp as the source of damage.

Identification of salt

Samples of efflorescence adhering to the surface of the stone were taken from several locations inside the tower. These were examined with the micro-analyser of a scanning electron microscope (SEMEDX). This showed the presence of the elements silicon (from the sandstone), sodium and sulphur. Elements such as oxygen, with an atomic number less than eleven, are not detected by this technique. No chlorine was detected, indicating that the damage was not caused by either sodium or calcium chloride from de-icing salt.

The efflorescence was characterized further by X-ray powder diffraction. This identified the efflorescence as anhydrous sodium sulphate (Na_2SO_4). This agreed with the microprobe results, which showed the presence of both sodium and sulphur.

Samples of spalling stone were removed from the damaged area inside the tower. These were broken in cross section and examined by SEMEDX. *Figure 7.7* shows a good example of the type of subflorescence found. The large crystals show the presence of silicon and are the quartz grains from the sandstone. The small crystals filling the pore in the centre of the field show the presence of sodium and sulphur and are sodium sulphate crystals. Thus sodium sulphate is being deposited in the pores of the sandstone.

Core analysis

The presence of sodium sulphate at the surface of the stone was a strong indication that the walls contained reservoirs of this salt in their cores. This, however, was not a firm conclusion; the sulphate may only be a surface phenomenon. If it is, then the problem of its removal is much simpler than if the sulphate is distributed throughout the walls. To determine the distribution within the walls and to help to identify the source of the sulphate, twenty-one core samples were taken with dry diamond drills from the points indicated in *Figures 7.4* and *7.5*. Wet drilling would have removed soluble salts. These cores were analysed along their lengths, to determine their sulphate and chloride content (*see Annex*).

The mean soluble sulphate content of the two walls was 0.07%, compared with a mean soluble chloride content of 0.007%. This reinforced the conclusion, reached from the study of efflorescence, that chloride de-icing salts were not a source of damage. Calculating the mean value for the sulphate concentrations of the cores from damaged and undamaged areas showed that the damaged areas had a higher average sulphate concentration than the undamaged areas. A plot of the mean level of soluble sulphate for these two groups is shown in *Figure 7.8*.

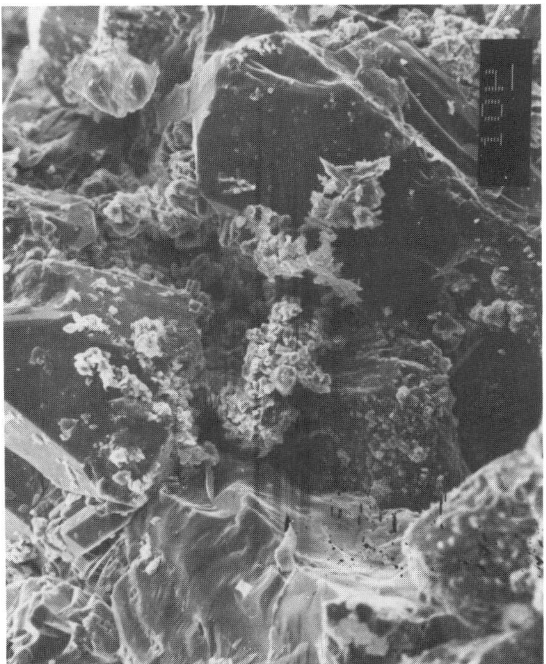

Figure 7.7 Scanning electron micrograph of fresh break surface of damaged ashlar (× 350)

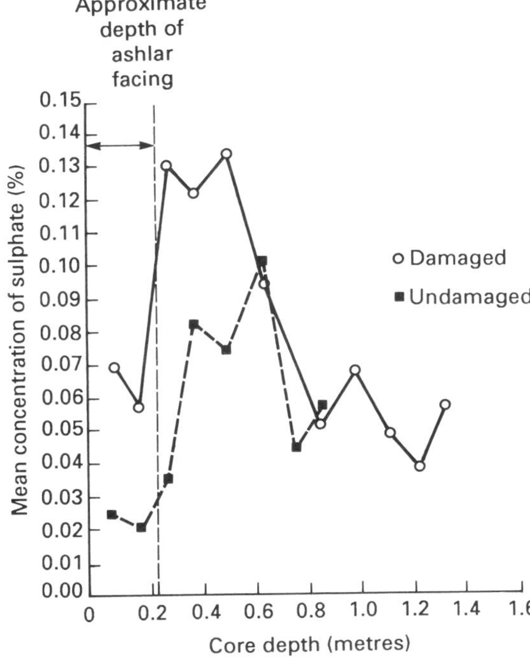

Figure 7.8 Mean levels of sulphate in cores

Dampness in walls

One method for measuring the dampness in a wall tried was the drilling and gravimetric technique.[2] Due to the heat generated by the coring operation in this method, samples were removed from the wall hot and steaming. Such samples were not suitable for any reliable gravimetric analysis of water. Conductivity measurements on the surface suffered from interference from the salts acting as electrolytes. Impedance measurements and thermal cooling techniques were not practicable due to lack of equipment.

As an alternative, three relative humidity probes were placed in the core holes at 250 mm (10 in) depth. This method does not tell the absolute water content of the wall, but it does give an indication of the relative humidity found within the walls.

These probes were left in place and monitored daily for a period of eighteen months. The results are shown for the two overlapping winter periods in *Figure 7.9*. Also shown is the relative humidity of the foyer air if it were cooled to the wall temperature found at the 250 mm (10 in) depth. The last number, RH_1, is derived from:

$$\% RH_1 = \% RH \times \frac{p_1}{p_2}$$

where $\% RH$ = relative humidity of foyer
p_1 = equilibrium vapour pressure of water at temperature of foyer
p_2 = equilibrium vapour pressure of water at temperature of wall

Figure 7.9 shows that the wall still has a moisture content higher than would be expected if it were in equilibrium with the foyer and, hence, is still damp. Furthermore, natural drying for an eighteen month period has done little to reduce the relative humidity in the walls.

Discussion of the wall study

To design a rational restoration plan, the examination of the walls was undertaken to answer three questions:

1. What is the nature of the damage to the stone?
2. What is its cause and source?
3. What factors influence the damage?

The spalling of the ashlar is a typical case of salt damage due to the crystallization and hydration of salt. The salt that is causing the damage is sodium sulphate. This conclusion is based on the fact that large quantities of sodium sulphate efflorescence and subflorescence were found in the walls and the damaged areas have a higher concentration of soluble sulphate than the undamaged areas. The

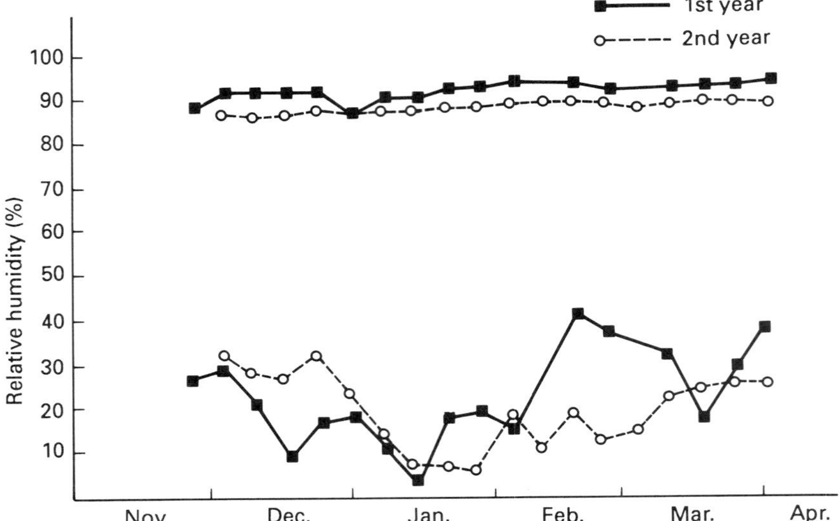

Figure 7.9 Top: Weekly averages of relative humidities at 250 mm depth within the walls. Bottom: Weekly averages of relative humidities in the foyer, adjusted to the wall temperature at 250 mm depth

problem is made more serious as the salt contamination is not localized on the surface. Instead, it is distributed throughout the wall, with a large reservoir of soluble sulphate at a depth of 200–750 mm (8–30 in) in both the damaged and undamaged areas (*Figure 7.8*). This means that, while the spalling is a surface phenomenon, the salt causing it is located deep with the walls.

The damaged ashlar inside the tower is associated with two factors:

1. A source of moisture from deteriorated external pointing.
2. A higher soluble sulphate concentration than found in the rest of the wall.

From these two facts, several sequences to explain the damage are possible. One such sequence would be the following: rain-water enters the masonry on the buttress and, as the presence of gypsum crusts on the exterior facade would suggest, this rain-water is polluted with sulphur oxides. The water leaches sulphate from the mortar in the masonry. This sulphate and the sulphate already in the rain-water travel in combination with sodium ions from the masonry and form sodium sulphate on the internal surfaces associated with the buttress. This sequence is sufficient to explain the association of the damage with both the damaged pointing and the higher than average sulphate content. However, the main facts are that the pointing has deteriorated and must be repaired; that the internal walls are suffering from spalling caused by salt damage; and that this salt is located throughout the depth of the wall.

The process by which sodium sulphate damages stones involves the formation of subflorescence. Sodium sulphate forms two hydrates,[3] the metastable heptahydrate ($Na_2SO_4{\cdot}7H_2O$) and the decahydrate ($Na_2SO_4{\cdot}10H_2O$). Of these two, only the decahydrate is stable and so is most probably the one that forms in the walls. Under sufficiently damp conditions, the sodium sulphate in the interior of the walls picks up moisture and forms a solution of sodium sulphate. If the moisture content of the walls exceeds the critical level (the level above which liquid water will move in the pores of the stone), the salt solution will migrate in all directions until it reaches a barrier. When it reaches the surface, the solution can travel no further and will start to evaporate and deposit salt as efflorescence. This, while unsightly, will do little damage to the stone, because the salt forms on the surface. However, when evaporation takes place a few millimetres behind the surface, subflorescence occurs.

Subflorescence is the growth of crystals in the stone pores. Initially, tiny crystals form, which then draw more salt from the solution and grow until they reach the pore walls. At this stage, the crystals still have a tendency to grow and exert pressure on the stone. When this pressure is greater than the mechanical strength of the stone, it will spall.

Crystallization pressure by sodium sulphate is one means by which stone is destroyed. The other is hydration pressure. The subflorescence found in the walls was anhydrous sodium sulphate, which is formed from the drying out of the decahydrate crystals and from the evaporation of the salt solution. As long as the salt stays as the anhydride, it should do no further damage to the stone. However, above a certain relative humidity, the anhydrous salt transforms into the decahydrate. The decahydrate has a volume 200% greater than the anhydride (reference 4, p.B-140) and, as such, the conversion to the hydrate exerts a hydration pressure on the stone pores, with subsequent spalling. When the relative humidity is over 93% at 20°C (reference 4, p.E-40), the decahydrate absorbs water from the air and goes into solution. Thus, even without liquid water present, a salt solution forms in the pores. As the relative humidity drops below 93%, recrystallization occurs, with more spalling. Thus, three factors are involved in the destruction of stone by sodium sulphate:

1. Deposition of sodium sulphate subflorescence from liquid water.
2. Conversion of the decahydrate to the anhydrate and back again, as the relative humidity cycles around the conversion point.
3. Deliquescence of the decahydrate at 93% relative humidity, with subsequent recrystallization when the relative humidity drops again.

The first factor should stop after the source of liquid water, i.e. the damaged pointing, is eliminated. The second, that of hydration–dehydration, will stop when the relative humidity in the first few centimetres drops below the relative humidity at which conversion occurs.

This relative humidity is dependent on temperature and can be calculated from equilibrium vapour pressure data,[5] using the Clausius–Clapeyron equation. The calculated values are shown in *Table 7.1*. Damage will continue to occur until the relative humidity in the wall drops below the 70–80% range. However, the data from wall relative humidity monitoring (*Figure 7.9*) shows this is not likely to happen in the near future.

The study of the walls has indicated that the spalling is due to the action of sodium sulphate. This has been transported to the damaged area by water entering from deteriorated pointing on the outside buttress. This water is also responsible for the high level of sulphate in the damaged area, because it is polluted with sulphur oxides. The salt is located throughout the walls and is not just a surface deposit. The spalling will continue to occur for as long as the walls remain damp enough to have a relative humidity greater than the conversion point of sodium sulphate to its hydrate.

Table 7.1 Relative humidities at which the reaction $Na_2SO_4 \cdot 10H_2O \rightarrow Na_2SO_4 + 10H_2O$ occurs at selected temperatures.*

Temp. (°C)	*RH* (%)
24	85
23	84
22	83
21	82
20	80
19	79
18	78
17	77
16	76
15	75
14	74
13	73
12	72
11	71
10	70

*Derived from equilibrium vapour pressure data using the Clausius–Clapeyron equation:

$$\log P = \frac{-\Delta H_{vap}}{2.303\,RT} + \text{constant}$$

where P is the equilibrium vapour pressure at temperature T, ΔH_{vap} is the heat of vaporization, and R is the gas constant.

Conclusions

At the time that the analysis work was undertaken, it was felt that the tower masonry could be restored and stabilized through a programme of poulticing to remove, or to appreciably lower the level of, the salts in the wall, coupled with replacement of some of the more damaged blocks. However, the results have shown that the situation is more complex and not so easily resolved. It is recognized that grouting the tower walls may well have compounded the situation by activating dormant salts deep in the wall, and has probably increased the time necessary for the masonry to dry out completely. Because the tower vestibule is the principal entrance to the building, it is still desirable to consider a programme of repair and replacement of the internal masonry.

Whilst replacement would be feasible, new stone blocks would quickly become contaminated by the salts behind the ashlar face. Coating the backs of new stones to prevent the transfer of salts would drive salt-laden moisture to seek other surfaces in the currently undamaged areas of the tower from which to evaporate and crystallize. Poulticing most probably would reduce salt levels in the surface layers, but could not hope to pull salts from deep within the walls.

For poulticing to be effective, thorough saturation of the wall with water is essential to ensure that all of the salts are put into solution. This, however, seems contrary to the overall desire to stabilize conditions by drying out the wall.

A more appropriate solution then would be to consider a longer-term poultice or render designed to act sacrificially, but avoiding the repetious saturation necessary with a series of poultice applications. This could be achieved by the use of a traditional lime:sand render with selective screening of the aggregate from 600 μm and below, in order to produce a micro-porous mix, which will more readily absorb moisture from the wall. Supporting this render with an alkali-resistant fibre mesh reinforcing will help retain it in place until saturated with salts. It is expected that this treatment will need to be replaced intially within a few months but subsequent applications may last up to a year. It is hoped that within four or five years conditions will be stable enough to contemplate repairs to the stonework.

Clearly the use of a sacrificial render in this situation has a number of advantages; it is a very simple approach, easily reversible, using traditional materials and techniques. It offers the least disruption to the building occupants and of all the options is truly a minimum intervention.

Annex: Analytical scheme for cores

1. The cores were taken using a diamond-tipped coring drill, without water as a coolant, i.e. dry.
2. The depth of the sample from the core was noted and the sample was put in a plastic bag. Generally, only the chunks were retained for analysis and the powder was discarded.
3. In the laboratory, the more friable chunks (sandstone and cement) were ground up in a mortar and pestle. No sieving was done. The limestone pieces were first crushed in a steel mortar, to a coarse size, and then pulverized in a spex grinder mill to pass a 30-mesh sieve (ASTM).
4. The total sample was weighed, put in an oven at 110°C for 24 hours and then weighed again. The per cent moisture content was calculated as follows:

$$\frac{\text{wt. sample before drying} - \text{dry sample wt.}}{\text{dry sample wt.}} \times 100\%$$

5. Approximately 10 g of each dry sample was exactly weighed into a 50 ml disposable beaker. Twenty ml of distilled water was added to each sample, using an Oxford Pipettor, and the beaker was covered. It was agitated periodically over the next 24 hours.
6. The resulting slurry was filtered through Whatman No. 40 ashless filter paper into another set of 50 ml disposable beakers.
7. For the $SO_4^{=}$ analysis, 5 ml of sample solution was measured using a calibrated Oxford Macroset pipette into a 100 ml volumetric flask. To this was added 10 ml of sodium chloride/hydrochloric acid reagent and 20 ml of glycerol alcohol solution, and then it was made up to volume with distilled water (after reference 6). In the analysis, 0.3 g of $BaCl_2$ (Fisher, Cert. ACS, (Crystal)) was added to the volumetric, then sealed and inverted once every 2 seconds for 1 minute. It was allowed to stand at least 3 minutes (up to 10 minutes). Light transmission measurements were taken using a Perkin-Elmer UV-Visible spectrophotometer (Hitachi 200). All measurements were taken at 600 nm with a slit width of 2.0 nm using a tungsten lamp. One cm cuvets were used and readings were taken in per cent *T*. The instrument was set to read 100% *T* on blank, and 0% *T* with the shutter in. It was found that a linear correlation existed between per cent *T* and the concentration of sulphate below 3.0 mg $SO_4^{=}$/100 ml. Standard solutions of sulphate were made ranging from 0–3 mg $SO_4^{=}$/100 ml and run with the samples. In cases where the amount of sulphates exceeded 3 mg/100 ml, the analysis was repeated, using only 1 ml of filtrate.
8. For the chloride analysis, a Buchler Digital Chloridometer was used. It was run using the small sample cup on the hi range. Two ml of sample (using 2 × 1.0 ml delivery from an Eppendorf pipette) was added to 4.0 ml of acid solution and 4 drops of gelatin/indicator solution.

References

1. *Canada Sessional Papers* 1863, No.3, p.3
2. Morton, W.B., 'Field procedures for examining humidity in masonry buildings', *Bulletin of the Association for Preservation Technology*, **8**, 3–19, 1976
3. Hougen, O.A., Watson, K.M., Ragatz, A.R., *Chemical Process Principals. Part I Material and Energy Balances*, p.142, Wiley, New York, 1967
4. Weast, R.C., *Handbook of Chemistry and Physics*, 52nd edn. p.B-140 and E-40, The Chemical Rubber Company, Cleveland, 1971
5. Hamad, S. El D., 'A study of the reaction $Na_2SO_4 \cdot 10H_2O$ $Na_2SO_4 + 10H_2O$ in the temperature range 0 to 25°C', *Thermochimica Acta*, **17**, 85–96, 1976
6. Vogel, A.I., *A Text Book of Quantitative Inorganic Analysis*, 3rd edn. p. 850–851, Longman, London, 1961

8

Cleaning masonry buildings

John Ashurst

Introduction

The Crafts Council *Science for Conservators* series defines dirt as 'material which is in the wrong place' and goes on to classify it in two categories:

1. *Foreign matter*, not part of the original object, such as soot, grease and stains, but which has become fixed with it.
2. *Products of alteration* of the original material, such as calcium sulphate on the surface of a limestone. A product of alteration forms through the chemical combination of the original material with chemicals from the environment.

It is apparent from these classification definitions that the removal of dirt which is a 'product of alteration' involves the removal of some of the surface. Even the removal of 'foreign matter', if pursued too far, may cause losses when, for example, dirt fills very fine cracks in a weathered surface. All cleaning of masonry buildings must, therefore, involve consideration of any immediate or induced possible losses which may be caused by cleaning, against the possible long-term losses associated with leaving the dirt alone.

Until the Clean Air Acts of 1956 and 1968 in the UK, smoke emissions from coal burning were seen as primarily responsible for the soiling of buildings. However, it is abundantly apparent that re-soiling of buildings cleaned since that time is quite significant, especially in urban environments. Vehicle emissions, especially diesel engine emissions, are seen as largely responsible for this rapid re-soiling with sticky particulate carbon deposits.[1] A survey carried out by the Urban Pollution Research Centre at the Middlesex Polytechnic[2] recently explored the relationship between the properties of these airborne particulates and the soiling of facades as a basis for the cost-benefit assessment of building cleaning. The indication was that there were benefits in maintenance cleaning in towns at 5–10 year intervals. The implications for building are considerable.

To clean or not to clean?

The motivation for cleaning a building is usually aesthetic. Although this is a very subjective issue, it is probably true that, as cleaning techniques have improved and the cleaned surfaces of buildings have become more familiar, there is less opposition to cleaning, at least in the United Kingdom, than there was ten or fifteen years ago. But there are often good, practical reasons for cleaning heavily soiled masonry buildings as part of a general maintenance and repair programme. Dirt fills cracks and open joints, obscuring pockets of decay; heavy encrustations on sheltered limestone or marble alter the surfaces on which they form and encourage their deterioration. If for aesthetic or maintenance reasons, it is decided that cleaning is desirable, what are the practical risks involved?

Ideally historic buildings should be cleaned with the same amount of care and attention to detail which is given to the cleaning of sculptures. However, the stone cleaning which has become a firmly established part of the building industry is not sculpture conservation and is not generally carried out by conservators. There is a very considerable wealth of stone cleaning knowledge and expertise in the building industry, which produces excellent results. Perhaps the important difference between the cleaning carried out by a sculpture conservator and a stone cleaner is that the conservator has been especially trained and has a personal reputation to protect, while the stone cleaner is not necessarily trained and will often be anonymous. It is his company's reputation, rather than his own, which will be enhanced or damaged by the quality of his work. There are incompetent practitioners in both fields, but the incompetent conservator can be more readily recognized and more quickly known. The practical risks in employing stone cleaning contractors will certainly be kept to a minimum if reputable companies are involved. These companies see the cleaning activity as inseparable from the maintenance and surface repair of the whole facade and are able to offer a range of cleaning techniques.

The selection and specifiction of a method is not all that needs to be considered. When any building surface is at stake, but especially the surface of any historic building, the level of expertise available must also be known. Regrettably this is not always high, and in some situations competitive tendering for cleaning work, with an obligation for the lowest price to be accepted, can work against the conscientious contractor who is not prepared to take short cuts or to accept low standards. A welcome development in the United Kingdom is the formation of the Stone Cleaning section of the Stone Federation, whose members are frequently in competition, but who share a common interest in the maintenance of high work standards. Members cooperate with the British Standards Institution in the production of the BS Codes, produce their own Code of Practice, and meet architects and other specifiers in the Standing Joint Committee on Natural Stones.

Cleaning methods

Whilst it is obviously better not to clean a building at all than to cause damage which will reduce its life expectancy, or adversely affect its appearance, in almost every case some cleaning is possible without significant risks, provided the right level of expertise is available. There is no cleaning category currently in use which should not be used in any circumstances. The wide range of results which has been obtained over the last two decades of cleaning accounts for the wide range of reaction which any discussion on the cleaning of buildings is likely to provide. It is quite common to hear architects refusing to have anything to do with chemical cleaning, or with sand-blasting, and some authorities have banned such techniques. In most such cases, these adverse reactions are based on first-hand experience of an inappropriate specification or incompetent work and supervision on site, or, alternatively, on misconception caused by ignorance.

Methods which will be described in this chapter include:

- *Washing*, used principally for limestone and marble
- *Mechanical*, used principally for sandstones, but also for some limestones and marble
- *Chemical*, used principally for sandstones and granites
- *Special cleaning techniques*, including cavitation, lasers and special poultices

The survey

Any proposal to clean the facades of a building must be preceded by a careful survey. Three levels of survey may be appropriate:

1. A relatively superficial inspection from existing vantage points. This survey will identify the general type and condition of the fabric and the degree of soiling. It should also look at the condition of adjacent buildings. Such a survey is appropriate in determining the desirability of cleaning at all. Some idea of how the cleaned building would look should also be formed.
2. A preliminary survey, designed to determine the best method of cleaning and to assess with some accuracy the extent of stone repair and replacement which will be involved and how the building will appear after cleaning. Problems which might be created by alternative methods and how access and programming can be planned to suit the occupants and public should be discussed and evaluated.
3. A detailed survey, possibly involving some trial cleaning, should be carried out to finalize the specification and to ensure that as many problems as possible involved in preparing the building and occupants for the cleaning contract are anticipated. Trial cleaning sites should not be on the most prominent part of the building, of course, but chosen to include as many typical problems as possible. Such problems may be experienced at openings, open joints, under overhangs and in the vicinity of old repairs and suspected staining. Cleaning contractors should not be expected to provide trial cleaning samples as demonstrations for no charge. Trial cleaning is a fact-finding exercise, which should have its own clear specification and be paid for separately from the main contract. The trial clean should also establish an 'acceptable standard' reference for the contract.

At the end of the survey, the following important questions should have been asked and answered:

1. Is the building dirty and, if so, is the presence of dirt damaging or only disfiguring?
2. What are the stones and other materials of the building?

3. What is the nature of the soiling? Are there evidences of previous treatments, such as oil or paint?
4. How much cleaning is desirable? How much dirt can be removed safely? How will the removal of dirt affect the appearance of the building now and in future years?
5. How will cleaning affect the weathering properties of the stones?
6. What method, or combination of methods, could be used to remove the dirt? How will these methods work and what hazards may be involved for the operatives and the public, as well as for the building?
7. How often is the building likely to need cleaning? Should some cleaning maintenance programme be established?
8. What remedial work, in the form of repairs to the stones and joints, should be included in the cleaning contract?
9. What surface treatments, if any, such as biocides, water repellants or consolidants, should be applied after cleaning, and to what areas?
10. What needs to be provided in the form of protection for windows and other openings, or for polished and painted surfaces?
11. What form of scaffold and what sheeting are required?
12. What water and electricity supplies are needed? What provision must be made for plant access, acoustic shelters, storage of materials and waste disposal?
13. Have the building owner and occupants been fully informed about the possible inconvenience, such as the nuisance from water, dust and noise which may be experienced? Have the necessary authorities been informed and all relevant permissions been obtained, especially if listed buildings are involved?
14. Having answered all the above, are the necessary skills available to carry out the cleaning to the required standard?

Note: Cleaning, like any other building craft, is a skill that is acquired to differing degrees by different individuals. Cleaning operatives must be able to demonstrate that they can clean to the 'acceptable standard' established during the trial clean. They should be named. Substitute operatives should not be accepted during the work unless they too can demonstrate their ability and experience.

The specification which is produced at the end of this preparatory work should cover all the foreseeable problems and be sufficiently comprehensive to make an accurate estimate possible. It may be advisable to write in a requirement that one of the cleaning team is to be stationed inside the building to maintain regular liaison with the team out on the scaffold, especially on a large and complicated building. In addition, regardless of the size of job, washing must never be left unattended and proper site security must be maintained. Regular site visits must be made at least weekly by the architect or professional supervisor.

Washing

Any soiled limestone building will exhibit the effects of regular rain washing on its exposed surfaces. Unlike sandstone, washing by rain inhibits the formation of dirt on limestone. The dirt which forms on limestone and marble tends to be soluble in water. Washing, whether by bucket and brush, multiple sprays, water lances or wet packs, is therefore a well established method of cleaning these surfaces.

Washing is a very simple process in principle. It requires only some sensible means of putting enough water in contact with the dirt deposits to wash them away directly or to soften them sufficiently to allow their release by brushing. Most problems associated with washing have to do with saturation. Unfortunately, most spray cleaning systems are insufficiently versatile to deal effectively with the different degrees of soiling usually found on a building with openings, projections and enrichments. A row of jets placed along a horizontal boom, or with their hoses looped along a scaffold ledger pole, may clean a flat surface within two hours, but a piece of carved cornice with encrusted dirt may well require two or three days of spraying before the stone is clean. Unless there is provision to modify the washing programme to avoid unnecessary general saturation, there may be a number of consequences such as:

1. Light to dark brown staining will take place as dirty water dries out from the stones and joints.
2. Staining, usually brown, and white efflorescences may appear as a result of salt migration to the surface.
3. The release of small flakes of stone, especially on small-scale and undercut detail, may occur as a result of the dissolution of salts. Such flakes may sometimes be attached to the surface only by water-soluble material present as the result of the activity of a polluted environment on the stone surfaces. Surface losses will also be incurred when the stone is powdery.
4. Weak jointing material may be washed out.
5. Water penetration through defective joints, or through cracks and contact with iron fixings, plaster, beam ends, bond timbers, panelling, electrical fittings and furnishings may take place. There is also the risk of water entering unsuspected reservoirs above vaults, in floor spaces or

in basements, which may result in direct damage or future problems with dry rot (*Serpula lacrymans*). In old walls, especially those of double skin and rubble fill construction, water from the outside may travel considerable distances before emerging in other parts of the building.

6. The development of disfiguring green, red or orange algae on recently washed surfaces, especially flat or inclined catchment areas, may be noticed.
7. In wintry conditions, considerable damage can result from the freezing of water trapped in the joints or in the pores of the stones. Ideally, no washing should take place during months likely to be frosty. If washing must continue, the work must be halted before sunset and be fully covered up. In exceptional circumstances, background heating on the scaffold will be necessary.

Washing with minimum risk

Successful washing programmes are those which put the minimum amount of water for the minimum time exactly where it is required and nowhere else. This may be achieved in different ways. Traditionally, water jets tied to the scaffold have been turned on and shut down as the surface response dictates, but this is difficult to control in practice and groups of sprays tend to be left on for as long as dirt remains in the most stubborn area. An experienced cleaner will get to work with small brushes of bristle, phosphor bronze or brass wire as soon as possible to cut down the saturation period. Steel wire brushes should never be used, because of their harsh action. Their design is usually inappropriate and there is a risk of leaving steel fragments on the building, which will later produce small, but vivid, rust stains.

The ideal condition for washing is a persistent wet mist over the soiled face of the building. This technique avoids the impact effect which large water droplets have when delivered by coarse sprays and the subsequent cascading which, when prolonged, can cause damage. To achieve the mist, or 'fogging', the sprays must be from fine nozzles situated at least 300 mm away from the masonry face. Enough water pressure and small enough orifices are required to atomize the water. In practice, this is rarely easy because, even on a tightly sheeted scaffold, draughts of air can carry the water mist away from the building. The effectiveness of the system therefore depends on how successfully the mist can be contained.

A more dependable system of washing was devised by R.H. Bennett in 1970 to reduce saturation and has since developed into an established method. It makes use of readily achieved fine sprays of water playing intermittently on the building surface. The water is controlled electronically by means of sensor heads or a pre-set clock. The sensor heads comprise twin carbon rods set in a non-conductive plastic body linked to an electrical control box. The sensors, about 20 mm (0.75 in) long, are pinned at intervals into the masonry joints with stainless steel staples. When a water bridge forms on the sensor head, the water is automatically cut off. When the water bridge is broken by drying out, the sprays are automatically switched on again. In most cases the clock control is preferred because it is more positive. With clock control a washing interval is established by preliminary trial and error. The clock is set to control a spraying time of, say, eight seconds, followed by a four-minute shut-down. The aim with either system is to supply just enough water to progressively soften the dirt without causing saturation and risking penetration through vulnerable areas. The system is usually referred to as intermittent or pulse washing. Close attention is still required to commence scrubbing as soon as the dirt becomes responsive to brushing.

A more recent development in washing is the use of flexible bars to position the nozzles exactly where they are required. Because of the difference in soiling conditions and variations in response times, the cleaner must constantly re-position the spray heads as the situation changes on the building face during cleaning. Because the fixed scaffold and any short battens secured to it are the only means of support for the sprays, it is very difficult to direct the water exactly where it is needed. Plastic-sleeved flexible bars are fixed to the scaffold with brackets and swivel mountings. These bars provide support for the nozzles and in this way a true three-dimensional flexibility in positioning water sprays is achieved. This enables the underside of a moulding or soffit of a niche to be cleaned as easily as a straight run of ashlar.

Brushes have also been the subject of some development and the variety in design has increased. Several sizes of scrubbing and stencil-type brushes are needed for all but the simplest facade. A light formation of phosphor bronze crinkle wire and synthetic bristle combination designed by Picreator is particularly useful. Small blocks of rubbing or abrasive sandstones can also be used to remove stubborn staining and encrustation from flat surfaces.

Water penetration risks may further be reduced, especially on high buildings, by the construction of splash or slurry boards of resin-bonded plywood, sheathed in polyethylene sheet, at intervals to form horizontal catchment to collect and carry off the water flowing down the building face. The water from these boards is collected in plastic gutters fixed at their outer edge and carried off in plastic downpipes. Similar constructions may be built over large openings which remain in use during the cleaning.

Cold water direct from the mains is normally used for cleaning facades of buildings. Hot water may be justified for particular situations, especially where detergents or de-greasing chemicals are used.

Water lances

Light soiling, especially where a high proportion is organic, may sometimes be removed by water lances without any preliminary softening by water spraying. Alternatively, they may be used in combination with water sprays, mechanical or chemical cleaning. Pressures are often in the 800–1200 psi range, and the lance is usually low volume, high pressure. Water at these pressures has a cutting action, however, and the design of the outlet and the technique of the operative both significantly affect the economy and the safety of the cleaning. Much higher pressures can be obtained enabling water jets to cut through concrete, so potential damage from indiscreet or careless lancing is a factor that must be taken into consideration.

A technique introduced approximately ten years ago mixes fine sand and water together at source for delivery through a lance at comparatively low pressures of between 18 and 30 psi. The water carrying the abrasive has a light scouring action. The abrasive can then be cut out to permit flushing with water alone. This system was used to clean the principal facades of the British Museum in London from a hydraulic platform, avoiding the need to scaffold. In common with conventional wet sand blasting, it will also clean sandstone.

Mechanical

Mechanical cleaning removes dirt by abrading the surface. The simplest form is dry brushing. This technique will remove loosely bound dirt and organic growth but little else. Sometimes it is practicable to use hand-held sandstone or carborundum blocks lubricated with water to improve the appearance of simple, flat surfaces, but only on resistant, tough materials that will not be scoured by the abrasive action. A harsher method is scraping the surface down with a suitable tool such as a mason's drag which is sometimes used to remove paint from flat surfaces. The most damaging cleaning in this category in the past has undoubtedly been 'spinning off', normally entailing the use of a power tool with an interchangeable set of heads including soft wire brushes, carborundum heads and discs. Flexible carborundum discs are also available. Unfortunately this technique removes some of the surface to achieve cleaning. It is also notoriously difficult even for an experienced operative to avoid scouring flat surfaces with shallow depressions and leaving wavy arrises on external angles. Good quality work is usually finished by hand. The surface is rubbed to remove the imperfections and is, in effect, re-dressed. In most situations it is a technique to avoid, unless there has been deep staining of a surface or a paint which will not yield to solvents must be removed.

Spinning-off has been largely superseded by the use of compressed air and abrasives. Wet or dry sand-blasting or grit-blasting have become very familiar methods of cleaning building facades. These systems were often used to descale large surface areas of iron and steel sheet. Their appearance in the field of building cleaning dates from the 1950s. In the United Kingdom these systems were very much in evidence during the decade 1965–1975. They were often used indiscriminately, unfortunately stimulated at the time by a government environmental improvement grant scheme.

A blasting system projects abrasive through a nozzle in a stream of compressed air. The basic equipment consists of a compressor, a pot for the abrasive and air and abrasive delivery lines. Some types of system introduce water by running a twin hose to carry water to the end of the abrasive delivery line and discharging several small jets of water through a ring adaptor into the air and abrasive stream. Other types mix the water, air and abrasive at source. Air pressures at the nozzle vary in practice from 15 to 80 psi and there are different orifice sizes and nozzle patterns available.

Abrasives are selected according to the toughness of the dirt to be removed, but cost and safety factors also have an influence. Sand is the cheapest abrasive, but the most hazardous, and is now banned in several countries. Harmful dust is always generated by dry blasting of sandstone, and the operatives must have the protection of helmets supplied with filtered air and should wear full protective clothing. Other tough abrasives are non-siliceous grits, such as copper or iron slag, carborundum and aluminium oxide powders. For less demanding or more fragile surfaces, olivine, dolomite, crushed egg or nut shells, minute glass beads or even talc may be used as the abrasive.

Factors which must be considered when the use of such a cleaning system is contemplated are:

1. The relative hardness of the abrasive and the surface and the likely risk of damage.
2. The size of the particles of abrasive. Coarse particles should be used for the preliminary cutting and fine for finishing.
3. The need for water to lubricate and cushion the impact effect of the abrasive and to reduce dust.

4. The risks of dust to the public and of penetration to sensitive areas of the building.
5. The available operative skills (see Appendix 3).

Problems associated with the air abrasive technique include:

1. The surfaces being cleaned and even the abrasive used can vary in hardness. Less resistant stones, or areas of the same stone, may be attacked by the air pressure and abrasive which cleaned a trial patch without damage.
2. Grits of sand and flint contain free silica, as do sandstone and granite. Dusts generated during cleaning which involves these materials can cause long-term, irreversible lung damage to inadequately protected operatives.
3. The vision of an operative wearing a protective helmet can be obscured by dust when large nozzles are used.
4. Dust can penetrate even small openings and damage furniture, fittings and machinery.
5. Compressor and air delivery noise can be a considerable nuisance to the occupants of a building which is being cleaned and may become intolerable in the immediate vicinity of cleaning.
6. Residual dust and spent abrasive will remain on the building, giving an unnatural appearance, unless the cleaning is completed by washing down. This is most conveniently carried out by using a high pressure, low volume water lance, which does not involve any soaking of the building.
7. Cheap, soft sands which are sometimes used can cause staining.

Advantages of the air abrasive technique, on the other hand, may be listed as follows:

1. Saturation of the building is avoided, even with wet-head blast cleaning and lancing off, so that cleaning can usually proceed through the winter, even in cold climates.
2. There are few risks of water penetration and staining or efflorescence, although wet-head blasting involves some risks.
3. On simple facades, the method is probably the fastest way to clean safely, assuming the necessary skills are available.
4. On small-scale, fragile detail, especially where there is a history of salt crystallization damage, small-scale air abrasive cleaning, if used skilfully, is safer than water cleaning or poulticing.

A range of equipment is now available which enables experienced operatives to clean a variety of surfaces safely, avoiding most of the mistakes of the past. The drawing shows some of the equipment currently in use. Of particular interest is the safety-conscious water injection system, which can largely avoid hazardous dust during large-scale cleaning. Small air abrasive pistols and pencils, using 50 mm, 100 mm or finer dusts, can be used very effectively as supplementary tools to cleaning with water or chemicals sometimes after the initial softening up.

Compressed air and abrasive may be used to clean in a vacuum chamber on site. Many buildings in Paris, for instance, have been cleaned in this way from a mobile platform.

The operators must be experienced and alert to changes in the surface on which they are working. Adjustments in pressure or abrasive or a change of method may be necessary. Work may have to be abandoned altogether if damage appears likely to a valuable surface. Work must never be hurried. Rushed air abrasive work, especially on flat surfaces, can result in a mottled 'gun-shading', which becomes apparent with subsequent weathering. Whether air abrasive cleaning is used wet or dry, the surface should always be finished with a water lance in order to remove all dust and spent abrasive. On small-scale detail, hand sprays or air jets may be used.

Cleaning with hydrofluoric acid

Hydrofluoric acid (HF) is the chemical cleaning agent normally selected for cleaning sandstone and unpolished granite. It is the traditional method which has been in use for over fifty years, although improvements in abrasive systems have introduced some competition during the last twenty years. Even so, because HF cleaning is quiet, generally efficient and avoids the risk of damage associated with abrasive discs, or unskilled compressed air and abrasive cleaning, it has held its position. Although HF is a particularly dangerous acid to personnel and will etch glass and polished surfaces, it hs the distinct advantage over other chemicals that it will not leave behind potentially damaging soluble salts.

Hydrofluoric acid cleans sandstones by reacting with the silica which forms the main constituent of the stone. As the silica dissolves, the surface dirt bound to it is loosened and may be washed away. If there is a delay in washing off, some of the dissolved silica may be redeposited and it will show as a white bloom or as white streaks from the joints. This redeposited silica is very difficult to remove. Although weathering generally improves the appearance, it is of little help if the disfigurement is excessive. These deposits can only be removed by mechanical means, i.e. by an abrasive disc or airbrasive unit, by water cutting, or by a further application of the acid, all of which make nonsense of the original intention to clean by chemical means.

Sandstones which contain iron compounds present another problem. Generally stones of this kind

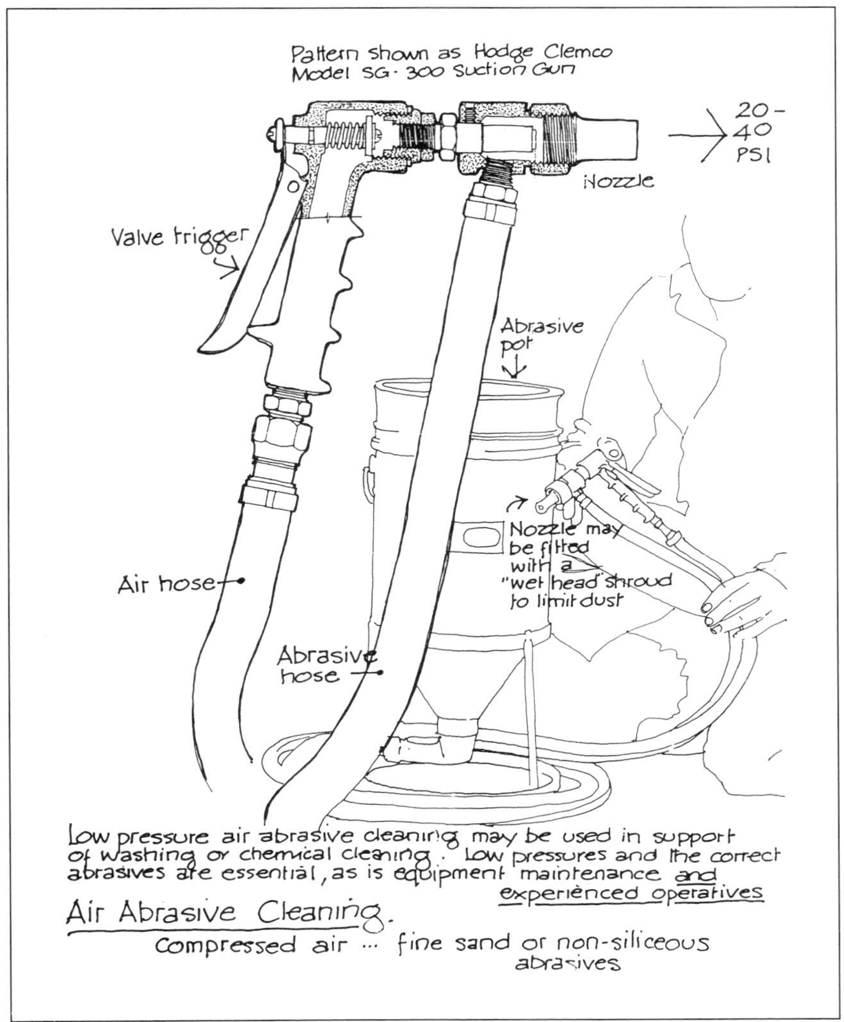

show the presence of iron in the form of light to deep brown staining in areas which have been subject to water percolation over a long period. Hydrated iron oxides appear as brown specks on the surface of the stone, even if staining is not apparent. Hydrofluoric acid will attack the iron and form soluble compounds, which then migrate to the surface and create deep brown stains. The risk of staining can be considerably reduced, but not eliminated, by adding phosphoric acid to the hydrofluoric acid. The phosphoric acid forms insoluble iron phosphates, which are unable to migrate to the surface. Before cleaning is undertaken, it is in everyone's interest to study the appearance of an iron-rich sandstone building, in order to assess the existing staining due to weathering. In this way, the building owner will be prepared, the contractor will not be unfairly blamed and the architect will be spared the unnecessary time and expense of investigation, reporting and arbitration, should further staining result from the cleaning. Although attempts have been made to remove iron staining with subsequent applications of phosphoric acid and mixtures of phosphoric and hydrofluoric acids, the results have been disappointing. It must be said that there is increasing concern and dissatisfaction with the colour changes brought about by ill-considered acid cleaning of sandstone.

Two further types of sandstones which are particularly susceptible to decay in polluted environments, are calcareous sandstones and dolomitic sandstones, in which the siliceous grains are cemented principally by calcite and dolomite respectively. Both calcite (calcium carbonate) and dolomite (magnesium calcium carbonate) are attacked by hydrofluoric acid and there will, in theory, be greater losses when these stones are cleaned with hydrofluoric acid, than when a sandstone with a siliceous matrix is cleaned. In practice, however, it seems that the commonly powdery surfaces of these stones are likely to lose as much from the washing-off process as from the acid application, unless the acid treatment is particularly prolonged or concentrated.

Sandstone with a largely siliceous matrix may still contain calcite or dolomite, but in this case hydrofluoric acid is no threat to the binding constituent of the stone. However, fears are expressed from time to time that a change in pore structure may result from the formation of calcium fluoride (an insoluble product formed by the reaction of hydrofluoric acid with calcite) and/or calcium fluoride and magnesium fluoride (formed by the reaction of hydrofluoric acid with dolomite). Modification of the pore structure might well affect the long-term durability of a sandstone cleaned in this way, but an examination by the Building Research Establishment, carried out on a sandstone building where claims of positive damage from hydrofluoric acid cleaning had been made, showed no evidence to support the claims. Microscopic examination of petrological thin sections, prepared from cores taken through the cleaned surface, was made and a piece of each sample was analysed by X-ray diffraction. The sandstone was composed of silica, with small amounts of mica, feldspar, dolomite and hydrated iron oxides. No calcium fluoride was detected and there were no signs of chemical attack on grains of dolomite at the surface. The opinion of the Building Research Establishment in this case was that no short-term damage from acid attack on the matrix, or long-term damage from pore blocking, had been caused. It would be foolish to say that, from this, hydrofluoric acid will not cause damage in any circumstances. Consideration must always be given to the constituents of the stone, and a sensible assessment must be made of the vulnerability of the stone to this type of cleaning.

Procedures for the commercial cleaning of a sandstone or unpolished granite building with hydrofluoric acid are described below. All personnel must be experienced in the use of the acid and equipped with full face and head protection, heavy duty gauntlets, and waterproof boots and clothing. They should be familiar with the appropriate first-aid procedures and the local hospital should be informed.

1. General procedures for protecting the building and sheeting the scaffolding apply, but particular care must be taken to protect contract personnel and the public from spillages or drift. First-aid boxes must be kept on site. All scaffold tubes must be securely capped to avoid the trapping of acid or acid vapour. Glass should be coated with two applications of a latex masking paint (remember that some solvents are effective paint strippers!). If the window glass is particularly valuable, it should be covered with a polyethylene membrane and resin bonded ply templates. Templates alone, without the latex, should not be used.
2. Use a proprietary, pre-diluted form of hydrofluoric acid; the concentration must be known and displayed on the container (between 2% and 15%). Do not store the industrial concentrate (which may be over 70%) on site, or permit on-site dilution. Keep the acid in a secure store, adequately labelled.
3. Pre-wet the area to be cleaned with clean water. A convenient way of achieving this is to use a low-volume, high-pressure water lance. The objective is to provide a damp surface, on which the chemical will spread. If the surface is dry, or only superficially wet, the chemical will be absorbed, especially at mortar joints. Thorough wetting will limit the activity of the chemical to the soiled face.
4. Apply the acid by brush to the damp surface, or by using a low-pressure garden spray. The application should be even and planned between architectural features, e.g. cornice to plinth or between internal angles of buttresses. The coverage rate should be in the order of 1 litre per 3.7 square metres of surface area (1 imperial gallon per 12–15 square yards). The contact period with the stone surface will vary depending on the amount and type of soiling and on the ambient temperature. Proprietary hydrofluoric acid cleaners which carry an Agrément Board certificate (pH 1–1.5 and pH 3.5–3.8) are recommended to be left between 20 minutes (Agrément Board), 30 minutes on a warm day (Neolith) and up to 1 hour on a cold day (Neolith). Repeated applications may be necessary. The cleaning material must never be allowed to dry on the surface.
5. The acid should be thoroughly washed off at the correct time. This can be achieved most efficiently with a low-volume, high-pressure water lance — a pump producing, say, 1000 psi at 4 imperial gallons per minute. It must be recognized, however, that even 1000 psi may be too strong for many surfaces, and the temptation to use the lance to 'cut' may be a hazard. 'Safe' pressures are below 500 psi, and it is generally wise to specify this limit. The technique recommended by Neolith is to hold the nozzle approximately 760 mm (30 in) away from the surface, while passing the lance to and fro, in sweeps of

760 mm (30 in). Rinsing for four minutes per square metre (1 square yard) is recommended as a minimum time, with extra attention paid to water traps, such as sills and strings, or weathered joints. The rinsing water must not be allowed to accumulate on such traps. At one site in London, dribble staining resulted from rinsing water left in recessed joints. As the water evaporated, the acid concentration increased and white streaks of silica were left behind.
6. The scaffolding boards must also be washed off thoroughly after each rinsing of the building and the scaffold tube capping checked.
7. Subsequent applications of the chemical must follow stages 3 to 6. At least half an hour should elapse before a second application.

Burns must be washed immediately with copious amounts of clean water for at least one minute, followed by rubbing calcium gluconate gel into and around the burned area, with clean fingers. The gel should be rubbed in continuously for 15 minutes after the pain has subsided and hospital treatment must follow. If gel is not available, washing must continue until it is. Eyes which have been affected should be irrigated with isotonic saline or clean water for at least 10 minutes. Hospital treatment may involve injections of calcium gluconate into and under the burn and further treatment in the case of large or severe burns.

The problems associated with this kind of cleaning may be summarized by saying that they are caused by little or no analysis of the surface to be cleaned, quite inadequate specifications and supervision, and too concentrated acid solutions.

Other chemical cleaning agents

An increasingly wide range of other acid or alkali cleaning agents is available, but they all involve some risk of soluble salt residues. The most common alkaline cleaning agents are based on sodium hydroxide (caustic soda) or potassium hydroxide (caustic potash). Some may contain surfactants and detergents to degrease a severely soiled surface before cleaning with hydrofluoric acid, in which case there is not likely to be a problem with residues. The same general procedures and safeguards as for cleaning with hydrofluoric acid should be followed, even though some hazards are less. In particular, prewetting and thorough washing off are vital if staining and damage are to be avoided. Unfortunately, examples of such damage can easily be found, especially on the underside of window and door heads. Caustic alkali cleaning of limestone should really be considered only as a last resort, when cleaning by other means is not possible.

Proprietary pastes are available containing ammonium hydroxides as a degreasing agent. Other proprietary pastes containing sodium hydroxide may also contain organic amines such as diethylene-triamine which make calcium sulphate skins more readily soluble. Methyl cellulose is a common thickener for these pastes.

In paste form, sodium hydroxide or potassium hydroxide have been used to break down multiple layers of unwanted paint, but these pastes must be covered by thin polyethylene film and lifted off dry, before thorough washing with clean water.

In a typical test using sodium-hydroxide-based paste on Bath limestone, samples analysed for the presence of water soluble sodium compounds showed that the sodium content of the outer 3 mm was increased by a factor of more than eighty. This would be quite unacceptable in terms of a residue on a building facade.

In one case application of sodium hydroxide paste was followed by washing and the application of a clean Attapulgite clay poultice, in order to encourage any harmful residues to dry out into the clay. This procedure produces a very good result, but is very labour intensive, especially if undercut detail is involved.

Another acid in common use for the removal of cementitious stains and deposits is hydrochloric acid. Ten per cent acid applied to a pre-wetted surface will remove calcium carbonate. It is more likely to be used on brickwork and limestone than on sandstone. Citric and acetic acids are used in 'neutralizing' washes after alkali cleaning.

First-aid treatment for potassium hydroxide ('caustic potash'), sodium hydroxide ('caustic soda') and hydrochloric acid ('spirits of salts') is washing with copious amounts of clean water. Severe burns must be treated in hospital as soon as possible. When burns from hydrochloric acid have occurred, a magnesium oxide paste should be applied.

Reputable manufacturers of proprietary cleaning materials produce full product data, dealing with all associated hazards, waste disposal methods, protective clothing, face and eye protection, handling and storage. It is imperative that such information is made available, read and acted upon.

There is little doubt that the chemical cleaning of buildings, at its best, shows an increasing versatility based on a proper assessment of the surfaces to be cleaned and the nature of the soiling present. In particular, improvements associated with dilute acid and alkali cleaning materials held in poultices of clay or carboxymethylcellulose (CMC) against the surface of the stone are extremely encouraging; so is the recognition that safe and efficient cleaning is (and perhaps should be) more expensive than hasty and ill-considered gambling with unsuitably concentrated materials and high-pressure jetting.

Special cleaning systems

The Hempel 'biological pack'

Certain clays, such as attapulgite or sepiolite, are very useful poultice media. The structure of the clays enables them to contain considerable amounts of moisture and to produce a sucking effect as they dry out. To prepare the poultice a 50 μm clay powder is added to enough clean water to produce a thick, sticky cream. The water should not be added to the clay, because a lumpy paste will result. This mixture may be applied to the surface of soiled limestone or marble without a solvent, and covered with a thin polyethylene film. The poultice may be effective within a few days, but it may need to be left for several weeks. The contact period can only be determined by lifting the edge of the poultice and testing the tenacity of the surface dirt by gentle scrubbing. When a promising result is obtained, the complete poultice can be removed with a spatula and the surface scrubbed clean with bristle or soft, non-ferrous wire brushes. Used in this way, such poultices are a development of the more traditional wet-packs composed of whiting, paper pulp or even bread. They may be mixed with various solvents to lift stains.

Hempel developed the idea of a 'biological pack', based on these clay bodies, which claims to assist the breakdown of sulphate crusts on marble and limestone by the presence and activity of micro-organisms. These packs include 25 g urea and 10 ml glycerol in 500 ml of water. Enough sepiolite or attapulgite clay must be added to form a thixotropic paste. In common with all poultice packs, the paste must be applied to have good contact with all the surfaces to be cleaned. Spray wetting of the surfaces should precede the application, and again thin polyethylene film should be used to prevent air reaching the surface of the pack. This biological pack may remain on the surface for several weeks (perhaps for up to two months) before it is lifted and brushing and rinsing takes place.

This technique is primarily suited to the cleaning of sculpture and small-scale detail on, for instance, church monuments.

The Mora poultice

An interesting system for cleaning limestone and marble based on a chelating agent was developed by Mora. The chelating agent is ethylene diaminotetra-acetic acid (EDTA). This weak acid facilitates the dissolution of calcium salts by complex formation. Complexing or sequestering agents separate or are cut off. The Mora poultice has been used with considerable success on marble and travertine which have had moderate soiling. The poultice contains 60 g ammonium bicarbonate, 60 g sodium bicarbonate, 25 g EDTA, 10 g surfactant disinfectant and 60 g carboxymethylcellulose in 1000 ml of water. The ammonium and sodium bicarbonate give a slightly basic mixture of pH 7.5 and facilitate the dissolution of some salts.

The poultice, in the form of a clear jelly, is applied to a pre-wetted surface by spatula or by brush to a thickness of 3–4 mm, and is covered at once with a thin polyethylene film to prevent drying out. The film is of utmost importance as the cellulose body of the poultice is very difficult to remove if it dries and hardens. The contact period may be twenty-four hours, and intermediate lifting and reapplication may be necessary. After cleaning and removal of all poultice material by the use of small trowels or spatulas the surface should be washed thoroughly with clean water.

The advantages and attractions of this system are principally that it is safe chemically and avoids any excessive use of abrasion or water. It cannot, however, be applied to friable or flaking surfaces (any more than any other poultice) without removing surface material. Surprisingly large areas can be cleaned relatively economically when the surface is not too detailed.

The Baker or lime method

The cleaning of limestone surfaces by lime poulticing as part of a total consolidation and protection programme was pioneered and developed by Professor Robert Baker (UK). The system is fully described in Chapter 9.

Soaps

Grease, oil, tar and pitch will frequently respond well to scrubbing with warm water and a suitable soap, especially on marble or limestone. Slate, granite and even sandstone may sometimes be cleaned, or partially cleaned, by this method as well. Any of the deposit which can be lifted by a scraper or spatula should be removed first. Powdered detergents must be avoided, because of the cumulative deposits of sodium salts which build up, particularly in joints, after repeated applications (maintenance cleaning, for example).

Experience has shown that a proprietary methyl cyclohexyloleate (pH 10.5–11.5) which is soluble in water and spirit, such as white spirit or trichlorethylene, is able to remove a wide range of soiling and has good penetrating effects into fine crazing and small cracks. This soap blend is non-foaming and remains active while it is on the surface, usually about 5 minutes. Thick deposits of greasy or oily dirt need to be worked on with bristle, synthetic fibre or soft brass wire brushes. Hand-warm water produces the optimum effect. After cleaning, all the soap should be rinsed away.

Suitable, economic proportions are between 3–9 parts water/spirit to 1 part of soap. No particular safety precautions are needed, but the efficient degreasing effect of the solution makes it advisable to wear protection gloves.

Alabaster, the surface of which is dissolved by washing with water, may be cleaned with the soap and white spirit and finished with white spirit alone on cotton swabs.

Iron and cuprous stain removal

Iron gutters and hoppers, roofing fixings and long-term scaffolding all can produce disfiguring rusty stains on masonry. Copper roofing and bronze statuary and plaques produce an unsightly green staining. These stains may be lightened and sometimes removed altogether by the poultices described below. In all cases, the surfaces must be pre-wetted and all poultice material must be lifted off with plastic spatulas and placed directly into disposal bins or sacks, before thorough rinsing off with clean water. The longer a stain is left untreated, the more difficult complete removal becomes. Before cleaning, means to avoid re-staining should be decided upon. This may involve, for instance, the painting or removal of iron, or the regular treatment of bronze with lanolin and wax.

Removal of iron stains

To remove or lighten iron stains (principally from limestone and marble), the following method should be used:

1. Add a solution of one part sodium citrate and six parts water to an equal volume of glycerin.
2. Add attapulgite clay to the solution until a smooth paste is formed.
3. Apply the paste to the stained surface and leave until dry.
4. Remove the paste with a wooden or other non-metallic spatula.
5. Reapply and remove the paste as often as required to lift or satisfactorily lighten the stain.

Very stubborn stains may require the following alternative treatment:

1. Wet the surface with a solution of one part sodium citrate and six parts water.
2. Apply an attapulgite wet clay pack, containing sodium dithionite.
3. Lift off and follow by washing the surface with copious amounts of clean water.

Removal of cuprous stains

To remove or lighten cuprous metal stains (principally from limestone and marble), the following method should be used:

1. Mix dry one part of ammonium chloride with four parts powdered talc or attapulgite or sepiolite clay. Add a 10% solution of ammonia water.
2. Pre-wet the surface with clean water, apply the paste and leave until dry.
3. Remove the paste with a wooden or other non-metallic spatula.
4. Rinse thoroughly with clean water.
5. Reapply, remove and rinse off the paste as often as required to lift or satisfactorily lighten the stain.

Ultrasonic cleaning

Ultrasonic cleaning uses vibration to achieve its effect. It is primarily a museum technique, applicable to relatively small objects. Electrically produced vibration is transmitted through metal plates to a liquid in a cleaning bath. Sound waves are carried by the alternate compression and expansion of the liquid. If this alternation is rapid enough, the intense waves of vibration travelling through the water 'tear holes' in it. Vapour cavities appear and collapse at an ultrasonic frequency, a phenomenon known as *cavitation*. The 'ultrasonic bubbles' have a brushing action on the surfaces of an object placed in the tank because, as the bubbles collapse, the liquid, locally, moves very fast. The process can be thought of as abrasion with molecule-sized grit.

The equipment used by dentists to descale teeth, developed some 25 years ago, is also used in conservation work. The tool has an ultrasonic vibrating head immersed in a spray of water, which flows around and through it. The vibration is transmitted into the water layer, creating movement, vibration and cavitation which cleans the surface. This technique is used in a similar manner principally by museum conservators in the workshop.

Laser cleaning

The first laser (Light Amplification by Stimulated Emission of Radiation) was built in July 1960, by the American physicist Maiman. Since then, the exploration of the potential of lasers in the fields of surgery, industry and warfare has been taking place. Since 1972,[3] laser radiation has been under investigation as a means of stone cleaning, specifically in the field of sculpture conservation. The attraction of the principle lies in the relative ease with which even encrusted dirt can be removed from the most fragile surfaces as a result of laser irradiation. Under the sponsorship of the International Fund for Monuments, a portable laser system was fabricated for use in Venice. Using Neodymium YAG as the active laser material and a 2 kV power supply yielding an output of one pulse per second, a heavily soiled small marble sculpture can be cleaned by an experienced operator in between one and three hours. A single pulse from the laser will clean a 25 mm (1 in) square area. This cleaning rate is comparable with the air abrasive pencil, when the few seconds interval needed for the laser operative to redirect the beam is taken into account. The advantage of the method is the absence of any mechanical contact with the surface of the sculpture.

Although this is an interesting and exciting development in the cleaning of fragile surfaces, and shows much promise, it is unlikely that laser cleaning will be of practical value outside the conservation studio for many years.

Removal of algal slimes, lichens, mosses

There are many circumstances in which lichen and some varieties of small plants may enhance the appearance of masonry without adverse effect. However in other circumstances sterilizing treatment is required for reasons of maintenance or appearance. Biological growths which should receive attention include unsightly algal slimes on vertical surfaces and especially on paving, and acid-secreting lichens which cause the deterioration of certain building materials, such as copper or lead sheet, or marble, limestone and glass.

An important point to remember when planning the consolidation and maintenance of many unroofed monuments, where the access to exposed wall heads is limited and expensive, is the function of lichens in nature as soil formers. Lichens, which are harmless in themselves, may assist the establishment of mosses, small plants and even trees. Complete cleaning of normally inaccessible areas during a consolidation programme is therefore of great importance. Due respect should be paid to the conservation of unusual or harmless flora where control and observation are possible.

Health and Safety regulations affecting biocides are becoming increasingly stringent, and obviously influence the use of some materials in some countries.

Treatment

In some situations, surface soiling by organic growth can be removed very simply by dry bristle or soft wire brushing, or by jetting with a high-pressure, low-volume water lance, provided that the substrate is sound enough to take this mechanical cleaning. However, rapid re-colonization is likely and some form of toxic wash will probably be needed.

A great variety of treatments which effect an initial kill is available. Unfortunately, some of the traditional treatments (for instance, the persistent use of calcium chloride or concentrated ammonia solutions) can build up residues of damaging soluble salts. Concentrated solutions of zinc or magnesium silicofluoride may produce hard surface skins on limestone, which are liable to spall off.

A long term inhibiting effect on biological growth on some walls may be obtained by the installation of narrow flashing strips of thin gauge copper. These strips are tucked into the length of horizontal joints in the masonry, approximately every metre. The effect of rain washing over the strips is to subject the face of the masonry to a mildly toxic wash. A certain amount of light green staining must be expected, which makes this system unsuitable for very light-coloured stones. In addition, it will not be effective where the detailing on the building tends to throw off the rain.

The best treatments currently available for controlling lichen are quaternary ammonium compounds ('quats'), used in conjunction with tin oxide (tri-*n*-butyl-tin oxide, TBTO) or other suitable biocides. The following method is suitable for masonry covered with algae, lichen, mosses and small plants. It is designed to give the maximum inhibition against recolonizing growth. Simpler specifications may be limited to a single application of a quat.

1. Remove as much growth as possible in the form of plants and thick cushions of moss, using knife blades, spatulas and stiff bristle or non-ferrous soft wire brushes. If the surface below the growth is delicate, or liable to be marked or scoured in any way, this preparation must be limited to lifting off the moss only.
2. Prepare a solution of quat by adding water to the manufacturer's specification.
3. Fill a pneumatic garden-type sprayer two-thirds full with the diluted biocide. Adjust the nozzle to a coarse spray setting. There should be sufficient pressure at the wand nozzle after pumping the compressor to saturate the surface of the masonry causing excessive bounce back and drift of the spray.
4. Apply a flood coat. Start at the top of the vertical surface to be treated and move across horizontally and slowly, to allow approximately 100 mm (4 in) run down. The next horizontal pass should be made across the previous run down.
5. Leave the treated area for at least one week. Brush off as much dead growth as possible with bristle brushes, making sure that any adjacent gutters and hoppers are kept clear.
6. Prepare a solution of a proprietary quat, including TBTO. A typical concentrate is delivered in 1 litre containers and should be diluted with 19 parts of water by volume.
7. Fill a second pneumatic sprayer with the diluted biocide and apply as before.
8. Allow the surface to absorb and carry out a second application of diluted quat as a growth inhibitor.

Protection of other areas

Provided that the applications are made carefully, there should be little risk to grass or flowers below the area being treated. However, as there is always a risk of spillage, it is sensible to lay a plastic sheet over plants on the ground whilst working. It is preferable to use only mechanical cleaning in areas which are in close proximity to buildings, areas occupied by farm animals, or ponds containing fish and other aquatic wild life.

Coverage

Coverage will vary with site conditions. As an approximate guide, one litre of biocide treats 1.5 m^2 (1.75 yd^2). There is some evidence that there will be a lessening of toxicity if the diluted biocide is stored for a long time. Only sufficient biocide for the day's work should therefore be prepared.

Failures with these treatments are not unknown, but, if the above procedures are followed, there should be no problems. In exceptionally dry periods it may be beneficial to revive dormant dry lichen, which tends to be water repellent, with light water spraying a day or two before applying the biocide. Applications of biocidal treatment should not be undertaken during wet weather, or when windy conditions lead to excessive drift of spray. It is important that products are applied in strict accordance with the manufacturer's recommendations, in order to ensure the safety and protection of the environment.

Removal of graffiti

The graffiti problem is not new, but since the availability of aerosol paint cans loaded with cellulose paint it has become an international nuisance of new proportions. Although most paints used for graffiti can usually be removed from the masonry surface it is very difficult to remove pigment which has been carried into the pores by a solvent. Sometimes the application of a solvent to remove the paint can drive the pigment more deeply into the stone, for example the application of cellulose thinners to freshly applied cellulose paint graffiti. Water-soluble paint strippers, 1:5 solutions of water and trisodium phosphate and pastes of sodium hydroxide in clay have all been used with varying degrees of success. The stripper must be left in contact with the paint for long enough to cause softening and to enable scraping and brushing to take place successfully. The application of a thick layer is essential, and a layer of thin plastic film may be necessary over the application. After the paint has been scraped off the surface must be washed thoroughly, preferably in warm water and liquid soap. Unfortunately, repeated attacks with paint and repeated removals build up an unsightly, patchy masonry surface which often results in despairing surrender to the apparently inevitable, either by inactivity or by overpainting.

Occasional graffiti attacks are not such a problem and may be dealt with as above (resorting to the caustic stripper only when all else fails), with the possible refinement of picking out some of the stubborn pigment with an air abrasive pistol or pencil and a fine abrasive such as aluminium oxide powder. Sometimes, as after the graffiti attacks on the sarsen monoliths of Stonehenge, the ghosting left behind after cleaning may be further obscured by encouraging the development of lichen with organic washes of animal dung in water. The application of such material is not recommended on fragile or highly sensitive surfaces. The graffiti vandal is normally attracted to a sound surface rather than to a friable, decaying substrate. Thus lichen not only obscures the visual scars left after cleaning but tends to discourage further attacks.

Areas liable to repeated attacks have sometimes been treated with a barrier application to try to prevent the migration of paint into the surface pores of masonry and to facilitate removal. These applications attempt either to block the pores, or to cause temporary blocking by softening and swelling in the presence of moisture, or to line the pores with a water-repellent coating.

A recent project carried out for the Department of Ancient Monuments and Historic Buildings by the Colebrand Research Unit in the UK has shown that the pore lining technique is the most successful. In a series of tests simulating repeated graffiti attacks on surfaces of varying porosity and permeability, either a single-pack, moisture-cured polyurethane or a two-pack polyurethane-based material on a colour stable isocyanate prepolymer appeared to be the most promising. Cellulose paint was entirely removed by swabbing with MIBK. No retreatment with the barrier was found to be necessary after any of the paint stripping stages, unlike some currently available barrier treatments. In addition the treatment is colour stable and need not change the appearance of the substrate. It will inhibit the formation of organic growth and has good abrasion resistance during repeated cleaning. It allows simple and fast paint removal with non-caustic paint strippers and allow the passage of moisture vapour.

These barrier treatments must not be used on surfaces which are decaying or where there are major moisture movements. In such a situation it would be wiser to leave the surface alone. If intervention is essential it is best to use a deeply penetrating silane treatment which will serve to consolidate and give protection against paint attack.

Colourless water-repellent treatments

Recommendations to apply a colourless treatment after cleaning are often made by professional advisors and contractors. Such treatments are only rarely necessary. General assumptions about the permeability of masonry walls can lead to expensive and unnecessary treatments with water-repellent liquids. In some situations these treatments can actually increase the incidence of water penetration and, where there is a concentration of soluble salts, they may accelerate decay.

Colourless water repellents are intended to improve the resistance of masonry to rain penetration. Modern water repellents line the pores of the bricks, stones and mortar with water-repellent material, which inhibits capillary absorption. Treated surfaces will still absorb water during prolonged rainfall, but will allow the evaporation of trapped water because the treated zone remains permeable to water vapour.

BRS Digest 125[4] states that 'water-repellent liquids should be used with discrimination, having regard to the cause of dampness and the suitability of the surface for treatment.' The cause of dampness is often inaccurately diagnosed. If walls are unusually thin, or unusually permeable, water penetration through bricks and stones may take place, especially in conditions of extreme exposure. If penetration persists after all other sensible remedial work has been carried out, such as correct tamping and pointing of joints and cracks and repair of defective copings, gutters, downpipes and flashings, then there may well be a case for the use of water-repellent treatment. However, water repellents are not a substitute for other maintenance work and can, in some cases, increase the incidence of water penetration where there are cracks present. Experience has shown that there are relatively few situations where a water-repellent treatment alone has solved a major damp penetration problem. It should be noted, however, that trials carried out by the Building Research Establishment in the UK (BRE Report *Rain Penetration through Masonry Walls*, 1988) demonstrated that better resistance to water leakage through a masonry wall was obtained when water repellents were applied to pre-wetted surfaces. Pre-wetting appears to have satified the porosity of the masonry so that when the water-repellent solution was applied it was to treat interface cracks efficiently instead of being drawn into the surrounding porous materials.

The application of water repellents may exacerbate decay in some situations. This can happen as a result of the evaporating of water which contains salts in solution from behind the treated layer leaving salt crystals in the pores behind the treatment. Repeated crystallization cycles can then lead to disruption and spalling of the treated surface. In addition to this hazard, the thermal and moisture movements of the thin, treated surface layer may be sufficiently different from those of the underlying stone to generate shear stresses which eventually lead to failure. For these reasons, silicone or other water repellents must not be used as consolidants or preservatives. They must not be applied to surfaces which are friable or spalling as the result of salt crystallization damage.

Sometimes colourless water repellents are applied after cleaning masonry surfaces as dirt inhibitors. Such treatments are successful in this role for the duration of the surface repellency. However, this tends to deteriorate relatively quickly even though the repellence may persist in the surface pores of the treated layer. Retreatment is possible, but is rarely carried out in practice because of the expense of access to most building facades. Unfortunately, the deterioration of surface repellency is rarely uniform and a patchy appearance can result. Even the short-term benefits of water repellents as dirt inhibitors are therefore debatable and rarely justify the costs of materials and labour.

Although caution is advised in diagnosis of damp penetration and in the use of water repellents on decayed surfaces or as dirt inhibitors, there are many other situations where their use does no harm, but is simply an unnecessary expense. It can double the cost of a small cleaning contract. Therefore, any proposal for their use requires very careful consideration.

Examples of situations where silicone water repellents have proved their worth include masonry close to the sea where decay is taking place on the inside face of mullions, tracery or lintels, but the outside face is sound. Here, water repellents can usefully be applied to the sound external face only. On extremely exposed sites, where rain is driven through permeable stones and mortar, the use of water repellents may be justified. They have also been used successfully on brickwork where there is a history of staining from limestone dressings, since they encourage the calcium carbonate and sulphate to run off the surface rather than be deposited in the bricks.

BS 3826[5] (now being superseded by BS 6477[6]) sets out performance standards and offers user guidance. It is advisable to use materials which are manufactured to BS 3826, or which meet its performance requirements. Classes of silicone water-repellent appropriate for various substrates are:

Class A for use on sandstone, clay brick, terracotta, cement and cement-like stucco.
Class B for use on limestones, calcium silicate bricks, cast stone.
Class C for use on limestones and cast stone.

Other water repellents are based on stearates, to which the same general comments on use apply.

Protecting buildings from birds

Bird droppings are a major disfigurement on some buildings and the accumulations of ledges can lead to decay of the masonry surface. Excreta can also be a hazard on paving. A recently cleaned building in a zone frequented by starlings or pigeons may quickly become resoiled unless measures are taken to control the nuisance. The various methods of attempting to effect this control are listed below.

1. *Netting*. Synthetic mesh of unobtrusive colour can be stretched across potential roosting sites such as pediments, capitals and entablatures or even window openings. These nets must be knotted mesh and securely anchored at adequate intervals to stainless steel eyelets. Whilst not obtrusive at a distance extensive areas of netting do not enhance the appearance of a building. Properly installed it is a basic but effective system although probably a last resort from a visual standpoint.
2. *Gels*. Strips of gel can be extruded from a gun applicator along all ledges where birds may roost. On wide ledges a number of gel strips must be laid. The object is to provide an insecure footiing which discourages the birds from settling. Unfortunately, although this system has been widely used, it requires fairly frequent re-application; when the gel attracts dirt it becomes harder and less effective. The dried gel is difficult to remove and can itself become a major cleaning problem. The solvent leaches into stone causing dark, disfiguring stains. Even the non-staining gels which have been developed have the same limited life.
3. *Spikes*. Spikes are commonly in strip form in aluminium or stainless steel secured by stainless steel screws through lugs into the stone. They are difficult to use effectively and have been known to be used as permanent shuttering for nests! To be effective a ledge must be covered with enough rows of spiked metal to prevent the birds from settling. Less obvious are almost colourless cones of plastic which are fixed with a resin adhesive to ledges and even to sculpture. Because these are single spikes they are more versatile than the strips but a large quantity are still required to form a defence. Single spikes in the form of fine stainless steel rods are sometimes used as antennae around, for instance, figure sculpture in niches. These antennae are set into prepared drillings in the stone in an epoxy adhesive at approximately 45° to the face of the stone. As local defence these kind of spikes are effective and maintenance free.
4. *Low-voltage wires*. A small electric charge is run through wires stretched between insulators along ledges. Whilst working these systems are moderately successful but are liable to breakdown, even as a result of being covered, locally, with bird droppings. Maintenance can be frequent and costly.
5. The most effective of the anti-roost devices appears to be stretched and sprung stainless steel wire. Fine stainless steel wires are supplied to purpose-made lengths terminating with a tight coil at each end. The coil terminals are secured to stainless steel eyelets and maintain tension in the wire. Even when a number of wires are stretched in parallel formation along a wide ledge they are unobtrusive and relatively maintenance-free. Stainless steel antennae are also available (see the drawing on page 140).

Other types of intervention which do not rely on the modification of building detail include:

6. *Trapping*. A labour-intensive exercise involving basket traps and bait installed, normally, on flat roofs requires the trapped birds to be removed from the site at daily intervals. It provides only very local control and has attracted criticism from bird protection groups.
7. *Noise*. Intermittent loud reports from a tape recording can be transmitted over a speaker system to keep birds on the move and discourage roosting. This type of system is only really suitable in confined spaces such as grain stores.
8. *Shooting*. This is a local solution which is only applicable to remote sites and requires a resident custodian or official competent patrols. Shooting at buildings is to be discouraged!
9. *Predatory birds*. Pairs of kestrels or other birds of prey can be effective locally if they can be interested in taking up residence, but they will move on if the food source disappears. Some success has been reported on isolated sites with artificial birds mounted on flexible wands which cast a moving shadow on the ground.
10. More ambitious controls relate to attempts to feed pigeon populations with corn coated with sterility-inducing hormones. The chemosterilant Ornitrol (22,25 diazacholeatenol dihydrochloride) was found to be effective in inhibiting reproduction in pigeons for three months after treatment and remained up to 75% effective from four to six months after treatment. The major problem in the field is the nomadic habits of pigeon flocks.

No note on pigeon control would be complete without reference to a distinctly Italian solution, the *Piccioncelli con olive nere*, a dressed pigeon dish with veal stock, pepper, salt, white wine, brandy and olives!

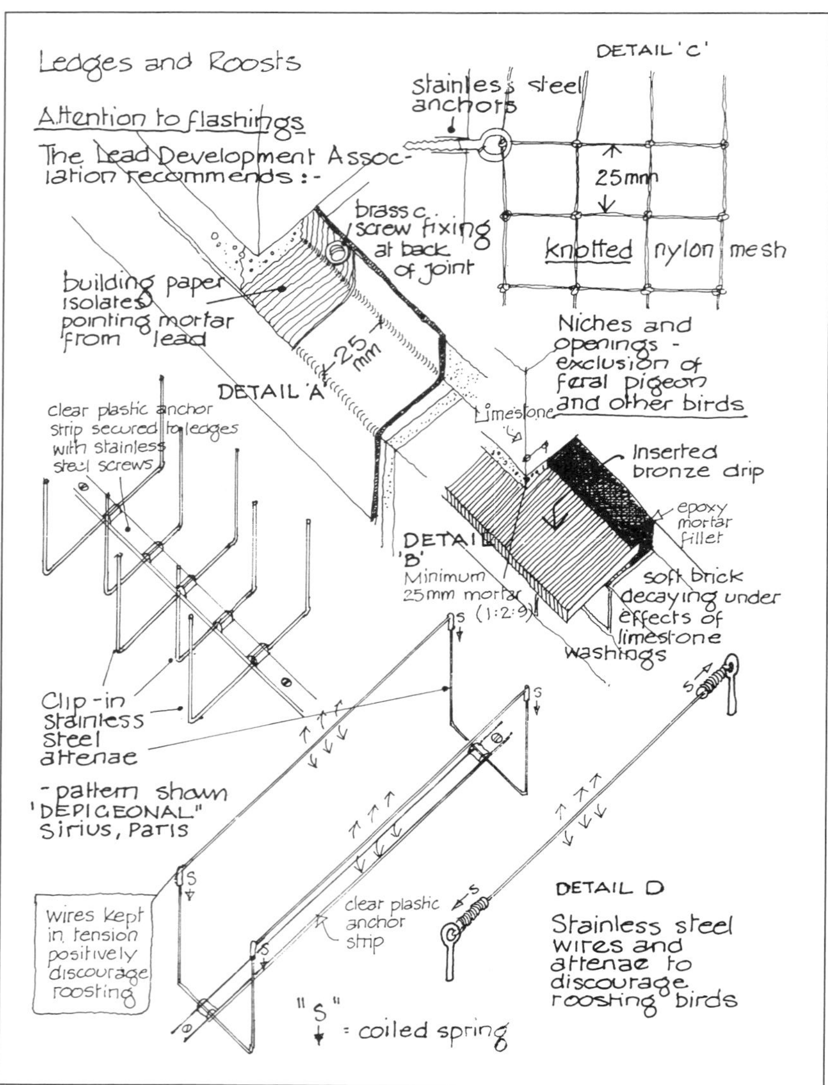

Removal of soluble salts from masonry

The capillary movement of moisture through masonry is often associated with salt deposition, which tends to be mainly concentrated at or close to the wall surfaces. The disruptive forces associated with the crystallization of these salts cause decay, usually seen as pitting, powdering and flaking of the masonry. Drying out of the walls associated with a damp-proofing treatment or the elimination of a groundwater source may also lead to an increase in the amount of salt at or near the wall surfaces. Deterioration may increase rather than diminish unless measures are taken to reduce the salt content of the masonry. Certain salts, particularly some chlorides, are hygroscopic and can take up moisture directly from the atmosphere. Dampness and deterioration may persist even after rising damp originating from the base of the wall has been stopped. In these circumstances the salts must be removed or at least substantially reduced from the masonry if deterioration is to be controlled.

Methods of removing salts

Two methods of removing some of the soluble salts from decaying masonry are the use of clay poultices and the use of a sand:lime sacrificial render. These systems have been used where the sources of soluble salts were rising damp, sea or estuarine sand in mortar, past flooding, storage of culinary salt, storage of gunpowder, storage of chemicals, human and animal urine, and caustic alkali cleaning and weed-killing treatments. The techniques are mainly suitable for large, plain areas of masonry or simple architectural detail. They should not be used (except in a limited way by trained conservators) on delicate, damaged surfaces of carving or sculptures, nor where the pre-wetting would create problems for plaster, painting or embedded wood or metal. Where poulticing or sacrificial rendering is considered to be appropriate it may need to be built into a long-term maintenance programme, perhaps every five or ten years, particularly if there is a persistent replenishment of soluble salts. In other situations, where the source of contamination has been removed, a single cycle of poultices may be sufficient to effect improvement.

Treatment of salt-contaminated masonry with a poultice

The form of deep washing of masonry which is usually described as desalination involves saturation and poulticing with an absorbent clay to try to reduce the level of potentially damaging soluble salts concentrated within the surface of decaying stone. To remove all soluble salts in a building is impossible, but a significant reduction in the outer 100 mm may have the effect of stabilizing a previously friable surface or may prepare the way for a consolidant whose curling process would be seriously inhibited by a high concentration of, say, sodium chloride. A further use of absorbent clay packs is as temporary plaster after the installation of a damp-proof course.

In principle the desalination technique is very simple. A wall is saturated for several days by spraying with mists of clean water, until wetting has occurred for the full, or a considerable, depth. During experimental work monitoring equipment is often set into the wall core. Plaster of Paris moisture gauges were used by the Building Research Establishment at the Salt Tower in the Tower of London in 1974.[7]

Fine sprays mounted on a boom delivering under 200 litres per hour are sufficient to feed six spray heads covering an area seven metres square. The setting up of the sprays should be designed to produce a consistent pattern of wetting. The wetting period is determined by construction of the wall and the porosity of the stone and mortar, but is likely to extend over three days and nights. Small areas may be persistently wetted from a back-pack sprayer, but this is labour intensive and tends to be less effective. In some situations it is sensible to carry out dry brushing before wetting. It is important to make sure loose material is removed from the site. During the wetting process temporary gutters are required to collect the run-off from the wall surfaces and to conduct it to a gully or run-off point well away from the treatment wall base and any other walls. Heavy-gauge polythene sheet, PVC guttering, timber battens and a siphon tube may be all that is necessary to provide an effective water catchment and drainage system. Sheeting should also be used to minimize splashing.

When the wetting process is complete the absorbent clay or diatomaceous earth (usually attapulgite or sepiolite clays, 50 mesh) is added to enough clean water to make a soft, sticky paste. Water must not be added to the clay or a lumpy, unworkable mix will be formed. The clay poultice can be mixed by hand or with a small mechanical mixer, depending on the quantity required. When free of lumps the poultice is plastered onto the wet treatment wall in a single layer 20–25 mm (up to 1 in) thick using a plasterer's float or broad trowel. A 50 kg bag of clay will cover approximately three square metres. In its freshly mixed state the clay has very good adhesion and can be levelled reasonably accurately, even by a relatively inexperienced person. An important part of the technique is the ironing on to ensure good contact at all points. To help the clay keep its bond for as long as possible a light-gauge galvanized wire mesh can be pressed into it and tacked carefully into joints with galvanized staples. Any springiness in the mesh can be reduced by localized cutting with wire snips and pressing the cut ends into the clay. In some situations, especially where the wall surface is heavily contoured as in core-work, the overall adhesion of the clay will be assisted by cutting strips of open weave hessian soaked in a runny slurry of attapulgite clay and pressing these into the poultice. These strips, approximately 75 mm (3 in) wide, may be used alone or with wire. Wire is essential on a large area of flat surface where the weight of the clay tends to induce pulling away from the wall.

When the treatment wall is fully plastered it must be protected from direct sun or rain or, if internal, from any heat source which will produce rapid drying. Externally a ventilated space can most easily be set up with a tarpaulin or reinforced plastic sheet as a tent.

As the poultice dries out it draws salt laden water from the masonry. Water evaporating from the clay face leaves behind salt crystals which are usually seen in the form of efflorescences on the clay or wire. Drying conditions and the thickness of the wall dictate the contact time, which varies considerably from a few days to weeks. One month is not unusual for drying out, during which the clay lightens in colour, cracks, shrinks and detaches from the wall. At this stage the staples should be withdrawn with pliers, and the bulk of the clay may be rolled up on its wire reinforcement. The spent clay should be put at once into plastic sacks or otherwise removed safely from the site. Small amounts of clay still adhering should be brushed off the wall with a stiff bristle brush. These sweepings must also be removed from the site.

The cycle of wetting and poulticing may need to be repeated several times to reduce the salts to an acceptable level. Salt sampling and analysis may need to be carried out to determine the levels present. Clay poultice desalination is a lengthy process but it does not require a lot of supervision, expensive equipment or highly skilled personnel. It is best scheduled in with other works on or near the site.

Clay poultice desalination has mostly been used on stone walling. On brickwork or rubble, where there are plenty of keys for the poultice, special care needs to be taken when brushing down to remove all traces of dry clay from the joints. Any masonry which has been subjected to extended periods of salt crystallization may well require pointing at the completion of the desalination treatment.

Treatment with a sacrificial render

Where it is not possible to remove excessive amounts of salts with the poulticing technique, the application of a porous sacrificial render may provide a more practical method of overcoming the problem. A porous render is applied to the wall and evaporation of moisture from the wall results in soluble salts being transferred from the masonry to the render. The render will deteriorate with time and may require renewal, but the masonry will be protected against continued decay. A sacrificial render can be used either to reduce the salt content of a wall where rising damp treatment will also be carried out, or it can be used to protect a wall against salt attack where rising damp cannot be prevented.

The wall is first wetted and a render of one part slaked and screened lime putty to four parts fine sand is applied at least 12 mm (½ in) thick to both sides of the wall, (if possible) to a height 50 mm (2 in) above the salt crystallization/evaporation zone. The render should not be overworked with a trowel as optimum moisture evaporation and salt transfer will be obtained when the render has an open texture and a rough finish to increase the surface area. A practical and visually pleasing way of achieving this is to scrape the surface down after rendering with the fine-toothed edge of a hacksaw blade. This should be carried out after the surface has begun to stiffen.

As salts transfer to the render and crystallize there, the render will begin to break down. Salt-contaminated render deposits at the base of a wall should be collected frequently. Where a contamination is severe, the application of only one render coat may be insufficient to reduce the salt context to a safe level and further treatment will be required. The remains of the first coat should be carefully removed, the wall re-wetted and the second coat applied.

Sacrificial sand:lime renders are a relatively slow method of masonry desalination. A period of several months may be required, depending on the level of salt and the amount of evaporation. Most success has been achieved on walls where rising damp was still present, before any damp proofing installation was carried out. The process is, however, inexpensive and easy to undertake. The method was developed in Australia where it has been used successfully on sandstone and brickwork.

Determining salt levels

If reasonable assessment is to be made of poulticing or sacrificial rendering, the level of salt within the masonry should be determined before, during and after a programme of work. Initially it may also be important to determine the types of salts and their hygroscopicity. The services of a laboratory will be required here. Samples should be taken at depths of 0–25 mm, 50–75 mm and 75–100 mm (0–1, 2–3 and 3–4 in), within the zone deterioration, which is usually about 900 mm (36 in) from ground level. After a clay poultice has been removed some drying and migration of salts will continue. Therefore the wall should be allowed to dry before further samples are taken for salt analysis.

References

1. Price, C.A., 'Industrial cooperation in the study of pollution effects', paper presented at the World Congress of the Heritage Trust in Toronto
2. Mansfield, T., 'Building cleaning and the stone cleaning industry', *Stone Industries*, April 1988
3. Lazzarini, L., Marchesini, L. and Asmus, J.E., 'Lasers for the cleaning of statuary: initial results and potentialities', *First International Symposium on the Deterioration of Building Stones*, La Rochelle, France, September 1972
4. BRS Digest 125, *Colourless treatments for masonry*, Building Research Station, January 1971
5. BS 3826, *Silicone-based water repellents for masonry*, British Standards Institution, 1969
6. BS 6477, *Water repellents for masonry surfaces*, British Standards Institution, 1984
7. Bowley, M.J., *Desalination of stone*, BRE Current Paper

Identifying soiling patterns

Figure 8.1 Soiling patterns indicate the nature of the stone. The limestone facade of St Margaret's, Westminster, in London exhibits clean parapets, cill and plinths. Wherever rain-washing is regular limestone is kept clean. Only the sheltered and semi-sheltered zones collect dirt

Figure 8.3 This limestone detail illustrates the two conditions very clearly. The rain-washed surfaces are roughened but sound and clean. The sheltered zones are crusted with dirt and the sulphate skin below is beginning to split, spall and blister. Maintenance washing could significantly overcome this problem in the sheltered zones

Figure 8.2 In some instances, as on the Old Palace retaining wall at Westminster, where there are repetitive elements, the light and dark contrasts have a strong architecture impact which is not always desirable. More importantly, the areas under soiling are the ones where acidic water sits in droplet form, reacting with the limestone to form a calcium sulphate skin

Figure 8.4 The soiling pattern in this illustration of a sandstone building in Leith (Scotland) is clearly different to that of Figure 8.1. In this case the most exposed features are the most heavily blackened

Figure 8.5 In contrast to Figure 8.2, repetitive elements on the sandstone of Lichfield Cathedral show reverse soiling. Cills, plinths and weatherings, the areas regularly washed by rain, are densely black, whilst the more sheltered zones remain clean

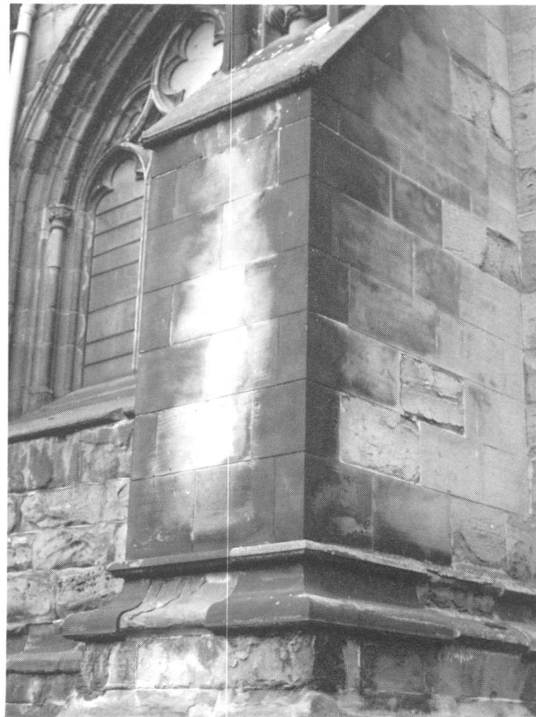

Figure 8.6 This detail illustrates the two conditions commonly to be found on external sandstone. Saturation zones, in this case the quoins of the buttress and the weatherings, are soiled in a way which clearly will not respond to water-washing. In these zones the dirt is bound to the surface with a siliceous matrix related to the etching of the stone by acidic rainfall. These are the same zones prone to suffer, through constant wetting and drying, from the decay phenomenon usually described as contour scaling. Failures of contour scaling related to pore blocking can be seen on the plinth weatherings. Although maintenance washing could not, by itself, avoid the development of contour scaling, there is some evidence that it could delay the problem if instituted from the early years of exposure and that it could, again if instituted early after exposure or mechanical or chemical cleaning, prevent the curious and unwelcome soiling patterns

Identifying soiling types

Soil types need to be properly identified and any associated deterioration accurately diagnosed before cleaning is advised. Figures 8.7 to 8.12 all involve soiled limestone, but each example requires a different treatment

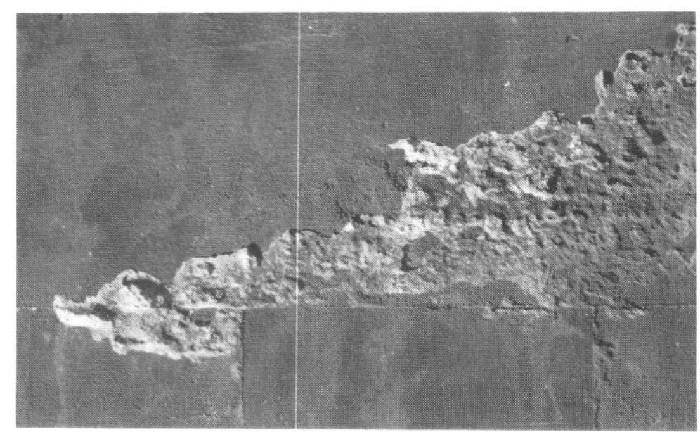

Figure 8.7 Carbon deposits form the bulk of the soiling but conceal a calcium sulphate skin which is being disrupted along a 'tide-mark' under a cornice. The cornice and coping need to be pointed to prevent further water migration, and the salt activity zone washed and poulticed with attapulgite clay packs after the wall has been washed with nebulous water sprays assisted by bristle brushing. A refinement would fill the decayed area with a lime:stonedust:casein sacrificial layer

Figure 8.8 The soiling and associated decay in this illustration is primarily affecting the brickwork but is in part caused by the presence and detailing of the limestone flush bands. Calcium carbonate and sulphate deposition in the pores of the brickwork bring about disruption and flaking as salt crystallisation develops. The increased surface area of the decaying brick provides ample key for wind- and rain-borne dirt. It must be acknowledged that any realistic dry abrasive cleaning will further increase the surface losses and that any saturation technique will further distribute soluble salts and increase, initially, the incidence of efflorescence. Heavy encrustation may be lightly dressed off with sharp chisels and hand-held carborundum blocks. Potassium hydroxide in CMC (see Figure 8.10) packs achieves the bulk of cleaning followed by warm water washing using lances at less then 150 psi. Whilst still wet, the areas affected by efflorescence are poulticed with clean water and attapulgite clay to draw out mobilised salts. When dry, the clay is lifted and dry brushed off. Lead drips must be inserted in the bottom bed joint of all flush limestone dressings

Figure 8.9 The limestone detail in this illustration is almost totally obscured by plate lichen, to the extent that it had been mistaken for limewash. It is not always necessary to remove such growths, even if there is some light etching of the surface from secreted acid, but since at this stage there is no possibility of seeing the stone or its condition removal is advisable. The area of stone exposed by the removal of a small section of lichen shows a split calcium sulphate skin. If this is typical the lichen could play a role in exacerbating local decay. Small, round-edged plastic and wood scrapers will remove most of the lichen, supplemented with orange sticks, and bristle or nylon toothbrushes. Wet scrubbing should be avoided. A flood spray application of a quaternary ammonium biocide followed after twelve hours by bristle brushing will remove tenacious areas of growth. A further inhibiting flood coat, applied to dry stone, will inhibit further growth and may become a maintenance treatment

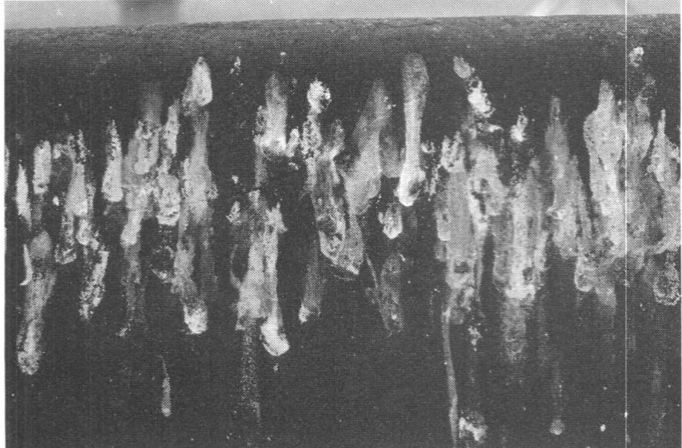

Figure 8.10 Dense, rather greasy soiling proved to be related to early linseed oil treatment (a ubiquitous water repellent/surface binder) which attracts particulate matter to it and inhibits natural rain-washing. Carbon deposits and especially soiling attributable to diesel emissions formed secondary deposits which were further soiled in some locations with bird excrement. Successful and safe removal of complex deposits of this kind inevitably involve more than one method. In this case a sequence of wood scrapers, non-ionic detergent and warm water used with bristle brushes was followed by potassium hydroxide in a carboxymethylcellulose pack and, finally, local areas of methylene dichloride poultice and efficient rinsing with clean water

Figure 8.11 The dark vertical staining is caused by rusting iron above the ashlar. Long-standing stains of this kind are not easily removed altogether but can usually be lightened satisfactorily by a poultice of clay (such as attapulgite or sepiolite) and sodium dithionite. The surface must be pre-wetted and several poultice applications may be needed before finally washing off. Of course, the source of staining should be treated to isolate it or removed before the cleaning process commences

Figure 8.12 The patchy appearance of this ashlar after washing was attributed to an earlier cleaning followed by the application of a silicone-based water repellent. The object of this application was apparently to encourage the wall to be self cleaning. Because the treatment had not been maintained and had begun to lose water-repellency unevenly, the new cleaning produced or enhanced a stain pattern. It is not wise to use water repellents for this purpose unless there is an assurance that regular retreatment (say 5–7 years) will take place

Feasibility studies for cleaning

Figure 8.13 For any but the most simple facade with an obvious soiling pattern some preliminary feasibility study including work on site as part of the diagnostic approach is highly desirable and may well be essential. Although valuable information may be gained by a cleaning demonstration such as the one shown in this illustration this must not be seen as a 'study' nor should any results obtained necessarily be regarded as typical. The clean area involves no real problems such as may be obtained at openings or in saturation zones

Figure 8.14 A carefully recorded feasibility clean of a piece of detail (top) which included oil, diesel soiling and paint and which showed (above) texture and mouldings unchanged in the process provided exactly the kind of information required for a detailed specification which required no speculation from contractors asked to submit competitive tenders

Figure 8.15 Feasibility studies should seek to anticipate all the problems which may be encountered during the main contract. These will include items on access, plant location and control of dust, water and noise. Left (above): shows window protection consisting of polyethylene sheets and heavy duty tape. Although cheap, during wet cleaning it may be confidently expected that this protection will peel off at frequent intervals risking water penetration and costly stoppages of the work. Left (below): shows alternative protection consisting of resin-bonded plywood templates set into tracery reveals in an improvised but effective gasket of pipe insulation. Although it was several times the cost of the sheet and tape, the study concluded that the template system was very much more effective and was likely to require no maintenance due to breakdown during the extent of the contract

Figure 8.16 The clean patches in this illustration are the result of trial cleaning with solvents and detergents in poultice media. Each patch has been placed on an area representative of the most difficult soiling problems and is referenced to a record sheet listing constituents, application method and conditions, contact periods and wash-off procedures. Results obtained in this manner are of real benefit in specifying and costing the work and reduce risks to the building

Washing

Figure 8.17 Removal of dirt from limestone by washing is traditional, often safe and often successful. Jets of water are played on the surface until the dirt is sufficiently softened to be removed by bristle or phosphor bronze wire brushes. Unfortunately, unless the building surface is very simple to clean, prolonged saturation can be involved in the process of removing substantial crusts of soil under projections or in detail, especially when the water jets are of the inefficient, large droplet type. The clean stone in the centre of the illustration responded to water spraying in five hours; the encrusted dirt in the detail required sixteen hours, during which time the building was subjected to considerable volumes of water

Figure 8.19 Unfortunately staining cannot be totally controlled by limiting the quantity of water, although this is a significant help. Staining shown in this illustration is random and was unpredictable, reflecting the surface condition and permeability of individual stones. Some staining, too, has already taken place during weathering. Light pre-wetting of the whole wall, to control absorbence, is advisable before concentrating water sprays on one horizontal lift. Much staining is encouraged by allowing soiled water to run down onto dry stones in the initial stages of cleaning

Figure 8.18 Other washing problems may be seen in the form of staining, especially of light coloured limestone and especially when the volume of water is left to do the work without any mechanical assistance in the form of brushing. Staining is usually the result of solubilised soiling being absorbed into some of the stones. As the wall dries out staining can become quite pronounced

Figure 8.20 Decayed stones, especially where small-scale detail is involved, are very vulnerable to washing with water sprays. Not only may water jets be responsible for mechanical damage, they will also mobilise soluble salts. Although the products of pollution, these salts may be performing a structural role in supporting critical flakes of weakened stone. On undercut, small-scale carving such as the example in the illustration, washing may actualy bring about the final destruction of some of the detail

Figure 8.21 The ultimate mechanical damage to stone by water is brought about by the use of high pressure water lances. Water lances used much in excess of 500 psi clean mechanically by cutting the surface; if the stone is already weak, or is characterised by soft, sandy beds as the limestone in this illustration, wholesale destruction may be brought about

Figure 8.23 At the British Museum in London, the whole of the main facade of limestone was cleared using low pressure (20–25 psi) water as a carrier for abrasive. Because so little repair was required, the whole operation was carried out from a mobile hydraulic platform (Cleanstone Ltd). In France, Thomann-Hanry use a similar access but enclose the cleaning platform on the end of the arm in a partial vacuum chamber, which 'sucks' itself to the surface of the facade. Within this chamber one or two operatives can work with low pressure dry abrasive guns to achieve safe dust-free cleaning with very low impact on the stone

Figure 8.22 Water lances operating at 20–25 psi with a small amount of fine abrasive are useful in cleaning simple ashlar. In this case the use of water is the vehicle for the abrasive, which distinguishes the technique totally from wet-grit blasting, where water serves only to contain dust generated by compressed air and abrasive

Figure 8.24 One of the most important washing developments of recent years has been the use of nebulous sprays. As the name implies, these nozzles are so designed to pass water through a fine brass gauze filter which atomises the water and delivers a wet mist through the nozzle. Nebulous water is easily caught by the wind and it is therefore necessary to place spray assemblies close to the wall surface and to screen the scaffold. There are many advantages to nebulous spraying. Dirt is softened progressively without cascades of water and the sprays can be mounted on straight booms, flexible bars or individual clusters just where they are most needed. A further refinement is to control the water by a pre-set timing device to deliver, for example, 8 seconds of water at 8 minute intervals. This 'intermittent' or 'pulse' washing is increasingly a feature of high quality washing

Abrasive cleaning

Figure 8.25 The simplest mechanical cleaning involves abrading or scraping a surface by hand. Even with care this must be acknowledged as to some extent destructive of the original surface. The most severe treatment, that of spinning off the surface with power tools and abrasive discs, should never be described as cleaning but as re-dressing. Removal of an oil-stained surface by the use of mason's drags or small blocks of carborundum lubricated with water may be appropriate in skilled hands if the staining or soiling cannot be removed safely by poulticing

Figure 8.26 Few cleaning methods have caused more damage or evoked so much criticism as the mechanical system popularly known as 'sand-blasting'. This illustration (above) shows the characteristic conditions of commercial dry blasting. The cleaning operative wears a helmet with a visor which is fed by an air line to maintain positive air pressure. The hose delivers air from a compressor, at pressures typically between 40 and 80 psi, and an abrasive which might be sand or a non-siliceous type such as copper slag. The abrasive spread is too wide to be selective and the dust generated after the first two minutes largely eliminates visibility

Figure 8.27 Even when the dust is contained by a 'wet-head' system the most serious problems remain. In this illustration (left) a water line is brought up to the nozzle and feeds a perforated ring ('water- shroud') clipped over the nozzle. By this means visibility is much improved and there may be some slight cushioning effect from the water, but the system is still crude and, in terms of slurry generated, very messy

Figure 8.28 On any surface other than the simplest and most robust, standard commercial sand or grit-blasting on the scale shown in Figures 8.26 and 8.27 should not be employed. In this illustration a reasonable clean of ashlar, columns and flat fascia can be seen at the top of the picture; but the composite capital, the moulded architraves and, above all, the sculpture have been excessively torn and pitted. Cleaning such detail by such crude means is impossible, and should never be attempted

Chemical cleaning

Figure 8.29 The chemical cleaning of sandstone is usually carried out with proprietary products containing hydrofluoric acid, orthophosphoric acid and surfactants. In less sophisticated forms hydrofluoric acid has been used as a cleaning agent since World War I, so that it has almost become a traditional cleaning material. Because it is extremely hazardous, even in many proprietary forms, to personnel and to building materials such as glass and some metals there is a strict code of practice governing its use. This illustration (above) shows the valuable crown glass of Holyrood Palace in Edinburgh prepared for cleaning. The glass has two coats of peelable latex, a marine ply template and heavy duty polyethylene masking. Because even acid vapour can etch glass, scaffold tubes must be capped and washed off regularly during the cleaning

Figure 8.30 Holyrood Palace after cleaning and removal of temporary protection (left). The deep brown staining of some of the stones in the fluted pilasters has been enhanced by the action of the acid on the iron constituents of the stone. This effect may be caused by reaction with the acid, but it is more likely that it was already present to some degree and can often be detected on the soiled building by a darker soiling pattern

Figure 8.31 The dark coloured parapet on the Corn Exchange in Leith is typical of saturation zone staining. Water can migrate freely through free-standing features such as this, carrying soluble, staining material to the surface. Often this goes undetected until cleaning, when blame is unfairly placed on the contractor or the cleaning material

Figure 8.32 Other situations, where the cleaning material is clearly inappropriate, can be demonstrated by this illustration (above) of staining up to the party wall line on a sandstone terrace. In this case the colour of the entire unit within the facade has been changed from a cream colour to a rich orange-brown in the course of removing dirt with a proprietary hydrofluoric acid cleaner

Figure 8.33 Successful cleaning with hydrofluoric acid based cleaners or any other chemical depends on a proper diagnosis of the soil type, identification of the stone/s, detailed specification based on site and laboratory trials, competent, experienced operatives and adequate supervision. In this illustration (left) the operative is properly dressed in full protective clothing, including face and hands. The water lance, a flat 15° v-jet operating at 500 psi, is being used to remove a cleaning agent after a dwell time of five minutes. The same lance is used to pre-wet the wall before application of the cleaning agent to avoid the risk of dry stones or joints absorbing cleaning material

Figure 8.34 Failure to remove certain cleaning agents successfully can result in disfigurement or damage, or both. This illustration shows staining and efflorescence resulting from residues of sodium hydroxide left in limestone detail. Salt crystallisation damage is likely as wetting and drying cycles promote the distribution growth of sodium salts

Figure 8.35 Failure to remove hydrofluoric acid will result in the formation of colloidal silica bound to the surface of the stone. This illustration shows carefully applied hydrofluoric acid formulation permanently bound to sandstone after being left for over twelve hours instead of 5–15 minutes. This disfigurement could only be removed by spinning, blasting or otherwise redressing the masonry to remove the outer 2 mm

Figure 8.36 Successful cleaning with proprietary chemical products is quite feasible, but must be based on proper investigation and diagnosis of the cleaning problem, and not on a 'hit-or-miss' basis influenced by a particular range of products available. In general, more applications of material diluted down from the supplier's recommendations will achieve a better standard of cleaning. Very dilute hydrofluoric acid formulation was used to clean the flush banded brick and stone of St Pancras Station, London, with excellent results

Figure 8.37 Chemical cleaning agents are increasingly used in poultice form to effect safe, successful cleaning. This sequence shows a poultice cleaning of a limestone facade in Londonderry, Northern Ireland, using a formulation of the 'Mora' type, based on EDTA with sodium and ammonium bicarbonate in a carboxymethylcellulose (CMC) body. The heavily stained facade is wetted up, poulticed and covered in plastic film for periods which may range from seven to 24 hours. When the staining has been mobilised and has migrated into the poultice the material is removed with wooden scrapers into bins and any residue removed with low pressure water lances. The final illustration of the sequence shows a very successful level of clean with no staining and no harmful disfiguring by-products

9

Surface treatments

David Honeyborne, John Ashurst, Clifford Price and Keith Ross

Introduction

> And as touching the stone of this cuntre, that shuld be for the jambes of your doores and windowes of your seid chapell, I dare not take upon me to sett no more therof upon your werkes, hit freteth and fareth so foule with himself, that, had I not ordained lynnessde oyle to bed hit with, hit wolde not have endured, ne plesed youre Highnesse. Wherefore I have purveyed xiij tons tight of Cane stone, for to spede youre werkes withall.

There is, of course, nothing new in the decay of building stones. The matter was as much of a concern to Roman builders as to Wren, and as much to us as to Henry V's Chief Mason writing his report on the building works at Calais in 1421, as recorded above. Writing in 1929, E.G. Warland gave the following summary on the subject of stone preservatives:

> *Preservatives* may be grouped under three headings – oils, wax, or solutions giving rise to the formation of insoluble salts.
>
> 1. Boiled oil has been used extensively, but its use is accompanied by discolouration of the face of the stone.
> 2. Paraffin wax is an effective preservative, especially if driven into the stone by heat, but this presents a difficulty not easily overcome in practice.
> 3. Those preservatives which come under the remaining heading are solutions which are intended to act upon the carbonate of lime making insoluble compounds, such as silicate of soda and fluosilicic acid and its salts. These silicon derivatives certainly have some value if administered correctly and at the right time.

Little had changed in several centuries because oil was still the most commonly used 'preservative' and even now is used in some rare instances. As we now know, oil can be the most difficult material to remove from old stonework, has in some instances contributed to decay and has almost always been disfiguring in some way. However, it must be remembered that ancient coatings may have been applied as a ground for paint, which is usually the case where they are found on sculpture or architectural detail. These coatings may be lime alone, lime and cheese or lime and animal fat, or may be more sophisticated such as one of the 'secrets' of Timoteo Rossello, mixing colophony, honey, wax and mutton tallow.[2] Investigation of old surfaces must always take this possibility into account. Such coatings are normally distinguishable from later applications whose role was evidently to arrest decay.

The caution we have learnt from the lesson of applied 'preservatives' must be exercised in any other treatment we are considering; we must always think in terms of side-effects and long-term effects and, if possible, what we use as a treatment must be reversible. The dilemma for the conservator comes when the only hope for a stone 'patient' is a non-reversible treatment. In this situation the conservator must always take a second opinion, must be convinced that there are no possible alternatives, and must be prepared for criticism.

Our objective in applying surface treatments must be to 'enhance durability', but not in a speculative or experimental manner. 'Medicine' should be a last resort, when all other sensible remedial and protective work has been carried out and still a genuinely unacceptable rate of decay continues. This situation and condition is not always well defined and is usually the subject of some controversy; but if we look first to good housekeeping in the form of sensible and thoughtful maintenance and not too soon to advanced technology to get our stones out of trouble we shall not make many mistakes and will not be guilty of creating worse conditions and more serious maintenance problems than we found.

In the first part of this chapter David Honeyborne describes the ways in which stone surfaces are treated to try to extend their life. As an ever-increasing number of proprietary products and pseudo-scientific trade literature assails us it is increasingly important to have some basic understanding of decay mechanisms and treatments.

J.A.

Part 1 Surface treatments in general

David Honeyborne

When all decay-inducing defects in a stone building have been repaired and the best possible maintenance procedures are being regularly carried out deterioration of the stone and other exposed building materials will still inevitably occur. This is a consequence of nature's subservience to the Second Law of Thermodynamics. Fortunately the rate of deterioration is often imperceptible over the span of a human lifetime. Therefore human beings do not become so discouraged that they give up fighting the rearguard action that must be the task of every conservator.

Where the rate of deterioration is more apparent, those caring for a stone building or piece of sculpture often wish to apply some proprietary product to the surface of the stone in a desperate attempt to arrest or at least slow down the change. Such surface treatments have sometimes proved to be beneficial, but sometimes they are positively harmful to the stone and are often quite ineffective. This chapter reviews surface applications that can usefully be made to building and decorative stone in existing buildings.

While it is possible to formulate general rules that might reasonably be expected to remain valid for many years to come, guidance at a more detailed level might become outdated quite quickly as new products are developed. To overcome this problem the following important conservation organizations in Italy have agreed to collaborate in producing progress reports on the subject[1].

The National Research Council Centres for the Study of the Causes of Deterioration and of the Methods of Conservation of Works of Art (CNR Centro di Studio delle Cause de Deperimento e Metodi Conservazione delle Opere d'Arte) in Rome, Florence and Milan.

The Central Institute for Restoration (Istituto Centrale del Restauro) in Rome.

The International Centre for Conservation (ICCROM) in Rome.

Up-to-date information may be sought from ICCROM, 13 via di San Michele, 00153 Rome, Italy.

Water repellents

When masonry walls are unusually thin or unusually permeable, rainwater will sometimes penetrate the wall and cause staining of and/or damage by salt crystallization to interior surfaces. When the building is near the sea and sea-salt is carried to it by strong winds the damage can be particularly severe. If this kind of penetration occurs even after full attention has been paid to the maintenance of pointing, gutters, flashings and other details that are essential to ensure longevity for the building, there is a case for using some colourless water repellent treatment on those parts of the building where water is entering the structure. This can lead to a reduction in the rate of decay, if not a cure. It is essential that any such treatment should be applied with the aim of preventing water *from entering* the structure. There are many cases on record of the failure of attempts to prevent further damage from occurring by treating already decaying areas of stonework with some colourless water repellent. This approach often makes matters worse.

Several types of water repellent have been tried for preventing or reducing the entry of water into stonework. Most notable are waxes and silicones applied as solutions in an appropriate organic solvent. It is usually considered essential that the stonework should be dry at the time of application. In some ways waxes present more problems than silicones. It is often difficult to obtain adequate penetration if the wax solution is too concentrated. On the other hand the use of very dilute wax solutions can result in a failure to achieve adequate repellency. Moreover, even if adequate repellency is achieved, the wax-treated wall tends to become discoloured in course of time, either because the wax becomes yellow as it is chemically changed by the action of sunlight or because the waxy surface picks up more air-borne dirt than an untreated surface. These effects are usually avoided by the use of silicone solutions in organic solvents though even with this system erratic results can be obtained.

Silicone-based repellents seem to be more effective on sandstones and other siliceous stones than on limestones. However, unpublished work at the Building Research Establishment at Watford, England, indicates that the effectiveness of such treatments depends very much on the presence or absence of pore water lying several millimetres below the relatively dry surface. Treatment after a pre-wetting and partial drying is said to give good repellency even with limestone. The water resists an unduly deep penetration of the silicone solution. The water-repellent barrier is therefore deposited in a concentrated form in the outer layer of stone and in the masonry joints[2]. After drying, a second treatment without a water barrier is said to produce an enhanced effect. In the absence of an initial water barrier, the resulting water repellency is sometimes poorly developed or evanescent. The writer does not know of any confirmation of this effect in full-scale treatments. Naturally those applying water repellent treatments in attempts to prevent damaging water penetration are normally unwilling to leave a substantial area untreated to enable fair comparisons to be made.

Once water repellency has been established by a silicone treatment the treated areas tend to remain dry-looking for a long time and the darkening associated with wax-based treatments does not occur. However, it is important that treatments are applied to all stonework between natural projections in the building. Otherwise the demarcation line between treated and untreated areas may become apparent soon after treatment, and more apparent as time goes on because the two areas will differ for quite a long time in their tendencies to pick up dirt, even though the *surface* repellence tends to deteriorate relatively quickly with most formulations. Retreatment is feasible.

A short discussion of silicone chemistry as applicable to stonework conservation is given later in this chapter. More details and many references have been given by Amoro and Fassina[3] and monographs on the subject have been written by Meals and Lewis[4] and by Freeman.[5]

A more recent approach to the problem of making sandstones water repellent involves the use of chemicals called perfluoro-polyethers. One of these materials, which has a molecular weight in the range 6000 to 7000 and is applied at a rate of $30 g/m^2$ in the solvent trichloro-trifluoro-ethane, is reported[6] to be particularly effective and causes no discoloration of the substrate.

Water repellents as preservatives?

Because water plays an essential part in the main processes of stone decay, it is tempting to believe that the application of a water repellent treatment to a decaying stone face will arrest the degradation processes. Unfortunately, the preliminary results often look very promising and this has led people to try this type of treatment on stonework of historical importance without waiting for the results of long-term trials on unimportant substrates. In fact, in the long term, wax-based treatments will give rise to often unacceptable discoloration, even in rural areas. Crystallizing salts will break through the treated surface or frost will cause a whole surface to break away. The final effects can be worse than those that would result from doing nothing. Schaffer[7] cites an example of stonework that was in a serious state of decay within a few months of being given a wax-based surface treatment. While silicone-based water repellents are unlikely to cause the same kind of discoloration when used in this way, the other consequences of their use are likely to be unsatisfactory. Clarke and Ashurst[6] reported the results of a comprehensive large-scale experiment which included 68 examples of the use of silicone-based water repellents on a large range of types of stone exposed under various conditions. Computations based on their report show that 92.6% of these treatments resulted in no change in or a worsening of the rate of decay; 75.4% resulted in no change in or a worsening of the appearance of the stonework and, of the cases that showed a reduction in the rate of decay, or an improvement in appearance, none showed a significant change. It thus appears that attempts to use colourless water repellents as stone preservatives are a waste of money. There is no reason to believe that the discovery of the value of perfluoro-polyethers as water repellents will lead to any modification of these conclusions.

Consolidants as preservatives?

It could reasonably be argued that since decay processes clearly weaken stonework, particularly near exposed surfaces, any kind of water-repellent treatment should be preceded by a treatment that would help to restore strength to the affected area and possibly give sound regions better strength to resist the weathering agencies. In fact, Clarke and Ashurst[6] included lime water and also silicon ester in their trials for this purpose. Lime water is a very dilute solution of calcium hydroxide which, on absorbing carbon dioxide gas from the atmosphere, is converted to calcium carbonate, the main component of limestone. The idea is that the calcium carbonate formed from the lime water will crystallize in critical positions in a limestone and strengthen it. Since calcium hydroxide has a low solubility, many coatings of lime water will always be necessary to achieve much in the way of strengthening, even if the crystals form at the most favourable positions in the stone. There is no value in applying lime water to a sandstone. Clarke and Ashurst reported[6] that 57% of the lime water treatments resulted in no change or in a worsening of the decay, and that all the treatments resulted in a worsening of the appearance of the stonework. In 43% of cases the treatment was successful in slowing decay, but none showed an improvement of any practical significance.

Silicon ester is a chemical product that is applied to stone in an alcoholic solution with the intention of hardening it. If some liquid water or water vapour is present, the silicon ester decomposes as the alcohol evaporates and a jelly-like material, silica gel, is developed which forms hard silica as it gradually loses water. Because silica is the main component of sandstones a treatment with silicon ester may seem more appropriately applied to sandstones than to limestones. However, Clarke and Ashurst's experiments[6] provide little evidence for this. Their results for silicon ester on all substrates show that 84.5% of all treatments resulted in no change or in a worsening in the rate of decay and 73.1% of the treatments resulted in no change or in a worsening of the appearance of the stonework. In trials involving only sandstone substrates 77.8% of treatments had no effect on the rate of decay and 100% had no effect on the appearance. The success in reducing the rate of decay was not of practical significance and in every case the effect on appearance was negative compared with the control panels.

A second reason sometimes put forward for the use of silicon ester on stonework is that, as a pretreatment, it will help a following silicone treatment to take better on limestone. Clarke and Ashurst's trials[6] were not intended to assess the efficacies of water-repellent treatments. However, of those treatments in their trials that involved the application of both silicon ester and a silicone to a limestone, 94.1% showed no improvement or possibly an acceleration in the rate of decay and 70.6% showed no change in or a worsening of appearance. Whether or not the silicon ester improves the effectiveness of the water-repellent treatment, it does not act as, or help the water repellent to act as, a preservative in these circumstances.

Is stone preservation by surface application impossible?

As long ago as 1932, Schaffer,[7] referring to failures of the stone 'preservatives' of that period, wrote:

> The properties demanded of a perfect stone preservative are many and conflicting. For instance, a waterproofing agent is required to prevent penetration of moisture, but, at the same time, it should allow water which has gained access at some unprotected point to escape. A common cause of failure is that, even in porous materials, and under the most favourable conditions, the preservative penetrates only to a relatively small depth and a surface skin is formed which differs in physical properties from the underlying material; dangerous stresses are likely to be set up and ultimately the skin may flake off. The penetration of the preservative solution can only take place when the stone is dry ... and in cases where the deposition of solids depends on the evaporation of a solvent, the process of drying causes much of the dissolved substances to be drawn back to the surface. Another source of danger is that certain forms of treatment introduce soluble salts as by-products of the reactions involved; these salts may be extremely deleterious.

Forty years later Schaffer's second and third points (the importance of deep penetration and the need to ensure that a solvent carrying a preservative material did not withdraw the material while evaporating) were no doubt taken into account when Clarke and Ashurst[6] recommended in 1972 that 'a study of deep penetration of stonework with materials likely to avert or compensate for the harmful effects of time and the environment' should be carried out. This idea is now widely accepted. Thus Price[8], writing in 1975 about the failures encountered by Clarke and Ashurst, has said:

> There are two main reasons for this. Firstly, water can invariably get behind the treated layer, either by passing through it in the vapour phase or by the absorption of rain or ground water at some unprotected point. This water evaporates from behind the water-repellent layer and any salts in the solution crystallize there. This can lead to spalling of the treated surface. Secondly, the thermal and moisture movements of the thin surface layer may be sufficiently different from those of the underlying stone to generate shear stresses that eventually cause failure. These effects would be reduced if the treated layer were sufficiently thick. The critical thickness is unknown but current research ... is aimed at impregnating stonework with a suitable material to a depth of at least 25 mm.

An impregnation treatment should serve both to consolidate friable stone and to prevent further deterioration caused by salt crystallization, either by making the salts inaccessible to water or by making the stone more resistant to crystallization damage. Increased resistance to crystallization damage could be achieved by an increase in the stone's tensile strength or by a modification of its pore structure. In order to achieve adequate penetration the treatment should have a high surface tension, a low contact angle and a very low viscosity at the time of application.

Schaffer's fourth point (that some treatments introduce soluble salts as by-products of the reactions involved) is certainly well recognized in authentic conservation work. Rossi-Doria, Tabasso, Torraca *et al.*[1] give a list of consolidants that they consider to be unsuitable for use on stonework, mainly because they give rise to soluble salts as by-products. This list and a list of materials they refer to as 'advisable consolidants' are presented in *Table 9.1*.

Is stone preservation by surface applications impossible? Probably not, if a suitable material can be found that will achieve adequately deep impregnation, will form a barrier against water movement but not against water vapour, and will not introduce soluble salts into the stonework either directly or as a reaction product. Available materials that are likely to meet these requirements are considered below.

Table 9.1 Consolidants for stone masonry

Recommended by Rossi-Doria et al.[a]	*Not recommended by Rossi-Doria et al.*[a]
Ethyl silicates	Sodium or potassium silicates[b]
Alkyl-trialkoxy-silanes	Sodium and potassium aluminates[b]
Mixtures of the above	Zinc or magnesium fluorosilicates[c]
Alkyl-aryl-polysiloxanes[d]	Epoxy resins[e]
Acrylic resins	
Barium hydrate (baryta)	

[a] Rossi-Doria, Tabasso, Torraca *et al.*[1]
[b] Because they give rise to soluble salts as by-products.
[c] Because they have poor penetration and give rise to soluble salts, mainly as a result of impurities.
[d] Either totally or partially polymerized.
[e] Because they penetrate poorly if they are not diluted with a solvent and block the surface pores. They also form shiny films which flake and turn yellow in time. Drawbacks substantially reduced if diluted with solvent, particularly with applications on very porous stone.

Conservation of stonework by consolidants

The first four recommended groups of consolidants in *Table 9.1* are chemical products that are related to one another and to the 'silicon ester' used by Clarke and Ashurst[6] in their stone preservation experiments. All are compounds of silicon, carbon, hydrogen and oxygen, yet each plays a different role in attempts to preserve stone. It is virtually impossible to provide any satisfying explanation of their functions and potential without understanding a certain amount of structural organic chemistry. We will start with the group that is simplest in terms of molecular structure.

Ethyl silicates

There are many ethyl silicates, but the one that has been of importance in stone conservation is more strictly called tetra-ethoxysilane. Its molecular structure is shown in *Figure 9.1(a)*. In this figure the short straight lines are used to represent chemical bonds and the symbol 'R' is used to represent the group of atoms C_2H_5–, which is usually called the 'ethyl radical'. When this ethyl radical is combined with one oxygen atom to form C_2H_50–, it is known as an ethoxy radical, hence the name tetra-*ethoxy*-silane. The simpler radical, CH_3–, is known as the methyl radical, and if the ethyl radicals in *Figure 9.1(a)* were replaced by methyl radicals as shown in *Figure 9.1(b)* the result would be known as tetra-*methoxy*-silane.

When tetra-ethoxy-silane has been used in stone conservation it has usually been fed to dry, or at least surface-dry, stone. If some water is present, either as a liquid or a vapour, the tetra-ethoxy-silane begins to decompose producing alcohol, C_2H_5OH (written as R–OH in *Figure 9.1(c)* since R– is C_2H_5– in that instance). The new product is called tetra-hydroxy-silane. This is unstable and each hydroxyl (–OH) radical will react if possible with an unchanged ethoxy radical or with another hydroxyl radical to form an –Si–O–Si– link and alcohol or water, respectively, as shown in *Figure 9.2(a)* or *(b)*. In either case the final solid product is silica, the crystals of which consist of a three-dimensional lattice of silicon and oxygen atoms in the ratio of 1 to 2. (Hence the common formula for silica is SiO_2.) This is the main constituent of sandstones. In the intermediate stages of these reactions, when the solid product is known as silica gel, a considerable number of water molecules are physically held in the silicon–oxygen lattice. The same solid product would have been obtained if the starting material had been tetra-methoxy-silane, but in this case the by-product would have been methyl alcohol rather than ethyl alcohol.

Amoroso and Pancella have shown that the compactness of the silica gel formed (and, by implication, the eventual binding power of the silica) is at its best if the reaction takes place very slowly as it would in dry stone in an atmosphere of low relative humidity. In practice, a very slow reaction might lead to an unacceptable loss of impregnating material by evaporation.

The product known as silicon ester differs from tetra-ethoxy-silane because some partial formation of a silica network has already been allowed to occur. The material is described as partially polymerized. It is fed to stonework in the form of a solution in alcohol, which must evaporate before hydrolysis and polymerization can take place.

Figure 9.1 Structural chemistry of an ethyl silicate

Because of the considerable differences in the thermal expansion coefficients of silica (the main constituent of sandstones) and calcite (the main constituent of limestone) ethyl silicates seem far more likely to consolidate sandstones effectively than limestones. In fact, chemical manufacturers of products of this kind now normally claim that they act only as sandstone consolidators (see for example reference 9).

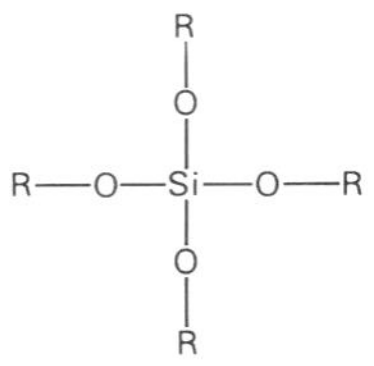

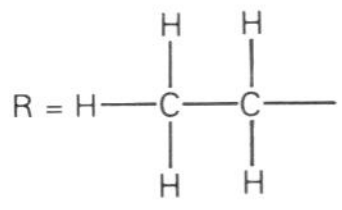

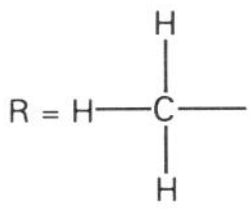

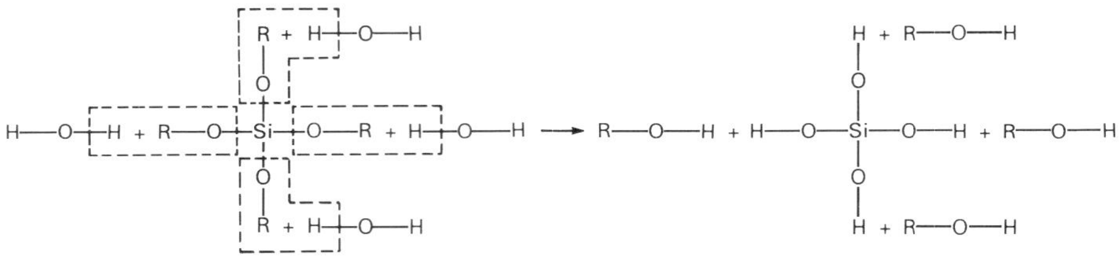

Alkyl-trialkoxy-silanes

The general structure of alkyl-trialkoxy-silanes is shown in *Figure 9.3(a)*, where R_1 and R_2 could independently be a methyl (CH_3-), an ethyl (C_2H_5-) or a propyl (C_3H_7-) radical, etc. The simplest member of this family would be methyl-trimethoxy-silane, the structure of which is shown in *Figure 9.3(b)*. Tetra-ethoxy-silane reacts with water

(a) By reaction between tetra-*hydroxy*-silane molecules. The dashed lines indicate where chemical bonds are broken.

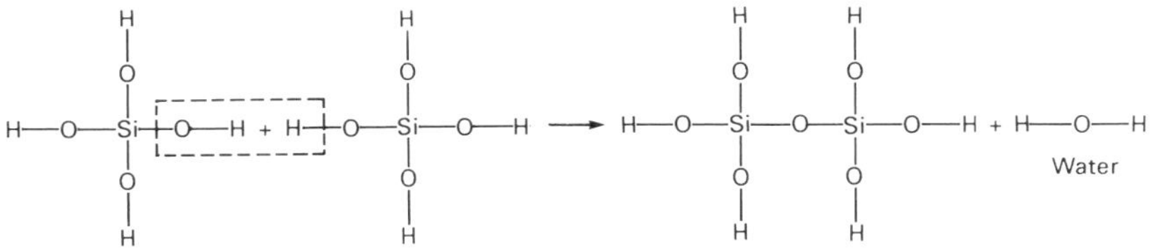

H—O—Si—O—H + H—O—Si—O—H → H—O—Si—O—Si—O—H + H—O—H
Water

Each stage reduces the proportion of hydrogen and oxygen relative to silicon until no more hydrogen is left and the silicon:oxygen ratio is 1:2 in terms of atoms. When dry the final product is silica dioxide.

(b) By reaction between tetra-*hydroxy*-silane molecules and remaining molecules derived from tetra-ethoxy-silane (for example, dihydroxy-diethoxy-silane).

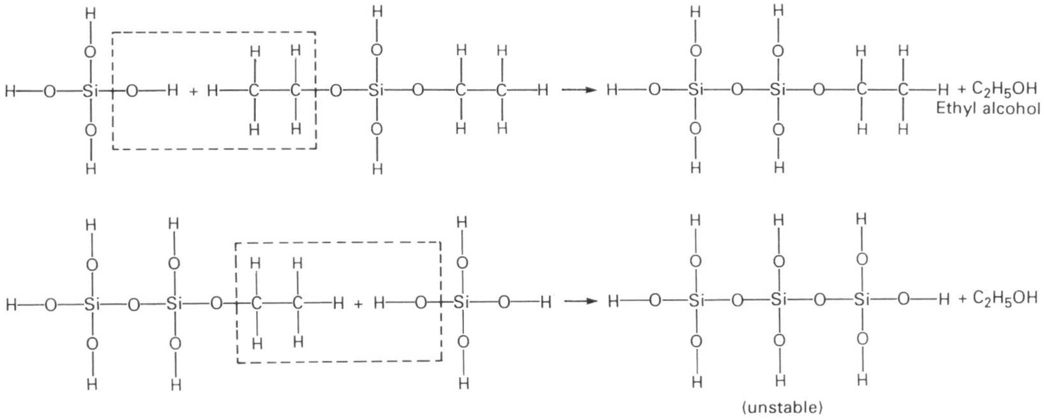

H—O—Si—O—H + H—C—C—O—Si—O—C—C—H → H—O—Si—O—Si—O—C—C—H + C_2H_5OH
Ethyl alcohol

H—O—Si—O—Si—O—C—C—H + H—O—Si—O—H → H—O—Si—O—Si—O—Si—O—H + C_2H_5OH
(unstable)

These and many other similar chemical reactions lead to reductions in the numbers of carbon, hydrogen and oxygen atoms present, relative to the number of silicon atoms, until nothing is left but silicon and oxygen atoms in the ratio of 1:2. This is silica.

Figure 9.2 Polymerization of tetra-hydroxy-silane

to form a network of silicon and oxygen atoms (silica). Methyl-triethoxy-silane or methyl-trimethoxy-silane also reacts with water to form a network of silicon and oxygen atoms. However, each silicon atom has one methyl radical attached to it and only three oxygen atoms. Because of the presence of the methyl radicals this material would have the property of water repellence at some sacrifice of consolidating power. An indication of the way the hydrolysis and polymerization reactions proceed is given in *Figure 9.3(c)*.

A material with these characteristics has considerable potential for use as a conservation treatment for stonework if it can penetrate the stone sufficiently deeply and in a satisfactory concentration. Conservators have tried several techniques to achieve this. The application of a silane on its own to dry stonework can result in deep penetration but water

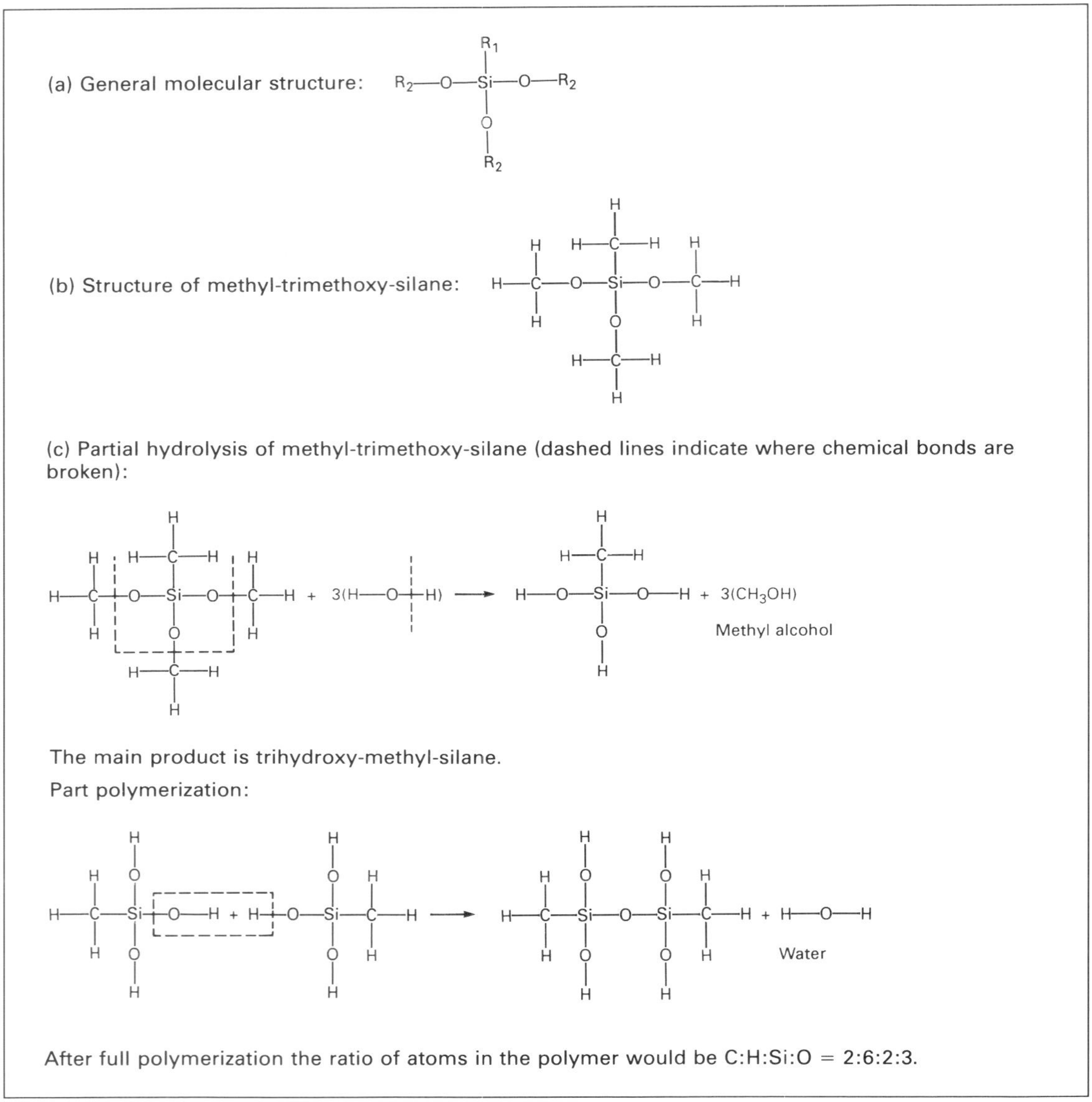

(a) General molecular structure: $R_2—O—Si(R_1)(O—R_2)—O—R_2$

(b) Structure of methyl-trimethoxy-silane: $CH_3—Si(OCH_3)_3$

(c) Partial hydrolysis of methyl-trimethoxy-silane (dashed lines indicate where chemical bonds are broken):

$CH_3Si(OCH_3)_3$ + 3(H—O—H) ⟶ $CH_3Si(OH)_3$ + $3(CH_3OH)$
Methyl alcohol

The main product is trihydroxy-methyl-silane.

Part polymerization:

$CH_3Si(OH)_2—OH$ + $H—O—Si(OH)_2CH_3$ ⟶ $CH_3Si(OH)_2—O—Si(OH)_2CH_3$ + H—O—H
Water

After full polymerization the ratio of atoms in the polymer would be C:H:Si:O = 2:6:2:3.

Figure 9.3 Structural chemistry of alkyl-trialkoxy-silanes

is needed for the hydrolysis. To wait for moisture in the atmosphere to achieve hydrolysis would result in loss of most of the silane by evaporation. On the other hand, if the stonework is not dry, hydrolysis will take place but the resultant resin might not be deposited in an advantageous position. In the treatment of objects housed in museums or other buildings such as churches, it has been found to be useful to add acrylic resins to the uncatalysed silane. The chemical significance of this is not entirely clear but it allows the conservator a long working time to deal with difficult jobs involving, for example, much surface readjustment of small pieces of stone that have become displaced by the decay process. It also allows for solvent cleaning of the surface. Solvent cleaning must be completed before the resin hardens, otherwise micro air-abrasive cleaning will be necessary.

Where consolidation is to be the last operation on stonework there is much to be said for using a *catalysed* silane system. In such systems water must be available from the start and additional substances must be added to make the silane and water miscible. Ethyl alcohol has been used for this purpose when caustic potash is used as a catalyst[10], and the rate of the reaction can be controlled by adjusting the amount of caustic potash used. This kind of system offers advantages for the treatment of external stonework, where conditions cannot be so well controlled as they can be in a museum laboratory or even in a church. However, one disadvantage is that the initial alcohol content can be as high as 38%. The alcohol takes no part in the reaction so it represents a severe dilution of the consolidant.

A later system which was developed at the Building Research Establishment and tried in Britain at a number of sites seemed to offer much greater advantages.[11] In this system, water sufficient for the hydrolysis is added to the alkyl-alkoxy-silane and the two liquids are rendered miscible by the addition of a very small quantity of acid. An organo-metallic catalyst is also added. The system is covered by a British Patent. The viscosity of the system remains low until a certain induction period has elapsed. After that it begins to rise rapidly as hydrolysis and polymerization take place quickly under the influence of the catalyst. This sequence reduces evaporation loss to a minimum and 'freezes' the advancing liquid so that it does not spread too far. The length of the induction period is controlled by selecting the appropriate initial composition. The system has been marketed under the trade name of Brethane since 1984. It is available only to licensed applicators who have successfully completed a two-day period of instruction.

Disadvantages of silane-based systems

The most important disadvantage of catalysed alkyl-alkoxy-silane systems is that once stonework has been treated and the silane has become hydrolysed and apparently polymerized there is a risk that any early retreatment with a fresh silane-based preservative will cause a previous immobile treatment to swell. This can be accompanied by such pressure that stone surfaces could suffer some disruption. For this reason conservators carrying out prolonged work on an object requiring more than one impregnation do not like to use silane systems. There is, however, reason to believe that polymerization continues for some time after the initial set of a catalysed silane system and it seems likely that a completely polymerized system would not swell in this way. Further investigation is needed.

In company with most other stone preservative systems, the residue left in the stonework after hydrolysis and polymerization is just a fraction of the amount of polymer absorbed by the stonework. *Table 9.2* shows the fraction by weight for four relatively simple alkyl-alkoxy-silanes. The best retention is obtained with trimethoxy-silanes. Unfortunately these evolve methyl alcohol during the curing process and this is poisonous. Greater retention could be obtained by increasing the size of the alkyl radical but various difficulties then arise, either because the raw material is prohibitively expensive or the substituted radical confers less advantageous properties on the resulting preservative. For example, a phenyl (C_6H_5-) radical in an aryl-alkoxy-silane confers flexibility on a polymer rather than water repellence. In any event, the proportion of solid retained will be diminished by the extent to which any of the preservatives has been diluted with a solvent.

Table 9.2 Theoretical maximum pore filling by some alkoxy-silanes

Preservative	*Theoretical proportion retained (%)**
Methyl-triethoxy-silane	37.6
Ethyl-triethoxy-silane	42.2
Methyl-trimethoxy-silane	49.3
Ethyl-trimethoxy-silane	54.3
Phenyl-trimethoxy-silane	62.6

* These figures are only a guide because in calculating them it was assumed that the densities of the preservative and the polymerized product were equal.

Because methyl alcohol is poisonous, all consolidation systems using an alkyl-methoxy-silane should be carried out under very well ventilated conditions.

Aryl-alkyl-polysiloxanes (partially or totally polymerized)

The fourth group of recommended consolidants listed in *Table 9.1* is the aryl-alkyl-polysiloxanes. The expression 'aryl' indicates the presence of a carbon ring radical such as phenyl, C_6H_5-. The phenyl radical confers flexibility on the product of polymerization of a silane. It also confers solubility on the polymer in organic solvents such as xylene or toluene. Therefore this type of silicone may be applied to stonework as a fairly concentrated solution. Nevertheless it is, in principle, less satisfactory than water-repellent/consolidation systems based on initially unpolymerized silanes to which no solvent has been added. Possibly Rossi-Doria *et al.*[1] recommend it because it has not been known to cause harm and because it was used with great success in stabilizing mural paintings on a gypsum ground at the Ghur Emir Mausoleum.[12] Poly-phenyl-methyl-siloxane was applied in solution in xylene to render

(a) For most purposes the starting point is an alkyl-methacrylate: $H-C(H)=C(CH_3)-C(=O)-O-R$

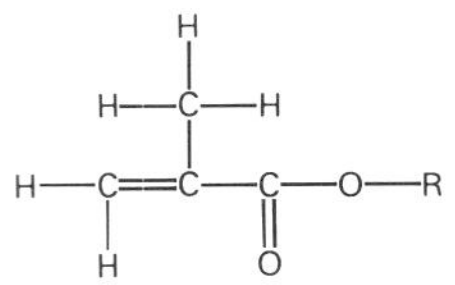

where R is an alkyl radical such as: methyl (CH_3–) ethyl (C_2H_5–) butyl (C_4H_9–)

This compound has a double chemical bond between two carbon atoms. This bond is easily broken and the material is very reactive. Under the influence of additives such as benzoyl peroxide and heat these double bonds will break and allow a large number of molecules to link up to form long chains. The result is a material that sets hard and is resistant to the weather when cold, but may be softened when heated again. Perspex is one example. The benzoyl peroxide is said to catalyse the reaction. It remains unchanged itself. Writing in a condensed form:

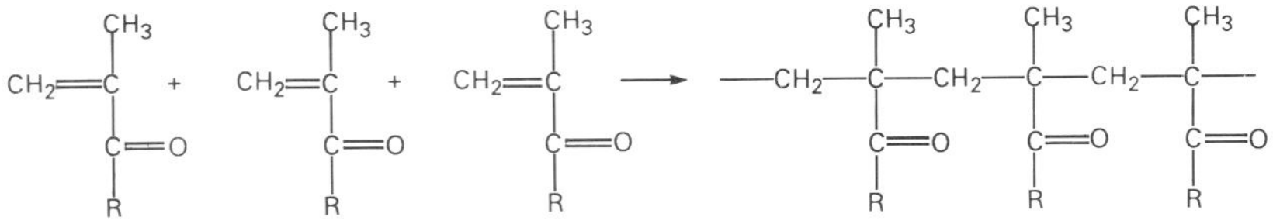

$$CH_2{=}C(CH_3)(C{=}O\,R) + CH_2{=}C(CH_3)(C{=}O\,R) + CH_2{=}C(CH_3)(C{=}O\,R) \longrightarrow -CH_2-C(CH_3)(C{=}O\,R)-CH_2-C(CH_3)(C{=}O\,R)-CH_2-C(CH_3)(C{=}O\,R)-$$

This is part of a chain molecule.

In consolidation work this thermoplastic material is usually introduced into the stone as a solution in a solvent such as tri-chlor-ethylene. The product is correctly referred to as poly-methyl-methacrylate or PMMA.

The solubility of PMMA is an advantage in consolidation work in some ways. An even more stable product can be formed by incorporating a cross-linking agent with the PMMA which will cause it to form a network of parallel chains.

Figure 9.4 Structural chemistry of acrylic consolidants

the gypsum ground-water repellent, and surface consolidation was then done by means of a suspension of 2-ethyl hexylacrylate in water. A solution of poly-phenyl-methyl siloxane was also recommended by Biscontin and Marchesini.[13] It was used to consolidate the terracotta facade of the Cathedral of S. Maria Assunta in Chivasso and for parts of the sandstone of the Re Enzo Palace in Bologna.

Acrylic systems

The essential structural chemistry of acrylic-based consolidating systems is given in *Figure 9.4*. A wide range of types are available, either directly or by blending. Methyl or ethyl methacrylates give rise to hard materials on polymerization; butyl methacrylate produces a softer polymer. The polymers formed are usually chain polymers, thermoplastic materials that are fairly easily dissolved in some appropriate organic solvent such as trichlorethylene. However, cross-linked (thermoset) polymers can be produced by incorporating a catalyst such as benzoyl peroxide.

Probably the commonest attempts to use acrylics in conservation have involved the employment of polymerized materials in an organic solvent such as trichlorethylene. The solution must be fairly dilute or the viscosity will be too high to permit reasonable penetration. However, such systems suffer from a defect common in conservation work. The consolidant tends to be drawn back as the solvent evaporates and the polymer is concentrated in a thin layer near the surface. There are many records of partially or completely unsatisfactory results from conservation attempts of this kind (see, for example, references 14 and 15). However, Domaslowski and Lehman[16] claim that choice of an optimum combination of solvent and type of polymer, e.g. with a greater than 10% solution of polybutyl-methacrylate in white spirit, can achieve good results.

To overcome the difficulties arising with acrylic polymer *solutions*, many attempts have been made to consolidate stone using acrylic *monomers* and arranging for them to polymerize once they have penetrated the stone to an adequate depth. In the Soviet Union, for example, it is claimed that objects made of deteriorating wood or stone can be made more resistant to decay by impregnation with a solution containing nine parts of inhibitor-free methyl methacrylate monomer and one part of xylene to which has been added 20 g of benzoyl peroxide catalyst for each 983 ml of the solution. Decaying objects are then impregnated under vacuum, wrapped in polyethylene foil to prevent evaporation and heated to 120°C (reference 17). Because of the need to evacuate and heat, this treatment can be applied only to objects of the kind normally kept in museums. Munnikendam has devised an easier experimental procedure by using technical quality methyl methacrylate monomer which sets in about one hour after the addition of 2% benzoyl peroxide and 0.6% dimethyl para-toluidine. The reaction takes place at room temperature. Spraying the treated object immediately with water thickened with starch or kaolin prevents loss of organic solvent or monomer. This coating can be removed with warm running water.[18] Under some conditions Munnikendam achieved 90% retention of polymer when impregnating a sandstone by this method. The use of gamma-radiation to polymerize the methacrylate is an interesting development.

This method seems very encouraging for museum conservation or the conservation of small externally exposed objects that may be removed from a building for treatment and then replaced. In general, however, acrylic materials do not yet offer the same hope as some silane-based systems do for the conservation of external stonework. Perhaps the most important use of acrylic materials for external conservation work at present is in the consolidation of loose flakes on carved stone. This is because acrylics weather well and have great transparency, and any excess can easily be removed from the treated surface by stroking it with solvent-saturated swabs. Nonformale[19] has developed a valuable restoration technique based on these properties.

Barium hydrate (baryta)

The barium hydrate shown in *Table 9.1* is more correctly called barium hydroxide or baryta. A solution of this material was proposed in the mid-nineteenth century by Church[20] as a preservative treatment for limestone or marble. Calcium sulphate, the sparingly soluble product of attack on limestone or marble by sulphur-based acids in the polluted air of industrial countries, will react chemically with a solution of barium hydroxide to form the nearly insoluble barium sulphate. The chemical reaction is:

$CaSO_4$	$+\ Ba(OH)_2$	$\rightarrow BaSO_4$	$+\ Ca(OH)_2$
Calcium sulphate	Barium hydroxide	Barium sulphate (insoluble)	Calcium hydroxide

The theory is that not only is the calcium sulphate, which is the basis of sooty incrustations on limestone, thus removed, but the coating of nearly insoluble barium which takes its place forms some barrier to further attack on the limestone by the acidic sulphur-based gases. In practice the system proved to be a failure, probably because the barium sulphate formed a barrier of insufficient thickness.

Just over a century later this method of conservation was given a new lease of life by Lewin[21] who showed that a treatment *in depth* could be achieved by soaking the limestone in a solution that contained urea and glycerol as well as barium hydroxide. By this process the surface of the limestone itself is converted to barium carbonate and the underlying stone is said to consist of solid solutions of barium and calcium carbonates which gradually decrease in barium content until, at some considerable depth, pure limestone is reached again. The chemical reaction in this case is:

$$CaCO_3 + Ba(OH)_2 \rightarrow Ca(OH)_2 + BaCO_3$$

Attack by sulphur-based acids would be expected to be brought to a standstill by the insoluble layer of barium sulphate that would develop *in depth*. If the regions have compatible coefficients of thermal expansion and rather similar wetting and drying movements this treatment appears to be promising. However, little more seems to have been published about it in recent years.

Epoxy resins

As shown in *Table 9.1*, Rossi-Doria *et al.*[1] placed epoxy resins in the 'not recommended' category mainly because no reasonable depth of penetration could be achieved unless the resin was greatly diluted with some suitable solvent. In fact, diluted epoxy resins can also prove to be disastrous as stone preservatives because small perforations in the film of set resin can be sufficient to allow the passage of acidic sulphur-based gases.[22] Nevertheless two developments in this field deserve to be watched with interest. Domaslowsky[23] appears to have achieved success with limestones and sandstones by immersing them in a 10% epoxy resin solution in an alcohol–hydrocarbon mixture. However, the operation appears to be rather tedious and more suitable for museum specimens than externally exposed stonework. In the second development Munnikendam[24] achieved promising results using a resin based on a special low-viscosity epoxy resin (1,4 butanediol diglycidylether) and diluted with a silica-producing silane such as tetra-ethoxy-silane. Unfortunately this system went out of favour when some of the ingredients were found to be carcinogenic.

Treatments based on lime

There is much to be said for the view that the composition of a surface treatment should be close to that of the stone to be conserved. In practice, it is seldom possible to achieve this, but the use of lime water, and lime wash in the conservation of limestone seems, in principle, to be an ideal approach. This system has been used, apparently with most impressive success, in the conservation of the limestone figures on the West Front of Wells Cathedral, Somerset, England. See Part 2 of this chapter.

There appear to be three mechanisms involved, namely, consolidation of the limestone near the surface by lime water, fixing of loose particles of stone to the surface by lime mortar, and sacrificial protection of the limestone by lime wash.

Lime water is a solution of slaked-lime (calcium hydroxide, $Ca(OH)_2$) in water. A litre (0.22 gal.) of this solution contains about 1.7 g of solid. Carbon dioxide gas in the air will react with the calcium hydroxide to form calcium carbonate (limestone). The chemical change is represented by the equation:

$$Ca(OH)_2 + CO_2 \rightarrow CaCO_3 + H_2O$$

The 1.7 g of calcium hydroxide will become nearly 2.3 g of calcium carbonate.

The average piece of building limestone has a porosity of about 20%. That is, a bulk volume of five litres would contain one litre of interconnected air-space. Thus the volume of limestone required to absorb one litre of solution would be five litres and the volume of solid limestone would be four litres. At the normal solid density for building limestones of 2720 kg/m^3 this would weigh 10.88 kg, i.e. 10 880 g. The 2.3 g of calcium carbonate deposited from the litre of solution on complete evaporation is thus little more than 0.02% of the weight of the dry stone. Clearly, an impracticable number of soakings and dryings would be necessary to have any appreciable effect on the strength of the stone, unless the calcium carbonate is deposited in exceptionally critical positions within the stone's pore structure. However, attempts to use lime water as a consolidant have failed. This suggests that even if conditions really exist that favour deposition of limestone in these critical positions, realization is difficult to achieve in practice.

Lime mortar is a thick paste of calcium hydroxide in water, with or without the addition of some inert sand as a filler. If the lime-mortar is to be used to fix back very small flakes on important carved stonework the sand will need to be very fine or omitted altogether. As the water evaporates from the mix the calcium hydroxide is converted by the carbon dioxide of the air to calcium carbonate (limestone), and this will join together all the limestone it is mutually in contact with (see equation above).

Unlike the deposits from lime-water, the position of the cementing deposit from lime-mortar is directly under the control of the conservator, who is responsible for the correct positioning of the flakes of stone in question.

Lime wash is a slurry of slaked lime, fine sand and stone dust in water to which casein has been added. It is applied to masonry that has otherwise been fully conserved. Its purpose is to fill small crevices and depressions caused by decay processes and then, by thinly coating the rest of the surface, to act as a barrier or sacrificial layer against future attack. Its use implies a rolling programme of conservation in which deteriorating sacrificial coats are renewed from time to time in the hope that this process will blunt the attack of aggressive gases and deposits and enable the precious masonry beneath to survive, or at worst decay more slowly. At Wells Cathedral, these are known as shelter coats. Coloured sands or stone dusts are included in the mix where this is necessary to moderate disturbing discrepancies between the colour of the shelter coat and that of the stone.

Lime mortar fillers and lime wash sacrificial coats appear to be useful conservation materials for use on limestones. They are not appropriate for use on sandstones because their conversion to calcium sulphate by sulphur-based acids in the air would soon enhance the rate of decay of all but the exceptionally weather-resistant sandstones.

Part 2 of this chapter describes the 'lime method' in detail.

Guidance through a maze

To those unfamiliar with chemistry and chemical terms, the range of chemical aids now available to those concerned with building conservation must often seem to be more confusing than helpful. *Table 9.3* is an attempt to clarify matters.

However, research aimed at the development of more effective aids is a more or less continuous process and better aids will no doubt appear as time goes on. The conservator will therefore be wise to keep in touch with international organizations such as ICCROM, as well as with national museums and building research organizations. However, it is the

Table 9.3 Consolidants in current use

1. *Acrylic monomers,* polymerized by (a) heat with a catalyst, (b) gamma radiation.

   Acrylic polymers, e.g. acrylic polymer dissolved in silane.
2. *Alkyl-trialkoxy-silanes*, can be used (a) without catalyst, (b) with catalyst (e.g. potassium hydroxide and metal soaps).
3. *Aryl-akyl-poly-siloxanes*, e.g. phenyl-methyl-poly-siloxane as solution in xylene.
4. *Ethyl silicates and silicon ester*
5. *Epoxy resins*, e.g. Domaslowski's method[22] with alcohol-hydrocarbon solutions.
6. *Lime water*, described in Part 2 of this chapter.

Notes
1. Although they are primarily museum treatments, acrylic polymers are used increasingly externally for securing flakes of limestone or marble.
   (a) Without a catalyst, requires handling by an experienced conservator.
   (b) Has behaved excellently with patented catalyst in trials on external limestones and sandstones and achieves good penetration. It was not commercially available until 1984. If an alkyl-trimethoxy-silane is used there must be good ventilation during treatment because poisonous methyl alcohol is released.
2. Success has been reported on terracotta and sandstone.
3. These are sandstone consolidators and are generally not very effective on limestones.
4. Successes have been reported but the method seems more suitable for museum work than external application
5. Successes have been claimed on limestones. Not suitable for sandstones.

unenviable lot of the conservator to be the one to decide whether to act now with any particular problem or wait for the better treatment to become available.

Philosophy of conservation by surface application

Ideally, any surface treatment applied to stonework of artistic or historical merit should be reversible. No present treatments are perfect and, judging by the past, better ones will be devised in the future. It is almost inevitable that the more effective and more long-lasting a treatment is in resisting the forces tending to destroy stone, the less likely it will be that the treatment can be removed without damage to or serious discoloration of the stone. Acrylic resins might seem to approach the ideal because they are normally removable by organic solvents, but at present they have not been proved to be as good at deep consolidation as treatments based on silane monomers. No safe methods have yet been devised to remove silane treatments once they have polymerized. Ideally, no conservator should make an irreversible mistake with any treatment, but unfortunately mistakes do occur.

Fears that the irreversibility of silane-based treatments and mistakes by conservators using them might cause irreparable damage to ancient stonework has led a number of people to ask if some conservators are not pressing ahead too rapidly. Indeed, the Society for the Protection of Ancient Buildings (SPAB) has gone so far as to call for a moratorium on the use of silane-based treatments on ancient stonework until sufficient experience of their use on unimportant stonework can give assurance that present fears are unfounded[25]. The Society has advocated, and is ready to initiate, a ***Register of Treated Stonework***. This would list all buildings or objects on which silane treatments have been used, together with all relevant information on date and type of treatment, method, etc. This might seem to be overcautious. However, the SPAB 'recognizes that those responsible for the care of stonework of historical importance are sometimes faced with the certain loss of stone substance if nothing is done. In such circumstances a choice has to be made between the short-term risk of possible loss of irreplaceable carving and the long-term risk' that irreparable damage will be caused. The Society goes on to recommend that the following procedure be adhered to in these exceptional circumstances.

1. Make sure that the deterioration causing concern is not caused or aggravated by faulty rainwater channels, decayed pointing or other defects that are causing the stonework to be wetter than necessary.
2. If the above does not apply there are two alternatives:
   a. Consider whether it would be feasible to remove the affected stonework to museum conditions and replace it with a cast copy to preserve the architectural concept. An alternative might be to provide temporary shelter for the historic stonework in its original position.
   b. Consider the use of a stone preservative system but only under the conditions outlined above.
   No system should be considered unless:
   i. It has support from at least one non-commercial body that does work in the field of conservation;
   ii. An example can be inspected of its use on exposed stone that is of the same kind or very similar to the stone in question;
   iii. The person who would apply the preservative can show an example of his or her work on similar stone. [The writer would add: 'carried out under at least as hostile ambient conditions'.]

The SPAB document continues: 'In these special circumstances silane-based preservatives would merit consideration together with other preservative systems. *It is essential* that all details are recorded of the use of any preservative system that is adopted.'

Although these conditions may always be met before any irreversible impregnation of historically important stonework is carried out, it is valuable to express this formally. It could well be argued that the Register should be kept internationally as well as nationally. Perhaps the International Centre for Conservation in Rome would be the best body to hold the International Register.

Silicone terminology

Since 1907, when Kipping made the first recorded synthesis of silicon–carbon compounds in which chains of carbon atoms occur, the terminology has evolved in several directions and some terms have changed their original meanings. Even those well acquainted with other fields of chemistry might become confused. The following is a brief description of what appears to be present usage.

Silane. The basic material in this branch of chemistry is silicon tetrahydride, commonly called silane. A molecule of silane is represented by:

```
    H
    |
H—Si—H
    |
    H
```

When any or all the hydrogen atoms in silane are replaced by some other atom or by a group of atoms including carbon the term silane is still retained in the name of the new material. Thus if one of the hydrogen atoms is replaced by a methyl radical, that is, a carbon atom with three hydrogen atoms attached to it, the new material is called methyl silane and the reaction could be represented by

```
    H            H                 H   H
    |            |                 |   |
H—Si—[H + R]—C—H   ——►   H—Si—C—H + R—H
    |            |                 |   |
    H            H                 H   H
  Silane     Methyl            Methyl
             radical           silane
```

R could represent the chlorine atom, for example. The dashed lines indicate where chemical bonds are broken.

If another of the hydrogen atoms attached to the silicon atom is replaced by a methyl radical dimethyl silane is formed, thus:

```
   H   H   H
   |   |   |
H—C—Si—C—H
   |   |   |
   H   H   H
```

Other silanes include tetramethoxy-silane and methyl-trimethoxy-silane.

Siloxanes. All materials with molecules containing the –Si–O–Si– group of atoms are known as siloxanes, except pure silica, the basic ingredient of sandstones, which contains nothing but silicon–oxygen links. An example is tetra-siloxane, which would have the following molecular structure:

```
    H       H       H       H
    |       |       |       |
H—Si—O—Si—O—Si—O—Si—H
    |       |       |       |
    H       H       H       H
```

Organo-siloxanes. When some of the hydrogen atoms in a siloxane are substituted by radicals containing carbon atoms, e.g. methyl radicals or methoxy radicals, the material is known as an organo-siloxane.

Polyorgano-siloxanes. When some of the radicals containing carbon atoms in a siloxane are radicals such as methoxy (CH_3O^-) which allows cross-linking of organo-siloxane chains the result of such cross-linking is known as a poly-organo-siloxane. An example is:

```
    H      ┌ H                  ┐ H   H
    |      | |                  | |   |
H—Si—O—[C—H          H—O]—Si—C—H
    |      | |                  | |   |
    O   H  | H                  | O   H
    |   |  └                    ┘ |
H—Si—C—H          +        H—Si—H
    |   |  ┌                    ┐ |
    O   H  | H                  | O   H
    |      | |                  | |   |
H—Si—O—[C—H          H—O]—Si—C—H
    |      | |                  | |   |
    H      └ H                  ┘ |   H
                                  |
                               H—C—H
                                  |
                                  H

         H                 H   H
         |                 |   |
      H—Si———O———Si—C—H
         |                 |   |
         O   H             O   H                 H
         |   |             |                     |
——►   H—Si—C—H     H—Si—H   + 2 X H—C—O—H
         |   |             |                     |
         O   H             O   H                 H
         |                 |   |
      H—Si———O———Si—C—H
         |                 |   |
         H                 H   H
```

The last term would normally be written 2 CH_3OH (methyl alcohol). The main product would be known as a *silicone.* Unfortunately the term silicone is also sometimes used to denote materials that consist of organo-siloxane chains *before* cross-linking. Most useful polyorgano-siloxanes have much longer chains than the example shown.

Alkyl. The term alkyl implies the presence of a radical containing straight chains of carbon atoms with hydrogen, e.g. methyl (CH_3^-) or ethyl ($C_2H_5^-$).

Alkoxy. The term alkoxy implies an alkyl chain plus an oxygen atom, e.g. ethoxy ($C_2H_5O^-$)

Aryl. The term aryl implies the presence of a radical in which carbon chains form an aromatic ring structure, e.g. phenyl ($C_6H_5^-$). This is represented formally as

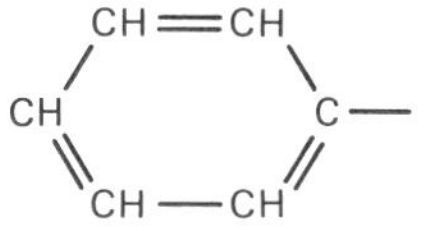

```
  CH══CH
 /      \
CH       C—
 \\     //
  CH——CH
```

Part 2 The cleaning and treatment of limestone by the lime method

John Ashurst

The West Fronts of Wells and Exeter Cathedrals and the ruined West Front of the Abbey of Crowland have undergone interesting transformations over the past few years. Heavily soiled, badly repaired limestone sculptures, which are fragile and have spalling sulphate skins, have been pulled back in some cases from the apparent brink of destruction. The dirt and all the wreckage of iron, copper and cement associated with past remedial work has gone. Some observers see a new warmth, clarity and stability in these façades; others see an unnatural uniformity, a blurring of detail and an uncertain future. These façades and others have been cleaned, repaired and consolidated using techniques generally known as the lime method.

In 1904, Lethaby examined the sculptures on the West Front of Wells Cathedral and commented: 'Sooner or later the question of preserving the statues from surface decay must be considered. It would, I believe, be desirable to cover them by degrees with distemper.' However, Lethaby did not have his way. The suggestion was rejected by the Dean and Chapter on the advice of their architect, Edmund Buckle, who foresaw a danger of blocking the pores of the stone if the surface was painted. The distemper suggested by Lethaby was probably a mixture of whiting (crushed chalk) and water, bound with a size made from parchment clippings and coloured with burnt umber or yellow ochre. However, in the absence of a precise specification for the distemper, it is difficult to estimate how much harm the execution of Lethaby's suggestion would have caused.

Lethaby's idea has some aspects in common with the lime method, especially the idea of replacing the protection once afforded by the gesso and polychrome with a substitute medium. Although distemper has been removed successfully from medieval polychromed sculpture elsewhere, for example from the figures of the Virgin and Gabriel flanking the Annunciation Door of Westminster Abbey Chapter House when it was cleaned in 1983, it is likely that damage would have been caused during the application of the distemper. Some of the effects of pore blocking would have exacerbated the decay of the sculptures, especially in sheltered areas.

Some critics of the recent work at Wells Cathedral have expressed similar doubts about the application techniques used and the possibility of pore clogging during the course of the recent restoration. Some do not find the finished work visually pleasing.

The lime method, which is also known as the Baker or Wells method, was developed on a few important sites over the past two decades. However, there is still much misunderstanding about what it really entails and what it sets out to achieve. Opinions which may have been formed about the lime method seven or eight years ago should be reviewed in the light of the evolution of the technique due to its increasing use and the accumulation of experience and discussion. Credit for this development must go to the originator of the complete lime method, Professor Robert Baker, to the architects, Alban and Martin Caroe, who were responsible for the West Front at Wells Cathedral, to members of the West Front Committee, and especially to the growing team of conservators who have shared their experiences and made their findings available.

What does the lime method involve? There is nothing new in the use of lime mortars for 'plastic repair' or in the use of lime washes for external weather protection. Although all these processes relate to the lime method, they do not actually describe it. The method is based on good common sense and traditional materials, but requires skill and experience to apply it successfully. Its lack of sophistication has led to great interest among conservators. However, all techniques, even those based on traditional materials, must stand close scrutiny and come under review from time to time. Success with one project should not stimulate unqualified commitment to the lime method as a solution to all stone problems, or even all limestone problems.

The lime method consists of several operations which are described below.

Preliminary survey

Any activity should be preceded by a careful survey of the general and detailed environmental influences and the condition of the subject. The survey should cover the following:

- *The environment:* the effects of the prevailing wind, exposure to direct sunlight, exposure to rain, water run and drip effects, humidity patterns, local pollution levels, proximity to heating outlets and nuisance from roosting birds.
- *The structural condition:* the presence of soft beds or open vents, failures due to edge or face bedding, damage from impact, diagnosis of other crack patterns, identification of position and type of fixings, especially ferrous fixings, type of any corset, existing stiffening or strengthening.
- *The surface condition:* the type of stones and description of any original covering, such as gesso and polychrome; pattern of decay and soiling; identification of existing repairs and fillings, especially those associated with decay; identification of later treatments, such as wax or limewash; description and analysis of any visible efflorescences; description of organic growth in the form of algae or algal slimes; identification of any areas too weak or too vulnerable to be cleaned by poulticing.

If the subject is very important and the conditions complex, the conservator may call in the services of other specialists. For instance, it may be advisable for an art-historian to make an assessment of a sculpture before it is touched, or a consultant to look at the conservation of fragmentary polychrome. What is vital for the conservator is thorough familiarity with the subject before work commences; for this reason, the survey should always be part of the conservation exercise and not carried out by someone other than the conservator.

The completed survey must include adequate photographs and drawings to record and explain all the information listed above, in addition to notes and appropriate measurements.

Structural repair

Although structural repairs are sometimes the first operation, most do not take place until the cleaning has been completed. They are not described here in detail, as they do not relate specifically to the lime method, but they commonly include the removal of at least one large iron dowel (in the case of figure sculpture) and other iron pins, copper straps, bars and nails. Where pinning and support is needed, it can be provided with threaded stainless steel dowels or non-ferrous pins, made of phosphor bronze, delta metal or fibreglass, set in a grout of synthetic or lime mortar. All dowel and pin heads should be set well below the surface of the stone and the outer part of the drilling filled with repair mortar. Removal of old fixings is normally carried out by careful drilling. Temporary support is provided as required. Staining from copper and iron is removed as much as possible during the cleaning operation.

Cleaning

Large areas of limestone, including ashlar and architectural moulding, are cleaned by traditional washing. Large amounts of water are very undesirable in situations where there is polychromed sculpture and many natural traps which will hold water. Various ways to protect vulnerable areas and figure sculpture have been devised, including polythene sheeting and rigid catchments, temporary gutters and downpipes. Experiments with controlled washing were commissioned by Alban and Martin Caroe at Wells Cathedral in about 1980 and some pioneering work was carried out by R.H. Bennett with sensor-controlled and clock-controlled washing.

Clock-controlled systems were subsequently developed by the Wells Cathedral conservators under the direction of Professor Baker and Mr Peter Cooley. They are still in use, on a four-second wetting time with dry intervals of four to five minutes. It is not sensible to specify the wetting-interval time too precisely, as it can only be determined on site by trial. The object is to achieve a progressive softening of the dirt deposits to enable them to be removed by brushing. Experience has shown that this does not require constant sheets and cascades of water running over the face of the building, with all the attendant risks of staining, loss of friable or fragile material and other problems associated with salt migration and water penetration.

Some areas of detail will require more positive protection from water than sheets or catchments. Obvious areas of polychrome, for instance, or areas likely to have surviving colour under dirt layers, should be covered with tissue pads under a thin plastic film, which is taped or tied in position. Delicate areas such as fleurons may now be cleaned with dry air abrasive and protected from subsequent washing. Once the washing of masonry has been completed, cleaning of the sculpture can begin.

The traditional method of cleaning associated with the lime method is by hot lime poultice. Quicklime should be used for the poultice. It should be broken into small pieces to pass a 12 mm (0.5 in) sieve and bound against the stonework with either sheet or strip sacking. This should be taped down so that no lime escapes at the bottom. The thickness of the lime should be 12–25 mm (0.5–1 in). The sacking should be covered with medium-heavy polythene, taped at the bottom and sides, but with a hole left in the top. Water should be poured slowly through the hole to allow the lime to slake. When the lime softens to the consistency of putty, sufficient water has been used. The hole should be covered and the poultice left for a week to ten days. The poultice may then be removed. It will be shaped like a mould of the object and will be stained by the bituminous material that covered the stone. The object should then be lightly sprayed for a few hours to remove any remaining deposits.

In the early days of the restoration of Wells Cathedral the lime was slaked against the surface of the stone. It is not surprising that Mr W.A. Wheeler, the Clerk of Works at the time, reported dramatic happenings during the slaking process when the string binding burst under the expansion of the lime and the hessian began to burn!

Hot lime is still in use, but it is now applied by gloved hand and trowel. The putty is pressed well into the surface of the pre-wetted stone. When a thick plaster is applied it is bound with scrim and wet sacking or underfelt which is secured with string. Finally, a heavy-duty polythene sheet is tied loosely in position. From time to time, over a period of two to three weeks, the polythene is lifted and the sacking surface is sprayed with water to ensure that the poultice remains damp and soft. If the poultice dried out it would render the lime useless, or bind it to the surface of the stone.

When the packaging is finally removed, the lime is carefully lifted off over small areas at a time with spatulas or small trowels, taking with it some of the dirt from the contact surface. Water sprays are used to assist in the removal of the lime and to further soften the dirt. In common with most other poultices, not very much dirt actually detaches with the poultice material. The softened deposit must be worked at with hand sprays, dental picks and small toothbrushes or stencil brushes to achieve a relatively clean surface. In the past, some areas were scraped down, but this practice no longer continues. The scrubbing stage is long and laborious. Added to perhaps three weeks of poulticing, the cleaning of a life-size figure may well take a month or six weeks before any repair work is undertaken. In 1965–66, Mr Wheeler was experimenting with alternatives to hot lime after the unsuccessful and literal baptism of fire, a line of enquiry which has still to be pursued.

A report by one of the Wells conservators draws attention to the fact that the air abrasive unit preserved more of the polychromy than a lime poultice would have done, particularly in view of the risks involved with water during removal of the poultice. With hindsight, it is a pity that the early use of small air abrasive tools at Wells Cathedral attracted so little interest and that superficial assumptions about the technique ruled it out on the grounds that 'sand-blasting' would be too destructive. (Statue 117 was cleaned by R.H. Bennett under the direction of the Directorate of Ancient Monuments and Historic Buildings with wet attapulgite clay packs, an air abrasive pencil and aluminium oxide abrasive in 1977.)

Wet poulticing combined with careful mechanical cleaning using dental tools and brushes or air abrasive seems to be the best option for both economy and the safety of the surfaces and operatives. Whether or not the poultice should be lime, hot or cold, or attapulgite clay, or some other medium is still open to debate. Any wet pack which can remain in intimate contact with the stone without drying out or adhering to the surface will have a softening effect on dirt and make it more responsive to gentle washing and brushing.

Does the lime poultice, which is initially hot, have any other beneficial effect during its two or three week contact period with the stone? It has been claimed that it increases the permeability of a sulphated layer and makes the surface more receptive to the lime water applications that follow. It is also claimed that initial strengthening of friable areas is noticeable after the poulticing and as the stone dries out. This phenomenon is related to the strengthening claimed to be achieved after multiple applications of lime water.

Removal of old fillings

The cleaning processes will reveal the full extent of the damage due to weathering and decay and the amount of filling of spalls and cracks which has been carried out in the past. Almost invariably these fillings, including some crude remodelling, were carried out in Roman Cement, a strong, brown coloured hydraulic cement much favoured in the nineteenth century for restoration repairs. More recently, equally strong Portland cement-based mortar has been used. These fillings are completely unsuitable as a visual match for the stone; but, more seriously, their dense, impervious nature encourages moisture and salt concentrations around them, thus extending the area of decay still further.

Removal of old fillings is essential, but it is slow and careful work. The old fillings must be drilled out, with only the minimum use of impact tools such as sharp masonry chisels and fluted plugging chisels on large areas. Small chisels and air abrasive tools should be used to assist cutting and to enlarge the cavities slightly by undercutting to improve the keying effect. The maximum amount of surviving surface should always be retained. Only where the original surface is already lost should any further dressing-off take place, to avoid the retention of water traps.

Once all old fillings have been removed, their cavities recut and new cavities formed where newer spalls and splits had developed, all loose dust and debris must be removed by flushing with clean water. If algae are present a few drops of formalin may be added to the water. This will provide a sound, clean and sterile area in which the new mortar can be placed. Flushing out is most conveniently carried out with trigger-operated hand sprays which have a simple adjustable nozzle to vary the jet from a fine pencil to a coarse spray pattern as required.

At this stage much of the sculpture looks very leprous, but all deleterious material which can be removed has been scrupulously excised. Once the cleaning has been completed any structural repairs can be carried out.

Consolidation by lime water

The cleaned surfaces with open cavities are next treated with lime water to attempt to consolidate the more friable areas. Lime water contains small quantities of calcium hydroxide (0.14 g in 100 ml of water at 15 °C.) Traditionally lime water is siphoned from the slaking tank after the lime has been slaked in an excess of water and after all slaking has ceased and the water is clear. Now the lime putty is usually stirred into a container of water and left to stand until the water is clear.

It is important to protect the lime water from the air, otherwise it will carbonate and become ineffective. A number of different methods have been used to achieve this. The most recent development is the covering of the surface of the lime water with a float of polystyrene sheet, pierced only by a siphon tube fitted with a filter. The lime water is drawn off when required by a hand pump into spray bottles or directly to a lance with a control valve and adjustable nozzle. It is necessary to check from time to time that the water has not accidentally become clouded through disturbance of the lime in the bottom of the bin. Any cloudy water should be rejected and the water allowed to stand until it is clear again.

Approximately forty applications of lime water must be flooded onto the surface of the limestone over a period of several days. Application can continue as long as the surface will absorb, but excess lime water should not be allowed to lie on the surface of the stone. It should be removed by sponges which are then squeezed out in clean water.

Over many years consolidation effects have been reported as a result of multiple applications of lime water to lime plaster, Doulting, Bath, Clunch, Barnack, Beer, Salcombe and Chilmark limestones. However, attempts to record or quantify the phenomenon have met with a disappointing lack of success. For example, in Wells Cathedral trial treatments with lime water (27 applications over a six-day period) were carried out by Mr W.A. Wheeler in 1967 on the south side of the south doorway and by the author and Mr Brian Clarke of the Building Research Station with Mr Wheeler on the blind arcading of the central tower in 1970. Neither of these produced any evidence that lime water had any strengthening effect on the stone.[6] The central tower experiment compared forty applications of lime water with forty application of distilled and of tap water.

Surface repair

The consolidation treatment is followed by the placing of mortar repairs. This is the stage in the lime method where perhaps the greatest skill and the most experience are needed. The mortar repair is the core of the method and, when well executed, is the work which evokes the greatest admiration.

All mortar repairs are based on lime; no Portland cement of any kind is used. If a weak hydraulic mortar is needed, then a small addition of high temperature insulation (HTI) powder, a pale coloured ceramic powder, is used as a pozzolana. At Crowland Abbey, Professor Baker used finely crushed Cambridge White brick dust as his pozzolanic additive in order to match the Barnack limestone of the building.

All limes should be of a high calcium, non-hydraulic type. Lime should be brought to the site after burning and be slaked as soon as possible in a suitable tank by adding it to water, raking and hoeing it through until all visible reaction has ceased. An excess of water should be used, so that the soft mass of lime putty formed during slaking is kept well covered. Experienced lime practitioners express preferences for different limes according to the kind of work and the type of stone they are working with. However, this should be an indication of very considerable practical experience and not an affectation! The lime putty must be left in its tank under water for as long as possible. It should be left for at least one week to ensure that all slaking is finished, but any days, weeks, months or even years that can be added to this period can be looked on as a bonus, especially if the lime putty can be mixed and stored in wet, air-tight conditions with the aggregates. The lime putty will never 'set' or harden too much if it is kept from the air, and even if it has stiffened it can easily be softened again when needed without the addition of water; with sufficient working it will soon become a soft gelatinous mass again. Pozzolanic additives must only be added just before use, and then mixed in very thoroughly.

Aggregates should be selected and graded for colour and function. Often considerable time must be spent in their selection and many sands and crushed stones will be tried in the process of finding the right combination. Stone pieces can be crushed by hammer or roller on a concrete slab, or even in a corn grinder, and then carefully sieved and graded for storing in a 'bank'.

The mortars have a number of different functions to fulfil. They are all likely to be a combination of lime and the same aggregates, but the lime:aggregate proportions may vary and so will the size of aggregate. A pozzolanic additive is required only for some functions. The basic proportions are summarized below:

	Lime	*Aggregate*
Repair mortar	1	2
Adhesive mortar (for fixing spalls)	1	1
Grouting mortar (for crack filling)	1	1.5
Shelter coating	1	3

A ten per cent pozzolanic additive (HTI powder) should be included in the basic aggregate proportion and in the adhesive and grouting mortar. A lower percentage is required in the repair and shelter coat mortars. Finer aggregates are used for adhesive and grouting mortars. The finest are used for shelter coating. Some examples of aggregate sizes related to mortar function are given in *Table 9.4*.

The lime putty should always be screened through a 1.18 mm mesh after slaking. Further screening takes place according to the function of the mortar.

The final colour of the repair depends on the selection and blending of the aggregates and the proportion of lime used, the method of placing the repair and the rate of drying out. Minor variations in colour continue to take place indefinitely just as the colour of a stone surface will continue to respond to variations in humidity. Successful 'instant effects' are not necessarily the most satisfactory after a period of weathering. Only with considerable experience can this be anticipated and the mortar constituents selected accordingly. At Wells Cathedral experience has been primarily concentrated on matching Doulting and Dundry stones.

Dundry and Doulting limestones weather in subtly distinct ways and are always distinguishable in colour. The workers at Wells Cathedral have developed a palette of mortars which can be used as repair mixes or as shelter coats and which make use of the same aggregates in varying proportions.

Dundry stone varies from a light cream to dark brown and light grey. Doulting varies from a pale buff to different and often darker browns and greys. The aggregates used to match these colours are not obtained by crushing stones of the same kind but rather, richer coloured stones with good staining properties. In particular, use is made of Hornton, a ferruginous limestone with a distinctive blue grey and golden brown colour from Edgehill in Oxfordshire, and of Guiting, especially the dark buff-orange Guiting from Gloucestershire.

Table 9.5 shows how typical colours are made up.

Before the conservator goes onto the scaffold to place the repair mortar a number of pre-mixed mortars, sometimes as many as thirty for two stone types, will have been prepared in separate plastic tubs and covered with a piece of wet cloth. The tools

Table 9.4 Mortar composition

Mortar function	*Lime*	*Aggregates*				*Pozzolanic additive*	
		BS sieve sizes					
		1.18 mm	600 µm	400 µm	300 µm	600 µm	300 µm
Mortar repair	3	1½	1½	¾	¾	½	–
	3	3	2	1	–	½	–
Adhesive mortar	6	–	–	–	6	1½	–
	6	–	1	1	4	½	1
Grouting mortar	3¼	3	–	1	1	½	–
	2	–	½	1¼	–	–	¾
Shelter coat	3	–	–	–	8	–	–
	3	–	–	2½	4½	–	–

Table 9.5 The composition of coloured mortars

Aggregates	*Dundry stone*		*Doulting stone*	
	Repair mix	*Shelter coat*	*Repair mix*	*Shelter coat*
Guiting	3	2½	2	2
Blue Hornton	¾	½	2¼	3
Brown Hornton	1½	1¼	2	1½
Gold sand	1	¼	1	1
Red sand	–	⅛	–	½
Lime	4	1	3¼	3
Pozzolanic additive	½	–	–	–

and materials necessary for the operation should be conveniently laid out on a board ready for use. These include hand-spray bottles full of water, cotton wool packs, a small trowel, dental picks and plugging tools, spatulas, two or three small bristle brushes and rubber gloves. The following sequence of working is typical.

1. Cavities and cracks are flushed out again with water from the hand sprays to avoid an otherwise dry stone surface de-watering the repair as it is pressed into position. The surface should be damp without water actually shining on the surface.
2. Deep cavities are treated at the back with a slurry of repair mortar followed by a filling into which small pieces of Bath or Doulting stone are inserted to reduce the thickness which needs to be built up in fine repair mortar.
3. A thin slurry of repair mortar containing HTI powder is brushed into the cavity or fracture to provide an additional key for the repair.
4. After one or two hours, when the slurry has dried, the cavity is wetted up again and the first repair mortar is kneaded and pushed into place with the fingers, exerting as much pressure as possible. With few exceptions, not more than 5–6 mm should be pressed in at one time. Dental plugging tools and spatulas are used to assist in the filling. Throughout the entire sequence compaction of the amalgam by pressure is absolutely essential to achieve good adhesion and minimum shrinkage.
5. As each filling is completed, precautions must be taken to avoid rapid drying out by protecting the area from direct sunlight or strong draughts. When dry, the cavity must again be wetted and step 4 repeated until the cavity has been filled completely. Overfilling is a useful aid to compaction and surplus mortar can be trimmed off with a spatula to the desired profile on completion. A texture matching the stone can be achieved with a dry sponge, hessian pads, stencil brushes and purpose-made plastic scrapers. It is important not to press hard and absorb moisture from the repair.

As a general rule no modelling is carried out using repair mortar. Its role is to fill cavities and cracks and to provide a weak, porous capping to vulnerable, friable areas. It is designed to draw moisture, and therefore soluble salts, to itself and finally to fail before any further stone is lost. Ideally it will then be replaced. To ensure slow drying, wet cotton wool packs are laid over the finished repair and left in position for as long as is thought necessary.

Shelter coating

The final stage of the work is to apply a thin surface coating to all the cleaned and repaired stone. This is intended to slow down the effects of weathering on the surviving surfaces by providing a sacrificial layer which may be removed by direct rainfall or disrupted by salt crystallization associated with wetting and drying cycles. In the case of stones which were once covered with gesso and coloured with tempera, the shelter coat may be seen as a substitute protection. It has been suggested that the shelter coat may also provide a warmer surface than the untreated stone and that this may inhibit the formation of condensation. Whilst this might conceivably be the case with a thick lime wash, it is difficult to believe that a fine shelter coat could have such an effect. One of the most obvious and striking developments of the technique is the increasing fineness and subtlety of the shelter coat. One observer, only slightly misquoting Hans Christian Andersen's story *The Emperor's New Clothes*, insisted that the stones 'had nothing on at all'! Thicker coats are still applied to ashlar and simple architectural mouldings, as they have been at Wells since 1980. Shelter coats have been applied to figure sculpture as a general policy since 1977, and were pioneered by Professor Baker twenty years before then.

Practitioners insist that a shelter coat is not a paint, largely because of the method of application. It is, however, a coloured surface treatment which requires periodic maintenance. The shelter coat is of similar or the same composition as the repair mortars, but the aggregate to lime proportion is slightly higher and sand and stone dust are crushed more finely (see *Tables 9.4* and *9.5*). Water is added to the fine lime and aggregate mix until a consistency of thin cream is reached. Thorough mixing continues for 20 to 30 minutes. At Wells Cathedral Mr Martin Caroe has introduced the use of a heavy-duty food mixer to carry out this part of the operation. At the end of the mixing period casein and formalin may be added.

More work needs to be carried out to establish the roles played by casein and by formalin in the shelter coat. Casein paints have been used since antiquity. Lime and casein form calcium caseinate, a useful binder for whiting and pigment. A readily available source of casein is milk, but there is some confusion on how best to obtain casein from milk on site.

Milk is the primary food for all young mammals. It is a mixture consisting of butter fats (3.8%), lactose (sugar, 4.7%), minerals (0.8%), water (87.4%) and solids (3.3%) which contain the protein casein. To ease digestion the milk is coagulated in the stomach by the enzyme rennin, which is secreted by the stomach wall. A similar process is used in the production of curds and whey. The addition of rennet (impure rennin) to milk will cause it to coagulate, forming curds (a calcium casein compound) which separate from the whey (a clear sugary solution with no casein present). Another method is simply to allow the milk to stale. In this situation coagulation is brought about by the action of bacteria digesting the protein, which leaves a clear liquid containing no casein.

Shelter coats gauged with whey have been used extensively at Wells Cathedral and elsewhere and have produced very satisfactory results. This suggests that perhaps casein has no role to play. Some lime method practitioners do not use any milk at all and include finely ground ceramic powder with the lime. However, lime casein mixtures continue to be of interest and skimmed milk or skimmed milk powder are still being used.

Skimmed milk is simply milk from which the cream has been removed. A typical composition for powder provided by the Milk Marketing Board contains lactose (52%), protein (mostly casein) (36%), ash (0.8%), moisture (3.2%) and fats (0.8%). Skimmed milk powder may be reckoned, therefore, to contain about one-third part of casein. Other experiments have used colostrum, the milk produced by cows for the first forty-eight hours after a calf is born, which contains more protein (casein) and less sugar and fats than ordinary milk.[26]

Lime casein paints use a proportion of about one part casein to ten parts lime. A paint with excellent binding properties was mixed at Old Gorhambury in 1979 for protecting weak badly decayed limestone based on three parts skimmed milk powder to ten parts lime putty. However, such applications are intended to lay on a relatively thick coat. Formalin is included in these paints and in shelter coats.

Formalin is a saturated solution of the gas formaldehyde in water. Casein plastics are produced by immersing casein in a solution of formaldehyde. A gelling effect occurs if formalin is added quickly to a solution of casein and lime. However, the minute proportions of formalin traditionally used in shelter coats are unlikely to have any effect other than a transitory sterilization of the milk and lime mixture. This is probably a useful property and 5 ml of formalin in one litre of lime and skimmed milk shelter coat seems to have an inhibiting effect on the development of mould spots.

Careful colour matching of cleaned, weathered stone should precede the full application of a shelter coat. This matching can be carried out on a separate piece of the same stone in similar condition, but it is better to lay the samples on the stone itself or on, for instance, an adjacent moulding. Considerable skill is required in colour matching, as it is in matching repair mortars. All trial colours must be completely dry before a decision can be made about its accuracy. Sometimes a hot air-blower may be used to hasten the drying of the trial colours.

The surface is prepared for application by careful but thorough spraying with water. Spraying is carried out with hand bottles until water begins to sit on the surface and is no longer absorbed into the stone. At this stage, as soon as the water has ceased to glisten on the surface, the shelter coat can be laid on with a soft bristle brush. A second, short haired or worn bristle brush is used to work the shelter coat into the texture of the stone. Traditionally, pads of hessian sacking were used for rubbing in to achieve the maximum compaction possible. The hessian must have been washed to remove the starch and any impurities. Compaction by rubbing is a very important part of the process and serves to fill the minute hollows of textured stone whilst wiping off all but a smear from the high spots. The treatment is always applied to complete stones, and sometimes, as in the case of sculpture, is carried across joints as well.

Drying out must be as carefully controlled as the drying out of mortar repairs. Polythene shrouds are often used, and intermittent mist spraying by hand during the first few hours avoids any risk of rapid drying which can result in a powdery and useless shelter coat and undesirable modifications in colour. During the first stages of drying out, small additions of colour in the form of finely ground stone dust or even powdered charcoal may be dusted on to achieve minor, subtle variations in the final appearance.

Shelter coating is the most visually striking part of the lime method but should never be too obvious. Inexpert handling can result in a bland, woolly appearance, which on the scale of the West Front of a cathedral would be an aesthetic disaster. However, properly carried out, with sufficient sensitivity to the colour and tonal variations of the worn stones, it can greatly enhance their appearance.

As with any other technique the principle of shelter coating can be misunderstood or misused. There is, in the stone cleaning trade, an expression used to describe covering up dirt, old paint and poor repairs with a lime and stonedust or coloured cement slurry. This technique, known as 'toshing' in England, is disliked by reputable cleaning contractors. However, in one recent case the covering up of the heavily soiled underside of a cornice, which should have been cleaned, with a thick cement slurry, was described defensively as 'shelter coating'!

The lime method is here to stay. Its continued use and the scientific scrutiny which is now being applied to it ensure that it will develop and will be refined. The following questions still have to be answered.

1. *Cleaning.* Should clay of the attapulgite type be used instead of lime and could the poultice contact period be much reduced? Would another poultice be more appropriate to delicate surfaces? Should more of the cleaning be carried out with air abrasive pencils?

2. *Consolidation.* How much consolidation is achieved by multiple lime water applications? Does a lime poultice have any consolidating effect? Could lime water be applied through long fibre tissue facings, enabling wet flakes to be gently pushed back onto the surface to achieve better consolidation?

The second question was taken up by Dr Clifford Price and Mr Keith Ross (both, at the time, of the Building Research Establishment). Which parts of the treatment had caused the changes observed, and how had they worked? How long would the apparent benefits last? An investigation was undertaken to provide a technical rationale for the treatment and to compare the performance of the lime poultice with air-abrasive and washing techniques.

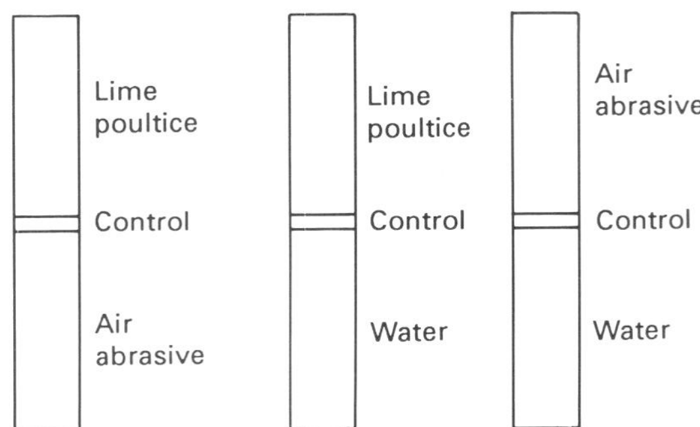

Figure 9.5 The design of the experiment permitted direct comparison between any two cleaning techniques on a single mullion

Technical appraisal of stone conservation techniques at Wells Cathedral

Clifford Price and Keith Ross

Ideally, the entire investigation should have been based on a single piece of stone, in order to eliminate variations in properties from one piece of stone to another. In practice, however, it was not possible to find a single piece of stone that was uniformly weathered and large enough to permit the necessary sampling. The investigation was therefore carried out on three pieces of stone cut from three mullions of the unglazed west cloister walk of the cathedral. They were each in Doulting limestone, the stone from which the majority of West Front figures are carved. The mullions were believed to have been installed around 1470, and were equally dirty and decayed. The pieces cut out for experiment were 900 mm (36 in) long, with a cross-sectional area of about 180 cm^2 (28 in^2).

The first stage of the experiment was to clean the mullions, using a lime poultice, air abrasion or water washing. The design of the experiment, shown in *Figure 9.5*, permitted direct comparison of any two techniques on a single piece of stone. A central portion, approximately 20 mm (0.8 in) thickness, was cut out using a dry saw and served as a control. The remaining six pieces were then cleaned by the conservation team; two pieces were cleaned using each technique. Every effort was made to ensure that the cleaning was carried out in a realistic manner. The lime poultice cleaning and the air abrasive cleaning were carried out on the scaffold alongside a figure that was being cleaned by the same technique. The water washing, normally used for the architectural stonework but not for the figure sculpture, continued until the stone was clean and lasted around two days.

When cleaning was completed and the stone had dried a 20 mm (0.8 in) slice was cut with a dry saw from the centre of each of the six pieces. This slice was set aside for laboratory examination. Of the two pieces that remained from each of the original six pieces, one piece was treated with around forty applications of lime water whilst the other was left untreated *Figure 9.6*. The lime watering was carried out by the conservation team in exactly the same way as the lime watering of the figure sculpture.

When the lime watering was completed, a 20 mm (0.8 in) slice was cut from the centre of each of the lime-watered pieces and set aside for laboratory investigation. One of the two remaining pieces was covered with a shelter coat. The blocks that had not been lime watered were simply cut in half and one half was covered with a shelter coat. A sample for

Figure 9.6 Quarter-length mullions after treatment with lime water

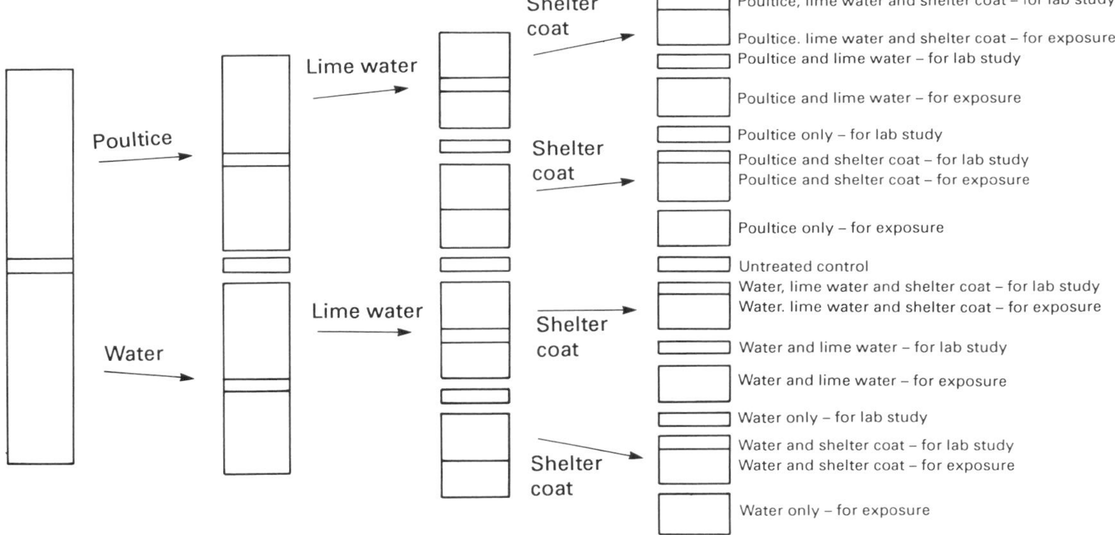

Figure 9.7 Stages in the treatment of one mullion

laboratory study was then cut from each of the shelter-coated pieces, and all the remaining pieces were exposed to the weather. Their condition will be monitored over the next few years. This seemingly complicated procedure, illustrated for a single mullion in *Figure 9.7*, enabled each part of the conservation treatment to be studied, either in isolation or in conjunction with other parts. End effects were eliminated in the cleaning and lime watering stages by cutting the specimens for laboratory study from the centre of each treated piece. This precaution was not necessary in the shelter coat stage.

Laboratory investigation of specimens

Each 20 mm (0.8 in) slice of mullion was sampled as shown in *Figure 9.8*. All cutting was done dry, to prevent any redistribution of calcium sulphate or calcium hydroxide.

Distribution of calcium sulphate

The majority of investigators agree that calcium sulphate plays a major role in the decay of limestones, the calcium sulphate being formed by reaction of the limestone with sulphur oxides in the air. There is remarkably little understanding, however, of the precise mechanisms by which the calcium sulphate causes decay, and little can yet be added to Schaffer's summary of 1932.[7]

On first sight, it would appear to be beneficial to the stone if all the calcium sulphate could be removed from it. However, this is not necessarily so. When stone is in a very advanced stage of decay, the calcium sulphate may actually be serving to bind the stone together. If the calcium sulphate were to be removed, the stone would disintegrate altogether (see *Figure 9.9* and *9.10*). This phenomenon was in

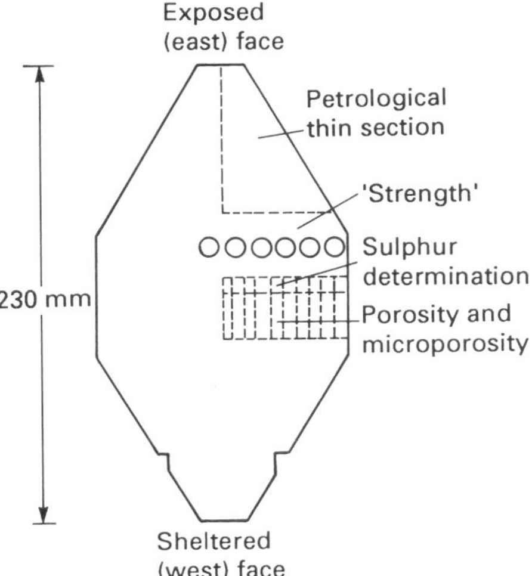

Figure 9.8 Sampling of mullion sections

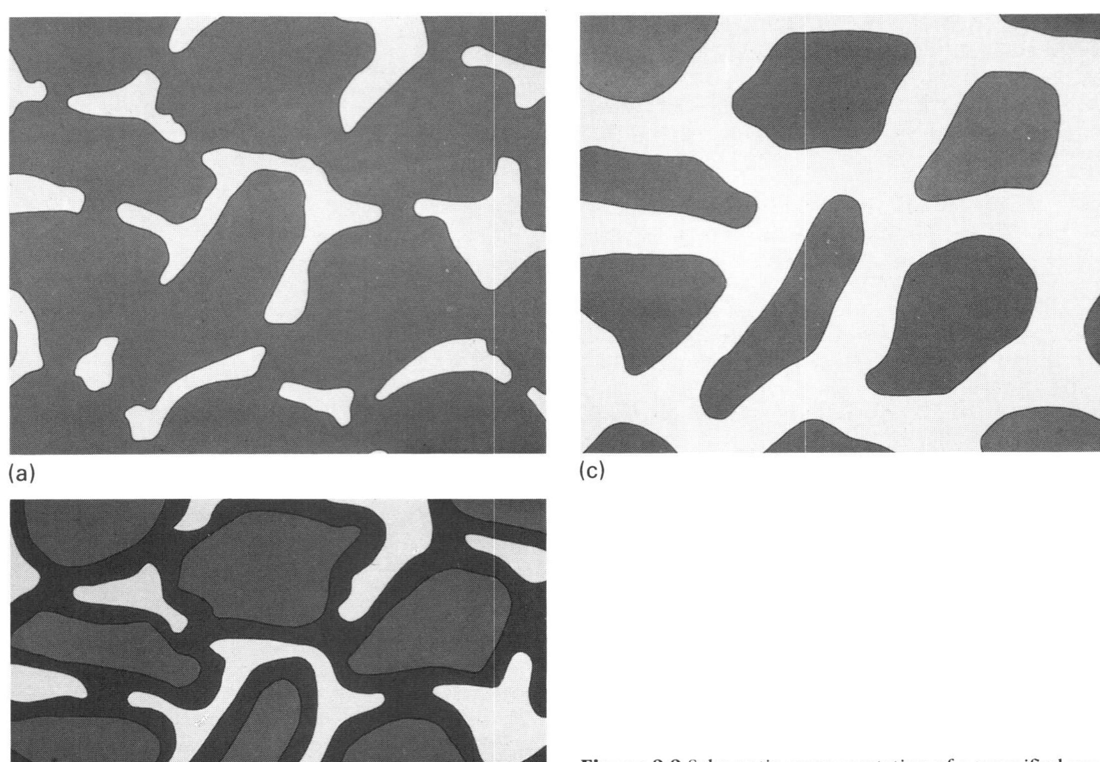

Figure 9.9 Schematic respresentation of a magnified cross-section through a piece of limestone. (a) The darker areas represent the grains of limestone cemented together by calcium carbonate. The lighter areas represent the pores. (b) After weathering in a polluted atmosphere, the exposed surfaces, including the cement, are converted to calcium sulphate. (c) After prolonged washing, the calcium sulphate dissolves and the stone disintegrates.

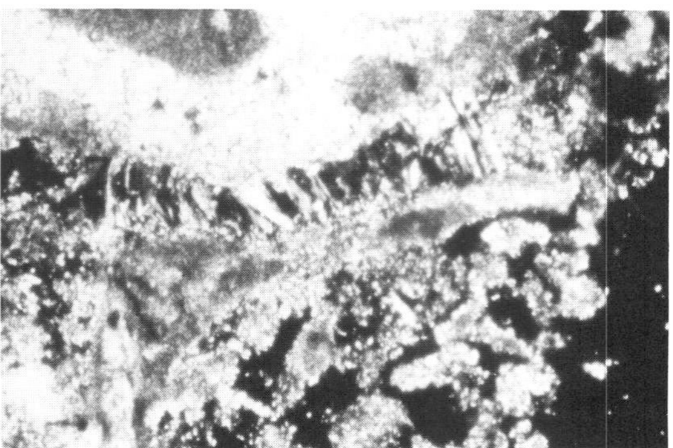

Figure 9.10 Petrological thin section: calcium sulphate crystals form a line of bridges between two grains of stone (× 130)

fact observed at Wells, when conventional water mist sprays were used to clean highly undercut architectural detail. The prolonged washing leached the calcium sulphate from the stone, which was reduced to a soft mass. (This experience led to a refinement of the technique for washing architectural stonework, in which water was sprayed onto the stone for only a few seconds at a time, with intervals of several minutes in between. The spray was controlled either by a time switch or by electronic sensors placed on the stone. This refinement enabled the stone to be kept wet, thus softening dirt, without the calcium sulphate being leached out.) One must conclude that removal of the sulphate is not necessarily beneficial, despite the fact that one would prefer the calcium sulphate not to be there in the first place.

The effects of the three cleaning techniques on sulphate distribution are shown in *Figure 9.11*, which gives the results for two of the mullions. The results show beyond doubt that none of the cleaning techniques has any influence on the quantities of sulphate contained *within* the stone. It should be remembered, however, that these results relate to specimens which are typically 7 mm (0.3 in) thick; they thus represent the average sulphate content within a 7 mm specimen. If there were to be any redistribution of the sulphate within such a specimen, it would not be discernible from these results. Nevertheless, the results clearly refute any claim that the lime poultice serves to draw calcium sulphate out of the depth of the stone.

The situation is different when the amount of sulphate on the *surface* of the stone is examined. *Table 9.6* contains the results of sulphate analyses on scrapings from the surface of the various samples. In both cases of water washing, the washing removes more than 80% of the sulphate skin. The effects of the air abrasive and the lime poultice, on the other hand, are more variable. In one case, the air abrasive reduced the sulphate content by 21%, in the other case by 51%. The lime poultice reduced it by 5% in one case and by 83% in the other, an even greater reduction than that caused by water washing. The variability of the results is not surprising, for some areas of stone will come clean more readily than others. In the case of the lime poultice, in particular, water is used to assist cleaning after removal of the poultice, so areas that had required a good deal of washing would be expected to give results similar to those for water washing alone.

Table 9.6 Sulphate content of surface scrapings, following the initial cleaning stage

	Cleaning technique	*Sulphate content* (% SO_3)
Mullion 1	Lime poultice	26.5
	No treatment (control)	28.0
	Air abrasive	22.1
Mullion 2	Lime poultice	4.4
	No treatment (control)	26.0
	Water	4.8
Mullion 3	Air abrasive	12.8
	No treatment (control)	26.3
	Water	3.8

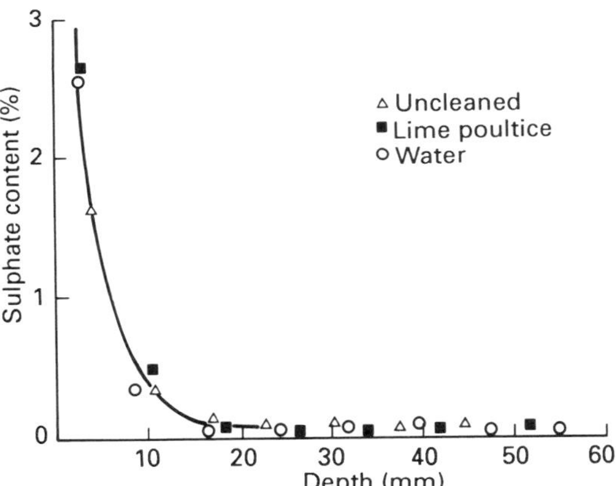

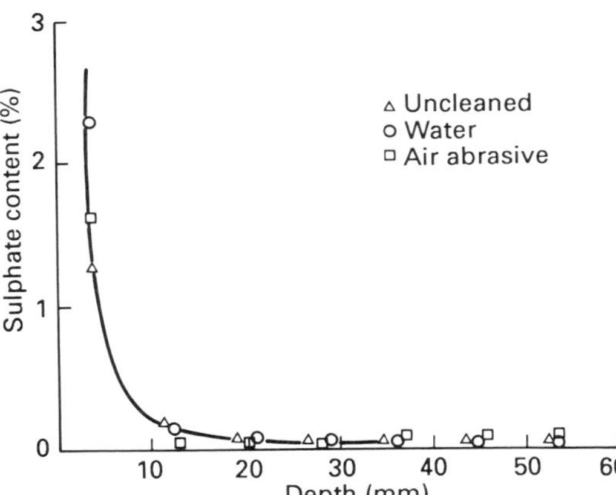

Figure 9.11 Variation of sulphate content with depth; analysis was by carbon/sulphate combustion, all sulphur being taken as sulphate

The results of *Table 9.6* are borne out by examination of petrological thin sections. The sulphate skin is largely absent from samples that have been water washed, whereas it is present in variable amounts in those that have been cleaned by air abrasive or lime poultice.

These data confirm that water washing is potentially harmful to the stone, because it can remove the sulphate that binds surface grains together. The air abrasive and the lime poultice, on the other hand, permit a reduction in the sulphate skin without disrupting the stone below. This will facilitate the subsequent absorption of lime water but will also make the stone more vulnerable to further attack by acid rain water unless the protective shelter coat is applied. One advantage of the air abrasive over the lime poultice is that the air abrasive is more selective. It is possible to clean around traces of pigment, for example, without affecting the pigment itself.

Deposition of calcium hydroxide

This part of the investigation was aimed at detecting any calcium hydroxide or calcium carbonate that had been deposited in the stone. The lime poultice consists of calcium hydroxide, and the lime water is a solution of calcium hydroxide. Either the poultice or the lime water could thus lead to the deposition of calcium hydroxide, which would subsequently react with carbon dioxide in the air to form calcium carbonate. Ultimately, the calcium carbonate would react with sulphur dioxide in the air to form calcium sulphate.

The search for calcium carbonate/hydroxide was based mainly on examination of petrological thin sections, in the expectation that this would reveal the precise points at which deposition had occurred and would also give some indication of whether the deposition had occurred largely at the surface or in depth. In the event, the search was disappointing. In the majority of specimens, no deposits could be seen in the treated specimens (after either poulticing or lime watering) that could not also be seen in the controls. *Figure 9.12* shows one of the few specimens in which deposition was possibly evident. This particular specimen had been lime watered after cleaning by air abrasion. Nevertheless, it was disappointing and puzzling that convincing evidence of deposition could not be seen in each of the specimens.

The failure to detect calcium hydroxide/carbonate does not necessarily mean that no carbonate or hydroxide has been deposited or that the lime treatment is worthless. It is possible that very small quantities of carbonate/hydroxide could have a marked effect on the strength of the stone if deposited in just the right places. The petrological examination may not have been sensitive enough to detect such deposits. Alternatively, it is possible that the calcium carbonate/hydroxide has already been converted to calcium sulphate, which is indistinguishable from pre-existing calcium sulphate.

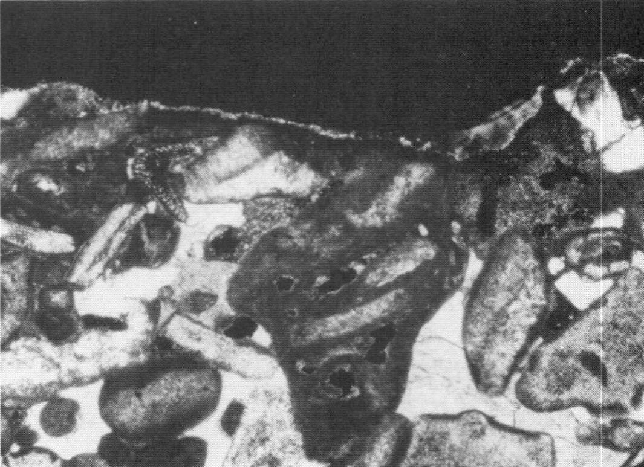

Figure 9.12 Petrological thin section of specimen after air abrasive cleaning and treatment with lime water. The calcium sulphate skin has been stained red, using Alizarin Red S in hot alkaline soloution. Magnification × 20; viewed under crossed polars. The white crust visible on the outer surface, and to some extent on the sides of the pores, may be a deposit of calcium hydroxide

Porosity and microporosity

The porosity of a stone is defined as the volume of the pores that it contains, expressed as a percentage of the bulk volume of the stone. The 'microporosity' gives a broad indication of whether the pores are mainly coarse or fine. Microporosity is defined as the volume of water retained (expressed as a percentage of the available pore space) when a suction equivalent to a 6.4 m head of water is applied to the specimen. The concept is discussed in reference 27; the detailed test procedure is given in reference 28. A high microporosity indicates a high proportion of fine pores and is normally associated with low durability; conversely, a low microporosity indicates a high proportion of coarse pores and is normally associated with high durability. In the present

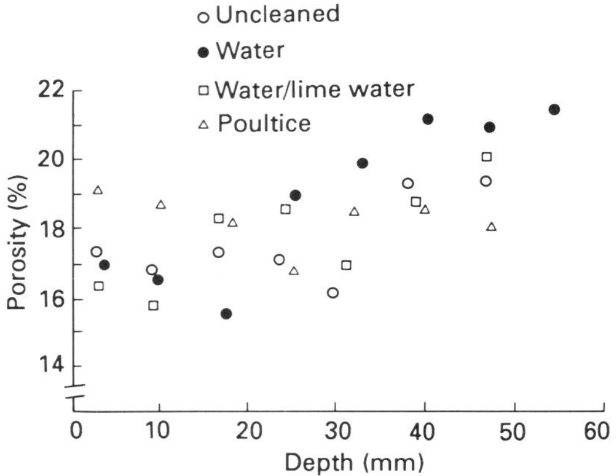

Figure 9.13 Variation of porosity with depth

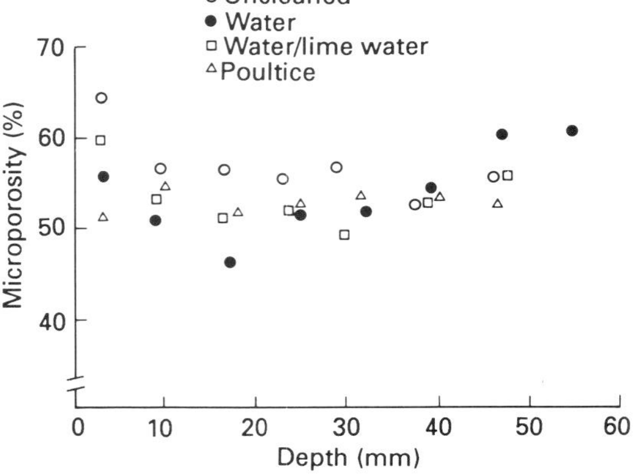

Figure 9.14 Variation of microporosity with depth

investigation, it is not so much the absolute values of microporosity that are of interest as the relative values, before and after treatment. Any marked change in the microporosity would indicate a significant change in the pore structure of the stone, with a consequent change in durability.

A representative selection of the results is depicted in *Figures 9.13 and 9.14*. As one would expect, particularly in the absence of major deposits in the petrological thin sections, neither the poultice nor the lime water has any discernible effect on the overall porosity of the stone. (Bear in mind, when examining the data, that the stone itself is not uniform and that fluctuations will inevitably occur from one part of the stone to another.) The microporosity data, likewise, show no effects attributable to the lime treatments.

Strength

One of the main benefits claimed for the lime treatment is the increase in strength that it brings about. Strength measurements, before and after treatment, are therefore essential to any assessment of the treatment. However, strength measurements are normally carried out on large cubes of stone, e.g. 80 mm (3.1 in) side, and many measurements must be made in order to eliminate statistical fluctuations. To avoid this a technique attributed to Butterbaugh[29] was tried instead. This entailed placing the stone in the jet of an air abrasive gun and measuring the size of the hole that was made in a given time.

The abrasive used was a silica sand of 100 FG mesh. The gun had a 5 mm (0.2 in) nozzle and was operated at 40 psi. It was held in a clamp 100 mm (4 in) away from the surface of the stone. A thin sheet of metal, with a 7 mm (0.3 in) diameter hole drilled in it, was placed on the surface of the stone. The gun was operated for two minutes, and the metal sheet was then moved on to another position. In this way, it was possible to make a line of holes, at approximately 10 mm centres, from the outer edge of each mullion slice to the centre. The size of each hole was measured by filling it level with 120 mesh carborundum grit, weighing the grit and converting to volume.

Examination of all the mullion slices by this technique is not yet completed, but the results for one of the mullions are shown in *Figure 9.15*. Disappointingly, the results are inconclusive. There appears to be a lot of scatter, which is not surprising in view of the inhomogeneity of the stone. Many more results would be required in order to confirm the statistical validity of any apparent trend. Even in the 'best' instance, the size of the outermost holes after lime watering is not very much lower than those of the control.

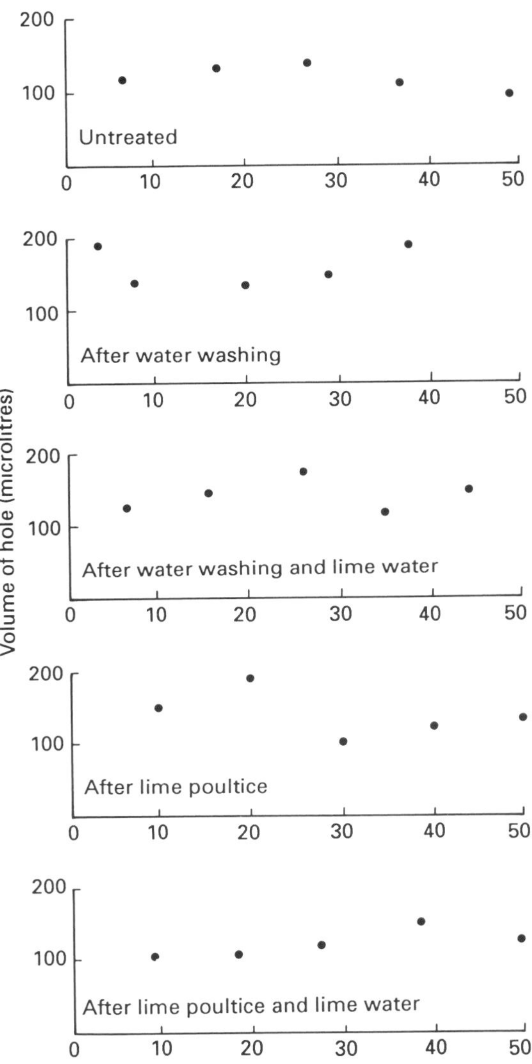

Figure 9.15 Estimation of strength by abrasion resistance

Consolidation of crushed stone

In the absence of conclusive data on strength, an attempt was made to consolidate crushed stone with lime water. Clearly, any consolidation so achieved would represent an increase in strength, since the initial strength was zero. Two types of stone were used, Doulting limestone and Monks Park limestone, which is an oolitic limestone mined near Bath. A silica sand (Ham River sandstone) was also tried. In each case, a carefully graded mix was prepared, in accordance with British Standard BS 1200. The proportions retained by standard meshes were as follows: 2.36 mm, 10%; 1.18 mm, 20%; 600 μm, 20%; 300 μm, 20%; 150 μm, 15%; 10% passed a 150 μm sieve. The moist mixture was placed into the filter funnel shown in *Figure 9.16*. It was next dried and weighed. The tip of the filter paper was then dipped into lime water until the crushed stone was all visibly wet. This took five to ten minutes. This procedure was adopted in order to avoid the fine particles in the mixture from being washed to the bottom, as would have happened if the lime water had been poured in from the top. The stone was then allowed to dry at room temperature. The drying period was never less than 24 hours and was usually several days. The cycle of wetting and drying was repeated thirty times over a period of six months. On each occasion, a control specimen was treated with distilled water.

At the end of the experiment, the Doulting and Monks Park specimens had increased in weight by 0.38 and 0.40% respectively. The sand had increased in weight by 0.22%. The control specimens had not changed weight significantly.

Despite the increase in weight, none of the lime-watered specimens showed any significant consolidation. All of them crumbled at the slightest pressure from a spatula. The Doulting specimen was perhaps marginally stronger than its control, but the Monks Park specimen was, if anything, even more friable than its control. Certainly none of the specimens showed the slightest degree of useful consolidation.

It is generally assumed that any consolidation would be achieved by carbonation of the calcium hydroxide, in a manner analogous to the hardening of lime mortars. Lime mortars harden when carbonation yields an interlocking mass of calcite crystals which binds the aggregate particles together.[30] By comparison with a lime-watered sample of stone, however, the amount of calcium hydroxide available for carbonation in a lime mortar is enormous. The reason for the failure of the lime water to achieve consolidation in this experiment may simply be that insufficient calcium hydroxide is deposited in the stone.

An alternative suggestion was contained in a Building Research Station Digest published in 1959 which reported that appreciable strengthening effects were obtained on friable stone by repeated applications of clear lime water. Repeated applications of lime water in the laboratory had no measurable effect on the strength of friable marble but it was suggested that any consolidation that might be achieved *in situ* might be due as much to the solution and redeposition of calcium sulphate already present in the stone as to the lime introduced into it. This tallies with the later observation that distilled water could sometimes achieve as much consolidation as lime water.[6]

It is clear that the mechanism by which lime water can consolidate porous building materials is not yet understood. There are certainly instances where useful consolidation has been achieved, especially with lime plasters, but equally there are some instances where there has been no apparent effect.[6] It is hoped that the present study will stimulate other workers to a further investigation of the general problem.

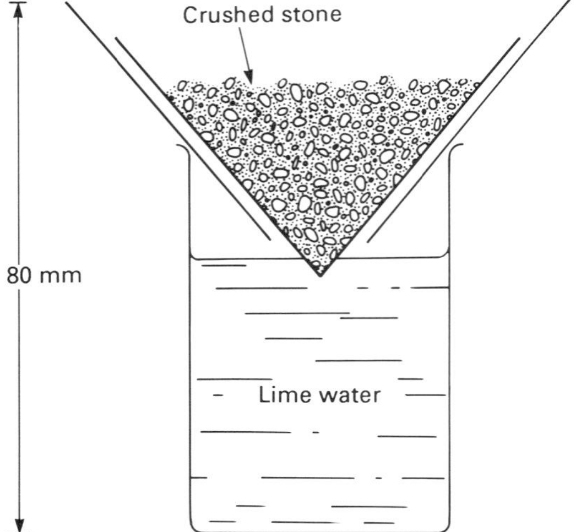

Figure 9.16 Attempted consolidation of crushed stone

Conclusions

1. A lime poultice, and associated washing, does not serve to extract calcium sulphate from the depth of the stone.
2. A lime poultice, and associated washing, can reduce or remove the calcium sulphate skin on the surface of the stone. This may assist the subsequent absorption of lime water, but it also makes the stone more vulnerable to attack by acidic rainwater unless a protective shelter coat is applied.
3. There is no evidence that a lime poultice serves to consolidate friable stone.
4. A lime poultice should be regarded as one of a range of possible cleaning techniques (e.g. clay poultice, air abrasive), each of which has its own strengths and weaknesses. It should not be regarded as a technique of unique stature.
5. On the basis of the laboratory experiments described, there is no conclusive evidence that multiple applications of lime water serve to consolidate friable limestone.

6. Despite these rather negative findings, the lime technique can undoubtedly produce a dramatic change in the condition of decayed limestone. It is possible that part of this change, at least, is attributable simply to the meticulous care and attention which the stone receives, principally the painstaking preparation of the stone and the placing of carefully designed mortars. In view of the evident benefits of the technique its continued use at Wells Cathedral is recommended, but it is clear that further investigation into the technique is required.

Acknowledgements

The work described has been carried out as part of the research programme of the Building Research Establishment of the Department of the Environment, and this section is published by permission of the Director.

The work would not have been possible without the collaboration of the conservation team and the masons at Wells Cathedral. In particular, gratitude is due to Mr Peter Cooley, Superintendent of Works, who supervised the work carried out at Wells, and to Mr Martin Caroe, architect for the West Front, who commissioned the investigation. The Dean and Chapter of Wells kindly gave their consent to the work. The use of grit-blasting for estimating strength was developed in collaboration with Mr Bob Bennett of Bennett Masonry Cleaning.

Further appraisal of the lime method

John Ashurst

A further appraisal of the lime method was made by Clifford Price, now head of the Ancient Monuments Laboratory of English Heritage, Keith Ross, still of the Building Research Establishment, and Graham White, lecturer in biochemistry at University College, Cardiff (Wales, UK).

They carried out an experiment on a limestone mullion removed from the cloister of Wells Cathedral (Doulting limestone) which had a typically decayed and friable surface. Cleaning and consolidation was carried out under the direction of Richard Marsh, then manager of the Wells Conservation Centre, to ensure that the techniques were correctly applied. After a light cleaning with an Airbrasive tool, the mullion was cut into five 100 mm lengths and treated with lime poultice (14-day contact) and forty applications of lime water (over 44 days). To enable the deposition of calcium hydroxide to be detected, a radioactive tracer, ^{45}Ca, was added to the lime. The experiment has been recorded in detail in *Studies in Conservation.*[32]

The conclusions of the experiment, and the experiment itself, are of interest. Important points were that some lime could be traced in every case to a depth of at least 26 mm and that at least half of the deposited lime was found in the outer 2 mm. The poultice deposited some lime, but four to five times more was deposited during the lime watering. How useful is this deposition in terms of consolidation? Based on the experiment and on observations of weight gains in limestone powder consolidated with lime water, the authors concluded that only the outer 1–2 mm can have experienced any appreciable consolidation attributable to lime. Further into the stone the amounts deposited are so small that no consolidating effect can reasonably be expected.

Overall, the results seemed to confirm observations and speculations made in previous years. The lime water application, by virtue of lime deposited, or soluble salt mobilisation and crystallisation, or a combination of both, created a surface firm enough to receive a shelter coat of lime, casein and stone dust. In all cases the vital element for success was the skill, patience and experience of the conservator.

References

1. Rossi-Doria, P., Tabasso, M., Torraca, G. *et al.*, Note on conservation treatment of stone objects, *UNESCO-RILEM Colloquium*, Paris, 1978.
2. Sharp, R.W., private communication, 1981.
3. Amoro, G.G. and Fassina, V., 'Stone decay and conservation', *Material, Science Monograph II*, Elsevier, Amsterdam, 1983
4. Meals, R.N. and Lewis, F.M., *Silicones*, Reinhold, New York, 1958
5. Freeman, G.G., *Silicones*, Iliffe, London, 1962
6. Clarke, B.L. and Ashurst, J., *Stone Preservation Experiment*, Building Research Establishment, Watford, WD2 7JR. England, 1972
7. Schaffer, R.J., *The Weathering of Natural Building Stones*, Department of Scientific and Industrial Research Special Report 18, HMSO London, 1932 (available from Building Research Establishment, Watford WD2 7JR, England)
8. Price, C.A., *Chemistry in Britain*, **11**(10), 350–353, 1975.
9. Herwig Fritsch, *The Preservation of Sandstone*, Central Research and Development Department, Thomas Goldschmidt AG, Essen, Germany
10. Stambolov, T. and de Boer, J.R.v.A., 'The Deterioration and Conservation of Porous Building Materials in Monuments', ICCROM, Rome, 1976
11. Price, C.A., *Brethane Stone Preservative*, Current Paper 1/81, Building Research Establishment, Watford WD2 7JR, England, 1981
12. Ivanova, A.V., Lelekova, O.V. and Filatov, V.V., 'Choosing materials for and developing methods of stabilisation of Mural Painting in Mausoleum Ghur-Emir',

Communication No. 21, United Central Laboratory for Research on Conservation and Restoration of Museum Valuables, Moscow, 1968, 42–54

13. Biscontin, G. and Marchesini, L., 'Techniques d'intervention pour la protection des oeuvres d'art en pierre: resultats obtenus', *Lithoclastia*, Special issue, 51–56, Sept. 29–Oct 30, 1975
14. Rossi-Manaresi, R., 'Causes of decay and conservation treatments of the tuff of Castel dell'Ovo in Naples', in Boloyannis, N. (ed.), *Proc. 2nd Int. Symp. on Deterioration of Building Stones*, Sept 27 to Oct 1, 1976, pp 233–248, NTU, Athens
15. Alessandrini, G., Giambelli, G. and Peruzzi, R., 'Prove sull'efficacia di un trattamento conservativo effetuato sul Duomo di Milano', RP 76/6/31, Politecnico, Milan, 1976
16. Domaslowski, W. and Lehman, J., 'Recherehes sur l'affermissement structural des pierres au moyen de solution de résines thermoplastiques', in Rossi-Manaresi, R. and Torraca, G. (eds) *Proc. Meeting of the Joint Committee for the Conservation of Stone*, Bologna, Oct 1–3, 1971, Centro C. Gnudi per la Conservazione delle Sculture all'Aperto, Bologna, 1972
17. Fedorovich, E.F., Khusnitdinkhodzhaev, Kh. and Ruzybaev, D., 'A new method for consolidation of archaeological objects of unbaked clay and other porous materials' *United Central Laboratory for Research and Conservation of Museum Valuables, Communication No. 17-18*, 113–116, Moscow, 1966
18. Munnikendam, R.A., 'Preliminary notes on the consolidation of porous building materials by impregnation with monomers', *Studies in Conservation*, **12**, 158–162, 1967; also Munnikendam, R.A. and Wolscgrijn, Th. J., 'Further remarks on the impregnation of porous materials with monomers', *Studies in Conservation*, **14**, 133–135, 1969
19. Nonformale, O., 'A method of consolidation and restoration for decayed sandstone', in Rossi-Manaresi, R. (ed.) *Proc. Int. Symp. the Conservation of Stone I*, Bologna, June 19–21 1975, Centro C. Gnudi per la Conservazione delle Sculture all'Aperto, Bologna, 1976
20. Church, A.H., 'Improvements in the means of preserving stone, brick, slate, wood, cement, stucco, plaster, whitewash and colour wash from the injurious action of atmospheric and other influences', British Patent 220, 28 January 1862
21. Lewin, S.Z., 'Preservation of limestone structures', United States Patent 3577244, 4 May 1971; also Lewin, S.Z., 'Rationale of the barium hydroxide–urea treatment of decayed stone', *Studies in Conservation*, **19**, 24–35, 1974
22. Gauri, K.L., 'Efficiency of epoxy resins as stone preservatives', *Studies in Conservation*, **19**, 100–101, 1974
23. Domaslowsky, W., 'Investigation on the consolidation of stones with solutions of epoxy resins', *Biblioteka Muzealnictwa i Ochrony Zabytkow*, Seria B, **15**, Warszawa, 1966
24. Munnikendam, R.A., *Studies in Conservation*, **18**, 95, 1973
25. Anon., *The Development of Silane-Based Preservatives—their Use and Abuse*, Society for the Protection of Ancient Buildings, (now at) 34 Spital Square, London E1 6DY, 1980
26. Henson, D., 'Experiments with milk and lime on limestone surfaces', 1983
27. Anon., 'The selection of natural building stone', *British Research Establishment Digest 269*, 1983
28. *Proc. Int. Symp. on the Deterioration and Protection of Stone Monuments*, Volume 5, Test I.4, UNESCO/RILEM, Paris, 1978
29. Phillips, M.W., 'Acrylic precipitation consolidants', *IIC Congress on Science and Technology in the Service of Conservation*, Washington DC, 1982
30. Lea, F.M., *'The chemistry of cement and concrete'*, 3rd edn, 252, Edward Arnold, London, 1970
31. Anon. 'Stone preservatives', *Building Research Station Digest 128* (First series), 1959
32. Price, C., Ross, K. and White, G., 'A further appraisal of the "Lime technique" for limestone consolidation, using a radioactive tracer', *Studies in Conservation*, **33**, 178–186, 1988

10

The conservation of stone monuments in churches

John Larson

Introduction

The term monument can cover a very wide range of carved memorials that can be as simple as an unadorned inscription tablet, or as complex as some of the great eighteenth century tombs that possess the scale of miniature buildings. However complex or simple the monument may be, all monuments share one basic feature: they are inevitably wedded to the fabric of the building that they inhabit and, of necessity, must suffer the same changes in fortune. Those architects and conservators who have to deal with decaying monuments and buildings must, if they are to succeed in preserving them, attempt to understand the complex interactions that take place, often over a period of centuries, between a monument and its environment.

It is fundamental to any sensible programme of monument conservation that hopes to achieve any enduring results to possess a knowledge of the basic forms of monument construction.

Monument construction

Tomb building in England, combining both sculptured and architectural detail, really began in the thirteenth century and carried through on an ever-increasing scale until the early years of the twentieth century. Throughout this time the basic pattern of construction remained similar. There is a supporting core surrounded by facings of carved stone, usually fixed to the core by cramps or, in a few cases, simply adhered with lime mortar. This basic simplicity of construction, however, has, over many centuries, been elaborated upon by architects and sculptors to the point where certain monuments attempt to achieve forms of construction that would be more suitable in wood than stone. Even in the most elaborate monuments, the same basic elements of construction recur and these can be categorized as follows.

The free-standing box tomb

The free-standing box tomb was very popular throughout the medieval period until well into the seventeenth century. The basic elements of this type of construction can be seen in *Figure 10.1*. A core of brick, stone blocks or rubble was constructed, to form a solid platform around which the monument was built. The core was usually built onto the floor of the church, and therefore may well stand on a bed of cut stone. In many cases, however, the core simply stands on earth, particularly if there is a vault below. With time this obviously creates problems of movement in the core and also allows the penetration of moisture and soluble salts.

Although the cores are usually hollow and make efficient use of mass to strength ratio, particularly clumsy constructions, where the core is a solid conglomerate of rubble, earth and mortar, are often found. It is obvious that there is little chance of either introducing air circulation or eliminating damp in such a structure.

Once the foundations, if they exist, and the core were constructed, the carved facing slabs of the monument were attached to the core. A wide variety of carving stones used for such monuments are found, ranging from Purbeck 'Marble' and alabaster, to limestones, sandstone and marbles. In general, the thickness of these facing slabs does not vary greatly. On average, they are 50 mm (2 in) to 75 mm (3 in) deep. Where the workmanship is poor, or the monument is very large, the stone may be 150 mm (6 in) to 300 mm (12 in) deep. The whole strength of this pattern of tomb lies in its core. The visible

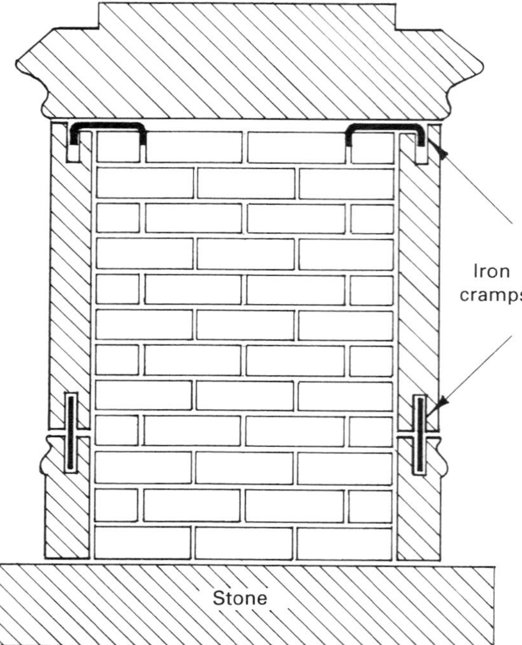

Figure 10.1 Traditional construction of box tomb. Although some medieval tombs have a brick core (as shown here) many are supported by a crude rubble, mortar and earth infill

elements of the monument rarely have a structural role; they are simply cladding.

The carved elements of the tomb are attached to the core by means of cramps and dowels. These are nearly always made of ferrous metal and little evidence is found to suggest that any other metal, such as copper, brass or bronze, was ever used on a regular basis. The cramps and dowels that are found in small medieval tombs vary little in character from those that are found in the enormous constructions of the eighteenth century. The cramps, whether retaining or supporting, fit into slots cut into the edges of the facing panel and are bedded into a suitable adhesive.

Insufficient research has been carried out to determine the difference in type between medieval and later adhesives, but it would be unwise to assume that the only adhesive available to masons of that period was lime mortar. In tombs of all periods, shellac and wax-resin mixtures are found being used as adhesives, but the constant moving and rebuilding of tombs that has occurred in so many churches over the years makes such evidence unreliable.

The box tomb acts as a support for a large slab on which there is often an embedded brass or, most commonly, a recumbent effigy or pair of effigies. The true box tomb is often further embellished above the level of the effigy with decorated finials, coats of arms, or other heraldic devices. However, when the construction goes beyond this, the structure really comes into the category of the canopy tomb.

The box tomb basically relies on the strength of its own construction and is therefore most often a free-standing monument. Tombs of similar construction are often built against walls in churches, but they are rarely fixed to the wall by cramps or other constructional devices. They simply lean against the wall and are fixed by mortar joints. In this case, there is no back panel to the tomb and the core is in direct contact with the wall of the building. In certain cases, notably St George's, Colegate, Norwich, where a tomb has been moved from a free-standing site, there is a carved panel facing into the wall, which would originally have been visible.

The wall tomb

This category of monument can be broken down into two types; the full wall tomb and the cantilevered wall monument. The full wall tomb, which has at its base the solid foundation of the box tomb, becomes a partially cantilevered construction as it ascends the wall, and derives its support from the wall behind (*Figure 10.2*). This type of construction can be found throughout the medieval period and is echoed in many Easter sepulchres and sedilias. It reaches its greatest technical extravagence in the vast tombs of the eighteenth century, constructed by such sculptors as Rysbrack and Roubiliac. The cantilevered wall monument (*Figure 10.3*) owes its origins to the sculpture of the Italian Renaissance, but is only fully exploited in baroque England.

The difference in construction between these two tomb types is very basic. The first relies on the firm foundation of the box tomb with its core to provide a platform for the elements of the superstructure, which are then tied back to the wall with cramps. The second has no support other than the cramps which secure it to the wall. In the seventeenth century, the cantilevered wall tomb tended to be very solidly constructed and relied heavily on large corbels (often penetrating 300 mm (12 in) deep into the wall) at the base of the monument to support the upper elements. Such a construction becomes very much a part of the wall into which it is constructed and often cannot be dismantled without considerable reconstruction of the wall behind. In the eighteenth century, when marble became the fashionable material for monuments, as opposed to limestone and alabaster, its inherent strength and expense led sculptors such as Francis Bird (*Figure 10.4*) to undertake daring experiments, whereby a monument was merely hung on the surface of the

Figure 10.2 Eighteenth century wall tomb by Roubiliac: Warkton Church

Figure 10.3 Example of eighteenth century cantilevered wall tomb

wall with cramps and was not corbelled back into the stone behind.

The canopy tomb

This type of monument employs the basic forms of construction found in the box tomb and the wall tomb. It was used throughout the medieval period, and is shown at its most elaborate in the Percy tomb, but reached its greatest constructional daring in the seventeenth century in tombs such as the St John monument at Lydiard Tregoze.

The free-standing canopy tomb usually has as its basis a box tomb construction and may have a reclining or kneeling effigy on top. Above this, the construction may rise to form an arched or domed canopy, although in many cases the termination is a stone tester supported on vertical columns. In this form, a pyramidal or rectangular format is essential to achieve stability in the tomb. However, when the tomb is adjacent to a supporting wall, the canopy may be cantilevered from the wall and may derive little support from the box tomb below. In such cases there is often a very complex arrangement of ironwork embedded into the canopy, in an attempt to replace the strength that would normally be derived from supporting columns. The ironwork in these tombs is not always original. Very often it is the work of the nineteenth century architect or engineer, who has tried to preserve the rash constructions of the seventeenth century.

Causes of decay in monuments

Structural problems

The very fact that monuments are of composite construction, containing a variety of materials of different thicknesses and weights bonded together by iron, is enough to ensure that they will, at some time, suffer some form of movement or collapse. Moisture in all its forms is the main agent of decay in all stonework. In monuments, moisture causes

Figure 10.4 Monument to Orlando Gee by F. Bird: Isleworth Church. This monument has a completely flat back and is only supported by irons in the walls. The corbel brackets at the base of the monument are not inset into the wall

disruption of the ironwork by the process of rusting and expansion. The expanding cramps and dowels exert an enormous pressure when they are trapped in stone; several tonnes of marble can be lifted by the expansion of a few iron cramps within a monument. This expansion causes such pressure that the brittle stone cracks and becomes structurally unsound. Movement in one part of a monument will also affect other parts of the structure and gradually create tension throughout the monument.

Structural pressures can also be exerted on a monument from outside. If the monument has inadequate foundations, or is built above a slowly collapsing vault, the shift beneath the monument will result in opening of the joints and the collapse of the core. If the monument is fixed by cramps to the wall, as well as to the ground, any movement will cause tremendous tensions that can result in the total collapse of the monument. The monument conservator may be the first to discover some serious weakness in the structure. Such weaknesses, even if only suspected, should be made known to the client immediately.

Pressures on the monument can also come from the wall into which it is fixed. Many churches have undergone structural alterations over the years and it is not uncommon for a door or window to have been blocked in to provide wall space for a monument. The filling of such an aperture is often of the roughest kind and sometimes consists of rubble bonded with mud and plaster. Monuments bedded into such structures, or sited above them, usually develop structural problems at a later date when the wall begins to sag under the weight of the monument.

One major factor in structural decay can often be blamed on the monument's designer. It is particularly apparent in some tombs of the seventeenth century, when alabaster was often the chosen medium, that the artist attempted to stretch the material beyond the limit of its tensile strength. In some cases this has resulted in partial collapse of the monument. In others alabaster has cracked or simply warped (*Figure 10.5*).

Figure 10.5 Alabaster monument: Bletsoe. One can see clearly that the support provided for the continuous alabaster architrave (1.5 m) has been inadequate and the stone has gradually warped

Decay from soluble salts

Perhaps the most insidious and least understood form of decay in stone monuments is that caused by the migration and crystallization of soluble salts. All old churches that do not have damp proof courses are contaminated by salts of one form or another. The most common types are sulphates and nitrates. Chlorides are less common and are most often found in maritime areas.

Salts in a monument tend to come from the ground on which they are built, although they can be introduced into a monument by the use of contaminated mortars. The classic pattern of salt contamination can, however, be broken down into several simple stages (*Figure 10.6*). If the source of moisture derived from rising damp caused by flooding, changes in the water table, blocked drains or, more commonly, from raising the ground level outside the church above that of the inside, then the salts will rise from the ground and be drawn into the walls of the church. If the cause is falling damp, e.g. broken gutters, decayed mouldings, or a damaged roof, then the rise of the salts will follow the moisture up the wet walls, but, because the monument may also be saturated with water from above, the breakdown will usually be even more rapid than that caused by rising damp.

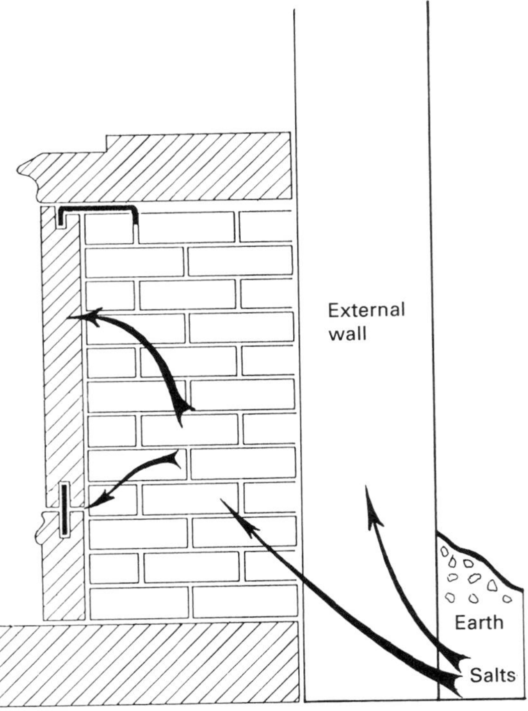

Figure 10.6 Progress of salt contamination. The most common source of salts is in the ground around or underneath the church. Where earth has been allowed to build up against an outside wall, the salts seep into the wall, gradually migrate into the core of the monument and then attack the mortar joints and fabric of the monuments. The mortar joints in both core and monument act as an absorbent pathway along which the salts can easily move

The progress of salt migration depends on cycles of wetting and drying to provide the migratory impetus. The walls of a church act as a wick. They are basically a column of stone standing on wet earth, and above ground level they act as a membrane between the outer and inner environments. As part of the outer environment, they are exposed to all the dramatic changes of weather, temperature and humidity. The inner environment changes less rapidly and may remain wet and cold, even when the outside environment is warm and dry. Generally the wall will be drier than the earth on which it stands. Therefore moisture will naturally tend to rise up into the dry stone above, carrying with it the salts in solution. While the salts remain in solution, they will cause little harm. However, when they crystallize near the surface as a subflorescence, or on the surface as an efflorescence (due to changes in temperature, or humidity, or wall thickness), damage will occur.

One thing that is certain about the presence of salts in a structure is that they will not simply disappear. Monuments do not mysteriously get better. It is possible to reduce salt activity in a wall by careful drainage of the ground, but as long as the salts remain they will always pose a threat. Once salts are in stone, the changes in relative humidity and temperature in the atmosphere around the stone will be sufficient to continue the growth of salts. Recent work in Switzerland[1] has shown not only that salts continue to migrate as long as moisture is present, but that the salts themselves will change the chemical balance of the stone they inhabit, attracting moisture to it. In some cases this will actively change the temperature within the stone.

Although salts display slightly different patterns of behaviour in different stones, their effect on a monument is equally destructive whether it be made of marble, alabaster, limestone or sandstone.

Condensation and heating

Unfortunately, the climate within most churches is not controlled in any way. Very few churches possess adequate ventilation and many of them are overheated for very limited periods of time. As a result, much of the damage that occurs to monuments is due to condensation and surface moisture. One of the stones most readily affected by condensation is Purbeck 'marble'. Because the stone presents a cold, polished surface, moisture condenses readily on it and, lying on the surface, slowly seeps into tiny fissures which are often found in this shelly limestone. The moisture is absorbed slowly into the surface, combining with salts from within the stone. Over a period of time the polish will disappear and the Purbeck 'marble' will become rough and take on a grey appearance, superficially similar to cement.

Black limestone and slate (usually used for inscriptions) will also be attacked by condensation; this often shows as dribbles etched into the surface where the moisture has formed persistently. Carrara marble and alabaster are also attacked by condensation, because they are both relatively impervious. However, most limestones, which are porous, will accept the moisture vapour into their pore structure without visible damage. The recurring movement of water droplets over a polished surface causes an erosion similar to that of a river in a valley, although a chemical reaction between water and stone is also involved.

Heating the interior of a church for a short period draws moisture through the walls and aggravates the condensation problem. Gas heaters are perhaps one of the worst forms of heating, as they give off many litres of water into the atmosphere in a few hours.

The greatest disasters occur when radiators or hot water pipes are placed near monuments. The heat will draw salts and moisture into and, eventually, through the monument. This creates an exaggerated rate of salt crystallization and an accelerating rate of stone decay.

Damage from restoration

A great part of the damage to monuments is manmade and not the result of natural causes. Whether a restoration is good or bad, whether from the aesthetic or technical viewpoint, is always debatable. However, on the technical side, there is positive evidence that certain treatments lead to decay.

Cleaning

Alabaster (calcium sulphate) is water soluble and therefore should never be cleaned with soap and water, which will slowly erode the surface. As alabaster is also very soft it should not be cleaned with abrasives, such as commercial abrasives containing pumice and bleach. Acid and caustic solutions should also be avoided because they will erode the surface and create, or exacerbate, staining.

Marble (calcium carbonate) is not readily soluble in water, and therefore the majority of cleaning treatments are based on water and liquid chemical treatments. It is unsafe, however, to use large quantities of water on marble for extended periods of time, because this can create iron-staining and will eventually cause loss of detail in fine carving. Acid and caustic solutions will both erode and discolour statuary marble. Abrasives such as pumice, or wet and dry paper, will remove any traces of original polish or fine detail.

Limestones and sandstones are used in a wide variety of types for monument construction. They differ from alabaster or marble in that some are porous. It is very noticeable in churches that it is the highly polished marble and alabaster monuments that suffer from surface erosion caused by condensation. The more porous limestones and sandstones absorb atmospheric moisture quite readily, and will also absorb any water from a cleaning treatment. Liberal washing can, for this reason, encourage salt crystal growths and staining from salts and iron. Similarly, the use of bleach, acids and powdered detergents can create problems in the surface pores of the stone which may not become apparent until several years later.

Generally, in the cleaning of all carved or decorative stone in churches, it is best to use a very controlled approach. Cleaning should proceed in small, manageable sections, using the minimum quantity of cleaning agent, so that there is never any danger of the treatment damaging a large part of the monument. Where a monument is still in contact with the fabric of the church during cleaning and has not been dismantled, great care should be taken not to saturate it with water, because this will create problems with salts that may eventually cause structural damage.

Pigmentation

One of the misunderstood areas of monument conservation, simply because it arouses strong aesthetic prejudices, is that which centres around the treatment of polychromy on monuments. If a monument is painted or gilded, it cannot be cleaned as though it were made of plain stone. It is surprising, however, how often this does occur and much of the understanding of the history of sculpture in this country has been blurred by such inept treatment. Water washing of painted stonework is a certain way of losing pigment, either from direct action of the water or from later salt growths. The cleaning of painted monuments is a specialized task and requires the expertise of a skilled conservator.

Although the current opinion is that monuments should not be repainted to simulate original colour schemes, a considerable amount of repainting does still occur. This is usually aesthetically disastrous because no one can hope to recreate the original painted scheme on top of decayed stonework. From the conservation point of view, it can also damage the monument. In some cases, oil paints and enamel paints have been used on monuments. These not only stain the stone, they also encapsulate the stone in an impervious film. Salts can build up under this film to cause irreparable damage. The application of new paint over original paint also creates problems and may result in the loss of the original paint fragments.

Cements

Portland cements should never be allowed to come into contact with old stone. So much damage has been caused to monuments by rebuilding with cement that it is surprising to find that this practice still occurs in churches. Long observation has proved that cements create or aggravate salt activity in old stone and will eventually lead to its destruction. Wherever cement or concrete has to be used near a monument, the monument should always be isolated from it by a suitable membrane.

Consolidation treatments and damp-proof courses

There have been many attempts over the past hundred years to consolidate crumbling monuments *in situ*. Materials such as wax, lime water, shellac, oil, epoxy resins and silicones have all been used for this purpose. In one way or another, they have all largely proved ineffective. The main reason is that deep-seated disruption, which is usually caused by soluble salts, cannot be treated by forming a casing of hardened stone on the surface. In fact, all research has shown that such impervious barriers accelerate decay. Even lime water, which remains permeable, can activate rather than neutralize salt activity. The injection of a liquid damp-proof course or the partial fitting of a solid one, will hasten decay, because salt is trapped and causes local tensions within the stone.

The treatment of monuments

The monument and the environment

When formulating a programme of conservation for a monument in a church, the problems that exist within its environment must be considered first. Faults in the building, such as bad drainage, broken gutters, decayed pointing, leaking roofs, condensation and structural movement, should all be dealt with before the monument is treated. The commonest failing is the gradual rise of the outside ground level above that of the floor in the church. This inevitably leads to problems with rising damp and salts. When all these problems have been dealt with, the treatment of the monument can begin.

The crucial question is really whether or not to dismantle. In most cases where a monument shows serious signs of breakdown, due to the presence of iron cramps or salts, there is very little choice but to dismantle. There are cases where local consolidation, removal of visible cramps, or partial dismantling, may solve or at least arrest the decay. However, it generally makes better long-term economic sense to carry out a full treatment, involving full dismantling, rather than to patch a monument and then undertake the full treatment at a later date. There are many examples where expensive surface treatments on salt contaminated monuments have not proved effective. As a result, the monuments have had to be dismantled and properly treated later. This makes monument conservation unnecessarily expensive and subjects the monument to further years of decay.

In cases of salt contamination (*Figure 10.7*), the monument can only be effectively de-salinated if it is fully dismantled and each individual block of stone is treated by poulticing. If the basic structure of a tomb is affected by expanding ferrous cramps (*Figure 10.8*), partial dismantling, or repointing of joints, would be ineffective.

To dismantle a large, finely carved monument by a sculptor such as Rysbrack or Roubiliac may be considered by some people to be vandalism.

Figure 10.7 Marble monument: Kirkleatham. Crystallization of salts has caused expansion in the core. Because the marble facings are cramped to the core, they have gradually cracked under the pressure.

Figure 10.8 Expanding iron cramp causing splitting in marble 12 cm thick

Figure 10.9 Seventeenth century painted stone monument: Colyton. The monument was originally painted and then repainted in the nineteenth century. All mortar joints had also been covered with paint.

However, with modern conservation techniques, it is possible to dismantle, conserve and re-erect such monuments without damage. Even large polychrome monuments with pigment actually covering the mortar joints, such as the monument at Colyton (*Figure 10.9*), can be dismantled without pigment loss. By 'facing up' friable stone (*Figure 10.10*) with a reinforced tissue before dismantling, the retention of all fragments of paint and stone can be ensured. This type of treatment allows the monument to be either partially or wholly transported off-site, if necessary, in order to be more fully treated in the safety of the conservation studio.

In any programme of monument conservation, record keeping is of the utmost importance. When a monument is to be dismantled, a complete record of the operation is vital. At the very least, good black and white photographs should be taken before, during and after the operation. These should be related to a measured drawing of the monument before conservation and to a written record of the condition before treatment. There should be a full record of treatment listing all the products involved, however basic. In some cases, photogrammetric surveys and corrected photography will be useful. Whenever polychromy exists, colour photography is essential.

Very few monuments contain buried remains. However, in some cases, bones or evidence of earlier remains do turn up during dismantling. Therefore it is wise to inform the local archaeologist when work of this nature is to be undertaken.

Membranes

Once a monument has been dismantled, the site that it occupies in the church should be treated so that damp or structural movement will not affect it again. The wall behind the monument should be repointed and any structural faults corrected. The floor beneath the monument may be perfectly sound, but the monument may be standing on little more than a bed of earth and rubble. In some cases, it may be supported only by the roof of a collapsing vault. In

Figure 10.10 Detail of Colyton monument, showing tissue 'facing-up'. By covering the painted surfaces with tissue and size (polyvinyl alcohol) the joints could be revealed by making incisions through the tissue and paint layers. When the paint had been peeled back on either side of the joint, the joints could be cut with a chisel. During rebuilding, the paint could be laid down and ironed with a heated spatula over the new joints

the majority of such situations it will be necessary to provide a new base for the monument. This usually consists of a concrete raft about 150 mm (6 in) deep. In some cases, slabs of stone are used for the base.

Whatever the condition of the wall or floor, all monuments must be isolated from them by a substantial waterproof membrane after refurbishment. There are many forms of membrane available today, ranging from thick polythene, epoxy resin and glass-fibre mat, to metal foils and bitumen laminates and even some polyester foams. Many of these membranes are suitable for small-scale domestic work or buildings where a life-span of thirty years is envisaged. However, when conserving church monuments, a life of a hundred years should be expected. Therefore, proven materials are needed that will ensure long-term service.

Lead has many advantages. A Code 4 to Code 6 lead sheet has sufficient thickness to keep out moisture and salts. It also has considerable flexibility, so that it will withstand compression without tearing. In one example, a two-hundred-year-old lead membrane which had been situated beneath a 15 m (45 ft) high medieval market cross was removed without any sign of damage. When coated with bitumen on both sides to protect it from alkali attack from mortar, a lead membrane will provide long-term protection for any monument and will isolate it from a potentially hostile environment.

Although lead can tear from its fixings when hung on a wall, this can be minimized if the lead is given adequate support, and is wedged and screwed into mortar joints. If this is done when it is pinned behind a monument, experience has shown that the movement is negligible.

Where a monument has to be cramped to a wall and the membrane has therefore to be pierced, the area around the point of pentration can be sealed with a suitable waterproof mastic such as Akemi, or 'General' resin mixed with sand.

Cores

The core is a basic structural feature of nearly all types of monument. When rebuilding a monument, the main concern is to produce a core that will not be a reservoir of moisture in the very heart of the monument. A dry system that does not use aqueous mortars has been evolved using Celcon blocks bonded with a sand and polyester mortar (*Figure 10.11*). In certain cases, where damp is not a great problem, a polyvinyl acetate emulsion (such as Unibond) and sand mix can be used. Apart from the obvious advantage of this system in excluding water, it also allows the core to be built up rapidly and does not require a long period for drying and settlement.

The core should be built slightly smaller than the internal dimensions of the monument, so that an air gap of 25–50 mm (1–2 in) can be allowed between the core and the monument. Where horizontal members have to bear directly onto the core, they should be isolated from the core by a lead and bitumen membrane (*Figure 10.12*).

Dowels, cramps and mortars

As there is a basic logic in the dismantling of a monument, in that it should be dismantled from the top down, so there is a logical pattern to reconstruction. Once the core has been constructed, building up is from the base mouldings. The individual elements should be cramped back to the core, making certain that the dimensions of the monument coincide with the original scheme.

Figure 10.11 Detail of monument at Lingfield during rebuilding. Here one can see the new core on its lead damp-proof course and the bottom stages of the monument during rebuilding. The monument is also on a damp-proof course and there is an air gap between it and the core of about 40–50 mm (1½–2 in)

Figure 10.12 Detail showing lead damp-proof course

When reconstructing a monument, the architect and conservator are faced with certain basic problems, arising from the use of both synthetic and traditional materials. The difficulty is in producing a balance between rigid and flexible materials, movement and stability. For instance, in traditional monument construction, the following pattern would be typical:

1. Core (brick and rubble and lime mortar), which is flexible
2. Monument (stone facings and lime mortar), which is rigid and flexible
3. Cramps (usually ferrous) which are rigid and brittle
4. Adhesives (shellac or wax/resin) which are initially soft, but become brittle

These materials, which are allied to the possible movement between the monument and supporting building fabric, are significant factors in the deterioration of monuments. When reconstructing a monument, all these factors must be taken into account and appropriate materials chosen.

None of the materials used in reconstruction must be affected by damp. Therefore, for cramps and dowels, the most satisfactory material is stainless steel. Non-aqueous, or at least water-repellent, mortars should be used for bedding the components of the monument. These are best made from mixtures of polyester, acrylic or PVA, mixed with silica sands.

Of course, stainless steel is highly inflexible. Some degree of movement around a cramp or dowel can be designed for, by sleeving in a thick polythene or nylon tube. Where necessary, the flexibility of the adhesive can be increased by using an acrylic or PVA resin instead of an epoxy or polyester resin. All of these changes will allow some small movement in the monument, but they will not weaken the retaining power of the cramps.

Whenever possible, the conservator should reuse the slots for cramps made by the original mason. Only where recent breaks have occurred will new

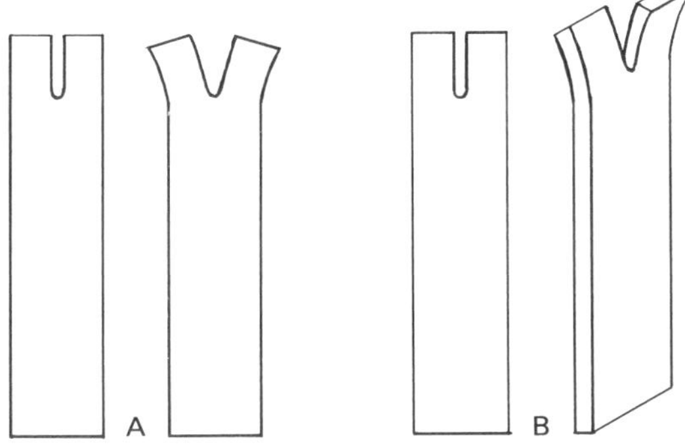

Figure 10.13 Two basic forms of cramp. Both cramps are made from flat stainless steel bar. A saw cut (about 15 mm long) is made at one end. In 'A' a chisel is inserted in the saw cut and tapped until a V-shaped is formed. In 'B' the two prongs are tapped away from each other with a hammer

holes be necessary. There are two basic shapes for cramps, which have not changed since medieval times (*Figure 10.13*). These can easily be cut on site in a vice and can be bent cold.

Fillings, repairs and retouching

There are widely differing views on the extent to which a monument should be restored. Some feel that it should look as new, while others feel that a strictly archaeological approach should be taken and no cosmetic work is necessary beyond essential structural repairs. The grant-awarding body of the Church of England, The Council for the Care of Churches, has a positive, though slightly flexible, view. In effect, it feels that the harmony of the monument should be retained, but no unnecessary cosmetic work should be undertaken, particularly if it is likely to blur the original intention of the artist. Thus recutting large areas of a monument, putting back garlands, hands, feet, armorials, or large areas of moulding, would be regarded as unethical. Generally, areas of moulding can be filled with a suitable filler when a disturbing break occurs in a line of moulding. Recutting a whole line of moulding and disposing of the original would not be sanctioned.

Over the years, considerable progress has been made in producing fillings that look very like marble, alabaster or limestone and will survive in a church environment for many years without deterioration. The advantage of a plastic repair, rather than splicing in new stone, is obvious. Plastic fillers can be modelled *in situ* and have a minimal effect on the original stone, whereas to piece in a new block of stone would require the loss of a certain amount of original material. The plastic filler has the added advantage that, from the ethical viewpoint, it will always be recognizable as a synthetic addition. A stone indent may look like an original repair, and possibly lead to historical confusion.

The most suitable fillings are based on mixtures of synthetic resins (polyesters and acrylics), mixed with ground stone dust, silica sands and alabaster powder. They can be mixed to a thixotropic putty and worked in place with a spatula. If carefully matched to the colour of the original, there should be no need to paint over the filling to blend it with the original. This is always an advantage for future maintenance, because it allows washing with water or some weak cleaning solutions at a future date.

In the past, plaster fillings could not visually match the marble or alabaster on which they were used. Their porosity also meant they were a breeding ground for salts and they tended to soften and crumble when attacked by rising damp.

Where re-touching is necessary, usually to preserve heraldic colour, or to tone down unsightly patches, the best medium is an acrylic. Acrylics produce a paint that will form a skin on the surface of the stone and will dry rapidly. These paints also have the advantage that they do not stain the stone and can easily be removed at a later date, should taste or practical necessity require it.

Consolidants and surface finishes

Stone consolidation is a subject which arouses a great deal of passion. There are many myths surrounding the treatment of decaying stone and the subject must be looked at logically if a sensible approach to the problem is to be formulated.

The basic factors that need to be borne in mind when looking at a crumbling stone monument include:

1. The major cause of all stone decay in churches is damp, either rising or falling.
2. Migrating soluble salts are the agency through which damp creates the greatest damage.
3. If stone is to 'breathe', it will go on absorbing moisture, salts and atmospheric pollutants.
4. It is dangerous to stop stone from 'breathing', when it is part of a major structure such as a church, if it does not have a damp proof course.
5. It is likely that, if a deteriorating monument is consolidated *in situ*, the damage caused by salt migration will be accelerated.

Once these factors have been assessed, a decision can be made on the desirability of full or partial consolidation. It is only possible to treat a monument successfully when full dismantling has been undertaken and the source of damp removed.

The consolidant must completely isolate each block against the further penetration of moisture, and the depth of penetration must be sufficient to ensure that the protection is not merely on the surface of the stone. Partial consolidation is only permissible where the element treated can be fully isolated from the rest of the monument, as in the case of an isolated figure.

The most widely used consolidants for marble, limestone and sandstone monuments are the silanes. These are deep-penetrating consolidants which give, on average, 3.5 cm (1.4 in) penetration. Silanes deposit silica in the stone and impart a high degree of water repellency. They can be applied by brushing, spraying, pipette and drip feed, but it must be stressed that they should *only* be applied by a skilled conservator who understands the full implications of this radical treatment.

There are two basic silane systems in use in the UK at the moment. One is a catalysed silane, which gels within a few hours and has a short working time. It is therefore mainly suitable for the treatment of large, plain surfaces. The second system is a mixture of acrylic and silane. This method allows the conservator a long working period and is suitable where more intricate work is involved, such as sculpture or ornament. It also allows a much wider range of cleaning treatments to be used, which is essential in cases where stonework has to be consolidated before it can be cleaned. The catalysed silanes, once cured, will only respond to air-abrasive cleaning: the acrylic-silane system allows the use of solvents and other more controllable treatments.

In cases where consolidation is not required, but where it would be advantageous to apply a protective coating to the stone after conservation, a varnish of cosmolloid wax, ketone 'N' resin and white spirit can be applied. This should only be used on the more impervious stones, such as marble, alabaster or compact limestone. It should never be applied to the more permeable limestones and sandstones. There is also a range of acrylics available, which can be mixed with wax or sometimes with silicones. These have proved very durable, even when subjected to external weathering tests. They have the added advantage that they can easily be removed with white spirit or acetone.

References

1. Arnold, A., 'Rising damp and saline minerals', paper presented at 4th International Congress on the deterioration and preservation of stone objects, 7–9 July 1982, University of Louisville, Kentucky
2. Larson, J., 'Conservation of alabaster monuments in churches', *The Conservator*, **3**, 28–33, 1979

11

The conservation of stone sculpture in museums

John Larson

Stone in the museum environment

There are many misconceptions regarding the role of the museum-based conservator. The greatest of these is that the sulpture in his care must be in good condition and will require little attention apart from cleaning. Nothing could be further from the truth. The origins of museum collections are threefold:

1. Objects from churches, castles or temples
2. Objects from tombs or archaeological sites
3. Objects from private houses and collections

In the first case, the objects will have been subject to many of the aggressive conditions mentioned in the preceding chapter. In the second, they will have been subject to burial and may be in an advanced state of decay when acquired by the museum. In the third, they will have been treated according to the whim of the owner and may well have been cleaned by unskilled staff over many years, usually with abrasives, bleaches and strong caustic solutions.

Therefore much of the stone sculpture in national museums is in a state of decay, and although much of it is housed in reasonably stable conditions it continues to decay.

The enemies of stone in museums are much the same as those in churches, namely moisture and salts. In the museum environment, however, these cycles of decay become extended and often produce less dramatic results. Even in very controlled conditions, only small changes in relative humidity and temperature are required to continue the cycle of salt growth. Even strict environmental control is unable to stabilize this condition. Therefore the stone conservator is required to take positive action to treat a great many of the stones in his care.

It is ironic that one of the main reasons why so much stonework in museums is deteriorating is not from neglect, but from too much attention. A stone that has been in a museum collection for a hundred years or more may well have been treated more than once during that time. In the past, waxes, baryta water, shellac, soluble nylon and all manner of synthetic resins were used to consolidate stone, often without any real understanding of the nature of stone decay. Large-scale installations, using cement for the fixing of large stones (*Figure 11.1*), were also responsible for the decay of many important objects.

The museum approach

One great advantage that the museum conservator has over the conservator working on his own in a church is that of continuity of practice and availability of records of treatment. The museum conservator can constantly reassess his treatments by comparing them with past treatments. He is also surrounded daily by his successes and failures. Such a concentration of experience, coupled with the demands of an active curatorial staff, allowed the museum conservator to develop techniques of examination and treatment that, until recently, were unknown in the world of the church conservator.

The use of the binocular microscope for the regular examination of sculpture surfaces (*Figure 11.2*) has heightened the conservator's awareness of the wealth of historical and artistic detail that cannot be seen by the naked eye. To preserve such detail, a more refined approach to stone cleaning and preservation has been evolved in museums. Many of the cleaning techniques listed below have been in use in museums for over twenty years. During that time, the results of their use have been monitored, so that some assessment can be made as to their long-term effect.

Figure 11.1 Detail of carved plinth, showing spalling caused by the migration of soluble salts in cement

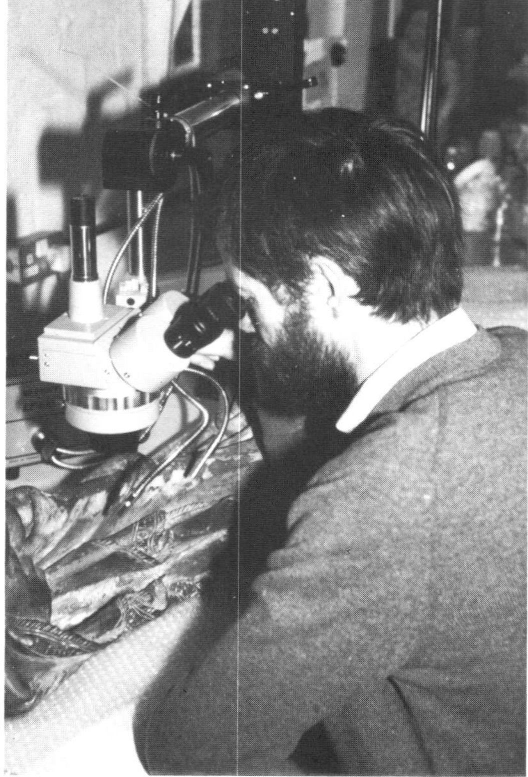

Figure 11.2 Sculpture being examined under binocular microscope: (magnification range ×10 to ×40)

Cleaning techniques

See pages 202–207 for case histories.

Poulticing

The idea of using a poultice to draw out dirt from stone evolved from a technique described by Plenderleith[1] for drawing salts out of stone with poultices of paper pulp. The advantage of using a poultice, rather than soaking, for cleaning is considerable. Cleaning a stone by soaking is not only dangerous, it is also unnecessary. Soaking may disrupt salt and minerals deep within the stone, thereby setting up salt movement, or iron-staining. It is also wasteful. In cleaning, only the stone surface need be wetted. Deep cleaning is rarely necessary. By using a poultice of deionized water and sepiolite (magnesium silicate), a layer of water can be suspended over the surface of the stone and kept there while it dissolves the dirt layer. As the poultice dries (*Figure 11.3*) the water evaporates and pulls the dirt back into the poultice. After about twelve hours, the mud begins to fall away. At this stage, the rest of the poultice can be removed and the stone cleaned with swabs and deionized water. This treatment may need to be repeated on badly blackened stone (*Figures 11.4, 11.5*), but careful use of this treatment is sufficiently gentle to allow even areas of painted stone to be cleaned without loss. The same sculpture immersed in a bath of water for several weeks, following the traditional treatment, would have lost much surface detail and a great deal of paint before it could be declared clean.

Water poultices are mainly used for cleaning marble, limestone and some sandstones. Alabaster can be cleaned with poultices composed of clay and white spirit.

Air-brasive

This machine (*Figure 11.6*) provides a dry abrasive cleaning, which is very useful in cases where water could be disruptive. However, the machine has severe limitations. It is essentially a micro-

Figure 11.3 Bust of Orlando Gee covered with clay poultice. One can see cracks in the clay as it begins to dry out

Figure 11.4 Sutton Valence reredos: before cleaning

sandblaster. Microscopic beads of aggregate (glass beads, or aluminium oxide are the most commonly used) are fired by compressed air from a tiny nozzle at the tip of a small, pen-like gun. Although in skilled hands this machine can be carefully controlled, it undoubtedly has a deleterious effect on the stone surface by weakening and causing surface abrasions. In many cases where thick sulphation layers cover the surface of a sculpture, it is the only tool available to conservators which will remove the encrustation without wetting the surface.

Cavitron

This machine (*Figure 11.7*) is an ultrasonic, dental de-scaling tool. It is a wet process and it functions by producing a delicate, ultrasonic vibration in the working tip, over which a jet of water is played. As the water runs under the tip it forms a gentle bubbling action, and when the tip is placed just above the surface of the stone, the machine will rapidly disperse the dirt. This machine is ideal when used in conjunction with poulticing techniques (*Figure 11.8*) and is very good for removing particles of dirt trapped in undercuts and crevices (*Figure 11.9*). It can be dangerous when carelessly used. If the vibrating point is pressed against a stone, then a small pit will result. This can be avoided if the point is kept moving over the surface.

Chemical treatments

Conservation of paintings is the conservation discipline with the longest history. Sculpture conservation has borrowed many of its techniques and materials from this discipline. The types of solvents and reagents used for removing dirt and varnishes on paintings have proved useful on sculpture. Also, the practice of cleaning only small patches at a time, using small cotton wool swabs, has proved effective in introducing a degree of care and delicacy into the treatment of stone surfaces.

Chemicals such as white spirit, liniment of soap and ammonia wax paste are very useful for cleaning

Figure 11.5 Sutton Valence reredos: poultice partly removed showing cleaned areas

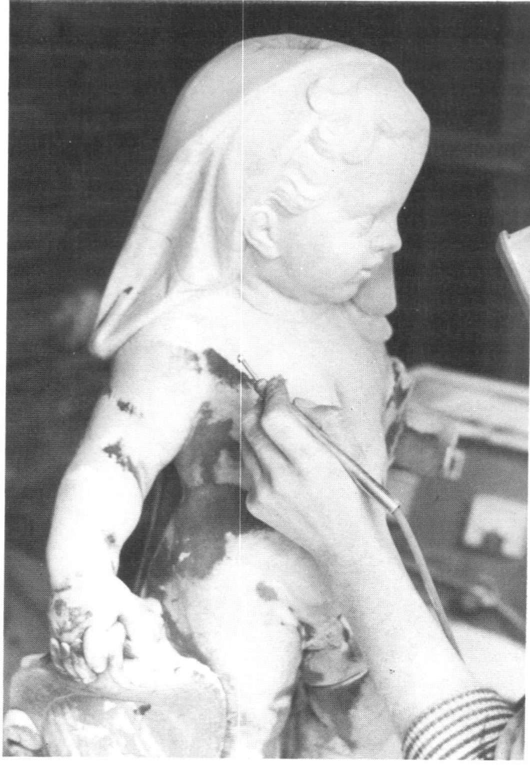

Figure 11.6 Detail of an eighteenth century marble putto, showing sulphation removal with air-brasive

alabaster because the surface is relatively impervious. On limestone, mixtures of acetone or white spirit with water are more effective. On marble, methylene chloride, solvol autosol, white spirit and acetone are all effective. Used in a disciplined manner, all these chemicals can be used safely, but brushed on carelessly and not properly neutralized, they can be very harmful.

Steam cleaning

Although steam cleaning has been an accepted method for the external cleaning of buildings, it is only recently that small-scale steam machines have become available for the cleaning of sculpture. Steam is an ideal cleaning treatment because it is controllable, causes minimal wetting and the pressure of the jet forces dirt out of undercutting and details that would otherwise be laborious to clean.

In England, the steam cleaner used most widely is a Derotor GV. This instrument is actually manufactured for use by dentists for degreasing and sterilizing their instruments. The steam pressure can be raised or lowered by the use of a regulating valve. When full steam pressure is reached the machine at first produces some excess water. This should be drained off before use. To clean effectively, the nozzle should be held near the surface of the stone so that dirt can be blown off. Although the steam pressure is not as great as on many large industrial models, it is dangerous to use the steam cleaner on powdering or friable surfaces. Where surfaces are damaged or fragments of paint remain, it is possible to lay Eltoline tissue on the suface and then pass the jet of steam over it. In this way the surface will be protected and the dampened paper will absorb the dirt.

The advantage of steam is that the surface dries rapidly after cleaning and therefore does not delay other processes such as consolidation or bonding. However, some water will be produced on the surface of the object, and this should be swabbed off with cotton wool or tissue to avoid pooling and possible staining.

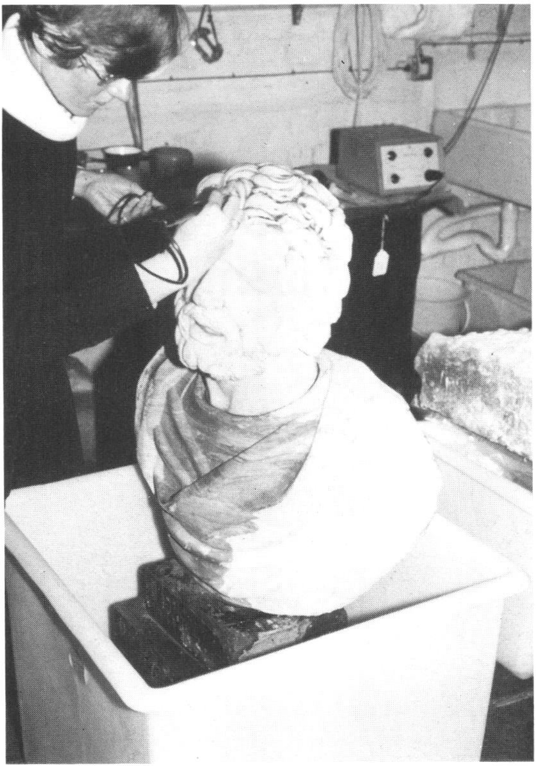

Figure 11.7 Cavitron being used to clean marble bust after poulticing

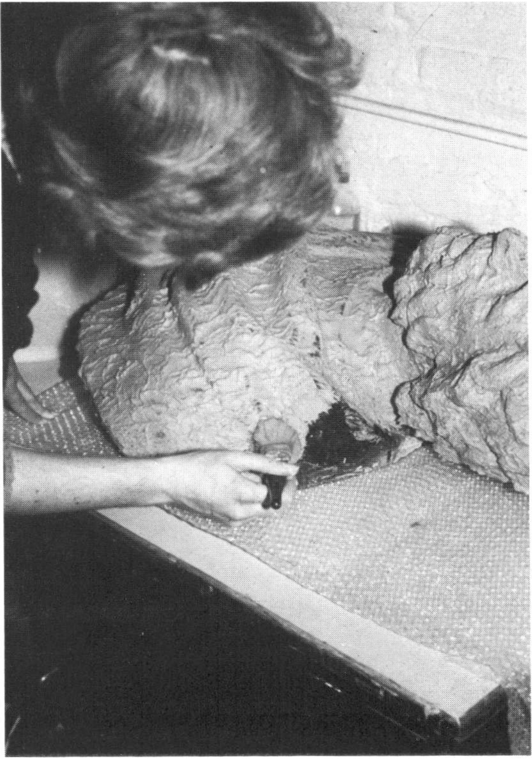

Figure 11.8 Clay poultice carefully applied to marble bust

Laser cleaning

Although this is not a widely available cleaning technique and may never become commercially viable, it can be used in the museum environment. The advantage of using a beam of laser light in contrast to an air-brasive or steam lies in the minimal contact of the beam with the stone surface. Most cleaning techniques leave dust or moisture on the surface, tending to obscure the conservator's view. The laser beam does not leave any deposit on the surface and simply removes the area of dirt at which it is aimed.

The use of laser energy for cleaning sulphated surfaces on decayed stone is not a new idea. Kenneth Hempel and John Asmus carried out experiments on blackened stone in Venice in 1970 and again at the Victoria and Albert Museum a year later. At that time Asmus was using a large, expensive and slow Ruby laser; although it produced impressive results it did not seem practical for museum use.

Over the years, as laser technology has advanced, more adaptable and cheaper lasers have been produced. The most suitable would appear to be a neodymium laser, and it is this type which is now the focus for cleaning research. The laser beam cleans by vaporizing the organic deposits contained in the black crust that forms on polluted stone. The beam will continue to burn away the black crusts until it meets the lighter stone surface beneath. When it does, the beam is reflected back and the laser automatically cuts out. It is this mechanism which makes the laser a very safe tool for cleaning. The laser beam can be focused down to very small sizes. In experimental work the beam size has been as small as 0.5 mm. However, the usual operating size is 4–10 mm.

It is possible, with care, to pass a laser beam over the most friable of surfaces, whereas an air-brasive or steam cleaner would damage the weakened surface. This is an advantage in that it does not constrain the conservator to use pre-consolidation, which is often necessary with other techniques and can inhibit the use of other consolidation treatments.

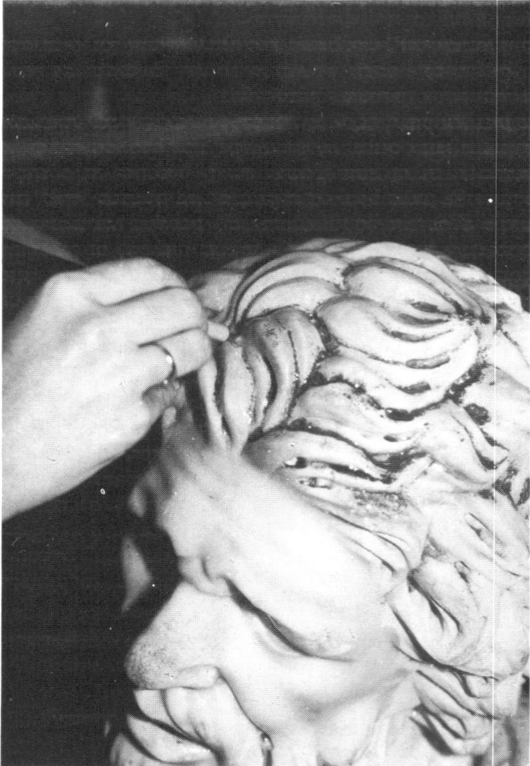

Figure 11.9 The cavitron is ideal for removing small areas of sulphation caught in undercuts

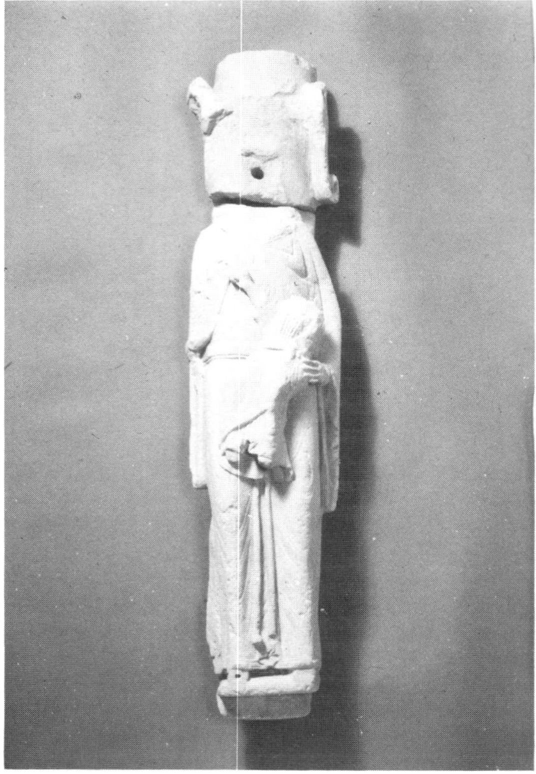

Figure 11.10 Sculpture of Virgin and Child from Minster-in-Sheppey (twelth century, English)

Case history A

A twelfth century figure of the Virgin and Child. English. Limestone (Caen stone). Dimensions: height 85.5 cm (33.7 in); width 19.5 cm (7.7 in).

This sculpture *Figure 11.10* was acquired by the Victoria and Albert Museum in 1973, from the church of St Mary and St Sexburgha, Minster-in-Sheppey, England. It was placed on display in the museum galleries without receiving any conservation treatment, as it was considered to be in a stable condition. The sculpture was re-examined in January 1979, because some concern had been expressed regarding the powdery nature of the surface.

Although originally described as a white sandstone, on re-examination with a magnifying glass (×8) it was clear that the stone was, in fact, a cream coloured limestone, covered by a dense layer of sparkling white crystals. The sculpture was then removed to the Conservation Department for further examination and treatment.

Examination

When examined under a binocular microscope, the crystals on the surface of the sculpture could be clearly identified as salt crystals (*Figure 11.11*). Samples of the crystals were tested in the laboratory and were found to contain sodium, potassium, calcium, sulphates, nitrates and some carbonates. The high concentration of nitrates was extremely worrying, as these are particularly damaging to stone. It was therefore obvious that the sculpture would have to be de-salinated.

Cleaning

Before any other treatment could take place, a careful surface cleaning of the sculpture was undertaken under a binocular microscope (×10–×40). The purpose was to remove the surface salts and to reveal any fragments of pigmentation that might remain on the surface. The cleaning was carried out by rolling small cotton-wool swabs, dampened with

Figure 11.11 Salts on surface of sculpture, seen at ×10 magnification

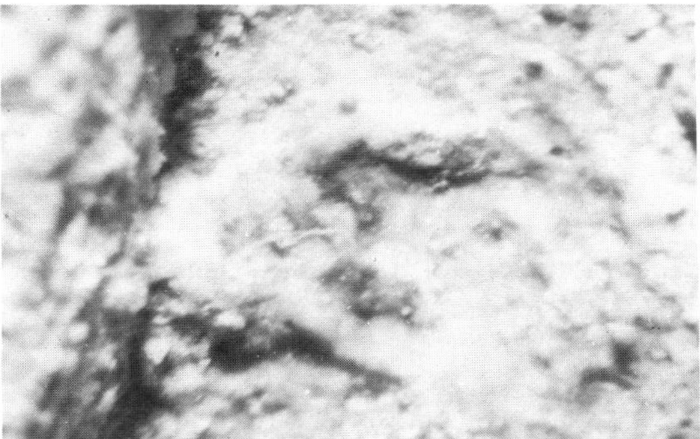

Figure 11.12 Pigment emerging from beneath salts during initial cleaning and examination

de-ionized water, over the surface of the sculpture. During cleaning, several traces of paint were discovered (*Figure 11.12*). These consisted of traces of vermilion and a dark iron oxide, less than 1 mm in width. The pigment was secured during cleaning by feeding an acrylic resin (Racanello E0057) under the flakes with a small pipette.

Cleaning revealed the true surface appearance of the stone and subsequent examination by the Geological Museum revealed that the stone was Caen stone.

Consolidation

The arguments for and against de-salination have already been discussed. In this case the surface of the sculpture was too fragile, and the fragments of pigmentation too precious, to attempt any form of de-salination. It was therefore considered that the least dangerous course of action was to attempt the encapsulation of the salts in the stone by introducing a deeply penetrating silane.

The real difficulty with using some silanes is that they will not allow any further treatment once the resin has cured. Experience with catalysed silanes in the past has revealed that attempts at re-treatment can be problematical. For a stone that has been previously consolidated with silane, the introduction of fresh resin can cause swelling in the gel that has already been formed by the cured resin. In some cases, this has caused noticeable disruption of the consolidated stone and produced cracks and surface flaking.

In an attempt to overcome this problem, tests were carried out with a silane (Dow Corning T 40149) to which a catalyst had not been added. By using silane in this way, it was found that it could be applied to decayed stone over a period of months without any signs of swelling or disruption. The only disadvantage was that the consolidation was not as effective as that obtained by using a catalysed resin. However, by leaving some T 40149 in a beaker, so that the solvent could evaporate, a more viscous solution was obtained. It was found that if the stone was first treated with the normal T 40149 and then with the more viscous T 40149 a more satisfactory consolidation resulted. Generally it was found best to apply the partially evaporated silane (reduced to half of its original volume) once the stone had begun to show signs of saturation, because it acts as a sealing coat, holding the volatile silane deep in the stone.

On the basis of these tests, it was decided to treat the sculpture in the same way, beginning with the larger figurative section.

Consolidation of the figurative section

Before consolidation began, a beaker containing 300 ml of silane was left in a fume chamber to partially evaporate. Unthickened silane was then carefully applied to the surface, using brushes and pipettes. The resin was measured out in 100 ml batches, and at the end of four hours 700 ml had been applied. The sculpture was then tightly wrapped in polythene and left overnight. This process, known as 'gassing', meant that the stone was completely enveloped in silane fumes for at least twelve hours. Over a period of years, it had been observed that this preliminary treatment greatly increased the capacity of the stone to absorb resin, presumably by ventilating the pores within the stone.

On the second day, a further 500 ml of silane was applied to the sculpture, including 100 ml of partially evaporated silane. Although at the beginning of the treatment the stone had quickly reverted to a dry appearance, now it was beginning to stay wet for much longer periods.

During the two following days, further batches of silane totalling 465 ml were applied. Of these, 165 ml was partially evaporated silane. As the absorption of resin was now extremely slow, it was decided to stop the treatment. The total quantity of silane absorbed was 1665 ml.

The sculpture was then left in the storeroom so that the resin could cure over the normal six weeks period. The sculpture was examined after four weeks, when it was, surprisingly, found to be covered by a film of tiny water droplets resembling dew (*Figure 11.13*). The relative humidity (RH) and the temperature in the room were noted as being 63% and 14°C (57°F) respectively.

The surface of the sculpture was carefully dabbed with dry cotton-wool swabs and all visible traces of moisture removed. The stone was left in the same room for a further week and, when inspected, was again covered with beads of moisture. The RH was then 45%, but the temperature remained at 14°C (57°F).

Samples of the water droplets were removed from the surface and tested for salt content. They contained nitrates, sulphates and chlorides. The tests produced very positive reactions, suggesting a fairly high level of concentration. Given such levels of contamination, it was considered dangerous to allow the formation of more droplets on the surface, as this would inevitably create disruption of the stone.

The formation of this surface moisture was at first puzzling. It was assumed that it was merely condensation. However, when the sculpture was removed to a much warmer and drier environment, the moisture still formed on the stone. The fact that this water contained large quantities of salts suggested that the silane had not completely encapsulated the salts in the stone and that moisture, or at least moisture vapour, could still enter the pores in the stone. The droplets resulted from the partial waterproofing of the stone by the silane. The normal transpiration of moisture, attracted by the salts, through the stone no longer occurred and the water was therefore settling on the surface in the form of droplets. At this time, the canopy section, which had not been treated, was showing no signs of similar disruption, even though it was exposed to the same humidity and temperature.

Figure 11.13 Moisture droplets on the surface of the sculpture

It seemed that the technique of salt encapsulation was, in this case, a failure. Although the silane had hardened the stone, it was obvious that the sculpture would never be stable without some form of de-salination.

De-salination

As the surface was now reasonably sound, poultices of de-ionized water and sepiolite (magnesium silicate) were applied to the sculpture, to draw out the salts. The poultices completely covered the sculpture to a uniform thickness of about 1 cm (0.4 in). They were allowed to dry to a craquelure over a period of about 48 hours. During this time, white salt crystals formed on the peaks of the clay poultice. When these salts were removed and tested, they matched those that had been found in the water droplets.

The poultice treatment was repeated ten times and, although some minute grains of stone were undoubtedly lost from the surface, the tiny fragments of pigment were still completely intact. Throughout the treatment, each poultice was tested for salt content and, by the tenth application, no evidence of salts could be found. At this point, it was assumed that a stable situation had been reached.

Re-consolidation

Once the sculpture had been allowed to dry, it was re-consolidated with an acrylic-silane resin, to give it greater strength and to seal it against moisture.

The decision to use an acrylic-silane mixture was based on the results of experimental work conducted at the museum during the previous year. This had shown that limestone consolidated by this method could be considerably strengthened without any noticeable colour change, or without the disruption that could occur when catalysed silanes are used for retreatment. Other advantages of this system were that it reduced the evaporation of the silane and that it allowed the use of other acrylic resins for the consolidation of paint, or large flakes of stone. It was also possible to use solvents, such as acetone, for cleaning, even after consolidation. With catalysed silane, cleaning is only possible with an air-brasive once the resin has cured.

For this consolidation, a combination of Racanello E 0057 (acrylic silane) and Dow Corning T 40149 (silane) was used. The materials were simply mixed together in the proportion of 5% E 0057 to 95% T 40149.

The consolidant was generally applied with a white bristle lacquer brush. In very fragile areas it was dripped from a pipette. During the first two days,

1270 ml of the 5% mixture was absorbed. Over the next two days, the rate of absorption declined and the 5% mixture was changed to one which contained 10% of the E 0057. The reason for this change was to reduce the evaporation of the silane and to ensure that the maximum consolidation was achieved at the surface. In all, 965 ml of the 10% solution was absorbed. The total quantity of acrylic silane used was 2.235 litres. This, added to the previous silane consolidation, meant that the sculpture had accepted 3.9 litres of consolidant.

Poulticing of the canopy section

At this stage, the canopy section had received no treatment other than local consolidation of one area of pigment and light cleaning with a swab and deionized water. No pre-consolidation of the sculpture was required, as the surface was very sound and it was thought that poulticing would not cause any damage. The same procedure for poulticing was adopted as had been used on the figure section. Ten poultices were applied until a neutral state was achieved.

Consolidation of the canopy section

As this part of the sculpture was in better condition than the rest, it was thought unnecessary to attempt complete penetration of the stone. A mixture of 10% E 0057 to 90% T 40149 was therefore used throughout the consolidation of this section. It was again applied by brush and, in total, 500 ml of resin was absorbed by the stone.

Humidity tests

Although no evidence of further salt movement could be seen during the curing period of six weeks, tests were carried out to establish the stability of the sculpture in the face of wide fluctuations of temperature and humidity. During the month of March, the sculpture was left in an unheated room and was subjected to humidity ranges of 40–70% and temperature changes between 8°C and 19°C (46–66°F). At no time during this period did any moisture appear on the surface of the stone, nor was there any sign of surface disruption.

Final cleaning

The sculpture was once again examined under a binocular microscope and any traces of sepiolite left on the surface were removed with a dry stencil brush and dental tools.

Case history B

Neptune and Triton. Bernini (1622). Carrara marble. Lifesize.

This important carving (*Figure 11.14*) was once the centrepiece of an elaborate water garden. It had functioned as a fountain and therefore, from its earliest days, had suffered from a certain degree of surface erosion. In the eighteenth century the sculpture was brought to England by Joshua Reynolds. It was displayed in various gardens during the next two hundred years and finally arrived in the collection at the Victoria and Albert Museum in 1950. Some cleaning and some minor repair work was carried out at that time, but the sculpture was never fully conserved.

Figure 11.14 Seventeenth-century Italian marble group: Neptune and Triton by G.L. Bernini

In 1979 the sculpture had to be moved due to redecoration of the Costume Court. As the condition of the sculpture was unknown, it was decided to examine the piece before removal. Once the sculpture had been scaffolded, the true condition of the marble became apparent (*Figure 11.15.*) The surface showed all the symptoms of Carrara marble that has long been exposed to weathering and pollution. The surface was very granular ('sugary') to the touch. The

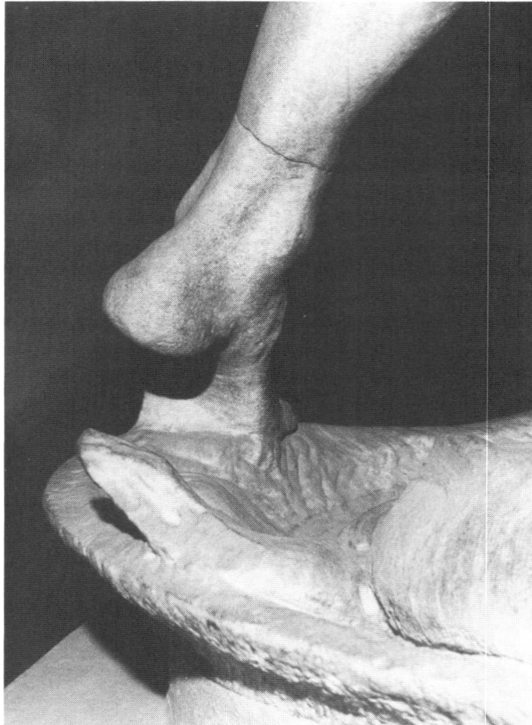

Figure 11.15 Neptune and triton: note the weathered condition of the surface

detail of the carving was blurred and a great many of the fine edges were completely blunted. Dirt had penetrated deeply into the very open structure of the marble and a thick brown film, resulting from pollution, covered the entire surface. There were cracks in the ankle of Neptune and it was obvious that the raised arm had been repaired at some time and had been incorrectly realigned with the shoulder.

Gamma radiography survey

Due to the lack of conservation documentation, it was decided to examine the sculpture as thoroughly as possible to try to uncover information regarding its past history. X-radiography is usually helpful when trying to reconstruct changes that might have taken place in the structure of an object. In this case, with 500 mm (22 in) of marble to penetrate, X-rays were insufficient. It was therefore decided to carry out a survey using the more powerful gamma radiography.

The work was carried out by a commercial company. They used a partial system in which the radiation source was an Iridium pill, which gives off a power of about 600 kV. Samples of sound marble with embedded iron dowels were given to the company so that they could make preparatory tests for material density and exposure time for the film. When they came to film the Bernini, the technicians were surprised to find that, on average, they only required about half the exposure time to penetrate the decayed Carrara that they needed to penetrate the sound samples.

Several important points could be deduced from the radiographs:

1. The raised arm had been dowelled on with a metal cramp, the end of which showed on the radiograph (*Figure 11.16*).
2. The cracks in Neptune's ankle did not penetrate right through the marble.
3. It had been known that the sculpture had functioned as a fountain and the radiograph showed the pipes clearly, still inside the body of Triton (*Figure 11.17*).
4. The ease with which gamma rays penetrated the marble gave some indication of its porosity and its very weak state.

Figure 11.16 Radiograph of left shoulder: the outline of the bent cramp; the white blob is the end of the cramp where it is embedded in mastic

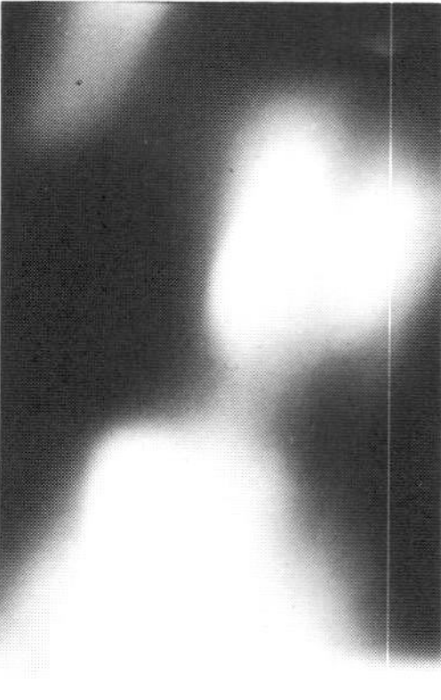

Figure 11.17 Radiograph of Triton's torso. The lead pipe still runs through the figure and can be faintly seen as two parallel lines running vertically through the centre of the body

Cleaning tests

A range of chemicals was tried on various areas of the sculpture. These were applied on cotton-wool swabs and included:

1. Acetone: little effect; some removal of surface dirt.
2. Acetone and water: slightly more effect; the brown staining remained unaffected.
3. White spirit/Lissapol/water solution: a noticeable cleaning effect, but the pollution staining remained unaffected.
4. Water soluble Nitromors: some cleaning effect, but really little more than the white spirit solution.
5. Sepiolite and deionized water: little or no effect.
6. Cellosolve (2-ethoxy-ethanol): used on swabs, this had the most promising cleaning effect. When left on wads of cotton-wool for one minute and then rinsed off with Cellosolve, it was even more effective.

On the basis of these tests, it was decided to use Cellosolve mixed with sepiolite and to poultice the sculpture in areas roughly 600 mm × 300 mm (2 × 1 ft) at a time. The poultice was left on the sculpture for an average of 12 hours before removal. The results were quite startling. Although the ingrained dirt could not be drawn out, the uniform brown layer on the surface was completely removed.

The final cleaning was completed by using an air-brasive with an aluminium oxide aggregate. This removed some traces of black sulphation that still remained on the sculpture from its external exposure. It also helped to pull the surface together, giving the sculpture a much greater sense of unity.

Consolidation

Before any cleaning had taken place, some minor areas of the sculpture, which were very weak, were treated locally with Racenello E 0057. This allowed cleaning to take place without hindrance and did not affect the final full consolidation.

For the complete deep consolidation of the sculpture, a mixture of 90% Dow Corning silane T 40149 and 10% Racenello E 0057 was used. The consolidant was applied with a brush and a total quantity of 8 litres was applied over a period of two days.

After a week, the sculpture was found to be firm to the touch, although the colour was still a little dark. After a period of a month, the sculpture was very hard, with no sign at all of powdering, and had returned to its natural colour.

Reference

1. Plenderleith, H.J. and Werner, A.E.A., *The Conservation of Antiquities and Works of Art: treatment, repair and restoration*, 2nd edn, pp. 304–305, Oxford, 1971

12

The museum display of architectural features

Deborah Carthy

Introduction

The removal of architectural detail from a building of historic importance fortunately is no longer common practice. Sometimes, however, such details are all that remain of buildings which have been demolished, having survived because of the interest and intervention of a collector, or because they have been removed through a less creditable acquisitiveness. Alternatively, an historic building may be so badly neglected that it cannot be saved. A detail such as a fireplace, a door case, a window or a balustrade may be all that can be preserved. Architectural details need to be re-used, or displayed, according to their importance and taking account of their original setting. If no record survives, informed speculation about the relationship of the architectural element to the building of which it was part may be all that is possible. If, however, a detail is to be salvaged from a derelict building, there are procedures to be followed if valuable information about the architectural context and history is not to be lost. Without this information, the rescued piece can become meaningless, or lose much of its architectural and structural significance.

Planning

Many factors may influence the decision on the best procedure to be followed. These may be structural, contractural, or simply physical, if the labour or equipment available for the project is limited. Since planned conservation work of this type has not taken place to any great extent, little has been written on the subject. The following procedures, therefore, have been based on experience gained in recent projects. A well-planned programme needs to be formulated at the start, in order to avoid much later investigation and researching of information.

The importance of recording and handing on information must be emphasized, particularly when the object to be conserved may pass through a number of hands before being reinstated in a new site. Even when the processes of taking down, storage and re-erection are in direct sequence, a project may take several years. Therefore detailed records should be kept throughout.

Survey

Ideally, a project begins with the architectural element concerned still in its original context. An architect, a conservator and a stone mason should be involved, because each has knowledge of the relevant conservation techniques. They should work closely together from the start. If further specialists are required for some aspects of the work, they should be consulted at the earliest possible stage. If the element to be conserved is free-standing, only the problems immediately relating to the element need be considered. If the element is an integral part of an already unstable structure, however, the situation is more complex.

A detailed survey of the element to be removed is of the utmost importance. This survey should include some, or all, of the following: a measured drawing showing all dimensions, including joint thicknesses and with all the stones numbered; photographs taken before and during taking down; a photogrammetric or corrected photography survey; use of a metal detector to indicate the positions of any iron fixings; the use of gamma radiography (X-ray) to indicate voids and all non-ferrous fixings, such as slate or timber dowels; consideration of

Figure 12.1 Back view of late 12th century English limestone doorway, dry built. In the Burrell Collection, Glasgow

relevant building techniques; and research into any historic accounts of the construction.

Before the scaffolding is erected, it is very important that all who are to be involved are properly briefed on site. Any particular requirements, such as areas to be kept free of scaffolding, whether or not the scaffold is to be tied to the structure surrounding the element to be conserved and any limitations on loading, should be discussed and understood. This is particularly important when stones are to be removed and lowered to the ground.

Some immediate stabilization of the surface of the stone may be needed in order to minimize the risk of damage during taking down. Most stabilization treatments require the stone to be as dry as possible and this must be allowed for in the programme. Further treatment may need to be carried out in a more suitable environment before the element is rebuilt.

At this point, the conservator should be able to make a realistic assessment of the visible problems and of the overall treatment likely to be needed, although the full extent of problems within the structure may not be revealed until the taking down is in progress. Surface problems are most likely to be those caused by weathering, atmospheric pollution, salt migration, iron stains from cramps or dowels within the structure, or cracking of the stone caused by movement or the expansion of concealed iron dowels and cramps. Any structural problems must be assessed as far as possible before taking down is started, in the interests of safety. Any temporary supports required should be put in position as soon as possible, and certainly before taking down is started.

Taking down

When an arch is to be dismantled, centering which is capable of taking the weight of the stone without deforming should be provided. It should be constructed just below the daylight size of the arch (the width of the opening at the springing line by the height from the springing line to the head), from the ground, or from a level surface below the arch. Final adjustments can be made with wedges at the springing line, to ensure that the stonework is fully supported; the wedges should be pushed in to make the adjustment but not forced in. Centering is not needed for a tympanum arch, unless the tympanum has been damaged in such a way that it has become structurally unsound. In principle, the same method of support applies to a split-lintel, but the supporting timber should be shaped to the profile of the lintel. In all cases, the stone must be protected from direct contact with the timber by a padding of polystyrene, or other non-slip, water-resistant material.

The original construction of the element to be conserved must be considered before taking it down. For example, when dismantling an arch, the keystone should be removed first and control then kept of the order in which the stones on either side are taken down. In some split-lintels, these stones act as a counter balance and this should be remembered when removing them. Equilibrium should be maintained and as little strain as possible put on the structure below.

The importance of marking stones as they are taken down cannot be emphasized too strongly. The method of numbering and marking should be recorded on the measured drawings and reference to compass points may be necessary when dealing with a free-standing structure. All identification marks should be made on the back, or the bedding, face of the stones; never, under any circumstances, on an exposed face. Marks need not be removable, but they must be readily distinguishable from any place or mason's marks already on the stones. The recording of any place or mason's marks will also help to identify the stones. This is important, since these marks may not be visible once the structure is rebuilt.

Transportation

When an architectural element has been dismantled and numbered, and is awaiting transportation, the stones should be stacked neatly off the ground on pallets and covered with black polythene, or tarpaulin, with air spaces in between. In wet conditions this will reduce condensation, help drying out and lessen the risk of algal growth on the stones. For transport, the stones should be packed in a non-staining material, such as polystyrene. Straw or wood shavings should not be used because these are likely to stain the stone if moisture is present. This staining can take place in a matter of days and, although superficial, is disfiguring.

An approximate estimate of the weight of the dismantled structure may be made at this stage for the purpose of designing foundations or calculating the loading on a new floor to carry the structure. This estimate can be obtained quite simply by driving first the unladen and then the laden transport onto a weighbridge.

Reassembly

If the architectural element has been dismantled already and detailed records of its original form are not available, the approach to reassumbly must be quite different and can be extremely time consuming. If the element has been numbered from the base upwards, it is likely to have been numbered on the ground and not in the sequence in which it was taken down. If the element has a complex structure, the dismantled stones may well be upside down or misleadingly positioned. All such possibilities must be anticipated and checked, either by laying out the stones in a sand box, or by erecting them without mortar in a 'dry-build'.

A sand box is a strong timber construction of sufficient superficial area and depth to contain the re-assembled stonework. The stones are laid out in the box on a bed of well-washed, dry, sharp sand. Iron or salts present in unwashed, damp sand can easily stain the stone, or even transfer soluble salts into dry stones. If, for any reason, it is impracticable to dry the sand, then a tough, easily flexible plastic film should be laid over the sand to avoid these risks. In some cases, additional support is provided in the sand box in the form of bricks, blocks, or timber framing. During laying-out, clues to the original bedding of the stones and their relationship to each other may be provided by the tooling pattern or building marks, all of which should be carefully recorded. Overall dimensions of the complete element can be taken once the stones have been set out, but allowances must be made for the width of bedding, vertical and radial joints.

If a 'dry-build' approach is made, rather than setting out in a sand-box, enough information must be available beforehand to determine the sizes of the supports and centering which will be required. Consideration must also be given to the ability of the stones to withstand the process. A dry-build with weak, fragile material would be most unwise. Dry-building is usually preceded by laying the stones out on a floor, to enable dimensions between jambs and the sizes of centering required to be established. At this stage, any missing stones can be sized and worked. These will be necessary for reasons of

Figure 12.2 Sixteenth-century sandstone arch from Hornby Castle, Yorkshire; new stones are Cat Castle sandstone. In the Burrell Collection, Glasgow

structural integrity or for completeness of a design element. They should be of a new or second-hand stone which will match the original, weathered material as closely as possible in colour and texture. The ideal replacement stone should not be obvious on casual inspection, but should be easily identifiable on closer examination. During the dry-build, non-staining wood slips or wedges can be used to cushion the stones and to take up the joint widths which will later be occupied by mortar. In some situations, new elements will have to be introduced to substitute for the function of masonry masses in the original structure. Stainless steel threaded tension bars, for instance, may be needed to take the place of masonry abutments opposing the thrust of an arch. Bars of this type are anchored to plates at springing level on, or near, the extrados of the arch and are tensioned *in situ.*

When setting out has been satisfactorily concluded either in the sand-box or as a dry-build, and all missing and new elements have been identified and supplied, erection, or erection and building-in to the new environment, can proceed. Because new masonry construction takes a long time to dry out completely and because there is likely to be differential settlement between, for instance, new brickwork and antique masonry (if only because of the difference in number of joints), it is essential that an isolating membrane and an air space are provided. If the architectural element is built in to a new wall, the foundation of the wall will need to be modified to take the increased size and loading. It may also be necessary to incorporate a new lintel or a brick relieving arch over the element, to ensure that loads from the new construction are not transferred to the museum piece. A 25 mm (1 in) air space is normally provided between new and old construction. The isolating membrane is usually of Code 4 lead, or of heavy-duty polythene. It must contain the historic element completely. When the element is free-

Figure 12.3 Lead being extracted from hole for hinge bracket (bracket visible at lower right). In the Burrell Collection, Glasgow

standing its base should be isolated from the ground surface with lead pads. All lead should be coated with bitumen where it will be in contact with fresh mortar and carefully lapped at least 50 mm (2 in). Where a membrane is pierced by ties or other fixings, a potential bridge for moisture and salt migration is established. This must be closed off. Polyesters, bitumen-coated polythenes and some of the silicone-based sealers have been used successfully for this purpose. When the element has an irregular surface, polythene is usually the most practical form of membrane since it can be easily cut and trimmed and the overlapped sheets heat-sealed or joined with a sealant. Where the surrounding walls are to be plastered, the membrane must be brought to the face of the plaster to avoid moisture bridging at the surface.

Any ties or dowels used should be austenitic stainless steel, or delta bronze. When stonework needs to be drilled through the beds, the mortices formed should be oversized to allow the dowels to fit loosely. The dowels should be no more than 70 mm (2.75 in) in length and should be dropped into the mortices dry, without mortar or mastic. This will provide a movement tolerance and will avoid any risk of localized stress.

The mortar used should be compatible with the stone; that is to say, it should not be too strong. A mortar such as one part of white lime, mixed with three parts of well-graded sand, to which a small proportion of white cement or pozzolanic powder has been added, will be quite adequate. If the architectural element concerned is to be completely protected from the weather, as in most museum environments, the cement or pozzolana is hardly necessary, but a weak hydraulic set may be necessary in order to take the loading imposed by heavy masonry units.

The planning stage of a museum project will have considered fire regulations and discussed the layout proposed with the regional authorities. If an historic element, such as an arch, is to be incorporated into a wall, fire doors may have to be inserted in the opening. If this is so, the doors must be designed to hang on an independent frame or pivots and be free of the historic element.

Free-standing structures

When the historic structure to be conserved is to be free-standing, different problems must be resolved. Some structures, such as arches, can stand quite satisfactorily on their own in many circumstances. Other elements, such as traceried windows, are difficult to display in isolation, without the physical and visual support of embracing walls. The physical support can be provided by a frame around all or part of the free-standing element, by floor to ceiling stanchions on either side, or by plating the back and top of the element. Physical and visual support together can best be provided by panels of stonework. Any metal used should be stainless steel or delta bronze. The method of support must, of course, be adequate for the size and weight of the element, and the design of the supports will need to be considered in relation to the relevant fire and building regulations. It should be remembered that regulations which may be waived in the context of an existing historic building may not necessarily be waived in relation to historic elements re-sited in a new building.

Conclusions

The conservation and display of historic details in a new environment is often a complex and always a challenging undertaking. It is essential for an experienced team and appropriate specialists to be consulted from the start of a project. Fortunately such an approach is increasingly adopted now. This follows significant developments in research on materials which are suitable for this type of work, and a greater general appreciation of the importance of conservation techniques.

13

The cleaning of painted stone

Clare Finn

Introduction

The purpose of this chapter is not to describe the treatment of polychromed sculpture, but to outline some of the problems and techniques which may be encountered in the cleaning and repainting of painted architectural detail and wall surfaces. In essence, the investigation of painted layers, their consolidation, cleaning and treatment, is the same whether the substrate is stone, plaster, or even wood. The process is often complex but for the sake of completeness this chapter will attempt to provide some information for those who find their masonry problems involve paint as part of a decorative scheme. This is particularly relevant to the large public buildings of the nineteenth century, such as town halls, museums and hotels.

Once it has been determined to clean, repair or refurbish a building which included painted stone, a careful survey and analysis of the painted areas should be put in hand as soon as possible. Without such a survey, much information about colours and techniques relating to different periods in the building's history may be lost. In addition, damage to the existing paint may be caused through ignorance about its type and the nature of discoloration and soiling.

Whilst there is little justification in most cases for carrying out extensive sampling as an academic exercise, by sensible and selective sampling it should be possible to establish, to some extent, the techniques and paints used to produce a specific finish at any given point in the history of the building. Additional examination of the stratification of the paint layers may be informative when structural alterations have taken place. Mistakes in re-colouring, based on assumptions made on the existing appearance, can be avoided by careful examination. The value and the extent of sampling carried out will vary with different situations and will need to be related to the information available on the history of the building and its decoration. Building records and other technical literature contemporary with the construction will often provide, in advance, a good idea of what the survey is likely to uncover. Sometimes a specification may survive from the period of building, but it should not be assumed without checking that the work carried out necessarily conforms with the printed intention!

Where samples are to be taken from should depend on:

1. The architectural detail
2. The known possibility of decorative paint
3. The amount of known alteration which has taken place

The sampling should be carried out only after available building records, or other literature contemporary with the building, have been searched. The more samples that can be examined, the more complete and accurate will be the picture obtained.

The survey should provide the following information:

1. An identification of the paint materials and the substrate
2. A description of the original colour schemes
3. A description of the paint stratification and characteristics of the surface finish
4. A description of the condition of the paint and substrate. Attention should be drawn to causes of deterioration and damage, alterations and additions

This information should be systematically recorded because it is the basis on which the restoration, or reconstruction, recommendations will be made. If a building has been altered it may be desirable to restore it to the historic finish dating from a particular alteration, and not back to the 'original' scheme.

Under item 4 above, the survey report must make clear which improvements are essential and which are desirable, before money is spent on painted surfaces. This may mean drawing attention to open joints, leaking gutters, soil levels and humidity problems. It may also mean advising that extra time must be allowed for drying out after remedial work before work on the painted surfaces can commence. 'Restored' paint can never hope to overcome basic environmental problems.

Temporary protection

In addition, measures such as improving ventilation and reducing humidity levels, and some 'first aid' protection of painted surfaces, may be necessary while other work is in progress.

Where the paint is more fragile, it will be necessary to secure it by a facing. This technique consists of brushing a suitable consolidant (see Annex) onto the wall through Japanese mulberry tissue, calendered eltaline tissue, or other suitable soft tissue. The paper remains in place, securing the paint, until work on the surface can be commenced. The paper can be removed by the appropriate solvent for the consolidant. However, there are some consolidants which cannot be removed, such as a catalysed silane system, and there are some solvents which would also remove the paint.

During major building works, it is expedient to cover the painted surfaces with thin sheets of hardboard, held in place with battens. Protective work of this kind needs close supervision to ensure that no avoidable abrasion or impact takes place and that no fixings are inadvertently made to the painted wall.

Paint types

Stone may be covered with thin gesso and painted, or prepared in some other way, or painted direct. Frequently, stone is part of a complex wall surface, and the colour scheme extends across stone and plaster.

Early production of building paint was largely in the hands of master painters, whose apprentices were taught to prepare colours for the craftsman's use. A prestigious market, however, often generated more organized production, as in the case of Richard de Welton of York, who was in business as a colour maker in 1591.

During the eighteenth century, paint production became more organized and centralized. Factories were established for the production of pigments, such as white and red lead, Prussian blue, vermilion and verdigris, in addition to various varnishes.

The nineteenth century saw the introduction of a wide range of pigments. Zinc oxide, lithopone, chrome yellows and Brunswick green appeared. Extenders, such as china clay and barium white, were added to reduce the yellowing tendency of pigments, by lowering their oil absorbency. Extenders increased and improved the durability of paints. However, sometimes they were added in such quantity that they became adulterants which significantly lowered tinting strengths. The range of binders based on modified drying oils alone, or combined with various resins, similarly increased.

Before 1930 there were two basic categories of building paint available: oil-based and aqueous. Oil paints, or oil/varnish paints, purchased in paste form for dilution on site, were mixed to the painter's own specification for the job in hand, although pre-mixed paint had been available from the eighteenth century. A wide range of materials were available, formulated from drying oils or modified drying oils, e.g. stand or blown oil, or combinations of drying oils with natural or fossil resins, such as rosin or Congo copal. All these were used for decorative purposes.

Thin oil mastic is another protective and decorative finish which was applied to stone externally from the last quarter of the eighteenth century. Although these mastics were most commonly used in the same way as stucco, lined out in imitation of masonry and painted with various stone colours, they were sometimes applied directly to stone after saturation priming with linseed oil, as a protective rather than a decorative finish. All were based on litharge (lead monoxide) and linseed oil, with fillers such as ground brick, porcelain clay, sand and glass.

Aqueous paint includes limewash and cement paints, lime-casein paints, and distempers and whitewashes based on whiting and glue size. Distempers and whitewashes were internal finishes. They had poor durability, but they were sometimes used externally and frequently renewed. This kind of repeated maintenance anticipated the kind of sacrificial coat now used to slow the effects of weathering on newly cleaned stone. Distemper was sometimes recommended as a preservative measure on external masonry which was decaying, although limewash, with or without tallow, was the more common treatment.

Generally speaking, the pigments found in building paints are cheap to produce. More costly pigments are sometimes included in interior schemes, such as the vermilion identified in the Morris Green Room at the Victoria and Albert Museum.

After the 1920s the development of the petrochemical industry brought about great changes with the introduction of vinyl, acrylic, alkyd and other synthetic resin-based paints.

Methods of application

Oil paint was usually applied to previously unpainted stone highly diluted with oil. When applied to previously painted stone, it was highly diluted with turpentine. The paint layer, as a rule of thumb, was built up in four to five layers. The first layer was the most dilute and subsequent layers increased in concentration as the stone became saturated. The first layer was the priming coat, followed by two or three undercoats and a finishing coat.

Over the base, a variety of decorative techniques might be applied including:

1. Striation with heavy brush marks
2. Hand rubbing to simulate enamel
3. Marbling to imitate marble (or porphyry or granite)
4. Graining to imitate wood (more common on plaster)
5. Stencilling with decorative motifs
6. Hand-painted elements
7. Gilding (generally oil mordant gilding or japan gilding)

The identification of these finishing techniques is as important as the identification of the colour scheme.

Sampling techniques

The simplest technique is to scrape 'windows' through the paint layers with a sharp scalpel, with the aid of suitable solvents if necessary. These 'windows' will expose the finishes *in situ*. Considerable care and experience are necessary to obtain the required information in this way. In addition to the visual information gained from the 'windows', analysis of samples removed from each layer may provide valuable supplementary data on the colour and material.

A study of the substrate layering, carried out by making cross sections, will provide a knowledge of the accumulated build-up of paint in different areas.

Ideally, these techniques should be used together. To use one method alone, especially the 'window' method, may lead to misinterpretation. The intensity of colour can be distorted, optically, by considering only a small sample area.

Cleaning and restoration

There may well be a considerable gap in time between the initial survey of a painted interior and the implementation of any remedial work, while proposals are considered, grants applied for, money raised and general building work put in hand. This time may well be useful, but it may also represent increasing danger to a threatened interior. The importance of the survey in drawing attention to causes of deterioration can be readily appreciated. Whilst it should not be the responsibility of the painting conservator to point out that a roof needs repairing, or that penetrating damp is the main problem, it should never be taken for granted that these items are all in hand.

Methods and dangers of cleaning

Cleaning should only begin when the maximum amount of information has been gained on the surfaces to be cleaned, and after careful visual examination and testing under good lighting conditions. Experience is crucial to the recognition of technique, aging effects, surface deposits and degree of attachment, and to the determination of what the original appearance and final aspect were and should be. There are specific practical limitations to cleaning. These are imposed by the sensitivity of the original surface (which may yield to cleaning more readily than the discoloration) or, for example, by the tenacity of a layer of oil paint laid over an aqueous distemper.

A basic decision must be made at the start on which layers are to be removed and which are to remain. Any necessary consolidation should be completed before cleaning commences, bearing in mind the problems of binding dirt layers to the substrate, on the one hand, and the risks of removing the consolidated layer during cleaning, on the other.

Loosely adherent dust should be removed first, by cleaning with a soft brush.

Greasy deposits, such as surface dirt associated with smoke from chimneys, lamps, candles, cigars and tobacco pipes, can usually be removed by swabbing gently with a mild alkali solution, such as ammonia water: 5% ammonia water (35% NH_3) in water. Suitable swabs for cleaning include sponges, soft paper tissue pads, or cotton wool. An alternative to ammonia water is a saturated solution of bicarbonate of soda, but ammonia is to be preferred. If the paint is sensitive to water, white spirit may be used.

Ingrained surface dirt can usually be broken down with a potassium oleate soap (Vulpex) in a solution of water, white spirit, or 1,1,1-trichloroethane. The solution may be applied, left for a short interval (determined by observation) and then removed with ammonia water. Both Vulpex and ammonia water solutions can be varied in concentration, as can the contact time. The cleaning action can be arrested with white spirit. Of course, extreme care must be taken to ensure that not more than is intended is being removed!

Wax can generally be removed with an aromatic solvent, such as xylene or toluene. If the wax has been applied recently, a less toxic petroleum distillate may be used. Unfortunately, if the wax was applied to a rather porous surface, it may not be possible to remove it all.

Resins, and oil-resin varnishes

Resins may be removed with a suitable organic solvent (see Annex for list of solvents in general use). Oil-resin varnishes may sometimes be swollen with solvents, in which case their removal must be carried out by careful scraping. The use of gelators may be helpful in holding a solvent in contact with a vertical or overhead surface. Methyl cellulose and laponite, which form a gel in water, are useful in this context. Sometimes, proprietary brands of paint strippers may be used successfully, but the constituents must always be known and great caution applied. An exact knowledge of what is supposed to be below the surface is absolutely vital, because too many layers can all too quickly be removed. It is essential to have adequate ventilation and to wear a filter mask, including eye protection, when working with solvants and toxic chemicals. Smoking is prohibited in such a work area.

Proteins, such as animal glue, milk, casein, or egg, may remain soluble in warm water. If they prove resistant, however, as may be the case with casein or egg white, small quantities of a dilute organic acid, such as formic or acetic acid, may be used.

Gum arabic is removable with warm water, if it has not been mixed with something such as egg or oil. If this is the case, then acid and alkali solutions, as described above, should be used alternately.

Organic deposits, such as bird and bat excreta or mould growth, may usually be removed by an alkali solution such as a weak ammonia solution.

Efflorescent salts should be removed, as far as possible, by gentle brushing, followed by washing in water or solvent, according to the sensitivity of the paint. If the paint is very fragile and friable, a poultice of soft paper tissue may be more appropriate. The reason for the efflorescence must be established at the time of the survey and a salt analysis carried out, if necessary. Remedial building work and humidity control may be required. Non-soluble efflorescences may sometimes be removed mechanically (see Chapter 8) bearing in mind the fragility of the paint layer.

Lime wash can be one of the most difficult surface coatings to remove, especially when sulphated. Gentle mechanical flaking is often the only answer.

Consolidation

In addition to consolidating areas of flaking and powdering paint before cleaning, it may be desirable to apply a weak fixative to the entire painted surface, once all dirt and unwanted deposits are removed, such as a weak solution of Paraloid B-72 (2% or 3% Paraloid in an aromatic solvent such as toluene). This not only improves the adherence of the paint to the surface, but will remove the white cloudy bloom, which may remain in patches after cleaning.

The choice of a suitable fixative should be governed by its surface gloss, flexibility, permeability to moisture, liability to discoloration, reversibility, and compatibility with the surface to be treated. Cost and availability will also influence the selection. In the past, beeswax or limewater were the usual consolidants and limewater is still used. However, beeswax is impermeable to moisture and should not be applied to a porous substrate. More commonly today the following materials are used as fixatives:

1. Acrylic resin, methacrylate in solution, e.g. Paraloid B-72 in xylene or toluene, or Bedacryl in xylene or toluene.
2. Polyvinyl acetate emulsion in water with a surfactant or in solution in alcohol or acetone, e.g. Vinamul, Mowilith, Gelva.
3. Soluble nylon in methanol, e.g. Calaton.
4. Polyvinyl alcohol in water.
5. Acrylic silane mixtures, e.g. Dow Corning, Racanelio.

Not all these consolidants meet the criteria listed above. For instance, both soluble nylon and polyvinyl alcohol cross-link and discolour. Both the methacrylates and polyvinyl acetate may darken the appearance of the surface in which they are applied. The consolidants may be brushed, sprayed or injected, depending on the detachment problem. The application of localized heat, using a heated spatula, aids reattachment.

Filling of losses

After consolidation, losses should be filled ready for reintegration with a material compatible with the original surface. Lime putty and sand should be used in lime plaster, or lime putty, sand, stonedust and ceramic powder in masonry. Such repairs must be built up in thin layers of 5 mm at a time and pressed well home. Smaller losses in stone may be better filled with synthetic filler (e.g. marble dust in a synthetic resin binder) which does not require water in the mixing process, nor pre-wetting of the repair area.

Reintegration

Reintegration should be carried out in paints compatible with the existing surface. Water colours or acrylic paints are the usual choice, although oil paint, from which the excess oil has been bled, is still used. Factors governing the choice are similar to those described for selecting consolidants. The reintegration of a decorative technique must be carried out by a suitably skilled technician, under the general guidance of a fully trained, competent conservator.

Very few buildings of importance have retained original colours and are rarely seen as they were intended. Regular maintenance, perhaps preceded by rubbing down or caustic washing, may have obscured or destroyed all evidence of original paintwork. New colours may also have been applied as determined by changing fashions. Soiling patterns may suggest a completely misleading range of colour and tone. Paint, such as distemper, may have disappeared altogether, except, for instance, under the protection of an oil-stencilled motif. Many repaintings fill the texture of the stone surface and affect the amount of reflected light. In all these situations, recorded descriptions or illustrations of the original interior may be the only guide as to how to proceed with a reconstruction. In many cases, interiors can only be restored by reconstruction because of the way in which they have been subjected to changing use. In these situations, the skill of the conservator is paramount in importance.

When trying to determine the colours to be used for a reconstruction, the metameric qualities of colour should be borne in mind. This should also be a major influence in designing the lighting system of an historic interior.

The artistic traits of all the parts of an interior should be matched with one another to the fullest extent possible, so that the complete effect, a single artistic unit, is achieved. Where some elements are to be conserved and others reconstructed, the approach to the reintegration exercise may be determined by the most seriously deteriorated areas.

Factors such as the intended use of the building, the new environment conditions and, in some cases, availability of the types required will also affect the choice of paints. Modern emulsion paint is wipe-proof, distemper is not. Pure mineral silicate paints have a better durability record than lime paints. These advantageous properties must, however, be weighed against the visual differences which will be involved. The sheen of a modern synthetic paint will look quite out of place in some historic settings.

Conclusion

The complexity, condition and importance of the painted surfaces will determine the appropriate approach to the cleaning, repair and consolidation of painted stone interiors. The cost of correct and careful cleaning, restoration or reconstruction may well be prohibitive, and a more economic option may have to be adopted. If this is the case, then priorities related to the survival of threatened areas must be established and original surfaces must not be jeopardized by the application of unsuitable, 'temporary' redecoration layers.

In some cases, where a full conservation scheme has to be postponed, displays of the sampling 'windows' can be made and left. Such displays may be seen in the cast court at the Victoria and Albert Museum in London. Alternatively, or in addition, economically produced reconstructions showing the original scheme, as at the Roman Painted House at Dover, England, may be commissioned. Both are ways of making use of necessary preliminary exercises to inform and create interest in the project.

Most important of all, short cuts imposed by the need to economize must not be allowed to destroy any historic material or potential source of information. Financial situations may improve, but surfaces damaged or destroyed by inexpert or unsuitable cleaning and painting cannot be recovered.

Annex

Some solvents in common use for the removal of resins and oil resin varnishes are listed below.

Aliphatic hydrocarbons
Petroleum distillates, e.g. white spirit, V M and P naphtha

Aromatic hydrocarbons
Xylene
Toluene

Alcohols
Methanol (methyl alcohol)
Ethanol (ethyl alcohol)
Industrial methylated spirit
Propan-2-01 (isopropyl alcohol, or isopropanol)
4-hydroxy-4-methylpentan-2-one (diacetone alcohol)

Ketones
Propan-2-one (acetone)

Ethers
2-ethoxyethanol (Cellosolve)

Chlorinated hydrocarbons
Dichloromethane (methylene chloride)

Amides
Dimethylformamide

Alkalis
Ammonia solution

14

The cleaning and consolidation of the stonework to the Annunciation Door, Chapter House, Westminster Abbey

Keith Taylor, Christopher Gradwell and Teresa McGrath

Introduction

The Chapter House of Westminster Abbey, which has been used as the meeting place of the English parliament and as a library since its original function became obsolete, was completed some time during the first half of the thirteenth century. It is approached from the cloister through an outer and inner vestibule. At the top of a flight of steps the Annunciation Door forms the entrance into the Chapter House itself. The entrance wall is largely filled by the doorway and is a mixture of thirteenth-century work and nineteenth-century restoration by Scott. Pevsner[1] has this to say about Scott's work: '. . . a last word . . . on Scott and his much attacked restorations. There is one thing at least that ought to be remembered. He found the Chapter House full of bookcases, staircases, galleries. If we have an idea today of its noble original beauty, Scott has given it to us'.

The Annunciation Doorway was cleaned and consolidated most recently during the period February to May 1983, by Ian Clayton Ltd.

The Annunciation doorway

The Gothic arched entrance to the Chapter House from the vestibule is made up of a double doorway divided by a central Purbeck 'marble' pillar, with a circular feature in the centre of the arch above. The jambs to the arch contain four large Purbeck 'marble' shafts on their outer side. On either side of the arch, facing the Chapter House, are sculptures of Gabriel on the left and the Virgin on the right. In the spandrels are two trefoils, each containing two angels: one large censing angel and one small angel. The orders on both sides of the arch are an extremely intricate design of openwork foliage containing small figures. The design continues in the jambs between the Purbeck 'marble' columns. In the central quatrefoil a Victorian addition, showing Christ in Majesty with angels, has blocked what was thought to be open tracery. This would have lit the stairs and given a view through to the Chapter House from the vestibule.

The entire Reigate Stone surface of the doorway, excluding the two large figures, was covered in a heavy limewash, which was later found to be a gesso mix applied in the 1950s. It was very dirty and dusty. After careful brushing of the surface with soft bristle brushes to remove dust, cleaning tests, using an S.S. White air abrasive machine at about 50 psi, with 50 μm aluminium oxide powder, were carried out on the right-hand trefoil, the upper arch order and the diaper flowers.

Fortunately, the tests showed that the gesso was soft and reasonably easy to remove at moderate air pressure and powder flow. The surface of the stone underneath the gesso was very friable with a great deal of flaking. However, with careful use of the air abrasive, the gesso could be removed gradually without disturbing the friable stone. Particularly friable areas were consolidated immediately, using Raccanello Acrylic Silane 55050. Pre-consolidation (applying the consolidant through the gesso and trying to clean back to the stone) was not successful because it hardened the coating too much and made it difficult to remove.

Tests also revealed that the stone was covered with a linseed-type oil, which presumably had been applied during the Victorian restoration, in an attempt to blend in the additions with the original work. Although this coating was lightened by air abrasion, the oil had penetrated the stone and was impossible to remove mechanically. Also, the need for immediate consolidation meant that the oil could not be removed by solvents, without disturbing the consolidant and the friable stone. Some tests were carried out with solvents such as white spirit, acetone and ethoxyethanol, but the results were not successful enough to risk damaging the unsound stone.

The method of work that evolved from these tests was to remove all limewash carefully and to consolidate where necessary, using Raccanello 55050. The possibility of re-limewashing certain areas after consolidation was discussed, because of the uneven appearance of the stone. However, as work progressed and the original detailing was revealed, it seemed inappropriate to obscure such fine detail as those on the front left-hand order by recoating. There was also some doubt about the compatibility of the consolidant and the limewash.

The working programme was planned by dividing the doorway into areas of differing conditions and for ease of working. These basic areas were:

The decorative arch orders and adjacent moulding and the four decorative jambs
The two trefoils with censing angels
The diaper flowers
The two large sculptures of Gabriel and Mary
The Victorian Christ in Majesty and surrounding moulding
The ashlar and niches
The Purbeck 'marble' columns

These basic areas are illustrated in *Figures 14.1* and *14.2*.

The arch orders and jambs

There are three intricately carved arches of moulding on the Chapter House side and two on the vestibule side. The dominant order of the arch on both sides of the doorway contains small figures surrounded by a continuous tendril of deep-cut foliage. Each order starts from a half figure on the Purbeck 'marble' capital and consists of 26 full figures (13 on each side), 270 mm (10.5 in) high. The order is 240 mm (9.5 in) wide.

Chapter House side

Arch orders

The arch orders figures were numbered from left to right as follows:

1–8. Original figures, with Victorian moulding on 2 and 7.
9. Head and shoulders are Victorian, as is adjacent moulding. The torso is original.
10. The figure is original with Victorian moulding.
11. Victorian figure.
12. Original figure, with some Victorian piecing in the moulding.
13. Victorian head.
14. Victorian figure, with some original moulding.
15. Original moulding and torso, Victorian head.
16–26. Mostly Victorian figures.

Figures in jambs

Left-hand jamb. The eleven figures, which were numbered 1 to 11 from top to bottom, are all original, with a great deal of surviving detail. By comparison, the original figures of the dominant order of the arch are in a much worse condition. They have none of the surviving crisp detail that can be seen on the figures in the jamb. There has been some flaking on the jamb figures, mainly on the fine detail such as the folds of garments and faces, and there is physical damage, with heads missing from figures 6, 7, 8, 9 and 11. Although the damage probably occurred before the Victorian restoration (as there is linseed oil and limewash covering the breaks), no attempt has been made to replace missing sections, leaving the whole jamb as original stonework.

Right-hand jamb. This jamb consists of deeply undercut foliage motifs, all apparently original, with a small architectural niche and a bird at the top. The detail is fairly good overall but there are some missing parts and some spalling.

Vestibule side

Arch orders

The vestibule side has a similar dominant order to the Chapter House side, with an outer order of foliage motifs. The left side of the foliage order is apparently mostly original and is in much the same condition as the original figures on the arch order on the Chapter House side. There are three badly damaged and missing motifs in the lower half. From the apex to the right the order is largely Victorian, but small sections of original work survive, for example a 15 cm (6 in) strip between the third and fourth motif from the apex. The inner order of figures is again made up of original pieces with Victorian additions, but on this side of the doorway most of the figures have been restored. The main part of the original work remaining seems to be on the right hand side of the arch. There is a section of foliage missing between the original figure 20 and figure 21.

Figures in jambs

The figures are similar to those on the Chapter House side. There are eleven small figures on the right-hand side and foliage motifs on the left. The condition of the carving is also similar to the Chapter House side. A great deal of untouched original detail survives,

A Decorative arch orders and adjacent moulding, and four decorative jambs
B Two trefoils with censing angels
C Diaper flowers
D Large sculptures of Gabriel and Mary
E The Victorian Christ in Majesty and surrounding moulding
F Ashlar and niches
G Purbeck 'marble' columns

Figure 14.1 The Annunciation Doorway, Chapter House side

Figure 14.2 The Annunciation Doorway, vestibule side

especially on the figures, which are not so damaged as on the Chapter House side.

The work carried out on these areas consisted of removing all limewash with air abrasive and then consolidating with Acrylic Silane where necessary (see *Table 14.1*). Fillings on larger fractures in the stone were made up of acrylic silane and dry Portland stone dust with pigment to match, and were mainly applied to the left-hand of the Chapter House side.

The two trefoils with censing angels

Each trefoil contains two angels; the larger angel (1090 mm (43 in) high) holds a censor towards the two life-size figures in the niches. To the inside of these are the smaller angels (560 mm (22 in) high).

Both panels have flaked badly, especially the left-hand side, which has lost most of its detail. The right-hand panel, despite a great deal of flaking, has quite a lot of detail remaining; the face of the large angel and the censor are still recognizable. The small angel has lost its head, but has a lot of detail remaining. The Victorian restoration is confined to the moulding of the trefoil.

The work carried out on the panels consisted of removing limewash with air abrasive and consolidating the surface with acrylic silane where necessary.

The diaper flowers

The diaper patterns which make up the background of the spandrel around the trefoils are original and, although badly flaked, have a reasonable amount of detail left, especially in the lower parts. The work carried out was similar to that on the trefoils.

The figures of Gabriel and the Virgin Mary

The two large figures, described as 'unique in importance and preservation among the whole body of Gothic sculpture in England' and 'perhaps the most significant surviving single works of English medieval sculpture,' stand on pedestals in niches and are fixed to the ashlar near the shoulders by overlapping wedged bars. Both figures are heavily waxed, and this has badly discoloured with age and surface dirt.

The figure of Gabriel is in almost perfect condition, with only one or two very small flakes on the drapery folds. The flakes reveal a chalk-like substance, probably gesso. This may have led to the belief that the figure was made from Chalk.

The figure of the Virgin is in a much greater state of decay. There are large areas of flaking on the face and hands and on many of the edges of the drapery. However, the flakes are not recent, as they are all obscured by the beeswax.

The finer surface detail on both figures was covered by the layer of beeswax. Therefore, test areas on both were initially carried out by fine air abrasion. These tests on the folds, the unfinished back and the scroll of Gabriel and the drapery areas of the Virgin did not reveal any pigment, but did reveal the possibility of a gesso covering.

The surface of the wax was cleaned, and was actually removed only in small areas. On Gabriel, the overall cleaning showed on inspection with a magnifying light a change of surface levels (especially on the face). This indicated the presence of some sort of covering on the stone below the wax. Inspection of the Virgin had similar results. After further wax was removed from the face of the Virgin, definite pigment layers were revealed. Several layers, with a flesh tone on top, are obvious on the forehead, as is an eyebrow in black. There are also details on the eye itself, to the left of a large flake. There is also a brown and black colouring on the hair, with a bright pink (probably undercoating) in two small areas. Tests, carried out by removing the wax slowly with a solvent as above, revealed a white layer, possibly gesso or pigment. On close inspection, two smooth 'high spots' are evident about knee level on the drapery, indicating further pigment layers.

The discovery of pigment on the figures was important, particularly when considering the significance of the sculpture, and it was essential that the pigment should be preserved. It was necessary to examine the surface of the figures carefully in order to determine the exact nature of the surface coverings and, from that information, to determine how to clean back safely to the original pigment layer. Discussions were held with John Larson, of the Victoria and Albert Museum Conservation Department, who indicated that an adequate examination could only be made by using microscopic techniques and by thorough testing in studio conditions. This would involve removal of the figures from the niches and their transportation to a suitable environment. This would be a complex undertaking, requiring careful supervision. Until this examination could be arranged, no cleaning work on the sculpture could be attempted because this could make future work difficult at best and, at worst, endanger the remaining pigment. If the figures were to remain in the niches for the time being, the test areas could be touched in so as not to detract from the overall appearance by sealing the surface with acrylic and then colouring with pigment. A photographic record of the test areas was made. Subsequently the sculptures were cleaned and conserved as described below.

Table 14.1 Acrylic silane record

Date	*Quantity applied*	*Area applied*
		Chapter House side
24/2/83	100 ml	Right-hand trefoil and sculpture: small angel. Mainly on right-hand wing and right arm and edges of folds around waist. Small spalls on left-hand wing and neck.
24/2/83	100 ml	Right-hand trefoil. Moulding of left lobe of trefoil in stone adjoining main arch.
25/2/83	50 ml	Left-hand trefoil. Small angel. Mainly wings, head and upper torso.
25/2/83	50 ml	Right-hand trefoil. Large angel. Mainly right arm and drapery fold edges.
25/2/83	50 ml	Right-hand trefoil. Larger angel. Head, left hand and right thigh.
26/2/83		Small figures in the dominant arch order of the Chapter House side, numbered from the left up over the apex and down the other side.
	20 ml	Figure 8: mainly upper half.
	35 ml	Figure 9: mainly lower torso.
	35 ml	Figure 10: foliage on right-hand side.
	150 ml	Figure 12: overall and foliage.
	25 ml	Figure 17: small exfoliations overall.
	25 ml	Figure 18: small exfoliations overall.
	20 ml	Figure 19: small exfoliations.
	35 ml	Figure 15: overall.
28/2/83	200 ml	Left-hand trefoil. Lower and right-hand moulding.
1/3/83	50 ml	Figures 21–26 on small sculpture.
	+50 ml	Dominant orders overall, small exfoliations.
	100 ml	Figure 8.
		Vestibule side
1/3/83	300 ml	Figures 1–4 of the dominant order.
	100 ml	Lower orders figures 1–3.
	50 ml	Figure 4 on lower order.
8/3/83	100 ml	Upper order rosettes.
9/3/83	350 ml	Lower left-hand rosette order. Small exfoliations.
9/3/83	300 ml	Upper rosettes and figures 8–13.
10/3/83		
(a.m.)	100 ml	Dominant order figures 13–18.
(p.m.)	150 ml	Dominant order figures 18–26. Small spalling.
11/3/83	150 ml	Reapplication dominant order figures 13–26.
15/3/83		
(a.m.)	100 ml	Right-hand lower dominant figures 5–8.
(p.m.)	100 ml	Lower dominant order figures 8–11.
(p.m.)	100 ml	Foliage order left-hand side.
16/3/83		
(a.m.)	100 ml	Foliage order left-hand side.
17/3/83		*Chapter House side*
(a.m.)	100 ml	Dominant order right-hand side figures 1–3.
	100 ml	As above, figures 4–7.
	100 ml	As above, 7–11.
(p.m.)	100 ml	Reapplication figures 1–11.
	100 ml	As above figures 1–11.
18/3/83	100 ml	Dominant order. Reapplication overall figures 1–26 where necessary.
20/4/83	100 ml	Dominant order. Reapplication to figures 10 and 12.
21/4/83		
(a.m.)	150 ml	Inner moulding above capital on left-hand side.
(p.m.)	100 ml	As above.
22/4/83	200 ml	Outer moulding overall and reapplication.

The Victorian Christ in Majesty

The space above the subarches has been blocked in by two large back-to-back seated figures of Christ, one facing the vestibule and the other facing into the Chapter House. On the Chapter House side Christ is flanked by two censing angels, on a similar scale to the large angels in the trefoils. The cusps of the circle contain the symbols of the Apostles. On the vestibule side the design is simpler, with four angels in the cusps.

The figures were covered in limewash. When this was removed in tests with air abrasive, there was also a layer of beeswax, similar to the wax on the Annunciation figures, underneath the limewash. The air abrasive removed the wax to a certain extent. However, the wax had obviously penetrated the stone, so a solvent cleaning method was thought to be more appropriate. The stone itself, on the whole, was in good condition with some flaking on the outer, presumably original, moulding. A dichloromethane type of paint stripper was found to remove the wax. This was swabbed off with white spirit. On flaking areas of moulding, it was considered safer to use the air abrasive pencil because the paint stripper had to be worked into the wax with stiff bristle brushes. No consolidation of any of the Victorian carving was needed.

The ashlar in the niches

The ashlar on the Chapter House side was brushed down with stiff bristle brushes to remove any old, flaking limewash. It was then recoated with lime–casein paint (see Appendix 1) using Mars Yellow and black artists' dry ground pigment to give a satisfactory colour. Care was taken not to interfere with the remains of wall paintings in the right-hand niche. Two stone columns on the vestibule side were also recoated with lime–casein paint.

The Purbeck 'marble' columns

These were treated with Renaissance wax after washing with Vulpex soap and rinsing with water.

Conservation work to the Annuciation Figures

Keith Taylor and Graciela Ainsworth

Following the conservation of the doorway, it was decided in 1988 that, because of the importance of the discovery and rarity of the polychromy on the sculpture the figures should not be worked on until they could be removed from their niches and be examined in a studio environment, where full and detailed analysis could be carried out under magnification. Only then could a specification for conservation be decided. The stone of the Virgin was very friable, with small areas of spalling stone evident particularly on the edges of folds in the drapery. Because of this, the more friable areas were treated in situ with acrylic consolidants as a holding operation until the detailed work could begin.

The difficult task of removing the sculptures without damage was achieved by sliding the statues on to the bases of travelling cases on the scaffolding. The figures were then braced into position with padded timber supports and the sides of the cases were constructed around them. In this way they could be lowered to the ground and safely transported in their frames without the need to touch the surface of the sculptures. They were transported to the studio for initial inspection. This inspection permitted the backs of the figures to be examined and photographed for the first time.[2] Both figures are flat and unfinished at the back. The figure of Gabriel has a large diagonal channel cut into the back behind the left shoulder and a slot with a dowel fixing hole in the right shoulder. Further fixing slots occur on the left arm, suggesting that originally the figure had wings (probably wooden) and possibly a scroll. The figure of the Virgin has a section of stone let into the top of the head above the hair line. This piecing-in does not appear to be a restoration and is probably an original addition to give the necessary height to the block of stone for the design.

The statues were carefully lowered into a horizontal position for the conservation work. The major part of the work was to remove the thick layer of beeswax covering the sculpture without disturbing the polychromy underneath and to consolidate this polychromy as it was exposed, as well as consolidating the extremely friable and spalling stonework of the Virgin. Cleaning tests were carried out to determine suitable solvents which would be required to remove the wax from a variety of conditions (e.g. friable stone, paint etc.) without disturbing any layers beneath the wax. Several solvents from white spirit, toluene and ethanol to dichloromethane were used overall to slowly remove the thick layer of wax until the stone and paint layers were clearly visible. Careful recording on a grid system with photography logged each minute trace of paint so that the remaining wax could be safely and thoroughly removed. It was found that although the surface of the figure of the Virgin was in a much more advanced state of decay, there were extensive areas of original polychromy. Gabriel, structurally, was in near perfect condition, with original tool markings still visible over the surface, but with only traces of polychromy in areas like the recesses of the nose and mouth.

The dissimilarity in the amount of surviving polychromy could be a result of the differing histories of the sculpture. The figure of Gabriel was taken down and placed in the vestibule, presumably after the Chapter House was turned into a Public Records Office in 1540, following the dissolution of the abbey. The Virgin, however, remained hidden behind a press until the Victorian restoration of the building by Sir Gilbert Scott between 1866 and 1872. It may be that Gabriel was cleaned before being put on display in the vestibule, resulting in the loss of the orginal polychromy in all but the deeper recesses.

The dissimilarity in the condition of the stone can be attributed to their differing origins. Core samples were taken from the bases of the statues and analysis (see below) has shown that the Virgin is carved from Reigate stone, a pale coloured calcareous sandstone from the Upper Greensand. Gabriel, however, is carved from Caen stone, a fine-grained French limestone widely used in England at the time. The reasons for the sculpture using different stones can only be guessed, but the size of blocks needed for the statues would have been difficult to obtain in Reigate (this might also explain why the top of the Virgin's head is pieced in) and as the figures were intended to be completely painted the choice of stone, as far as its appearance was concerned, would have been immaterial.

Six paint samples were taken from differing areas of the figures and polished cross sections were prepared and examined at × 175 by Jo Darrah of the Victoria and Albert Museum. The sections from both figures have been confirmed as simple, finely applied and consistent with a medieval date.

The very friable surface of the Virgin was locally consolidated as the wax was removed using an acrylic consolidant (Raccanello 55050). The Caen stone of Gabriel was sound over the whole surface and did not require any consolidation. The paint layers were also consolidated using the acrylic consolidant.

When all the wax had been removed from the Virgin and the stone was sound, the hollow edges of the spalled areas were carefully filled with finely sieved stone dust in acrylic binder to give maximum protection to the surface. The completed figures are now reinstated in the Chapter House at Westminster Abbey.

Determination of samples from the Annuciation sculptures

Francis G. Dimes

As received the specimens comprised two small cylinders of stone (identified as RTAS/88/1/S The Virgin and RTAS/88/8/2/S Gabriel) each about 14 mm in diameter and each with an axial hole about 7 mm in diameter, not symmetrically drilled along the axis of the cylinder. That of RTAS/88/2/S Gabriel did not penetrate the length of the cylinder.

The specimens were first inspected 'by eye' and with the aid of a ×10 lens and a stereoscopic microscope. Simple non-destructive physical and chemical tests were carried out. In veiew of the statements made that the determination of the stone was of archaeological and artistic importance, permission was sought, and received, to have thin-sections cut for microscopic examination to support and confirm the determinations made by eye. The thin-sections were prepared by GAPS of Putney, London. The petrographical descriptions are given below. The pieces of stone removed from the cylinders (to prepare the thin-sections) were impregnated in blue-dyed epoxy resin. The thin-sections were then made. They were stained with Alizarin Red S and potassium ferricyanide in order to differentiate between carbonate phases present. The photomicrographs were shot in plane polarized light.

The Virgin Mary (Figure 14.3)

Fine- and even-grained, highly calcareous, mostly of fine grains of quartz. Abundant grains of dark-green colour determined to be the mineral glauconite. Scattered planar flakes of the white mica muscovite may be seen. From its general appearance and mineral content, and from direct visual comparison with material from known provenance and geological horizon, the specimen is determined as being a piece of 'Reigate Stone', from the Upper Greensand, Cretaceous in age. Around Reigate, Gatton, Godstone and Merstham, Surrey, the Upper Greensand occurs as a pale-coloured calcareous sandstone. In this area it was commonly referred to as Malmstone or Firestone and it was extensively used for major building works during the Middle Ages in and around London. The stone taken from the Upper Greensand of the Reigate area is recorded under a number of names such as Reigate, Gatton, Merstham and Godstone stone, which ostensibly indicates its source area. However, these names probably are sheer guesswork. The rock is lithologically similar along considerable distances of its outcrop and no absolute technique is currently available to distinguish stone from one quarry from that of another in this area.

The petrographic description given below supports the determination of the specimen as 'Reigate Stone'.

Archangel Gabriel (Figure 14.4)

Fine-grained, highly calcareous evenly-granular, homogeneous, yellow-white coloured, with areas of crystalline calcite commonly in optical continuity.

Figure 14.3 Sculpture of the Virgin Mary (Courtesy John Larson)

Figure 14.4 Sculpture of Gabriel (Courtesy John Larson)

The specimen was compared with material from known geological horizons and provenances and for overall appearance and mineral content matches specimens of 'Caen Stone'.

Caen Stone is the name given to stone extracted from beds of middle Jurassic, Lower Bathonian age found in the Caen plain, Calvados, Normandy, France. There were three main areas working in Caen and the adjoining communes:

La Maladrerie – Bretteville/Odon – Corpiquet belt
Fleury/Orne or Allemagne – Grâce de Dieu belt
Rue Basse – rue de Calix – eastern Caen Hérouville belt

Caen Stone has been used since Gallo-Roman times, with large-scale exploitation developing in the 11th century boosted by the conquest of England by William, which opened up a huge new export market. Trade with England continued into the nineteenth century with production effectively ceasing in 1914, although there is some record of extraction up to 1930, up to 1952 and up to 1966 at various quarries.

Petrographic descriptions

Archangel Gabriel. Fine grained well sorted biopelsparite (Folk) or grainstone (Dunham) containing many small micritic peloids (?fecal pellets), typically 100 μm across, and brachiopod valves and spines. These lie in a medium to coarsely crystalline sparry calcite mosaic zoned to ferroan calcite in places. The brachiopod fragments show internal structures characteristic of spiriferoids or pentameroids, and punctate forms are also observed. Other skeletal grains identified include echinoderms (echinoid spines and plates), foraminifera and rare bryozoa and ostracods. The foraminifera comprise trocospiral, planispiral and biserial as well as undiagnostic types. A minor micritic matrix is stained with carbonaceous impurities. Minor quantities of phosphate are also observed. The sparry calcite is probably a cement; some, at least, occurs as epitaxial outgrowths from echinoid fragments.

Virgin Mary. A sandy biomicrite (Folk) or wackestone (Dunham) containing, in approximate order of abundance, very fine quartz sand and silt grains, siliceous spicules, glauconite pellets, planktonic foraminifera, calcispheres, muscovite and biotite flakes, bioclast moulds, phosphatic clasts and ?bivalve fragments in a calcareous matrix consisting of ?microspar crystallites, typically 15 μm across. The spicules are mainly monaxon, but also include diaxon and triaxon forms and may show ribbing. The foraminifera include *Heterohelix*, *Hedbergella* and *Praeglobotruncana*. Carbonaceous materials occur locally dispersed within the matrix.

References

1. Pevsner, N., *The Buildings of England: London*, Volume 1, 3rd edn, Penguin, London, 1973
2. Williamson, P., 'The Westminster Abbey Chapter House Annunciation group', *Burlington Magazine*, **CXXX**, February 1988

Appendix 1

Limewashing

John Ashurst

The practice of limewashing is very ancient. Limewash is one of the simplest, but also one of the most effective external 'paint' treatments which can be applied to historic masonry, rendering or plaster. Frequently it is the only treatment which should be applied. Limewash cannot be matched in appearance, except in the most superficial way, by any paint system, whatever claims may be made to the contrary. First-time limewashing should not be carried out on sandstone, even though there are good historical precedents for this. Limewash should also not be used as a preservative treatment on sandstone, as recommended in the earlier part of this century, unless regular maintenance can be guaranteed. Flaking limewash on decaying sandstone will only exacerbate the situation, because water washing off the lime is carried into the sandstone. This encourages the stone to behave as a calcareous sandstone, with less resistance to a polluted atmosphere.

The milky suspension of hydrated lime in solution with water is mildly antiseptic. It was used extensively in the past for this reason, as well as for decorative reasons and its light-reflecting properties.

Limewashes

Slaked lime mixed with water will rub off rather easily, so some additional ingredients are usually needed. Whiting (crushed chalk) and lime were traditionally mixed with glue, or size water, to bind them and to improve adhesion. Sometimes common salt, or crude commercial calcium chloride, would be added to tallow washes to assist the emulsification of the tallow. Because salt is hygroscopic, it can also assist the carbonation of the lime on exposure. A common proportion was 7 kg (15 lb) of common salt to 27 kg (50 lb) of hydrated lime. These salt mixes are not recommended for historic fabric; apart from the risk of introducing an unwelcome soluble salt crystallization cycling, such mixes are not strongly adherent. Mixes which include tallow are not recommended for interior situations, where they may inhibit the drying out of a damp plastered wall. Walls liable to development of mould growth should be treated with a quaternary ammonium fungicide, such as Murosol 20, rather than by the traditional inclusion of carbolic acid.

Lime–glue formulations are another traditional wash which should be discarded, even when improved with the addition of alum (for better working properties) and formaldehyde (for resistance to rubbing), because they require frequent maintenance.

Recommended washes are of three types:

1. Lime–tallow
2. Lime–casein
3. Lime–cenosphere (PFA)

Lime–tallow limewash

Ingredients

High calcium lime, in the form of lump lime: 5.0 kg

Tallow: 0.38 kg

Pigment (if required): as much as necessary to produce the intended colour.

Quantities given here and below are those recommended in references 1 and 2.

Procedure. Break the fresh quicklime into small lumps and shred the tallow. Fill a galvanized tank with about five litres of hot water, to a depth of about 300 mm and add the quicklime slowly, taking all necessary protective precautions. While stirring the boiling liquid, add the shredded tallow and pigment. Keep stirring until all activity has ceased. Screen the limewash through muslin. A consistency of thick cream is required to start with. Subsequent thinning with water may take place.

Lime–casein limewash

Ingredients
High calcium lime, in the form of lump lime as above, or soak 12.5 kg hydrated lime in 14 litres of water.

Casein:	0.9 kg
Trisodium phosphate:	0.57 kg
Formaldehyde:	0.5 litre

Pigment as required

Procedure. Soak the casein in hot water for two hours. Ordinary commercial quality casein, prepared from separated milk, is adequate. Dissolve the trisodium phosphate in two litres of water. Add the pigment to the lime, stirring vigorously. When the solutions are quite cool, add the trisodium phosphate solution to the casein solution and then, as slowly as possible, mix in the lime solution. The formaldehyde should be dissolved in seven litres of water and added just before use, stirring constantly. Rapid addition of the formalin will result in a gelling of the whole mixture. Thin with water as required. This mix should be used at once and not stored for more than one day. A simpler lime–casein limewash can be produced by substituting skimmed milk for the commercial quality casein and trisodium phosphate. Both lime–casein washes have excellent rub resistance.

Lime–cenosphere (PFA) limewash

A form of ready-mixed limewash, which has shown itself to be useful over the past six years, is composed of hydrated lime with 10% of pozzolanic PFA added (cenospheres). Powdered pigment may also be added to the mix. A 'polyox' thickening agent is also incorporated. This mixture is bagged and delivered by Pozament Cement Limited. It only requires the addition of cold water. This limewash is quite resistant to rubbing and to normal external exposure. Adhesion is markedly better on porous surfaces, such as old lime plaster or brickwork, than on fresh gypsum plaster. Because of the variations which occur in fly ashes, fine, light-coloured ash should be specified.

Pigments

Lime-fast pigments, complying with BS 1014, should be used. Trial samples are always advisable. Traditional colours for limewash may be prepared with the following mixes:

Cream: 1.8–2.7 kg (4–6 lb) of ochre to 36.3 litres (8 gal) of lime putty.
Fawn: 2.7–3.6 kg (6–8 lb) of umber, 0.9 kg (2 lb) indian red and 0.9 kg (2 lb) lamp black to 36.5 litres (8 gal) of lime putty.
Buff: 2.7–3.6 kg (6–8 lb) raw umber and 1.35–1.8kg (3–4 lb) lamp black to 36.5 litres (8 gal) of lime putty.

Hydraulic limes

Hydraulic limes should not generally be used for limewashing. They tend to flake on drying out, and have poor resistance to rubbing.

Application of limewash

Brush down the surface to be limewashed with a stiff bristle brush to remove dust, old scaling limewash and loosely adhering particles of stone. Treat with a quaternary ammonium fungicide if there is any evidence of organic growth. The surface should be damp on application, and direct heat on a warm day should be avoided. The limewash should be applied when cool, in thin applications, with a large 100 mm brush (grass brush). Four and a half litres (1 gal) should cover approximately 18 square metres (200–300 square feet). An application rate of 17 to 32 square metres per hour, with the above size brush, is average. The limewash should be worked well into the surface and allowed to dry. A second and third application may then be made in the same way.

References

1. Building Research Establishment, *Lime and Lime Mortars*, DSIR Special Report No. 9 (Cowper), HMSO, London, 1927
2. Anon., *Lime in Building*, British Quarrying and Slag Federation Ltd, Croydon, 1968

Appendix 2

Effects of large numbers of visitors on historic buildings

David Honeyborne

People can inadvertently harm buildings in the following ways:

- By direct contact (feet, hands, clothing)
- By polluting the air inside the building with tobacco smoke
- By increasing the relative humidity of the air inside the building to an extent that causes some kind of condensation of moisture on the fabric

Minor effects

Minor risks arise from vibration, if many people step in unison, or from an increase in the concentration of carbon dioxide in the air inside the building. Vibration risks can normally be eliminated, however. Also the risk from an increase in the carbon dioxide content of the air is unlikely to be serious; this is partly because people become noticeably physiologically affected if the carbon dioxide content of the air rises very much, and partly because the only significant effect on the building of a higher concentration of carbon dioxide in the air would be an increase in the rate of dissolution of very wet limestone surfaces. Limestone inside a building normally has a nearly dry surface unless severe rain penetration or rising damp is occurring or the wall is subject to condensation of moisture. Even then, the rate of dissolution caused by the acid-forming sulphur oxides in polluted air and its natural carbon dioxide content will far outweigh any effects caused by the carbon dioxide exhaled by people.

Effects of direct contact

The wearing away of paving and flooring materials by the passage of many feet is a well-recognized hazard. In general, the damage is done mainly by hard particles embedded in the soles or heels of shoes or boots. Damage will tend to be greatest where people turn sharply. In some circumstances the damage can be minimized by arranging for people to have to take smooth curves rather than sharp turns. In others, it may be possible to lead the visitors along routes paved with hard-wearing contemporary materials of no historical value. Eventually it might be necessary to require visitors to replace their outdoor footwear with slippers before entering some historic buildings. This will pose many problems and probably necessitate the introduction or the raising of entry charges. In churches, where right to free entry is more than just a custom, the problems of policy will be particularly difficult to solve, but they concern matters of policy rather than technology and will not be further discussed here.

The rubbing of clothes against the fabric of a building can produce a polishing and staining of the fabric. This is often particularly noticeable in spiral stairways. Even granite can be affected in this way, but limestones and lime- and gypsum-based plasters are more quickly polished. Sandstones are relatively immune. Lighter coloured materials naturally show staining more readily than darker ones. Staining in these circumstances is generally attributed to oil from woollen clothing. However, some of the staining may well be due to a polishing in of dirt particles already on the surface.

Oil naturally present in the skin has a similar effect to oil from clothing. This may often be seen on stone hand-rails and on carved features that people tend to finger out of curiosity. Some of the stains to be seen on marble, particularly on white statuary marble, no doubt originate in this way. There is no reason to believe that oil stains of this kind will lead to any deterioration of the building material. Indeed, there is some evidence that the oil has a tendency to preserve the material. However, such stains are usually considered to be unsightly and there are sometimes calls for their removal.

The relatively cheap methods available for cleaning the masonry of ordinary buildings are seldom appropriate for cleaning the general masonry, much less the carved work in historic buildings. The special methods required instead, for example micro-scale grit blasting or poulticing with special solvents, are slow and need very skilled people to operate them. Hence removal of stains caused by visitors can involve considerable expense and may absorb money that is needed for other conservation activities.

Effects of tobacco smoke

The staining that may be caused on marble counter and table tops by cigarettes that are left smouldering in contact with them is well known. It is not so generally realized that a more wide-spread staining may occur as a result of large numbers of people smoking inside buildings. This has been established as being the most likely cause of otherwise unexplained staining of marble in at least one large building in London. There is no reason why tobacco smoke should not cause similar stains on porous stone or brick surfaces, though stains are likely to be noticeable only on a light-coloured limestone or marble. The removal of such stains from a porous limestone building would present grave difficulties. If an area of polished marble of no great historic value is involved, the best method of removing the stains is by repolishing the surface. Where, for historical or other reasons, this method is not appropriate, poulticing methods must be used. These will involve the use of organic solvents which may well present a health hazard if inhaled.

The removal of stains may absorb money needed for other purposes.

Effects of increasing relative humidity

Air is able to absorb a certain amount of water vapour and hold it invisibly, but its capacity is limited. When air contains the maximum quantity of water vapour it is capable of holding, it is said to be saturated. The amount of water that a given volume of air can hold varies with the temperature of the air, rising as the temperature rises and falling as it falls. In air that is not saturated, the amount of water present is usually expressed as a percentage fraction of the amount that would be present if the air were saturated at that temperature. This is the *relative humidity* of the air.

When unsaturated air is cooled, its relative humidity rises. When the relative humidity reaches 100%, the air will be saturated and further cooling will cause a separation of moisture. This takes the visible form of mist if the air is being cooled by radiation of heat to a cold region (such as a clear night sky), but if the air is being cooled by an impervious surface, moisture will appear on that surface in the form of water droplets. This process is called condensation and the cold body is called a condenser. Window glass is the commonest condenser in buildings with single glazing. The temperature at which condensation first appears is known as the dew point of that body of air. If the air is initially nearly saturated with water the dew point will be high. That is to say, the dew point will be near the air temperature and little cooling will be needed to produce condensation. If the air is initially rather dry its dew point will be far below the air temperature. If the dew point is below the freezing point of water, any condensation will appear as frost.

With every breathing cycle people exhale air that contains more moisture than the air they inhale. They also pass some moisture into the air in the form of perspiration. Hence, if people enter a building in sufficient numbers they will cause the relative humidity of the air to rise significantly, particularly if the ventilation rate of the building is relatively low. In consequence, the dew point will also rise and so will the probability that condensation will occur on the coldest parts of the building. The greater the number of people involved, the greater the risk.

In his analysis of the moisture balance in King's College Chapel, Cambridge, Lacy[1] assumed that, on average, a person walking around an historic building produces 50 g of moisture per hour. A large building of internal air capacity of 50 000 m^3 (rather larger than King's College Chapel) with air at 15 °C and relative humidity 65% will contain 8.26 g of water per cubic metre of air. The dew point will be about 8.1 °C. If, over a period of three hours, 1000 people move quietly round the building they will contribute 3 g of moisture to each cubic metre of air. Assuming negligible loss by ventilation, the total moisture content will become 11.26 g per cubic metre of air, the relative humidity will become 88.6% and the dew point 13 °C. Thus, before the visitors came in, a window would have needed to be at least 6.9 °C below the air temperature to cause condensation. At the end of the three hours in question, condensation would form on the window if it were just over 2 °C below air temperature. The basis of this calculation is given in *Table A2.1* to illustrate how to carry out analogous calculations with data appropriate to other buildings. What happens to the additional moisture introduced by visitors will depend not only on the temperatures of the solid surfaces within the building but also on the nature of those surfaces.

Table A2.1 Calculation of effect of a heavy influx of visitors on the moisture conditions in a large building with a negligible ventilation rate

In this example the building has an air capacity of 50 000 m^3 and the relative humidity of the air is 65% before the entry of the visitors. The temperature of the air is assumed (rather unrealistically) to remain at 15°C throughout the period under examination.

From tables of physical constants (e.g. Kaye and Laby), saturated air at 15 °C contains 12.71 grams of water per m^3. Thus, at 65% RH the air must contain 0.65 × 12.71 = 8.26 grams of water per m^3. The dew point is then found by inspecting the table below to find the temperature at which 8.26 grams of water per m^3 will saturate the air. This is found to be 8.1 °C.

For three hours after opening, there are an average of 1000 quietly moving people in it. If each visitor contributes moisture at the rate of 50 g/h the total moisture added to the air in the building by the end of the three hour period will be 50 × 1000 × 3 = 15 000 g. The contribution per cubic metre of air will then be 150 000/50 000 = 3 g so the moisture content of each m^3 of air goes up to 3 + 8.26 = 11.26 g. The air at 15 °C will still require 12.71 g for saturation, so the new relative humidity will be 11.26/12.71 × 100 = 88.6%.

From the table below, 11.26 g of water will saturate one m^3 of air at 13°C, which is the new dew point.

Temperature (°C)	*Water* (g)
5	6.76
6	7.22
7	7.70
8	8.21
9	8.76
10	9.33
11	9.93
12	10.57
13	11.25
14	11.96
15	12.71
16	13.50
17	14.34
18	15.22
19	16.14
20	17.12
21	18.14
22	19.22
23	20.35
24	21.54
25	22.80

Effects on impervious surfaces

Moisture condensing on an impervious surface will normally be very pure and initially very reactive chemically. Some attack on window glass may take place. If this is repeated often it will cause deterioration of some medieval window glass, particularly glass with a high content of potash. Modern glass is unlikely to be affected significantly.

Condensation running down window panes can also cause damage to putty and to timber framing in the long run. If condensation runs over gypsum-based plaster it can cause softening or the appearance of blisters. If it runs into brickwork it can often transfer soluble salts from the brickwork to other building materials which may be damaged if the salts crystallize on subsequent evaporation of the water. Staining of the surface from which the evaporation occurs may also take place.

Effects on porous surfaces

It may be shown by thermodynamical reasoning (see for example Croney *et al.*[2]) that water held in the pores of a porous material has a lower vapour pressure than water at the same temperature lying on a plane impervious material. It follows that moisture from humid air will condense in the porous material at relative humidity below 100% and at temperatures above the dew point. Condensation will occur first in the finest pores. The relative humidity at which water will begin to condense in a pore of given diameter may be calculated if the angle of contact of the water surface with the solid surface of the pore is known (see *Table A2.2*).

Unfortunately the angle of contact when water is advancing in a pore is not precisely known for any porous masonry. In consequence, only a crude estimate of the relative humidity at which moisture will condense in a pore of any given size can be made. However, it is possible to calculate the relative humidity below which water will *not* condense in pores of a given diameter. This is the relative humidity at which water will just begin to leave the pore. This calculation is possible because, under drying conditions, the angle of contact becomes so near zero that its cosine is 1 for all practical purposes. The relative humidity required to cause condensation in this pore will theoretically always be equal to or greater than that calculated in this way.

To obtain a picture of what will happen in a real porous material, as opposed to a single pore, under given conditions of relative humidity it is necessary to know the pore size distribution. The equations in *Table A2.2* were used by Croney *et al.*[3] to obtain estimates of pore size distributions in soils. Honeyborne and Harris[4] obtained estimates of pore size distributions by carrying out similar analyses on some British building stones. However, too few were examined to allow conclusions to be drawn from their results. The only other workers in Europe known to have employed this technique are in Portugal (see, for example, de Castro[5]); their work naturally concerned Portuguese stone. Owing to the lack of sufficient experimental data it would be better to obtain data about British stones by direct

Table A2.2 The relationship between the maximum diameter of the pores that would be filled with water when the material is in equilibrium with air of a given relative humidity

Croney *et al.*[3] state that:

$$h = -\frac{R\,t}{M\,g}\log^{e}\frac{H}{100} \qquad \text{(A2.1)}$$

where h is the height (cm) of the column of water that the pore will just support by capillarity
H is the relative humidity (%)
R is the universal gas constant (8.315 J/mol K)
M is the molecular weight of water (18.0 g/mol)
t is the absolute temperature (K)
g is the gravitational acceleration (cm/s^2)

From Laplace's equation:

$$h\rho g = \frac{4\sigma\cos\theta}{d} \qquad \text{(A2.2)}$$

where σ is the surface tension of water (dyn/cm)
d is the pore diameter (cm)
θ is the angle of contact between water and solid
ρ is the density of water (g/cm^3)

Rearranging this equation:

$$d = \frac{4\sigma\cos\theta}{h\rho g} \qquad \text{(A2.3)}$$

Combining Equations A2.1 and A2.2:

$$d = \frac{4\sigma\cos\theta M}{\rho t R\log_e(100/H)} = \frac{4\sigma\cos\theta M}{\rho t R 2.303(2 - \log_{10} H)} \qquad \text{(A2.4)}$$

At a temperature of 20°C t = 293; ρ = 0.9982; σ = 72.8. Hence:

$$d = \frac{0.00000009359 \cos\theta}{2 - \log_{10} H}$$

If the diameter is expressed in micrometres we have

$$d = \frac{0.0009359 \cos\theta}{2 - \log_{10} H} \qquad \text{(A2.5)}$$

The amount of residual water in the pores is often plotted against a factor designated as *pF*. This is the common logarithm of the value of h in cm. Thus:

$$d = \frac{4\sigma\cos\theta}{\rho g\ \text{antilog}(pF)}$$

measurement of the amount of water taken up by initially dry test pieces when exposed to controlled atmospheres covering a range of relative humidities. The simple desiccator/sulphuric acid system used by Croney *et al.*[3] and by Honeyborne and Harris[4] for studying the drying cycle can be used just as easily to study the wetting cycle, as shown by de Castro[6]. There seems to be scope for even small conservation laboratories to carry out useful work along these lines. *Table A2.3* gives the densities of the sulphuric acid solutions that may be used to give a range of useful relative humidities.

Table A2.3 Relationship between relative humidity and density of sulphuric acid solution in a closed vessel

Relative humidity (%)	*Density of acid at 20°C* (kg/m^3)	*Suction (pF)* $\log_{10}$ (cm)
20	1475	6.34
30	1416	6.22
40	1377	6.10
50	1336	5.98
60	1293	5.85
70	1245	5.69
80	1194	5.49
90	1130	5.16
93	1103	5.00
98	1030	4.45

Source: references 3 and 6.

A limited amount of useful information can be drawn from published results. Because de Castro[6] gives simple water absorption properties of the stones tested as well as their cumulative pore size distributions (CPSD) it is possible to judge if any of them are sufficiently like any British stone for useful comparisons to be drawn. The limestone from Anca is sufficiently like Monks Park limestone from Wiltshire to justify examination of the results obtained when de Castro tested it. *Figure A2.1* shows CPSD graphs for Monks Park stone and Anca stone. The Portuguese results have been recalculated to fit the unit system usually employed in this field of work in Britain. The graphs have a similar shape, but the Portuguese stone has a finer pore structure (Monks Park stone has the finest pore structure of any British limestone so far studied). De Castro's moisture take-up measurements for Anca stone at a range of relative humidities have also been recalculated to fit the unit system usually employed in Britain. They are shown in *Table A2.4* together with an estimate of the diameters of the pores involved. Column 4 is the most informative.

Over the range of relative humidities from 50% to 70% the pick-up is relatively small. Even at 90% relative humidity the volume of water taken up would occupy only 0.35% of the bulk volume of the stone. Since British stones generally have coarser pores, their moisture pick-up at these relative humidities will probably be distinctly lower.

In his examination of moisture conditions at King's College Chapel, Lacy[1] deduced that about 15 tons (15 240 kg) of water exhaled by visitors passed into the walls of the building during the summer and about 5 tons (5080 kg) of this passed back into the building during the winter when the heating was on. It seems most likely that the water was held in the pores of the masonry. It might also be of interest to note that at equilibrium with an atmosphere of 90%

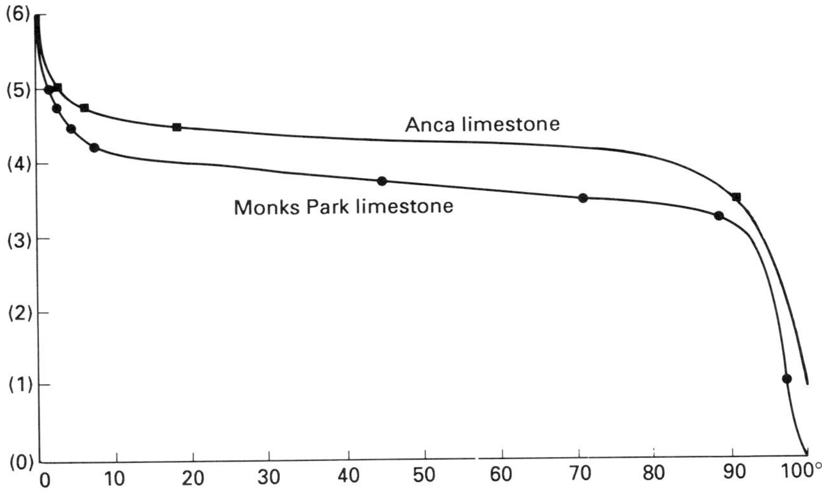

Figure A2.1 Suction-based cumulative pore size distribution (based on reference 4, Figure 8, and reference 6, Figure 3)

Table A2.4 Hygroscopic properties of limestone from Anca, Portugal

Relative humidity (%)	*Moisture absorbed*			*Max. pore diameter affected* (nm)
	g water per 100 g stone	*% saturation*	*% volume of stone*	
20	0.013	0.09	0.025	1.3
30	0.022	0.15	0.043	1.8
40	0.031	0.22	0.061	2.4
50	0.038	0.27	0.074	3.1
60	0.048	0.34	0.094	4.2
70	0.063	0.44	0.12	6.2
80	0.102	0.71	0.20	9.7
90	0.18	1.2	0.35	20
95	0.56	3.9*	1.1*	42

Data taken from ref. 6, figure 19
*Value less certain

relative humidity each cubic metre of Anca stone would hold 3.5 kg (3.5 litre) of water and in an atmosphere of 50% relative humidity it would hold 0.74 kg.

It is debatable whether water held in this way causes harm to the stone, even if it is a limestone and the ambient air is polluted with oxides of sulphur. De Castro[6] assumes that there must be a connection between the amount of hygroscopic moisture, as she calls it, and the rate of attack by aggressive agents in the air. However, there does not appear to be evidence to support this view. Intra-porous condensation must occur in the stonework of many older churches, yet damage to interior stone can seldom be found away from areas suffering from rising damp, rain penetration, massive dew-point condensation, or the action of some of the more aggressive soluble salts. Any liquid held in very fine pores (see *Table A2.4*, column 5) will be subjected to intense molecular forces. Crystallization of any salts present will be highly suppressed and the normal chemical behaviour will be much modified, so abnormally passive behaviour is possible.

Effects on walls when hygroscopic salts are present

The situation is entirely different when hygroscopic (i.e. moisture-attracting) salts are present on the surfaces or in the larger pores of the stonework. Such salts will induce condensation of moisture from the air at relative humidities well below 100% and at temperatures well above the dew point. In this respect they resemble the fine pores. However, instead of being held harmlessly, the water so condensed will dissolve part or all of the salts involved. Damage to the fabric will almost certainly occur on subsequent drying out, if the accompanying crystallization takes place within the coarser pores. Such damage can occur with nearly all kinds of porous building materials.

Unfortunately there is no available theory that can quantify hygroscopic condensation. Each salt or mixture of salts is characterized by an equilibrium relative humidity (ERH) above which hygroscopic condensation will occur. The ERH is affected by temperature as well as by the kinds of salts involved. *Table A2.5* lists the ERH for a few simple salts at room temperatures. However, mixtures of salts

Table A2.5 Equilibrium relative humidity (ERH) of a number of simple common salts

Salt	*Chemical formula*	*EQRH* (%)
Calcium chloride hydrate	$CaCl_2 \cdot 6H_2O$	31
Magnesium chloride hydrate	$MgCl_2 \cdot 6H_2O$	33
Potassium carbonate hydrate	$K_2CO_3 \cdot 2H_2O$	44
Potassium chloride	KCl	85
Potassium nitrate	KNO_3	93
Potassium sulphate	K_2SO_4	98
Sodium carbonate hydrate	$Na_2CO_3 \cdot 10H_2O$	90
Sodium chloride	NaCl	76
Sodium nitrate	$NaNO_3$	75
Sodium sulphate hydrate	$Na_2SO_4 \cdot 10H_2O$	93

The ERH of a salt tends to rise with a fall in temperature. The effect is more striking with some salts than others. The EQRH may sometimes reach a maximum at some mid-range temperature. The values given have been rounded off and apply approximately within the temperature range 20–25°C.

behave in anomalous ways and it is not possible to deduce the ERH of a mixture from the known properties of its constituents. When a mixture of salts is present in a building material and changes of relative humidity are believed to be causing damage, the best way to investigate is to measure the ERH of the mixture experimentally. This can be done using a small sample and the same kind of controlled-humidity vessels as are used for measuring the hygroscopicity of materials. The initially dried and weighed test sample is placed in the driest atmosphere first and, after an appropriate time, is removed, weighed and placed in the vessel with the next higher relative humidity, and so on. A plot of gain in weight against RH will soon reveal the ERH of the material. (This measurement can be done more precisely with an absorption balance, if one is available.) If the ERH found is within the RH range normally found in the building, crystallization damage is likely to occur.

Different salts have different degrees of aggressiveness when crystallizing. For example, sodium sulphate tends to be more damaging than sodium chloride, which tends to be more damaging than calcium sulphate. However, mixtures of salts have an aggressiveness that appears to be unrelated to the aggressiveness of the constituents. These properties are not yet understood.

Changes in relative humidity that lead to the solution and recrystallization of salts and mixtures of salts are likely to be as damaging to the internal fabric of a building as rain penetration or rising damp.

References

1. Report of special investigation No. 2143 on atmospheric humidities in King's College Chapel, Cambridge, Building Research Station (Department of Scientific and Industrial Research), 1963 [No author of this report is named but it is well known that the principal investigator was R E Lacy.]
2. Croney, D. and Coleman, J.D., Soil thermodynamics applied to the movement of moisture in road foundations, *Proc. 7th International Congress for Applied Mechanics*, **3**, 163–177, 1948
3. Croney, D., Coleman, J.D. and Bridge, P.M., 'The suction of moisture held in soil and other porous materials', *DSIR Road Research Technical Note No. 24*, HMSO, London, 1952
4. Honeyborne, D.B. and Harris, P.B., 'The structure of porous building stone and its relation to weathering behaviour', *Proc. 10th Symposium of Colston Research Society*, pp. 343–365, Butterworths, London, 1958
5. de Castro, E., 'Determination of pore size distribution in stones by means of moisture suction', *Memoria No. 441*, Laboratoria Nacional de Engenharia Civil, Lisbon, 1974
6. de Castro, E., 'Evaluation de l'hydroscopicité des pierres', *Memoria No. 526*, Laboratoria Nacional de Engenharia Civil, Lisbon, 1979

Appendix 3

The use of air-abrasive cleaning techniques for stone building surfaces

Peter Moss

Air-abrasive or 'blast' cleaning is not an appropriate technique for all stone building surfaces, and there is no doubt that bad experiences associated with poor specification and inept operatives have, on many occasions, led to prejudice against the system. Successful cleaning with compressed air and abrasive, with or without water, depends on a correct and detailed specification, properly trained operatives and well maintained equipment. A full understanding of the principles of the 'blast' methods, by both specifier and operative, will ensure that they are used only in the correct way on appropriate surfaces, in a safe and cost-effective manner.

'Blast' cleaning methods include (in descending impact effect):

1. Wheel type (electric). Metallic grit or shot abrasive. Suitable only for removing surfaces, descaling and cleaning of some pavings.
2. Air pressure blast (portable). Various abrasives. Typical pressures at the nozzle range from 20 to 100 psi. When air-abrasive cleaning is used, most building surfaces are cleaned by this method.
3. Air suction blast (lightweight portable). Fine abrasives only. Typical pressures at the nozzle range from 20 to 100 psi, but the design type has the effect of reducing impact to about half that of the air pressure blast at the same air pressures. Architectural detail, especially if small-scale or multi-faceted, is frequently cleaned by this method.

All air blast cleaning equipment should be fitted with a pressure regulator, complete with a (working) gauge. High pressure water may also be used with suction-feed abrasive, but is generally only suitable for lightly soiled, flat surfaces.

Applications and use

The pressure machines can be fitted with water injection or water shroud type fittings. The 'Kleanblast' water injection unit need only inject one litre per minute, which is ideal for damping down dust, without the use of running water, on the surfaces or base of a building. Generally, the work rate is equal to that of dry blasting.

The wet blast head (water shroud) uses substantial amounts of water, because it has six or eight jets of water around the nozzle. The centre area is dry, but the water volume washes the surface. The work rate is slower and general visibility less than with the water injection unit. The water injection unit is preferred by most contractors.

The advent and availability of water injection units such as the KB80 means that there should be no reason for a dust nuisance to be experienced on any site cleaned by this system, even when the scaffolding is unsheeted. Suction blast guns, such as the SG300, can only be fitted with the shroud type water attachment.

For safety reasons, all blast cleaning machines should be fitted with remote control. Building cleaning requires a system capable of enabling the operator to shut the abrasive flow off and on as required, in order to avoid the risk of damage to the surface. Electric or electronic remote controls are available, and they give instant response even on the longest of high-blast hoses. These controls are not affected by liquids and always fail-safe. A common malpractice is to check the flow of abrasive by folding the blast hose. This is extremely dangerous and should be absolutely prohibited. Remote control grit valves are also available, which enable operators to blow or wash down the surface intermittently during the cleaning process.

Table A3.1

Nozzle diameter (in)	*Nozzle pressure* (p.s.i.)						*Compressor size* (cubic ft/min)
	50	60	70	80	90	100	
1/8	11	13	15	17	18	20	25
3/16	26	30	33	38	41	45	60
1/4	47	54	61	68	74	81	100
5/16	77	89	101	113	126	137	160
3/8	108	126	143	161	173	196	250
7/16	147	170	194	217	240	254	325
1/2	195	224	252	280	309	338	450

Abrasives and nozzles

Abrasives, nozzle types and sizes and air pressures must be selected and specified for particular applications. In general, round abrasives, such as shot, beads and some types of sand, hammer the surface. These are ideal where the soiling is hard and brittle on a fairly hard substrate, for example a sulphated film on granite. Angular abrasives, such as blasting grits, quartz sand or flint grit, have a cutting effect. These are suitable where a soft or resilient soiling covers the substrate.

Blast cleaning uses kinetic energy (1/2 mass × velocity^2). The size or the specific gravity of an abrasive and its impact velocity will determine the cleaning work rate. In building cleaning, the emphasis should be not on the fastest, but on the most effective work rate. Therefore, a trial area should be specified and the contractor should always start with the lowest pressure and the smaller, lighter abrasives. These factors can then be modified to determine the optimum work rate, abrasive type and size and pressure.

The 'Health and safety and the blasting of castings' Act and others forbid the use of abrasives containing 'free silica' (sands and flint grit). Even the use of water does not prevent dust risks. There is some evidence from the USA that wetted sand is absorbed more easily into the lungs than dry dust. The ready availability of building cleaning grits, such as Stonegrit, in many different sizes, now means that there is little need to use banned grits.

Nozzles must be chosen carefully. Long venturi nozzles are more efficient and give an even particle spread over a greater impact area (at a constant distance from the surface) at any pressure. They are ideal for flat areas, or consistent soiling conditions. Long and short straight nozzles, whilst less efficient, provide a more pencil-shaped blast, which is ideal for window seals, channels and taking out poor pointing. Angled nozzles are also available.

An important aspect of nozzle choice, for consistency of application and economic reasons, is the selection of nozzles which will stay the same shape throughout the job. The design life of some nozzles is only 20–25 hours. With a constant air-feed pressure, the abrasive will cut differently between the start and the finish of a 25 hour job. If the air supply is constant, the pressure will be reduced. This will gradually reduce the impact on the surface. If, as is more common, air is available to maintain pressure, then the impact area will be reduced and more energy will be expanded within this reduced area. This means there will be a greater chance of substrate damage. These nozzles are generally of the cast alloy or ceramic type.

A comparison of work carried out with venturi nozzles of different orifice sizes shows:

If 1/4 in = 100% area:
- 5/16 in = 157% more area than 1/4 in nozzle
- 3/8 in = 220% more area than 1/4 in nozzle
- 7/16 in = 320% more area than 1/4 in nozzle
- 1/2 in = 400% more area than 1/4 in nozzle

This relates to any specific nozzle pressure. A comparison of air requirements, nozzle size and pressure for pressure machines is given in Table A3.1.

Suction gun jets require approximately 28% more air, but are only available in 1/16 inch to 1/4 inch sizes. Suction gun nozzles should be at least twice the diameter of the jet size.

The air/grit mix at any pressure should be as lean as possible, but should give an even, constant flow of abrasive to the work. All blast cleaning machines used for building cleaning should be fitted with a flat 'sand' valve, not a 'steel' grit valve.

Summary

Both clients and specifiers must insist that work is carried out at specific and appropriate pressures, and site supervision should ensure that these are adhered to. 'Blast' cleaning can be considered as an even area cleaning method, which is fast and suitable for much building cleaning. It is not a spot cleaning method. The characteristics of soiling on buildings are infinitely variable, particularly the tenacity of adhesion to the substrate. Although 'blast' cleaning systems are very flexible, they cannot be expected to provide a total cleaning of all areas. Other techniques and methods may be used in conjunction with 'blast' cleaning. This includes the use of fine water sprays as a preliminary treatment, where the soiling has been absorbed and the substrate is not at risk from water damage. If the substrate is weak and friable, with a hard dirt crust on the surface, a chemical cleaning agent may be appropriate as a preparation for careful air abrasive treatment. In this case pre-wetting is essential and some washing on completion will also be necessary. Flame cleaning should precede the use of air abrasive where hard paint films or resilient bitumen paints have to be removed from weak substrates.

Note Peter Moss is a member of Hodge Clemco Limited of Sheffield, England, a company which supplies the stone cleaning industry with most of its blast cleaning equipment and materials. The equipment and abrasives mentioned are trade names of Hodge Clemco Limited. The company provides a free advisory service to customers and specifiers on application and techniques, and has a training school for operatives and supervisors.

Appendix 4

The analytical approach to stone, its cleaning, repair and treatment

Nicola Ashurst and John Kelly

The belief that the identification of a stone as, for instance, 'sandstone' is sufficient basis for an understanding of the processes of alteration or decay is an erroneous one. It is equally inadequate in the formulation of a program of remedial work. The term 'sandstone' is a generalized term for those rocks representative of a section of the arenaceous rocks–that is, those detrital, quartz-rich sediments with a grain size of 2.00–0.0625 mm. This does not reflect the wide variation of chemical, mineralogical and physical characteristics found within the generalization. A failure, or inability, to recognize this variation prior to cleaning or other remedial treatments can often lead to damage in the form of discoloration or accelerated decay rates.

An analytical approach, involving a geologist and a competent architect experienced in stone weathering deterioration and repair, can avoid many of the problems which have become all too familiar. Their correct interpretation of on-site factors and laboratory analysis, and the meaningful and accurate synthesis of the data obtained, may be translated into appropriate recommendations for remedial work.

On-site investigation/analysis

On-site investigation of stonework should be directed towards obtaining visual identification of the apparent stone types present. This will, of necessity, be based on colour and such characteristics as may be observed with the naked eye or hand lens–for example, grain size or other large textural features such as banding or lamination. The occurrence of any alteration of the stone surfaces due to the action of algae, lichen, pollutants or efflorescence, together with granulation, scaling or exfoliating elements, should also be noted.

Above all, no local consideration of a particular problem should exclude an assessment of the condition of the whole facade. Decay and staining frequently relate to poor building maintenance and remedial work to joints, flashings, copings and rainwater disposal goods. The effect of these as well as the design of the facade should always be taken into account.

Sampling

On the completion of preliminary assessment of stone types present and the range or nature of their alteration, samples should be taken which reflect these variations and will be useful in the proposed program of analysis. With due consideration for the aesthetic integrity of the masonry, it is usual that the larger the number of samples available the more the results of analysis will be representative of the materials present. However, even relatively small, carefully selected samples, with proper preparation and analytical techniques, can provide an adequate data base.

The location of samples on the structure and their relationship to any failures of structure or detailing should be noted. A description of the sample methods should accompany each sample. Also, each sample should be packed separately and be clearly labelled with all relevant information.

It is preferable that the sampling is carried out by personnel from the analysing facility who can be expected to be responsible for correct sampling. This should, of course, always follow discussion with the owner or the owner's delegated agent.

Laboratory analysis

While some simplified analysis may be carried out on-site as an aid to sampling procedures, meaningful results can only be obtained by proper laboratory-based work to fully elucidate the physical and chemical characteristics of the stones.

Petrological analysis[1]

This basically entails the systematic examination of stone sample, both in thin section and hand specimen. The purpose is to identify or classify the stone type under consideration. Even where the stone type is identified in historical records such an investigation is recommended for the purpose of confirmation or to note any variation from an expected norm.

The work is generally carried out using a stereoscopic and petrological microscope with plane-polarized light. Due to the limits of magnification and resolution inherent in light microscopy, the analysis may need to be supported, where appropriate, by other methods. Those most commonly employed are X-ray diffraction (XRD) and the scanning electron microscope (SEM). From the application of these techniques the mineralogy of the individual elements and their textural relationships can be determined.

The identification and quantification of the mineralogy allows the determination of the gross chemistry of the stone; it also clearly indicates the direction of further analysis and the choices available for the future remedial work. At this stage of analysis the fundamental classification of the sandstone is established.

Physical analysis

While the differences apparent in the various sandstone types will be determined from petrological analysis, it is the physical characteristics which will largely control the ingress and movement of water. The majority of processes which are detrimental to stonework require the presence of water for their operation, and it is the physical characteristics of porosity and capillarity which determine the rate and amount of water uptake.

Capillarity determination

The capillary characteristics are generally calculated from the uptake of deionized or distilled water into a stone sample by surface contact with a wetted, absorbent pad. The amount of water taken up is calculated against the dry weight of sample and recorded against time. From these measurements a capillary curve may be plotted. When such measurements are carried out under similar conditions, a graphic illustration of the capillarity of a sample may be compared to other stone types or to modified samples of same stone. Furthermore, from these results the capillary coefficient of the stone type may be determined. The observations may, of course, be applied to the determination of a drying curve.

Porosity determination

The uptake of water into a stone will be determined largely by its capillary system. However, the effect of the water within the stone, either alone or together with contained contaminates, will depend on the extent and nature of the pore system.

Two methods may be used to determine the porosity:

1. Water uptake at atmospheric temperature and pressure (APT) and under vacuum. Unlike capillary testing, these tests are carried out by controlled immersion and saturation of the sample.
2. Mercury porosimetry. Using this method mercury is forced into a small sample. The amount of mercury intruded and the force required are indicative of the volume of pores penetrated and their diameter.

Both these methods have positive and negative aspects, which must be correctly interpreted.

With the water method the pores are either filled completely or not. From the amount of water taken up under both ATP and vacuum, effective and total porosity may be determined together with water absorption coefficient, saturation coefficient and density. This information is useful in several ways, particularly for assessing the susceptibility of the stone to frost damage. The use of mercury porosimetry allows the determination of both the total porosity and the relative amounts of pores of known diameter. This allows a calculation of the relative amounts of macro-pores to micro-pores. The division between these is an arbitrary one based on earlier petrological work. The present division at 5 mm diameter is under review. Again, this data is significant as an indicator of the ability of the stone to withstand internal pressure originating from either freezing water or salt hydration. The shortcomings of the mercury porosity method are that certain assumptions must be made concerning the pore geometry of the stone, and that the size of the mercury molecule limits measurements to pores of 32 Ångstroms (3.2 nm) diameter or greater.

However, both methods have their application in determining the characteristics of the stone and with careful interpretation can provide a valuable insight into the material and its alteration.

Chemical analysis

This involves determination of the water-soluble, acid-soluble and solvent-soluble contents of the stone.

Chemical analysis can be developed to a considerable extent by interpretation of the results of petrological analysis. Unfortunately, contaminants, whether derived from alteration of the original chemistry of the stone or by ingress of extraneous matter, are often extremely fine-grained. They may be dispersed through an area relatively large in relation to their amount. In addition, the amount of contaminants present may be small relative to the damage caused by their presence. These factors tend to make their identification by direct observation time-consuming and problematical.

With few exceptions the stones utilized for building and monumental work do not contain appreciable amounts of water-soluble material, and therefore where such material is present it may be regarded as a contaminant. Similarly, by the use of other solvents the chemistry relevant to decay processes may be more closely defined.

Water-soluble content

Using deionized water, soluble materials may be extracted for analysis. Total analysis may be carried out, but it is considered sufficient to determine the cations and anions which constitute the main classes of soluble salts known to occur within inorganic building materials. It is essential, however, that such analysis be quantitative with regard to the total water-soluble contaminants and to their relative amounts. The techniques most readily available for this determination are atomic absorption and inductively coupled plasma spectroscopy and ion chromatography.

Acid-soluble content

The acid-soluble content is relevant where the stone type under analysis has been previously noted as having a calcareous content. The determination of the total calcareous content is needed in order to assess the response of the stone to a polluted environment. The loss of a calcareous mineralogy will have a direct effect on the stone, owing to loss of its cementing mineralogy or its conversion to a different mineralogy. In the latter respect the dissolution of the stone in acidic water may also have a detrimental effect on adjacent non-calcareous stonework, similar to that observed at times between limestones and sandstones. Futhermore, sandstones with a clay content may have a greater susceptibility to acidic waters.

Sovent-soluble content

The solvent-soluble content aspects of the chemical analysis is mainly directed to the nature of soiling of pollutants other than those mentioned above. While the presence of unburnt fossil fuels and their residues is thought of largely in terms of surface disfigurement, they can contain materials which catalyse or assist other decay mechanisms. As their presence as the dark components of soiling crusts is often the reason for the intiation of an intervention program, determination of their nature is an important preliminary to the selection of appropriate cleaning methods.

Conclusions and the approach to cleaning

With the completion of a sequence of analysis as outlined above, an understanding of the nature of the stone substrate and its alteration will be available, upon which a programme of intervention may be reasonably based. This will allow a choice of methods and materials applicable to the problems of the stonework as determined rather than as perceived. It will also preclude the use of inappropriate stone for replacement or indenting repairs based on a superficial assessment of colour alone.

From the examination of correctly selected thin sections and from the use of chemical profiling it will be apparent that soiling or alteration are not confined to the surface of the stonework. Furthermore, cleaning as the removal of damaging as well as disfiguring contaminants may have to be carried out on delicate or weakened stonework. The damage caused by the widspread and seemingly indiscriminate use of abrasive or harsh chemicals has led to radical reassessment of cleaning methods.

There are no universal sandstone cleaners, just as there are no universal limestone or granite cleaners. Note must be taken of the nature and the specific condition of the stone substrate so that the cleaning approach can be tailored to suit.

In the light of this it may be seen that building cleaning should, ideally, be an extension of museum cleaning methods based on extremely weak solutions of the appropriate chemicals. Serious consideration should also be given to the use of chemicals together with absorbent packs to form gels and poultices, as these allow a much greater control of the chemical action.

Poultice cleaning

The principles of a poultice are that it not only acts as a vehicle for the chemical but also functions as a capillary system exterior to the stonework but intimately associated with it. This means that, once the soiling is dissolved, it is absorbed by the poultice and drawn away from the stone rather than moving into the body of the stone, Using the poultice approach, combinations of chemical solvents can be brought into contact with the soiling; these combinations will relate to the nature of the substrate and the nature of the soiling. The intimate contact of the cleaning materials means that smaller quantities of chemicals have to be used, and these may be of much lower concentration. Typically, concentrations of less than 0.5% hydrofluoric acid in poultice form have been effectively used on sandstone against levels of 5% to 10% hydrofluoric acid used in many other available systems. In addition, the use of poultice techiques greatly reduces the amount of water required.

To conclude, it is very important that the testing of any proposed cleaning materials is viewed as an integral part of the programme of analysis and assessment. In addition, a post-cleaning analysis of all affected stonework is another essential element in the analytical approach to sensitive and proper stone cleaning.

It must be reiterated that the success of the process described relies heavily on the quality of the professional interpretation given to the many factors.

Reference

1. Kelly, J., 'The petrographic microscope as an aid to stone conservation', *Microscopy and Analysis*, June 1989

Index

Page numbers in *italics* refer to illustrations or tables. Some textual matter may also occur.

Aberthaw (Glamorgan) lime, 82
Abrasive cleaning, *see* Mechanical cleaning
Acropolis, 34
Acrylic consolidation, 164–5
Acrylic paints, 195
Additives to mortars, 83
  air-entraining agents, 84
  antifreeze, 83–4
  brick dust, 81, 84, 172
  HTI powder, 15, 18, *19*, 81, 84, 172
  PFA, 81, 84
  pigments, 84
  surfactants, 84
  water-reducing agents, 84
  waterproofers, 84
Adhesives, 186
  epoxy adhesive, 15–16
Adze, 100, *101*, 102
  tool marks, 103, *104*
Aggregates for mortars, 173
  grading, 85
  materials, 84
  summary of requirements, 85
  washing, 84–5
Ainsworth, Graciela, 224–5
Air abrasion, *see* Mechanical cleaning
Air pollution, 59
  building zones, 73–4
  environmental effects on tombs, 191–2
  limestone durability and, *73*, 74
  microclimate, 73
  Parliament Buildings, Ottawa and, 118–20
Air-entraining agents, 84
Alabaster, 135, 188, 190
Algal slimes, 136–7
Alkyl-trialkoxy-silanes, 160–3
  structure of, *162*
All Souls College (Oxford), 16
Ammonium hydroxide cleaning, 133
Ammonium sulphamate, 10
Analysis
  chemical, *see* Chemical analysis
  chloride, 124
  dating structures and, 88
  laboratory, 240–1
  of core, 120–1, 124
  of mortars, 88–93
  on-site, 88–90, 240
  petrographic, 98, 225–227
  petrological, 241
  physical, 241
  recordings, *91–2*, 93
  sampling, 90, 93, 214, 216, 240
Anca stone, 234, 235
Anchor bolts, 69
Ancient monuments, *see* Monument sites
Ancona (Italy), *109*
Annunciation Door, *see* Westminster Abbey, Annunciation Door
Antifreeze additives, 83–4
Arches
  arch springers, 11
  structural failure, 58
Architect's plan of approach, 1, *2–3*
Architectural feature displays, 208–13
  free standing structures, 211–12, 213
  information, 208
  packaging, 210
  planning, 208
  reassembly, 210–13
    dry-build, 210–11
    isolating membranes, 211–12
    setting out, 210, 211
  scaffold, 209
  site briefings, 209
  surveys, 208–9
  taking down, 209–10
    marking stones, 210
    temporary supports, 209, 210
  transportation, 210
Arequipa (Peru), *112*
Aryl-alkyl-polysiloxanes, 163–4
Ashlar, 11, 98
  boasted or axed, 98
  measurement of dressed stonework, *99*, 100
  plain or rubbed, 98
  punched, 98
  rock-faced, 98, 104–5
  rusticated, 11, 98
  spalling, 118, 121, 123
  tooled or batted, 98
Ashurst, John, 1–54, 78–96, 124–54, 229–30
Ashurst, Nicola, 240–3
Atmospheric pollution, *see* Air pollution
Attapulgite clay, *52*, *54*, 134, 141, 171
Axed ashlar, 98

Baker method, *see* Lime surface treatment method
Balderrama, Alejandro Alva, 107–13
Balvac process, 29
Banker-mason, 100
Barium hydrate (baryta), 165, 197
Barnack limestone, 172
Baryta water, *see* Barium hydrate (baryta)
Basalt setts, 33
Bath limestone, 133, 172
Batted ashlar, 98
Bedding surfaces, checking of, 99
Beer limestone, 172
Bees, damage from, 88
Beeswax, 223, 225
  see also Wax
Bench marks, 63, *64*
Benzoyl peroxide catalyst, 165
Berea sandstone (Ohio), 115
Binders, 24, 25, 215
Binocular microscopy, 197, *198*, 202, *203*
  see also Stereoscopic microscope

Biological growth cleaning
  coverage, 137
  protection of other areas, 137
  treatment, 136
Bird droppings, 139, *140*
Bird, Francis, 186, *188*
Bituminous roofing felt, 30
Blades, Keith, 114–24
Block-in-course masonry, 98, *99*, 100
Boasted ashlar, 98
Boaster, 97, *101*
  tool marks, 103
Bolsover Castle (Derbyshire), *42*
Bonders, 12
Bonding timbers, in walls, 60
Boulogne cement, 82
Bowing, 59
Bracing, diagonal, 58
Brick dust
  Cambridge White, 172
  mortar additives, 84
  red, 81
  yellow, 81
Bristol Temple Church, *47*
British Geological Survey, 71
British Museum (London), *149*
British Museum (Natural History), 71
Buchler Digital Chloridometer, 124
Budva (Yugoslavia), *109*, *111*
Building Research Establishment, 12, 60, 63, 71, 72, 157
Building Research Station, 69, 141
Building zones, 73–4, *75*
Bulging, 59, *116*
Bull-nose chisel, 103
  tool mark, 103
Burrell Collection (Glasgow), *209*, *211*, *212*
Butterbaugh technique, 181
Buttress caps, *42*
Buttressing, 58

Caen stone, *43*, 202, 203, 225, 226
Calaton, 217
Calcination, 81
Calcite, 132
Calcium casein, 174–5
Calcium fluoride, 132
Calcium hydroxide, 179–80, 182
Calcium sulphate, 177–9, 182
Calderwood cement, 82
Capillarity, *76*, 140, 241
Carbonation, 80
Carboxymethylcellulose (CMC), 133
Carrara marble, 205–6
  condensation and, 190
  sculptures, 30
Carthy, Deborah, 208–13
Casein, 174
  lime-casein paint, 22, 215, 230
Cast stone, 25, *50–1*
Castle Acre Priory, *35*
Castle Drogo, *95*
Casts, 1
Cathedral Works Organization, 71
Causey Arch (Tanfield, Co. Durham), 29
Caustic potash cleaning, 133, *145*, *146*
Caustic soda cleaning, 133
Cavitron, 199, *201*, *202*
Celcon blocks, 193, *194*
Cellosolve, 29
Cement and Concrete Association, 62
Cement paints, 22
Cements
  Boulogne, 82
  Calderwood, 82
  damage from, 191, 197, *198*
  high alumina, 83
  Louisville, 82
  masonry, 83
  Medina, 82
  natural (Roman), 82, 171
  Portland, 82, 171, 191
    waterproofed (OPC), 84
    white, 82–3
  pozzolanic, 83
  Rosendale, 82
  Rugby, 82
  Sheppey, 82
  sulphate-resisting, 83
  Weymouth, 82
  Whitby, 82
Chemical analysis, 241–2
  acid-soluble content, 242
  chloride analysis, 124
  mortars, 90
  solvent-soluble content, 242
  water-soluble content, 242
Chemical cleaning, *151–3*, *151–4*, 199–200
  caustic potash, 133
  caustic soda, 133
  hydrochloric acid, 133
  hydrofluoric acid, 130–3, *152*, *153*
    commercial procedures, 132–3
    personal protection, 133
    staining, 131
  poultices, *see* Poultices
  proprietary pastes, 133
  sandstone, *151*
Chichester, medieval market cross, *43*
Chilmark limestone, 172
Chimney caps, cast stone, 25
Chisels, *101*, 103
Chloride analysis, 124
Churches
  tombs in, *see* Monumental tombs
  see also Wells Cathedral; Westminster Abbey, Annunciation Door; *and individual churches*
Claw-tool, *101*, 102–3
  tool marks, *105*
Clay
  attapulgite, *52*, *54*, 134, 141, 171
  sepiolite, 141, 198, 204
Cleaning, 242
  abrasive, *see* Mechanical cleaning
  Baker or lime method, *see* Lime surface treatment method
  biological growths, 136–7
    coverage, 137
    protection of other areas, 137
    treatment, 136
  bird droppings, 139, *140*
  cavitron, 199, *201*, *202*
  chemical, *see* Chemical cleaning; Poultices
  damage to monuments from, 190
  expertise, 126, 127
  feasibility studies for, *147–8*
  flame cleaning, 239
  graffiti removal, 137
  Hempel 'biological pack', 134
  identifying soiling patterns, *143–4*
  identifying soiling types, *144–6*
  iron and cuprous stains, 115, 135, 170
  laser, 135–6, 201
  masonry buildings, 124–54
  mechanical, *see* Mechanical cleaning
  Mora poultice, 134, *154*
  motivation for, 125
  painted stone, *see* Painted stone
  poulticing, *see* Poultices
  risks involved, 125
  soaps, 134–5
  steam cleaning, 200
  survey preceding cleaning, 126–7
  ultrasonic, 135, 199, *201*, *202*
  washing, *see* Washing
  water lances, 129, 130, *149*
  water-repellent treatment after, 138, *146*
  see also Desalination
Cleeve Abbey (Somerset), *36*
Climbing frames, 10–11
Clunch limestone, 172
Cobbles, 33, *51*
Colebrand Research Unit, 137
Combs, 16
Commonwealth Experimental Building Station (Sydney), 25
Compression failure, 58
Compressive strength, 57
Concrete stitch insertion, 6, 7, *60*
Concrete tiles, 29
Condensation
  impervious surfaces, 233
  monuments and, 189–90
  porous surfaces, 233, *234*, *235*
Conservation, *see individual method e.g.* Consolidation
Consolidation
  acrylic systems, 164–5
  alkyl-trialkoxy-silanes, 160–3
  aryl-alkyl-polysiloxanes, 163–4
  as preservation, 157–8
  barium hydrate (baryta), 165, 197

Consolidation (*cont.*)
  crushed stone, 181–2
  damage from restoration, 191
  epoxy resins, 165–6
  ethyl silicates, 159–60
  lime method, *see* Lime surface treatment method
  monumental tombs, 195–6
  painted stone, 217
  sandstone, 160
  sculpture in museums, 207
  silanes, *see* Silanes
  silica gel, 159
  silicon ester, 158, 159
Contour scaling, 17, *46*
Copings, 6, 25
Copper, staining, 135, 170
Corbelled out, *40*
Core
  analysis of, 120–1, 124
  cementitious grout injection, 59
  consolidation, *41*, *42*
  monumental tombs, 193
  'reading' corework, 4
  rubble, 115
  taking down and rebuilding, 6
  voids, 59, 115
  water penetration, 115
Corfe Castle (Dorset), *35*, *36*
Corn Exchange (Leith), *152*
Cornice, 24, *42*
  lead flashing over, *42*, *44*, *46*, *48*
Corrosion, 58
  iron and copper staining, 115, 135, 170
Corsetting, 58
Council for the Care of Churches, 195
Cracking, 59–61
  differential settlement and, 59
  epoxy resin treatment, 68–70
  flushing out cracks, 16, 69
  in Parliament Buildings, Ottawa, 118
  in plastering and rendering, 59
  monitoring, *see* Monitoring cracks
  planes of weakness, 59
  pointing, *94*, *95*
Cramps, *14*
  corrosion of, 58
  in tombs, 186, 188, 191, *192*, 193–4, *195*
  replacement of, 69
  stainless steel fishtail, 12, *14*
Cross walls, 58, 60, *61*, 69
Crowland Abbey, 169, 172
Crystallization test, 74
  alternatives to, 76
Cutting out stones, 11–12
  alternative treatment, 11
  cramps, 12, *14*
  criteria for deciding to replace, 11
  estimating life, 11
  physical process of, 12
  piercing-in, *12–13*, 12, 17
Cutting out stones (*cont.*)
  recording and marking, 11–12, *14*
  timing of replacement, 11

Damp-proof courses, 191
Dampness, 121, *122*
  falling damp, 189
  rising damp, 115, 189, 191
  see also Drainage; Humidity
Decahydrate, 122, 123
Delamination, 58
Delta metal, 6, 170
Demec strain gauge, *62*, 118
Dentistry repair, *see* Mortar repair
Desalination, *52–4*, 118–19, 123–4, 140–3
  determining salt levels, 142
  museum sculptures, 203, 204
  sacrificial render, 124, 140, 142
  see also Poultices
Dichloromethane, 224
Diethylene-anamine, 133
Dimes, Francis G, 225–7
Directorate of Ancient Monuments and Historic Buildings, 60, 69, 137
Dirt
  definition, 124
  see also Cleaning
Distemper, 22, 169, 215
Dolomite, 132
Domaslowski's method, *167*
Doulting limestone, 172, 173, 176, 182, 183
Dow Corning T 40149, 204, 207
Dowels, *14*, 16
  in monuments, 193–5
  in tombs, 186, 188
  stainless steel, *42*, 69, 170
Drags, 16
Drainage, 115
  damp-proof course, 191
  see also Dampness
Drawings, 1
Dressed stonework, *44*, 104–6
  hand-dressing, *44*
  quoin angles, 100
  rock-faced ashlar, 104–5
  squareness test, 99–100
  stone size dimensions, 100
  straightness test, 99
  surface finish, *99*, 100
Drought, foundation failure and, 55
Drumlanrig Castle (Scotland), *49*
Dry rot (*Serpula lacrymans*), 128
Dundry limestone, 173
Durability
  building zones, 73–4, *75*
  crystallization test, 74
    alternatives to, 76
  granites, 75–6
  limestone, *73*, 74
    Magnesian Limestones, 75
  marble, 75
Durability (*cont.*)
  sandstones, 74–5
  selection of stone for, 72–6
  slate, 75
  structural parameters and, *76*
Durham Cathedral, *43*
Dutch tarras, 81

Earthquake damage, 107–13
  building structural characteristics, 107–8
  earthquakes, 107
  foundation condition, 111
  quality of construction and, 108, 109
  seismic stress absorption, 109
  strengthening buildings, 108, *109–12*
Efflorescence, 118–20, 141, 189, 217
Emulsions, 22
English Heritage, 83, 88
Environmental effects, *see* Air pollution
Epoxy quartz sand blends, 25
Epoxy resin
  anchor bolts in, 69
  application, 68
  chemistry of, 66–7
  consolidation using, 165–6
  external reinforcement, 70
  gravity techiques, 68
  mortar joint repairs, 69
  physical properties of, 70
  pressure techniques, 68
  repair techniques, 65–70
  safety precautions, 68
  setting stainless steel in, 69
  surface repairs, 70
  vacuum injection, 68
Ethanol, 224
Ethyl silicates, 159–60
  structural chemistry, *160*
Ethylene diaminotetraacetic acid (EDTA), 134
Eton (England), *51*
Exeter Cathedral, 169

Facing, 12, *42*, 98
Facing up, 192, *193*
Failure, *see* Cracking; Foundation failure; Structural failure; Superstructure failure
Falling damp, 189
Fibre glass pins, 170
Finn, Clare, 214–18
Fire damage, 15–16, *47–8*
Firestone, 225
Flame cleaning, 239
Floors
  'Fox and Barret' fireproof, 114
  iron joists, rusting of, 115
  suspended, 59, *60*
Flushing out, 16, 69
Fly ash, *see* PFA

Fogging cleaning, 128, *149*
Formalin, 175
Formwork support, 4
Fort George (Scotland), *44*
Foundation failure, 55–7
  chemical grouting of soils, 55
  micropiles, 56, *57*
  piling systems, 55–6, *57*
  settlement, 55, 56, 59, 62–3, 118
  shrinkable clays, 55
  signs of, 55
  tree and shrub removal, 55
  underpinning, 55, *56*
  water table alterations, 56
Foundations
  damp-proof course, 191
  grouting of, 115
  rising damp, 115
  weeping tiles, 115
Fountains Abbey (Yorkshire), *37*
Fracture, *35*
  broken arches, *8*
  jointing fractured stones, *7*
  vertical, of walls, *7*, *35*
Francois Cementation process, 25
Freeze-thaw cycle, 115

Gabion, 6
Gamma radiography, 206–7, 208
Gassing, 203
Gelva, 217
Geotextile sheets, 4
Gesso, 17, 174, 215, 223
Ghur Emir Mausoleum, 163
Goodrich Castle, *36*
Gouge, 97, 103
  tool mark, 103
Gradwell, Christopher, 219–28
Graffiti removal, 137
Granite
  cleaning with soap, 134–5
  durability assessment, 75–6
  HF chemical cleaning, 130–3
  kaolinization, 76
  setts, 33
Gravity grouting system, 26, *27*, 28
Grouting, 26–30, *38–9*
  Balvac process, 29
  chemical, of soils, 55
  detailed investigations, 26
  Francois Cementation process, 25
  gravity system, 26, *27*, 28
  liquid Portland cement grout, 25
  masonry walls, 26
  of foundations, 115
  Parliament Buildings, Ottawa, 118
  PFA, 115–16
  placing new stones, 15
  pouring and proving holes, 15
  pumped system, *27*, 28–9, 115–16
  vacuum grouting, 29
Grouts, 15
Guiting limestone, 173

'Gun shading', 130

Halving technique, 16
Ham River sandstone, 182
Hammer, *101*, 102
Handworking of stone, 97–106
  dressed stonework, *99*, 100
    quoin angles, 100
    squareness test, 99–100
    stone size dimensions, 100
    straightness test, 99
    surface finish, *99*, 100
  hand-dressing, *44*
  masonry types and descriptions, *see* Masonry
  stone type identification, 97–8
  tools, *see* Tools
Hardening, freshly quarried stone, 17
Heating, 190
Heptahydrate, 122
High alumina cement, 83
High temperature insulation, *see* HTI powder
Hill, Peter, 97–106
Holyrood Palace, *151*
Honeyborne, David, 71–7, 156–69, 231–6
Hornton limestone, 173
Howden Minster (Yorkshire), 25, *49*
HTI powder, 15, 18, *19*, 81, 84, 172
Humidity, 121, *122*, 123, 215
  measurements, 121, *122*, 123
  tests, 205
  tourist effects, 232–5
Hydraulic limes, *see* Mortars
Hydrochloric acid cleaning, 133
Hydrofluoric acid cleaning, 130–3, *152*, *153*
  commercial procedures, 132–3
  personal protection, 133
  sandstone, 130–3
  staining, 131
Hygroscopic properties, 234–5

ICCROM, 83, 156, 168
Inner cities, monument sites, 4
Interference problem, 1
International Centre for Conservation (ICCROM), *see* ICCROM
International Fund for Monuments, 135
Iron, corrosion stain, 115, 135, 170
Iron oxide wash, *43*
Irrigation, *52–4*
Ivy (*Hedera helix*), 10

Jambs, 17
Jervaulx Abbey (Yorkshire), 10, *35*, *36*, *40*
Joggles, *14*, *44*
Joints
  architect's plan of approach, *3*
  beak joint, 86
  double struck, 86
Joints (*cont.*)
  jointing fractured stones, *7*
  'joints jointed', 86
  masonry bees damage, 88
  sounding, 26
  see also Grouting: Mortar joints; Mortars

Kaolinization, 76
Kelly, John, 240–3
Kerbs, 32
Ketone 'N' resin, 196
King's College Chapel (Cambridge), 232, 234
Kingstone Church (Dorset), *51*
Kirkleatham, 191
Kotor (Yugoslavia), *109*, *110*, *112*

Laboratory analysis, 240–1
Larson, John, 185–96, 197–207
Lasers, 65
  cleaning with, 135–6, 201
Lateral stability, 58
Lead
  code 4, 25, 30, *49*, 193, *194*
  code 5, 26, 30
  code 6, *48*
  for stone roofs, 30
  isolating membranes, 211–12
  lead lined sump on wall, 6
  protection using, 25, *49*
  waterproof membrane, 193, *194*
Lead flashing, 25, 26, *48*, *49*
  mortar repair protection, *23*, 24, *48*, *49*
  over cornices, *42*, *44*, *46*, *48*
Leith (Scotland), *143*
Lewis pins, 33, 34
Lichens
  cleaning, 136–7
  graffiti and, 137
Lichfield Cathedral, *144*
Lime-casein paint, 22, 215, 230
Lime gesso, 17, 174, 215, 223
Lime (hydraulic), 81, 230
Lime (non-hydraulic), 78–81
  hardening of lime mortar, 80
  mixing, 79–80
  pozzolanic additives, 81
  production of, 78–9
  slaking, 79
Lime putty, 79, 172–3
  alternative sources, 80–1
Lime surface treatment method, 134, 166, 169–85
  Annunciation Door, Westminster Abbey, 169
  cleaning, 170–1
    air abrasion, 171
    hot lime method, 171
  lime mortar, 166
  lime wash, *see* Lime wash
  lime water, 157–8, 166
    consolidation, 172

Lime surface treatment method (*cont.*)
  lime water (*cont.*)
    strengthening, 157–8
  old fillings removal, 171–2
  preliminary survey, 170
  shelter coats, 166, 174–6
  structural repairs, 170
  surface repair, 172–4
  Wells Cathedral, 166, 169, 176–83
Lime wash, 22, 166, 215, 219, 229–30
  application of, 230
  lime-casein, 230
  lime-cenosphere (PFA), 230
  lime-glue formulations, 229
  lime-tallow, 229–30
  pigments, 230
  removal of, 217
  whiting (crushed chalk), 229
Limestone
  Anca stone, 234, 235
  argillaceous, 82
  Barnack limestone, 172
  Bath limestone, 133, 172
  Beer limestone, 172
  black, 190
  Caen stone, *43*, 202, 203, 225, 226
  Chilmark limestone, 172
  Clunch limestone, 172
  condensation and, 190
  decorative paving, 34
  Doulting limestone, 172, 173, 176, 182, 183
  Dundry limestone, 173
  durability asssessment, *73*, 74
  Guiting limestone, 173
  Hornton limestone, 173
  Monks Park limestone, 182, 183, 234
  Purbeck limestone, *51*
  redressing, *45*
  Salcombe limestone, 172
  setts, 33, *51*
  washing by rain, 127
Linseed oil, *146*, 219
Lintols, secret, *8*
Loading
  earthquake stresses and, 108
  eccentricity, 58
Louisville cement, 82
Lump lime, 79

McGrath, Teresa, 219–27
Magnesian Limestone, 75
Mallet, *101*, 102
Malmstone, 225
Marble
  Carrara, 30, 190, 205–6
  cleaning damage, 190
  durability assessment, 75
  paving, 34
  Purbeck 'marble', 189–90, 219
  washing by rain, 127
Market cross (Chichester), *43*
Marking stones
  for cutting out, 11, *14*
  for removal, 210
Masonry
  ashlar, 98
    boasted or axed, 98
    plain or rubbed, 98
    punched, 98
    rock faced, 98
    rusticated, 98
    tooled or batted, 98
  block-in-course class, 98
  coursed rubble, 98–9
  defects and weaknesses, 58–9
  facing stones, 98
  polygonal or rag walling, 99
  providing protection for, 25–6
  random rubble, 99
  types and descriptions, 98–9
  see also Walls *and individual aspects of treatment e.g.* Cutting out stones; Replacement of stones
Masonry cement, 83
Mastic plug, *96*
Mechanical cleaning, 129–30, *150–1*
  abrasion, 219
  abrasives, 129, 239
  air abrasion, 171, 198–9, *200*, 237–9
    abrasives, 238
    advantages, 130
    in museums, 198–9, *200*
    nozzles, 238
    problems, 130
    remote control, 237
    water injection or water shroud, 237
  blasting system, 129
  factors requiring consideration, 129–30
  'gun shading', 130
  personal protection, 129
  range of equipment, 130, *131*
  sand blasting, *150*, 171
  spinning-off, 129
  wheel type, 237
Medina cement, 82
Methacrylate, 217
Methyl cellulose, 133
Methyl methacrylate monomer, 165
Methyl-triethoxy-silane, 161
Methyl-trimethoxy-silane, 161
Methylcyclohexyloleate, 134
Micropiles, 56, *57*
Microporosity, *76*
Microscopy
  binocular, 197, *198*, 202, *203*
  scanning electron, 120, *121*
  stereoscopic, 225
Milk, 174–5
Mills, Ralph, 55–71
Minster-in-Sheppey, Virgin and Child sculpture, *202*, 203–5
Mist cleaning, 128, *149*
Modern Practical Masonry (Warland), 17
Moisture measurement, *52*
  see also Humidity
Monitoring cracks, 59, 62–5
  actual displacement, 63
  autoplumb, 64, *65*
  choice of system, 62
  Demec strain gauge, *62*, 118
  differential movement, 62–3
  in Parliament Buildings, Ottawa, 118
  lasers, 65
  movement out of vertical, 64–5
  plumb bobs, 64
  recording results, 65, *66–7*
  strain gauges, 62–3
  theodolite, 64
  vernier callipers, *63*
  vertical movement, 63–4
Monks Park limestone, 182, 234
Monument sites, 4–6
  inner cities, 4
  temporary reburial, 4
  walls
    above ground level, 4–6
    below ground level, 4
    see also Walls
Monumental tombs, 185–96
  canopy tombs, 187
  causes of decay, 187–91
  condensation, 189–90
  construction, 185–7
  cramps and dowels, 186, 188, 191, *192*, 193–4, *195*
  damage from restoration, 190–1
    cements, 191
    cleaning, 190
    consolidation, 191
    pigmentation, 190–1, 192
  free-standing box tomb, 185, *186*
  heating, 190
  polychrome, 190–1, 192
  sculptures, 186, *188*
  soluble salts and decay, 189
  structural problems, 187–8
  treatment of
    consolidation, 195–6
    cores, 193
    environmental effects, 191–2
    fillings, repairs and retouching, 195
    record keeping, 192
    surface finishes, 196
    waterproof membranes, 192–3, *194*
  wall tombs, 186, *187*, *188*
Mora poultice, 134, *154*
Mortar joints, *94*
  cleaning, 86
  filling, 86
  foam backing rod in, *96*
  masonry bees damage, 88

Mortar joints (*cont.*)
  pointing, 85–6
    cutting out, 85–6
    raking out, 85, 116
  remedial treatments, *87*
  resin repairs, 69
  special joint treatment, 86, 88
  see also Joints
Mortar repair, 22, *23*, 24, *43*, *46*, *46–7*, *47*
  binders, 24, 25
  decision to use, 22, 24
  dentistry repair, 22, 25
  failure of, 22
  lead flashing, *23*, 24, *48*, *49*
  lime mortar, 169
  moulding repair using, *23*, *46*, *47*
  patch repair, *23*
  procedures, 24
  proprietary mortar repairs, 24
  protection of, 24
  resins, 69
  sandstone, 24, 25
Mortars, 78–96
  additives, 83
    air-entraining agents, 84
    antifreeze, 83–4
    brick dust, 81, 84, 172
    HTI powder, 15, 18, *19*, 81, 84, 172
    PFA, 81, 84
    pigments, 84
    surfactants, 84
    water-reducing agents, 84
    waterproofers, 84
  aggregates, 173
    grading, 85
    materials, 84
    summary of requirements, 85
    washing, 84–5
  analysis, 88–93
    chemical, 90
    dating structures and, 88
    on-site, 88–90
    recording, *91–2*, 93
    sampling procedure, 90, 93
    X-ray diffraction, 90
  cements
    artificial, 82
    high alumina, 83
    masonry cement, 83
    natural (Roman), 82, 171
    Portland, 82, 171
    pozzolanic, 83
    sulphate-resisting, 83
    white Portland, 82
  coloured, 81, *173*
  for remedial work, *89*
  lime (hydraulic), 81, 230
  lime (non-hydraulic), 78–81
    hardening, 80
    lump lime, 79
    mixing, 79–80
    pozzolanic additives, 81

Mortars (*cont.*)
  lime (non-hydraulic) (*cont.*)
    production of, 78–9
    quicklime, 79
    slaking, 79
    unslaked lime, 79
  lime putty, 79, 172–3
    alternative sources, 80–1
  repair and maintenance, 85–8
    see also Mortar joints
  staining from, 15, 86
  strength, 57
Moss, Peter, 237–9
Moulds, 1
Mowilith, 217
Muchelney Abbey, *53*
Mullions, 15–16, 17
Museums, *see* Architectural feature displays; Sculpture in museums

Natural (Roman) cement, 82, 171
Natural Stone Directory, 71
Nebulous sprays, 128, *149*
Nylon, soluble, 197, 217

Old Palace, Westminster, *143*
On-site investigations/analysis, 88–90, 240
Organic amines, 133
Organic growth, *40*
  see also Biological growth control; Plant growth; Weed removal
Ottawa, *see* Parliament Buildings, Ottawa

Packaging, 210
Painted rendering, 22
Painted stone, 22
  application methods, 216
  cleaning, 214–18
    methods and dangers of, 216–17
    oil-based paints, 217
    resins, 217
    solvents for, 218
  consolidation, 217
  filling of losses, 217
  monuments, 190–1, 192
  reintegration, 218
  sampling, 214, 216
  sculpture, cleaning and, 202–3
  survey and analysis, 214–15
  temporary protection, 215
  Virgin Mary sculpture, 222, 224, 225
Paints, 215
  acrylic, 195
  aqueous, 215
  binders, 24, 25, 215
  casein paints, 174
  distemper, 22, 169, 215
  emulsions, 22
  extenders, 215
  isolating paints, 15

Paints (*cont.*)
  lime-casein, 22, 215, 230
  oil based, 215
  pigment range, 215
  resin based, 215
  sanded bitumen, 15
  silicate, 22
  see also Lime wash; Pigments
Pantiles, 29
Paraloid B-72, 217
Parapets, 6
Parliament Buildings, Ottawa, 114–24
  construction, 114–15
  core analysis, 120–1, 124
  cracking, 118
  dampness in walls, 121, *122*, 123
  desalination, 123–4
  efflorescence, 118–20
  freeze-thaw cycle, 115
  grouting, 115–16
  pointing, 115
  programme of repairs
    masonry repairs, 115–17
    roof level, 115
    south-west tower, 117–23
  salt damage, 118–23
  salt identification, 120, 121
  south-west tower, *117*, *118*, *119*, 120–3
    construction, 117–18
    structural problems, 118–19
  subflorescence, 119–21, 122, 123
Pattern of English Building, The (Clifton-Taylor), 30
Paving, 32–4, *51*
  access to services, 33
  cobbles, *51*
  in light traffic areas, 34
  kerbs, 32, *51*
  lewis pins, 33, 34
  limestone setts, *51*
  marble and decorative limestone, 34
  pavements, 32
  paving specifications, 33–4
    cobble stones, 33
    granite or basalt setts, 33
    limestone and sandstone setts, 33
    stone flags, 33–4
  roads, 32
  setts, 33, *51*
  stairs, 32
  thresholds, 32
  wear problems, 34, 231
Perfluoro-polyesters, 157
Pesticide Safety Precautions Scheme, 88
Petrographic analysis, 98
  Annunciation figures, 225, 227
Petrological analysis, 241
PFA, 81
  lime-cenosphere (PFA) limewash, 230
  mortar additives, 84

Phosphor bronze, 170
Photogrammetry, 1, 11, 192
Photography, 1, 11
Physical analysis, 241
  capillarity, 241
  porosity, *76*, 180–1, 233, *234*, *235*, 241
Pick, *101*, 102
Piercing-in, *12–13*, 12, 17, *43*
Pigments, 225
  cleaning and, 202–3
  mortar additives, 84
  see also Painted stone; Paints
Piling, 55–6, *57*
  micropiles, 56, *57*
Pitcher or pitching tool, *101*, 102
Placing new stones, 15–16
  bedding, 15
  flushing out, 16
  grouting, 15
  isolating paint, 15
  spot securing, 15–16
Planning permission, 62
Plant growth, *40*
  climbing frames, 10–11
  coexistance with masonry, 10–11, *40*
  see also Weed removal
Plant removal, *see* Biological growth cleaning; Weed removal
Plaster, *50*
  cracks in, 59
Plastic repair, *see* Mortar repair
Plinth courses, 77
Plumb bobs, 64
  autoplumb, 64, *65*
Pointing, 85–6, *94*, *95*
  cutting out, 85–6
  maintenance, 115
  raking out, 85
  repointing, 118
  spalling and, 58–9
  tuck pointing, 88
Pollution, *see* Air pollution
Poly-phenyl-methyl-siloxane, 163–4
Polychrome, *see* Painted stone
Polyester resins
  application, 68
  chemistry of, 67–8
  gravity treatment, 68
  mortar joints, 69
  physical properties of, 70
  pressure pots, 68
  pressure treatment, 68
  repair techniques, 65–70
  safety precautions, 68
  vacuum injection, 68
Polyethylene shroud, 29
Polygonal walling, 99
Polymerization, 159, 160, 161
Polypropylene mesh, 29
Polystyrene 'duvets', 4, *5*
Polyvinyl alcohol, 217
Pompeii, 34
Porosity, *76*, 241
  condensation and pore size, 233, *234*, *235*
  Wells Cathedral, 180–1
Porta della Carta (Venice), 30
Portland cement, 82, 171, 191
  air-entrained, 84
  waterproofed (OPC), 84
  white, 82–3
Portland stone, 76
Potassium hydroxide, 133, *145*, *146*
Poultices, *52–4*, 123–4, 140–2, 171, 242–3
  attapulgite clay, *52*, *54*, 134, 141, 171
  desalination, 204, 205
  hot lime method, 171
  in museums, 198, *199*, *200*, *201*
    sculptures, 204, 205
  mixing, 141
  Mora poultice, 134, *154*
  of clay or CMC, 133, 134
  repeated applications, 142
  sepiolite clay, 141, 198, 204
  tobacco smoke stain removal, 232
  wetting process, 141
Pozzolanic additive, 15, 18, *19*, 81, 90, 172, 173
Pozzolanic cement, 83
Preservatives
  consolidants as, 157–8
  water repellants as, 157
  see also Surface treatments
Profiles, 105
Protection
  for buildings, 25–6
  of walls, 4, *5*, 6, *9*
  temporary, of painted stone, 215
Pulverized fuel ash, *see* PFA
Pumice, 81
Pumped grouting system, *27*, 28–9, 115–16
Punch, *101*, 102
  tool marks, *104*
Punched ashlar, 98
Purbeck 'marble', 219
  condensation and, 189–90

Quats, 136
Quicklime, 79
Quirk, *94*
Quoins, 11, 17, *44*
  checking angles, 100

Raccanello 55050, 219, 225
Raccanello E 0057, 204, 207
Rag walling, 99
Raking out, 85, 116
Records, 1, 4
  before cutting out stones, 11
  monitoring of cracks, 65, *66–7*
  mortar analysis, *91–2*, 93
  of monument treatments, 192
  of museum treatments, 197
Records (*cont.*)
  stones for cutting out, *14*
Recrystallization phenomena, 34
Redressing stone, 16–17, *45*, *46*
  contour scaling, 17
  hardening of freshly quarried stone, 17
  reasons for, 16
  tools, 16
  water traps, 17
Register of Treated Stonework, 167–8
Reigate stone, 219, 225
Relative humidity, *see* Humidity
Rendering, 17–22
  cracks in, 59
  matching, 18
  mixes for, 18, *19*, 20
    strong impermeable backgrounds, 20
    thick, rough textured, 18, *19*
    thin, smooth textured, 18, *19*
  mixing and application
    rough textured, 20
    smooth textured, 20, 22
  painting, 22
  sacrificial render, 124, 140, 142, 215
  thick, to weak background, *21*
  thin, to rubble, *21*
  wall preparation, 18
Repairs
  epoxy resins, *see* Epoxy resins
  polyester resins, *see* Polyester resins
  stone selection for, *see* Stone selection for repairs
Replacement of stones, 12, 15, *43*
  profiles, 15
  templates, 15
  with cast stone, 25, *50–1*
Repointing, 118
Rescue archaeology, 4
Ribs, decayed, 11
Richmond Terrace (London), *44*
Richmond (Yorkshire), *51*
Ridges, cast stone, 25
Rising damp, 115, 189, 191
Roads, 32
Rock-faced ashlar, 98, 104–7
Roman cement, 82, 171
Roman Painted House (Dover), 218
'Roof-bond' system, 32
Roofs
  asbestos, 29
  bituminous roofing felt, 30
  copper, 114
  slate, 32
    deterioration, 32
    pegs, 32
    resin block, 32
    slating hooks, 32
  stone slates, 30–2
    failures, 30–1
    laying of, 30
    signs of defects, 31

Roofs (*cont.*)
  stone slates (*cont.*)
    specification for, 31
    waterproofings, 30
  tiles, 29
Rosendale cement, 82
Rubble
  coursed rubble, 98
  coursed squared rubble, 99
  random rubble, 99
  thin rendering to, *21*
Rugby cement, 82
Rusticated ashlar, 11, 98

Sacrificial render, 124, 140, 142, 215
St George's (Colegate, Norwich), 186
St Margaret's (Westminster), *143*
St Maria Maggiore (Rome), 34
St Mary the Virgin (Iffley, Oxford), *49*, *50*
St Pancras Station (London), *153*
Salcombe limestone, 172
Salt damage, *43*, 118–23
  in monumental tombs, 189, *191*
  salt identification, 120, 121
  see also Desalination; Poultices
Sampling, 90, 93, 214, 216, 240
Sand blasting, *150*, 171
  see also Mechanical cleaning
Sandstone
  Berea formation (Ohio), 115
  calcareous sandstones, 131–2
  chemical cleaning, *151*
  cleaning with soap, 134–5
  consolidation, 160
  dolomitic sandstones, 131–2
  durability assessment, 74–5
  Ham River sandstone, 182
  HF chemical cleaning, 130–3
  mortar repair of, 24, 25
  redressing, 17
  Reigate stone, 225
  setts, 33
  stone slates, 30
  washing by rain, 127
  water repellants for, 156–7
Saturation, 127–8
  coefficient, *76*
Scaffold, 11, 209
Scanning electron microscope, 120, *121*
'Scotch work', 115
Sculpture
  cast stone replacements, 25
  laser cleaning, 135–6
  lime gesso plaster, 17
  vacuum grouting, 29–30
  see also Sculpture in museums
Sculpture in museums, 197–207
  binocular microscopy, 197, *198*, 202, *203*
  case studies
    Neptune and Triton, *205–6*, 207
    Virgin and Child, *202*, 203–5

Sculpture in museums (*cont.*)
  cleaning techniques
    air-abrasion, 198–9, *200*
    cavitron, 199, *201*, *202*
    chemical, 199–200
    cleaning tests, 207
    de-salination, 203, 204
    laser cleaning, 201
    pigmentation and, 202–3
    poulticing, 198, *199*, *200*, *201*
    salt encapsulation, 203–4
    steam cleaning, 200
  consolidation, 203–4, 207
  museum based conservators, 197
  reconsolidation, 204
  records of treatments, 197
Sedgwick Museum, 71
Sepiolite clay, 141, 198, 204
Settlement, 55, 56, 59, 62–3, 118
Setts
  granite or basalt, 33
  limestone, 33, *51*
  Purbeck limestone, *51*
  sandstone, 33
Shear strength, 57
Shellac, 197
Shelter coating, 166, 174–6
  application of, 175
Sheppey cement, 82
Shoring, 4
Silanes, 196, 203
  alkyl-trialkoxy-silanes, 160–3
    structure of, *162*
  catalysed silane, 24, 163
  consolidation by, 24, 159–63
  disadvantages of, 163
  maximum pore filling, 163
  methyl-triethoxy-silane, 161
  methyl-trimethoxy-silane, 161
  Raccanello 55050, 219, 225
  silicone terminology, 168–9
  surface treatment by, 167
  tetra-ethoxy-silane, 159
  tetra-hydroxy-silane, *160*, *161*
  tetra-methyloxy-silane, 159
Silchester, *41*
Silica gel consolidation, 159
Silicate paints, 22
Silicon ester strengthening, 158, 159
Silicone, *146*, 196
  terminology, 168–9
Siloxanes, 168
  aryl-alkyl-polysiloxanes, 163–4
  organo-siloxanes, 168
  poly-phenyl-methyl-siloxane, 163–4
  polyorgano-siloxanes, 168
Site analysis, 88–90, 240
Site observations, 1
Slate
  cleaning with soap, 134–5
  condensation and, 190
  durability assessment, 75
  Welsh slates, 29

Slate roofs, 32
  deterioration, 32
  pegs, 32
  resin block, 32
  'Roof-bond' system, 32
  slating hooks, 32
Slenderness ratio, 57–8
Society for the Protection of Ancient Buildings (SPAB), 17, 167
Sodium hydroxide cleaning, 133
Sodium sulphate, 118, 120–3
Soluble nylon, 197, 217
Solvents, 218
Sounding, 26
Sources of stone, 97–8
Spalling, 118, 123, 158
  compression failure and, 58
  pointing and, 58–9
  sodium sulphate and, 118, 119, 120–3
Spinning-off, 129
Squareness test, 99–100
Staining
  from mortars, 86
  iron and cooper corrosion, 115, 135, 170
  removal by hydrochloric acid, 133
Stainless steel, 170
  fishtail cramps, 12, *14*
Stairs, 32
Steam cleaning, 200
Stereoscopic microscope, 225
  see also Binocular microscopy
Stewart, John, 114–24
Stitching, 6, 7, *60*
Stone Federation, 126
Stone flags, 33–4
Stone mason, meaning of, 100
Stone selection for repairs
  durability, 71–6
    building zones, 73–4
    crystallization test, 74
    limestone, *73*, 74
    sandstones, 74–5
    structural parameters and, *76*
  for plinth courses, 77
  granites, 75–6
  guide flowchart, *72*
  limestone, *73*, 74
    Magnesian Limestone, 75
  marble, 75
  matching for appearance, 71
  slate, 75
  weathering characteristics, 72–6
  workability, 76–7
Stone slates, 30–2
  failures, 30–1
  laying of, 30
  signs of defects, 31
  specification for, 31
  weatherproofings, 30
    touching or tiering, 30
Stones
  architect's plan of approach, *2–3*

Stones (*cont.*)
  hand-dressing, *44*
  handworking, *see* Handworking of stone
  mortar repair, *see* Mortar repair
  painted, *see* Painted stone
  redressing, *see* Redressing stone
  repairing, *see* Stone selection for repairs
  repairing with tiles, 17
  replacement, 12, 15, *43*
    profiles, 15
    templates, 15
    with cast stone, 25, *50–1*
  roofs, *see* Stone slates
  selection, *see* Stone selection for repairs
  source identification, 97–8
  type identification, 97–8
  see also individual aspects of treatment e.g. Cutting out stones; Placing new stones
Straightness test, 99
Strain gauge, 62–3
  Demec strain gauge, *62*, 118
Straw 'duvets', 4, *5*
Strengthening
  lime water, 157–8
  silicon ester, 158
Stress-release, 34
Strings, 24
Structural failure
  arches, 58
  compression failure, 58
  cracking, *see* Cracking
  external reinforcement, 70
  foundations, *see* Foundation failure
  in Parliament Buildings, Ottawa, 118–19
  masonry defects and weaknesses, 58–9
  superstructure, *see* Superstructure failure
  see also Fracture
Structural frame, 58
Strutting, 4
Subflorescence, 189
Sueno's stone (Aberdeenshire), 25
Sulphate skins, 17
Sulphate-resisting cement, 83
Superstructure failure, 57–8
  bracing, 58
  compressive and shear strength, 57
  cross walls, 58, 60, *61*, 69
  eccentricity of loading, 58
  lateral stability, 58
  mortar strength, 57
  slenderness ratio of component, 57–8
  structural frame, 58
Surface treatments, 155–84
  consolidation, *see* Consolidation
  lime method, *see* Lime surface treatment method

Surface treatments (*cont.*)
  objective of, 155
  philosophy of conservation by, 167
  possibility of preservation by, 158–9
  preservatives, 155, 157
  tools, 174
  water repellants, 156–7
Surfactants, 84
Suspended floors, 59, *60*

Taylor, Keith, 219–28, 224–5
TBTO, *see* Tri-*n*-butyl-tin oxide (TBTO)
Templates, 1, 15, 105
Temple Church (Bristol), 15–16, *47*
Temple of Saturn (Rome), 6
Tetra-ethoxy-silane, 159
Tetra-hydroxy-silane, *160*, *161*
Tetra-methyloxy-silane, 159
Theodolite, 64
Therian Earth, 81
Thresholds, 32
Tie-marks, *144*
Tiering, 30
Ties, 58, *60*, *61*
Tiles
  concrete tiles, 29
  plain tiles, 29
  repairing stone with, 17
  weeping tiles, 115
  see also Slate; Slate roofs; Stone slates
Tilestones, *see* Stone slates
Tintern Abbey (Monmouthshire), *41*, *49*
Tito (Italy), *110*, *111*, *112*
Tobacco smoke, 232
Toluene, 217, 224
Tool marks
  adze, 103, *104*
  punch, *104*
  see also Tools
Tooled ashlar, 98
Tools
  adze, 100, *101*, 102
  boaster, 97, *101*, 103, *105*
  chisels, *101*, 103
  claw-tool, *101*, 102–3
  drove, *see* Boaster
  gouge, 97, 103
  hammer, *101*, 102
  mallet, *101*, 102
  pick, *101*, 102
  pitcher or pitching tool, *101*, 102
  punch, *101*, 102
  surface treatment, 174
  see also Tool marks
Touching, 30
Tourist effects
  carbon dioxide concentration, 231
  clothes and building fabric, 231
  humidity, 232–5
    hygroscopic properties, 235–6

Tourist effects (*cont.*)
  humidity (*cont.*)
    impervious surfaces, 233
    porous surfaces, 233, *234*, *235*
  oil from skin, 231–2
  tobacco smoke, 232
  vibration, 231
  wear on pavements and floors, 34, 231
Tower of London, Salt Tower, 141
Trachyte, 81
Transportation, 210
Trass, 81, 90
  see also Pozzolanic additives
Treasurer's House (Yorkshire), *42*
Trees, root removal, 10, *41*
Tri-*n*-butyl-tin oxide (TBTO), 136
Trichloro-trifluoro-ethane, 157
Tuff, 81
Turf wall tops, 6, *9*
Tutbury Castle, 97

Ultrasonic cleaning, 135
  cavitron, 199, *201*, *202*
Underpinning, 55, *56*
Unibond, 193
Unslaked lime, 79
Urban Pollution Research Centre, 125

Vacuum grouting, 29
  Balvac process, 29
  sculptures, 29–30
Vacuum injection of resin, 68–9
Vault springers, 11
Ventilation, 215, 231
Vents, 59
Vertical movements
  bench marks, 63, *64*
  independent datum, 63
  levelling sockets independent datum, 63
  precision level, 63, *64*
Vibrations, 231
Vinamul, 217
Virgin and Child sculpture (Minster-in-Sheppey), *202*, 203–5
Visitors, *see* Tourist effects
Voids, 59, 115
  testing for, 26
Volcanic materials, 81

Walls
  above ground level, 4, 6
  architect's plan of approach, *2*
  below modern ground level, 4, *5*
  bonding timbers, 60
  bowing, 59
  broken arches, *8*
  bulging, 59, *116*
  capping, *9*
  consolidation of monument sites, 4–6
  copings, 6
  core, *see* Core

Walls (*cont.*)
- cross walls, 58, 60, *61*, 69
- fencing, *4*
- formwork support, 4
- initial surveys, 4, 6
- jointing fractured stones, *7*
- lead lined sump, 6
- leaning, *37*
- parapets, 6
- plant growth and, 10–11, *40*
- polygonal walling, 99
- protection of, lead, *49*
- rag walling, 99
- random rubble, 60
- rendering, *see* Rendering
- secret lintols, *8*
- soft wall top, *9*, 10–11
- stitching, 6, *7*, *60*
- strutting and shoring, 4
- taking down and rebuilding, 6
- temporary protection, 4, *5*
  - capping, *9*
  - mortar blankets, 6
  - 'stable and moist', *5*
  - turf, 6, *9*
  - 'warm and dry', *5*
- ties, 58, *60*, *61*
- vertical fracture, *7*, *35*
- wall heads, 4, 6, *39*, *40*, *41*
- water traps and pockets, 6
- weed removal, 6, *9*, 10
- *see also individual aspects of treatment e.g.* Cutting out stones; Placing new stones; Replacement of stones

Warkton Church, *187*

Washing, 127–9, *148–9*
- brushes, 128
- by rain, 127
- intermittent or pulse washing, 128
- mists and fogging, 128, *149*
- nebulous sprays, *see* Mists and fogging
- saturation, 127–8
- splash or slurry boards, 128–9
- staining, *148*
- water lances, 129, 130, *149*
- water temperature, 129

Water barriers, *54*

Water lances, 129, 130, *149*

Water penetration, 115

Water repellants, 138, *146*
- as preservatives, 157
- perfluoro-polyesters, 157
- silicone-based, 156–7
- surface treatment, 156–7
- trichloro-trifluoro-ethane, 157
- wax based, 157

Water table level changes, 56, 189

Water traps, 6, 17

Water-reducing agents, 84

Waterproof membranes, 192–3, *194*

Waterproofers, mortar additives, 84

Wax, 197
- discolouration, 157

Weathering, 72–6
- *see also* Air pollution

Weed removal, 6, *9*, 10, *40*
- foundation failure caused by, 55
- glyphosphate, 6
- ivy, 10
- plant growth coexistence, 10–11, *40*
- root removal, 10, *41*
- *see also* Biological growth cleaning

Weeping tiles, 115

Wells Cathedral
- calcium hydroxide deposition, 179–80, 182
- calcium sulphate distribution, 177–9, 182
- crushed stone consolidation, 181–2
- lime treatment, 166, 169, 176–83
- porosity, 180–1
- strength, 181
- technical appraisal, 177–81

Wells method, *see* Lime surface treatment method

Welsh slates, 29

Westminster Abbey, *42*

Westminster Abbey, Annunciation Door, 219–227
- acrylic silane record, *223*
- arch orders and jambs, 220, 222
- ashlar in niches, 224
- Chapter House side, *221*
- diaper flowers, 219, 222
- Gabriel sculpture, 219, 222, *226*
  - conservation of, 224–5
  - determination of samples from, 225–6
  - petrographic description, 227
- lime surface treatment method, 169
- lime wash removal, 220, 222, 224
- pigment layers, 222, 224, 225
- structure, 219–20
- trefoils with censing angels, 219, 222
- vestibule side, *221*
- Victorian Christ in Majesty, 219, 224
- Virgin sculpture, 219, 222, *226*
  - conservation of, 224–5
  - determination of samples from, 225
  - petrographic description, 227

Westminster Hall, 15, *48*

Weymouth cement, 82

Whey, 175

Whitby cement, 82

White Portland cement, 82–3

Windows, traceried windows, 15–16, *47*

Woburn Abbey, 16, *45*

Workability, 76–7

X-ray diffraction, 120
- mortar analysis, 90

Xylene, 165, 217